fully acknowledges
the generous contribution provided by the Director's Circle
of the Associates of the University of California Press
whose members are

JOLA AND JOHN ANDERSON

ELAINE MITCHELL ATTIAS

JUNE AND EARL CHEIT

MARGIT AND LLOYD COTSEN

PHYLLIS K. FRIEDMAN

SUSAN AND AUGUST FRUGÉ

HARRIETT AND RICHARD GOLD

ELLINA AND ORVILLE GOLUB

JANIE AND JEFFREY GREEN

FLORENCE AND LEO HELZEL

LISA SEE AND RICHARD KENDALL

NANCY AND MEAD KIBBEY

YVONNE LENART

LISA SAWYER AND JOHN T. LESCROART

SUSAN AND JAMES MCCLATCHY

HANNAH AND THORMUND A. MILLER

MR. AND MRS. RICHARD C. OTTER

JOAN PALEVSKY

SHIRLEY AND RALPH SHAPIRO

JUDY AND DONALD SIMON

SHARON AND BARCLAY SIMPSON

MAGDA AND FRED WAINGROW

MELINDA MCCARRY WULFF

CREATING THE CORPORATE SOUL

ROLAND MARCHAND

CREATING THE

CORPORATE

THE RISE OF PUBLIC RELATIONS

SOUL

AND CORPORATE IMAGERY

IN AMERICAN BIG BUSINESS

THE UNIVERSITY OF CALIFORNIA PRESS

Berkeley Los Angeles London

University of California Press
Berkeley and Los Angeles, California

University of California Press, Ltd.
London, England

First Paperback Printing 2000

Library of Congress Cataloging-in-Publication Data

Marchand, Roland.
    Creating the corporate soul : the rise of public
relations and corporate imagery in American big
business / Roland Marchand.
        p. cm.
    Includes bibliographical references (p.   ) and
index.
    ISBN 0-520-22688-7 (pbk. : alk. paper)
        1. Corporate image—United States—History.
2. Public relations—Corporations—United States—
History.   3. Big business—United States—History.
4. Advertising—United States—History. I. Title.
HD59.2.M368   1998
659.2′85—DC21   97-50098
                                            CIP

Printed in Hong Kong

09   08   07   06   05   04   03   02   01   00
9   8   7   6   5   4   3   2   1

To Betsy

CONTENTS

8 LITTLE TOWNS AND BIG CORPORATIONS:
THE WARTIME IMAGERY OF A NATION UNITED

ACKNOWLEDGMENTS

After more than a decade of research into the history of corporate public relations, I owe many debts of gratitude. Although it is impossible for me to name all who have assisted me in so many ways, I welcome the opportunity to thank those to whom I am most indebted. The American Council of Learned Societies provided me with a generous fellowship at a crucial stage in my work. Fellowships and research grants from the Humanities Institute of the University of California, Davis, and from the Academic Senate Committee on Research at the University of California, Davis, provided me with time for writing and helped defray the expenses of many archival explorations.

Many colleagues have made an indispensable intellectual contribution with their critical reading of drafts of this study. David Nye of Odense University, Denmark, offered marvelously detailed advice on one version of the entire manuscript. Several readers for the University of California Press helped me recognize strengths and weaknesses in the penultimate drafts. James Baughman, Michele Bogart, David Brody, Daniel Brower, Lizabeth Cohen, Karen Halttunen, Howell Harris, Sheldon Hochheiser, Lawrence Levine, Charles McGovern, Michael L. Smith, and Richard Tedlow all read portions of the manuscript or my related essays and papers and prompted me to consider wider perspectives and alternative interpretations. I also garnered insights from exchanges of ideas and work-in-progress with Heather Allen, James Baughman, William L. Bird, Sally Clarke, Catherine Cocks, David Glassberg, Sally F. Griffith, Daniel Horowitz, Richard John, Austin Kerr, Nikki Mandell, Leon Mayhew, Jeffrey Meikle, Daniel Robinson, Joan Shelley Rubin, David Sicilia, John Staudenmeier, Elizabeth Toon, Margaret Walsh, and Joanne Yates. Marc Richards enabled me to broaden and deepen my research forays into several topics.

Many companies generously granted access to their records and archives. For their time and invaluable assistance, I am indebted to Elizabeth Adkins of Kraft General Foods in Morton Grove, Illinois; Julian E. Aurelius of E. R. Squibb; Larry Eubank of the Sarnoff Corporation in Princeton; Lois Gauch of Eastman Kodak;

Kristin Henson and Cindy Whittaker of Aluminum Company of America; Sheldon Hochheiser and others of AT&T and Western Electric; Warren Hull of the U.S.X. Corporation (formerly United States Steel Corporation) in Pittsburgh; Greg Lennes of the Navistar Company; Daniel May of Metropolitan Life Insurance; Charles Ruch of Westinghouse; and George Wise of the General Electric Research Laboratories. Hubert L. (Bart) Snider not only gave me access to the General Electric Corporate Library and its public relations archive in Fairfield, Connecticut, but also shared his own research into the company's history.

Richard Scharzburg, Bruce W. Watson, and Beth Wickham welcomed me on several visits to the GMI Alumni Collection of Industrial History in Flint, Michigan. I am particularly indebted to Bruce Watson for helping me locate materials in the Charles Kettering collection before it was catalogued and arranging for reproductions. Kim Schroeder of the GM Media Archives in Detroit helped me obtain permissions for illustrations. At General Motors headquarters, Nettie Seabrooks gave me access to the corporate library and the company's historical collection of public relations materials.

Both the Young & Rubicam and BBDO advertising agencies granted me access to historical files, publications, and reports in their company libraries. At N. W. Ayer, Annamarie Sandecki, Brad Lynch, and Howard Davis helped me uncover relevant materials among those historical files that remain in the company's basement (a large collection of Ayer materials resides at the National Museum of American History at the Smithsonian). At the J. Walter Thompson Archives, formerly at the corporate offices in New York and now housed in the John W. Hartman Center for Sales, Advertising, and Marketing History at Duke University, I was first assisted by Cynthia G. Swank and later by Ellen Gartrell and Marion Hirsch. All scholars in this field are indebted to them for their work in developing a model agency archive and their missionary efforts to persuade corporations and advertising agencies to preserve and make available their historical records.

I am grateful for the assistance of archivists at numerous universities and institutes housing the papers of companies or executives, especially to Mary Ann Bamberger at the Century of Progress and Lenox Lohr Papers at the University of Illinois, Chicago; Florence Bartowitz, Barbara Dailey, and Linda McCorkle of the Baker Library of the Harvard Business School; Matt Blessing and Virginia Mattern at the State Historical Society of Wisconsin and the Mass Communications Collection at the University of Wisconsin, Madison; Vanessa Broussard-Simmons, Stacey Flaherty, John Fleckner, and Mimi Minnick at the National Museum of American History; Diane Carothers at the D'Arcy Collection and Maynard Britchford and Arathi Kylasam at the Advertising Council Papers at the University of Illinois, Champaign-Urbana; David Crippen and Cynthia Read-Miller of the Ford Motor Company Papers at the Edison Institute, Dearborn, Michigan; Lynn Ekfeld and Darlene Leonard at the Owen Young Papers at St. Lawrence University; John V. Miller of the B. F. Goodrich Papers at the University of Akron; Prentiss Moore and Melissa Miller-Quinlan at the Norman Bel Geddes Papers at the Harry Ransom Humanities Research Center, University of Texas, Austin; Michael Nash, Marjorie McNinch, and Jon Williams at the Hagley Museum and Library; and Thomas Rosenblum at the Rockefeller Archive Center.

A number of people shared with me their own recollections or their particular knowledge of certain materials. Chaplin Tyler recounted the early planning of fair exhibits for Du Pont, and James Worthy discussed with me his experiences at Sears during a slightly later period. Catherine Heinz provided indispensable help in locating items in the Broadcast Pioneers Library, and Richard Prelinger invited me to review several relevant industrial films from his extensive collection. Homer Sharp familiarized me with the historical artifacts and documents retained by Marshall Field in Chicago.

My family knows only too well how incessantly I have drawn upon them for both intellectual and emotional support. To my daughters, Sue and Jeannie, I have turned again and again with the most momentous and most trivial of queries. Their advice on matters extending from phrasing and argument to choice of illustrations has been critical. Throughout my academic career, my wife, Betsy, as a politician of consummate skills (twenty-four years in elective office), has given me the opportunity to glean insights from vicarious participation in the "real world." More than that, she has favored me with unreserved love and confidence, constant patience, and intellectual stimulation that have sustained me through this prolonged undertaking. This book is dedicated to her.

The line of glittering windows swiftly vanished behind the big tree by the river bridge as the night mail train thundered out of Lambert Hollow. Few townsfolk were awake to note the flashing passage of the dependable Pennsylvania Railroad local. But as it dropped the mail and snagged the outgoing packet, once again it linked this tiny community with the rest of the nation. The opportunity to play this crucial role in the life of small-town America inspired the giant railroad corporation to paraphrase Abraham Lincoln: "The Lord must have loved the little towns. He made so many of them."[1]

Through such sentimental imagery, evoking countless touching instances, in both sacred and secular lore, of powerful figures bestowing tender and beneficent attention upon frail subjects, the Pennsylvania Railroad Corporation suggested a way in which a modern industrial society's great disparities in scale might best be understood. The very size, efficiency, reach, and power of the corporation enabled its local trains to "make the little towns" by carrying to them "life, and news, and interest." In its tributes to the service of its "puffing locals," so "close to the people of America," the company found a satisfying way of bonding itself to small-town America. If Lambert Hollow desperately needed the Pennsylvania Railroad for its ties to the "cities and towns and villages of the world," so too did the public relations departments of giant corporations need the "Lambert Hollows" of America to afford them a gratifying sense of rootedness and legitimacy. And it was all for the better that an actual Lambert Hollow did not exist; nothing could mar the idyll that the Pennsylvania Railroad had created.[2]

This fable of the efficient and benevolent giant, ever attentive to the welfare of the tiniest entity, was simply one of a myriad stories that pervaded corporate publicity during the first half of the twentieth century.[3] Other fables recounted the corporation's discovery of its grand mission amid the humble surroundings of its founder's tiny shop or described the salutary working milieu within which it had nurtured the skill and loyalty of its workers. Some related the corporation's sense of exaltation upon becoming infused with the "service ideal"; others told how its sponsorship had retained during wartime "those educational and cultural activities which have so enriched Americans in all walks of life."[4] All these fables, and a host of others, attributed to the corporation virtues that stood apart from purely business values. Emulating those organizations responsible for the education, health, religious practice, and cultural enrichment of the nation's citizens, the giant business corporation of the early twentieth century aspired to become an institution.

Qualities befitting an institution were demonstrated in services both great and small. Catering to the needs of each Lambert Hollow and each small town's Main Street counted just as fully toward institutional status as did perpetuating the work of the great medical geniuses through a commitment to "serve mankind forever" (the promise of an E. R. Squibb & Company institutional ad). To the large early twentieth-century corporation, becoming an institution meant more than simply acquiring the status of a customary, established entity. It meant rising above mere commercialism and removing the taint of selfishness. As a leading AT&T executive proclaimed in 1916, "We have lofty purposes and we are entitled to have them known." Or as the Goodyear Tire Company put it in 1926, "We like to think of the Goodyear business as something more than a successful commercial enterprise. We like to look upon it, in all its magnitude and variety, as the creation of a grateful public for its own service." From the Ford Motor Company to Metropolitan Life Insurance, the corporate giants savored such self-bestowed characterizations as "serving a nation" and "a national institution."[5]

Such aspirations, as political scientist Neil J. Mitchell has observed, would have been inappropriate had the classic theory about the nature of businesses within a competitive market economy remained persuasive. In that view, no business could rightly be expected to rise above purely self-interested endeavor. None would seek institutional status, because businesses could not exercise discretionary social power. All real power lay in the market, governed by the iron laws of supply and demand; individual corporations, no matter how large, could only respond to its decrees.[6]

But as major corporations expanded at a bewildering pace at the end of the nineteenth century, the notion of corporate powerlessness became untenable. Many companies, through mergers and other forms of vertical integration and horizontal consolidation, so dominated their industries that they now controlled the market as much as they were ruled by it. And they threatened to control much more than that. The pure size of many corporations—their number of employees, the magnitude of their production, their capital resources, their national scope in distribution, and their capacity for political influence—persuaded many Americans, classic economic theory notwithstanding, that the nexus of social institutions within which they lived had been radically transformed. The traditional potency of the family, the church, and the local community suddenly seemed dwarfed by the sway of the giant corporations. This momentous shift in the balance of social forces created a crisis of legitimacy for the large corporations.

At question was not primarily their legal legitimacy. Although antitrust legislation and litigation abounded, the legal form of the corporation had stood unchallenged for decades.[7] Nor was the moral legitimacy of the business corporation as such at issue. Despite intermittent anticapitalist sentiments, hundreds of thousands of nineteenth-century business corporations had enjoyed comfortable moral legitimacy in communities throughout America. Norman Cooley Angell once astutely observed that "as the property principles of capitalism work out in the family farm or the small store, few find them suspect." But with the appearance of "the large capitalist enterprise," he noted, "even the foundation stone of capitalism" came to be "critically examined."[8] The crisis of legitimacy that major American corporations began to face in the 1890s had everything to do with their size, with the startling disparities of scale.

In his portrait of American life in the 1870s, Robert Wiebe characterizes the social nexus as one of "island communities" in which "family and church, education and press, professions and government, all largely found their meaning by the way they fit one with another inside a town or a detached portion of a city." Significantly, this model describes the roles of small businesses and market-oriented farming, not that of the large corporation. In fact, that emerging entity became the focus for antimonopoly sentiment—the ultimate expression of "the desire for community self-determination."[9] It was not the issue of the corporation's legitimacy per se that stirred passionate protest during the late nineteenth and early twentieth centuries in the United States. It was the threat of these huge new entities to the "fit," or nexus of relationships epitomized by those "island communities."

The corporate quest for social and moral legitimacy spurred an array of public relations initiatives. Many of these aimed at immediate political, marketing, and organizational goals. But wider purposes permeated each of the disparate endeavors in image creation and linked them, however unconsciously, with each other. Although the first impulse for a public relations campaign was often a defensive response to actual or anticipated external criticism, even those within the corporations perceived a lack of sufficient legitimacy. Corporate executives, however confident in the rightness of their expansion and their new scale of operations, still acknowledged some remorse for having shattered old relationships, particularly those with their employees. As Mitchell observes, they "needed to make sense of their [new] environment . . . , to know that their work was of social value. . . . They not only needed to prove the legitimacy of their power to others, they also needed to prove it to themselves."[10]

In addition to recognizing the complex motives of those who shaped corporate imagery, we need to consider the complexity of the images themselves. As David Nye observes in *Image Worlds,* the new corporate images of the early twentieth century were rarely single images.[11] The earliest examples already show an awareness of different audiences, displaying a slightly different aspect of the corporate profile to each. Furthermore, the corporation itself cannot be seen as a single entity. The economist Oliver Williamson calls it "a nexus of treaties," but even viewed in more concrete terms, it is an organization subject to internal contests for dominance among various individuals, divisions, and functional elements.[12] The large business corporation often struggled to define its image for itself as much as to present it to the public. Thus, when I speak of what General Motors or U.S. Steel said or thought or did, I do not imply a unified or organic entity but rather refer to the dominant voices within the company at a particular moment or the outcome of internal debates.

In shaping their corporate images, the great business giants of the early twentieth century were not only seeking to legitimize their newly amassed power within the nexus of social institutions, they were also constantly renegotiating their position along a series of increasingly fuzzy boundaries within business itself. The most ominous and ambiguous of these boundaries lay between two broad modes of business practice. The first mode, previously dominant, favored a "stick-to-business" attitude: a serious, "masculine," production-oriented sense of independence, a legacy from earlier decades and smaller businesses. The second, to many disconcerting yet increasingly necessary, employed new, more "feminine," practices, consciously catering to public opinion, adopting show-business techniques of display and publicity, and institutionalizing welfare and public relations programs.

Despite the trepidation of business leaders as they scouted such boundaries, the quest of large corporations for enhanced social and moral legitimacy went forward with an almost evangelical ardor. In the process, the rhetoric of big business reflected the extreme mood shifts, from grave apprehension to sanguine expectancy, that accompanied these transformations in conventional practice. As late as the mid-1920s, the Cassandra-like business journalist Amos Stote lamented that "our great institutions, as institutions," were unknown to a public that gave them nothing but "passing patronage without appreciation, without loyalty."[13] But only two years later the advertising executive Bruce Barton, a true business evangelist, stressed the ultimate possibilities in the transformation of corporate imagery. Although people no longer feared "these large aggregations," they still "only tolerate[d] them," he acknowledged. That they did not "fully understand" the giant corporations, did not "fully trust them," and did not yet "love them," however, was no cause for pessimism. Even public "love" for these great business institutions, Barton ventured, should not lie beyond the realm of corporate aspiration.[14]

Some corporate leaders had already taken up that challenge. In the early 1920s an AT&T public relations executive frankly aspired "to make the people understand and love the company. Not merely be consciously dependent upon it—not merely regard it as a necessity—not merely to take it for granted—but to love it—to hold real affection for it."[15] In our more secular, less naive contemporary world, we see such attempts to augment moral legitimacy as campaigns to gain corporate prestige or a reputation for social responsibility. But in the late nineteenth and early twentieth centuries, both advocates and critics of the giant corporation spoke of similar aspirations as quests for a "corporate soul."

Diverse actions, from launching an employee welfare program to re-creating an intimate neighborliness across long distances through telephone service, could manifest such a "soul." But the Pennsylvania Railroad's godlike regard for the well-being of little Lambert Hollow conveyed a particularly poignant notion, one that persisted over several decades of the early twentieth century as a supremely appropriate display of corporate soul. After all, it was the strong tradition of localism, the awareness of community as expressed geographically in the small town, that the new power of the giant corporations had disrupted.[16] The "web of interests" that had bound earlier businesses into local communities, Kenneth Lipartito has observed, provided those small businesses with moral legitimacy, whereas "the tendency of modern business to sever the connection between the firm and its location" stirred anxious protests against the new corporations.[17]

In the chapters that follow, as we trace the quest for a corporate soul over the first half of the twentieth century, we will encounter a great variety of stratagems and initiatives as one major company after another discovered the need for a more favorable and distinct corporate image and more self-conscious public relations. No two companies faced exactly the same needs and circumstances; each defined its purposes and strategies in different ways. The striking diversity of these many case studies enriches this story of emerging corporate cultures and public relations strategies. Yet engaging as these individual narratives are, it is also intriguing to observe the ways in which they subsequently converged. Halfway into the twentieth century, at the end of World War II, the prevalent association of the great corporation with small-town Main Street once again recapitulated the Lambert Hollow mystique, only in somewhat more modern form. A contrived sentimentalism seemed adequate, even then, to address the disproportions in size and power that the giant corporation still signified.

In what follows, I survey first the array of tactics that some companies had already explored by the onset of the twentieth century, as they came to recognize a need to enhance their social and moral legitimacy. In Chapters 2 through 5 I then examine, through extended case studies of such corporations as AT&T, the Pennsylvania Railroad, General Motors, General Electric, E. R. Squibb, and Metropolitan Life Insurance, the maturation in styles and strategies of corporate image creation through the 1920s. Chapters 6 through 8 focus on the responses of giant corporations to a second major crisis of legitimacy in the 1930s, carrying the story from the Great Depression to the victory by both the nation and those corporations during World War II. Legitimacy, of course, can never be a fixed and permanent condition. But by the mid-1940s, the great corporations had attained a conventional, largely uncontested standing that most corporate leaders could recognize as an acceptable substitute for soul.

CONFESSIONS AND REBUTTALS: THE PLIGHT OF THE SOULLESS CORPORATION

In 1886, in the case of *Santa Clara County v. Southern Pacific Railroad,* the Supreme Court bestowed upon the business corporation, under the Fourteenth Amendment to the Constitution, the legal status of "person." Through subsequent judicial opinions and scholars' treatises, this initially indeterminate notion developed into a concept of the corporation not as a creation of the state (as it had once legally been) but rather as a "natural entity"—"as just another rights-bearing person . . . a *fait accompli,*" in the words of Morton Horowitz. For all the legal legitimacy and "inevitability or . . . naturalness of large-scale concentration of capital" that this doctrine implied, however, the great corporation of the early twentieth century still conspicuously lacked a comparable social and moral legitimacy in the eyes of the public.[1] If the Court had assumed almost godlike powers in conferring "personhood" on the inanimate business corporation, still its juristic finger—unlike that of God in Michelangelo's Sistine ceiling—did not have the authority to bring this commercial entity to life as a moral "person." The big business corporation, as a rising chorus of American voices chanted insistently from the 1890s onward, had no soul.

These denunciations intensified with the great merger movement of 1895–1904, during which some 157 major consolidations brought the eclipse of over 1,800 existing companies.[2] The vulnerability of the new corporate giants to charges of soullessness emerged again and again in the titles of their wounded rebuttals: "The Heart of a 'Soulless Corporation'" (1908), "Corporations and Souls" (1912), *United States Steel: A Corporation with a Soul* (1921), "Puts Flesh and Blood into 'Soulless Corporation'" (1921), "Refuting the Old Idea of the Soulless Corporations" (1926), and "Humanizing a 'Soulless Corporation'" (1937).[3] Although the expression gradually lost currency, business spokesmen confronted its implications well into the 1940s, as it continued to highlight an array of potential frailties in any large corporation's quest for consumer favor and moral legitimacy.

What specific defects might the accusation of "soullessness" imply? Prominent among them was a perceived lack of conscience on the part of the corporation. If some of the great entrepreneurs of the 1870s and 1880s had proved greedy and ruthless in their pursuit of profits, the new corporations of the 1890s and 1900s would have even fewer scruples. After all, one might appeal to the conscience of an individual businessman. But the soulless corporation, driven by a cold economic logic that defined its every decision as a money equation, had none. This charge gained force in the mid-1890s, as the new, popularly priced mass-circulation magazines featured exposés of the harsh competitive practices and corrupt political manipulations of some of the nation's largest corporations. Americans had long taken to heart Lord Acton's warning that "power corrupts." When immense power was coupled with the relentless drive for efficiency and profits that had impelled business expansion, how could moral indifference fail to result?

"Soullessness," however, more often referred to the coldness and aloofness of the giant business corporation, and in that sense it was often ascribed to scale alone. The personal relationships that had depended on face-to-face contact were no longer possible in corporations that operated multiple plants, with tens of thousands of employees. "Mere bigness," Vice President Edward Hall of the American Telephone and Telegraph Company (AT&T) would later reflect, tended "to squeeze out the human understanding, the human sympathy, the human contacts, and the natural human relationships."[4] In 1923 General Motors, although eager to have its employees "look upon our organization as a human rather than a corporate institution," had to recognize that "it is one of the limitations of a large organization that the men charged with guiding its destiny cannot maintain a direct personal contact with all of its employees."[5]

Familiar images of massive factories contributed to popular perceptions of the corporation's soullessness. Workers seemed mere cogs in immense machines, oblivious to any connection between their narrow, repetitive tasks and the company's larger operations. Distant from the guiding minds and purposes of the corporation, how could they recognize it as other than a soulless thing? Similar effects of scale might also shape the customer's view of the corporation, an advertising executive later reflected. As the manufacturer lost all direct contact with his customers, "by degrees he ceased to think of them as people, but merely as so many units of consumption, a set of impersonal figures on a chart." Gone were the days when "the maker of goods dealt personally . . . with the customer and was known and understood by him, as man to man." As Vice President Hall of AT&T lamented in a 1909 address, "The public does not know us. . . . It has never seen us, never met us, does not know where we live, who we are, what our good qualities are. It simply knows that we are a corporation, and to the general public a corporation is a thing."[6]

The fear of being perceived as only "a thing" suggests another aspect of corporate soullessness: the failure to project a distinct personality. The problem lay not only in size but also in abstractness. Of course, companies still governed by a dynamic founder, or still dominated by his aura, carried the distinctive imprint of his individual personality into their relations with the public. But others might seem unfamiliar and remote—just another of the faceless trusts whose executives and financiers worked behind the scenes. Reports of an apparent dwindling of employee morale, sometimes voiced by corporate leaders themselves, revealed a lack of internal vitality within these large-scale operations, an absence of a recognized, animating purpose.

Nearer, My God To Thee

FIGURE 1.1
In 1880 the Trinity Church steeple still topped the lower Manhattan skyline. By 1913 it was completely dwarfed by skyscrapers twice its height. Art Young's 1913 cartoon, "Nearer, My God to Thee," dramatized the perception that this change signaled a transposition in social values.

Beyond their amoral conduct, impersonal size, and lack of a humanizing personality, the intense secrecy and zealous autonomy of many of the largest corporations seemed actually to invite charges of soullessness. J. P. Morgan broke his habitual silence only to comment that "I owe the public nothing," and John D. Rockefeller complacently adopted the maxim "silence is golden" as his response to unwanted public inquiries. Glaring instances of the refusal of corporate leaders to acknowledge any responsibility for public welfare, as in William Vanderbilt's famous "the public be damned" remark, further contributed to the soulless image.[7]

Above all, the notion of soullessness reflected the giant corporations' incomplete social legitimacy.[8] Even into the early twentieth century, public suspicions went beyond narrow moral reproaches or uneasiness with the impersonalities of scale. A more general concern was the appropriate standing of large corporations within the nexus of major institutions in society. How were Americans to understand the relationship of these commercial leviathans to the family, the church, the local community, and the nation itself? A giant corporation might exercise control over the activities and opportunities of an individual family through employment or welfare programs. Its assets, influence, and geographic reach might surpass those of one of the states and even challenge those of the entire nation. As for the church—the institution most distinctly associated with the word "soul"—what citizen could ponder, without unease, the numerous sketches, photographs, and cartoons that depicted skyscrapers towering, both literally and symbolically, over the highest of steeples (Fig. 1.1)?

These traditional institutions each represented some loftier principle, some moral claim to loyalty and sacrifice—some element of soul. Yet all of them seemed to have lost standing beside the giant business enterprises. As Mansel Blackford has observed, the emergence of big business—unlike that of the smaller corporations—"was so sudden and so disruptive of traditional ways of work and life" that the new imbalance among social institutions filled many Americans with dismay. In particular, in the wake of the corporate mergers of 1895–1904, the United States found itself, in Naomi Lamoreaux's phrase, "transformed overnight from a nation of freely competing, individually owned enterprises into a nation dominated by a small number of giant corporations."[9] The fundamental amorality of market relationships was magnified by this glaring disproportion in the institutional nexus, as corporations controlled resources and sometimes even necessities.

In short, the phrase "soulless corporation" quickly amassed a multitude of meanings. While some of these could be differentiated in the ways I have suggested, in practice the epithet often gained force through its capacity to evoke a variety of overlapping impressions. The corporate response took on even more diverse configurations. For instance, a corporation worried about an image of moral irresponsibility might initiate and publicize benefit programs for its employees, associate itself with some current moral or patriotic crusade, or seek to characterize its operations as public service. One dismayed by its apparent lack of personality might erect an impressive new corporate headquarters, disseminate a "humanized" image of its chief executive, affix a striking logo to all its products, or link its identity with its research laboratories.

Whether a corporation responded through a merchandising mode, an employee relations initiative, or a public relations campaign, each tactic could be bent to multiple purposes. Thus AT&T would eventually discover effective merchandising and employee relations benefits in its public relations campaign against government ownership; the Metropolitan Life Insurance Company would instruct its agents to use its altruistic public service advertisements to solicit new business; and General Electric would promote new products and foster internal morale by implanting in the public consciousness the image of its research laboratories as a "house of magic" in the service of social progress.

These varied responses accumulated fitfully over the first half of the twentieth century, as one corporation after another recognized the need to devote resources to the systematic construction of a corporate image. In the aggregate their responses constitute the "creation story" of corporate imagery that I wish to tell. After exploring strategies that had emerged by the first decade of the twentieth century, I will turn to major case studies that reveal their subsequent evolution. From these individual corporate sagas, and the larger visual and rhetorical patterns they helped to shape, we can gain insights into the social, economic, and cultural consequences of the myriad quests to create a corporate soul.

The Giant Retailers: Conspicuous Pioneers, Dubious Models

At the end of the nineteenth century the creation of a corporate image was hardly a new enterprise. The display of corporate images by organizations of commerce goes back to classical antiquity, as evocative, logolike mosaics still intact in the Foro delle Corporazioni in Ostia, the seaport of ancient Rome, attest. Nor was the endeavor simply a response to perceptions of soullessness. During the last three decades of the nineteenth century the great urban department stores successfully cultivated distinctive identities and favorable images. Despite the laments of shopkeepers in nearby communities and acrimonious charges of unfair competition by smaller and more specialized urban retailers, the department stores had rarely been seen as soulless. Attempts to legislate limits to their operations persisted into the 1890s but were readily overcome.[10] In fact, the public quickly came to treat the most successful department stores as civic assets. In 1868, as John Tebbel has noted, the grand opening of Marshall Field's "dazzling edifice" attracted "the largest audience ever seen in Chicago." Chicagoans, John Dennis Jr. remarked in 1906, regarded the store "an institution to which they take visitors and of which they boast as does Boston of its culture."[11]

These magnificent urban emporiums enjoyed distinct advantages in evading imputations of soullessness. Although many of them loomed large in the consciousness of specific cities, few ranked among the largest corporations in assets or national power and influence. Few had grown through mergers; none exerted monopoly power, although several clearly held a dominant position in local retailing over significant periods. John Wanamaker took care to distinguish his business from the emerging trusts. His early Depot store, which "once was thought so big," was, he pointed out, "but a shoestring" in relation to a Standard Oil plant. Moreover, his store was "not the creature of capitalists, or the result of monopoly." Its "iron purpose" was "to be worthy of the City, and useful to its citizens."[12] Above all, thanks to their direct daily contact with consumers, the grand retailers such as Wanamaker, Field, and Rowland Macy could convey—through architecture, furnishings, style of merchandise, and customer policies—a distinctive presence and manner. No one faulted the leading department stores for a soulless lack of personality.

The high-profile presence of an irrepressible proprietor could further enhance this personality. In Philadelphia, Wanamaker never strayed far from center stage, either in his store or in the city. According to the pioneer public relations man Ivy Lee, Wanamaker "made it his policy to wander about the store and perform himself little services for customers." Such actions, Lee observed, "served to personify an organization which might otherwise have been looked upon merely as a corporation." An early proselytizer for the YMCA, Wanamaker believed that religion and business should work "hand in hand in the service of humanity." Every Sunday, at the huge Bethany Mission School building that he had helped finance, Wanamaker provided another highly visible service to Philadelphians by leading four thousand people in Bible lessons, calling these assemblies the world's largest Sunday school. He made his store the venue for choral and orchestra concerts as well and declared it one of the nation's foremost art galleries. He furthermore claimed to teach history through exhibitions on Napoleon, on great rulers and great beauties of the past, and on the French Revolution—displays that made the store appear au courant with Paris fashions and the tastes of European aristocracy. Wanamaker also wrote and signed much of his own advertising and delivered public speeches on every possible occasion.[13]

Field, by contrast, avoided the public eye and largely spurned civic service. Yet despite his personal reticence, according to biographer John Tebbel, "the store and its workers were fashioned in the image of Marshall Field, and his spirit dominated the place." Field's "sheer presence" during daily scrutinizing circuits of his store and his careful attention to the deportment of the sales force imbued the operation with his own "unobtrusive, polite presence which charmed the ladies and made the store run like a fine watch." This air of luxury blended with dignity, observed John Dennis Jr. in *Everybody's Magazine,* afforded even the Marshall Field clerks an enhanced status as "aristocrats of their trade."[14]

Department store magnates shaped conspicuous identities for their businesses in dozens of ways, from featuring the founder's signature on merchandise labels to appropriating the hallowed aura of stained glass (in Field's Tiffany Dome, Fig. 1.2). Often their strategies linked distinctiveness with an image of public service or cultural uplift. Field promised visitors to a 1907 "public reception" that the displays in the windows of his new store would be of "unusual educational and artistic in-

FIGURE 1.3

John Wanamaker claimed to instruct customers in artistic and cultural styles through the varied designs of lavish courts and display rooms in his Philadelphia department store. The "lesson" here was in the baroque.

terest." The immense clocks that he erected at two corners of his block-long store served as landmarks and meeting places for Chicago pedestrians, identifying the store as a provider of useful information to the public.[15]

In Philadelphia, Wanamaker also erected a clock tower outside his store. Inside, the ornate Grand Court, the exotic Egyptian Hall, and the stately Greek Hall not only lent a refined air to the merchandise, but they also provided the setting for uplifting art exhibits and concerts. To visit the Byzantine Chamber, the Empire Salon, and the Art Nouveau Room was to be schooled in artistic and cultural styles, Wanamaker declared (Fig. 1.3). Was education in art not served, he asked, simply by entering his store? Were not the thousands who passed "daily through the great portals supported by . . . lofty Corinthian pillars" inspired with "a larger appreciation of the fitness and nobleness and sincerity of true art"?[16]

In one sphere, however, the department stores found themselves on the defensive. Beginning in the 1890s and continuing for the next two decades, a host of social reformers and government investigators published unflattering accounts of the debilitating working conditions and the low pay of department store employees. In response to, or occasionally in anticipation of, such charges and out of concern for both employee loyalty and public image, department stores became some of the first large businesses to experiment with corporate welfare programs. Already in 1882 Wanamaker had set up a benefits association for death and sickness; he proceeded to establish a hotel for women employees in 1887, a borrowing library and a commercial school for employees in 1896, a "seashore camp" for store boys in 1900, and a women's league "for study and mutual improvement" in 1902.[17] Filene & Company in Boston was among the first corporations to foster employee representation associations. Well before 1910 many other leading department stores, including Marshall Field, Siegel Cooper, and Macy's, had developed welfare benefits ranging from free or low-cost medical care and "gratuity lunches" to country vacations and Thanksgiving turkeys.[18]

Despite these efforts, the department stores never served as effective models for other corporations seeking to respond to the charge of soullessness. As we have seen, their physical circumstances made their quest for a personal identity and an image of service too easy. Unlike Field or Wanamaker, the producers of steel, machinery, chemicals, or electrical equipment could not develop "intimate" daily contact with a mass public. But the differences were philosophical as well. The indefinite borders of the corporation were a persistent, if not fully conscious, concern. Gender stereotypes, aspirations to an image of independence, and the work ethic demarcated the corporate identity. A "good businessman," by the accepted standards of peer judgment in the late nineteenth and early twentieth centuries, was serious, rational, self-controlled, manly, and direct. He was not swayed by passing fancies or emotional impulses. His self-image was that of an efficient producer, a devotee of economic independence, hard work, steadiness, and frugality. He had little time for diversions or public posturing, since his vocation, and therewith his service to society, called for tending "strictly to business."

The department store entrepreneur, on the other hand, was not a producer, and the lavishness of his store displays suggested a contempt for austerity. The exhibitions and events through which he cultivated a personality for his store were often reminiscent of the promotions of P. T. Barnum; they seemed more like show business than "serious business." Worse still, the mass retailers had to pander to a fickle public, to adopt a dependent, almost servile attitude toward customers who were "always right." And those customers, more to the mass retailer's humiliation, were overwhelmingly women. Thus, by the standards of manliness, autonomy, and austerity, the department store executive was a dubious model, even if he had found ways to give his large business an identity and a soul.

Some department store entrepreneurs did assiduously patrol these cultural boundaries and guard their reputations as serious and virile businessmen. Macy "worked indefatigably" and established a reputation as a hard-bitten economizer. Field, in his personal comportment, maintained a penchant for austerity, a contempt for frivolity, and a "steely cold" disdain for any decision not based on fundamental business principles. No work ethic–minded businessman could fault him.[19] And the executives of the bigger department stores largely displaced the "feminine" subservience of catering to the whims of customers onto their increasingly female staff of clerks.[20] But the boundary-threatening taint of a role that involved submitting to fashion and acquiescing to popular demands for titillation still made department stores unacceptable models for corporate behavior. Skirmishes along this gendered boundary, complete with spirited defenses and attempts to take the high ground, would continue to characterize business attitudes toward public relations for the next half century.

Buying Soul through Welfare Capitalism

One way for a large corporation to prove it possessed human feeling was to demonstrate compassionate concern for its employees. A paternalistic display of kindness might so alter public and employee perceptions that the abstract corporation would seem more like a big family. As Charles Dellheim has demonstrated for the Quaker-directed chocolate firm Cadburys in Britain and Michael B. Miller for the Paris department store Bon Marché, gemeinschaft values or a family feeling could effectively be cultivated as more than mere rhetorical veneer. This was particularly the case when welfare programs were accompanied by other familial modes and by an intention to create a distinctive corporate culture.[21]

Personal interactions, gifts, and other social rituals induced workers at Cadburys to idealize their employers, "Mr. George" and "Mr. Richard," as "kind fathers, supportive friends, or generous benefactors." At Bon Marché the *grande famille* image through which Aristide and Marguerite Boucicaut smoothed the passage toward a rationalized bureaucracy drew strength from their "deeply felt ties and responsibilities," as well as from "the need for integration and control." Moreover, because the paternalistic image of the Bon Marché as an enlarged household "went to the heart of public uneasiness over the passing of traditions and of community values," Miller observes, its welfare beneficence offered the perfect publicity to legitimize not only the store's transition but also the emerging bureaucratic corporation in general.[22]

Certainly many American firms looked to these foreign examples of "company spirit" (as it was commonly termed during the early twentieth century) and model community. Like Cadburys and the Bon Marché, they publicized their welfare programs as a safeguard against perceptions of soullessness. But they also had to confront the apparent failure of George Pullman's highly publicized model factory community, the image of which had been severely damaged during the 1894 railway strike.[23] Moreover, here too loomed a "boundary problem." To carry welfare programs to the point of philanthropy, or even to accept the notion that paternalistic practices might give their employee-children the right to make claims on their benevolence, violated the precepts of good business practice. A man who seriously attended to his business could not confuse the sphere of business with that of philanthropy or allow sentiment to interfere with rational business decisions.

The majority of corporate welfare programs in the United States originated to address concrete and immediate needs. Mills and mines were often established far from existing communities. Extractive industries required proximity to resources, but even such urban manufacturers as the McCormick Reaper Company in Chicago found it advantageous, when it rebuilt and enlarged its factory after the great fire of 1871, to locate on cheaper land that was not easily reached from the city center. From the outset, then, a number of companies found themselves in the business of providing convenient housing or inexpensive transportation for some or all of their employees. In the many company towns a variety of ancillary services for employees had emerged. By the beginning of the twentieth century, companies began to factor their corporate image into such necessary provisions for amassing a satisfactory labor force. Thus, when Tennessee Coal and Iron, a subsidiary of the image-conscious United States Steel Corporation, sought to combat union organization and reduce turnover at its mining sites in 1908, it experimented with welfare programs designed for an amalgam of labor control and image purposes.[24]

A prime example of such a course of development, fully within the context of the extractive industry's convention of company towns, was the welfare work of the Colorado Fuel and Iron Company (CF&I). These activities, begun in the late nineteenth century, would later generate highly favorable publicity for the Rockefeller family. Under John Osgood, the manager before the Rockefeller interests obtained full control in 1903, CF&I had provided nursing services and, in 1882, a central hospital for its geographically scattered employees. Employees were assessed a monthly fee to cover such services. In the 1890s the company added other, more paternalistic, benefits: kindergartens in many of the company's towns and occasional reading rooms and musical and recreational groups. In 1901 CF&I enjoined the chief surgeon of the hospital to manage a corporate "sociological department." A recent strike had called public attention to CF&I labor policies, and a subsequent state investigation had severely criticized them. The firm's new welfare initiatives, a sympathetic historian of the company observes, may have aimed to "reestablish . . . harmonious relations with employees" and "improve the corporation's public image."[25]

Through articles with such cavalier titles as "How Young Rockefeller Is Making American Citizens by Trust Methods," the company began to gain wider publicity in 1904 and 1905 for its efforts to concoct a soul through welfare. Meanwhile, it had launched an employee magazine to "help develop a strong esprit de corps among employees." By 1904 its "sociological" work encompassed a normal school for its teachers and a clubhouse for employees in its model community of Redstone. The houses built for kindergarten teachers at its various towns and camps had evolved into local headquarters for social work and medical outreach, as well as model cottages in which workers' wives were taught to be frugal housekeepers and skillful cooks. (These cooking schools, according to the *Chicago Tribune,* were the brainchild of "the wise men of the Colorado Fuel and Iron Company's Sociological Department," who reasoned that the best way to combat drunkenness was to recognize that "to a hungry man the attractiveness of home begins at the table.")[26] So comprehensive were its medical and social services, the company boasted, that it stood third in the world—exceeded only by the Bon Marché in Paris and the House of Krupp in Essen, Germany—in the scope and proficiency of its welfare work.[27]

CF&I anticipated a payoff more significant than mere publicity or image enhancement. Through its welfare policies it sought to secure a more permanent, contented, and efficient workforce.[28] Whatever its temporary gains in that respect, however, the company did not achieve sufficient long-range harmony in labor relations to avoid one of the bloodiest labor conflicts in American history: the infamous Ludlow massacre of 1914, in which militia attacked and killed men, women, and children in a camp occupied by striking workers. Critics would later wonder whether it was CF&I's neglect of welfare programs after 1905, the inherent ineffectiveness of all such efforts in insuring employee loyalty, or the antilabor arrogance of its management that brought this destruction of the earlier CF&I public image.[29]

Another problematic aspect of such welfare practices emerged in concerns about the deleterious effects of too generous and "philanthropic" a program. CF&I, like many another company, took satisfaction in the praise it received for requiring its employees to pay for each benefit they received. The company exacted fees for medical care and club participation; it netted 16 percent on its investment in rental homes in its camps. A plant manager at International Harvester in 1905, worried that his own company was "tending . . . toward too much paternalism," commended the head of the CF&I Sociological Department for stating forthrightly that "the company treats this whole matter simply as a matter of business and do not pay for anything for which they do not receive full benefit."[30] Yet if such a stance preserved the manly and businesslike boundary between philanthropy and "matters of business," it might also diminish the capacity of company welfare programs to prove the existence of a corporate soul.

"A Sermon in Steel and Glass": Welfare at the National Cash Register Factory

Far more energetic and successful than CF&I in gaining favorable public recognition for its welfare programs was the National Cash Register Company (NCR) of Dayton, Ohio. Even before the turn of the century the showmanship of NCR president John H. Patterson had won this company of modest size an international reputation as a pioneer in corporate welfare. No company was more inventive in devising new employee amenities nor more lavish, albeit erratic, in dispensing them. Yet Patterson seemed to reject any credit as a philanthropist. To assure his workers that they were not being patronized, he posted terse signs proclaiming "It Pays" throughout the NCR shops and offices.[31]

Even so, a hardheaded businessman might observe (and several did) that Patterson did not rely on cost accounting to assess the returns from this largesse. Rather, he looked to such intangibles as employee loyalty and morale. In 1899, at the height of his early welfare undertakings, Patterson pontificated to his employees that "while it is the duty of the company to show to its people that it is not a corporation without a soul, so it is fair for the people to show . . . that they too have a soul, a spirit which responds to considerate treatment."[32]

If Patterson was quick to deny any penchant for unbusinesslike philanthropy, he and his welfare directors were equally prompt to insist that none of the NCR welfare programs had been initiated for advertising and public relations purposes. This may well have been true, since motivations such as the desire to reduce labor turnover and to thwart unionization spurred most corporate ventures in welfare capitalism. Yet once having invested in welfare programs, employers like Patterson often came to relish the enhanced public image, for both their companies and themselves, that these policies could bring. Through energetic and flamboyant public-

FIGURES 1.4 & 1.5
The National Cash Register
Company boasted such welfare
amenities as cooking and sewing
classes and calisthenics during
morning and afternoon recesses.
President Patterson even invited
employees to a "factory cotillion"
on the wooded grounds of his estate.

ity of his welfare measures, Patterson soon defined the NCR, both in the United
States and abroad, as a pioneer in benefit programs. "Welfare work is the heart of
this business," asserted the slogan on an NCR pamphlet entitled *The Human Side
of Industry*.[33]

Using recently improved equipment for projecting slides, Patterson and one of
his sales managers created a "factory lecture." When they took it on tour in Great
Britain in 1905, showings before large audiences won the company accolades as
"the home of 'welfare work.'" On his return to Dayton, Patterson proclaimed that
the presentations had transformed attitudes toward welfare work from "the cold-
house of indifference to the hot-house of enthusiasm."[34] Earlier tours had already
cultivated a welfare-pioneer corporate image for the NCR within the United
States. Jane Addams and Jacob Riis applauded the NCR programs; the National
Civic Federation publicized them as a model for other enlightened corporations.
The journalist Frank Crane would later glorify the NCR factory in florid prose as
"a sermon in steel and glass," a "Temple of Work" in which machinery rather than
an organ provided the music and the choir "was the glad laughter of happy workers."[35] As early as 1900 the NCR at Dayton had become the mecca of potential converts to employee welfare work. In 1901 and 1902, when the McCormick Reaper
Company began to consider its own major welfare program, it sent social worker
Gertrude Beeks on several national tours to survey the salient models. Her reports
devoted twice as much attention to the NCR as to any other company. Moreover,

those managers whom she interviewed at other companies frequently commented on the NCR programs or compared their own work to that at Dayton.[36]

The NCR's welfare practices, most of which were instituted between 1893 and 1905, included such typical amenities as a women's lunchroom, industrial and domestic education programs, factory beautification (both external and internal), health and recreation programs, and an employee suggestion box with prizes (Fig. 1.4). Among the more imaginative initiatives were a gardening program for neighborhood boys, noon entertainments for the workers, and a neighborhood beautification program, with prizes for the best-landscaped homes in the surrounding community. Twice annually the "happy family" of the NCR, including "representatives of every class of labor," gathered in a wooded area of President Patterson's estate for a "supper . . . served to thousands on the greensward" and the distribution of prizes. Patterson made the grounds around his home available to employees for picnics and recreation and, in 1905, hosted an evening cotillion for factory workers on his estate. The "white-gowned girls in their hats and scarfs of rainbow tints," according to one Dayton newspaper, made the scene seem "more like a French or English garden party than a dance by American factory employees" (Fig. 1.5).[37]

If anything united these diverse endeavors, it was the irrepressible, even manic, personality of the company's founder, John H. Patterson. One observer described him as "a little man with a dynamo inside"; the popular writer Paul de Kruif christened him "the cash-register Napoleon." The authors of a detailed, adulatory account of Patterson's contributions to salesmanship depicted him as "an authentic genius" who "probably loved arbitrary power too well."[38] Others, who lionized him as an innovator in sales techniques and a master in the inculcation of a strong corporate culture, could not keep from describing him as a man of vagaries and obsessions, using such words as "tyrannical," "autocratic," "temperamental," "arbitrary," "capricious," and "a mass of contradictions" to characterize Patterson's managerial style.[39]

With ardent enthusiasms and utter assurance in his own judgments, Patterson sporadically subjected his employees to such regimens as required horseback riding at dawn for all executives, salt-free and fat-free diets for all employees, and a "forty-chews-to-the-mouthful" drill for all who ate in his presence.[40] He was famed for arbitrary firings and equally impulsive favors. Lena Harvey, a nondenominational deaconess and settlement-house worker who became the NCR's first welfare secretary in 1897, described Patterson in Svengali-like terms as she recounted how he had enlisted her with a mesmerizing onslaught of fervor and flattery.[41]

Having entered the inauspicious and totally undeveloped cash register business almost by chance in the 1880s, Patterson succeeded by dint of intense sales efforts and zealous attention to the business. His dramatic and unpredictable actions generated the kinds of company legends often associated with a strong corporate culture. Foremost among these was an incident in which $50,000 worth of defective cash registers were returned to the factory in 1894, the result of either poor workmanship or sabotage. Patterson, according to the oft-repeated tale, immediately moved his office desk into the midst of the factory floor, so he could find out what was going wrong. His awakening to the deplorable working conditions there—the filth, the cold, the inadequate lighting, the uncomfortable stools, the absence of decent washing facilities for the men or lunch facilities for the women—led to a "clean-up that was to have not only factory-wide but nation- and world-wide results." By the time Welfare Secretary Lena Harvey heard this tale, in 1897, it had grown beyond this single incident to represent what Patterson "sometimes" does, as if the founder regularly shared the workers' conditions to glean insights in managing his company.[42]

Another recurrent story recalled how Patterson and Harvey had discovered how to divert "bad boys" in the factory neighborhood from window-breaking and other "hoodlumism" by developing a program of "boys' gardens," in which the NCR provided the land, seed, tools, and instruction. Such narratives contributed to the conclusion of recent analysts of corporate culture that "NCR was never just a factory; rather [it was] a living organization. The company's real existence lay in the hearts and minds of its employees . . . a cohesion of values, myths, heroes and symbols."[43]

As he fought his way to success, Patterson persuaded himself that the promotion of the cash register—one of whose main functions, in early years, was to prevent theft by employees—was an all-important moral crusade. He brought the same "almost fanatical" sincerity, along with the promotional flair of a "great egoist," to the publicity of his initiatives in factory welfare. At one point he invited the trustees and entire faculty of the University of Chicago to travel to Dayton as his guests to tour the NCR factory and learn in person why "welfare work is the germ of the solution of labor problems." Two later celebrators of Patterson's genius in sales promotion upheld company legends by insisting that none of his welfare programs "was created or maintained for the sake of publicity," yet they also admired how "virtually everything that the company did, particularly in the line of factory welfare work, was capitalized and exploited" by the NCR's "highly efficient press bureau." Patterson himself observed privately to Gertrude Beeks that "[some] people say we do it for advertising. We do not do it for that purpose although it has advertised us."[44]

For all the public recognition that Patterson generated from his welfare programs, he still occasionally revealed some ambivalence. In 1901, in the wake of a major strike and lockout, managers of other companies speculated that he had cut back on "frills" or "entirely abandoned" the welfare programs.[45] A few months later a welfare worker at the NCR told Gertrude Beeks that one employee, at the time of the strike, had bluntly informed Patterson that the workers "did not care a damn for flowers, grass, etc." and "would rather have the money for such amenities divided up among them" in increased wages. Other workers were said to distrust the welfare activities as "simply . . . an advertisement." Although Patterson soon resumed welfare work at the NCR, his vacillations reflected a concern that perhaps he had been too altruistic, once again raising the issue of the dangers of philanthropy in business. Had employees become resentful at being patronized or "bought off" by inconsequential amenities? Had Patterson's "prodigal, and even reckless" spending confirmed warnings about the pitfalls of engaging, as Patterson's brother complained, in unbusinesslike practices that were "too expensive and not needed"?[46]

As an avowed model for the creation of a corporate soul through welfare capitalism, the NCR design could not easily be separated from Patterson's idiosyncrasies. Henry Dennison, himself noted for welfare and employee relations programs at the Dennison Manufacturing Company, recalled that although the NCR's employee suggestion program and "intelligently selfish attitudes" had impressed him on his visit there, he could not help recoiling at "much that struck me as conceited paternalism and insincerity."[47] Such subsequently prominent business figures as Thomas Watson of IBM and Charles Kettering of General Motors Research Laboratories derived ideas and methods from their service under Patterson at the NCR that they later employed to infuse a cohesive corporate culture into their organizations.[48] But they, like many other talented young businessmen, had not remained long under Patterson's arbitrary reign. They might well have wondered—along with others—whether so authoritarian a beneficence was the answer to the image problem that increasingly beset American corporations. While no one described the NCR as soulless, still its welfare policies were too entangled with Patterson's imperious style and too suggestive of unbusinesslike indulgence in personal whims to offer a persuasive formula for the creation of a corporate soul.

Manufacturing a Good Trust

Far more plausible prototypes were such corporate giants as United States Steel and International Harvester. Here the welfare programs were more expressly calculated to counter the most politically menacing of the charges of corporate soullessness—those flung by antimonopolists at the emerging trusts. From the moment of its creation in 1901 as the nation's first billion-dollar corporation, the United States Steel Company had recognized its political need to develop a favorable public image. Under Elbert Gary it avoided aggressive competition with smaller firms, explicitly departed from the older corporate mode of secrecy and silence, and expanded and publicized its welfare activities. International Harvester—also, like U.S. Steel, the product of a J. P. Morgan–devised merger—faced even greater popular suspicion.[49] As striking embodiments of soullessness, in both their depersonalizing size and their monopolistic power, the Steel and Harvester trusts were likely proving grounds for the efficacy of welfare programs in the infusion of soul.

The exigencies of their situation as large employers of labor at remote mining sites as well as in major manufacturing communities such as Homestead, Pennsylvania, had already involved the Carnegie Steel Company and other component companies of the new steel trust in a variety of welfare activities. These included employee housing initiatives, visiting nurses, courses in "practical housekeeping" for employees' wives, and even a "day nursery" for child care. The new, publicly suspect United States Steel colossus multiplied such efforts until, by the second decade of the century, it was approaching expenditures of $10 million per year on welfare programs.[50] Instrumental in this bid to enhance the company image through welfare and labor relations initiatives was George W. Perkins. A leading insurance company executive and, after 1910, a prominent figure in Progressive Party politics, Perkins served as the representative of J. P. Morgan & Company on the board of directors of United States Steel.

It was Perkins's resolute strategy to prove United States Steel a "good trust" in the eyes of President Theodore Roosevelt and subsequent administrations. After a brief period of "internal friction" within the new corporation, Elbert Gary, who shared Perkins's views, emerged in 1903 as chairman of the board. Meanwhile, Perkins had kept Roosevelt informed of his "fight for publicity" within the company.[51] By the beginning of 1903, as a result of his successful campaign to persuade the corporation to announce an employee stock-sharing plan, Perkins was reaping accolades from United States Steel stockholders and his business peers for his farsighted program "to disarm the prejudice against the trusts." Correspondents praised Perkins and United States Steel for this step toward "the peopleizing of the great corporations" to protect against adverse legislation. Such welfare initiatives, another correspondent added, would contribute to "the public belief that the Steel Corporation is one of the good trusts."[52]

Perkins was also the prime mover behind International Harvester's similar campaign to prove itself a good trust through welfare capitalism.[53] As the J. P. Morgan deputy who had contrived this ticklish corporate merger in 1902, Perkins was well aware of the political vulnerability of a trust that controlled the manufacture of 85 percent of the nation's harvesting machinery. Members of the McCormick family, owners of one of the major firms in the merger, worried that making the trust a public company, thus expanding stock holdings beyond the various family groups involved in the merger, would expose the new combination to attacks for overcapitalization. They also feared that farmers, "as a rule still quite hostile to the idea of a trust," would generate injurious legislation. But Perkins dismissed their fears as "unnecessary alarm." By following the model of United States Steel, which now counted many "farmers and especially women" as sympathetic stockholders in the corporation, and at the same time demonstrating the magnanimity of the Harvester Corporation through stock-sharing plans and other welfare programs, the trust could gain public approval. It would come to seem, in the historian John Garraty's characterization of Perkins's reasoning, "almost . . . a publicly owned business."[54]

Although welfare programs multiplied at International Harvester after 1902, their genesis predated Perkins's quest for a "good trust" image. The original stimulus, as Stuart Brandes has discerned for many of the early corporate welfare initiatives, was the paternal sensibility awakened in management as large numbers of women were employed.[55] At International Harvester this impetus was strikingly evident. In 1901 the McCormick Reaper Company in Chicago—soon to be incorporated into the Harvester Trust—opened its first twine mill, hiring four hundred women as the operatives. Up to this time, Robert Ozanne observes, the McCormicks—with a factory workforce of nearly five thousand men—had introduced none of the new welfare and employee relations ventures that were being tried elsewhere. But the new circumstances created by the "girls" at the twine mill made all the difference.[56]

At the urging of Nettie McCormick, the widow of founder Cyrus McCormick, the company immediately engaged Gertrude Beeks, previously a settlement-house worker and reform advocate in the Civic Federation of Chicago, to act as "social secretary." Her assignment was to guard the health and moral reputations of the twine mill workers. But, as Ozanne notes, also at stake were "the McCormick clan members' Presbyterian consciences and the proud McCormick name, known for substantial gifts to religious education as well as for the reaper."[57]

Beeks gathered ideas through extensive tours of other corporations known for welfare programs. She immediately built a reputation for ingenuity by introducing mirrors in the women's dressing room at the twine mill to boost their morale. She also moved briskly to have fresh drinking water piped into the factory, to reduce the lint in the air, and to provide towels and hot water in the women's dressing room. She arranged for noon entertainments and a summer outing and even helped workers stage an operetta. Beeks insisted, somewhat to the company's discomfiture, that high wages were an indispensable part of any successful welfare program. Her frustration in this sphere, along with the resistance of the plant superintendents as she extended her work to the fifteen thousand male workers, led Beeks to resign at the end of 1902.[58]

International Harvester nonetheless pressed forward in cultivating a corporate image through welfare work. On the board of directors, Perkins energetically presented a pension plan (1908) and a profit-sharing plan (1909). S. M. Darling, another in the rapidly shifting corps of "social secretaries" for International Harvester, continued to look frequently to the NCR as a model. He proposed an ambitious and wide-ranging program of recreation and welfare work and reported enthusiastically on the effectiveness of employee athletic associations in "promoting a feeling of unity and identity with the corporation."[59] Meanwhile Stanley McCormick, the youngest of the founder's three sons, convinced the family in

1903 to initiate stock sharing with a gift of stock to employees. He then proceeded, after consulting with the social worker Henry Bruere, to launch a men's club for the workers at the McCormick works.[60]

Despite the corporation's conventional denials that it sought publicity for its welfare efforts, International Harvester gained considerable press attention for some of its programs. An internal report in 1904 observed that "the advertising the Company will get will be very great after having put in operation the profit sharing plan with factory employees." At fairs and expositions the company presented lectures and exhibits on its welfare work. Bruce Barton would later praise Stanley McCormick's clubhouse as "the only place of gathering in the neighborhood which is not connected with a saloon," and *Harper's Weekly* would feature it in an article subtitled "The Heart of a 'Soulless Corporation.'" Barton also praised the corporation's entire welfare department for having become "the heart" of the organization, "pumping good will and sympathy to all the members."[61]

Did the plethora of welfare programs at International Harvester thus prove successful in promoting a favorable public image? The question would be difficult enough to answer even if image-polishing had been the exclusive motive behind Harvester's efforts. But, like many other corporations, International Harvester looked to an immediate payoff from welfare programs in preventing strikes and thwarting unionization.[62] Early press coverage of Gertrude Beeks's activities measured her success by the company's "freedom from labor disturbances." The *Chicago Evening Post* reported that Beeks "is called an angel of peace, so free have the factories been from strikes since her employment." With teasing condescension, it wondered whether "any woman [could] have the heart to strike in a factory which gives her plenty of looking-glasses." Other newspapers picked up the "angel of peace" label, which must have come from a company press release, since it appeared simultaneously in both the *Chicago Tribune* and the *Evening Post*. While the company gained plenty of publicity for its inventive labor "diplomacy," the *Tribune*'s characterization of Beeks as an "Anti-Strike Social Agent" added a note of ambiguity to the humane and benevolent portrait.[63]

Then again, how benevolent did the corporation wish to appear? Although a laudatory newspaper article described the McCormick men's club as "philanthropy of the kind that abhors almsgiving," International Harvester, like other self-respecting businesses of the era, flinched at having the term "philanthropy" applied to any of its corporate activities. Perkins protested that the measures, although costly, had been undertaken in "a purely business spirit." In a private letter to Cardinal Gibbons, Perkins avowed of his welfare advocacy that "I do not claim for it anything in the way of charity or philanthropy." Elsewhere he asserted that welfare work was "as much a business branch of the company as any other division." Even Gertrude Beeks disparaged any "theoretical sentimental efforts."[64] Cyrus McCormick Jr., the president of International Harvester, very likely found it personally flattering in 1908 to be held up as the disproof of corporate soullessness because employee welfare was "really rather nearer to his heart than the making of more money." But he also undoubtedly appreciated the reporter's assurance that no "softness" underlay Harvester's welfare initiatives. "In truth," the obliging reporter added, "there is a degree of hard business sense in it, of which any man in industrial or commercial life . . . will probably discern the soundness."[65]

International Harvester's stance reflected a frequent pattern in the corporate world: on the one hand, the recognition of the need for "feminine" measures to attend to workers' welfare, for the sake of both labor stability and public relations; on the other, the insistence, fueled by a masculine contempt for policies tainted with emotionality or softness, on the rational exclusion of anything philanthropic from the company's business considerations.[66] Similarly, at General Electric, President E. W. Rice—having rhetorically asked what the motive had been behind improved working conditions in the GE Schenectady works—disingenuously observed, "Whatever it was, it was not philanthropy or paternalism."[67] And Swift & Company, the meatpackers, after describing in its 1916 *Year Book* how it had provided employees with garden plots and a summer camp, quickly added that it was merely putting to use otherwise wasted land and an "idle boarding house." Just as it utilized the by-products of its slaughtering processes, it boasted, here too it demonstrated that "waste and unproductiveness are abhorrent to the spirit of the organization." Self-sacrifice, as Kathleen McCarthy points out, was traditionally seen as crucial to women's charity work but inappropriate to men's philanthropy. Even less should any such feminine quality find justification, legal or moral, in the masculine world of business.[68]

The case of International Harvester also epitomized the internal tensions that welfare programs often created. Beeks, Bruere, and several of the other "social secretaries" at International Harvester enjoyed personal connections with members of the McCormick family. Plant managers and foremen resented having their authority undermined by welfare workers, especially when such interlopers could appeal over the managers' heads to company executives. They closed ranks against "outsiders" whose welfare initiatives might result in "upsetting, in a measure, the authority of the superintendents."[69] Such tensions were exacerbated when the welfare workers were women, as they often were.[70] While recognizing that a woman might better understand the needs and grievances of women workers, they were abashed that a woman should restrain their control. That their responsibilities stemmed from the serious business of production reinforced their discomfiture with "feminine" restrictions on plant operations and supervisorial authority. So thoroughly had welfare come to be perceived as feminine, and so threatening was such gendered activity to status within the ranks of serious business, that male publicists at International Harvester found themselves defending the men's club at the Deering works from contempt by protesting that the club rooms were no "namby pamby pink tea arrangement."[71]

For all its welfare programs, International Harvester did not attain the "good trust" image that Perkins had hoped for, at least not sufficiently to escape antitrust prosecution by the attorney general under the Taft administration in 1912. Nor did it apply its welfare measures broadly enough throughout the corporation to avoid revelations that same year of deplorable working conditions at one of its twine mills.[72] But given the acute public suspicion of the Harvester Trust upon its founding in 1902, it is quite possible that the company would have become the target of adverse legislation and more abrupt antitrust action had it not sought to cultivate a benevolent image. Robert Ozanne concludes that the company's success in persuading Jane Addams of its concern for workers' welfare at the McCormick plant helped it survive one strike, and its implementation of certain welfare plans among select groups helped it thwart union organization. If one of its internal reports on labor relations had been leaked to the public, Ozanne concludes, the company would actually have been "revealed as the epitome of the soulless corporation, its goal the pursuit of power and profit!"[73] But the visibility of its welfare activities established a public image of a company that seemed to be trying to be more humane.

Forging a Corporate Personality

Building a company reputation was but one defense against charges of soullessness. Another approach was to cultivate a corporate personality. Of course, no clear boundary distinguished the two projects: some business leaders insisted that a reputation for paternalistic benevolence and fair dealing was exactly what constituted their company's personality. Still, the attempt to distinguish reputation from personality may illuminate the different ways in which giant corporations came to fear being perceived as soulless. It also helps reveal the differences between corporate public relations based primarily on "good works" and those PR strategies more closely allied with merchandising.

Concern about the lack of a distinctive corporate identity was usually a direct motive for strategies in this second category. One evident tactic was to project the personality of the company founder, particularly if he still commanded the firm. A number of successful big businesses of the late nineteenth century had demonstrated how this asset could be turned to account regardless of scale. Montgomery Ward, conscious of the need "to compete with the country storekeeper in folksiness and in the personal touch," managed to convey an image of such neighborly, yet authoritative, concern that customers wrote to ask his advice on the most mundane and intimate matters. In the early years of Sears, Roebuck & Company, mailings of thousands of postcards carried convincing facsimiles of Richard Sears's signature. Customers were urged to send their orders to "Richard W. Sears, President, personally."[74] A writer for *Printers' Ink Monthly,* recounting the success of the creator of the Erector set, described how the company founder and president, A. C. Gilbert, conveyed the "personal touch." "When a boy writes in to the company," he observed, "he is made to feel that he is writing direct to A. C. Gilbert." The reply, which might include Gilbert's folksy reminiscences about his own boyhood, was signed by Gilbert himself. In his catalog Gilbert casually reminded boys, "When you are in New Haven don't forget to come and see me, and I'll show you just how Gilbert toys are made."[75]

Some entrepreneurs infused the image of their companies with their own personalities in the manner of Henry Ford, by participating in newsworthy events (such as automobile racing), by championing causes (such as Ford's fight for the "common man" against the Selden patent), and through pure showmanship.[76] Others followed the lead of the indefatigable shoe manufacturer W. L. Douglas, who persistently published ads in the national magazines with his picture, his signature, and an account of his rise to success through integrity and hard work (Fig. 1.6). Douglas not only gained gratifying sales results from this intense personalization of his company's image, but he further parlayed his celebrity into a winning campaign for governor of Massachusetts.[77]

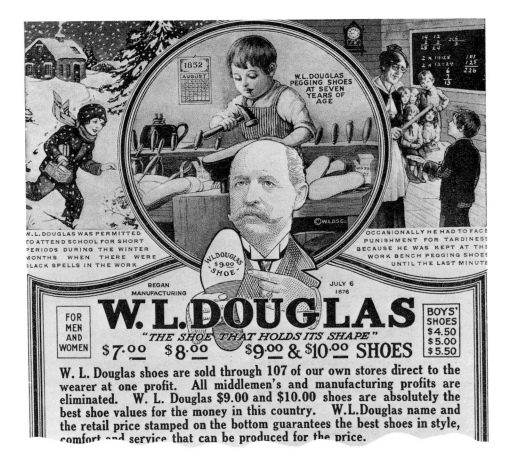

FIGURE 1.6

Through moralistic recollections of his youthful quest for success through hard work, W. L. Douglas merchandised *himself* as his company's image. Having pegged shoes since age seven, he claimed both long experience and exemplary character.

Long before the new giant corporations provoked charges of soullessness, manufacturers had used their portraits to introduce themselves to distant customers. Even if fostered by egotism, such advertising tactics reflected the perfectly reasonable assumption that customers would find it more comfortable to deal with a seller whose personal image was familiar—and perhaps carried an aura of dignity, integrity, or friendliness—than with an anonymous corporation. The image seemed to guarantee that a real person, with his identity publicized and his reputation thus placed on the line, stood behind the product. King Gillette made his appropriately clean-shaven visage a regular element in his ads, and Mennen's Toilet Powder adopted the slogan "Mennen's face on every box." The redoubtable Smith Brothers replicated their trademark images on each box of cough drops.[78] The advertising likeness of Lydia Pinkham, which also appeared on every jar of her

"Vegetable Compound," testified to the effectiveness of a familiar face in instances where the manufacturer doubled as personal counselor to remote customers.[79]

But the largest corporations of the turn of the century, whether in manufacturing, transportation, or public utilities, did not usually focus on a single person to advertise themselves. Some were inhibited from doing so because of their origins in mergers; in others the founder was no longer the active chief of the company. Given the public attacks on such figures as John D. Rockefeller, William Vanderbilt, and J. P. Morgan, some business executives recognized advantages in relative anonymity. Yet a statement of company principles or a rebuttal of muckrakers' attacks carried little weight when delivered by an invisible, anonymous corporation. The best answer on such occasions, advertising experts agreed, was a statement by the president himself (see Fig. 3.1). This strategy, as early advertising expert Claude Hopkins has described it, would assert that "a man is talking—a man who takes pride in his accomplishments—not a soulless corporation."[80]

Although specific occasions demanded the authority of a personal presidential statement, other modes of forging a favorable identity seemed more desirable over the long run. The trade press during the second decade of the century began to badger companies to seek more imaginative ways to establish a company "voice," to "find the personality of the institution." Like other department stores, Wanamaker's could creditably assert that "the Wanamaker Store's personality is but the composite individuality of the Founder . . . and of those he has gathered about him."[81] But founders were mortal. What of the company after the founder's death, when the impress of his personality became less obvious? The business itself, warned *Printers' Ink,* "must be given a character of its own, which is still recognizable after the human personality is removed."[82]

To this end, some followed the example of another department store, one less favored with a renowned founder. Greenhut & Company, as New York's newest department store in 1906, adopted a standard format for all its advertising and the single, thematic "Greenhut color" of "Mignonette Green" for all its stationery, boxes, decorations, wrapping papers, and delivery wagons. A consistent appearance, even in such mundane matters, could at least project a definite, and ultimately familiar, image. Henry Heinz had done this with his green pickle pins and his "57 varieties" logo. His willingness to be dubbed the "Pickle King" had contributed to a unified, humane, and memorable corporate image.[83]

Another source for a distinctive corporate identity was that jewel of the manufacturer's eye: his factory. Of course, the actual buildings were often in a remote area, and even if the corporation had more than one major manufacturing plant, their visibility remained entirely local, affording no national publicity. A few notable companies strove to make showplaces of their factories; Chapter 7 will examine their image-creating strategies as they first welcomed visitors to their facilities and then sought to take their companies on the road. But most corporations relied instead on the wide circulation of images of their factories, ranging from advertising illustrations and trade cards to logos, letterheads, and fair displays.

The use of factory pictures to define and publicize the image of the company enjoyed a robust legacy from the nineteenth century. Lowell, Massachusetts—the first newly created industrial city in the United States—had initiated this strategy in the 1820s and 1830s. Paintings, lithographs, and engraved business stationery depicted the mills of the Middlesex Company, the Boston Manufacturing Company,

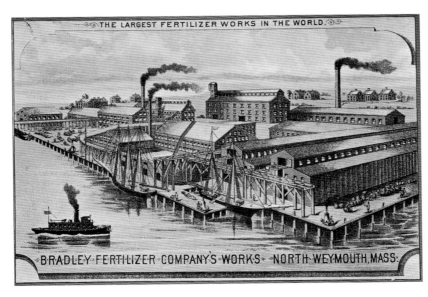

THE LARGEST FERTILIZER WORKS IN THE WORLD.

BRADLEY FERTILIZER COMPANY'S WORKS · NORTH WEYMOUTH, MASS.

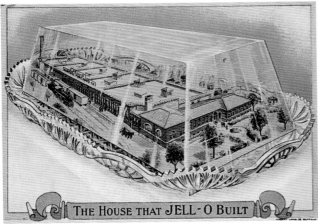

THE HOUSE THAT JELL-O BUILT

FIGURES 1.7 & 1.8
In trade cards of the 1880s and 1890s an impressive view of the company's vast factory connoted stability and a successful product. Bradley Fertilizer Company underscored the size and power of its operations, while Jell-O suggested the purity and radiance of its product.

and the Merrimack Manufacturing Company. More significant than the image of any individual corporation, as Helena Wright has observed, was that of the city of Lowell as a whole. Idealized scenes of Lowell's factories, as well as those of other emerging industrial cities, sold the "new system"—the basic "idea of industrial capitalism"—while also publicizing the individual companies.[84]

The factory as the palpable personification of the corporation became a prevalent theme in one of the widespread modes of advertising during the 1880s and 1890s: the trade card. Here, even before its soullessness was at issue, manufacturers found a way to evade the seeming abstractness and anonymity of the distant corporation. A factory panorama embedded their name in a concrete image of a particular place. Moreover, the idealized image of the factory could convey whatever claims they might wish to make for their products and their entire enterprise—whether of size, stability, efficiency, or cleanliness (Figs. 1.7 and 1.8).[85]

FIGURES 1.9 & 1.10

Business leaders engrossed in building massive manufacturing plants and consolidating corporate empires might logically feel that their factories put forth the most desirable public image. Even for marketing yeast and flour, largest equaled best.

Sophisticated advertising agents would later bemoan their clients' fixation on their factories. A writer for *Printers' Ink Monthly* in 1920 described a familiar experience—the advertising agent's typical "shudder" when the client "swings around to that sentimental hour of factory talk, and looks upward to the framed view on the wall of the one spot on earth that's dearest to him, because he made it possible" (see Fig. 1.19).[86] The manufacturer had so invested his ego in his factory, complained the agents, that it was hard to convince him that consumers were interested in what his products would do for them, not in his cherished manufacturing plant. Never depict your factory, they exclaimed to dramatize their point, unless it itself is for sale![87]

But during the late nineteenth century and even later in some cases, as industries rapidly expanded, the factory image made good sense as a merchandising and public relations vehicle. Impressive and often romanticized, it assured customers that they were dealing with a stable, competent firm. "There the factory stands," remarked a contributor to *Printers' Ink* in 1910, "a most tangible and conclusive proof of the advertiser's ability to cope with demand. . . . Suspicions of irresponsibility, of fly-by-night policies, are allayed before they are born." Interior factory scenes, as well as those showing the expanse of factory windows or its rural location, could help reinforce selling points about the clean, sunny, healthy conditions under which the products were manufactured (see Fig. 1.4). Moreover, the immensity of the plant would attest to the previous success of the enterprise and thus, presumably, to the quality of its products. Such an image suggested large capacity, well-developed expertise, ample capitalization, and modern production techniques.[88]

Factory pictures in ads and trade cards, while usually retaining considerable verisimilitude, often featured panoramic or bird's-eye perspectives, "sprawling the factory back toward the vanishing point," in Frank Fox's phrase, "in order to dramatize its vastness." Pamela Walker Lurito has noted how these depictions sought to hearten executives and impress viewers by displaying billows of (productive) black smoke spouting from a multitude of chimneys.[89] These were signs, as John Stilgoe observes, of "permanence and prosperity."[90]

While such images did not unmistakably individualize each company, since all tended to convey a similar message, they did provide one possible answer to the lament of Edward Hall of AT&T that "the public does not know us, . . . has . . . never met us, does not know where we live."[91] The corporation that showed where it "lived" on its letterhead, trade cards, and advertisements at least gave the public a concrete, even iconic, image of itself, however romanticized. It also appealed to that commonsensical American popular judgment that whatever had become the biggest must be the best. Corporations selling products as varied as yeast, razor blades, fertilizer, and underwear all greeted the public with pictures of the factory. Even food processors, who later might stress the "home-cooked flavor" of products from their "kitchens," sought to impress the early twentieth-century public with factory portraits over such captions as "the largest flour mill in the world" (Figs. 1.9 and 1.10).[92]

For the manufacturer no identification of the company with its factory could be more personally gratifying than one that united his visage, in a cameo portrait or marble bust, with a monumental rendering of his factory as the backdrop (Fig. 1.11). Even more flattering—to the founder or to a corporation that wished to revitalize its founder's legacy—was a montage juxtaposing the company's imposing modern plant with the little shop, house, or shed in which the enterprise had begun.[93] Cast in the model of "Great oaks from little acorns grow," such visually powerful moral narratives found a cherished place in the musings of American businessmen (Fig. 1.12). *System* magazine reflected that fascination in 1915, when it published a multi-issue illustration series entitled "Where They Started— The Humble Structures That First Housed the Great Industrials."[94]

In 1904 the H. J. Heinz Company went so far as to locate and purchase the brick house in Sharpsburg, Pennsylvania, in which Henry J. had first bottled preserves. The company transported the "House Where We Began" down the Allegheny River by barge to the site of the immense modern plant in Pittsburgh, installing it

"An institution is the lengthened shadow of one man"

QUALITY *for Half a Century*

HALF A CENTURY ago a man of high ideals, far-seeing vision, and rare courage dedicated his life to the work of making shoes fit better. That man was George E. Keith, and his life work became an American institution, for George E. Keith created Walk-Over.

He surrounded himself with men who believed in him and who shared his high ideals. Together they worked, and together they succeeded. Today, wherever shoes are worn, in

The first Walk-Over shoe plant, where George E. Keith founded Walk-Over

workers of the Walk-Over family will join with hundreds of Walk-Over dealers from all over the world in a glorious memorial pageant.

In the pageant will be a special group of 160 men who worked with George E. Keith from twenty-five to fifty years. Leading the pageant will be Harold C. Keith, who, surrounded by able men of long experience, with the high ideals set before him by his father, is successfully carrying even

FIGURE 1.11

A marble bust seemed appropriate when a company claimed status on the basis of a visionary founder. Note the inscription and the morally

instructive contrast of the current factory with the "first Walk-Over shoe plant," shown in the tiny vignette.

at the heart of the factory complex (Fig. 1.13). Here employees and visitors could contemplate the hortatory visual juxtaposition of the quaint house with the modern plant and reconstruct for themselves the appropriate moral narrative. In its ads Heinz disseminated to a wider audience this instructive linkage of successful personal struggles with the attributes of the corporation (Fig. 1.14).[95]

If one strategy for humanizing both factory and company was to associate them with the life story of the founder, another was to employ the element of beauty to associate both with uplift and enlightenment. Since the era of the mill towns of Lowell and Lawrence, American companies had often sought to ameliorate the ambience of the factory through landscaping that suggested a natural or parklike

FIGURE 1.12

Here Burroughs worked its tiny first shop, its founder's portrait, and its massive factory into a single visual story—one that identified the huge corporation with a corporate culture of artisanship.

setting and architectural embellishments such as cupolas and decorative towers.[96] In the late nineteenth century, as urban corporations looked for larger and cheaper manufacturing space, a few welfare-oriented companies such as Procter & Gamble, H. J. Heinz, National Cash Register, and Eastman Kodak hoped to distinguish themselves from the operators of grimy, cheerless factories by creating new industrial "parks." Procter & Gamble built Ivorydale on the outskirts of Cincinnati in 1886–87, George Eastman began developing Kodak Park in Rochester in 1890, and the National Electric Lamp Association of General Electric created Nela Park near Cleveland in 1912 and 1913. They counted on the lawns, ornamental shrubs, and flower gardens to attract workers of a higher caliber (especially among women laborers) and to reinforce their other efforts toward worker uplift, such as paintings on the walls.[97] A factory so embellished might symbolize, for both employees and the public, a corporation that put refinement and culture above cold, avaricious calculation.

FIGURE 1.13
The Heinz Company was so intent
on drawing moral lessons from its
rise from small beginnings that it
transported its original "little house"
by barge to Pittsburgh, at great effort
and expense.

Nonetheless, most large corporations never relied on factory images in their bid
to personalize or humanize their operations. They looked primarily for efficiency
and functionality in their buildings. In Berlin the modernist architect Peter Behrens envisioned the AEG Turbinenfabrik as a "Cathedral of Work," enclosing the
functional plant within "the envelope of a Classical Temple." But even those
American factory architects like Albert Kahn, internationally recognized for his
modern steel and glass creations for Ford, declined to emulate Behrens and departed little from a narrowly utilitarian devotion to production efficiency.[98] And
when the Ford Motor Company publicized images of its River Rouge plant in
1924 advertisements and fair exhibits, it accentuated the visual qualities of impressive size and raw power, not aesthetic or humanizing details (see Figs. 5.1 and
7.16). Finally, many large corporations either operated multiple plants—and thus
preferred not to base their self-image on a single plant—or did not operate a factory at all.

This old building, erected in the fifties, was moved half a mile overland, placed on a barge and towed five miles down the Allegheny River. To get it under a low bridge the barge was sunk, pumped out, floated again, and moved on down the river to Pittsburgh, where it was placed in the center of the Heinz plant.

Where the "57" began
The LITTLE HOUSE *that was floated down the* RIVER

WHEN YOU visit the "Home of the 57" you see the little "House where we began" —surrounded, overshadowed by large modern buildings. To the visitor the little house may seem but an interesting relic— a thing of purely historical interest, signifying growth and prosperity. To us, this homely little brick building stands as a symbol—a constant reminder of the ideals established there, the principles on which the Heinz business has been built.

It was because of this, of what the little house meant to us all, that we moved it from its original location, floated it five miles down the river on a barge, and placed it where its inspiration would be most manifest. Loyalty to the standards which the little house represents is reflected in the spirit of service, care in preparation and pride in workmanship which characterize the whole Heinz organization.

H. J. HEINZ COMPANY
57 *Varieties*

FIGURE 1.14

Nestled amid the massive structures of the modern plant, Heinz's "little house" acquired a radiant moral glow. It became the visitors' entrance and also held the time clock where workers punched in each day.

The Corporation as Skyscraper

For many corporations in the early twentieth century, the skyscraper office build-ing came to offer an even more potent identity than the factory. Like the princi-pal factory, the corporate headquarters could occupy only one location; thus its na-tional visibility depended on the dissemination of its image through various media. But the skyscraper transcended the functional factory building in projecting mo-dernity, success, power—and even civic stature—through an aesthetically striking image. Although companies did need space for expansion, many executives al-lowed their broader ambitions to carry them beyond mere utilitarian needs as they aspired to more elevated civic profiles. When the cost of urban real estate made taller buildings more attractive economically and the development of structural steel and the elevator made them more feasible and practical, entrepreneurs defied the early bias toward horizontal monumentality for civic structures. Blending per-sonal ego with a greater consciousness of public relations, they came to favor the tower as an architectural expression of the corporate image.[99]

Two industries dominated the early skyscraper frenzy in its most nationally con-spicuous setting of lower Manhattan: the metropolitan newspaper publishers and the giant life insurance companies. The Equitable Life Insurance Company kicked off the race toward the skies in 1870. Henry B. Hyde, the company's president, sought personal renown and increased rental profits with an innovative, elevator-equipped seven-story office building. Momentarily, at 130 feet, it claimed the title of tallest building in New York City. But by 1875 both the 230-foot Western Union building and the 260-foot *Tribune* building had surpassed it. The spire of Trinity Church, previously the pinnacle of the city skyline, was suddenly eclipsed (see Fig. 1.1).[100]

After a scramble by newspaper publishers in the 1880s and 1890s to overtop each other, something of a showdown ensued between 1906 and 1913.[101] First the Singer Sewing Machine Company surpassed all precursors in 1908 with a 47-story sky-scraper that reached 612 feet. Its primacy lasted eighteen months. By the end of 1909 the Metropolitan Life Insurance tower held bragging rights at 700 feet, only to capitulate in 1913 to the Woolworth building, at 792 feet. At three times the height of the Trinity Church steeple, the Woolworth skyscraper inspired "feelings too deep even for tears," wrote the Reverend S. Parkes Cadman, who dubbed it "the cathedral of commerce."[102]

The newspaper publishers, who played a prominent role in the early dash for sky-line supremacy, quite possibly projected their personal feuds and circulation battles into this contest. The *Tribune* obtrusively cut its name into immense granite blocks near the top of all four sides of its building, just below the tower and spire. Joseph Pulitzer, in planning his dominating *New York World* building at the end of the 1880s, made it one of his specific goals to look down, literally, on James Gordon Bennett and his *New York Herald* building. With their expanded overviews of the city, the metropolitan newspapers made symbolic claims to superiority in knowl-edge of the city's happenings and moral authority in championing the city's bet-terment. A lofty vantage point could reinforce other architectural elements that as-serted their legitimacy as institutions of "public enlightenment."[103] Moreover, given their marketing focus on a local constituency, a striking corporate visibility in a single city suited their needs.

THE
PRUDENTIAL
HAS THE
STRENGTH OF
GIBRALTAR

THE MASSIVE BUILDING PICTURED ABOVE IS OWNED AND OCCUPIED BY

THE PRUDENTIAL INSURANCE CO. OF AMERICA

AS ITS HOME OFFICE AT NEWARK, N. J.,   JOHN F. DRYDEN, President.

FROM WHICH IS CONDUCTED ITS VAST BUSINESS OF LIFE INSURANCE FOR MEN, WOMEN, AND CHILDREN.

FIGURE 1.15
This dominating image from an 1890s magazine embedded one impression of corporate strength and stability within another. The caption stressed that "the massive building pictured above is owned and occupied by . . . Prudential . . . as its home office at Newark, N.J."

The great insurance companies, while requiring a national image, found ample rationale in financial and marketing considerations for investing in showpiece edifices. Insurance was a relatively new and often controversial enterprise; they needed to persuade a suspicious public to place confidence in their financial soundness and their ability to withstand economic depressions. With immense funds to invest, large clerical staffs to house, and a reputation for strength and stability to cultivate, insurance companies could see advantages in erecting spacious, landmark buildings at highly visible metropolitan centers. The Prudential Company turned to metaphor, vaunting endurance and protective strength in its Rock of Gibraltar logo. But rival companies envisioned their skyscraper offices as carrying the same message while serving as real estate investments besides. Even Prudential, in an 1896 ad, coupled its depiction of Gibraltar with an illustration of its massive home office in Newark (Fig. 1.15)[104]

The skyscraper not only represented a claim to strength, modernity, and protective dominion; it was also designed to signify service. As early as 1870, Equitable Life underlined its dedication to public service by establishing a weather bureau on the roof of its building. Later, businesses ranging from department stores to insurance companies signaled their service role by placing huge clocks on their structures. That of the Metropolitan Life Insurance Company was visible from a mile away, set in a striking tower that was modeled on the Campanile of St. Mark's in Venice (Fig. 1.16). This association with traditional culture conferred greater legitimacy on the company, while a beacon light in the tower pointedly symbolized the company's watchful guardianship over the city and its people.[105]

Metropolitan Life was not content to rely on architectural symbolism to carry the message of service. The Metropolitan tower, under the inscription "The light that never fails," soon emerged as the company's logo on its letterhead and in its advertisements and brochures. A company pamphlet described the tower as standing "high and lofty, like a great sentinel keeping watch over the millions of policyholders and marking the fast-fleeting moments of life." As historian Mona Domosh has observed, such expressions of the corporate personality as that of "a tower that in its style harked back to the precapitalist, civic values of medieval Venice" conveyed "a civic as well as a commercial message."[106] Since the insurance industry had assumed certain functions previously associated with the family, the church, and the state, it seemed an apt public relations gesture to accentuate the social responsibility undertaken by a major insurance company as a "quasi-public institution." This image was particularly appropriate for a mutualized life insurance company like Metropolitan, which could claim simply to serve its members, not external shareholders. AT&T similarly saw the allegorical sculptures it commissioned for its new headquarters building in 1914 as a contribution "to the public good" that would reflect the company's public service.[107]

While the Singer and Woolworth skyscrapers could not credibly exemplify social guardianship and civic service, their exquisite appointments, and particularly the gothic style of the Woolworth tower, intensified a rhetorical association increasingly prevalent in descriptions of impressive commercial architecture, from department store palaces to corporate headquarters skyscrapers—the metaphor of the cathedral. With its huge rotunda, its ornate fixtures, its immense Tiffany Dome (described by one art critic as "in a class with the nave of St. Peter's in Rome" and by the editor of *Dry Goods Economist* as "exceeding in its iridescent radiance the famous Taj Mahal in India"), and its pretensions to uplift and inspiration, Marshall Field's store in Chicago had taken to calling itself "the Cathedral of all the Stores" (see Fig. 1.2). Wanamaker encouraged this perception of his store, telling his employees in 1906 that as he contemplated the plans for remodeling he glimpsed "a great cathedral of magnificent opportunity." When he and his son installed "the finest organ in the world" in the Grand Court of the Philadelphia store, Wanamaker's biographer observes, they transformed the building "into a veritable cathedral."[108]

The skyscrapers, especially when their skyward-aspiring towers were linked to claims of corporate benevolence, evoked a similar terminology. A company historian spoke of the "cathedral-like quality" of the Prudential headquarters building in Newark. Similarly, the board of directors of the New York Life Insurance

FIGURE 1.16
The Metropolitan Life tower was
intended to connote civic beneficence as well as corporate power. Its
huge clock provided a public service,
and observation platforms afforded
visitors imperious, edifying views.
Metropolitan did not hesitate to
boast of its preeminence, although
it would last only four years.

Company observed that the resemblance of its remodeled building to an "ancient
temple" was quite fitting for an institution that was itself a "temple of Humanity."[109] The publicist, advertising advisor, and frustrated former clergyman Gerald
Stanley Lee extolled the Metropolitan tower, with "its great bell singing hymns
above the dizzy flocks of skyscrapers," as exemplifying "the soul of New York."[110]
In the context of such rhetorical evocations of divinity, it hardly seemed presump-
tuous to christen the even taller, night-illuminated Woolworth building a "cathedral of commerce." By giving "the Gothic quality of lace in stone to a building of
supernormal proportions," the architect Cass Gilbert made the Woolworth tower
the epitome of the emerging effort to confer a charismatic legitimacy on business
corporations through architectural allusions to the sublime (Fig. 1.17).[111]

FIGURE 1.17
In its gothic splendor, the Woolworth
building claimed a role in the cultural
enrichment of New York City. It symbolized high ideals but at the same time
constituted an immense advertisement.
Just to its left, the spire of Trinity
Church (see Fig. 1.1) had virtually
disappeared from the skyline view.

Still, as William Taylor concludes, this "civic gothic tower" mainly reflected Frank Woolworth's effort to communicate his "sense of civic obligation" and "the grandeur of his own commercial triumph." Drawing on the civic and ecclesiastical associations of the gothic style, Woolworth sought to provide society with a culturally enriching monument as well as create a "super billboard" on behalf of his company's merchandising.[112] Daniel Bluestone notes how the "grand, ennobling" entrances of skyscraper office buildings elevated the status of the work performed therein, and Kenneth Turney Gibbs alerts us to the importance of conspicuously wasted space in the design of skyscrapers. In providing rich, refined ornamentation and giving "over to the architect a certain amount of untenable space" for the symbolic tower, bell, beacon, and other embellishments, companies pointed to "ideals higher than those of business enterprise." "Honorific styling" made it safer for a corporation to call attention to its size and power through a massive skyscraper, because it emphasized the desirable aspects of those qualities—the presumed stability, efficiency, and security—while symbolizing the company's role as a "social service institution."[113]

While huge expenditures on skyscrapers might seem dubious by the standards of hardheaded business decision making, this strategy of image creation did not involve the pitfalls often attributed to too liberal a company welfare program. No skyscraper was accused of instilling employees with false values and unrealistic expectations or of confusing serious business with "feminine" benevolence and sentimentality. The competition to erect higher and higher corporate and personal monuments—with its indubitably male, specifically phallic component of entrepreneurial egotism—shielded this "edifice complex" from any taint of femininity. Moreover, it would appear that most of the ventures in creating a visible corporate personality through architectural heroics repaid their costs in their merchandising value.[114] Whether they proved cost-effective in realizing greater moral legitimacy for the corporations that employed this strategy, or afforded them increased protection from public suspicion and unwanted legislation, is a much more difficult question to answer. Certainly there is no evidence that business leaders of the era applied cost-benefit calculations to a strategy so sacred as that of erecting business cathedrals.

Muckrakers and Crises Spur an Organized Response

It seems inevitable that the brief epoch of great corporate mergers between 1895 and 1904 should have ushered in both the escalation of muckraking exposés of big business and the rise of organized corporate public relations. Americans had long been suspicious of the dangers of centralized power. For many the new corporate giants violated all sense of proportion, all notions of democratic rule.[115] For their part many corporate leaders acquired a new awareness of the import of public opinion, of the vulnerability of their operations to the whims of an uncomprehending public. Still, the corporate response to public agitation was neither instantaneous nor consistent. The process by which more specifically organized, deliberately focused, and often defensive campaigns of public relations came to supplement the scattered experiments in creating corporate images—through welfare programs, promotions of executive personalities, and the impress of factory and skyscraper images—was less a sweeping movement than an accumulating series of isolated incidents.

One such event, often recounted as a backdrop to the rise of organized public relations in the United States, was the anthracite coal strike of 1902. Some 150,000 miners walked out for six months while the nation's coal supply dwindled, winter approached, and President Theodore Roosevelt called for compromise. Meanwhile the mine operators, under the leadership of railway president George F. Baer, arrogantly ignored the press, defied public opinion, and refused to cooperate with Roosevelt. In the single press statement issued by the operators, Baer infamously asserted that "the rights and interests of the laboring man will be protected and cared for not by the labor agitators, but by the Christian men to whom God in his infinite wisdom has given the control of the property interests of the country." The union, gaining the sympathy of the public and the assistance of Roosevelt, came away with a substantial victory. Having been forced to make unpalatable concessions in 1902, Baer chose another tactic four years later, when another strike loomed. He employed Ivy Lee, soon to emerge as the nation's first professional public relations counselor, to speak exclusively for the operators and to deluge the press with "advance information."[116]

Lee had formed a partnership in 1904 with the experienced journalist George Parker. They began to contract for publicity work with the manufacturer George Westinghouse and the financier Thomas Fortune Ryan. In 1906, while serving as a temporary public relations department for the coal operators, the Parker & Lee Company also contracted with George Perkins to promote International Harvester's "good trust" image. On behalf of the trust Lee responded to a Bureau of Corporations probe by welcoming the investigation and promising to supply all information requested. He also wrote an article entitled "An Open and Above-Board 'Trust'" for *Moody's Magazine,* in which he explained (while neglecting to be above-board about his contract with International Harvester) the economies of large size in an agricultural machinery corporation and the beneficence of Harvester's many welfare programs.[117]

During the few years just preceding and following the panic of 1907, corporate public relations clearly crossed a threshold.[118] It was no coincidence that during these same years the muckraking of corporate America reached an apex. During 1905 *Everybody's Magazine* featured Charles Edward Russell's exposé of the beef industry in a series entitled "The Greatest Trust in the World." The next year it carried not only Thomas Lawson's "Frenzied Finance" but also "The Condemned Meat Industry," by Upton Sinclair, and a series by Hartley Davis on the coal trust. Meanwhile, *McClure's* took on the railroads in a series by Ray Stannard Baker. *Collier's* unnerved its readers with a series by Samuel Hopkins Adams that muckraked the proprietary drug business. Before 1906 was over, Upton Sinclair had published *The Jungle.*[119] One of the first specific corporate crises triggered by this spate of muckraking ensued after Thomas Lawson, in *Everybody's,* exposed fraudulent dealings by the "big three" of the life insurance industry—Mutual Life, Equitable Life, and New York Life—revelations that were reinforced by additional attacks in Joseph Pulitzer's *New York World* and by Burton Hendrick in *McClure's.* An entire industry reeled from the subsequent probe by the Armstrong Committee of the New York legislature and prosecutions by the state attorney general.[120]

This scandal involved outrageous violations of the companies' responsibilities to the public. Secret connections between the insurance companies and trust companies had allowed insiders to milk some corporations for the benefit of others. Company presidents had paid themselves enormous salaries, unbeknownst to the trustees; they had padded company payrolls with idle and inept relatives. The insurance companies had plied the state legislature with money and dispensed "huge sums" with no authority or accounting. All of the big three responded by cleaning house in top management; some insurance executives began to worry that the public would agitate for government-sponsored insurance.[121] Equitable Life quietly employed Parker & Lee to present "the best side of life insurance" in the nation's press. In May 1906 they arranged for the president of Equitable Life to send some seven hundred letters to the editors of various newspapers. Parker succeeded in getting most of these "printed in the papers to which they were addressed as news matter in a conspicuous place without any payment or undue influence of any kind on the part of the Equitable."[122]

More significantly, Mutual Life Insurance purchased advertising space for a major, highly visible image rehabilitation campaign. It employed N. W. Ayer & Son, the largest and most respected of the advertising agencies, to develop a series of ads for the national media as well as dramatic half-page ads in metropolitan newspapers. Under massive headlines proclaiming "The Truth about Mutual Life," "The Great Difference in Life Insurance Companies," and "There Is No Good Reason Against Good Insurance," the agency undertook damage repair by assuring readers that "extravagance has been stopped," that "a new management has been installed," and that "the solvency of this Company has not for a moment been affected." *Printers' Ink,* the advertising trade journal, reported that Mutual had appropriated an immense $100,000 for the campaign. A conspicuous precedent had now been created, under the guidance of a highly reputed advertising agency, for using paid advertising space in a focused effort to enhance a corporation's image.[123]

Soon thereafter, a major corporation within the industry most incessantly under attack, the railroads, undertook its first significant public relations initiative. In the wake of the passage of the Hepburn Act, in mid-1906, President Alexander Cassatt of the Pennsylvania Railroad contracted Parker & Lee to advise the railroad on its publicity problems.[124] The contract launched Ivy Lee into an intermittent but protracted relationship with the Pennsylvania Railroad that would propel him to the forefront of the nascent public relations profession. Meanwhile, eager to promote any expansion of public relations that would result in corporate advertising, *Printers' Ink* reported in 1906 that United States Steel had just organized a "publicity bureau" and that Standard Oil, "after years of obstinate silence," had appointed a press representative. Only a few months later the journalist James Ellsworth resigned from the Publicity Bureau in Boston, just as the J. P. Morgan interests triumphed in a battle for the control of AT&T. When the victors in that battle installed Theodore Vail as head of the company, and when Vail then appointed Ellsworth as his personal advisor and coordinator of publicity for AT&T, the stage was set for a pivotal event in the history of corporate image creation.[125] In 1908

AT&T launched a three-decade-long, multifaceted public relations campaign to shape the nation's image of one of its largest corporations. That precedent-setting campaign will be the subject of Chapter 2. First, however, it is important to review the recurrent issues and tensions that would arise within corporate councils as company after company set out self-consciously to create a corporate image.

Emerging Tensions in Image Strategies

One problematic issue in the creation of a corporate image was that of audience. Was the corporate image being constructed primarily for the public or for the company's own employees? Would the same image work equally well for both? As figurative makeup artists, could public relations officers carry out their work in backstage privacy and then usher the resulting corporate persona directly from dressing room to front stage for a selected audience? Or would other audiences—composed of business peers, retail distributors, or special interest organizations—glimpse the same performance from the wings? David E. Nye, in his study of General Electric, has shrewdly concluded that any analysis of corporate "image worlds" must recognize a plurality of corporate identities.[126]

Another source of tension derived from the gender implications of businessmen's attention to corporate imagery. From the outset public relations was gendered female in the male business world. Welfare capitalism, often associated with public relations in these early years, was so viewed because of its nurturing image and because women often served as the welfare "secretaries." Moreover, virtually all public relations activities were superfluous to the processes of production. The need for them stemmed instead from the potential power of a mass public, a public that business leaders often characterized as emotional, ignorant, and irrational—and thus, by the tenets of the day, feminine. Those who did the work of public relations could not escape some taint from their responsibility to pander to this audience. Even after decades of accepted legitimacy among the functions of the corporation, the work of public relations would still be understood, by contrast to other operations, to belong to the "soft" side of business and thus to partake of the feminine.[127]

These more "feminine," but seemingly necessary, corporate activities emerged at a critical moment in the forging of corporate imagery. Many major corporations were in the process of shifting from family firms or companies based on the leadership of a single dominant entrepreneur to modern, bureaucratically managed entities. The nation had recently experienced a crisis of masculinity—a mounting fear at the end of the nineteenth century that peace, prosperity, and urban living were endangering those manly qualities associated with a more aggressive, outdoor life. Concurrent with these changes, the print media began to form a conventional picture of the businessman as steely-eyed and square-shouldered, with a broad, sharply etched jaw. Patterned roughly on Charles Dana Gibson's drawing of Richard Harding Davis, the dauntless, romantic war correspondent and symbol of the independent adventurer, this jutting-jaw image of the business executive would predominate over the next two decades. In describing Marshall Field as a "born commander" among captains of industry, a reporter in 1906 noted particularly that Field's "dominant quality was expressed in a jaw of extra-ordinary width." That was exactly the image adopted in the standardized vignettes of exemplary business-men that accompanied each major article in the magazine of business moderniza-tion, *System* (Figs. 1.18 and 1.19).[128] Perhaps this stereotype was an unconscious compensation for the new developments—an increasing cadre of office workers and such activities as public relations and welfare—perceived as introducing sub-versive feminine elements into the manly world of business.

Intertwined with this gender-related tension over the status of public relations among other corporate activities was the issue of businesslike demeanor. Early cor-porate leaders retained a strong attachment to the values of hard work, indepen-dence, seriousness of purpose, and hardheaded practicality. A self-respecting busi-nessman should be a "no-nonsense" person, one who would simply "get down to business" and "attend strictly to business." Yet the activities involved in the cre-ation of a corporate image often seemed unserious, even trivial, and hardly "busi-nesslike." While cultivating public favor and a good impression came to seem both wise and necessary to many corporate leaders, the vast majority were also apt to deplore these unmanly concessions, feeling they had been forced to divert some of their efforts to aberrant activities. At the extreme, business seemed disconcertingly to segue into show business.

Finally, deciding on the scope of functions to be asserted through a corporate image and assessing what responsibilities these might entail brought further ten-sions. The giant business corporation was a very new aspirant to an acknowledged place among society's basic institutions of family, church, community, and state. Confronted with the quandary of how to secure social legitimacy—that is, pub-lic acceptance of its moral right to occupy a major, even dominating, place within the nexus of fundamental social structures—the corporation was tempted to ab-sorb some of the functions of traditional social institutions. The NCR, for in-stance, observed in 1899, after adding a neighborhood improvement program to its many welfare activities, that the company, "by thus touching every side of the life of all its people . . . both in the factory and in their homes," had become far more than "only a great business concern."[129]

But business corporations needed to consider how fully they wished to accept the roles implied by the rhetoric of leadership, guardianship, and service. Vice President James Deering of International Harvester might proclaim expansively, "Our responsibility to the world is great in proportion as our power is great," without implying commitment to any particular responsibility. But when images of service and leadership were less vaguely drawn, they could invite burdensome public expectations. In their quest for a corporate soul, business leaders would fre-quently talk of how their enterprises aspired to accomplish "something higher than money profits." They strove for an image, as Joseph Kett puts it, "of a service in-stitution rather than that of a mere convocation of dollar chasers."[130] They trum-peted their contributions as patrons of the arts, beneficent providers of welfare for their employees, builders of progress through civic leadership, and creators of the inspirational "cathedrals of commerce." In all these endeavors, they sought an ad-ditional moral legitimacy for themselves and their corporations, a legitimacy they feared they had not secured through their bounded, explicit business activities.

But did they really wish to blur so protective and reassuring a boundary as that, staked out in recent years, which separated business—with its presumption of ra-

SYSTEM
THE MAGAZINE OF BUSINESS

tionality, its aura of masculine practicality and seriousness, and its ethics-evading discipline of the "bottom line"—from the realms of philanthropy and stewardship and from the moral, social, and spiritual functions of family and church? In their anxiety to gain legitimacy for their companies as morally sanctioned basic institutions within American society, corporate leaders often referred to themselves as patrons, statesmen, and the patriarchs of contented corporate "families." At times, however, they had to consider whether they could indulge in such rhetoric without subsequently incurring unwanted costs. Was the security of greater moral legitimacy worth the risk of promising to serve more than purely business functions?[131]

Many of these tensions found expression in explicit corporate decisions, as well as in less conscious responses, in selecting among various elements of a corporate image. Should the company encourage the public, and its own employees, to see it as an efficient industrial army or more as a collaborative family? Did it wish the public, in thinking of the company, to conjure an image of its president, its factory, or its skyscraper headquarters, or perhaps a heroic image of its "typical" worker? Should it cultivate an aura of power and dignity or one of folksy "humanity"? Should it confine its image to an association with excellent products, or should it lay claim to a wider service of social betterment or aesthetic progress?

All these dilemmas would have made strategies for the creation of a corporate image complex enough if the choices had consisted merely of such distinct, binary

options. But the possible tactics were never so narrowly circumscribed, nor even so clearly delineated. A corporation did not opt simply for a more aloof or more personalized, a more masculine or more feminine, image; it often drew, both consciously and unconsciously, on a variety of symbols and impressions, some of which carried contradictory connotations. Moreover, each element of a corporate image, and each audience for which it was projected, carried a consequence for every other element. As if these variants did not make the creation of corporate souls sufficiently enigmatic, changes in the array of possible media through which an image might be shaped presented even further opportunities and dilemmas.

We can best explore the differing strategies in the quest for legitimacy by examining in detail such seminal campaigns as that on which one of the nation's largest corporations, AT&T, embarked in 1908.

2

AT&T:
THE VISION OF A
LOVED MONOPOLY

In 1908 the leaders of the N. W. Ayer & Son advertising agency took a deep and worried breath as they embarked on a significant new task for one of the nation's largest corporations, the American Telephone and Telegraph Company. To launch an advertising campaign touting the virtues of a private monopoly—and to do so amid the political atmosphere of muckraking exposés and trust-busting rhetoric—seemed a bold and possibly foolhardy venture. But the Ayer agency was eager to prove its mettle, and AT&T's new president, Theodore Vail, was distressed by his company's unfavorable public image. The formidable obstacles only reinforced Vail's resolve to fund the forging of a corporate image at a level unprecedented among American corporations.[1]

Thus began the first, most persistent, and most celebrated of the large-scale institutional advertising campaigns of the early twentieth century. Its primary purpose was political—to protect a corporation with an odious public reputation against threats of public ownership or hostile regulation. Among the methods deployed to publicize Vail's new emphasis on quality and service were measured argument, emotional appeal, and transformed corporate behavior. Certainly AT&T was not the first major American business corporation to recognize, for good or for ill, that it had an image, and that its image could affect its long-term welfare. But never had a major corporation so systematically and decisively set out to create a new corporate image for itself as did AT&T in 1908.

And never did a corporation so triumphantly accomplish that task—at least that was the verdict of experts some three decades later. At the end of the 1930s, as large corporations again faced intense public suspicion, AT&T emerged virtually unscathed from an extensive antitrust investigation by the Federal Communications Commission. When observers asked why investigations of the telephone monopoly had elicited almost no public support during the perilous mid-1930s, corporate analysts almost unanimously gave credit to AT&T's thirty-year campaign of coordinated institutional advertising and public relations.[2] They marveled at AT&T's astute integration of multiple elements of successful public relations and the effectiveness of its various rhetorical strategies in countering the mistrust of business bigness. In the pantheon of great corporate public relations feats, L. L. L. Golden reflected in the late 1960s, the campaign that AT&T initiated in 1908 had been "The Granddaddy of Them All."[3]

The success of this institutional advertising campaign cannot simply be attributed to the genius of its original conception. AT&T's venture in corporate imagery was a long process of gradual, and sometimes sporadic, incorporation of rhetorical and strategic elements that were often unperceived, underplayed, or only vaguely glimpsed at the outset. If one single aspect of the campaign stands out as most consequential, it was the early decision of AT&T executives—only two years into the initial campaign—to view the deliberate shaping of a corporate image no longer as an experiment but rather as a policy they would doggedly pursue. Sometimes clever, and eventually well-integrated, the AT&T campaign was, above all, relentless.[4]

From Arrogance to Service: AT&T's "New Voice"

Fresh leadership and a corporate reorganization at AT&T in 1907 precipitated the new strategy.[5] In 1894 the patents that had given AT&T a monopoly over telephone equipment in the United States had expired. The giant corporation, renowned for its arrogant attitude, suddenly found itself locked in an intensely competitive struggle with a multitude of independent commercial companies and small cooperative systems. Up to this time, as a Boston lawyer and advisor to AT&T had remarked, the company had enjoyed "a monopoly more profitable and more controlling—and more generally hated—than any ever given by any patent."[6]

Always a remorseless defender of its patent rights (it had initiated more than six thousand successful lawsuits against infringers), AT&T responded to direct competition after 1894 with the harshest tactics at its disposal: price-cutting (including below-cost pricing in competitive regions), denigration of its rivals' service and financial soundness, the use of its financial connections to cut off needed capital from its rivals, isolation of independent competitors through its control of access to long-distance lines, and buyouts of key companies to prevent independents from establishing national or regional links. In response AT&T's competitors, who were invariably smaller and often locally owned, cultivated sentimental support and local political favoritism through their underdog status and hometown connections. As a result AT&T usually played the role of the "heavy"—the "foreign" corporation—in municipal and regional contests against "'home' institutions."[7]

By 1907, after more than a decade of competition, AT&T still could not claim a substantial victory over the independents, despite its superior resources and ruthless tactics. Managed by a group of conservative Boston financiers, the company had given higher priority to high rates and short-term profits than to improvement and expansion of the system. Meanwhile, independent companies, often mutual in form, had emerged in markets that AT&T had dismissed as less immediately profitable. Although it had won many of the head-to-head local wars with competitors, AT&T found its share of the market reduced from 100 percent in 1893 to only 51 percent in 1907, when the market was much larger. For this very modest "success" in preserving its dominant position in the industry, it had paid a heavy price in public suspicion and antagonism. By 1907, in Robert Garnet's words, AT&T

was "strapped by burgeoning financial obligations, troubled by intense competition, haunted by a reputation as an insensitive, ruthless monopoly, and hounded by the specter of regulation and municipal ownership." To cap this inglorious epoch in AT&T's career, the financial panic of 1907—which further inflamed anti-monopoly sentiments—brought the corporation to the brink of disaster.[8]

At this point J. P. Morgan & Company stepped in to take control. Morgan ousted the old leadership in favor of sixty-two-year-old Theodore Vail, a president of AT&T in the 1880s (when it was merely the long-distance subsidiary of the American Bell Company) and a general superintendent of railway mail under the postmaster general in the 1870s. Vail moved the corporate headquarters from Boston to New York, undertook a major internal restructuring, and began to pay close attention to the company's publicity operations. He shared Morgan's distaste for competition. Any reasonable customer, in Vail's view, wanted the broadest service with the widest network of interconnection. Competing companies meant duplication, inconvenience, inefficiency, and barriers to interconnection. Thus the telephone was a "natural monopoly"—only a single, "universal" system could provide maximum benefits to each subscriber.[9]

Although the very mention of monopoly stirred deep public fears and resentments, Vail concluded that AT&T should meet that issue head-on, although with one discreet concession. The inescapable reality of monopoly would be cloaked in more palatable language, with phrases like "a single system" and "universal service" invoked. A persistent campaign of public relations would surely win approval for this reasonable concept. Under Vail's leadership the giant utility increased its market share in five years to 58 percent. By 1912, in Claude Fischer's phrase, it was "clearly in ascendance." Already, according to the *New York World,* financiers in New York were ranking Vail along with J. P. Morgan and Judge Elbert Gary of U.S. Steel as "the three biggest men in big business today."[10]

The daunting obstacles to success justified unprecedented spending for institutional advertising. AT&T's previous "take-it-or-leave-it" attitude toward the public and its heavy-handed competition against the independents had left a legacy of public suspicion. Many people considered AT&T's dominance in telephony as simply a temporary holdover from the patent era and did not share Vail's vision of the telephone as a natural monopoly. Indeed, the independent telephone companies ridiculed that notion and denounced the Bell system as a "piratical enemy to every Independent company."[11]

Moreover, advocacy of public ownership of various utilities reached its height between 1905 and 1915. Vail deplored the dangerous example set for American reformers by government ownership of nearly all the telephone systems of Europe. Closer to home, in some Canadian provinces, ominous trends were emerging. There private utilities were confronted by the forces of what Christopher Armstrong and N. V. Nelles have characterized as "civic populism." A protest movement built on angry reactions to "the dawning of a new era in which large corporations would dominate economic life," civic populism represented the most clearly organized expression of those concerns that large business corporations would have to overcome if they were to attain full popular legitimacy. In Canada civic populism took the specific form of protests "against inadequate service by arbitrary, self-serving monopolies."[12]

AT&T had looked to extend its natural monopoly throughout Canada as well as the United States, but Canada had terminated the company's patent rights earlier, ushering in a season of severe competition. Its experiences in Canada made AT&T highly conscious of the power of grassroots resistance and of potential threats from the kinds of "large-scale ventures in public ownership" that had forced it into retreat in the prairie provinces of Manitoba, Saskatchewan, and Alberta.[13] Fears that Canadian models of public ownership would contaminate opinion in the Midwest and plains states continued to perturb AT&T executives for nearly two decades.

When Vail assumed the leadership of AT&T, he threw his support behind those on his staff who sought to recast the corporation's public image and find means for AT&T to speak directly to the public in its new voice. At one point even the Ayer agency, which stood to gain a sizable commission from the company's proposed new advertising campaign, warned nervously that open advocacy of monopoly, particularly during the 1908 presidential election campaign and in the wake of the panic of 1907, might provoke a backlash. But Vail overrode these concerns. His philosophy of service rather than competition, he believed, was crucial to the long-range interests of the company and the nation. AT&T should begin forthrightly to advocate the virtues of corporate bigness; it should reshape its image in accord with the slogan "One Policy, One System, Universal Service."[14]

In taking this bold initiative Vail committed AT&T to a program of image building that the company had begun to explore in recent years, ever so tentatively, through local experiments and publicity advisors. Early in the century the previous AT&T president, Frederick Fish, had started a public relations program; he engaged a press agency to check on press coverage (in the first survey 90 percent of the clippings were antagonistic to the Bell companies) and to "scatter seeds of real information."[15] Then, in 1906, the New York Telephone Company, a Bell affiliate, was confronted by the challenge of an independent company seeking to "invade" its New York City domain and obtain a competing franchise. This rival attacked AT&T's affiliate for its inadequate service and extortionate rates.

At a time when "the public was beginning to become pretty thoroughly inoculated with the muck-rake germ and was ready to believe ill of any large corporation," the New York Telephone Company concluded that it would be unwise to ignore this threat. In what *Printers' Ink* characterized as "a new way to lobby," the company purchased display ads in the New York and Brooklyn newspapers for the ten days preceding the hearings scheduled on the issue. The ads condemned the evils of "telephone duplication"; they did not flinch from quoting those who fearlessly used the term "monopoly" in explaining the advantages of a natural monopoly over the vexations and wastefulness that would arise from competition.[16] By directly putting its case "before the whole public," AT&T's New York affiliate not only defeated its challenger but also inspired supporting editorials in several major newspapers. The success of this effort, it reported to the AT&T publicity director in May 1907, "indicated the possibilities of a broad policy of publicity."[17]

Early in 1908 James Ellsworth, who had left the corporation's Boston press agency to join the AT&T headquarters staff, persuaded Vice President E. K. Hall to allocate several thousand dollars for a similar campaign in Rochester. In what Vail and Ellsworth were to term a "laboratory experiment," Ellsworth masterminded an operation to turn the tables on a rival that was making inroads among Bell subscribers. First he defused resentment against outside intervention from AT&T headquarters by offering prizes for advertising copy submitted by local journalists.

Then he developed a series of ads that explained the advantages of Bell service, with its long-distance linkages. When the loss of subscribers ceased and complaints about service lessened, AT&T deemed the experiment a success.[18]

While this series was still in progress, the parent corporation signed its first contract with an established advertising agency to prepare a national campaign. Unsurprisingly, its choice was N. W. Ayer & Son. One of the largest and most reputable agencies of that era, Ayer had recently devised a campaign of institutional advertising aimed at corporate image rehabilitation and political protection—namely, on behalf of the Mutual Life Insurance Company in the wake of the sensational insurance scandals and investigations of 1905.[19] Ayer's work for AT&T, however, would differ radically from that momentary rescue mission. Indeed, it would extend over half a century.

Of Innocence and Image

With a heightened appreciation of public opinion AT&T now committed itself to the creation of a new public image. This move reflected President Vail's emphasis on system building, his confidence in the public's ability to see the logic of a natural monopoly, and his recognition that the company's image was important enough to warrant the employment of a professional advertising agency. But AT&T's notion of what that new image would be, and how it could best be conveyed, remained very rudimentary. Even though the company had gained some experience in the clandestine tactics of manipulating public opinion, its initial efforts to shape a corporate image through institutional advertising betray a staid and lofty innocence.

Negative public attitudes toward the large corporation, businessmen habitually surmised, stemmed from a single problem: "They do not know us."[20] By contrast, anyone who saw AT&T at close range, asserted Publicity Chief Ellsworth, "became a supporter and friend." That was the fundamental premise of AT&T's naive approach. Since it was not practical to bring the entire public into the company to gain this understanding, Ellsworth explained in retrospect, "we tried to take the Company to the public, hoping for similar results."[21] With the same naïveté AT&T assumed that the public understanding that was needed was purely rational. If public opinion was unfavorable, Vail observed in the company's 1911 annual report, "it is wrong because of wrong information." Public hostility, Ellsworth noted, arose simply from "lack of knowledge." The leaders of AT&T had devised a logical and systematic approach to the development of telephony; they had come up with rational responses to the problems and constraints that they faced. If only the public could be brought to understand the problems and to see the rationality of the solution, AT&T would henceforth operate with the public confidence that its policies warranted.[22]

The first five institutional ads, which appeared monthly in a large selection of magazines beginning in June and July 1908, impeccably reflected the lofty tone of this appeal to rationality. Embellished, at Vail's insistence, with nothing more than a prominent headline and a very modest logo or illustration, the long texts extended from 350 to over 500 words (Fig. 2.1). Sometimes awkwardly defensive, they argued that AT&T's "widespread work should clear your mind of doubt, if any exists, that the associated Bell companies are working *with* and *for* the public."

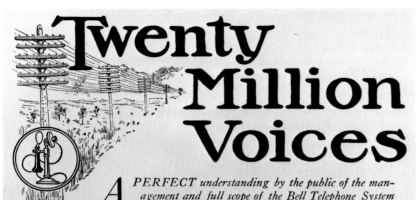

Twenty Million Voices

A PERFECT *understanding by the public of the management and full scope of the Bell Telephone System can have but one effect, and that a most desirable one—a marked betterment of the service.*

Do you know what makes the telephone worth while to you—just about the most indispensable thing in modern life?

It isn't the circuit of wire that connects your instrument with the exchange.

It's the Twenty Million Voices at the other end of the wire on every Bell Telephone!

We have to keep them there, on hair trigger, ready for you to call them up, day or night—downtown, up in Maine, or out in Denver.

And to make the telephone system useful to those Twenty Million other people, we have to keep *you* alert and ready at this end of the wire.

Then we have to keep the line in order—8,000,000 miles of wire—and the central girls properly drilled and accommodating to the last degree, and the apparatus up to the highest pitch of efficiency.

Quite a job, all told.

Every telephone user is an important link in the system—just as important as the operator. With a little well meant suggestion on our part, we believe we can improve the service—perhaps save a second on each call.

There are about *six billion connections* a year over these lines.

Saving a second each would mean a tremendous time saving to you and a tremendous saving of operating expenses, which can be applied to the betterment of the service.

The object of this and several succeeding magazine advertisements is *not to get more subscribers*. It is to make each one of you a better link in the chain.

First, give "Central" the number clearly and be sure she hears it. Give her full and clear information in cases of doubt. She is there to do her utmost to accommodate you.

Next, don't grow fretful because you think she represents a monopoly. The postmaster does, too, for the same reason.

The usefulness of the telephone is its *universality, as one system*. Where there are two systems you must have two telephones—and confusion.

Remember, the value of the service lies in the number of people you can reach *without* confusion—the promptness with which you get your response.

So respond quickly when others call you, bearing in mind the extensive scope of the service.

The constant endeavor of the associated Bell companies, harmonized by one policy and acting as one system, is to give you the best and most economical management human ingenuity can devise. The end is efficient service and your attitude and that of every other subscriber may hasten or hinder its accomplishment.

Agitation against legitimate telephone business—the kind that has become almost as national in its scope as the mail service—must disappear with a realization of the necessity of universal service.

American Telephone & Telegraph Company

And Its Associated Bell Companies

One Policy—One System Universal Service

UNITING OVER 4,000,000 TELEPHONES

FIGURE 2.1
Long-winded and didactic, AT&T's early ads favored argument over imagery. Proclaiming their intent to "make each one of you a better link in the chain," they explained testily why "agitation against legitimate telephone business . . . must disappear."

That being the case, the October ad concluded pompously, "the less the working conditions are made inflexible by legislative proscription, the better will be the solution of the constantly-changing problems incident to maintaining the universal telephone service wisely demanded by the public." In an implicit response to public criticism AT&T insisted that its rates were fair, because they were based on costs openly stated.[23]

Contentious and often didactic, these AT&T messages shifted part of the blame for telephone problems back onto the public. The July 1908 ad, for instance, instructed subscribers to give "full and clear information" to the operator and then lectured them: "Don't grow fretful because you think she [the operator] represents a monopoly. The postmaster does, too, for the same reason." Rational understanding, the ads asserted, would reveal why the telephone had to be a single, universal system. AT&T's aspirations for monopoly status thus should be regarded not as a "fault" of the company but rather as its frank and upright acceptance of "The Telephone's Burden." As the initial ad observed: "The Bell companies are not responsible for the fact that a nation's convenience demands the use of one telephone system, any more than they are that *one language* for a nation is better than a collection of provincial dialects."[24]

Some aspects of this high-toned yet argumentative style persisted in AT&T copy for nearly two decades. Perhaps that was only to be expected from a company whose president was engrossed in the structural rationalization and system building and whose vice president could matter-of-factly declare: "We have lofty purposes, and we are entitled to have them known." Consciously designed to convey order and respectability through balanced and dignified layouts, the AT&T ads included ample white space and no visual gimmicks. They used genteel, noncolloquial phrasing, frequently resorting to metaphor, allegory, and historical allusion to present the telephone as an agent of civilization. These ads clearly reflected the "stability, order, security and predictability" that George David Smith identifies as having become "embedded in the Bell System's corporate culture since Vail's regime." But were these qualities sufficient to create a new corporate image that would, as the initial Ayer proposal had prophesied, "sink down deep into the hearts of all classes of people who use the telephone"?[25]

The Ayer agency's response to this question set the predominant tone of early institutional advertising. As its passageway to the public heart Ayer looked to the grandiose vision. People would be stirred by seeing how directly the telephone was connected with the greatest of personal and societal aspirations. Thus the AT&T ads regularly glorified the telephone's role in advancing civilization, promoting human harmony and national unity, and contributing to personal power (Fig. 2.2). Eventually AT&T would establish tactical models for many a giant corporation. It would push beyond primary reliance on such grandiose visions and explore a variety of other ploys, both visual and rhetorical, for subduing popular misgivings about the power embodied in the new corporate leviathans.

The Politics of the Continuous Campaign

The results of institutional advertising are notoriously difficult to measure.[26] Even so, AT&T quickly found reasons to extend and enlarge its initial campaign. The

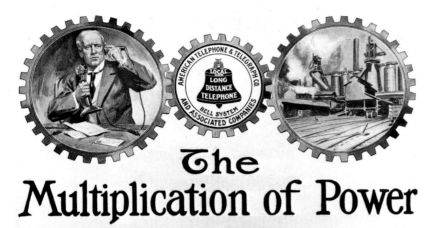

The Multiplication of Power

There is no higher efficiency in the world than that of the American business man.

The multiplication of *power* in a business man—if he has the ability within him—depends upon the *increased number* of people whom he can, *by personal contact,* interest in his purposes.

He does this by telephone, and the multiplication of *the telephone's* usefulness depends on the *increased number* of persons whom he can reach.

Has the vast development of industries since 1890—the greatest period of advance in the world's history—*when America has advanced faster than all the rest of the world,* been the force that has built up this great, unified, efficient telephone service; or

Has the increased ability of the American business man to bring people to him from every locality, far and near, *over the Bell Telephone System,* been the cause of the multiplication of his power and his principality?

... ichever ... se and

FIGURE 2.2

AT&T highlighted the telephone's role in making business more efficient. Promising the businessman a "multiplication of his power and his principality," the company depicted itself providing power, not amassing it.

Ayer agency assured AT&T (without providing any specific evidence) that it was "manifest in many ways" that the public, especially "the more important classes," displayed a strong interest in AT&T's "monthly communication." It would be best, the agency added when proposing an expanded campaign in 1910, if the new 1909 format of "strong, effective illustration, a forceful headline, and a short, pithy, well boiled down text" was adopted as a uniform style. "Our idea," Ayer's account executive had confided in 1909, "is to make the AT&T advertising an institution and have the advertisements so attractive that the people will begin to look for the monthly story about the telephone." Through cumulative effect the series would "get the people acquainted with the magnitude of the work the AT&T Company is doing" and inspire the habit of reading the monthly messages "with a friendly eye." [27]

More important than the agency's promptings were encouraging signs that the drive for a new corporate image was moving forward on several fronts and with myriad effects. Not only had there been no political backlash from the advertising, but the campaign seemed to be serving as an excellent marketing tool as well. Although Vail had insisted that the series "get away from the commercial idea" and avoid any appeal to purchase telephone service, it had apparently produced substantial new business. Moreover, the campaign coincided with what Leonard Reich describes as Vail's drive to "transform a loosely organized, poorly managed group of semi-independent companies into a truly integrated national system." The obstacles to such integration, and to the achievement of greater efficiencies through functional specialization, were often the "longstanding traditions of local company autonomy," as Robert Garnet points out. But the national advertising campaign helped convey Vail's rationale of systemwide cohesion and order to local executives as well as to the public.[28]

Beginning as early as 1909, AT&T executives badgered the associated Bell companies to adapt their advertising to the style of the national campaign in order to create an "appearance of uniformity." This would impress the public with the unity of the Bell system and "increase in geometrical proportion" the effect of all advertisements. AT&T headquarters began supplying illustrated ads to its associated companies to adapt for local use. The coordination of national and local advertising and publicity led to conferences between headquarters and regional executives, which Publicity Chief Ellsworth described as "worth while for the purpose they serve of amalgamating, of bringing together, the eyes, ears and mouth-pieces of the Bell System." Such meetings of regional executives with the same specific functions became a major structural means of coordination within the Bell system. The surge of publicity and centralizing activity even inspired one headquarters executive to propose a new AT&T magazine to supplement all the local company publications. Although his proposal was not immediately adopted, his zeal to promulgate "sane and sound doctrine" to all regional executives clearly reflected the company's enthusiasm for the infusion of a new national image, both internally and externally.[29]

For all the eagerness of AT&T leaders to see in the new advertising a vehicle of corporate cohesion, the basic purpose of the campaign remained political. As one of the corporation's vice presidents had observed as early as 1909, "unwise legislation" was "the only serious danger that lies ahead of the company."[30] Agitation for progressive reform continued to mount after 1909; popular discussion of municipal ownership of utilities did not subside. In Canada several victories in public ownership campaigns suggested that the tide might be turning against the private utility companies. In Great Britain the government completed its takeover of the telephone system at the beginning of 1912.[31] Even more ominously, President Woodrow Wilson came into office in 1913 with views favorable to public ownership of the telephone system, and in November Wilson's postmaster general, Albert Burleson, proposed government ownership and operation. Although no legislation ensued, AT&T remained highly sensitive to the issue. As Neil Mitchell observes, the company dedicated "about half of the sixty-eight pages in [its] 1913 annual report" to arguments against public ownership. Moreover, it initiated a maneuver—both a public relations venture and a shift in corporate behavior—that may well have undercut the prospects for the challenge momentarily contemplated in the Wilson administration.[32]

In December 1913 AT&T announced a significant revision of corporate intentions. In what came to be known as the Kingsbury Commitment (in recognition of AT&T vice president Nathan Kingsbury, who signed an agreement with the Department of Justice), AT&T promised to divest itself of its stock in Western Union, to provide connections with its long-distance lines for non-Bell companies in areas that AT&T did not serve, and to desist from acquiring independent telephone companies without explicit approval of the Department of Justice. This commitment was widely recognized as a deal by AT&T to avoid antitrust prosecution. What it meant, as Garnet observes, is that AT&T had "traded away future acquisitions for government approval of Bell's existing and powerful position in the market." AT&T would no longer seek an ownership monopoly over the entire national system. Rather, through cooperation with independent companies, it would oversee the creation of a national network. As Claude Fischer notes, competition now rapidly gave way to the creation of local and regional "geographic monopolies" (mostly under Bell companies but with a significant minority of independents), all linked by the Bell long-distance lines.[33]

In many respects the 1913 commitment represented a logical unfolding of Vail's corporate strategy. Certainly it paved the way for further cultivation of AT&T's new corporate image of fairness, stability, and paternalistic responsibility. Vail had consistently accepted the validity of public regulation. Far from attempting to evade such control, he had contrived to foster regulation at the state level (by expert commissions, not political bodies) as a backfire against local regulation or municipal ownership. As early as 1908 Vail had conveyed his views to another AT&T executive by citing an instance in which AT&T had chosen to submit to regulation rather than incur public disapproval. Instead of fighting a proposed state regulatory commission, the company had used its energies to obtain "as good a Commission law as possible." Cooperation and interconnection with the independents actually served this strategy better than competition. Not only did all the telephone companies acquire the same interests, but the decline of competition removed some of the internal controversies in the industry that could attract public attention. During an era characterized by a corporate search for stability and rationalization, AT&T stood at the forefront of this pursuit.[34]

One might assume that the Kingsbury Commitment of 1913 would have eased AT&T's concern about the threat of public ownership. But as visible agitation for public ownership in the United States subsided between 1914 and 1916, AT&T actually grew more concerned—about the dangers of a loss of vigilance, if not about substantive threats. During its national publicity conferences of 1914 and 1916, which advertising and public relations executives from all the associated companies attended, AT&T focused on "government ownership sentiment."[35] Several regional officers noted both the vulnerabilities and possibilities among AT&T employees. A Nebraska executive recommended "the strongest work . . . with our own employees." He had talked with men laying cable in the field, he reported, and learned that they assumed workers were better treated under government ownership. A New York representative observed that AT&T employees, if given all the facts, could be the company's greatest PR assets. At the very least, AT&T publicity agents concluded, a continuing program of "education without irritation" was "essential . . . to keep misguided agitation from growing into misguided legislation." In 1917 *Printers' Ink* would credit the complete subsidence of the "decided movement toward Government ownership of telephone systems" of "only a few years ago" to the effects of AT&T's "comprehensive advertising campaign."[36]

Another aspect of the essentially political orientation of AT&T's campaign, as Ellsworth made clear to the associated companies in 1916, was an emphasis on farm publications. As late as 1927 AT&T still spent approximately one-third of its appropriation for institutional advertising in the agricultural press. The "good reason for specializing on this particular class of people," Ellsworth noted, was that they were both numerous and "politically powerful." Another reason, of course, was that rural residents were expensive to serve and had therefore been largely neglected by the AT&T regional companies in their expansion. It was from rural areas that political attacks on AT&T were most likely to be launched.[37]

The choice of periodicals clearly reflected both the range and duration of AT&T's political objectives. It published its regular monthly advertisements not only in popular magazines but also in obscure farm publications, trade journals, and even — as a long-range investment — such magazines as *American Boy.* Although some other institutional advertisers would explicitly take the N. W. Ayer list of publications for AT&T ads as their model, those with smaller public relations budgets and more pressing political agendas usually dropped the farm and juvenile publications and focused on a smaller number of prestigious or high-circulation periodicals. But AT&T continued to spread its campaign very broadly. Behind this strategy lay the usually unspoken but persistent assumption, voiced by Ellsworth during the experimental upstate New York campaign of 1908, that the magazines and newspapers that benefited from AT&T advertising revenues would also be influenced thereby in their editorial policy. They would carry the Bell companies' numerous self-serving "news releases" because "there would be the pressure of advertising patronage" behind them.[38]

In 1926, reflecting on the absence of measurable results from its two decades of institutional advertising, Ellsworth would philosophize that "advertising is like bullets and bird shot." If there was a specific, immediate target, he observed, you would use a bullet. But "to bring down as many birds from a flock as possible," bird shot was the better choice. "Institutional advertising is like bird shot," he concluded. "It is not for a one time effect but for a long pull."[39] Ellsworth was certainly right in ascribing prime significance to the broad, relentless quality of AT&T's "bird shot" campaigns over several decades. Still, the tactics embodied in each of the tiny pellets, the individual ads, were crafted with careful attention to their intended effects. And many of these tactics, like AT&T's campaign as a whole, would serve as models for subsequent converts to the mission of corporate public relations.

The Issue of Power

In no area did AT&T deal with a more fundamental strategic problem, or explore a greater variety of approaches, than in its representations of corporate power. AT&T constantly sought ways to evoke public appreciation of the extent and complexity of its system (and thus its power to serve). But its politically vulnerable

Annihilator of Space

To be within arm's reach of distant cities it is only necessary to be within arm's reach of a Bell Telephone. It annihilates space and provides instanta-~ ~~~~~~~ ~~~~n, both near and far.

An exchange which is purely local has a certain value. If, in addition to its local connections, it has connections with other contiguous localities, it has a largely increa~~~ value.

FIGURE 2.3

AT&T designated the businessman the proper figure to wield the power to annihilate space. When women, as telephone operators, reached over vast areas (see Figs. 2.13, 2.14), they did so only in the service of others.

position as a private monopoly made it especially sensitive to the need to tell the story of its vast size in a nonthreatening way. Other large corporations would soon benefit from observing AT&T's tactics for brandishing impressive size while ignoring, understating, or ennobling corporate power.

AT&T did not shy from using the word "power." But it shifted the focus to its subscribers' exercise of power via the telephone. Under headlines such as "The Multiplication of Power," "In Touch with His World," "Annihilator of Space," and "Your Telephone Horizon," AT&T consistently placed the subscriber (always a man, and usually a businessman) in a position of command. Again and again the ads identified the telephone as an instrument of power. It afforded a command over distance—and, by implication, over people and things. AT&T conveyed this concept most forcefully through dramatic images of businessmen looming over the land, reaching out to extend their control to new, distant horizons (Fig 2.3).

Although AT&T ads beguiled men with talk of their personal power, they resorted mainly to numbers to brag of the company's own magnitude and resources. The early ads exhibited a decided penchant for the recitation—to the point of incantation—of large figures. Over the first ten years some 70 percent of the ads cited at least one figure in the thousands, millions, or billions. Sixty percent included one or more figures in the millions or above. Between 1908 and 1912 the

In The Public Service

The President of the United States works for 80,000,000 people all the time.

He needs rest and change to keep him fit for his work, and yet he cannot neglect his official duties, he must always be within reach.

When Washington was president he

A Highway of Communication

It goes by your door. Every Home, every office, every factory, and every farm in the land is on that great highway or

This service adds to the efficiency of each citizen, and multiplies the power of the whole nation.

FIGURE 2.4 *(top)*
Standing in the foreground between the White House and the summer mansion, the telephone was the first central corporate image of a company that imperially represented itself as the embodiment of telephony.

FIGURE 2.5 *(bottom)*
Through overpowering size and patterned repetition, along with imposing statistics in the text, AT&T ads aimed to impress the public with the company's enormous effort to provide extensive service.

texts of seven individual ads incorporated "million(s)" and "billion(s)" at least four times. In 1914 the corporation outdid itself by including figures in the millions or billions some fourteen times in its April advertisement and nine times in August.[40]

Such litanies of figures would be awe-inspiring, AT&T and its ad agency seem to have assumed. They would impress readers with the size and capacity of the system and perhaps even evoke gratitude for the work involved in constructing and maintaining so elaborate a network.[41] These numbers, of course, were always presented in the context of a capacity to serve. Although they also conveyed a notion of power, it was power placed in the hands of telephone users. As if fretful that the almost-ritualistic reiteration of huge numbers had not completely accomplished its intended effect, or perhaps sensitive to the need to move beyond an engineering mentality, copywriters after about 1914 frequently enhanced these lists with such adjectives as "vast," "myriad," "wondrous," and "marvelous."

As enumerations of figures increased, verbiage declined. The argumentative copy of the first year's ads soon gave way to radically reduced texts (from an average length of over 350 words in 1908 to fewer than 150 words by early 1911).[42] Metaphor and pictorial imagery assumed the responsibility for educating a lay audience in the logic and beneficence of a unified system—the telephone as highway, as "clear track," as ancient runner or pony express, as nervous system, as "sign board of civilization."[43] While the numbers continued to stress the pure size of the corporation's undertakings, the metaphors reduced that vast system to familiar terms and emphasized its functionality.

Illustrations soon expanded to occupy at least one-third of the space in each ad. Repeatedly AT&T promulgated two simple, striking images, that of the telephone itself (Fig. 2.4) and that of receding rows of poles and wires (see Fig. 2.1). Even though images of the telephone were virtually proscribed from the many ads based on allegories and historical metaphors, still some 60 percent of all AT&T institutional advertisements over the first four years depicted at least one telephone. Eight times during 1909 and 1910 the image of the telephone appeared in such disproportionate size as to acquire iconic status (see, e.g., Fig 2.4). On three other occasions during these same two years, it gained equivalent visual power through patterned repetition (Fig. 2.5).

This iconomania went beyond print advertisements. At the 1915 Panama-Pacific Exposition AT&T mounted an archetypal telephone, some ten feet high, atop its "Attended Pay Station" building. At the same event Western Electric, AT&T's manufacturing arm, called attention to its exhibit with a gigantic reproduction of a telephone desk set (Fig. 2.6).[44] A variety of reasons—including technical problems and a fear of higher costs—underlay AT&T's hesitancy in adopting the differently configured "French phone," with receiver and mouthpiece in the same unit. But one wonders whether part of its resistance to this change, perhaps subconsciously, stemmed from a reluctance to abandon so visually embedded a cultural icon as that serious, utilitarian, black desk set.[45]

Early on AT&T equated itself with all telephony; representations of the company through the image of the telephone conformed to that stance. AT&T ads virtually never mentioned the independent companies; rather, they credited to the Bell system the benefits of all telephone communication. When AT&T identified the telephone with the advancement of civilization, the unity of the nation, or broad technological and economic progress, it neglected to differentiate the social

FIGURE 2.6

The telephone as icon found its ultimate expression in what the Western Electric Company described as a "Brobdignagian instrument" in its 1915 Panama-Pacific Exposition display. Twenty people could fit on the upholstered seat constructed around its base.

Union Increases Use

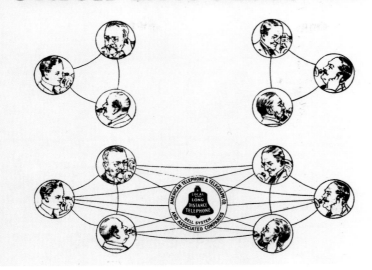

FIGURE 2.7

In the first five years of AT&T institutional ads women had little visibility. Not even a female operator intruded into this diagram of a network of male subscribers, who were linked instead by the company logo.

and economic effects of telephony from the achievements of the Bell system. The public was encouraged to imagine AT&T as something like an immense telephone hovering over the nation and linking all its citizens. Certainly such an image promised to dispel any notions of the corporation as a clique of greedy, monopoly-seeking capitalists, connoting instead a relatively abstract provider of power-as-service through functional technology. But it did not yet approach the goal, proclaimed by one AT&T executive, of inspiring "real affection."[46]

Operators and Linemen: AT&T's Human Face

Only after five full years of institutional advertising did AT&T begin to experiment with a major new visual strategy in its ads, one aimed at humanizing the company's image though illustrations of its employees. While it had not neglected other avenues for publicizing the heroism, loyalty, and courtesy of its employees—especially the operators—its ad campaign up to that point had been devoted to preaching the virtues of a single, nationwide system.[47] Nearly every ad had sought either to celebrate the concept of a system through metaphor or historical comparison or to flatter the consumer by portraying him (rarely her) extending his power through the telephone network. Not once between 1908 and 1913 did an ad include the image of a telephone employee. When a connection between users was depicted, wires, the company logo, or the telephone itself signified the linkage (Fig. 2.7).

The Spirit of Service

WHEN the land is storm-swept, when trains are stalled and roads are blocked, the telephone trouble-hunter with snow shoes and climbers makes his lonely fight to keep the wire highways open.

̄ ̄ ̄ ̄ he ̄ ̄ ̄ ̄d to f̄ ̄ ̄

telephone forces, who are finally responsible to the public for good service.

This spirit of service is found in the recent rearrangement of the telephone business to conform with present public policy, without recourse to courts.

T̄ ̄ Bell ̄ ̄ ̄ ̄ has ̄ ̄ ̄ ̄ ̄

FIGURE 2.8

In this 1913 heroic painting the lineman, dwarfed by the storm to underscore his courage, emerged as the first humanized embodiment of AT&T's "spirit of service."

But in March 1914 the monthly AT&T ad broke with tradition to feature the romanticized image of a lineman. As a heroic figure he struggled against wind and snow to carry out his dangerous mission of emergency repairs. Entitled *The Spirit of Service,* the painting used for this ad was long displayed in "an honored place" at AT&T's New York headquarters (Fig. 2.8).[48] After another two years of rather slight attention to employees, during which operators were occasionally depicted in small drawings or as parts of a montage, AT&T granted its operators their own glorified stature as the embodiment of the company. In *Weavers of Speech,* a painting first reproduced in a December 1915 ad and soon accorded the status of another of AT&T's aesthetic treasures, the archetypal operator gracefully and competently gathered up a profusion of wires as she offered human connection to factory, city, and rural household (Figs. 2.9 and 2.10).[49] The metaphor of the operator as "weaver of speech" (or in an earlier version, as "spinner of speech") evocatively associated women's historic domestic role as spinners or weavers with their new function as facilitators of communications technology.

Weavers of Speech

Upon the magic looms of the Bell System, tens of millions of telephone messages are daily woven into a marvelous fabric, representing the countless activities of a busy people.

Day and night, invisible hands ⸍⸍ the shu⸍⸍⸍⸍ ⸍⸍nd fro

the subscribers, these weavers of speech sit silently at the switchboards, swiftly and skillfully interlacing the cords which guide the human voice over the country in all directions.

Whether a man wants his neighbor in town, or some one ⸍⸍⸍⸍ ⸍⸍ ⸍⸍⸍ ⸍⸍⸍

FIGURE 2.9 *(above)*
Romanticized and ennobled in this sumptuous painting, the operator as "weaver of speech" brought to the corporate image the aura of her traditional feminine role as weaver of the family's bonds of kinship and caring.

FIGURE 2.10 *(left)*
Now, by 1915, AT&T's network had attained a human, and specifically female, persona (cf. Fig. 2.7). The operator gained stature, but mainly though service to men. Of the three sites depicted, only the rural homestead could be assumed to encompass female subscribers.

Loyalty to Public Service

From this point forward AT&T regularly presented itself to the public through the images of operator and lineman. The corporate giant had long recognized that its public standing depended heavily on its users' satisfaction with their many personal contacts with its employees. In the earliest years a desire to improve public relations had spurred the company to replace boys as operators with young women, who were presumably more patient, courteous, and deferential to subscribers and whose gendered cultural roles included mediation and personal service.[50] President Vail, as Richard Tedlow observes, had long "recognized the importance of making employees ambassadors to the public"; Vice President Hall, in a warning about the need to protect the company from "unnecessary legislation," had stressed the promise that employee contacts with the public held for a big company. "No man is going to get very friendly with a corporation," Hall admonished his listeners. But he might get friendly with a person who served him and put "the personal element into it."[51] By the time the "Spirit of Service" and "Weavers of Speech" ads appeared, AT&T had also clearly recognized that public glamorization of its workers might enhance their morale and performance, thus making them better public relations "ambassadors."

Of AT&T's two humanized personas the lineman initially enjoyed greater visibility. He served admirably as a symbol of employee loyalty, heroism, and public service. Although AT&T's March 1921 ad, "Loyalty to Public Service," gave him a recognizable face and an endearing family (Fig. 2.11), the lineman thereafter specialized mostly in more emblematic appearances, featuring intrepid action atop

The continent that became a neighborhood

An Advertisement of the American Telephone and Telegraph Company

THROUGH slim wires etched against the sky . . . through cables laid in the earth under cities and fields . . . millions of Americans, miles' or days' journeys apart, speak to each other as readily as though they stood face to face.

Over her telephone, a housewife in a Wis-

System is the vital one of making it possible to maintain social and business contacts in cities that contain many times more people than this nation once boasted . . . in a neighborhood which the Census reports to hold 127 million people. Year after year from its beginning, the Bell System has incr   'rs
fo   'te p   nd i-

FIGURES 2.11 & 2.12

Humanized in domestic and on-the-job close-ups here, the lineman—as heroic persona of the corporation—would eventually appear mainly in

middle-distance profiles, dramatically etched against the sky, to portray the company's courageous loyalty to public service.

telephone poles (Fig. 2.12). By the beginning of the 1940s an allusion to "snapshots of linemen against the sky" would denote this now-routine corporate image.[52]

   Even at a distance the lineman made an excellent persona for a large corporation, as an executive for the Pacific Gas and Electric Company testified in 1922. Determined to put "some flesh and blood" into its own "soulless corporation," PG&E adopted for itself the figure of the "red-blooded man at the top of a thirty-foot pole, covered with snow and ice, fighting a . . . mountain gale and literally 'hugging an icicle' to repair the power line." Soon thereafter Western Electric created its own heroic repairman, "hard at it night and day" to restore service in stormy weather. AT&T had shown other public utilities, as the PG&E executive suggested, "the way in which the company wants to visualize itself to its patrons." It did not want to be conceived as some "unseen power which squeezes the most

Where Woman's Service Looms Large

War gave woman her supreme and glorious opportunity to enlarge her field of service. She won her share of the laurels for patriotic achievement.

In counting house and chemical laboratory she has loaned her brains to the cause.

In telephone service, also, a host of capable. loyal daught⯑

out of people." The lineman not only gave the corporation a human form, he also epitomized loyal service.[53]

The telephone operator eventually proved her capacity to outshine even the lineman as representative of the corporation. She could effectively symbolize even more than heroism, loyalty, and dedicated service. From her first major appearance in AT&T institutional advertising she emerged as a symbol of human communication itself, both as a vast national system and as an intimate personal connection. Only in this role during the 1920s and 1930s did women in advertisements gain the prestigious position—one conventionally afforded to businessmen—of looking down over vast urban and rural landscapes, even over the entire continent (Fig. 2.13; see also 2.3). Of course, the operator did so only as the agent of the corporation and the adept servant of its male customers, but the corporation thus afforded her a vital self-image, one that aimed to reinforce the satisfactions she might draw from providing an essential service. By suggesting, through its ads as well as its direct communications with employees, that they "should feel a sense of special pride" in their employment by "a great institution devoted to public service,"

AT&T endeavored, as historian John Schact observes, to fortify its workers against the appeals of labor unionization.[54]

The aesthetic qualities of the archetypal operator's image earned recognition in corporate discussions of the AT&T exhibit at the 1933 Century of Progress Exposition in Chicago. Not only did the company offer visitors a view of *Weavers of Speech,* it also erected a display in which operators at a switchboard were illuminated for the public only through overhead spotlights. Against a background of "dead black," the lights created a "most artistic and arresting" effect. The company was delighted that "thousands of people" had taken "this picture of a telephone operator away with them." Six years later, at the 1939 New York World's Fair, the corporation would grant its employee icons an even more awesome stature. There a lineman on a telephone pole and an operator at a switchboard, each fifty feet high, occupied the "two heroic-sized panels" that framed the colossal entrance to the Telephone Building.[55]

What Gender the Corporation?

In 1915 AT&T devised an emblem that placed one of its major technological achievements in the service of its central image—that of a corporation that amassed power only to put it at the disposal of others. The occasion was AT&T's completion of the first transcontinental telephone line, a dramatic moment for rendering to the nation "an account of its stewardship." In an image that metaphorically depicted this accomplishment of man-to-man communication through technological wizardry, AT&T elevated a woman, draped like a goddess and wearing a tiara labeled "SCIENCE," to a height from which she could span a map of the continent with her arms. She gazed at the viewer invitingly as she held out a telephone to each coast to anchor the connecting line between them (Fig. 2.14).[56]

In historical hindsight we can discern an underlying tension, probably only half-conscious, in the gender properties of corporate imagery. Although by the 1960s many Americans would refer to AT&T, either contentedly or sardonically, as "Ma Bell," that nickname did not originate before the 1930s. Still, the concept of service carried a feminine ambience. Could an organization that was imbued with an engineering mystique and prided itself on rationality accommodate so problematic a self-image?[57]

In two intriguing studies the sociologists Claude S. Fischer and Michele Martin have provided significant insights into the gender dimensions of the Bell system's self-image. Various forms of evidence indicate that the telephone, from early in its dispersion, was frequently used for purposes of "sociability," especially by women. In congruence with their culturally ascribed role as the sustainers of the family's social networks, women used this new technology for conversations with friends and family members, or—as such usage was framed by those unsympathetic to the actual work of weaving the fabric of the community—for "gossip." However, the sales advertising of the Bell system companies, as Fischer points out, emphasized business uses of the telephone. When it did present home uses, it focused on the telephone's serviceability in emergencies and its contributions to practical home management, not on its nurturing dimensions. Only after many decades, in the late 1920s and 1930s, did Bell sales advertising begin to recognize and endorse

Making a Neighborhood of a Nation

THE TRANSCONTINENTAL
TELEPHONE LINE

FIGURE 2.14
The woman (or goddess) whom
AT&T labeled "Science" in its 1915
celebration of the achievement of
transcontinental service also connoted both the operator and
the nurturer of "neighborhood."

the social use of the telephone. Fischer astutely concludes that "telephone sociability" was "long ignored or repressed by industry leaders . . . because such conversations did not fit their understandings of what the technology was supposed to
be for."[58]

The gender issue was crucial in industry leaders' evasion of the social qualities of
the telephone. The telephone "facilitate[d] an activity that women typically both
enjoy and are good at," Fischer observes, but one that businessmen with an engineering bent found too unserious and "feminine" to deserve positive recognition.[59]
And if local Bell companies considered such usage too frivolous to publicize, even
when trying to promote sales, it should not be surprising that it found no place in
AT&T's quest for a corporate image. Institutional advertising, even more than the
local sales advertising, insisted on a serious, managerial image for the corporation
and its system—one commensurate with AT&T's status as a national "institution."

But women were part of a public whose political views could affect AT&T's
destiny. As early as May 1909 the Ayer agency proposed the inclusion of a specific
appeal to women in AT&T's institutional campaign. The tenor of the proposal,
and the advertisement that resulted, testify eloquently to the discomfort of AT&T
leaders with anything that might introduce a feminine or unbusinesslike aura into

THE SATURDAY
EVENING POST

An Illustrated Weekly Magazine
Founded A° D. 1728 by Benj. Franklin

MAY 29, 1909   5cts. THE COPY

ALONZO · KIMBALL

THE CURTIS PUBLISHING COMPANY, PHILADELPHIA

FIGURE 2.15
The ostensible model for
AT&T's female user of the
telephone carried a warm

ambience and assumed a
relaxed posture, suggesting a
social conversation.

the corporate image. The Ayer account executive proposed a group of three ads. Two would deal with men and power; the third, billed as "The Human Side of Universal Service," would depict a woman at home. "Up to this time," he noted, "we have not paid as much attention to the woman end of this advertising as we could." He attached a copy of the cover of the current *Saturday Evening Post* to indicate the type of "strong" woman the ad should depict (Fig. 2.15).[60]

FIGURE 2.16

When AT&T's advertising agency altered the *Saturday Evening Post* "cover girl" for institutional service, it gave her a desk and a more businesslike pose, consistent with the serious use of an essential implement.

AT&T did approve the proposed ad "for the ladies." But when it appeared the title had shifted to "The Comfort of the Telephone," and the prototype woman on the *Post* cover, with her flowing, slightly clinging dress and her casual demeanor, had been converted into a starchily attired, managerial housewife. Obviously, AT&T's female subscriber did not use her telephone to gossip; rather, she carried out businesslike calls from her household desk. The cover girl's divan had given way to a straight-backed chair, and the soft texture of the cover portrait had been replaced by sharper lines (Fig. 2.16). Here the "comfort" of the telephone had nothing to do with sociability. The telephone, as the "nervous system" of the business and social world, simply allowed a mother to keep track of her children and to hear from her husband while he was away on business.[61]

This bias toward utilitarianism and no-nonsense masculinity, while manifestly blind to the cultivation of a female market, did reflect a consciousness of contemporary political vulnerabilities. A monopoly utility company, one charged with supplying a functional service, needed to assume a dignified civic stature; it had reason to shun any association with frivolous indulgences. Thus, the engineering mentality of AT&T executives and their masculine self-conceptions called for an austere notion of public service. Female consumers would not gain much visibility in AT&T institutional advertising for some time. Over the first ten years of these ads, depictions of male consumers outnumbered those of female consumers by more than 10 to 1. From the outset men were regularly depicted in conversation with other men, and more rarely with women. Not until 1934—after more than twenty-five years of monthly institutional ads—would AT&T finally bestow upon two female subscribers the privilege of conversing privately with each other.[62]

The Neighborhood Image

While AT&T resisted too explicit a feminine image, it did not shrink from the nurturing aura associated with the concept of neighborhood. In fact, it heralded the telephone—and, by extension, itself—as a restorer of community. Unquestionably the telephone had contributed to industrial growth, geographical mobility, economic interdependence, and the complexity of economic and social relationships, as AT&T ads often pointed out. But the exceptional quality of the telephone—its special contribution to progress, as the ads frequently reiterated after 1910—was that it provided a means of overcoming both distance and complexity while reestablishing simple, immediate person-to-person contact.[63]

Although the social cohesion of the old local neighborhoods of the past had been disrupted by the industrial advance of which the telephone was a part, telephone service provided an antidote for the social ills brought by such changes. "It has banished loneliness," AT&T reminded the farmer. "Binds together the human fabric," it avowed. "The Bell System has made America a nation of neighbors." In "The Meeting Place" (see Fig. 2.20), AT&T sought to reinforce the reader's image of the close-knit social order of older, small communities, with their town halls and village stores. It implied that all that had been best in this nostalgic scene was now being retained even as the telephone enabled people to retreat into privacy and "discuss matters with one another without leaving their homes." The telephone "speeds and eases and simplifies living," AT&T promised. "It offers you gaiety, solace, security. . . . Helps the individual man and woman to triumph over the complexities of a vast world."[64]

AT&T first turned to the neighborhood metaphor in December 1910, with "The Neighbor-Maker." Soon it was not only celebrating the telephone's "step-by-step extension" across the continent, "from neighbor to neighbor," but also claiming to have acted as "a great cementing force" in bringing together East and West, North and South into "one great neighborhood of the whole country." As war engulfed Europe, AT&T proclaimed its "neighborizing" influences under such headlines as "The Telephone Unites the Nation" and "The Agency of a United People."[65] Although AT&T's claims to a unifying influence and the restoration of community were anchored in some plausible realities (telephone service did greatly facilitate cross-country communication, and relatives and good friends who moved apart physically could retain a semblance of their former personal contacts by telephone), the notions that the company conveyed through such phrases as "making a neighborhood out of a nation" surely obscured—if they did not directly falsify—both the conventional meanings of the word "neighborhood" and the actual social effects of the telephone.

In the nostalgia-tinted view of "neighborhood" and "community," physically contiguous clusters of people—whatever the chance circumstances or deliberate choices that have set them side-by-side—demonstrate gratifying capacities to sustain each other materially and emotionally and to enrich each other's lives. But relationships in actual neighborhoods in twentieth-century America, as Constance Perrin suggests, have usually been too attenuated to fulfill such expectations. And telephone connections, as Claude Fischer indicates, have rarely served to create new social links or to make "neighbors" out of strangers. As for the implication that the telephone would bring a new cosmopolitanism, a wider neighborly embrace of distant and diverse people, Fischer concludes that in actual usage the telephone was more apt to serve as "a device supporting parochialism."[66] The promise of AT&T to "make a single community out of our vast, busy continent," to make one neighborhood of the entire country, simply manipulated these value-laden terms in ways that evaded their basic meanings.[67]

AT&T first employed the "telephone neighborhood" metaphor to encourage farmers to recognize their particular benefits from a telephone connection.[68] Eventually, however, AT&T executives would discover a more significant use for the idea of neighborhood, as the institutional campaign evolved to encompass a new imperative—that of humanizing the corporation. At its inception, in 1908, Vail envisioned the corporate image project as "more or less . . . a scheme of publicity . . . as to what the Bell System stands for," and his emphasis on the "one policy and one system" message never mentioned "humanization."[69] In fact, in focusing on the efficiencies of the single large system, Vail seemed to slight the human element.

But by 1927 AT&T's vice president for public relations, Arthur W. Page, was reporting disturbing news. In "one or two towns," people had "spoken of AT&T as a foreign corporation." Two years later Page talked frankly about the small-town anti–chain store movement and its roots in the "point of view of these towns toward organizations which are managed from places foreign to them." As part of a strategy to divorce itself from any association with the chain stores, AT&T began to emphasize the role of the local AT&T affiliate as "a home town enterprise" and to remind people that its local employees were their "friends and neighbors."[70] For a corporation with "the largest aggregation of capital and resources that had ever been controlled by a single private company in the history of business," this paradoxical self-portrayal as a local, hometown friend and neighbor carried a special attraction.[71]

An Investment Democracy

Of all the themes that AT&T explored in its search for antidotes to the taint of monopoly and the "curse of bigness," none proved as satisfying to company executives or found such resonance in other corporate image campaigns as the concept of "investment democracy." Expressed most directly and dramatically in AT&T's ad of November 1921—"Democracy—'of the people, by the people, for the people'"—this theme equated the corporation with its hundreds of thousands of stockholders. A focus on "typical" stockholders among this multitude legitimized the company's exercise of power as truly democratic. Rather than asserting a rightful, dominating power for huge corporations within the nexus of social institutions, the concept of investment democracy denied that the corporation represented any nucleus of power distinct from the public at large (Fig. 2.17).[72]

As was true for many of its other image profiles, AT&T only gradually perceived the full possibilities for shaping and exploiting a democratic self-image. The company first introduced the word "democracy" into its institutional ads in February 1911, in the context of the phrase "a telephone democracy." Through this terminology AT&T sought initially only to convey such notions as the equal opportu-

Democracy

"—of the people, by the people, for the people"

People of every walk of life, in every state in the
Union, are represented in the ownership of the Bell
Telephone System. People from every class of tele-

FIGURE 2.17
Although male figures suggestive of
businessmen and investors appear
among this democratic throng of
AT&T "owners," workmen are also
conspicuously present, as are women
in roles ranging from office worker
to maid to housewife.

nity of all to subscribe and use the telephone ("the telephone is for everyone") and
the equal participation and responsibility of all subscribers in making the system
work ("each individual must do his part").[73] Even in this modest variant the theme
of democracy clearly appealed to the leaders of a corporation whose monopoly
power represented its major political vulnerability. To have moved in only a few
years from argumentative defensiveness ("don't grow fretful because you think she
[the Bell system operator] represents a monopoly") to the confident aplomb of
an ad with the headline "In the Bell Democracy" was certainly to have turned the
corner, rhetorically, toward a more auspicious corporate image.[74]

Several years later, in January 1915, AT&T ads advanced a somewhat broader
term, "business democracy." Even here the meaning of the phrase was at first
quite narrowly delimited. In describing the complexity of its system Bell explained
how its vast army of loyal employees worked together harmoniously in a business democracy to supply a valuable service. Although AT&T had mentioned its
large number of stockholders in an August 1914 advertisement, it did not proceed directly to associate widespread stock ownership with the democracy theme.
Throughout the prewar and war years it continued to link that theme to notions
of equal access to the neutral power of technology ("essentially democratic; it carries the voice of the child and the grown-up with equal speed and directness") and
of the telephone's contribution to a unity of language and understanding within
the "true American democracy."[75]

Our Stockholders

In mid-1919, however, in an ad entitled simply "Our Stockholders," AT&T now set forth both visually and verbally the basic elements of the message it would reiterate endlessly over the next three decades. AT&T constituted an "industrial democracy," it claimed. The 135,000 stockholding citizens of this democracy were represented by a young mother (presumably a widow) with two young sons at her knee, opening her dividend check, and by a receding throng of farmers, butchers, tradesmen, and a variety of other folk ranging from an immigrant woman and a maid to a wealthy couple and a banker. All those depicted were "partners" in a company represented not by its management but by its subscribers and service employees (Fig. 2.18).[76]

Subsequent ads in December 1920, November 1921, and November 1922 augmented the democracy argument with refined phrasing and additional details. AT&T had attained "a new democracy of public service ownership," in which the company not only served the people but was "owned directly by the people—controlled not by one, but controlled by all." The large number of shareholders (over 200,000 by the end of 1922) meant that the average share holding was small. The typical shareholder, the various illustrations averred, was a widow with children or an average, middle-class couple with children and parents to provide for. Alternatively, the model AT&T owner and controller might be a young worker "in the car shops at Orenville" who had learned from his plant superintendent, after he was promoted to foreman, "the difficult art of economy" through safe investments in AT&T stocks. Shareholders were "mechanics and merchants, teachers and bankers, laborers and lawyers." They came "from every walk of life," "from every rank and file in every state." Far from a dangerous monopoly, AT&T represented an "investment democracy." It was "owned by those it serves."[77]

AT&T and the Ayer agency astutely blended dry statistics and homey imagery to convey this notion of an investment democracy. Relentlessly, the company employed the phrase "no one person owns as much as one per cent of the total stock" to draw a sharp contrast between the broad ownership of AT&T and the small cliques of business titans who stereotypically, in the public's mind, controlled and profited from monopolies. Luckily for the company, Arthur Page pointed out, "nobody could point to a single big telephone fortune."[78] As an investment democracy, Page and his associates assured readers in 1930, the Bell system represented "a new type of ownership in American business," one that had no incentive to seek "speculative or large profits." Rather, AT&T recognized a particular "responsibility to further the nation's welfare and prosperity." In fact, its "widespread ownership" entitled the corporation to recognition as "a public trust."[79]

AT&T proved particularly adept at bringing conventional assumptions about gender to the support of its claims of democracy. As early as 1917, even before it had begun to advance a full-fledged doctrine of investment democracy, AT&T observed in passing that "about half" of its current seventy thousand stockholders were women. By the beginning of the 1920s women became the prototypical stockholders in AT&T advertising illustrations;[80] the texts of its ads now hastened to remind readers that women constituted over 50 percent of the huge corporation's owners. AT&T assumed, probably quite correctly, that most readers would think of women as modest housewives or needy widows, not as rich investors. By 1936 AT&T had carried the gender ploy to truly remarkable lengths. It now presented itself to the public in the persona of the plain, aproned, salt-of-the-earth farm woman of modest circumstances, dutifully shelling peas as she grinned at readers under the caption, "She's a partner in a great American business" (Fig. 2.19).[81]

If one way of implying a representative democracy was to emphasize the parity of women with men as investors, another was to emphasize a dubious parity of rural and urban investors. Without ever setting forth precise statistics, AT&T regularly asserted that "The People's Telephone" both served and was owned by numerous people on farms and in small towns as well as in metropolitan centers. Thus, as a counterweight to lingering images of corporate investors as big-city plutocrats, the corporation tapped into conventional notions of the farm and town as the self-evident abodes of democracy. To reinforce this democratic aura, ads featuring the democracy theme were likely to carry such illustrations as that, in November 1924, of a country store (Fig. 2.20).[82]

AT&T did not manufacture the theme of an investment democracy out of whole cloth. Forging a model for a number of other major corporations, it had deliberately set about broadening its stockholder base. By the 1920s AT&T stock was more widely distributed among a greater number of stockholders than was that of any other major American corporation. Its regular dividends (paid out even during the Great Depression, despite massive employee layoffs and high rates that

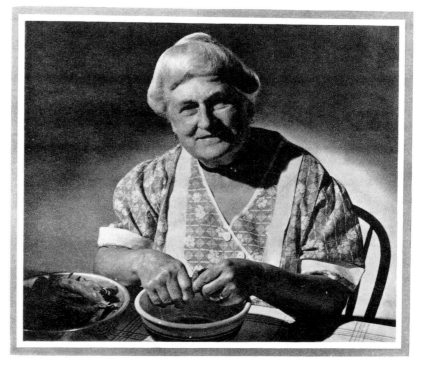

SHE'S A PARTNER IN A
GREAT AMERICAN BUSINESS
SHE is one of 850,000 owners of Bell System securities. They are typical Americans—some young, some middle age, some old. They live in every part of the nation.
One may be a housewife in Pennsylvania. Another a physician in Oregon—a clerk in Illinois—an engineer in Texas—a merchant in Massachusetts—a miner in Nevada—a stenographer in Missouri—a teacher in California—or a telephone employee in Michigan.
For the most part, Bell System stockholders are men and women who have put aside small sums for saving. More than half of them have held their shares for five years or longer. More than 650,000 of these 850,000 security holders own stock in the American Telephone and Telegraph Company—the parent company of the Bell System. More than 225,000 own five shares or less. Over fifty per cent are women. No one owns as much as one per cent of the stock of A. T. & T.
In a very real sense, the Bell System is a democracy in business—owned by the people it serves.
More than 270,000 men and women work for the Bell System. One person out of every 150 in this country owns A. T. & T. securities or stock and bonds of associated companies in the Bell System.
BELL TELEPHONE SYSTEM

FIGURE 2.19 *(above)*
During the 1920s corporate use of women as typical investors became conventional in evading association with rich investors. The deliberate choice of a rustic, heartland figure in this 1935 ad may have reflected particular depression-era sensibilities.

FIGURE 2.20 *(opposite)*
The setting of country store or village post office connoted the preservation of democratic relationships on a human scale in the operations of massive corporations.

The Meeting Place

An Advertisement of
the American Telephone and Telegraph Company

IT IS not so long ago since people met in town hall, store or at the village post-office, to talk over matters of impor- in completing seventy million calls daily depends upon the efficiency of Bell System employees and equipment as well

forced millions to forfeit service) gained it a reputation as the preferred stock for investors who sought stability and secure earnings. Moreover, the rapid expansion of corporate shareholding between 1900 and 1930, actively fostered for employee relations and public relations purposes as well as for raising capital, had been of sufficient magnitude to leave a deep impression on corporate leaders. So engrossed were they in observing this expansion that they easily and conveniently disregarded the masses who still did not figure among the stockholding classes.

Thus, AT&T's promotion of itself as an investment democracy constituted an understandable, if myopic, extrapolation from an underlying reality. In its ardor to exploit the democracy theme, however, the corporation pushed the idea to the point of duplicity. In one critic's words, the AT&T figures, constantly reiterated, were "correct as to arithmetic, false as to implication." The company boasted that the average holding was only twenty-six shares but deliberately overlooked the fact that a minority of 5 percent of the stockholders owned some 50 percent of all AT&T shares. And while the claim that no one person owned "as much as one per cent of the total stock" was true, this phrase suggested the absence of large investors only because most readers failed to comprehend the size of AT&T. The ownership of even one-half of one percent of all AT&T stock, at a value of $130 a share, would have represented an investment of approximately $12 million in the 1930s.[83]

AT&T ads certainly did not help readers grasp such realities of scale. Moreover, in implying that the "average Americans" shown receiving their dividend checks in cozy living rooms or at modest bungalow doors not only owned but also controlled the giant phone company, the ads relied on a popular misconception of control. In fact, the wider distribution of stock holdings placed more power in the hands of professional management. But the image against which both corporate leaders and the public measured a presumed tendency toward democracy in business was that of the autocratic firm of the gilded-age entrepreneur. Taking advantage of this standard of comparison, other corporations seeking a democratized image copied AT&T's personalizations of highly selective statistics.

Beginning in the years just before World War I, a number of large corporations—including United States Steel, Swift & Company, General Electric, Du Pont, and the Pennsylvania Railroad—had taken steps to distribute their stock more widely. They did this partly to raise capital, partly to enhance labor relations through employee stockholding plans, and partly to counteract their images as trusts. In the 1920s they and others would follow the lead of AT&T, publicizing the increasing number of their stockholders to suggest the identity of their interests with the public interest.[84] AT&T's effective tactics for blurring the meaning of democratic ownership and control found many an imitator among corporations eager to evade the "curse of bigness." And the telephone giant might well have claimed an unacknowledged tribute in 1933, when the BBDO advertising agency, in explaining to a client how stockholder statistics might best be personalized, advised that "a plain ordinary citizen, *preferably a woman,* should . . . present the case of the small investor."[85]

Hammering Away

By the early 1920s AT&T had already proved itself a pioneer in devising the themes and arguments that would characterize corporate institutional advertising for decades to come. Adopting such motifs as investment democracy, corporate neighborliness, the company as employee, or power as service, a number of major corporations accorded AT&T the flattery of imitation. But the influence of such individual themes, however important in modeling tactics in the shaping of corporate imagery, never approached that of AT&T's public relations program as a whole.

As early as 1909, when AT&T leaders deemed their national institutional advertising no longer an experiment, Publicity Chief Ellsworth advocated the perpetuation of this campaign, "without extravagance or over-display," as the way to "keep on hammering until the cumulative effect is realized." Three decades later both admirers and critics of the company's campaign were more apt to emphasize the scope and resoluteness of AT&T's corporate image promotion than to extol any of its specific tactics or messages.[86] It was AT&T's persistence over the long run that marked its campaign as exemplary. Together with N. W. Ayer & Son, whose early motto had been "Keep everlastingly at it," AT&T had adopted a standard format for its ads that would persist for more than two decades, despite changes in the size of the illustrations and the length of the text. In recognition of the seemly fit between AT&T's cultivation of an image of stable, dignified helpfulness and the staid reputation of the venerable N. W. Ayer & Son agency, some ad agents labeled the standard AT&T format "Ayer #1."[87]

This stately form consisted of a "large squared-off picture . . . and rectangular block of copy," crowned by a simple headline. AT&T ads appeared only in black and white; their illustrations expanded only slightly between 1910 and 1928, usually covering no more than 40 percent of the space in each ad.[88] Rarely, before 1927, did the entire ad occupy more than one-third of a magazine page. Such modest dimensions and decor were intended to dispel any suspicion of lavish expenditures by AT&T. With cumulative impact over the long haul as AT&T's central objective, as Ellsworth noted in 1926, it seemed "best to use a modest space steadily."[89]

AT&T's standard format aimed at public familiarity and confirmed a long-range commitment to corporate image building. Designed to argue for the advantages of a single, nationwide system, the ads relied on uniformity to project AT&T as stable, dependable, cohesive, and systematic. In 1921 William Banning of the Corporate Information Department sagely defended the uniformity of style that AT&T had maintained since an Ayer account executive had proposed it in 1909. The distinctive mode of arrangement in AT&T ads, he argued, made them instantly recognizable; many readers would identify them with AT&T even if the company's signature were left off. Two years later a speaker at an AT&T publicity conference recommended incorporating the same standardized stylistic elements in the advertisements of all AT&T affiliates. While it might not be practical to make all the advertising of the local companies "look as much alike as 'two peas in a pod,'" he remarked, still they should strive for the "general uniformity" that characterized the national campaign.[90]

In addition to the national advertising campaign and the parallel campaigns run by each of the numerous regional affiliates of the Bell system, the parent corporation developed a massive, integrated system of public relations activities. It subsidized books and magazines, showered newspapers with press releases, and inundated schools with free information, including educational films.[91] Dozens of brochures and special publications, such as "Boy's and Girl's Book of the Telephone" and "On Telephone Duty—Heroism of Operators," flowed from its public relations offices, both national and local. Especially after World War I, AT&T donated generously to local causes and participated widely in community organizations, for which it spent some $5 million between 1925 and 1934 on memberships.[92] And the unstinting attention that both AT&T and its manufacturing arm, Western Electric, gave to fair exhibits and special events also played a significant role in image creation and promotion.

Within the boundaries set by AT&T's commitment to uniformity, modesty, relentlessness, and a focus on such targeted audiences as farmers, investors, regulatory commissioners, and its own employees, the corporation eventually altered the tone and tactics of its messages. Without relinquishing its claims to a serious, respectable image, AT&T gradually moved away from the heavy-handed argumentativeness of its early advertising and from the fact fetishism dear to its technically oriented managerial circle. In a hortatory address at the company's publicity conference in 1921, Banning noted that although the telephone business was an "engineered business" in which its leaders took pride in being rationally oriented, "literal men," still its publicity men had to deal with an audience less susceptible than such executives might imagine to a factual, scrupulously accurate, and "strenuously" didactic approach. While maintaining its dignity, AT&T had to sway an audience that "would much rather be amused than instructed."[93]

AT&T ads, Banning argued in 1921, were now rightly being pitched at a median level. Since the telephone served "the mass of the people," the degree of refinement characteristic of ads for Steinway pianos might offend "folks of modest means." On the other hand, the coarser, more blatant pitches of a typical ad for Prince Albert pipe tobacco might cheapen the company's image and constitute "a lowering of the standard of appeal necessary to both the financial and social stability" of an institution like AT&T. The right tone, Banning concluded, was one of restrained but straightforward friendliness. AT&T advertising should envision the audience in terms of the "ball park crowd," and then make its pitch—not to the box seats or to the bleachers, but rather to the main grandstand.[94]

With the assistance of the local Bell companies, which could advertise their services to their friends and neighbors in "far more 'folksy'" language and imagery than could the more stately national institution, Banning concluded, AT&T could attain the goal of its image campaign: a public that would say, "'I like that company; it seems so friendly, so pleasant, so accommodating, so modest.'" From there it might even go on to accomplish the ultimate objective of its search for legitimacy: "to make the people understand and love the company. Not merely be consciously dependent upon it—not merely regard it as a necessity—not merely take it for granted—but to love it—hold real affection for it—make it an honored personal member of their business force, an admired intimate member of their family."[95]

But Did It Work?

By the time of World War II, AT&T had pursued its institutional advertising campaign for one-third of a century. What did the company have to show for an effort at image creation that, although not a large expense year-by-year, had cumulatively absorbed significant corporate resources and represented the most visible part of a much larger effort in the cultivation of public favor?

Early assessments of the campaign were highly self-indulgent. AT&T executives contented themselves with the praises of their corporate peers and the trade press. Vail and his top AT&T lieutenants gained great satisfaction from seeing the philosophy of "universal service" propagated widely in such dignified discourse.[96] When other corporate campaigns of institutional advertising, usually less comprehensive and less sustained, began to appear, the trade press almost invariably gave credit to AT&T as the inspiration and model.[97] These, however, were not measures of the impact of institutional advertising on the public. Nonetheless, many AT&T executives joined in the staunch defense of cumulative, intangible results from a type of advertising that had been "considered on faith" and "continued on faith." One sought to cinch the case by identifying the AT&T ads with the "song shot into the air" that Longfellow had sentimentalized as having been found, "long afterwards, in the heart of a friend."[98]

Ironically enough, an event that initially appeared as the ultimate threat to AT&T's long-range goals was to furnish a different kind of proof for the effectiveness of the institutional advertising. In July 1918, ostensibly to meet wartime emergencies, the federal government assumed control of the telephone system. Logic suggested that wartime control could well lead to permanent nationalization. But a year later AT&T leaders easily persuaded the Post Office Department to return the telephone monopoly to their private hands. The leading AT&T executives, Vail and Kingsbury, freely attributed the success of their negotiations to the previous ten years of AT&T advertising. Considering that they had not only regained control but had also reaped the advantages of higher rates, a new right to make charges for service connections, and the political leverage of being able to say that government operation had been tried and found wanting, their victory seemed an indisputable endorsement for institutional advertising.[99]

Soon the campaign was augmented to address new purposes, which further justified its costs in the eyes of AT&T executives. By the early 1920s employee cultivation and morale building had emerged as one of AT&T's central objectives. Partly to ward off unionism and partly to enhance its public image, AT&T devised within its institutional advertising a "centrally directed personnel program" that complemented its public relations campaign.[100] Subsequent assessments of the prolonged AT&T institutional advertising campaign often noted its role in setting "the pace for employee performance." It had modeled courtesy and good service, generating high morale as well as "pride in workmanship and loyalty."[101] Already in 1924 a business publicist in *Printers' Ink,* singling out AT&T as the best exemplar of institutional advertising, remarked on how the ads had exerted "a direct and active influence over the loyalty of its great army of employees."[102] As one executive put it at the 1927 publicity conference, the corporation's personnel and publicity departments had come to work so closely together that "sometimes you can't tell which one is which."[103]

By the end of the 1920s changes in AT&T's leadership had both intensified the corporation's commitment to conscious image building and inspired a somewhat more rigorous attention to measuring the results of institutional advertising. In 1927 Walter S. Gifford, who had served as director of the Council of National Defense during World War I, took over the presidency of AT&T. He hired as vice president of publicity Arthur Page, editor of the *World's Work* and the son of a former ambassador to Great Britain, to bring more prestige and energy to the corporation's public relations efforts. Both Gifford and Page took seriously the theory of entropy as a warning to a business monopoly. Perhaps legitimately, people were suspicious of monopolies—not only because of their power and reputed greed but also because of their tendencies toward "slothfulness." Without the "spur of competition," Page warned, "dry rot" might develop. During 1929 the corporation both reassured the public and admonished itself by injecting a terse sentence into the text of its institutional advertisements: "There is no standing still in the Bell System."[104]

Under Gifford and Page, both of whom sought to reinvigorate AT&T's corpo-

IT BELONGS TO MAIN STREET
—and to every other street in this country. Everybody uses the telephone. Over 300,000 people operate the business. And more than twice that number own it.
The interests of all are the same. Good telephone service—good wages —and a fair return to the owners.
BELL TELEPHONE SYSTEM

rate culture through a more sales-oriented sensibility, AT&T's institutional advertising took on a somewhat less austere style. The ads expanded to full-page; illustrations became more dominant, but without sacrificing the balance and dignity of AT&T's traditional, squared-off style.[105] As Page expanded this and other elements of the corporation's public relations, he introduced a new concern for measuring results. In 1929 he commissioned an independent study by David Houser, Inc. "We had been doing institutional advertising for some twenty-five years and the advertising fraternity said it was a grand job and that it was entirely responsible for the good reputation of the Bell System," Page observed. But he was "anxious to find out, if possible, what we really did accomplish."[106]

When the Houser survey of 2,500 people in Pittsburgh revealed that 17 percent of readers could recall the specifics of what they had read in the AT&T ads, Page declared himself satisfied with the impact of the institutional campaign.[107] Still, throughout the 1930s, Page continued to pursue every avenue of possible measurement, from monitoring free long-distance calls at the company's fair exhibits for information on consumer preferences to subscribing to the Psychological Corporation's emerging project of public opinion polling on favorable or unfavorable views toward major corporations. So intently did Page aim to prove the effects of his public relations activities that he designated a unit within the corporation's Chief

FRIEND AND NEIGHBOR

CLOSE to those who live in small towns, and farther out upon the farms, is the helpful service of the telephone operator.

In the truest sense, she is both friend and neighbor. Ties of kinship and association bind her to those whose voices come across the wires. Through her switchboard pass many messages that are important to the life and business of the community.

Bright and early in the morning she puts through a call that helps a farmer locate a drill for sowing oats. Another connection finds out if Jim Thomas, "over near Bogard," is feeding a bunch of calves and needs any shelled corn. Another gets the latest price on heavy hogs for Bill Simpson.

Through the day she aids in calling a doctor for Mrs. Moore, whose baby is ill. Plugs in an emergency call

that sends an ambulance east of town. Puts through a long distance call for Bob Roberts, whose boy attends the state college. Then, through the night, stands ever ready to help those in need.

Constantly in her mind and activities is one fixed, guiding purpose . . . "*Speed the call!*" And the further thought that she serves best when she serves with courtesy and sympathetic understanding.

In the bustle of the city, as in town and country, that is the established creed of every employee of the Bell System. Its faithful observance in so large a percentage of cases is an important factor in the value of your telephone service.

AMERICAN TELEPHONE AND TELEGRAPH COMPANY

FIGURES 2.21 & 2.22
The phrase "friend and neighbor" characterized not only the helpful operator but also the giant corporation she represented. Far from distant and aloof, it belonged to Main Street.

Statistician's Division to conduct and monitor public relations surveys. This office would, for instance, develop a fine-grained analysis of the effects of AT&T's exhibit at the Century of Progress Exposition in Chicago in 1933.[108]

The tribulations of the depression years hardly decreased AT&T's concern for maintaining its highly favorable public image or for monitoring the effectiveness of its public relations programs. Having chosen to retain high rates and protect the level of its stock dividends, the telephone giant was forced to make severe cutbacks in employment and to accede to a massive loss of less affluent subscribers. AT&T employees declined from approximately 435,000 to about 270,000 between 1929 and 1933; over 15 percent of its customers discontinued service during the same period. The calculated loss of subscribers and AT&T's greater sales emphasis on services—such as long-distance calling—to those who could afford them may actually have reinforced the telephone monopoly's concern to protect itself politically by reaffirming a friendly, folksy, democratic image.[109]

During the 1930s AT&T continued its themes of neighborliness and democracy, with special emphasis on the cheapness of AT&T rates and on the corporation as a "hometown" entity. "It Belongs to Main Street," affirmed a 1937 institutional ad (Fig. 2.21).[110] New, striking formats, often featuring full-page photographs, now dramatized the personal qualities of telephone service through "just folks" images of AT&T stockholders and subscribers. These ads also increased the visibility of the switchboard operator, the "Voice with a Smile," as the company's most familiar public face. The small-town telephone operator best epitomized the company, a 1933 ad suggested, because she was "in the truest sense . . . both friend and neighbor" to those she served (Fig. 2.22).[111]

In 1935 the seemingly inevitable government challenge finally came. Congress authorized the Federal Communications Commission, staffed with "reformers eager to expose and correct the misdeeds of corporate institutions," to undertake a major investigation of AT&T. The resulting report revealed the massive extent of the corporation's public relations apparatus and its huge investment in swaying public opinion and political bodies, local and national. But the FCC's relatively harmless specific recommendations, at a time when many corporations felt themselves gravely threatened or impaired, clearly represented a victory for AT&T. Vice President Page pointed to AT&T's good public reputation as the reason such a "natural target" had escaped attention earlier in the "investigating craze," and he took delight in the public's apparent indifference to the investigation reports. *Fortune* magazine buttressed the judgment of AT&T executives that the investigation had "produced only the most trivial accusations" against the company. It credited the absence of any public outcry to the success of the corporation's tireless advertising and public relations campaign.[112]

Once again, as when the corporation had regained control from the government in 1919, events had vindicated the long-run effectiveness of AT&T's institutional advertising campaign. In a 1940 address entitled "Industrial Statesmanship," Page confidently invited his audience to ponder the fact that in a society that held "an instinctive fear of large aggregations of power," his company had attained full public legitimacy. AT&T's success in eluding any damaging effects from the federal investigation in 1937–38 only amplified the penchant of enthusiasts for corporate image advertising to point to AT&T's long-standing campaign as an admonitory example. "If only . . . ," the wistful refrain was heard again and again, if only that company (or *our* company) had gone in for educational advertising like AT&T; if only, like AT&T, it had started early to protect itself from government interference rather than waiting until a moment of crisis.[113]

What most impressed AT&T's admirers was not so much the style and content of the ads as the foresightedness and persistence of the campaign. Members of the FCC staff had sought to rebuke AT&T by declaring it "unique" in the extent to which its public relations had been "based on the long-range cultivation of public opinion through constant and unrelenting propaganda and advertising." But it was just that quality of relentlessness that inspired praise from AT&T's disciples and advocates. AT&T itself never apologized for the repetitiveness, both stylistic and thematic, of its advertising.[114] "In order to convince people," an AT&T vice president affirmed in 1915, "we have to keep reiterating it over and over again in thousands of different ways." The "it" that was to be so inculcated comprised the lofty ideals of the company and its slogan of "Universal Service."[115]

This slogan, as one longtime AT&T public relations officer put it, had been "sent forth to do battle with the slogans of the 'curse of Bigness.'" At a succession of AT&T conferences on corporate publicity, company executives continued to reaffirm the "advantage through constant repetition" of a standardized format and the focus on "certain central ideas at which we . . . hammer away during the year." The result of this steady publicity, AT&T PR executive Norton Long claimed in 1937, had been the thoroughgoing transformation of the public image of a "soulless . . . corporation . . . of the trust-busting era." AT&T had gained a soul, he concluded, by clothing itself in "the radiant raiment of a . . . service ideology."[116]

3

CORPORATE MORALE IN WAR AND PEACE: ADVOCACY, INDUSTRIAL STATESMANSHIP, AND HUMANIZATION

The experiences of American corporate leaders during the World War I era had a profound impact on their ideas and practices. Active participation in the United States' war effort, sometimes in government agencies, awakened up-and-coming executives to broader horizons for business as a public service and convinced many of the promise of the "associative state." [1] Labor traumas, extending from the 1914 Ludlow massacre and wartime worker shortages to post-1917 fears of the influence of bolshevism, prompted many executives to recognize an insufficient loyalty and dedication within their expanding, high-turnover labor forces. At the same time the efficacy of wartime propaganda, which demonstrated the power of words and images to impart ideas and stir emotions, deeply impressed business leaders. They now looked increasingly to the cultivation of a corporate image as the key to both solving internal problems and maximizing new marketing opportunities.

The war effort, as the historian Morton Keller has recounted, brought a "revelation as to how people, goods, and beliefs could be mobilized and organized for an overriding public purpose." Businessmen, often working as "dollar-a-year men" on loan to the federal government from major corporations, provided the visible leadership for this mobilization. Despite some initial chaos and dubious experiments, they ultimately constructed an effective network of private and public industrial cooperation, one made possible by temporary antitrust immunity. Amid the rhetorical celebration of cooperation, the movement toward trade associations flourished. Big businesses, in particular, thrived as the favored recipients of war contracts. And a new merger movement ensued as the war service of large corporations inhibited the resurgence of antitrust sentiment. As the wartime utility and even the institutional permanence of huge corporations won greater acceptance, the public now came to view them, as Louis Galambos notes, in more impersonal terms, and less as the dangerous instruments of "flesh and blood villains." [2]

Many top corporate executives took part in the wartime network of government agencies and boards. Walter Gifford, who would become president of AT&T in the late 1920s, served as director of the Civilian Advisory Commission to the Council of National Defense. Daniel Willard of the Baltimore & Ohio Railroad and Julius Rosenwald of Sears joined him on the commission. Willard went on to serve on the War Industries Board, as did Gerard Swope, subsequently the president of General Electric; Owen D. Young, GE's future chairman of the board; Frank A. Scott, CEO of Warner & Swasey; and Paul Garrett, the future vice president of public relations at General Motors.[3] Businessmen from diverse fields, including many younger executives, became closely acquainted through cooperative wartime work. In his study of the War Industries Board, the most significant of all the wartime agencies, Robert Cuff astutely comments that the businessmen on the board reflected the decisive contemporary shift in executive leadership from "economic entrepreneurs" to "business politicians." Their role in managing the massive wartime mobilization spurred many corporate executives to larger visions and long-term planning. Having known, amid wartime unity and enthusiasm, "the uncommon experience of a transcendent national purpose," these businessmen aspired to broader goals and responsibilities.[4]

Mobilizing for World War I

Because they were heavily involved in war production during 1917 and 1918, many corporations lacked consumer goods to peddle. But advertising was a legitimate business expense under wartime tax policies, so rather than allow their high profits to be taxed away, companies could funnel them back into advertising.[5] Moreover, the success of wartime campaigns for bonds, food conservation, and other public sacrifices led the advertising trade journal *Printers' Ink* to recall that "it is possible to sway the minds of whole populations, change their habits of life, create belief, practically universal, in any policy or idea."[6] The crux of that assertion lay in its final phrase. The business community was now prepared to believe that not just products but also policies and ideas could be sold. Wartime publicity so impressed the rising generation of advertising professionals that in subsequent years their trade journals would claim that institutional advertising had been "born in World War I."[7]

The federal government's Committee on Public Information (CPI) and War Industries Board (WIB) provided convenient opportunities for advertising agents and business corporations to associate themselves with the national cause. The Advertising Division of the CPI prepared ads for Liberty Bonds and the Red Cross and appeals for food and fuel conservation. For the patriotic service of buying newspaper or magazine space for such an ad, any company could have its name featured in the credit line at the end of the war message, "This page contributed to the Winning of the War by. . . ."[8] By the time of the Third Liberty Loan, in the spring of 1918, the Advertising Division of the CPI had further merged corporate interest with national service through a new "duplex plan." Now a corporate advertiser could promote both its product and the war bonds in the same ad, furnishing its own copy with "a slant that shows how his product is affiliated with Liberty Bonds in the scheme of national affairs."[9]

Printers' Ink reported that corporations like the U.S. Rubber Company had recognized in the duplex plan "the possibilities for impressing the public with the idea that business and Government are one and inseparable." The journal thus identified an expansive form of advocacy, one on behalf of large business interests generally. It predicted confidently that such ads would imply "that the interests of business are inseparably linked with the interests of the Nation." At a time when citizens were willing to see the federal government assume, at least temporarily, much greater relative power within the nexus of social institutions, large corporations could only gain in moral legitimacy through advertisements that would help in "breaking down any imaginary, artificial barrier between private industry and the national cause."[10]

Beyond their roles in encouraging the conflation of business and national interests, the CPI, the WIB, and other government agencies contributed an important experiential element to business thinking about corporate imagery. A host of advertising agents and emerging public relations professionals served the CPI in some capacity; Ivy Lee later commented that the CPI scheme of having Liberty Bond ads prepared by advertising professionals for company sponsorships had ensured that "every advertising man in America was enrolled." Edward Bernays, Ivy Lee, and Carl Byoir, the most prominent figures in public relations over the next dozen years, all served on the CPI. Future leaders in the advertising profession—Bruce Barton, Arthur Kudner, John Benson, Henry Ewald, Helen Resor, William Day, and Thomas Logan—worked on wartime ads and messages. William Johns, the head of the George Batten advertising agency, became the director of CPI's Division of Advertising.[11] George Creel, the chairman of the CPI, credited the war service of advertising agents with removing them from the class of the morally suspect and gaining them new prestige as professionals.[12]

Without doubt, the war also inspired many companies to be more aware of their corporate image. War propaganda had saturated the nation in emotion-laden imagery; few remained unimpressed by the power of those images to stir the public to action. Ivy Lee called attention to the potency of British propaganda, confronting the corporations, which had been "almost apologetic about appointing men to interpret them to the public," with the challenge "Look what nations are doing."[13] Although the effectiveness of institutional and advocacy advertising was notoriously difficult to test, the apparent success of wartime propaganda spread faith in advertising that sought to mold opinion. The enthusiasm of some business leaders for broader horizons of social authority was thus reinforced by a war-bred sense of their capacity to persuade the masses. Having provided a national service at no expense to their corporate loyalties and goals, they returned with a vision of the future of their companies as great public institutions.

An article in *Judicious Advertising* in 1919 captured this burgeoning mystique. The war, the author argued, had "wrought great changes in the whole business structure." These had set the stage for the rise of the "business statesman," the new corporate leader who "comprehends his business as a public institution." President Walter Teagle of Standard Oil of New Jersey had suggested this notion when he told a reporter that Standard was "essentially a public service corporation and today more than ever."[14] The Burroughs Adding Machine Company joined the chorus in a particularly inspirational ad entitled "Our National Objective." Describing eloquently the wartime effects of "unity of effort" on behalf of "an ideal untainted by purely selfish purpose," Burroughs foreshadowed the 1920s corporate quest for an image of "business statesmanship." It called for a new vision of "business achievement as public service, . . . business management as a great human responsibility." Going beyond a recent prediction in *Forbes* that "business hereafter will be conducted on a higher plane than . . . before the war," Burroughs frankly doubted whether "commercial success . . . will ever again satisfy American business men."[15]

Fighting Back: Bethlehem Steel and the Meatpackers

Wartime experience and claims to war service became significant themes even in the crisis campaigns of those few major corporations that had to wage defensive battles on the public relations front. In 1916 the Bethlehem Steel Company, frustrated when traditional lobbying failed to prevent the U.S. Senate from passing a bill for a competing $11 million government armor plant, mounted its own narrowly focused advocacy campaign to sway the House of Representatives through an appeal to public opinion. "In desperation," *Printers' Ink* reported, the company recruited Ivy Lee to mastermind this eleventh-hour campaign. With the Senate already on record and Woodrow Wilson's secretary of war ardently supporting the government armor plant, Bethlehem Steel and Ivy Lee faced a truly formidable challenge.[16]

Lee confronted this challenge by running a series of twelve ads in 3,257 city and county newspapers, an effort that may well have been, as *Editor and Publisher* declared, "the biggest publicity campaign ever undertaken anywhere in the world." Lee hoped to influence many of these newspapers to editorialize on behalf of Bethlehem's position. He deliberately chose a style with "technical demerits," hoping to contrive an amateurish—and thus "warmly human and persuasive"—voice for the giant steel corporation.[17] Unadorned and starkly argumentative, the first ad in the series boldly "confessed" to "a mistake in the policy of the Bethlehem Steel Company" (Fig. 3.1). The "mistake" had been to remain silent in the face of "irresponsible assertions." With a bravado that most subsequent advertisers would consider themselves too sophisticated to employ, Bethlehem bluntly reiterated its critics' charges of gouging and profiteering. Then, over the names of its chairman and president, Charles Schwab and Eugene Grace, the company refuted the charges. In a final gutsy maneuver, Bethlehem offered to sell armor plate to the government at whatever price the Federal Trade Commission might set.[18]

In contrast to the steady cultivation of a corporate image by AT&T, here was advocacy advertising in its most direct, unsubtle form. Contrary to conventional American expectations about underdog efforts, Bethlehem achieved no "come-from-behind" victory. In fact, a number of newspapers took the occasion to upbraid the steel company.[19] The House of Representatives passed the bill for the government armor plant handily and President Wilson signed it into law. The advertising trade press sought to use this failure to good purpose, however, by arguing that through long-term cultivation of its corporate image, Bethlehem might well have achieved a different outcome. The 1916 emergency campaign would never have been necessary, one AT&T official remarked, if Bethlehem had gradually educated the people through word and deed. Ivy Lee, looking to the future, emphasized his success in making this company seem less faceless (by publicizing its chief executives) and providing it, through the man-to-man sensibility of its all-print advocacy ads, with an image of straightforward honesty. For Lee the campaign ushered in "a new era in the conduct of American corporations" in

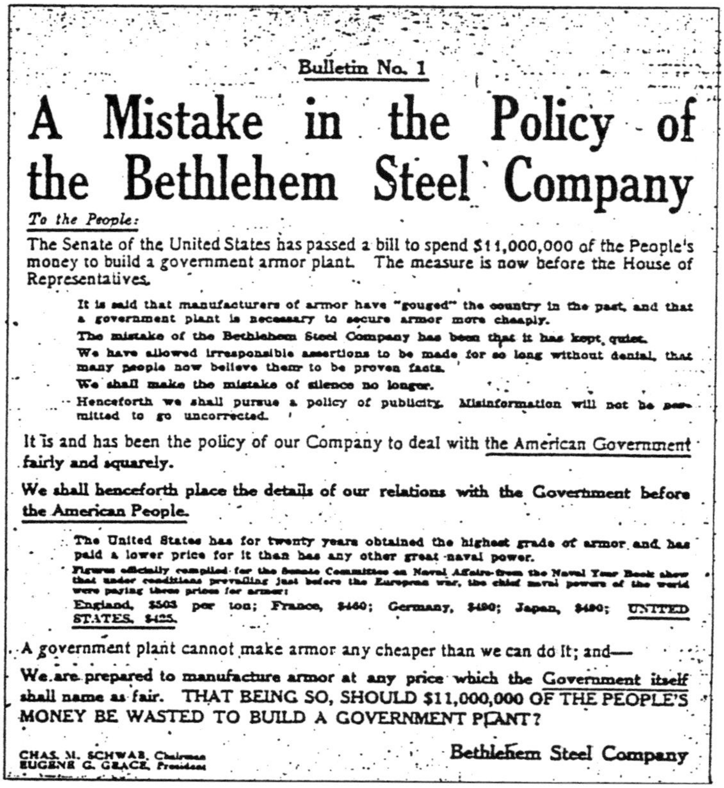

> ### Bulletin No. 1
>
> # A Mistake in the Policy of the Bethlehem Steel Company
>
> *To the People:*
>
> The Senate of the United States has passed a bill to spend $11,000,000 of the People's money to build a government armor plant. The measure is now before the House of Representatives.
>
> It is said that manufacturers of armor have "gouged" the country in the past, and that a government armor plant is necessary to secure armor more cheaply.
>
> The mistake of the Bethlehem Steel Company has been that it has kept quiet.
>
> We have allowed irresponsible assertions to be made for so long without denial, that many people now believe them to be proven facts.
>
> We shall make the mistake of silence no longer.
>
> Henceforth we shall pursue a policy of publicity. Misinformation will not be permitted to go uncorrected.
>
> It is and has been the policy of our Company to deal with the American Government fairly and squarely.
>
> We shall henceforth place the details of our relations with the Government before the American People.
>
> The United States has for twenty years obtained the highest grade of armor and has paid a lower price for it than has any other great naval power.
>
> Figures officially compiled for the Senate Committee on Naval Affairs from the Naval Year Book show that under conditions prevailing just before the European war, the chief naval powers of the world were paying these prices for armor:
>
> England, $503 per ton; France, $460; Germany, $490; Japan, $490; UNITED STATES, $425.
>
> A government plant cannot make armor any cheaper than we can do it; and—
>
> We are prepared to manufacture armor at any price which the Government itself shall name as fair. THAT BEING SO, SHOULD $11,000,000 OF THE PEOPLE'S MONEY BE WASTED TO BUILD A GOVERNMENT PLANT?
>
> CHAS. M. SCHWAB, Chairman
> EUGENE G. GRACE, President
>
> Bethlehem Steel Company

FIGURE 3.1
By forgoing a slick format and having the corporation's chief officers speak directly in their own names, Bethlehem's PR advisor, Ivy Lee, hoped to create amateurish ads that would convey an ingenuous sincerity.

which they would eschew inside lobbying.[20] Schwab and Grace proved so gratified with their increased personal celebrity and their company's image of greater frankness, earnestness, and aggressiveness that they agreed to continue institutional advertising.[21]

Less than two years after Bethlehem Steel's abrupt, extensive advocacy campaign, wartime circumstances magnified the crisis faced by the corporate giants of another industry. During 1917 and 1918 the nation's major meatpackers came under investigation by the Federal Trade Commission. Seething with outrage at the packers' incorrigibility, the FTC reacted with alarm to their wartime entry into non-meat lines, a move that could gain them control over the nation's food supply. That the packers' profits had escalated by some 350 percent during the war year of 1917 further excited the ire of the FTC, which called for criminal indictments. The packers, the FTC charged, had conspired to exploit a monopoly position through the use of "practically every tried method of unfair competition known to this Commission." They had even "invented certain new and ruthless methods to crush weaker concerns" and "extort excessive profits." To counteract the packers' power grab, the FTC proposed that the government take over their refrigerator cars, stockyards, and branch houses and "operate them as a public monopoly."[22]

An odious public image was, of course, nothing new for the meatpackers. Except for the railroads, few industries had drawn such frequent attention from the

A business
that is as big as its job

FIGURE 3.2

The war proved, Swift insisted, that
the nation needed corporations
large enough to handle "a big
and complex job." Invoking
the "Lambert Hollow" narrative
of corporate attentiveness, Swift
also recounted its service to "the
smallest out-of-the-way village."

muckrakers in the early twentieth century as had the "Big Five" of the "Beef Trust" (Armour, Swift, Morris, Cudahy, and Wilson). Of these the dominant two, Swift and Armour, loomed largest in the public's suspicions. Between 1902 and 1910 the packers had been the targets of no fewer than six antitrust suits. Yet although the government had brought criminal indictments against them in 1909 and 1910 for "conspiracy and combination in restraint of trade," they had nonetheless withstood all charges with little damage.[23] But the gravity of their situation in 1918 persuaded the packers to attend more earnestly to their corporate images.

The advocacy campaigns that Armour and Swift mounted in response to this crisis drew on both Bethlehem Steel's blunt and narrowly focused advocacy ads and AT&T's more broadly conceived institutional campaign. Armour adopted the Bethlehem approach, with attacks on its critics and unsubtle, straight-from-the-shoulder defenses of its policies. Swift opted for AT&T's modulated, positive style of argument, establishing a more genteel tone through dominating illustrations, wide margins, and lots of dignified white space. In mid-1918, just as the FTC issued its denunciatory report, Swift opened its case for the defense. Calling on its wartime service as witness, it advertised that the pure "size of the job" of providing perishable food products to the Allies and to American soldiers had "dictated the size of America's packing industry" (Fig. 3.2). Only an organization with an integrated system—including refrigerator cars and branch distributing houses—

ACHIEVEMENT

THE ACHIEVEMENT OF TODAY BUT POINTS TO THE PATHWAY OF TOMORROW. THROUGH SERVICE COMES GROWTH, AND THROUGH GROWTH COMES GREATER SERVICE.

FIGURE 3.3 *(right)* Adopting the hues of a Sunday school reader, complete with a central allegorical figure, Armour and Company proudly displayed its smoking factory chimneys and stockyard trains as the backdrop to this grandiose yearbook illustration.

FIGURE 3.4 *(opposite)* Swift & Company splurged on color covers for its widely distributed yearbooks. Perhaps it hoped, through such a bucolic scene, to deflect attention from its feared power and chided practices.

could have met this emergency. Thus, Swift argued, the war had underscored a principle that remained valid in peacetime. The nation, and individual consumers, were best served by a total system. Dismemberment of that system would destroy coordination and efficiency.[24]

Armour initially assumed a more truculent tone. In "Forced to Be Big!" the company bluntly confronted the issue of size. "The packers are frequently accused of being large," Armour's statement began. "If bigness is a crime, Armour and Company are guilty of the charge." But why should the corporation be apologetic for its all-American story of growth from small beginnings, it inquired. Did not its efficient wartime service prove the wisdom, even the public utility, of its vast ex-

Swift & Company
Year Book 1921

pansion? In other ads, such as "Why Armour Cannot Fix Meat Prices," the company aired other charges and set about refuting them through long, argumentative copy.[25] Given the emergency situation they faced, the highly polemic mode of the packers' institutional campaigns was hardly surprising. But subsequently, having recognized the crucial need to win public approval, both companies embarked on multifaceted and persistent campaigns of corporate image cultivation.[26] Both exalted themselves in lavish yearbooks (Figs. 3.3 and 3.4); Swift's was now distributed far beyond its stockholders because of an increased "demand from the general public," and Armour's even indulged in cartoon caricatures of its assailants (Fig. 3.5). And both continued, through institutional advertisements, to confront—at least

Hindering the operation of Industry with destructive criticism is the favorite diversion of numerous malcontents and theorists, who give no heed to the chaos that would follow their success.

FIGURE 3.5

In this richly tinted yearbook illustration, Armour seemed to relish turning the weapon of the political cartoon against its enemies.

obliquely—the issue of business bigness.[27] Swift mimicked AT&T's constant stress on its large number of stockholders (and sought wider distribution of its stock for just this purpose).[28] The company also occasionally parroted AT&T in its attempt to remove the curse of bigness by speaking in a small-town, "jes' folks" vernacular, chatting familiarly with housewives about "bringing the country to you" and linking "your ice box—and ours" (Fig. 3.6).[29]

The results of Armour's argumentative advocacy and Swift's more genteel persuasion are obscured by concurrent events. The packers' executives were spared from criminal trials by signing a "Consent Decree" in 1920. In it, without admitting guilt, they agreed to divest themselves of their interests in stockyards, meat markets, market newspapers, and terminal railroads. They also agreed to refrain from using their distribution system to handle specified nonmeat foods. But they were allowed to retain those "bastions of monopoly," the branch houses and refrigerator cars. In effect, they accepted major barriers to any extension of their power into other sectors of the food industry but maintained completely their

THE SATURDAY EVENING POST

S W I F T

*A vital
nation-wide service*

Bringing the country to you

FIGURE 3.6
Swift & Company emphasized its
bigness through homey motifs. The
"huge tasks" undertaken by the
corporation became simply familiar,
small-scale chores writ large.

dominant, oligopolistic power in meatpacking. The FTC's government takeover proposals were shunted aside, but whether the packers had won or lost remained just as uncertain as did the impact of their advertising on the outcome.[30]

In typical response the advertising trade journals affirmed the efficacy of institutional advertising and publicized Swift's own claim that it had warded off "self-seeking agitators." They contended that the meatpackers had put themselves beyond the reach of public criticism. Swift concluded that it had "made headway" and that this publicity drive had been "well worth the effort and the expense involved." It resolved to continue its "educational" advertising until it had both convinced the public that Swift's profits were so small as to have "practically no effect on prices" and convinced itself that it had removed "the last vestige of suspicion and prejudice."[31] For its part Armour anticipated negative public reaction when it consummated a merger with Morris in 1924—a move almost certain to rekindle antitrust sentiments. It successfully shielded itself by mounting a massive image and advocacy campaign with advice from Ivy Lee.

Employee Representation as a Public Service

War mobilization brought high labor turnover and anxious attention to worker morale. These, in turn, quickened awareness of yet another function of corporate imagery: its potential effects within the large corporation. And labor unrest, allegedly stimulated by indulgent government wartime labor policies and the radicalism the Russian Revolution had inspired, now stirred many a corporate executive to worry about internal morale. The extent to which many union members had come to see some form of worker-empowering "industrial democracy" as an essential part of war and postwar goals unsettled employers, including those who occasionally used such terms but blanched at seeing them so interpreted.[32] The promotion of a consummate solution to the "labor problem" quickly became one of the salient motifs in the service mystique of postwar corporate imagery.

The most prominent solution was one that John D. Rockefeller Jr. had modeled in 1915: the employee representation plan. In the wake of the Ludlow massacre of 1914, in which the Colorado Fuel and Iron company militia opened fire on a camp of striking workers and their families, killing a number of men, women, and children, Rockefeller—the absentee owner of the company—had discovered a personal mission. He promoted employee representation as "a tool for the modernization of corporate public relations." By 1917 Rockefeller had succeeded in inducing Standard Oil of New Jersey, which had previously dismissed his ideas on corporate publicity as too idealistic, to adopt such a program in the wake of two successive strikes at its refinery in Bayonne, New Jersey, in 1916 and 1917. Near the end of 1918 Rockefeller championed employee representation at a national conference of the U.S. Chamber of Commerce and gained endorsement of a creed that incorporated his scheme for "bridging the gap between employers and employees in large scale industry." By this time employee representation suffered no lack of prestigious patrons.[33]

During the war, with many workers in the military and employees at a premium, corporate employers had become more keenly aware of the costs of high labor turnover. Increasingly apprehensive about the government's support for labor unions during the war, many also worried about how to restore greater discipline to their labor forces. Above all, as business managers recoiled from the impact of wartime strikes and labor shortages and observed the power of patriotic fervor in boosting the rates of wartime production, they perceived, as David Brody points out, that their workers' level of performance was not "a fixed item" but was governed by morale. Welfare capitalism gained a new momentum, as did the various employee representation plans.[34]

This war-bred intensification of the corporations' quest for an esprit de corps among their workers, together with their dismay over strikes and domestic "bolshevism" in 1919, led to widespread interest in the use of advertising to cultivate worker loyalty. Such advertisements as the Addressograph-Multigraph Corporation's "You Want No Bolsheviki in Your Plant" capitalized on these anxieties. Promoting its printing services for house organs (one of the "solutions" that Ivy Lee had persuaded the Rockefellers to introduce at Colorado Fuel and Iron), the company reminded employers: "The very thought of them [bolsheviki] makes shivers chase each other up and down your spine."[35] In a more positive vein, other companies took their cue from Rockefeller and sought to cultivate an image of busi-

"Let us put our own House in Order"

SOME seven or eight years ago, a number of manufacturers met for their annual convention at a city in the middle west.

After the usual routine business had been disposed of, the meeting drifted into a discussion of labor problems. A number of speeches were made, most of them emphasizing the word "fight"; all of them proposing to let somebody else do the fighting—either through associations, committees or special legislation. The last speaker to get to his feet was especially bitter, although it was well known that he had been anything but fair in his treatment of his own men.

Suddenly, a big, wholesome specimen of a man jumped up. "This is all damn rot," he said. "It gets us nowhere. I happen to know that three or four of you fellows who have done the most talking don't know the first thing about conditions in your own plants—or else you are side-stepping. You can have all the meetings and committees you want—I'm through. I'm going home to 'put my own house in order'—to make dead sure that my superintendents and foremen are as square with my men as I want them to be. If every man here will take the trouble to find out what a square deal to his own men means, and then see that they get it, we won't have to listen to many more speeches like we have heard here today."

* * * *

WE went home from this meeting, deeply impressed. We looked ourselves squarely in the face—and found shortcomings.

Through an earnest and increasingly successful application of this simple suggestion, in our relations with our own people, we have come to have an utter faith in it. It has paid us—and by us we mean our men at the forge and the hammer; the men who work at their desks and the men and women who own our stock. It has paid in quality and quantity of product. It has paid in added profits. It has paid in daily growing content.

To all those whose interests lie in Industry, we can say with confidence born of experience, that the principle of the square deal with your own people, *based upon a thorough knowledge of all conditions affecting them*, works—and works well.

If there was a brush big enough, and a hand big enough to wield it, we would like to paint across the face of the heavens, "*Is Our Own House in Order?*"

This is the third of a series of articles in this publication. On April 19 will appear "What *is* a House in Order."

HYDRAULIC PRESSED STEEL COMPANY
of Cleveland

HYDRAULIC
PRESSED STEEL COMPANY

FIGURE 3.7

As the scale of factory operations increased and the workforce came to be seen as more "foreign," corporate concerns with employee morale intensified. Hydraulic cultivated a statesmanlike image by declaring its good intentions to give workers a "square deal." It imagined no loss of managerial autonomy in the process.

ness statesmanship and public service by publicizing their plans to solve the "labor problem."

Hydraulic Pressed Steel, for instance, launched a series of monthly full-page advertisements in the *Saturday Evening Post* and the *Literary Digest* in January 1919, in which it urged other companies to adopt its model for humanized labor relations and worker benefits. Entitled "Out of the Ashes of War," the first ad explained that Hydraulic had moved "to express in the conduct of our own business that spirit of Democracy which this great world struggle has developed." In the long, self-congratulatory texts of the series, Hydraulic described how it had encouraged thrift and promoted wholesome recreation for its workers. Democracy in industry, it avowed, did not require "sympathy . . . with combinations of Labor as they exist today" and thus entailed no recognition of unions. But it did mean some form of employee representation and a recognition of the workers' need for self-respect (Fig. 3.7).[36] The Goodyear Tire and Rubber Company, which devised a

FIGURE 3.8

The internal publicizing of corporate image ads (here, on a profit-sharing plan) might foster cohesion, a feeling of "we" and "us," while also grati- fying the penchant of corporate officers for an image of business statesmanship.

pseudoparliamentary structure for its highly publicized program of employee rep- resentation, offered itself as a model of public service in labor relations in such ad- vertisements as "A Man and His Work."[37]

Most of the companies that publicized their contributions to industrial democ- racy did so to garner public appreciation. They sought to command the respect of notable citizens and other corporate leaders by portraying themselves as modern pacesetters in industry. A few—including suppliers, like Hydraulic Steel, of un- finished products to larger corporations—undoubtedly saw their prominence in promoting enlightened labor relations as a way to catch the favorable attention of large corporate customers. But increasingly executives recognized a further mis- sion for such publicity: it could be used to build internal morale. One company vaunted the effects of a series of advertisements that "credits the men in the shops." When these ads were enlarged and posted in the plant, the response of the work- men "was even more gratifying than the public good will that their widespread circulation crystallized." A Hydraulic vice president extolled his company's cam- paign in a business convention address titled "How an Industrial Institution Can Secure Labor Co-Operation through Publicity." The Hammermill Paper Com- pany made explicit the double purpose of institutional ads that praised company workers or described company welfare plans. In its December 1918 advertisement a group of workers proudly examined an ad posted on the plant bulletin board. "That advertisement ought to sell paper for us," proclaimed the caption (Fig. 3.8). The text of the ad explained the company's profit-sharing plan, the "we" and "us" character of its employer-employee relationships, and the positive results in quality and service.[38]

As they envisioned generating a "we" and "us" solidarity that would unite labor and management in loyal service to a single goal, corporate leaders of the immediate postwar years revealed the extent to which their wartime worries about labor turnover, their fears of postwar labor "bolshevism," and their continuing distress over the violence of labor strife had fused the impact of the war with another of their mounting concerns—the impact of corporate size on employee morale. The same dramatic increases in the scale and scope of operations that had created new political vulnerabilities and market opportunities for large corporations had also brought a troubling sense of distance between management and workers. Although executives did not initially view this as a problem of corporate imagery, the issue of effective internal communications preyed on their minds. The rapid growth of their firms had undermined those relationships within the company that, in the warm glow of nostalgia, they now remembered as human in scale and highly satisfying. With the efficacy of corporate imagery and the advertising of ideas seemingly validated by the war experience, this rising concern about labor morale prompted some business leaders to give their corporate image a new thrust inward.

The Lament

Nostalgic ruminations about employer-worker relationships in the "old days" became a staple of businessmen's discourse in the late nineteenth and early twentieth centuries. Repeated with each new perception of the impact of an increasing scale of operations, these audible musings acquired so ritualized a form and role that I have chosen to designate them, categorically, as "the Lament."

As elaborated in 1923 by AT&T's vice president for personnel and public relations, E. K. Hall, the Lament typically unfolded like this: During a fondly remembered earlier era, the manufacturer had "owned his own tools, bought his own materials, completed his product, and marketed it. The factories were small. The employes all lived in the same small town and were generally well acquainted." The employer, in Teddy Roosevelt's earlier version of the same story, had "known every man in his shop; he called his men Bill, Tom, Dick, John; he inquired after their wives and babies" and "swapped jokes and stories" with them. As the enterprises grew, however, employers came to realize that they had "lost contact" with their workers. "That was their [the workers'] loss to some extent," Hall reflected, "but it was our loss most of all. We had lost these valuable contacts by getting so big."[39]

For almost a century, at various stages of corporate expansion in diverse industries, executive voices like that of E. K. Hall could be heard intoning similar refrains about the passage of a golden age of human relations in industry. "When the business was smaller," the Swift & Company Year Book recalled in 1926, "management and men were in closer contact and could discuss their material problems face to face." Only the year before, Vice President W. W. Atterbury of the Pennsylvania Railroad (PRR) had bemoaned the loss of the "family spirit" under modern conditions where "we are so separated from each other by the mechanical partitions which divide us; we see each other so seldom." It was now imperative to restore that spirit and "get closer to our men."[40]

This estrangement was not new, as the president of the N. W. Ayer & Son agency reminded his audience of national advertisers in 1937. As early as 1900, he observed, employers "had begun to arrive at a precariously exposed and isolated position." In contrast to the "old days," when the employer knew everyone by name and "men dealt with each other face to face and on equal terms," there was now a "widening breach between manufacturer and employees." Procter & Gamble made the same confession about a loss of the "close personal contact" that had existed when it had operated only one plant.[41] The subheadings that a Pennsylvania Railroad executive chose for an article on public relations in the employee magazine in 1926 succinctly outline the formulaic quality of the Lament:

> "The Old Era of Personal Contact"
> "Passing of the Intimate Touch"
> "Seeking an Effective Substitute."[42]

The Lament not only brooded over the lost satisfactions of personal contact and "hands-on" comradeship with rank-and-file employees, but it also frequently ruminated on the employees' distrust of management and their flagging morale as they lost sight of the "big picture" in the company's operations. As Hall of AT&T put it, the worker knew that "somehow he was losing his status in industry. He was lost in the shuffle somewhere . . . just a cog in the machine . . . nobody paid any particular attention to, or took any particular interest in him. . . . He did not even know who he was working for. He did not know, in the great big corporation, just who the real boss was."[43] Companies as diverse as General Motors and J. C. Penney reflected on the problem of bringing workers in geographically scattered operations to see themselves as "vital and important units" in a "big nationwide institution."[44]

Most expounders of the Lament saw rapid increases in the company's scale of operations as the sole cause of these problems. J. Carlisle MacDonald, the head of public relations at U.S. Steel, compared his company's challenge with the "ideal situation"—one in which the manager of a small business could "know each employee personally and . . . talk to him at frequent intervals." In a 1917 speech entitled "The Personal Relation in Industry," John D. Rockefeller Jr. evoked the days when the owner or manager not only "actually worked with his employes" but knew them as "his companions in school days, his friends and neighbors, often calling him as he did them by their first names." Bayard Colgate, of Colgate & Company, contrasted his circumstances in 1934 with those of his grandfather, who had worked a century earlier with three or four employees who "were almost like members of his family" in a single building that served as factory, office, store, and home. Obviously, such interactions were no longer feasible in a business that had expanded to twelve plants and 7,500 workers.[45]

AT&T's Vice President Hall examined more carefully the causes for alienation. Confronted with the sudden requirement to organize people in large groups, he explained, industry had "looked around for a precedent." Quickly and unthinkingly, it seized upon the military as the available example. "The big industrial corporation was organized like the army," with a line-and-staff system, general managers instead of generals, and foremen instead of lieutenants. Manufacturers had failed to realize that "the spirit of the military organization and its methods are ill adapted to industry." The army was simply not an adequate model, given the pressing need to "get back into industry the normal, human relationships that bigness in anything tends to squeeze out." The proper model, Hall suggested indirectly, was the family.[46]

The Corporation as Army and as Family

Could a vast corporate enterprise such as General Motors, as one of its executives proposed in 1922, both solve its internal problems and reconstruct its public image merely by presenting itself "not as resembling an octopus, but as being the parent of a large and creditable family"?[47] Certainly the rhetoric of corporate familialism enjoyed widespread favor among company executives and in employee magazines in the 1920s and 1930s. But it did not immediately displace the imagery of the workforce as army. Rather, both of these metaphors figured in early twentieth-century corporate imagery. Most executives seemed unfazed by their dissonance.[48]

The metaphor of the corporation as army reflected the striking changes in the size and structure of large businesses in the late nineteenth century. In ways that Alfred Chandler has elucidated, the railroad companies were leaders in this trend. Not only did the army model fit the process of railroad building quite well, but railroad executives further adopted the line-and-staff pattern of military command to bring large-scale coordination and centralized administration to their mushrooming industry. Moreover, in their need for exact timing in complex operations, railroad officials strove for "military precision" in their maneuvers.[49]

As Peter Drucker has noted, the great armies of the past had served as the main prototype of the large organization up to the twentieth century. Thus the model of the army easily found applications beyond the railroads. The spiraling demand for detailed information in all kinds of complex business operations encouraged executives to see their systems of internal reporting as similar to those in a military hierarchy. Alfred Sloan took satisfaction in General Motors' adoption of the army model for a general staff; Alfred Hunt of Alcoa, according to George David Smith, was "fascinated by military discipline."[50]

In a narrow sense, as Drucker observes, the army model defined the corporation as an organization composed of "a tiny group of generals at the top, who made all the decisions, and a vast mass of illiterate soldiers underneath, who were rigidly drilled to obey a few repetitive commands." But more generally, it reflected the perceived need for discipline and coordinated control to assure that a large, complex organization would function effectively. Even the managers of such seemingly unmartial businesses as telephone service and department stores turned to military imagery to convey their high level of coordination. AT&T's publicity brochures referred proudly to the leadership of President Theodore Vail over "the army of his employees." And reporter John Dennis Jr. seemed to find the military metaphor inescapable in his 1906 essay on Marshall Field. Referring regularly to the store's employees as the "Field army," with its "long line of division commanders and subcommanders, captains and lieutenants," Dennis concluded that "no army was ever more carefully drilled . . . [or] more skillfully disposed on the battle-field."[51]

Apart from its implications of intricate control, the military image enjoyed huge popularity simply as the most vivid and immediately comprehensible metaphor for large numbers of people efficiently acting together for a common purpose. In 1915 and again in 1916 AT&T used the phrases "an army of loyal men and women," "the army of telephone employees," and "an army of telephone workers" in advertisements that proclaimed its "spirit of service." And Charles Ripley, in his romanticization of life in the main General Electric factory, referred constantly to GE's "great army of industrial workers." The frequency with which the term "army" was applied to a company's customers, subscribers, or stockholders, as well as to its employees, suggests that to most speakers it was simply a way of connoting pure size.[52]

The metaphor of the corporation as family was used far more self-consciously. While it certainly could claim valid descent from the origins of most corporations as small family businesses, this metaphor only became more popular as the reality of family-like scale vanished. Business leaders frequently drew upon the imagery of the corporate family to rebut the Lament through an act of will. Although they might supplement it with various welfare initiatives and more personalized media of internal communications, the metaphor remained largely a rhetorical denial of precisely the opposite trend in internal relationships. Beyond the effects of expanding size and increasing geographical reach, the systematization of information flow, as JoAnne Yates has remarked, was promoting impersonality and a "strictly businesslike tone" within the corporation.[53] The "rational, objective, calculated approach to business problems," Alfred D. Chandler Jr. and Stephen Salsbury have pointed out, epitomized the shift from the particularistic values associated with the family to the ethos of the modern industrial corporation. In the face of these changes the family metaphor expressed the sentimental hope of many executives, and perhaps even of some employees, that the large corporation could still offer its workers, in the words of Standard Oil president Walter Teagle, "some meaning and some definite reward in addition to the daily wage."[54]

Some corporate leaders called their companies "families" only in passing. But others seized on family imagery almost compulsively. In its company newsletters the Aluminum Company of America (Alcoa) consistently referred to employees as "The Family" or "Aluminum Family." A typical article might begin, "Aluminum Family will be interested to learn. . . ." The large N. W. Ayer advertising agency urged its employees to greet newcomers and visitors with "the Family Smile," and Caterpillar Tractor's booklet for new employees declared that "the relations between 'Caterpillar' employees and the Company are like those of a happy family." Metropolitan Life Insurance Company executives competed in voicing filial tributes to "Mother Metropolitan." Some corporations found ways to apply the concept of family to virtually every company function. Meetings of executives and engineers became "family reunions"; at banquets, managers and agents "gathered . . . about our family table." Births and graduations of employees' children were announced as "family" events.[55]

In a perceptive analysis of gender conceptions within one of the corporations (and industries) most zealous in its attachment to the family metaphor, Angel Kwolek-Folland has coined the terms "corporate motherhood" and "corporate domesticity" to characterize the pervasive family rhetoric and ideology of the Metropolitan Life Insurance Company.[56] But while the extensive family imagery that defined the company as "Mother Metropolitan" challenged prevailing views that "business was a public, male arena driven by men and masculine values" and presaged a broader shift in business to a service model, most images of the corporate family, including Metropolitan's, were also fully compatible with a patriarchal ideal and a hierarchical company structure. President Haley Fiske clearly identified himself as Metropolitan's "father . . . grandfather . . . great-grandfather." When Fiske sought to add a "motherly" component to his portrait of this corporate family, he turned "with a [patriarchal] bow" to Mrs. Brockway, the company's decidedly subordinate welfare matron for the female employees.[57]

The use of familial imagery may also have stemmed from business leaders' consciousness of the increasing number of female employees within many large corporations. In its connotations of warmth and softness the image of the corporate family offered a feminine counterpart to the stern, masculine image of the corporate army. Still, the highly sentimental family imagery of Metropolitan Life's rhetoric did not preclude simultaneous use of the military metaphor. In fact, Metropolitan frequently referred to both its employees and its policyholders as "armies." It called its 15,500 white-collar workers an "army" in 1912 and again in 1915, in welfare pamphlets that praised their "loyalty and efficiency" and sought to convince them of the company's concern for their welfare. Even as it addressed such family-like needs as care during illness and old age, the company seemed drawn to the army metaphor whenever it talked about loyalty or efficiency, or simply when it contemplated the vast size of its workforce.[58]

Loyalty—the employee's devoted, enthusiastic participation with the employer in a common endeavor—was the quality for which the Lament had most wistfully yearned. It was also the bridge that surmounted all the incongruities between the army and family metaphors. The image of an army evoked selfless sacrifice in the service of a higher cause. But the family, too, ideally bound its members in unselfish loyalty. The first issue of the *Ford Man* exhorted workers to see the factory as "just as much yours as it is ours," and thus as an institution to which all members of the corporate family should devote "every ounce of loyalty we possess." A business journalist in 1919 observed that "the spirit desired in industrial organizations . . . the ideal . . . [is] that all workers from the president to the office boy shall feel that they belong to one big family and have the loyalty which that relationship implies." Hinting at the psychological as well as economic advantages in a corporation that acted like a family, he added, "The employer wants his men to work not for him but with him."[59] When corporate executives expressed pride in the achievements and preeminence of their companies, they often pointed to the loyalty and esprit de corps of their employee armies or employee families with particular satisfaction.[60]

Some corporations persisted in their penchant for company-as-family rhetoric even when the nuances of that metaphor contradicted other aspects of their desired image. Thus, the president of the Pullman Company declared it "the height of my ambition that the Pullman Company shall be known as the embodiment

Photo of National Cash Register Plant and Employees, Taken June 5, 1923, showing Four of the Twenty-six Factory Buildings

The people *and* plant that stand behind *every* National Cash Register

THOUSANDS of men and women workers! Enormous modern factories, covering 46 acres of floor space! Millions spent in research! 41 years devoted solely to making National Cash Registers! All with one great purpose.

To build cash registers for you. Cash registers that protect your profits, stop losses, reduce expenses, help business grow.

Cash registers that fit your business exactly, no matter what it is. No matter how large or small.

National Cash Registers do it. They do it for every kind of business in the civilized world where money and records are handled.

How we have made them do this is a wonderful story.

A story of progress! The first National Cash Register met the needs of forty years ago. The present National Cash Registers meet the complex needs of our day. There are more than 500 different types and sizes. When business requires more—and it will—we will build more.

It's a story of service! Making cash registers save money and earn money for their owners. Nationals quickly repay their cost.

And another kind of service! Putting National Cash Registers within reach of all with low prices, easy payments, liberal allowances on used machines.

These thousands you see have the National Register ideal of progress and service. From the president

to the office boy, each is working to make the best cash registers in the world, to be sold at the lowest prices.

The giant factories behind them are a monument to their success—a guarantee of the permanence of their work.

While, in every quarter of the earth, representatives of the National Cash Register Company are daily meeting the business world, studying business problems with business men, blazing the way for greater achievement.

The National Cash Register Company
Dayton, Ohio, U. S. A.
Offices in all principal cities of the world

National Cash Registers

FIGURE 3.9
Enormous factories and massive workforces connoted progress, but such images also challenged the notion of the corporation as family.

of efficiency and a happy family." But here, just as with the seemingly opposed metaphors of army and family, a certain pragmatic linkage undercut the contradiction between family feeling and efficiency. A lack of loyalty and enthusiasm did affect the efficiency of the company, as virtually every corporate leader realized. It had once seemed feasible to obtain the desired harmony, energetic performance, and wholehearted cooperation from workers through leadership based on a military model. But as the twentieth century advanced, workers responded less to authoritarianism than to persuasion.[61]

One striking vogue in corporate imagery can provide us with an insight into the gradually shifting balance between army and family metaphors and the ultimate difficulties by the 1930s in maintaining the previous conflation of images. With the developing capacities of wide-angle photography by the second decade of the century, a number of companies chose to personify themselves through panoramas of the factory plus the workers (Fig. 3.9; see also 3.10).[62] While such photographs gave more agency to the workforce than had illustrations of the factory alone, their bias toward pure magnitude undercut the corporation-as-family paradigm. Labeling such a crowded scene a company's "family picture" could only accentuate the challenge of scale to the family metaphor. How could a sea of faces (or hats) convey those qualities of closeness and affection that a corporation sought through family imagery?[63]

Despite their attention-grabbing visual power, panoramas of the workforce gained only sporadic use, mainly between 1914 and 1927.[64] In the early 1930s this genre disappeared almost completely, as employers increasingly linked negative associations to images of huge numbers of people congregated outside their factories. Interestingly, it was also during the 1930s that public relations officers began to cultivate a new kind of family image for the corporation—one that stressed identifiable individual employee families, real or fictional. Some companies publicized the continuity of specific families among the workers in their plants; others showed how their local plants provided neighborly, extended-family functions for their workers. By that time almost no one talked about the "industrial army" or the company's "army of employees." During World War II photographic panoramas of massed workers were seen again, often depicting actual ceremonies honoring the plant for meeting some production goal and receiving a government "E" (for "excellence") award.[65] But despite the ease of association afforded by the war and the engagement of workers in war production, the word "army" appeared surprisingly seldom as a metaphor for the workforce.

As the popularity of familial corporate rhetoric during the first three decades of the century suggests, many corporate executives, in their desire to move as far as possible from the sense of a merely contractual or expedient nexus between themselves and their mass of employees, looked for models more congenial than the army, disregarding even the team in favor of the more consecrated image of the family. Howell Harris surmises that the team metaphor appealed "to the 1940s generation of senior executives" because of "their upbringing in the first great age of organized sport," but their predecessors lacked this experience. For their generation the hegemonic image of the ideal Victorian family was a more powerful model, with more emphatic connotations of moral sanctity than those suggested by the concept of the team—an important benefit for a company that wished to be recognized as "A Corporation with a Soul."[66]

The idea of family was also more compatible with the hierarchical image of the company. It conveyed a more paternalistic concern for the welfare of subordinates than did the notion of a team. The family's relations were more intimate than a team's, and its bonds of loyalty deeper and less situational, while the father's moral authority was greater than that of any coach. As one executive described the relationship with workers established through the employee magazine, "Of course, as in the household, 'father' should direct the conversation so that it will be harmonious and helpful to all." The tension between such a concept of managerial control and the occasional, perhaps inadvertently egalitarian, expressions by corporate executives of their desire to "sit down and talk with you as a fellow employee" could be comfortably obscured in family imagery, which encompassed both closeness and a tradition of hierarchical status.[67]

Of course, the image of the corporation as family could hardly withstand critical analysis, even though some employees—as well as many executives—appear to have valued the sense of security, collaboration, and united moral purpose that it sometimes supplied. What family would "fire" its children when expediency so dictated? How did stockholders, who might dispose of their interests in the company at any moment, fit into a model of ongoing moral unity and commitment? Could workers be expected to buy into a language and symbolism that so blatantly denied both the scale and the contractual nature of the relationships that characterized the large modern business corporation? Undoubtedly, some executives counted on employees and the public to take the improbable metaphor of the corporation as family with a certain grain of salt, allowing for the extent of poetic license that Leo Spitzer so elegantly described as inherent in the "language of advertisement." The success of the metaphor also depended on differing elements of scale and policy within individual companies: personal recollections indicate that employees during certain eras at such firms as Kraft, Alcoa, and Eli Lilly truly felt themselves to be working within a "family atmosphere." But those who testified to such feelings seem largely to have occupied white-collar and managerial positions.[68]

The corporate leaders who promulgated this family rhetoric were responding to the breakdown in communications outlined in the Lament—the loss of face-to-face conversation and familiarity with their employees. Their use of the family metaphor was one aspect of their search for a new mode of communications with their masses of workers that would convey the imagined humaneness and benevolence of an earlier personal relationship. One test of the credibility of the corporation-as-family model would lie in the effectiveness of the corporate family—however extended—in devising adequate substitutes for those bygone workplace conversations and thus recreating family feeling through modern means.

The Employee Magazine and the Restoration of the Corporate Family

Almost as predictably as the movies' irrepressible Andy Hardy reacted to a crisis by exclaiming, "Let's put on a show," corporate leaders responded to the revelations of the Lament by proposing, "Let's put out an employee magazine." Given the significance they had nostalgically attributed to face-to-face relationships between employers and workers, it is astonishing how readily many corporate executives and public relations officers concluded that the printed word could accomplish the same results. Their eagerness to find a happy ending for the Lament narratives encouraged them to take at face value the assertions of how-to articles that claimed employee publications had "cut through this tangled and thinning web of communications and re-established a direct line between the men at the big desks and the workers and their families in their homes."[69]

As though the extent of the need ensured the adequacy of the response, employee magazines and internal corporate memos shimmered with enthusiastic predictions about the effects of the "mutual communication" between employer and employee that these publications would promote. Although the vaunted American "can-do" philosophy was now being applied not to technical or production issues but to subtle matters of employee psychology, corporate optimism remained undaunted. In its first issue, in March 1912, the *Western Electric News* described itself as "the answer to the universal demand of the employees for an opportunity to know more about this wonderful organization." Ivy Lee spoke confidently of "employee publications that take the place of heart-to-heart talks." Even in 1932 a General

Motors public relations officer could still propose a corporation-wide employee magazine as "the ideal, economical medium for establishing a *friendly, personal* relationship between General Motors and its divisional employees."[70]

Corporations introduced employee magazines at different times in their course of development and in response to a variety of considerations. Some of the earliest coincided with paternalistic welfare initiatives in companies like Heinz, Procter & Gamble, Dennison Manufacturing, and National Cash Register.[71] Others emerged in the wake of strikes or extraordinary worker-management tensions. A Westinghouse public relations official surmised years later that the *Westinghouse Electric News* had been launched in November 1914 as a direct result of a "bitter strike" that year against the company. No such surmises were needed to connect the 1915 origins of the *Industrial Bulletin* of the Colorado Fuel and Iron Company with efforts of John D. Rockefeller Jr. and Ivy Lee to counteract the effects of the Ludlow massacre of 1914.[72]

David Nye remarks that General Electric "published nothing" for factory workers until 1917, when, "at a moment of internal crisis," it "responded to an apparent threat to control over the labor force." The emergence of a large number of employee magazines between 1917 and 1920 suggests that the particular labor problems of the wartime period, together with the culmination of labor turnover rates in major industries, had inspired employers to look to internal publications to bind employees more closely to the corporation.[73]

In recognizing the need for an employees' magazine, employers departed from their predecessors, who typically, in the words of Sanford Jacoby, "regarded workers as brutish or machine-like and paid no attention at all to motivation, preferring to leave that to their foremen." The house organ of Standard Oil of New Jersey frankly observed that "it is only human nature that the individual will work harder and more effectively when he is a partner." Therefore, employees were encouraged to think of themselves as "member[s] of the family rather than . . . servant[s] of the family," concluded Standard's president, Walter Teagle. Editors of house organs often reported how eager they were to receive employee contributions and make the magazine "truly representative."[74]

Still, many editors also revealed a compulsion to sermonize. After proclaiming in its first issue that it would be "no pulpit of preachment," the *Pullman News* regularly appropriated the sayings of figures from the biblical Abraham to one of its own "recruit porters" to moralize on the virtues of loyalty, ambition, and "the dignity of work." The *Ford Man* carried such front-page editorials as "How Many Days Have You Lost?" and observed that "too many employees . . . stay away from work without good reason." It reminded blue-collar workers that "cheerfulness and enthusiasm make monotony in work impossible" and chided them for envying their superiors: "Don't think for a minute that the foreman, or superintendent, or any of the executives nor any of the workers in the Administration Building have any easier time than any others in the army of Ford workers."[75] Other editors instructed workers on everything from economics to dental hygiene and admonished them not to "grumble over . . . things you do not understand." The *Westinghouse Electric News* steadily sermonized on thrift, the evils of envy, and the advantages of being a "self-starter." It did not hesitate to advise workers on "how to live a perfect day." Nothing would foster a "sunny mental attitude" as much as a "cheery whistle." To get a perfect day off to the proper start, it counseled, "when you arrive at the factory, greet the Boss with a breezy, cheery, 'good morning.'"[76]

Such stiltedness and condescension reflected the tensions inherent in publications provided *by* the corporation but (at least ostensibly) *for* the employees. Although the first issues of employee magazines often assured workers that "this paper is your paper" or urged them to take the magazine "as your own, for it was sincerely planned and designed for you," employee magazines were vehicles of downward communication and could hardly be anything else. Their editors were headquarters employees who reported to top management. No matter how folksy their touch, many of these editors felt compelled to print lectures on the virtues of free enterprise, especially when those lectures came from the company president. As JoAnne Yates has noted, however, employee magazines usually communicated "general values" rather than "specific orders." And in seeking to convey these values, editors frequently adopted some pretense of facilitating a conversation through which "the members of your business organization [will] feel a family interest and pride in their work."[77]

Whether or not employees ever recognized the company as family, the employee magazine often did. If the object of the house organ was "to cement the relationships of the big family," as a review of the genre in *Printers' Ink* in 1916 advised, "human interest must be the bait." The board of editors of the *Western Electric News* declared itself "ever on the hunt for 'human-interest stuff.'" Many of the house organs found such material, as Yates observes, in the "home lives and personal interests" of the employees, as well as in "their roles in the company." Thus, the organ of the Chicago Telephone Company included not only news on dances, social events, and weddings but also a regular page devoted to "the Girl who Sews." Ivy Lee described the optimum employee magazine as "just like a small town weekly which tells the news about the neighbors." Its goal, he added, should be "to bring into its columns as far as possible mention of every man on the railroad who does anything of consequence." The desire of each employee "to see his name . . . or the names of his friends in print" was sometimes put forward as an argument in favor of many local plant magazines rather than a single corporation-wide publication. The best formula seemed to be one that Lizabeth Cohen has noted in the house organs of Chicago industrial concerns in the 1920s: the inclusion of "as many . . . employee names as could possibly be dropped."[78]

Employee magazines cultivated the image of the corporate family in a variety of ways. Some, like the *Alcoa News* and Postum's *Wellville Post,* incessantly used the term "family" to refer to company employees. Others displayed the term in their titles, like the *RCA Family Circle,* the *American Sugar Family,* the *Minute Family,* and *Monitor Family Circle,* or in special subsections like "In the Hawthorne Family." Still other magazines adopted a "chatty, informal style," one that the editor apparently hoped would convey the atmosphere of a family "conversation." The employee magazine of the Endicott Johnson Corporation, as Gerald Zahavi observes, emphasized a sense of "collective bonds" by labeling the firm the "Happy Family." Its manual for new workers extended the cheerful greeting: "You have now joined the Happy Family."[79]

Even more self-consciously than they cultivated family imagery, the employee magazines sought to enhance workers' morale by bolstering their sense of place within their own extensive factory and within the corporation as a whole. In large organizations, particularly those with plants in several regions, workers lacked a sense of the scope and purposes of the entire corporation. They would take more pride in their work, managers concluded, if they could see where they fit into the organization. The employee magazine of the Fort Wayne Works of General Electric surmised in 1920 that "only a comparatively few of the 5,000 employees of this plant have a good idea of its greatness, the variety of its products."[80] *Printed Salesmanship* praised the Northwestern Bell Company for "keeping alive . . . the human side of personal acquaintance" through its employee magazine; "the larger the corporation," it observed, "and the more scattered its people, the more need there is for fanning this community of interests."[81] The *Ford Man, Westinghouse Electric News,* and *Alcoa News* all made a point of informing employees about the activities at other plants. The *Erpigram,* a house organ of the film division of Western Electric, asserted that an organization with people "stationed all over the country" needed something like a town newspaper to give them a feeling of community. General Electric proclaimed the mission of its *Monogram,* aimed at the company's sales force, as "the bringing home to the man out in the remotest outpost of our far-flung commercial army the realization of the fact that he is as much a part of the G-E family as the man in the home office." Thus would the corporate army become family.[82]

In the quest both to unite their entire, often geographically widespread, corporate families and to restore greater intimacy of communications, corporate leaders looked beyond the printed word of the house organs whenever other media promised a greater impression of "closeness." International Harvester particularly noted the value of company fair exhibits for publicizing its welfare activities and giving employees "a keener interest in their work and broaden[ing] their scope of vision as to what they are working at." Some promoters of new technologies for bridging the gap between employees and remote executives must have taxed the credulity of corporate leaders. One such promoter hoped to interest Alfred Sloan of General Motors and Lammot du Pont of the Du Pont Company in loudspeaking equipment that, through long-distance telephone lines, could be connected to a microphone on the president's desk. From this seat of authority, the top executive could then "talk regularly with all your employees at the same time." This "human touch method of communication," the enthusiast promised, would allow all of the workers at the corporation's vast operations to "feel that they [know] you personally." A motion picture agent assured General Electric president Gerard Swope that a film carrying his "personal Yuletide greetings" could promote "friendship and amity" through this "friendly intimate manner."[83]

Dubious as such propositions might seem, corporate executives proved very willing to experiment with technological solutions to the Lament. By 1922 the Western Electric Company was publicizing a new technology that enabled the company's president to speak directly from his desk in New York to thousands of assembled employees in Chicago. The employees derived particular satisfaction from this contact, the company implied, because they themselves had made the wires, cables, and the loudspeaker (Fig. 3.10). The following year Metropolitan Life linked fifteen thousand of its agents by radio into "one great audience" for the officers' addresses at the annual company banquet. Howard Heinz rejoiced in 1930 that a "radio banquet" had enabled the employees in "widely scattered units" of the Heinz Company to be "all brought into a family circle" and to "sit at a

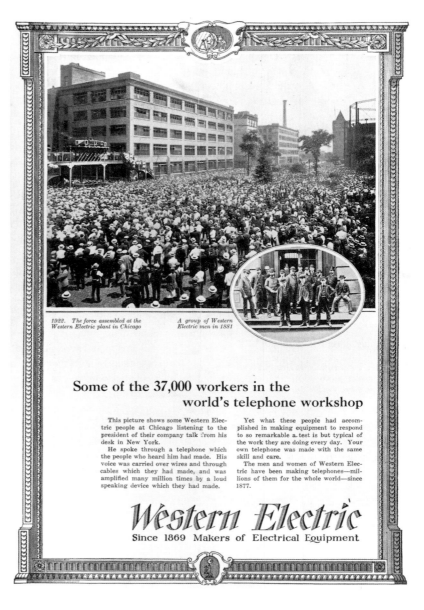

1922. The force assembled at the Western Electric plant in Chicago

A group of Western Electric men in 1881

Some of the 37,000 workers in the world's telephone workshop

This picture shows some Western Electric people at Chicago listening to the president of their company talk from his desk in New York.

He spoke through a telephone which the people who heard him had made. His voice was carried over wires and through cables which they had made, and was amplified many million times by a loud speaking device which they had made.

Yet what these people had accomplished in making equipment to respond to so remarkable a test is but typical of the work they are doing every day. Your own telephone was made with the same skill and care.

The men and women of Western Electric have been making telephones—millions of them for the whole world—since 1877.

Western Electric

Since 1869 Makers of Electrical Equipment

FIGURE 3.10
Western Electric proposed a technological fix to the problem of scale: from New York headquarters the company president could talk directly to his massive Chicago family through a telephone-loudspeaker hookup "which the people who heard him had made."

common table." Such a "family gathering" ensured the preservation of "a proper place in business for sentiment."[84]

If radio could reunite the family at one great dining table, film might also provide a technological fix for the Lament. In 1920 *Printers' Ink Monthly* reported on the use of motion pictures in several factories to "carry over to the individual workers the same understanding which the owner could produce were he able to talk to each man personally." Such films, the journal exulted, could convey economic lessons, gain the employee's empathy by telling "the honest-to-goodness troubles of the modern owner of a big plant," and show each man "where his little piece of work fitted into the finished product put out by the company." *Printers' Ink* confidently titled the article "Bringing the Hand-shake Back to Our Factories." By 1929 the employee magazine of the film division of Western Electric Company was predicting that before long "many officers of the big corporations will be addressing their employees through the talking pictures, thus saving the time of long trips to meet personally with them." The "hand-shake" of the earlier, silent corporate films could now be joined by a hearty vocal greeting.[85]

Particularly dramatic and intimate, the leaders of the Pennsylvania Railroad assumed, were the radio-linked family Christmas parties they initiated in 1925. These "family gatherings" were held in a number of the cities on the Pennsylvania Railroad lines. Broadcasts from the Edgewater Beach Hotel in Chicago and from the Metropolitan Opera House in Philadelphia, company press releases promised, would "link the 200,000 Pennsylvania employees and their families for one simultaneous holiday party." It would probably rank as "the biggest family Christmas celebration in the world" and would, in the words of Vice President A. J. County, demonstrate that the Pennsylvania Railroad was emphatically "something more than a mere machine without heart or soul." Vice President Elisha Lee told the listening participants that the corporation's new president, General W. W. Atterbury, had conceived of the idea of a huge family party and, "if he could have found a hall big enough, . . . would have invited every man, woman and child in this big family of ours to be with him." Atterbury himself radioed a wish to his "fellow workers" that "on this occasion we could really feel like one great big family . . . not that we are working for a corporation, but that we are engaged in an endeavor, the primary purpose of which is to make one another happy."[86]

Did employees take to heart the earnest efforts of these corporations, through company magazines, films, and radio parties, to reestablish "that vanished personal contact between management and man . . . [which had] existed when enterprises were smaller"? In their discussion about how best to disseminate company magazines, even the irrepressibly optimistic house organ editors revealed doubts about their impact on rank-and-file employees. The cheapest means of mass distribution was simply to hand out the employee magazines at the factory. But did workers really take the magazine home and read it? Did they encourage their families to become part of the company family by reading it also? When Western Electric noted that it distributed its magazine "as near 'whistle time' as possible" so that it would immediately be carried home, we may surmise disappointment with other times of distribution. Metropolitan Life's deliberate decision in 1931 to absorb the extra cost of mailing its magazine directly to employees' homes, in the hope that members of their families would "develop a personal interest in it—and, parenthetically, in the organization," also suggested some fears of a lack of employee interest.[87]

We may justifiably remain skeptical of the power of the family metaphor— whether repeated in company publications or enacted in such technological feats as radio-linked corporate Christmas parties—to reshape worker consciousness. But this imagery often functioned in tandem with efforts to decrease worker alienation through humanizing systems of employee representation and paternalistic welfare programs. In fact, programs in which the company "became a partner in providing basic family needs, such as medical care, relief, recreation and housing," provided much of the content of company magazines. As Gerald Zahavi argues, "The company attempted to do more than merely cultivate an image of a corporate family. It also sought to unite the functions of corporation and family."[88]

The Concerned Corporation:
Welfare and Employee Representation

Leaders of a number of large businesses stepped forward during the 1920s to shoulder new responsibilities for their workers' welfare. A great variety of motives, ranging from calculations of workplace efficiency to aspirations to transcend detached, purely contractual relationships, prompted these initiatives.[89] The extent to which such measures seemed to counter the attractions of labor unionization, of course, counted heavily in their favor. Whether or not the company couched them in the language of family relationships and responsibilities, welfare activities reinforced the particular distinction between "us" and "them" that corporate executives desired—not one between managers and workers but rather one that separated all inside the company from alien forces.

The Pullman Company expressed this conception vividly in its imagery of "Joining Hands in the Pullman Circle." Through company-sponsored recreational activities it hoped to realize the adage that "those who worked together should also play together." Such a "circle" not only suggested warm inclusiveness but further implied a shared understanding of the moral divergence between inside and outside—with the union organizer on the outside. "The employee has a closer bond between himself and his company than he has or can have between himself and some outsider," the corporation avowed. "Any outsider who attempts to break this bond is an enemy of both."[90]

As hedges against labor unrest, unionization, and excessive worker turnover, corporate welfare programs were often primarily defensive in purpose. But some, particularly in the 1920s, represented a more expansive gesture. Providing special employee benefits reinforced the corporation's moral legitimacy; it made the company's social obligations more commensurate with its economic power. The growing willingness of large corporations to take on this wider responsibility coincided with their aspirations to the status of institutions. Upon their acceptance of certain social responsibilities rested their claims, increasingly asserted in the 1920s, to be recognized as the institutions most fit to be entrusted with the public welfare. Companies so dominant that "we can today rightly list [them among] the great powers and principalities of this world," as one business journalist remarked, might well consider it appropriate for their "business statesmanship" to encompass wider areas of human welfare.[91]

But some executives also understood their programs of welfare capitalism on a more personal basis. The Lament had focused on the loss of personal communication, a breakdown that could imply an evasion of responsibility. That legendary old-time employer, who had known each worker individually, was presumed to have felt paternalistic concern for the worker's needs. Perhaps, some corporate leaders mused, the loss of that element of "human connection" had helped foster the notion of corporate soullessness. Out of an amalgam of personal sensibilities and tactical calculations, executives expressed a naive hope in the "restoration" of a fundamental "kindly feeling" among all the people in the corporation.[92]

Defying the obvious barriers of scale in the huge modern corporation, some business leaders imagined that they could successfully recreate the old atmosphere by occasionally fraternizing with their employees. Those executives who had at least once engaged in the exercise of mingling with the common workers (as had John D. Rockefeller Jr. at Colorado Fuel and Iron in the wake of the Ludlow massacre, at the urging of Ivy Lee) obtained a special status among their peers by telling "war stories" from their tours of the shop floor. But most corporate observers accepted the limitations of scale. Corporate concern for the worker, they concluded, could best be displayed through the "closer contact" afforded by employee representation plans and through the institutionalized beneficence of company welfare measures.[93]

Early corporate welfare programs had not necessarily been linked to extensive size. At places like Heinz and National Cash Register they owed their origins primarily to the extreme paternalism of rather idiosyncratic company founders; in England, at Saltaire in Bradford and at Cadburys in Birmingham, Quaker entrepreneurial families, suffused with paternalistic responsibility, had nurtured welfare-oriented company cultures. In many instances, ranging from the kitchens of Heinz to the counters of Filene's department store in Boston and of the Bon Marché in Paris, particular concern for the exposed circumstances of a workforce of young women had inspired a sense of moral responsibility in employers (see Figs. 1.4 and 5.5). Of course, all these employers also anticipated increased loyalty and productivity in response to these measures.[94]

By World War I, pragmatic considerations had largely supplanted religious influences and idiosyncratic enthusiasms as the basis for corporate welfare programs. In some instances, as with the United States Steel Corporation, a consciousness of political vulnerabilities had, at least marginally, sensitized the corporate conscience.[95] More commonly, the larger scale and greater integration of their highly mechanized plants, together with the labor shortages of the war years, had made leaders of large businesses attentive to the costs of labor turnover. Apart from any paternalistic considerations, corporate leaders saw a need for incentives—ranging from profit sharing to factory restaurants—that would attract the best employees and bind them to the company.[96]

The variety of programs and activities encompassed by welfare capitalism by the early 1920s was sweeping. Any given corporation might offer a few benefits or many, from medical care and organized recreation to pensions, company housing, and profit sharing. Many programs, such as bonus systems, pension plans, employee stock-purchase programs, and vacations with pay after ten years, aimed to reduce turnover by offering conspicuous financial rewards for long service. Others, from company theater groups and choruses to athletic teams, cooperative garden plots, hobby clubs, and summer camps, sought to give employees a feeling of community within the company. Such leisure and recreational programs gained extensive coverage in the employee magazines. Whatever they may have thought of the company's motives in subsidizing these activities, many employees readily incorporated them into their lives and thus accepted at least this degree of paternalistic nurturance as part of their image of the company.[97]

Of course, as was true for the earliest programs described in Chapter 1, these welfare efforts were often intended for public consumption as well. Corporations occasionally touted their employee housing or pension plans in their institutional advertisements, fair exhibits, and company publications. Most publicized were the employee stock-owning programs, which afforded a company the opportunity to advertise its broad "public ownership" while taking credit for internal benevolence. Firestone Tire & Rubber Company claimed in a 1928 ad that "today every employee in this great corporation is a stockholder," with "more than a wage interest" in the company. The *Pennsylvania News* proclaimed that the oversubscription of Pennsylvania Railroad stock offered for employees gave evidence that American industry was no longer "owned by the so-called rich." Not only had railroad ownership moved from "Wall Street" to "Main Street," but it had also extended into the "side streets . . . where live the clerk, the mechanic, the track workers, the brakeman, the engineer, the carpenter, the telegrapher and the conductor."[98]

Employee representation, eagerly embraced by some corporate leaders and warily ventured upon by others, also gained a place in corporate public relations programs, often as an answer to the Lament. Largely precipitated by the rising tide of American Federation of Labor (AFL) unionization during the World War I era, these schemes of employee work councils and company-funded unions became quite fashionable among self-consciously "modern" large employers by the beginning of the 1920s. By the mid-1920s, Kim McQuaid calculates, nearly five hundred corporations, including such giants as AT&T, International Harvester, Bethlehem Steel, Goodyear, and Standard Oil of New Jersey, had established some form of nonunion works councils.[99] The mixed motives with which leaders of major corporations adopted these programs for employee representation were vividly captured in the arguments presented at top management meetings of International Harvester. Harold McCormick, the brother of the company president, Cyrus McCormick, and a convert to works councils as a new business necessity, presented employee representation as a way for the company to "maintain its standing among the other, forward-thinking, large institutions in this country." Cyrus reinforced this argument by pointing out that the leaders of International Harvester had "always claimed to be leaders . . . in welfare work" and should not relinquish that leadership. But defensive motives could prove more powerful than appeals to corporate stature and rectitude. Turning to the analogy of a "bomb under the bed," Harold McCormick urged his fellow executives not to run away from the problem of labor's demand for less "autocracy" in the workplace but also not simply to "stand and take the consequences." By instituting employee representation, they would recognize the inevitability of a change in industrial relations while "stoop[ing] down and put[ting] out the fuse" of independent unionization.[100]

In a similar vein the Pennsylvania Railroad set up a system of employee representation just as AFL unionization was advancing among its employees during the period of government operation in 1917 and 1918. Such plans not only provided a corporation-controlled channel for adjudicating employee grievances, but, like the employee magazines that were sometimes initiated simultaneously, they also attempted to restore the lost qualities of personal two-way communication between manager and employee. Representation programs, AT&T's Vice President E. K. Hall observed, offered management the occasion to extend a "cordial, hearty, man-to-man invitation" to workers, while solving the dilemma of how to "get close" to such large groups of employees as "the men in the ranks." General W. W. Atterbury, president of the Pennsylvania Railroad, hailed his company's employee representation system as central to his ambition to restore the old family spirit among railroad employees. The system was "not a plan to exclude unionism from the railroad," he insisted, but "a plan to enable us to get closer to our men."[101]

Although the idea of "getting closer" through employee representation plans was largely illusory, corporate managers soon recognized the value of such systems as conduits of corporate imagery and as instruments in cultivating employees to further disseminate that imagery.[102] At AT&T, a company highly dependent on the impressions its rank-and-file employees made on the public through millions of individual contacts, regional executives competed in offering tributes to the representation system for infusing employees with a sense of "their relation to the large objectives of the business." Moreover, local supervisors, who spoke on behalf of the company in meetings with employee representatives, began to educate themselves more thoroughly about the company in order to interpret it to its employees. In return for listening to employee grievances (and thus keeping them within the corporate family), management had gained an effective medium through which "to tell employees more about the business" and propel its messages internally through the "several steps in the line of supervision" to the "general forces."[103]

AT&T was not alone in discovering fringe benefits in employee associations and shop councils. Daniel Nelson cites the comments of several corporate executives who believed they had been successful in guiding their employees "into thinking of things from the company's standpoint" and convincing them that "the company—its success, its politics and its reputation—belongs as much to them as it does to the management." In 1925, Cyrus McCormick would observe how useful International Harvester's work councils had proved as "a forum for the discussion of management problems as well as employee problems" and how they had brought "management and men . . . closer." In addition, he reported, although any idea of publicity had been "furtherest from our thoughts" in initiating employee representation, it had "turned out to have publicity value of an extraordinary character."[104]

Several recent accounts have suggested that employee representation plans and other programs of welfare capitalism eventually served to school employees in organizational techniques, helping them surmount departmental barriers to labor unity and insist on their new "entitlements." When frustrated workers came to feel betrayed during the depression years, their organizational experience under employee representation enabled them to move toward militant unionism. Whatever these ultimate results, the programs also helped provide an additional medium of internal communication, one that was often used effectively to infuse the corporate image within the company. A survey on association conferences in one company during 1926 and 1927 counted "more than twice as many public relations discussions (mostly initiated by management) as there were wage discussions (mostly worker initiated)." At the risk of fostering expectations it might be hard pressed to fulfill, management used employee representation and welfare programs to make manifest its "friendly interest" in employees, to inspire "a feeling of confidence in the organization," and to enhance the corporation's public image.[105] Perhaps it was only natural for the question to arise: If internal programs could make good PR, couldn't good PR likewise boost internal morale?

Bank Shot: Ivy Lee, General Atterbury, and the Pennsylvania Railroad's Campaign for Morale

In the early 1920s Ivy Lee ranked highest in prominence among pioneer professionals in public relations. For more than a decade Lee had both voiced the Lament and pondered a variety of responses. The cleavage between management and workers in big businesses, he observed ruefully, was "one of the most unfortunate things in the world today." The large employer desperately needed to find ways to interpret himself "to the large number of people . . . impossible to reach with his voice." Out of the struggle against railroad unionization and the vicissitudes of the crucial railroad shopmen's strike of 1922, Lee concluded that "some means in advertising must be found of selling the employer to his employees."[106] As advisor to the giant Pennsylvania Railroad (in "publicity and public relations," at $20,000 a year), Lee devised his most inventive strategy—a deliberately oblique approach to workers. In a much-lauded institutional advertising campaign of 1927–28, which featured workers as both the content and the targets of the same ads, the Pennsylvania Railroad undertook an ambitious experiment in linking employee morale with corporate image.

Essential to this venture was the ascendance of "General" W. W. Atterbury to the presidency of the Pennsylvania in November 1925. As vice president of operations for the PRR during its period of greatest struggle over federal regulation and as head of the trade association for American railroads from 1916 to 1917, Atterbury had come to appreciate the importance of public relations. Ivy Lee had worked closely with Atterbury during these years, finding him the most sympathetic of all the company's executives toward Lee's various proposals. With Atterbury as president, Lee enjoyed direct access to a corporate chief who was both a long-time associate and a particularly vigorous leader.[107]

Having "risen from the ranks," Atterbury considered himself a fitting model for all railroad workers. From apprentice in the Altoona shops he had advanced to assistant road foreman, assistant engineer, master mechanic, and then onto the vice-presidential ladder. He took pride in reminding his employees that he had "worked at the bench the same as any other man on the system." During World War I he had been appointed brigadier general to coordinate railroad transport in France under General Pershing, and he wore the martial title very comfortably throughout his subsequent career. The constant references to the Pennsylvania's new president as "General Atterbury" conformed well with the organizational culture of the railroads. The "mobilization" of men and equipment to build and run a railroad, the deployment of relatively unskilled crews of track repairers and construction workers, and the necessary attention to timing and logistics all invited analogies to the operations of an army.[108]

Atterbury's special concerns for discipline and morale made the military title particularly apt. He often assumed a resolute and rigid position, as in his pugnacious resistance to railroad unionization. Like nearly all railroad executives, Atterbury wished to avoid any bargaining with independent unions; also like many others, he saw the necessity of accepting employee representation as a backfire against inroads by the AFL, particularly after the federal government had upheld employee bargaining during World War I. But Atterbury stood out among railroad executives in the early 1920s for his truculence in defending managerial prerogatives. In contrast to Daniel Willard of the Baltimore & Ohio and other railroad executives who proposed various forms of conciliation, Atterbury gained prominence among the "hard-boiled" group.[109] In what the Pennsylvania Railroad's company magazine later characterized as a heroic lonely fight, Atterbury "ignored and even flouted" the rulings of the federal government's Railroad Labor Board "in key cases involving union-smashing practices and union recognition." Peter Lyon described the General's dauntless stance bluntly: "Under the slogan, 'No contracts with labor unions,' [Atterbury] . . . plunged into the work of crushing them utterly."[110]

Like AT&T, the Pennsylvania turned the government's brief control of the railroads during World War I to its advantage in public relations, incessantly grumbling about the damage done to its workers' morale. "When I returned from France," Atterbury recalled in 1926, "I was confronted with a situation that nearly stunned me. I found that the Pennsylvania Railroad Company was no longer in a position to work with its employees in a manner that gave the freedom of expression we enjoyed before. . . . The more I studied the situation the more calamitous it appeared." The essence of the "calamity" was that the AFL, encouraged by federal edicts, had organized some thirty thousand of the Pennsylvania's workers. Not only had their wages nearly doubled between 1917 and 1920, but worse yet, they had received their paychecks not from the individual railroad companies but from William McAdoo, the federal coordinator. "From the moment the government took charge of the railroads," Ivy Lee fumed, "he [McAdoo] disseminated the thought that the loyalty of the individual railroad employee should not be to his employing officer but to the U.S. government." As a result "the morale of the employees had been absolutely shattered."[111]

Interpreting the wartime history of the railroads as an age of horrors, Atterbury and Lee introduced conspicuous villains (the federal government and the outside unions) into the Lament, making it more a vehicle for righteous indignation than for anxious reflection. The government had destroyed the "enviable esprit de corps" of the prewar Pennsylvania Railroad, a "big railroad family" in which "employees as a body were satisfied and worked in close cooperation with their officers." The "family spirit" of the old "direct, frank and friendly relationships" could be restored only if there were no further outside interference. With the battle cry "Let railroad men run the railroad business," Atterbury vigorously promoted his own company unions, cultivated the conservative railroad brotherhoods, and defied the federal government's Labor Board in carrying out employee representation elections. He looked to the day, he announced, when "our family will not be a broken family."[112]

By 1922 the railroads' cost-cutting measures, including wage cuts and the increased use of nonunion contract shops for repair work, had precipitated a strike by the shop unions. Atterbury resisted conciliation, breaking with several other railroad leaders. By reaching an agreement with his own company unions on the Pennsylvania Railroad, he managed to keep the majority of his workers on the job and break the strike. Afterward PRR spokesmen recalled with relish how the Pennsylvania, "where the labor unions were supposed to bitterly oppose . . . management," had commanded the greatest employee loyalty during the strike.[113] By mid-1926 the Pennsylvania could rightly claim success in its project to erect an employee representation system as a barrier to unionization.[114]

The employee-oriented institutional advertising campaign on which the company now embarked, at Ivy Lee's instigation, thus stemmed mainly from concerns about employee efficiency rather than labor policy. The Pennsylvania had regained a measure of prosperity in 1926, with a profit of over 13 percent on capital stock. But this did not diminish Atterbury's commitment to an ongoing program of cost cutting and morale boosting. Instead, it provided him with a sufficient margin of confidence to support Lee's ingenious proposal for an experiment in behavior modification through corporate imagery.[115]

General Atterbury had ample reason to concern himself with both Pennsylvania's corporate image and its employees' performance. Aside from the effect its public image might have on future labor issues before Congress and on rate-setting bodies, the Pennsylvania was suffering from invidious comparisons with other railroads in the quality of its service. When the J. Walter Thompson advertising agency surveyed frequent rail travelers as it prepared to devise an institutional campaign, it uncovered a miasma of negative impressions toward the PRR. Of some sixty respondents, only a few expressed praise. The others, at best, used words like "slump" and "deterioration" to characterize PRR service. One noted "an utter disregard of passengers and a total lack of common politeness," while another observed that "the employees seem to think that the public is working for the Pennsylvania." Other complaints focused on discourteous station guards; roadbeds that were "poor," "rough," or "a disgrace"; "abominable" dining service; and the lack of a "human quality."[116]

Whereas such public impressions called for image rehabilitation, the Pennsylvania's hopes of making up for a slow start in reaping a share of 1920s prosperity rested mainly on cost cutting. Ivy Lee went to Atterbury with a plan that would serve both purposes, while carrying forward Lee's own favored projects—creating a more human image for the railroad and "selling" that image to its employees. In his vision Lee hoped to do for the railroad "what Billy Sunday has done for religion." By speaking the language of the people, Lee promised, the Pennsylvania might lead its employees and the public to see the railroad "not as so many miles of track and so many locomotives but as so many human beings."[117] Together with Pennsylvania vice president J. L. Eysmans, Lee called for the commitment of $50,000 a year for at least three years to an institutional advertising campaign "directed primarily at raising the esprit de corps of the personnel of the Company."

Refusing to accept the inevitability of the trends so often recounted in the Lament, the railroad would embark on a crusade to "restore the Pennsylvania Spirit."[118]

Atterbury endorsed the idea of a humanizing institutional advertising campaign, infusing it with his own cost-cutting emphasis. With two hundred thousand employees in its service, the Pennsylvania could gain much from "a little additional effort" by each worker. "Now if we can increase the efficiency of these employees by even so little as 5 per cent," Atterbury explained, "you can see that we would reduce our operating expenses by twenty-five million dollars." *Printers' Ink* quoted Atterbury as describing the objects of the campaign in the following order: cutting operating expenses, improving service, increasing efficiency, and making employees "understand the ideals of the company."[119]

Having successfully promoted the J. Walter Thompson advertising agency to carry out the Pennsylvania campaign, Ivy Lee then cooperated actively with the agency in developing a multifaceted approach. To humanize the freight side of its service Lee induced the Pennsylvania, amid loud fanfare, to bestow nicknames on all its freight trains. Instead of merely a number, each train would now have "a name that the public would remember and come to have a personal, friendly feeling for." Some trains, PRR advertisements and pamphlets pointed out, would carry names that typified their speed or reflected the territory they crossed. The Yankee, for instance, was a freight with "a New England Conscience." Others, such as the Blue Goose or Uncle Remus, imparted an "amusing and whimsical" touch.[120]

The railroad carefully instructed its employees in the logic of humanized public relations. To the prototypical "old railroader," it acknowledged that numbers were more practical for designating the trains, noting that "the point of these names is not that the railroad should use them in running the trains." But shippers might take a fancy to such names and identify with them. "Numbers lack something," the *Pennsylvania News* noted. That "something" was "the human touch, a most desirable quality that everyone likes to see creep into the business world." Although the Pennsylvania downplayed the significance of the nicknames for its internal operations when it spoke directly to its employees, *Printers' Ink* noted that the railroad hoped not only to stir up public interest but also to "build up an internal esprit de corps among the men responsible for the performance of these trains." By constantly seeing what the ads were telling the public, through reproductions in employee magazines, in pamphlets, and on posters, the workers would recognize that "the public's attention is being directed toward them, that they're not merely automatons behind the scenes, and of no great importance, but rather that they are part of a great operating body which is making history for transportation." So pleased was the Pennsylvania with the free publicity it earned as the first railroad to nickname its freight trains that it went a step further in 1928, giving such nicknames as Sarah Bernhardt and MacBeth to its theatrical scenery cars and Pimlico and Saratoga Springs to its horse express cars.[121]

Meanwhile, Ivy Lee cultivated the human touch within the company as well. He constantly sought ways to promote Atterbury as a thoroughly human, knowable friend of the employee. Undoubtedly at Lee's instigation, the company magazines began this work in early 1927 with articles carrying such headlines as "President Atterbury Tells Employes Intimate Story about His Life" and "Finds Atterbury Is a Human Sort Like All Other Employes." Employees learned from such accounts that Atterbury was "just a 'Regular Fellow'" whose life was "just about the same as [that of] the average employee."

The company's annual Christmas party, begun in 1925 and connecting all regional employee parties by radio to the central celebration, enabled Atterbury to preside in fatherly benevolence. He assured employees that although it was not possible for him to be present in person at each local celebration, "I feel you are as much a part of this gathering here in Philadelphia as though I were looking into your faces." When Lee discovered a candid photograph of Atterbury cheering for his railroad's team at a baseball game against the New York Central, he immediately wired a request to the editor of the company's employee magazine to reproduce it "so well and in such size that many employees might be induced to cut it out and paste it on their walls." To Atterbury, Lee explained that this laughing, one-of-the-boys photograph would be "worth a million dollars" to the railroad. "I want to have this picture printed in poster form," Lee declared, "and have you write under it 'A Happy New Year to Every Worker on the Pennsylvania Railroad—W. W. Atterbury,' and send it just after Christmas to every employee of the system." This picture, which Lee also sent to all the rotogravure papers in the nation to promote a personalized image for the corporation, would "do more to enspirit [sic] and enliven the men on the road than all the words that could be uttered," he asserted.[122]

But the centerpiece of the Pennsylvania's new thrust in public relations was not the image of Atterbury as the company personified. Rather, it was the idealized image of its workers. In the railroad's new, well-funded magazine advertising campaign, Lee drew on a small, earlier campaign in which the Statler Hotels, in a series of ads addressed, sequentially, to each category of its employees, had reminded them of the company's regulations for their specific duties and of their obligation to act with courtesy. As a result of such ads, the Statler promised its potential customers, each Statler employee would be more "watchful" of his quality of service because "every assistant manager, every room-clerk, every waiter, bellboy or other employee of these hotels *knows that you know* just what instructions he works under" (Fig. 3.11).[123]

Like the Statler—only on a grand scale and with less heavy-handed emphasis on corporation rules—the Pennsylvania used its ads to place models of courteous and efficient performance before its own employees. As Ivy Lee explained the strategy, "Often it is effective to make a statement to the public, when the corporation is aiming not so much at the public, but at getting an idea over to its own employees." The idea, he noted later, was "to make them feel conscious of their positions in the railroad, make them proud of it and make them feel through the ads . . . that they wanted to get behind the service."[124]

The major magazine campaign, internally labeled "Stories of the Day's Work," got under way late in 1926 with advertisements in *Time,* the *Literary Digest, Saturday Evening Post,* and intermittently in several other national magazines. In turn the redcap, the yard master, the gateman, the baggage master, the engineer, the "track walker," and even "the man with the pick" appeared before the public in idealized portraits. The track foreman became a "Guardian of the Rails"; the fireman, described lyrically as ensuring safe, swift passage with "the rhythmic swings of his shovel," was said to view his labors not as "just a job" but as "a fine expression of

man's triumph in tirelessly meeting, with the muscles of his body and the steadfastness of his mind, the ever-growing needs of civilization." Several ads in the series fused idealized portraits with humanizing anecdotes about special service. In "Gimme a Ticket to Texas," a ticket taker gently persuaded a boy not to run away from home (Fig. 3.12). Another ad sketched the profile of the archetypal redcap through a customer's letter to the president of the Pennsylvania. This grateful woman, who had arrived late for her train, described the porter's extra effort to get her baggage on board. Her letter concluded: "So you see I'm not sure who is responsible but somebody on the Pennsylvania road has insisted on service until even the red caps are marvels of intelligence and the ushers are the finest kind of gentlemen" (Fig. 3.13).[125]

"Gimme a
Ticket
to
TEXAS"

HE was perhaps eleven, and he made
his request with elaborate carelessness. "Gimme a ticket to Texas."

"Where to in Texas?" the ticket seller
asked smiling.

"Oh, anywhere in Texas."

"Half fare to Texas," he was informed
with mock gravity, "will cost you $35."

The young man produced a roll of
bills.

Later, under the kindly but firm ques-
tioning of station authorities, he confessed that he had taken French leave
from home after scraping together enough
cash to get to Texas. He was, he said, going
to fight Indians.

He, with the money, was returned to his
send money and a ticket to her runaway son.
Hundreds of such cases come to the ticket

*The ticket agent had been a boy
himself. He understood—too well,
from the standpoint of this young
adventurer!*

ticket sales and Pullman reservations made
at any railroad station in the world—ready
at all times to call into play knowledge of
transportation facilities to the four corners
of the globe and to make suggestions that
save the traveling publ¹   ¹s of doll——

FIGURE 3.12

As the corporation's most visible
public face, employees who dealt
with customers could endow the
company with a caring, common

touch. Ads like this one promoted
that "human and helpful" image
while instilling employees with
the responsibility to uphold it.

In seeking to glorify the work of the most menial railroad employees, the advertising copywriters gave eloquent voice to mute gestures and even appropriated
the heroic images of socialist realism. In "Not a Signal—*A Salute!*" the narrator
recalled seeing a member of a section gang, "a big fellow with a pick," look up as
a train passed "with something like admiration lighting up his face." Noting that
the worker's right hand was raised, the narrator confided to readers, "I don't think
it was any sort of signal. No, he was a railroad man instinctively saluting the spirit
of *his* railroad. He seemed as proud of that Pennsylvania train as if he owned it"
(Fig. 3.14). In a number of the "Stories of the Day's Work," the Pennsylvania also
managed to incorporate messages about the immense size of its operations, its
stock-purchase plans for employees, and the widespread ownership of its stock
among "business men, widows, laborers, orphans, . . . [the] well-to-do and comparatively poor." These everyday people, "not some mythically cold corporation,"
owned and supported the Pennsylvania Railroad. The simultaneous emphasis on
the vastness of the corporation ("6,700 trains per day"; "over one million, seven
hundred thousand employees") and on human interest details about the activi-

A RED CAP who called forth a letter to the President of his Railroad . . .

Miami, Florida, Dec. 8, 1925

W. W. Atterbury, *President*,
The Pennsylvania Railroad,
Philadelphia, Pennsylvania

MY DEAR SIR: I am taking the very great liberty of writing you because I have just experienced one of the finest acts of service which I have ever heard of happening to anyone on any railroad. And I thought perhaps you might like to hear about it, as a change from the great American pastime of complaining about railroads.

On Monday, the 30th of November, I was to leave New York on the 12:30 noon Florida Special for Miami. I had four heavy and awkward pieces of hand luggage, and a lunch engagement. So I checked the luggage in the Pennsylvania Station check place, and went off to lunch. At lunch, as women will, and my kind especially, I quite forgot to notice the time until some one told me it was 12:10. This was at 34th Street and Park Avenue. I made a flying dive for a taxi and prayed for no traffic jams. We got to one at Herald Square but at that it was 12:28 when we dashed down the ramp into Pennsy Station, I flourishing my deck of checks. I burst out of the taxi, threw the checks at a red cap—any red cap—and gasped "The Florida Special."

"Mah Gawd, lady", said the porter, "you gotta run."

I RAN. The red cap ran. Officials in buttons, beholding us, urged us to run faster. I flashed my ticket at the gate, galloped down stairs, and below me the catacombs of the Pennsy were re-echoing "Allll abo-ard."

Well, I found my coach. "Get on, lady", said the porter of it (K 95), and I wailed, "But my bags—my bags."

"If you're going you'd better get on", he said, and with no red cap anywhere in sight, I got on. And the train began to glide with that awful finality of New York trains, out of the station. I might have jumped off, except that the K 95 porter put a long muscular arm across the doorway. And there I was, everything I owned . . .

Ten years' service to the Pennsylvania Railroad is the average record of the 360 Red Caps employed in the Pennsylvania Terminal in New York. Many have been on the job continuously for twenty-five, thirty-five, even forty years. A very real esprit de corps has grown up in those years of service together as a body of trained, disciplined men, and a real pride in their railroad and the beautiful building in which they work.

FIGURE 3.13

The Pennsylvania sought to inspire other employees to similar service by recounting this redcap's strenuous efforts to reunite a woman with her luggage. But the actual exemplar of such company esprit de corps remained anonymous (and unrewarded).

ties of individual workers engendered an atmosphere of solicitous paternalism that the railroad captured specifically in its Lambert Hollow advertising copy (see the Introduction).[126]

The image of a humanized corporation emerged most dramatically in one of the most celebrated ads of the Pennsylvania series, "An Old Man and a Corporation." A man of about eighty, enjoying the surroundings of "a beautiful park in a far Western city," confided a touching story of corporate concern and recognition to the narrator of the ad. A retired engine operator, who "for years now" had "received a gratuity from the road," had recently been visited by a stranger who explained, "'Mr. . . . , I have been sent here to hunt you up and to ask you if there is anything the company can do for you.'" The old man protested that he had no needs but inquired what the company might have done if he had needed something. "'Well, the company sent me especially to talk with you,'" replied the railroad's representative, "'and if there is anything lacking in your welfare that gives the company an opportunity to help you in a reasonable way, I am sure it would be done with pleasure. You had a good record and you have not been forgotten.'"

NOT A SIGNAL–*A SALUTE!*

The Pennsylvania takes another step forward
—it fosters pride of ownership in its employees

The Pennsylvania's New Army of Employee-Owners

Through its Board of Directors, the Pennsylvania Railroad this year set aside $17,500,000 of common stock and offered this to its employees at *par*. The issue was over-subscribed.

Over 100,000 employees took advantage of the opportunity. This will represent the highest percentage of employee-ownership

"M Y rookie days in the army were brought back to me recently as I looked out from the observation platform of the Broadway Limited," said a recent traveler on that train.

"At first we hated to salute. Then an old army sergeant put snap into us. He told us we weren't saluting just our officers. We were saluting the government—something long ourselves

lighting up his face ... His right hand was raised. I don't think it was any sort of signal. No, he was a railroad man instinctively saluting the spirit of *his* railroad. He seemed as proud of that Pennsylvania train as if he owned it."

Today, that man with the pick is only one of the scores of thousands of Pennsylvania Railroad employees wh w se ship

FIGURE 3.14

Claiming that even unskilled workers had eagerly embraced its new stock-sharing plan, the Pennsylvania betrayed its penchant for viewing its workers as soldiers, who expressed their loyalty with a salute.

After reflecting a while the old man mused, "'And they say corporations have no souls.'"[127]

Whatever feelings of goodwill or incredulity such exercises in self-congratulation may have stirred among the public, the Pennsylvania focused primarily on promulgating the ads among the company's employees. Beginning early in 1927 the *Pennsylvania News* carried large reproductions of virtually every ad in the institutional series. Internally, it distributed handsome booklets such as *The Limiteds of the Freight Service* and *Stories of the Day's Work*. As the campaign debuted in the national magazines, the *Pennsylvania News* warned workers that they would now be "subjected to more critical examination by the average citizen"; it urged them to "set out to make yourself worth more" as employees and to avoid any "let-down" in friendly attitudes toward the public.[128]

Anyone who had read J. Walter Thompson's 1926 survey or was privy to the continuing reports of serious problems with the Pennsylvania's facilities and service might have wondered how the company and its agency could be so hypocritical as to extol services they knew to be deficient. What could bring the corporation to glorify employees whom its own executives considered to be working "at a fraction of their capacity"? One commentator in *Printers' Ink*, noting the actual performance of some railroad employees and the current news that porters were discussing a strike, dismissed the campaign as "hooey" and questioned whether the railroad actually believed that "the traveling public will digest any such piffle."[129]

But the Pennsylvania and its agency possessed a buffer against such cynicism. The theory of enhancing both image and performance through a psychological tug on the company's own bootstraps rationalized a disregard for current realities. When the employees viewed these portraits "over the shoulder of the public," they "would have constantly forced upon them what they were expected to do" and thus would grow to resemble their images. Moreover, by praising its workers (no matter how unjustifiably or insincerely) rather than itself, the railroad would presumably avoid the offensive narcissism of earlier institutional campaigns while reaping the benefits of its own benevolence. "It does not place its laurel wreaths upon the forehead of an inanimate corporation," observed the trade journal *Tide* in lauding the campaign, "but lays them upon humble brows that are moistened with honest perspiration."[130]

In 1928 Ivy Lee and the Thompson agency added yet another dimension to the Pennsylvania campaign. To convey to the public the image of a knowable, human company, they frankly copied a technique from Gordon Selfridge, the proprietor of an immensely successful London department store. Lee admired the public relations and merchandising results that Selfridge had obtained through "regular intimate chats with the public" in columns in the London papers. Twice each week, in newspapers in New York City and Philadelphia, the Pennsylvania Railroad bought space in which to run its own column of human interest news. Signed "PRR," these anecdotes related such incidents as that of a Pennsylvania train accommodating a tearful mother by making a special stop for a baby's bottle or that of a brakeman wiring trackworkers to find the pocketbook that a "quiet grey-haired little woman" had let slip out the window. This series "made of the public a confidant" and responded to Ivy Lee's call for the company to "look for those little things . . . which will be read as news and which will dramatize the spirit of the institution." Frequent attention to special acts of helpfulness by exemplary railroad employees reinforced the behavioral modification strategy of the "Day's Work" campaign.[131]

Corporate Publicity and Managerial Morale

Was the Pennsylvania's multifaceted, employee-targeted campaign a success? Did the railroad's employees imitate those images that they were given so many opportunities to view "over the shoulder of the public"? The available answers are grossly incomplete and come from suspect sources. Atterbury and the other Pennsylvania executives declared themselves fully satisfied. The *Mutual Magazine* confidently asserted that "the public has unmistakably endorsed" the Pennsylvania's policy of "proclaiming to the world pride in the faithfulness and achievements of its men and the dignity and responsibility of their jobs." An article in the J. Walter Thompson house organ later claimed that Atterbury had stated that "no money ever spent by the company had paid better as an investment."[132] Ivy Lee reported in 1930 that one superintendent of an operating division on the Pennsylvania, a confirmed skeptic of advertising, had pronounced the campaign one of the few "from which you could see money results." Finally, in 1930 the Baltimore & Ohio Railroad paid the Pennsylvania the ultimate compliment of launching its own humanizing campaign of indirection, likewise seeking to stimulate its workers' efforts through human interest stories about exceptional employee service.[133]

Neither the railroad nor the advertising agency considered a follow-up survey on the attitudes of Pennsylvania employees. Whatever such a survey might have revealed in short-term responses during the campaign, it seems clear that any measure of long-term results would have confirmed the observations of many emerging public relations professionals—that words without reinforcing action would accomplish little among the railroad's blue-collar workers. By 1933 the Pennsylvania Railroad had fired sixty-seven thousand workers and reduced others to occasional work. The year before, it had cut the pensions of its most loyal and favored former workers by 10 percent, and Atterbury was thanking those who had "cheerfully consented to take a share of our present burden." No Pennsylvania executive would then have wanted to be reminded of the sentimental promises of "An Old Man and a Corporation." During the depression the Pennsylvania had become, in Peter Lyon's words, "easily the most hated railroad and General Atterbury the most hated railroad executive."[134]

Despite these clues to the apparent futility of the inward thrust of the Pennsylvania's corporate imagery, the celebrated 1927–28 campaign may actually have achieved its greatest impact through an indirect effect even more complex than Ivy Lee had envisaged—the boosting of managerial morale. The ads had depicted rank-and-file employees; it was their performance that corporate leaders had hoped to elevate. Acting under the spell of the Lament, with its vision of an army or family of loyal, dedicated, zealous employees, the architects of this morale campaign scarcely mentioned that smaller segment of employees who were likely to pay the most attention to the corporation's public standing and gain the most inspiration from its external messages—its cadre of middle and top managers. For more than two years Pennsylvania Railroad executives basked in the plaudits of the wider business community for having devised pioneering strategies to boost employee performance.[135] Like other corporate leaders, they seemed able, at least momentarily, to convince themselves that they had re-created the old bonds with employees.[136]

Thus, somewhat ironically, such campaigns for improved morale only ratcheted up the executives' identification with the corporation and pride in its activities. When Vice President Hall of AT&T sought to persuade other corporate managers of the workers' desire for a sense of belonging, status, pride, and "joy of work," he turned intuitively to an appeal to these managers' own feelings and aspirations: "Where do you people in this room get your real fun? You get it on the job . . .

working at the problems of your industry." As if in direct response, one executive of an AT&T regional subsidiary remarked of the parent company's institutional advertising, "It does me good to see its flag waving high."[137] The executives of Bethlehem, Armour, and Swift took similar satisfaction in showing the company's flag through their advocacy campaigns.

The famed Pennsylvania Railroad Christmas parties, at which General Atterbury effusively applied the rhetoric of family to all the company's interrelationships, were attended primarily by managerial staff and white-collar employees. At such gatherings a corporation could most emphatically demonstrate, in the words of one Pennsylvania Railroad executive, that it was "something more than a mere machine without heart or soul."[138] The General Electric Company, through the inculcation of corporate culture and the male-bonding shenanigans of its annual "Association Island" camps, could credibly claim similar success in boosting executive morale. Although *Printers' Ink* had observed in 1913 that nobody was as likely to read a company's advertising "so carefully as its own rank and file," this trade journal was simply among the first to wistfully overestimate the corporation's capacity to energize its lowliest employees through corporate imagery. It was among the cadre of corporate managers, not its section gangs, that one might discover the psychological impact of "the expression in public print, of the aims and purposes of the institution."[139]

4

A "CORPORATION CONSCIOUSNESS": GENERAL MOTORS, GENERAL ELECTRIC, AND THE BRUCE BARTON FORMULA

During 1923 and 1924, ads in the *Literary Digest, American Magazine,* and *Saturday Evening Post* persistently prompted readers to get to know a "Famous Family," assuring them that this family—like any close, united family—was "more than the sum of its members." Moreover, this famous family was linked intimately with other families throughout the nation because it "*completes* the home, broadening its circle of friendships and opening its doors to a larger world." Citizens of each local community were urged to recognize how they shared "directly or indirectly" in this famous family's income. They also learned how this family's activities had improved the everyday lives of pastors, farmers, country doctors, and housewives, and how the family had succeeded in the humane task of "making the nation a neighborhood." This "famous family," which invested over $600,000 in "making friends for the family" through such messages, was the General Motors Corporation.[1]

Was it plausible for a gigantic holding company—comprising five passenger car divisions, more than a dozen parts and accessories subsidiaries, a workforce of nearly ninety-eight thousand, and assets of $593 million—to presume to introduce itself to the public through notions of family, neighborhood, and ministry?[2] General Motors thought so, and the company never flinched in its strategy of building a corporate image through kinship and community metaphors. Neither did its primary counselor, Bruce Barton, the popular writer and advertising executive whose vision shaped the style and tone of the campaign. Rarely recognized by historians except as the author of the fatuous *The Man Nobody Knows,* a mid-1920s bestselling interpretation of Jesus as organizer and businessman, Barton was legitimately hailed within business circles as the "boy wonder" of American advertising in the early 1920s.[3]

At the end of 1922 Barton won not only this challenging General Motors project but also another "glittering account," that of the General Electric Company. Virtually simultaneously, two of the emerging corporate giants of the new era of business dominance and welfare capitalism had committed themselves to a visionary young agency for major, innovative advertising campaigns.[4] The stories of the

Barton–General Motors and Barton–General Electric collaborations reveal the concerns and aspirations that led a number of the giant corporations to undertake sophisticated programs for creating a corporate image.

Two Needs: A Corporate Soul and Corporate Cohesion

At General Motors the quest for a corporate image arose in the wake of the company's financial crisis in 1920, when the Du Pont interests stepped in to protect their sizable investment and restructure the company's management. By that time the Progressive Era's muckraking attacks on big business had subsided. Business leaders were now more inclined to fret about labor radicalism and about a diffuse problem that affected their internal functioning as well as their external repute and political security: the widespread perception of the giant corporation as impersonal, aloof, and devoid of any "human touch."

Whereas attacks on the soulless corporation had once alluded mainly to immoral behavior, often manifest in the actions of a prominent mogul, the focus of the term now shifted to the remoteness that came with operations of immense scale. Giant corporations still had to worry that their very size would draw antimonopoly attacks, a consideration that dominated the policies of companies like United States Steel.[5] But in the 1920s many of these companies worried even more about the external and internal problems that their indistinct, bureaucratic images might provoke: insufficient marketing clout and poor coordination and morale.

Early in 1922, very soon after assuming the presidency of General Motors, Alfred P. Sloan Jr. commissioned a study of the corporation's public image. The findings, he reported bluntly, revealed it had none. "People throughout the United States, except at the corner of Wall and Broad Streets, didn't know anything about General Motors," he later recalled. In 1924 he was still complaining to Charles Kettering, head of the GM research laboratories, that even potential investors did not know that Chevrolet was part of the General Motors Corporation. GM vice president Alfred Swayne, who directed the 1922 survey, noted that if General Motors was known at all, it was only as "the name of a security." People recognized such GM brand names as Cadillac, Buick, and Chevrolet, but hardly anyone associated these with the parent company.[6]

If General Motors lacked a public presence in 1922, it suffered an even greater defect in the eyes of its executives: it lacked adequate integration and coordination. Since its origins in 1908, GM had existed primarily as a holding company composed of independent manufacturers. GM's dynamic early leader, the irrepressible high-stakes speculator Billy Durant, had displayed little interest in systematic management. As Alfred D. Chandler Jr. and Stephen Salsbury observe, Durant believed that he could manage his conglomeration of diverse operating divisions as if they constituted a "relatively small company." Despite three "penetrating reports" in 1919 by Sloan, who was then his top assistant, Durant ignored the need for internal reform and rationalization. Sloan, in retrospect, characterized the GM operations under Durant as "management by crony, with the divisions operating on a horse-trading basis." *Printers' Ink* observed in 1923 that the actions of the "practically independent managements" of the pre-1922 General Motors divisions had revealed that they were "not particularly concerned with the interests of the corporation as a whole." Some of its car divisions competed intensely against each other. Thus General Motors, at the outset of the 1920s, was really something less than the sum of its individual parts.[7]

To make matters worse, 1920 had marked the depth of a severe postwar economic recession. Durant had been caught short of cash, and his financial maneuvers brought General Motors to the brink of disaster. Late that year, to protect the large Du Pont investment in GM, Pierre du Pont and his allies forced a financial reorganization of the corporation and pushed Durant out. A reluctant Pierre du Pont accepted the presidency temporarily, adopting Sloan as his right-hand man. At this point, Sloan later recalled, the market for automobiles had nearly vanished and most of the GM plants had closed. The company had a surplus of high-priced inventory and a scarcity of cash. Moreover, the 1920 reorganization, despite positive steps toward better coordination and inventory control, did not bring immediate competitive gains. In 1921 General Motors' combined production of Chevrolets, Buicks, Oaklands, Oldsmobiles, and Cadillacs constituted only 13 percent of the nation's total automobile production, compared to Ford's 61 percent. Market shares favored Ford by an overwhelming margin; Ford's Model-T eclipsed GM's Chevrolet in the low-priced field.[8]

In 1922, as the economy began to recover, Pierre du Pont and Alfred Sloan accelerated their push for internal rationalization and greater centralized control. This effort did not proceed without resistance. As Ed Cray has observed, "There were men all around who knew only Durant's way of doing business, men who pulled long faces whenever Sloan talked about rational managerial controls." There was also "resentment down the line" toward the managerial cadre imported into GM from Du Pont. Although GM's sales manager, Norval Hawkins, had worked out a unified approach for advertising, sales techniques, and dealer relationships for the various divisions, his program, in spite of Pierre du Pont's support, was largely ignored. When *Printers' Ink* disclosed Hawkins's grand plan in September 1921 under the headline "General Motors to . . . Administer Publicity of All Its Companies under One Head in Centralized Drive," it felt obliged to add the cautionary note that his scheme was "not yet worked out in full." At this point Sloan began to search for structural reforms to promote greater cooperation and coordination.[9]

Sloan looked first to areas where cooperation might be fostered most easily and where the large size of General Motors offered evident efficiencies of scale. Surely centralized purchasing to meet the common needs of the various divisions could bring down costs through volume orders. When division managers remained skeptical about such coordination, Sloan proposed forming an "interdivisional committee" to carry it out, in order to improve communications (and, subtly, to circumvent divisional autonomy and stimulate a corporate consciousness). As Donaldson Brown, a major strategist in GM's drive for centralized control, observed discreetly several years later, interdivisional committees offered a means for "gaining a widely diffused knowledge and understanding of corporation policies, and a sympathetic compliance." Early in 1922 the Executive Committee approved Sloan's plan for the creation of a General Purchasing Committee.[10]

Shrewdly, Sloan structured this committee to include the purchasing agents of each of the divisions (but not the division heads) and a number of general headquarters staff, including himself. This design would ensure the efficiencies of volume purchasing, Sloan promised, yet preserve the control by the divisions over buying decisions. While that was ostensibly true, the committee bypassed the powerful division heads, linking top corporate executives directly to specialized staff members within the divisions. Chaired by a headquarters executive and supported by headquarters staff, this new interdivisional committee gave the corporation's leaders an arena for promoting cooperation. Moreover, since this approach averted the need for blatant challenges to divisional autonomy, it provided Sloan—whose managerial style was to avoid having to "dictate a course of action"—with effective means to rationalize internal operations.[11]

With his strategy for gaining control over internal operations cautiously under way, Sloan took the step that would bring Bruce Barton into a significant role as corporate counselor. To address the public invisibility of General Motors that the recent image survey had revealed, Sloan laid the groundwork for a second interdivisional committee—one on institutional advertising. Since all General Motors funds ultimately derived from moneys "taxed" away from the individual producing divisions, Sloan and other corporate executives recognized that the divisions would resist a diversion of funds for corporate publicity (nearly all did, to some extent, oppose his plan). In a carefully worded memo, he circumspectly requested the advice of the division managers as to whether or not the company should do anything to enhance its visibility. When they did not advocate a policy of inaction, he interpreted this as their assent to an institutional advertising campaign, doing his best to present it as something of a "free" supplement for the divisions and promising that the campaign would be "properly coordinated with what I term the product advertising of the Divisions."[12]

The division managers reluctantly acquiesced. The Finance Committee voted to contract with Barton's agency for a corporate image campaign and created a new interdivisional committee to advise on the campaign. Pierre du Pont, as president, warmly endorsed this initiative. He remarked to Sloan that even if the measurable value of the advertising carried out by Barton's agency—Barton, Durstine, and Osborn (BDO)—was negligible, "the other benefits accruing to the corporation by the development of a General Motors atmosphere and the working together spirit of all members of the Committee" would fully justify its costs.[13] While public familiarity with the "famous family" would undoubtedly bring some benefits in stock values, general prestige, and even the merchandising of individual automobiles, Sloan and du Pont primarily hoped that the enhanced internal legitimacy of the corporation's central headquarters would result in greater cohesion and coordination. In tributes to the GM family in the ensuing ads, Barton never lost sight of his key audience—the managers within the GM divisions.

As with the General Purchasing Committee, Sloan stacked the Institutional Advertising Committee with headquarters staff. The divisions were represented largely by their sales managers. Privately BDO leaders speculated that their agency had been selected because "we recognized the problem of getting the units to be enthusiastic about the parent company's campaign."[14] They also recognized that Barton had "won" this account and that, whatever other members of the agency contributed to the subsequent campaign, General Motors viewed him as its mastermind. A 1928 BDO status report on the GM account indicated that Barton continued to attend all the meetings with the General Motors Institutional Advertising Committee. And Sloan, when he recounted the campaign years later, spoke of having conferred "full responsibility" on Barton (rather than on BDO).[15]

It seems probable, although I have not been able to discover any large body of his correspondence with GM, that Barton personally carried on most of his agency's ongoing counsel with General Motors executives. Internal GM documents mention only Barton when they describe the BDO agency's strenuous efforts to merchandise the institutional campaign within the GM organization. And a BDO account summary notes that Barton met with Sloan every other week and frequently went to Detroit "to keep in touch with the division people." Moreover, the archives of the General Electric Company reveal that Barton played just such a role—as original cultivator and persistent counselor—in BDO's very similar corporate image campaign for GE during these same years.[16] More than any other figure in this era, Barton empathized with the aspirations of corporate executives for an ennobling sense of their businesses as agencies of great public service. He recognized their impatience to infuse an esprit de corps within their increasingly distended and bureaucratic organizations. The style of the GM institutional program was vintage Bruce Barton. It reflected a sensitivity to the problems of coordination within complex corporate structures while cultivating public esteem and internal loyalty through a homespun yet expansive language of service.

Bruce Barton: Forger of Institutional Souls

In Barton, General Motors executives and other corporate leaders discovered one of the "great communicators" of the 1920s. As one observer noted, Barton "had few equals as a persuasive spinner of words." The son of a preacher and grandson of a small-town pharmacist and doctor, Barton never allowed his Madison Avenue surroundings to cloud his image of himself as a country boy and ordinary American who could instinctively reflect the tastes of the typical consumer. Moreover, as John Caples, the early genius of mail-order advertising, commented, Barton exuded the "three qualities most important in a writer: 1) Sincerity; 2) Sincerity; 3) Sincerity." Even James Rorty, a caustic critic of advertising in general and Barton in particular, paid sardonic tribute to Barton's efficacy: "Like a modern Sir Galahad, his strength was the strength of ten because his heart was pure. He was sincere."[17]

As the youthful editor of *Every Week* magazine from 1915 to 1918, Barton had developed a knack for evoking a sense of intimacy in distant readers. Hundreds wrote Barton personal letters in praise of his inspirational editorials. One asserted that "it seems as if I almost knew you personally." Instead of receiving a magazine, another correspondent wrote, "I feel as if a personal friend had dropped in for an informal chat." At the age of thirty-six, already known as a gifted writer of biographical vignettes, morale-boosting editorials, and human interest stories for popular magazines, Barton had perfected a genre of magazine essays that one General Electric official felicitously dubbed "business sermonettes."[18]

During World War I Barton experienced the joys of sacrificial labor while chairing the publicity committee of the United War Work Campaign, a war service confederation that linked various religious and secular organizations. He gloried in playing an active part in the nation's war-born "larger idealism" and fulfilled his editorial exhortation that a person "truly finds his life who first loses it in the service of a great ideal."[19] The Victory Loan campaigns provided the forum for one of his early rhetorical exercises in breathing life into an abstract collective entity

JOSEPH PENNELL, DEL.

I AM NEW YORK AND THIS IS MY CREED

BY BRUCE BARTON

FIGURE 4.1

As a wartime fund-raiser, Bruce Barton penned a poetic "creed" that enshrined the city in grandeur and high principle. Later he would craft tributes to giant corporations as venerable public institutions.

dedicated to a greater cause. In such ads as "I Am New York and This Is My Creed," Barton summoned New Yorkers to make larger financial contributions to the war effort. He recruited the noted illustrator Joseph Pennell to etherealize New York City as a misty yet monumental backdrop to the Statue of Liberty and then turned his own poetic talents to endowing it with a voice and a heart (Fig. 4.1). Even the disparate mass of a city, Barton presumed, might discover in itself a soaring spirit that transcended the mere sum of its mundane parts. In Barton's peroration the city cried out: "For I am New York, the dwelling place of HONOR. 'A city that hath foundations'—whose corner-stone is FAITH." [20]

After the war, now a partner in an aggressive new advertising agency, Barton participated in the campaign of the Interchurch World Movement (IWM) to raise enough money to "win the world for Christ." [21] In ads with an unmistakable Barton ring, the IWM combined the image of a huge cross towering over the Manhattan skyline with a text that proclaimed, "We're hungry and thirsty for Faith."

Both churches and "hard-headed business men" agreed, the text added, that economic problems ultimately called for a spiritual solution. But "spiritual problems," as Barton had already assured the IWM, also had business solutions. The extent to which "the cult of business [had] penetrated American Protestantism," Eldon Ernst observes, could be seen in the bureaucratic organization adopted by the IWM as well as in its ads, from which "church-going readers learned that they were 'stockholders in the greatest business in the world.'" Although the IWM's fund-raising efforts failed disastrously, Barton had displayed his talents for fusing the methods, aspirations, and languages of religion and business.[22]

For both internal and external purposes the expanding, often-disjointed corporate giants of the early 1920s needed just what a gifted wordsmith like Barton, who was also a sincere and fervent "believer," could help them attain: a larger vision of themselves to which internal struggles could be subordinated. Here was a very practical use for what might be romanticized as the soul of the corporation. And nobody brought more enthusiasm to the task of infusing businesses with souls than did Bruce Barton. In an expression he attributed to an unidentified banker (but which he may well have drafted himself), Barton supplied General Motors with an affirmation that President Pierre du Pont fondly passed along to the GM stockholders when he announced the corporation's new venture in institutional advertising: "I like to think of advertising as something big, something splendid, something which goes deep down into an institution and gets hold of the soul of it. . . . Institutions have souls, just as men and nations have souls."[23]

The Begetting of a Corporate Family

Barton astutely shaped GM's early corporate image advertising with an eye as much to its internal effects as to its external impact. And with Barton's eager cooperation, Sloan merchandised the new advertising program to his own divisions with solicitous care. Nothing that General Motors had undertaken, Sloan assured his divisional chiefs, had been given more "mature deliberation" and "thorough consideration" than this image advertising. Seeking to protect himself and the program from inevitable complaints, he warned that "there is no single function of the average business in which there is liable to be a greater difference of opinion than in the subject of what constitutes proper advertising." The corporation could not adopt everyone's advice, Sloan continued, but it earnestly solicited suggestions and criticisms. Sloan's cautious wording typified his overall managerial style, which was nicely complemented by the subtle tactic of bolstering a drive for internal rationalization with a corporate image campaign.[24]

Meanwhile Barton sought to involve the GM car divisions in the campaign by asking their sales managers and other executives to contribute ideas. Henry Weaver, the secretary of the new Institutional Advertising Committee, distributed thousands of brochures to stockholders, board members, divisional managers, and local dealers "as a means of bringing about the internal unification which was an essential part of the program." His committee sent the individual divisions articles on the institutional ads (for use "in your house organ or elsewhere") stressing "the principles of cooperation" that governed GM activities and its "conviction that each of its companies is better able to serve by reason of its association with the others." It also supplied division chiefs with multiple enlarged copies of each ad for posting on bulletin boards. Even GM's research laboratory chief, Charles Kettering, who had initially expressed great skepticism about the campaign, soon reported that "we are making very good use of this material" and requested additional copies for distribution to employees.[25]

It was not long before Sloan, who had succeeded du Pont as president in the spring of 1923, was waxing eloquent over the psychological effects of the Institutional Advertising Committee and the General Purchasing Committee. "It is wonderful to see how the boys have got together and given up their own individuality for the sake of a constructive result," he enthused. When the invaluable Kettering threatened to resign in mid-1923 — because the opposition of division managers and engineers had thwarted his plan to mass-produce his cherished copper-cooled engine — Sloan dissuaded him by promising to create yet another interdivisional committee. The new Technical Committee would facilitate better communication and centralized control over engineering issues. "Forcing the issue" would accomplish little, Sloan protested to Kettering, but there was "nothing that can not be accomplished along cooperative lines in the General Motors Corporation today." The experience of the interdivisional committees on purchasing and institutional advertising had demonstrated that "every time we take up something the boys begin to see the light."[26]

When the Technical Committee proved successful, Sloan carried the idea of the interdivisional committee as a centralizing agency into such other fields as sales, works management, and maintenance. Even so, he remained sensitive to the divisions' power of resistance. If the ultimate goal of General Motors' management was "decentralized authority with central control," its primary effort in the early 1920s, Arthur Kuhn effectively argues, was centralization. As Richard Tedlow points out, "the actual adjudication of the relationship among the divisions and between the divisions and the market was extraordinarily difficult and became the very stuff of management." Sloan was "100% for co-operation and co-ordination," he commented in 1924, but knew "no other way of doing it than by these Inter-division Relations Committees."[27] With his conviction that corporate leaders could "not order a co-operating spirit to be developed in the organization," Sloan was predisposed to appreciate whatever an institutional advertising campaign could do to promote "a corporation point of view."[28]

Barton had astutely sized up the internal politics of General Motors. He perceived that the ostensible by-product of the institutional advertising campaign — a reorientation of divisional leaders to the big corporate picture — was actually its primary function. When BDO summarized its work in a successful quest for an advertising award, it listed the early campaign's first objective as fostering "a unification of spirit and interest among GM's manufacturing and distributing units."[29]

In his inimitable way Barton found just the analogy to flatter himself and his client with the greatness of the work they were about. General Motors, he observed, had very recently been in a condition similar to that of the American states immediately after the ratification of the federal Constitution: "citizenship in the state" still meant more than "citizenship in the new nation." At that point George Washington carried out the great institutional advertising campaign of his era. By traveling and "showing himself to the people," he personally convinced the states of their gains as members of a mighty union. General Motors was now following Washington's example with the same august prescience. Barton's own enthusiasm for seeking fulfillment in grandiose causes and inspiring unity by discovering the soul of an eminent institution thus found a perfect outlet in the General Motors project.[30]

Attentive as they were to merchandising the campaign to GM's divisional officers, Barton and his agency also took pride in the public image they were creating for this Wall Street agglomeration. To humanize a complex and remote entity Barton seized on the metaphor of family and put it to double service. General Motors became a large family of people and divisions that in turn produced a family of vehicles. The strategy that Pierre du Pont had initiated to rationalize the GM product line—to "bracket" the market by eliminating various makes and repositioning others so that one GM car, and only one, would be offered within each price range—provided the nominal basis for Barton's family metaphor. But instead of lining up all the members for a conventional "family portrait," Barton thought they should be introduced to the public one at a time. That way the family would become known and respected, "with no waste motion," as less-known relatives were associated with its "already famous members." For any too laggard to grasp the idea, Barton and his colleagues provided an example. If you wanted to lead the public toward the most favorable impression of the Lee family, you would begin by announcing, "This is Robert E. Lee, one of the family of Lees." Thus, the choice for the first advertisement in the series was obvious: "What Cadillac brought to General Motors."[31]

Getting Cadillac to agree with this approach was no easy task. Barton later recounted that the head of the Cadillac division had greeted the plan for institutional advertising with the sneer, "Cadillac is a famous name in American life; General Motors means nothing." An agency colleague who wrote Barton's eulogy in 1967 made a point of celebrating that moment when Barton had "talk[ed] Cadillac into admitting that it was related to Chevrolet, so that the first advertising for General Motors could appear." In *Conspicuous Production* Donald Davis has convincingly shown how the links between their personal social prestige and the quality and price of their cars led many early automobile manufacturers to eschew any association with low-priced models. GM "escaped the class-consciousness" of many Detroit manufacturers and managed to make "the organization, rather than the product, its hallmark" largely because of its wider split between ownership and control, its domination by eastern (not Detroit) capital, and the geographical dispersion of its manufacturing units. But the persuasive influence of Barton's vision and strategy quite likely played a crucial role in inspiring GM's deliberate quest for the "corporation point of view."[32]

Having appropriated Cadillac's prestige for GM's advertising debut, Barton and BDO then introduced the GM family through each of its other best-known members. Oldsmobile took credit for bringing "the courage of the pioneer" to the corporation in the form of "Old Scout," a car that had made an early coast-to-coast run. For the struggling Chevrolet division Barton borrowed stature by returning to his fond analogy between the task of GM and the situation that had faced the new American nation. As founding father, George Washington had wisely foreseen that "distance was the enemy which menaced the new republic most." In that revered tradition Chevrolet helped vanquish distance as the enemy of community.

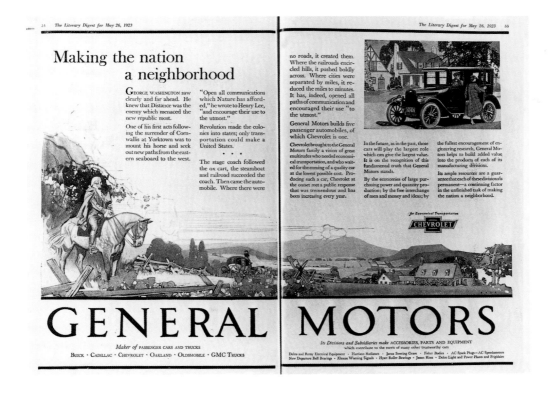

Making the nation a neighborhood

GEORGE WASHINGTON saw clearly and far ahead. He knew that Distance was the enemy which menaced the new republic most.

One of his first acts following the surrender of Cornwallis at Yorktown was to mount his horse and seek out new paths from the eastern seaboard to the west.

"Open all communications which Nature has afforded," he wrote to Henry Lee, "and encourage their use to the utmost."

Revolution made the colonies into states; only transportation could make a United States.

• • •

The stage coach followed the ox cart, the steamboat and railroad succeeded the coach. Then came the automobile. Where there were no roads, it created them. Where the railroads encircled hills, it pushed boldly across. Where cities were separated by miles, it reduced the miles to minutes. It has, indeed, opened all paths of communication and encouraged their use "to the utmost."

General Motors builds five passenger automobiles, of which Chevrolet is one.

Chevrolet brought to the General Motors family a vision of great multitudes who needed economical transportation, and who waited for the coming of a quality car at the lowest possible cost. Producing such a car, Chevrolet at the outset met a public response that was tremendous and has been increasing every year.

In the future, as in the past, those cars will play the largest role which can give the largest value. It is on the recognition of this fundamental truth that General Motors stands.

By the economies of large purchasing power and quantity production; by the free interchange of men and money and ideas; by the fullest encouragement of engineering research, General Motors helps to build added value into the products of each of its manufacturing divisions.

Its ample resources are a guarantee that each of these divisions is permanent—a continuing factor in the unfinished task of making the nation a neighborhood.

GENERAL MOTORS

Maker of PASSENGER CARS AND TRUCKS

BUICK · CADILLAC · CHEVROLET · OAKLAND · OLDSMOBILE · GMC TRUCKS

Its Divisions and Subsidiaries make ACCESSORIES, PARTS AND EQUIPMENT which contribute to the merit of many other trustworthy cars

Delco and Remy Electrical Equipment · Harrison Radiators · Jaxon Steering Gears · Fisher Bodies · AC Spark Plugs—AC Speedometers
New Departure Ball Bearings · Klaxon Warning Signals · Hyatt Roller Bearings · Jaxon Rims · Delco Light and Power Plants and Frigidaire

for Economical Transportation
CHEVROLET

FIGURE 4.2

Barton enlisted no less imposing a figure than George Washington on behalf of the "making the nation a neighborhood" trope, one favored by giant corporations to both idealize and familiarize their public service.

It "brought to the General Motors family a vision of great multitudes who needed economical transportation"—thus committing GM to the "unfinished task of making the nation a neighborhood" (Fig. 4.2). Successive ads introduced every other car and truck division in turn.[33]

General Motors should not only advertise itself as the sire of a "family of products," Barton insisted, but it should also realize that its own various components constituted a corporate family. As his agency's subsequent summary of the campaign emphasized, "one objective . . . is to personalize the institution by calling it a *family*." Alfred Swayne, the chairman of the Institutional Advertising Committee, elaborated on the idea. "The word 'corporation' is cold, impersonal and subject to misunderstanding and distrust," he observed. "'Family' is personal, human, friendly. This is our picture of General Motors—a big congenial household." By the end of 1923, this happy household embraced 66,000 stockholders, over 100,000 employees, and 12,500 dealers. In light of the continuing hostility and distrust by some of the operating staff, especially the "Durant men," toward the corporate executives, as well as President Sloan's disinclination to call even the other

FACTS ABOUT A FAMOUS FAMILY

Mothers, sisters, wives

A CORPORATION is often regarded as impersonal—great plants, great resources, which are owned by only a few.

More than 68,000 investors own General Motors and divide its earnings. They live in every state in the Union, in Canada and in 16 foreign lands.

Of these General Motors stockholders, 58,000 own 100 shares or less.

More than 18,000 stockholders are women —mothers, sisters, wives.

GENERAL MOTORS

BUICK · CADILLAC · CHEVROLET · OLDSMOBILE
OAKLAND · GMC TRUCKS

FACTS ABOUT A FAMOUS FAMILY

The family's home

NATURALLY when you purchase a motor car you ask, "How permanent is the company which manufactures it?"

Buick, Cadillac, Chevrolet, Oldsmobile, Oakland, and GMC Trucks are built by companies strong in themselves, with long records of continuous service. But back of them are the resources of the General Motors family to which they belong. Of these resources the General Motors Building in Detroit is a symbol—the largest building of its kind in the world.

GENERAL MOTORS

BUICK · CADILLAC · CHEVROLET · OLDSMOBILE
OAKLAND · GMC TRUCKS

FIGURES 4.3 & 4.4

General Motors advanced the family metaphor partly to counter notions of its impersonality and its control by rich (male) investors. The rational strategy of emphasizing its size and resources, however, led to such incongruous images as that of the giant headquarters office as a family home.

top executives by their first names (he was always Mr. Sloan to them), the notion of Sloan as the fond paterfamilias in a warm, congenial household must have seemed dubious.[34]

But the wish was father to the belief at corporate headquarters. If General Motors needed the aura of family to overcome its impersonality and absence of internal cohesion, then a family it would proclaim itself. A 1927 institutional ad explicitly defined the company as "a family of PRODUCTS and PEOPLE." When Sloan came to summarize the company's achievements during its enormously successful year of 1926, he spoke recurrently of the unity of employees, stockholders, and managers in the "General Motors Family" and used this imagery to refute those who were "apt to think of big business as a piece of automatic machinery—soulless." To further humanize its image, the BDO agency concluded, GM's signature on all ads would omit the impersonal "Corporation" and simply use the company's "popular name," General Motors.[35]

The informality of the ads in the "Facts about a Famous Family" series aimed to build a "feeling of friendliness" for GM and to bring about "the personification of General Motors as a family—something personal, warm and human." The ads thereby sought to assuage fears about the power of the giant corporation; furthermore, they invited readers to see themselves as members and beneficiaries of the family rather than as outsiders (Figs. 4.3 and 4.4).[36] As the series evolved, even assertions about the immense size and productive power of the General Motors family were couched in this friendly mode. Ads featuring the GM Proving Grounds, for instance, explained such testing as a cooperative undertaking made possible only by the resources of "a very large corporation like General Motors." GM was thus a *big* family, whose very size ensured the consumer's benefit.[37]

While institutional advertising campaigns conventionally sought the goodwill of the public, this campaign—with its internal thrust—also sought explicitly to cultivate the goodwill of each division, or "family member." Each institutional ad, claimed a GM pamphlet aimed at stockholders, dealers, and division personnel, would benefit both General Motors and the individual division. Moreover, it would "add to the prestige of our other units by binding them together more closely and emphasizing the strength and efficient service made possible through such a union." All the ads carried the General Motors "signature"; BDO designed a "ribbon" that read "product of General Motors" to appear near the division emblem on all product advertising. In his letter announcing the campaign to the corporation's stockholders, Pierre du Pont had observed that "just as a family is more than the sum of its separate members," so General Motors would now be recognized as "more than the sum of its parts."[38]

In 1924, after a year of introducing General Motors through its "family members," Barton won approval for a campaign that reflected even more truly his instinct for the expansive and ingratiating gesture. The "famous family" would now win friends and goodwill by "the indirect but graceful procedure" of praising the nation's most important unsung heroes and heroines. In tributes that simultaneously aggrandized the company, General Motors described the indispensable contributions of the automobile to the work of the doctor, the teacher, the postman, the engineer, the mother, the farmer, and the minister. BDO contracted with the high-priced illustrator Leone Bracker, who was famous for his Red Cross and Woman Suffrage posters, for all the illustrations in this series. It had taken great care in this selection, BDO explained, both to provide physical continuity in this "goodwill" series and to ensure that the powerful, emotional human interest copy in the ads would not be diminished by "an atmosphere of insincerity and weak sentiment."[39]

The Problem of Size

In GM's "goodwill" ads of 1924 and 1925 Barton found an opportunity to highlight that aspect of General Motors that was simultaneously its most marketable quality and its greatest political liability: its immense size. "It is always a temptation to emphasize bigness," Barton's agency warned. "But mere size sells no cars and begets no affection." Still, as the agency's own surveys would shortly reveal,

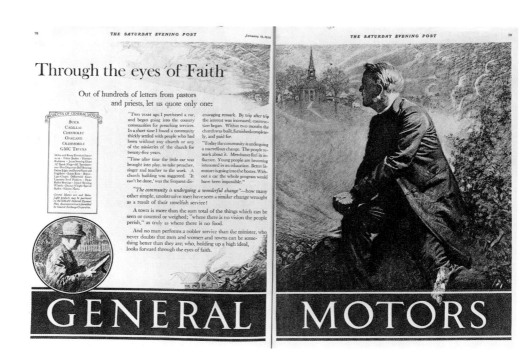

Through the eyes of Faith

Out of hundreds of letters from pastors
and priests, let us quote only one:

PRODUCTS OF GENERAL MOTORS

BUICK
CADILLAC
CHEVROLET
OAKLAND
OLDSMOBILE
GMC TRUCKS

Delco and Remy Electrical Equipments · Fisher Bodies · Harrison Radiators · Jaxon Steering Gear · AC Spark Plugs · AC Speedometers · New Departure Ball Bearings · Delco Light and Power Plants and Frigidaire · Inland Bros. · Brown-Lipe-Chapin Differential Gears · Lancaster Steel Products · Hyatt Roller Bearings · Inland Steering Wheels · Dayton Wright Special Bodies · Klaxon Horns.

General Motors cars and Delco Light products may be purchased on the GMAC Deferred Payment Plan. Insurance service is furnished by General Exchange Corporation.

"Two years ago I purchased a car, and began going into the country communities for preaching services. In a short time I found a community thickly settled with people who had been without any church or any of the ministries of the church for twenty-five years.

"Time after time the little car was brought into play, to take preacher, singer and teacher to the work. A church building was suggested. 'It can't be done,' was the frequent discouraging remark. By trip after trip the interest was increased; construction began. Within two months the church was built, furnished completely, and paid for.

"Today the community is undergoing a marvellous change. The people remark about it. Merchants feel its influence. Young people are becoming interested in an education. Better literature is going into the homes. Without a car the whole program would have been impossible."

"The community is undergoing a wonderful change"—how many other simple, unobtrusive men have seen a similar change wrought as a result of their unselfish service!

A town is more than the sum total of the things which can be seen or counted or weighed; "where there is no vision the people perish," as truly as where there is no food.

And no man performs a nobler service than the minister, who never doubts that men and women and towns can be something better than they are; who, holding up a high ideal, looks forward through the eyes of faith.

GENERAL MOTORS

FIGURE 4.5

In this 1924 series of striking double-page ads, Barton's agency melded the noble service of the minister with that of the automobile industry.

size was a selling point. People felt assured that GM divisions would not suddenly fold, as had some of the numerous small automobile manufacturers over the previous decade, leaving their cars without adequate repair service or resale value. From 1921 to 1926, as fifty-five auto manufacturers went out of business, this was no small consideration for the consumer.[40]

Barton recognized that it was important to communicate large size without flaunting it. In his view the solution lay in accepting large responsibilities and promising large service. The BDO agency now proposed impressive double-page spreads to dramatize Bracker's illustrations, indirectly suggesting the corporate size and stature underlying such capaciousness. Moreover, General Motors, through a typical Barton association of bigness with benevolence, would show itself big enough to assume the burden of "more than a campaign for itself." It would imply its dominance by speaking for the entire industry and heralding the motorcar as "a great contributor to human effectiveness, an enlarger and enricher of human life." Thus the ads proclaimed the higher service not simply of General Motors but of the automobile. This ploy, BDO affirmed, would "evoke that spontaneous response which always comes when a strong man or institution does a big, generous thing."[41]

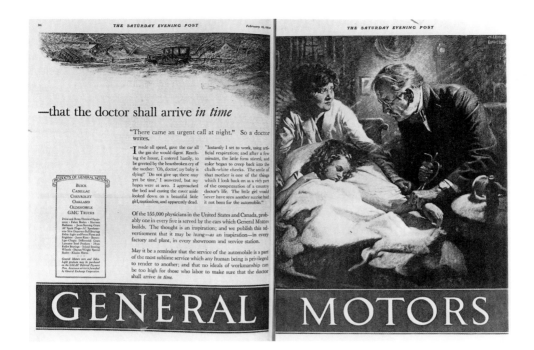

FIGURE 4.6

If it were not for the motorcar, General Motors dramatically disclosed, this child "would never have seen another sunrise." By celebrating the automobile rather than General Motors, the company positioned itself as the representative for the entire industry.

Barton, Durstine, and Osborn won a Harvard Advertising Award in 1924 for the General Motors campaign. One letter to General Motors praised the tribute to ministers in "Through the Eyes of Faith" as "one of the must stunning spreads I have ever seen anywhere" (Fig. 4.5). In another melodramatic ad in the series, "That the Doctor Shall Arrive *in Time*," a country doctor, by "pushing his automobile to the limit," reached "the bedside of a dying child" just in time to revive her and "bring [the girl] back to life" (Fig. 4.6). These reverent portraits recall Barton's own father, a minister, and his grandfather, a self-sacrificing pharmacist and country doctor, whom he portrayed in a similar light in a speech several years later. *Printers' Ink* described this series as one of "much feeling and an occasional heart-throb" and thus "strongly reminiscent of the effects you see on the silver screen." As if Hollywood wished to acknowledge this flattery by imitation, the director of Famous Players—Lasky remarked of one ad in the series, "A mighty industry like General Motors seems coldly and mechanically inhuman. . . . Yet what romance and human appeal was represented in this ad!"[42]

Meanwhile, recognizing that Sloan was both averse to promoting himself as GM's human face before the public and ill suited for it, Barton turned to Charles F. ("Boss") Kettering, the head of the General Motors research laboratories and an enthusiast for the popularization of science and technology. He interviewed Kettering and prepared an article for *American Magazine* that cast him in the role of pioneering hero in the saga of industrial progress. Barton took care to mention General Motors only very discreetly in the article; he certainly did not reveal to the reading public that he was simultaneously masterminding GM's corporate image campaign. But this venture was integral to Barton's larger strategy for humanizing GM while giving publicity to its research capacities. Alfred Swayne, the chairman of the Institutional Advertising Committee, went out of his way to urge Kettering to set aside his apparent distaste for personal publicity and accept this role as a corporate personality. Kettering eventually became GM's most visible public figure of the 1930s and early 1940s.[43]

In cultivating a marketable public image for Kettering, Barton ostensibly drew on the conventional notion that the way to humanize a large and distant corporation was to conjure a popular, folksy image of its leaders—a technique that has been applied from the days of Henry Ford to those of Lee Iacocca. Barton had created ads aimed at just this purpose for such corporations as the Bankers Trust Company and Marshall Field; for General Electric he devised retrospective celebrations of the accomplishments of Thomas Edison and Charles Steinmetz. But the main thrust of the GM campaigns was, in fact, quite different, and its goal was more formidable—to give the corporate entity a soul.[44]

In an age of large bureaucratic private business it made less sense to try to create charismatic leaders as figureheads than to infuse charisma into the organization itself. As Barton explained in a letter to Sloan (a copy of which he also sent to Gerard Swope, the president of his other major institutional client, General Electric), "For us to capitalize individuals would be to do the cheaper thing." In modern society people needed to be given ways to relate to bigness that were more stable than mere identification with an individual, Barton eventually concluded. Exalting the corporation, while subordinating individuals, was "the sound and permanent way" for a corporation to build its image, both internal and external.[45]

In Barton's mind no goal surpassed the internal mission—that of forging a corporate consciousness. Barton's agency steadily pressed a "resale" scheme—a campaign to "sell" the institutional advertising within GM itself. Ads from the goodwill series were posted in factories and supplied as jumbo posters for the car dealers to display in their windows. Reproductions of these ads, with their purposes explained, appeared in sales bulletins and divisional publications. GM's headquarters staff used reams of paper to duplicate and circulate multipage compilations of commendatory letters evoked by the campaign. Personnel managers were enlisted to spread the "new consciousness."[46]

Barton appealed directly to division representatives and editors of divisional publications to cooperate with him in the campaign. He urged them to pass along to him, from letters and their own experiences, "dramatic instances" of car performance and of lives transformed. Such stories might arise, he suggested, from the experiences of workers who now owned cars and, "instead of living right beside a smokestack" as before, could now "work beside one and live in the country." Whether Barton actually obtained useful material from the GM rank and file we do not know, but he put his own example to use in mid-1924 for an ad that related the story of a foreman who now lived healthily in the countryside and commuted to work. Entitled "The Whole Family Enjoys Life Much More," the ad

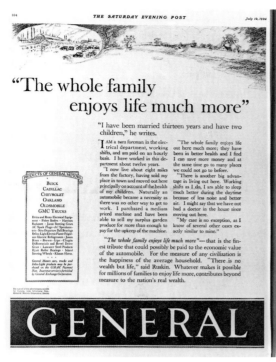

FIGURE 4.7

Here a worker testified to the auto–
mobile's enrichment of his family's
life. Even on hourly pay, he
could afford to commute to work,
moving his family away from the
city to healthier surroundings.

concluded that such "happiness of the average household" was "the finest tribute that could possibly be paid to the economic value of the automobile" (Fig. 4.7).[47]

Intimations of Success

The program of internal resale represented an effort both to realize the central objective of the institutional advertising campaign—the stimulation of a corporate consciousness among the various divisions—and to assure BDO of a continuing account. The GM institutional advertisements were certain to encounter that perennial enigma—how to prove results. BDO anticipated inevitable criticisms in several ways. It convinced Sloan and other GM executives at the outset to make a long-term commitment. Citing the fifteen-year-old, continuing institutional campaign of AT&T as a model, BDO explained that the desired results could not be expected "in a single year or in several years." Barton seized on a comment by Kettering that "it takes four years to develop an organization spirit." He also impressed upon GM's Institutional Advertising Committee that such campaigns were "iceberg" campaigns: their most significant impact came from "under the surface," through word-of-mouth promulgation by the entire network of corporation employees.[48]

A "Corporation Consciousness" 145

BDO and the GM committee assiduously collected any letters that commented on the campaign, eagerly passing the most favorable along to the divisions. For instance, the committee presented as "typical of many that arrive daily" a letter from within the GM organization that praised the goodwill series for demonstrating that GM had the "strength of character . . . to blaze the way for . . . higher ideals in business." Early in 1924 BDO conducted a survey of GM dealers in the Buffalo area to test the impact of the campaign within the organization. In a sense this tactic undermined the thesis that the effects of institutional advertising could be assessed only over the long run. The survey did indicate some short-term results, primarily in marketing. Most of the dealers agreed that the campaign had probably improved sales, but only one mentioned the ideals of public service celebrated in the campaign. Most focused on a single impression that the ads had successfully conveyed—"that GM is a big organization—here to stay."[49]

By the beginning of 1925, although the company had no systematic evidence of its effectiveness, GM corporate leaders obviously deemed the institutional advertising a success. That year they doubled the appropriation, now advertising in newspapers as well as in magazines. In 1927 GM increased funding for the campaign to $1,275,340; the following year the amount rose to $2,796,118.[50] By this time the institutional campaign was also serving such auxiliary purposes as touting the GM installment-buying plan and seeking to bolster the market for used cars. The price of GM stock had been rising most agreeably since 1923. In 1926 and 1927, GM led all manufacturers in profits; in 1927 its dividends to stockholders surpassed all previous records for industrial firms. Wall Street, at least, had gained a favorable impression of General Motors, although profit figures surely counted far more in its esteem than corporate imagery.

The Harvard Advertising Award, which BDO and GM received for the 1924 campaign, offered the added imprimatur of academic and cultural authority to the image of service. Moreover, Sloan's desire for greater integration, cooperation, and control had largely been realized by 1925. It was impossible to measure just how much the corporate image campaign had contributed to that process. But given Sloan's preference for avoiding confrontation and seeking the right psychological atmosphere for cooperation, he very likely agreed with Pierre du Pont's assessment that institutional advertising was worthwhile even if it accomplished nothing beyond its contributions to internal cohesion.[51]

Beginning in 1925 General Motors also sought to capitalize on the more tangible public effects of its corporate image campaigns. That year the Oakland division launched the Pontiac, advertising the new car as "reflecting 17 years of General Motors experience." Early ads for the new model mentioned the Oakland division only in tiny print and did not, at first, even include the brand name "Pontiac." Banking on the prestige of the parent corporation, the ads proclaimed, "Only General Motors could achieve such a Six" (Fig. 4.8). *Printers' Ink* affirmed the success of the entire 1923–26 institutional campaign by observing how, "backed by General Motors' prestige," the Pontiac had instantly taken hold.[52]

When it stepped up its activity in the electric refrigeration field in the mid-1920s, General Motors seemed even more convinced of the power of its corporate title. Its production of household mechanical refrigerators soared from roughly 16,000 in 1925 (about 21 percent of total U.S. production) to more than 70,000

Only General Motors could achieve such a Six ⌐ ⌐ ⌐

FIGURE 4.8

Less than four years after a survey had reported that the name "General Motors" was virtually unknown to the public, the company felt confident enough to phase out its old Oakland brand by promoting its eventual replacement, the Pontiac, simply as a "product of General Motors."

(and by the calculations of its own order department, as many as 95,000) in 1926. Suddenly it commanded at least one-third of the market and perhaps as much as 45 percent.[53] "Only Frigidaire can give you General Motors value," it announced to *Good Housekeeping* readers in March of 1927. *Printed Salesmanship* noted the effectiveness of a Frigidaire ad that displayed a composite picture of all the GM plants in the background. "Surely an organization of the size illustrated in the picture would see that purchasers got a run for their money," the journal observed. The accompanying slogan, "Frigidaire—the only electric refrigerator made and guaranteed by General Motors," bolstered consumer confidence that "here is an organization one can depend on." Other ads accentuated the GM-Frigidaire association with headlines reading, "Frigidaire is the *name of the* Electric Refrigerator made *only* by GENERAL MOTORS" (Fig. 4.9).[54]

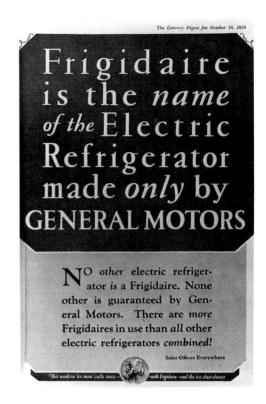

The Literary Digest for October 16, 1926

Frigidaire
is the *name*
of the Electric
Refrigerator
made *only* by
GENERAL MOTORS

N O *other* electric refrigerator *is* a Frigidaire. None
other is guaranteed by General Motors. There are *more*
Frigidaires in use than *all* other
electric refrigerators *combined!*

Sales Offices Everywhere

This modern 'ice man' calls once— *—with Frigidaire—and the ice stays always*

FIGURE 4.9
To establish itself in a new industry
in 1926, GM drew on the prestige
of a corporate name assiduously
cultivated through four years of
institutional advertising.

In its eagerness to exploit this affiliation General Motors even urged *Saturday Evening Post* readers, in a dubious gambit, to envision its Frigidaire as "the car in the kitchen" (Fig. 4.10). The Frigidaire, it explained, had come from "the same great Research Laboratories which have helped perfect its cars." Just as GM offered "a car for every purse and purpose," so it now could provide "a suitable Frigidaire model for every family." Billboards for Frigidaire proclaimed in large type: "IT'S A PRODUCT OF GENERAL MOTORS." Sloan might well have pointed out that such ads would have been ludicrous in 1922, when GM had been known only on Wall Street.[55]

Corporate Identity and Mass Merchandising at GE

An irony surfaced when General Motors sought to use the corporate image that Barton had helped it craft to capture the electrical refrigeration market for Frigidaire in the late 1920s. It was quickly bested by another giant corporation, fresh from its own intense corporate image campaign, under the counsel of none other than Barton. The General Electric Company had relied on Barton's agency to develop its institutional advertising campaign between 1923 and 1926; the refrigera-

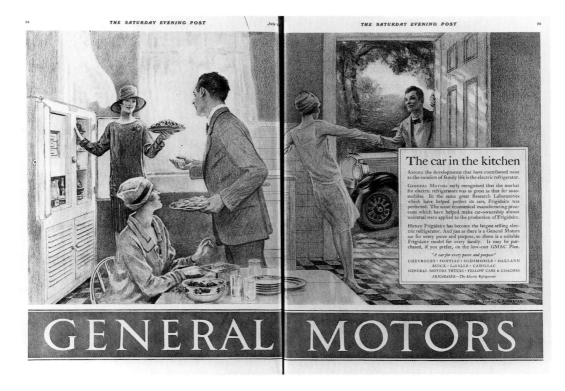

FIGURE 4.10

In 1927 General Motors introduced its Frigidaire as "the car in the kitchen," apparently believing its corporate image could easily vault the gap between driveway and breakfast nook.

tor it brought out in 1927 soon dominated the market.[56] At General Electric, as at General Motors, Barton had associated himself with those executives pushing for greater corporate cohesion. And in a mode that also recalls his counsel at General Motors, he had successfully urged GE to link an image-building, "unselfish," broad-visioned national campaign for an "electrical consciousness" with an internal campaign for a "corporation consciousness."[57]

Barton's command performance had carried the day at General Motors through his astute reading of the internal needs of that corporation. His tour-de-force at General Electric again displayed his capacity to promote service and business ideals while anticipating merchandising strategies and internal dynamics. Barton approached the company's prospective clients with a sensitivity to what would now be termed its "corporate culture." He relished the opportunity to help shape that culture.

At General Electric 1922 was an auspicious year for such a project. In May the seventy-eight-year-old Charles F. Coffin had closed out his lengthy term as company president (1892–1913) and chairman of the board (1913–1922) and persuaded President Edwin W. Rice to retire along with him in favor of a new leadership team. The two successors Coffin picked were to epitomize the new era of business

A "Corporation Consciousness"   **149**

statesmanship of the 1920s. Owen D. Young, a lawyer of international outlook and diverse public interests, became chairman of the board; Gerard Swope, a former executive at Western Electric and one-term resident in Jane Addams's Hull House, took over as president. Coffin had been a respected, if remote, corporate head. But everyone expected new initiatives and directions under the more youthful, vigorous, and service-oriented leadership of Young and Swope. Advertising agencies were so confident of change at GE that Swope found himself immediately bombarded by their proposals for new directions. At the first corporation-wide conference ever held on advertising and sales at GE, Swope invited the various ad agencies that were presently handling accounts for GE and its divisions to present proposals before some sixty of the corporation's executives at the Schenectady golf club. Barton's agency, with a typically majestic plan for institutional advertising, vanquished the competition.[58]

Institutional advertising was less of a novel idea at GE in 1922 than it was at GM. The first GE corporate ad, an avowal of the company's commitment to use electricity to improve people's lives, had appeared in 1916. By 1918 some voices in the advertising department had raised the cry for a full institutional campaign. They warned that the company's main rival, Westinghouse, was spending "enormous sums" for magazine ads that presented all its products "in a bold, impressive way" under its single corporate title. By contrast, none of the advertising for GE-produced appliances was signed by GE, so the ads did "[not] a particle of good toward creating good will for the General Electric Company." A market survey in 1918 revealed that to most consumers "the name of the General Electric Company has only an extremely vague significance." What was more, despite GE's much more extensive advertising in the business press, Westinghouse nearly equaled GE in positive impressions among prospective buyers. None of these arguments, however, proved sufficient to spur a corporate image campaign.[59] GE profits were high, and its leadership was conservative. Before 1920 the company still primarily produced large electrical equipment—motors, turbines, and transformers—for railroads, public utilities, and other industrial enterprises. Its sales often depended on its ability to supply specially designed apparatus for particular needs. The only GE products sold directly to consumers were fans and light bulbs (then universally known as "lamps").

General Electric's need for a popular corporate image early in the century arose more from political than marketing purposes. Challenged by a federal antitrust prosecution in 1911, GE had escaped major damage through a consent decree. Young, who took over the firm's legal department shortly thereafter, sent "a group out into the highways and byways to find out what the plain citizen thought of General Electric." The public thought well of GE's products, research, and engineering but knew none of its officers; it perceived the company, which had been forged through a J. P. Morgan–contrived merger in 1892, as an impersonal Wall Street corporation. "The owner or master of most of the public utilities of the country" and an organization of "tremendous power," GE readily came to mind among the public as the "head and front . . . of a 'power trust.'"[60]

Young had beseeched President Coffin ("one of the most modest and retiring of men") to make himself known to the public and thus give the corporation a human face. Coffin absolutely refused. Although the company encouraged publicity about its leading engineer, the brilliant hunchbacked dwarf Charles Steinmetz, as a fascinating, "gnomelike wizard," it had largely adopted a low-profile strategy, on the assumption that any media attention was apt to prove unfavorable.[61] For many years, according to one GE executive, the company avoided all newspaper advertising because "we were then constantly on the defensive and anything and everything we said in public print was apt to be misconstrued and made the basis of unfriendly, and in many cases vicious, criticism."[62]

One of the keys to GE profitability had been its control over crucial lamp patents—patents its lawyers defended aggressively against all infringers. Up until the 1920s, one of GE's advertising agents observed, the patent situation had always commanded "the best thought of the higher officials," while merchandising and advertising were neglected. Another significant dimension of GE's success had stemmed from its early financial assistance to local utility companies, a "generosity" that usually made them steady purchasers of its large apparatus. In the course of this assistance, GE had acquired and consolidated within its subsidiary company, Electric Bond and Share, considerable financial interests in a variety of utility companies. Faced with changing markets, political attacks on its "power trust" influence over utility companies, and complaints of its price-fixing of lamps through patent control, GE's response remained conservative: keep quiet, exploit the lamp patents, and concentrate on selling large apparatus in a seemingly captive market. A paragon of the old school of management, which concerned itself greatly with production and very little with "image," Coffin defined the GE agenda succinctly: "A company's job is simply to make goods and sell them."[63]

But Swope and Young swept into office in 1922 with enhanced visions of vigorous merchandising, statesmanlike business stature, and public service.[64] Of the various advertising agents with small pieces of the business of GE and its subsidiaries in 1922, Barton, who for two years had produced institutional ads for the Edison Lamp Works, one of GE's two light bulb manufacturers, was best positioned to carry out this mission of public edification. Barton not only spoke the language of ideals and service more fluently than any of his advertising contemporaries, but he was also quicker to grasp the "big picture" and propose a dramatic campaign commensurate with expansive new visions. Why should a manufacturer settle for hawking light bulbs, he asked, when it could claim credit for light itself—and for promoting qualities such as health and ambition that might feasibly be associated with light?

Preferring, like most GE divisions and subsidiaries, to produce its own advertising, Edison Lamp had contracted with Barton and Norman Rockwell in 1920 to create the decade's dream team of popular persuasion. Rockwell's sentimental vignettes for Edison Lamp ads strove mightily to reverse the process that Wolfgang Schivelbusch has called the "disenchantment" of light.[65] In them the light from stark, inert bulbs acquired a misty, shimmering glow, with something of the poetry and mystery that had once linked light with flame. To accompany Rockwell's poignant scenes Barton supplied such heart-stirring headlines as "The Stuff of Which Memories Are Made" and texts that sought to touch deep chords of emotion. One of these mused that "from the first candle of youth to the twilight of life, the moments that mean most are etched in memory by the glow of a lamp." Another confirmed that "a friendly lamp invites confidences" (Fig. 4.11). In "The

The party *after* the party

BACK of every Edison MAZDA Lamp is Mazda Service, centered in the Research Laboratories of the General Electric Company, whose ceaseless search for better lamps at lower cost has, in the short period of eleven years, resulted in six times as bright a lamp for the same amount of current.

HIS ONLY RIVAL

EDISON MAZDA LAMPS

THE strains of the music still sing in her ears; her pulses beat to its rhythm, her cheeks are aglow—So, flushed and happy, she slips into her mother's room, to live through the evening again.

They are very rich, those *after* hours—when the hearts of mothers and daughters draw close, and sons discover that fathers are pals. A friendly lamp invites confidences. In every such family party it plays its silent part.

YOU have noticed how, on the stage, a gloomy room is changed into a cheerful room by merely rearranging the lights.

Your Edison MAZDA Lamp dealer knows something of the application of the stage manager's art to the home. He will tell you which Edison MAZDA Lamp will light each room of your home to make your comfort greater and your work easier.

EDISON MAZDA LAMPS
EDISON LAMP WORKS OF GENERAL ELECTRIC COMPANY

FIGURE 4.11
The team of Norman Rockwell and
Bruce Barton provided this GE lamp
division with the powerful appeal of
sentimental associations.

Great Things in Life," a subsequent 1921 campaign by Edison Lamp, Barton supplied effusive tributes to work, health, home, anticipation, and ambition, as evoked in sentimental illustrations of the contributions of artificial light to human civilization (Fig. 4.12).[66]

Having already displayed his flair for idealization on behalf of one segment of GE, Barton won GE's new institutional advertising account for his agency in 1922

FIGURE 4.12

Already in 1921 Barton displayed his penchant for the grand vision. Why should a corporation merchandise mere fixtures when it could take credit for light itself—and for all other noble qualities that could be associated with light?

by proposing to merchandise something even more comprehensive than light—an "electrical consciousness." Other agencies also proposed greater unification in GE advertising, but Barton upstaged them with a particularly lofty plan. Shrewdly identifying himself (through the collective pronoun) as already part of GE's leadership cadre, Barton set forth a challenge: "If we do anything we ought to take our courage in our hands and do a very unusual thing." To settle for "timid, orthodox advertising," he continued, would amount to just "one more 'institutional campaign.'" But a dramatic departure would "capture national attention." As General Motors had obliquely claimed leadership in its industry by showing itself big enough to advertise on behalf of the automobile's contributions to civilization, so General Electric should seize a leadership role by glorifying electricity. The subject of the first series of ads, Barton insisted, should be nothing less than "human progress."[67]

Barton's proposal corresponded propitiously with Swope's belief that the future of General Electric lay in the expansion of its mass consumer market. Even though

GE presently sold few consumer goods under its own name, it now seemed logi-cal to consolidate its affiliates' products under the GE trademark and to augment its line of appliances by purchasing other companies. General Electric had invested in one of the nation's most highly developed research laboratories. By utilizing its research capacity GE could improve the appliances of its new subsidiaries and mer-chandise them under the GE brand. During his years as a Western Electric execu-tive Swope had envisioned putting the WE brand "on everything electrical going into the American home," only to see his ambition thwarted by Western Electric's agreement to give priority to AT&T's equipment needs. Now, as David Loth has noted, the only difference was that instead of "WE," the omnipresent monogram in the American home would read "GE." [68]

GE's large commitment to research and development promised a future parade of new consumer products onto the market. These could be launched more ef-fectively if introduced with a prestigious family name. Part of the new institutional campaign, Swope and Barton agreed, would be an ongoing effort to ensure that the GE logo would be displayed in a uniform way on all advertising by General Electric and its affiliates and on all the factories. Over the next five years Swope followed through with intense scrutiny of the fine details of the advertisements and factory signs of all GE divisions and affiliates. [69]

A classic 1923 GE advertisement sought to embed not just the design but the meaning of the company logo in the consciousness of all who viewed it, defini-tively identifying the GE logo as "the initials of a friend" (Fig. 4.13). Since the purpose of the new campaign, Barton repeated, was "to personalize the Company in the minds of important people who now regard it as a purely impersonal and rather overwhelming machine," the word "company" was dropped. Replicating his advice to General Motors, Barton argued that just plain "General Electric" was a "more colloquial," and thus more friendly, signature. With time, Barton confi-dently predicted, the phrase "initials of a friend" would quietly work itself into the public consciousness. It would give the organization "something to live up to." After years of constant reiteration, Barton suggested, people would come to think of "the initials of a friend" as "something that has been said about us, not merely something that we have said about ourselves." [70]

Barton also grasped the role that the new institutional campaign could play in the company's internal dynamics, as he had at General Motors. In 1922 General Electric, too, constituted an insufficiently integrated amalgam of manufacturing operations. Its two light bulb manufacturers—the Edison Lamp Works and the National Lamp Works—suspiciously maintained primary allegiances to their dis-tinct origins and seemed barely to tolerate visible association with General Elec-tric in their advertising. As soon as he gained the GE account Barton sought to impress upon Swope the irrationality of the "private little campaigns" of the lamp divisions. Other segments of the company also relegated GE to invisibility in their publicity, he pointed out. The current advertisements of Premier Vacuum Clean-ers, Thor Washing Machines, and all Hot-Point products revealed "no connec-tion" with GE. Swope and Young, who were vigorously yet patiently striving to unify the company's lamp manufacturing "beyond the point of unscrambling," and encountering many bruised egos and much "sparring for positions" in the process, had good reason to favor Barton's vision of cooperation among all GE units in the pursuit of elevated common goals. [71]

The initials of a friend

You will find these letters on many tools by which electricity works. They are on great generators used by electric light and power companies; and on lamps that light millions of homes.

They are on big motors that pull railway trains; and on tiny motors that make hard housework easy.

By such tools electricity dispels the dark and lifts heavy burdens from human shoulders. Hence the letters G-E are more than a trademark. They are an emblem of service—the initials of a friend.

GENERAL ELECTRIC

FIGURE 4.13
Even a logo could convey a sense of corporate soul. Through the notion of personal initials Barton reduced the corporation to a familiar scale, one comfortably compatible with the concept of "friend."

Barton allied himself with Swope and other GE executives who pushed for greater corporate unity. He used his influence to get Martin Rice, one of GE's most vocal internal critics of decentralized operations, appointed head of a new corporate publicity department. Whereas one competitor for the GE institutional account had warned that an agency would need to be sensitive to the special problems of "each decentralized sales organization" within the corporation, Barton planned to merge the various GE campaigns. He made certain that the new national campaign for an "electrical consciousness" was accompanied by an internal campaign for a "corporation consciousness."[72]

"Electrical Consciousness" and "Corporation Consciousness"

As at General Motors, Barton worked to ensure that the new campaign was reproduced and explained in the local divisional newsletters. He helped promote a new companywide publication, the very title of which (*GE Monogram*) proclaimed an increasingly predominant role for the company logo. These efforts facilitated the "resale" of the institutional advertising to the various departments of the company, which were "taxed" (as GE executives put it) to pay for the advertising and "could not understand why the company should spend *their* money to 'educate the public.'" BDO's sensitivity to the importance of "reselling" its corporate advertising campaigns within its clients' organizations and overcoming local resistance to a more centralized corporate culture is revealed in a confidential internal BDO status report on the General Electric account in 1928. One particular GE executive, the report noted, "has been frank and serviceable in interpreting to us political factors in [the] G-E organization, such as attitude of unit sales heads to [the] G-E institutional program." Identifying himself with the other GE executives, Barton declared one of the major objectives of the new campaign to be the "stimulation of *our own people* to a large vision of the Company's service and opportunity."[73]

From GE's advertising manager, Barton exacted cooperation in a plan for "making our own organization advertising conscious." The electrical consciousness campaign would not be effective, he argued, unless it created "in every representative of GE . . . a larger pride in his work and self confidence born of the knowledge that he is backed up by the force of a great national understanding." The company's elaborate internal brochure on 1924 publicity promised local managers, the sales force, and distributors that the prominent role given to the large GE monogram in the institutional campaign would make a major contribution to their individual marketing efforts. The electrical consciousness campaign, all GE personnel were assured, would thus simultaneously produce "a General Electric consciousness." Without measures to sell the institutional advertising within the organization, Barton warned Swope, some executives would be certain to undermine it, attacking it as "merely an expensive bit of self-exploitation."[74]

Although Barton recognized the same need to promote a unifying corporate image internally at GE as he did at GM, he perceived the different implications of an emphasis on size for the two corporations. General Motors was still thoroughly overshadowed by Ford in 1922; it confronted a host of smaller competitors in its battle for even a modest share of the market. It had not yet suffered public attacks on account of its size. As BDO's survey of car dealers had suggested, GM would only benefit from public perceptions of its extensive size and resources (and thus, presumably, its stability).

General Electric, by contrast, had frequently come under attack, as in the 1911 antitrust case, for the extent of its control over the industry. Quoting one GE top executive to another, Barton discreetly warned Swope: "The one danger, as Mr. Young has so often said, is that your growth will outrun public appreciation of the necessity for that growth." A business as immense as GE, Young had warned, could not remain a "purely private" business if it expected to endure and grow. It had to become an "institution," with its leaders serving as trustees. As late as 1925 Young was still worrying that GE had not done enough to cultivate a favorable impression as "a public service concern" and looked ahead wishfully to a day when the company would enjoy such public goodwill as to stand "invulnerable to the attacks of politicians."[75]

While Young and Swope moved promptly to remove one element in GE's "power trust" image by formally divesting the company of any ownership in Electric Bond and Share, Barton advised Swope on how to downplay GE's size and power in its institutional advertising. Its campaign should start with modest-sized advertisements, not the dominant ones Barton had proposed for the less politically vulnerable GM (see Figs. 4.5, 4.6, and 4.7). And it should avoid signs that might "give the impression that it has a great deal of money to spend." Swope was easily convinced. At the end of the first year's campaign he passed on to Barton the praise of one outside observer for the wisdom of using less-than-full-page ads and thus avoiding any suggestion of "lavish effort."[76]

As GE's electrical consciousness campaign took shape from 1923 through 1926, it adopted a consistent style while addressing several audiences. One series defined "what electricity is doing for human life" and attributed this progress to the efforts of General Electric's largest customers: the railroads, the central power stations, and the street railways. "We can afford to be very generous in the text," Barton noted of these advertisements, since "we will have the signature at the bottom of the advertisements and will get the glory without urging our claim to it." The railroads were "getting very few kind words these days," he noted, and would be "particularly appreciative" of a message that explained that their use of electricity was not selfish but "greatly benefits the public." Another series of closely related ads highlighted GE research while also reporting on "dramatic progress from all sources, including competitors." This second form of ingratiation, Barton observed, again enabled GE to occupy the high ground. Without claiming credit for all contributions to advancing civilization, General Electric, "by sponsoring this report to the nation, . . . would create in people's minds the belief that it is the headquarters of progress."[77]

Other GE institutional advertisements, such as "A Child's Cry in the Night" and "The Life of One Little Child," were reprises of the General Motor's country doctor ad (see Fig. 4.6), providing a "human touch." Another series, which included "The Suffrage and the Switch," reminded women that their civic and political progress was intertwined with electrical progress (Fig. 4.14). All these ads sustained a single pattern: a dominant illustration, lots of white space to enhance visibility, a concise "editorial" in a single block of large type, and the GE signature. Reflecting back, a recent GE advertising executive has characterized them as "crisp, clean, inviting." A 1925 article in the trade journal *Printers' Ink* praised their texts as "always intensely practical and 'of the soil.'"[78]

Barton might well have seen in these assessments a tribute to his insistence that the copy of institutional ads be kept "short and simple." By the advertising standards of that era, the GE ads were remarkably concise; their main texts always contained fewer than seventy words, sometimes barely fifty. They could thus be set in large type and still allow for ample white space to help give drama and focus to the ads. If they seemed "of the soil," that was perhaps because each ad featured a single idea, approached with that "deep and glowing conviction" that Barton could seemingly conjure at will. "I am getting religion on this subject," he wrote Swope in December 1922, as he pondered how to convey the noble work of emancipation that was taking place as electricity lifted burdens from human shoulders.[79]

After illustrating this theme in scores of ways throughout the series, Barton found its consummate expression in a 1926 ad, which compressed electrical conscious-

Millions of American women voted for President in 1920 and are finding time to take active interest in civic affairs

The suffrage and the switch

Woman suffrage made the American woman the political equal of her man. The little switch which commands the great servant Electricity is making her workshop the equal of her man's.

No woman should be required to perform by hand domestic tasks which can be done by small electric motors which operate household devices.

The General Electric Company is working side by side with your local electric light and power company to help lift drudgery from the shoulders of women as well as of men.

FIGURE 4.14
In its championship of progress and an "electrical consciousness," GE took on the responsibility of emancipating American women from drudgery. The parallel motion of the two hands foreshadowed an emphasis on democracy through consumption.

GENERAL ELECTRIC

ness in the home into a single slogan: "Any woman who does anything which a little electric motor can do is working for 3¢ an hour!" The illustration, as dramatic as the text was pithy, cast the electricity-deficient housewife as a stunted menial, entombed in the looming shadow of her own drudgery (Fig. 4.15). Barton's "any woman" formula—with minor adaptations for specific circumstances ("Any woman who irons by hand . . ."; "Any woman who beats a rug . . ."; "Any industrial worker who moves things by hand . . .")—often evoked the specter of drudgery with similar "shadow pictures" and always included the graph of declining costs. This pattern became so frequent that the entire electrical consciousness series would later be called the "Any woman campaign." With this series the BDO agency repeated the triumph of its 1924 General Motors campaign: the 1926 segment of the GE electrical consciousness campaign won the agency another Harvard Advertising Award.[80]

Any woman who does anything which a little electric motor can do is working for 3¢ an hour!

There are few hard tasks left in the home which electricity cannot do at trifling cost. You will find the G-E monogram on many electrical household conveniences. It is a guarantee of excellence as well as a mark of service.

Ask your electric company or dealer to help you select the labor-saving electrical appliances best suited for your home.

GENERAL ELECTRIC

FIGURE 4.15

Here, with dramatic simplicity, the woman's shadow connotes the bleakness of a life of drudgery. GE, in Barton's strategy, would reap rewards of gratitude and prestige for bringing people these messages of available emancipation, written with "deep and glowing conviction."

Assessing the Results

At the height of 1920s prosperity both General Motors and General Electric found reasons to applaud themselves for their institutional campaigns. Both companies were enjoying unprecedented profits; the price per share of GM and GE stocks steadily advanced. Although corporate imagery may not have been a main factor, business executives were inclined to read this success as certification of all their strategic moves. Moreover, top executives in both corporations now had greater control over operations that were increasingly coordinated and integrated. If institutional advertising had also contributed to a related "corporation consciousness" within all elements of management, it had certainly demonstrated the value that Pierre du Pont had prophesied.

Ironically, if Barton had then wished to boast of his agency's accomplishments in institutional advertising, he would have had to describe how he helped his client, General Electric, score a victory over his former client, General Motors. The name General Motors might still convey size, power, massive resources, and stability for products other than cars, and prospective customers might respond to ads that re-called images of General Motors Research Laboratories and Proving Grounds. But in selling electric refrigerators, a company that had identified itself broadly with the services of the automobile to civilization could simply not match a company that credited itself with progress through electricity.[81]

General Electric began advertising its refrigerators in 1927. By the end of 1929 it was producing nearly 30 percent of the refrigerators made in the United States, compared with 37 percent for GM's well-established Frigidaire and only 12 percent for the third-ranking Kelvinator. By the end of the next year General Electric's share had leapt ahead of Frigidaire's, at 34 percent versus 25 percent, according to figures compiled by Frigidaire's Market Research Department. An ad agency pro-fessional recalled in 1932 that General Motors' reputation had made Frigidaire so formidable a presence in the electric refrigerator market that it had suffered very little from competition by Copeland, Majestic, and Kelvinator. "It was a terribly bad day, however, for Frigidaire, when General Electric came on the market," he concluded.[82]

Other factors, including technical soundness and a good distribution system, may well have played a larger role than the previous four years of institutional advertis-ing in the triumph of the GE refrigerator. Still, it is difficult to imagine that same degree of success if GE had enjoyed no greater public visibility in 1927 than it had back in 1922, when the GE research laboratories were little known and when sales executives were reporting to top GE officials that "the GE trademark meant little to the average housewife." In the mid-1920s, by contrast, BDO agency studies re-vealed that more people were now aware of GE's activities in research than they were of those of any other corporation. Institutional advertising had increased that visibility.[83]

Barton and his agency were not too modest to claim both practical and intan-gible achievements for the corporate image campaigns of GM and GE. In solicit-ing other accounts the BDO agency recounted the success of its work for both in-dustrial giants.[84] By 1929 Barton was declaring that one-third of all people who entered the showrooms of General Motors dealers had already decided to buy *some* GM car because of their impression of GM's size and competence. Barton's asser-tion was largely corroborated by an independent survey of twenty-five thousand people, commissioned by GM in 1932, that attributed to the company's institu-tional stature "more than one third to one half of all buying influences at work in the public mind."[85] Nor did Barton hesitate to claim that "every dollar ever spent" by General Electric in institutional advertising had been "repaid many times over" by the rapid success of the GE refrigerator alone. Moreover, GE's own sales man-ager, Barton reminded Swope, had concurred that the long-range electrical con-sciousness campaign had been "the best possible foundation for the bigger sales that are to come."[86]

Additional testimony to the repute of the Bruce Barton mode within the trade was voiced where neither Barton nor his clients could overhear it—at the strategy meetings of a rival agency. In 1931 and 1932 top executives of the J. Walter Thompson advertising agency lamented that its new major client (the Johns-Manville Company) had not followed the GE model years earlier to develop a background of "institutional strength," a background that had primed the public to respond favorably whenever "GE puts out anything."[87]

The Charisma of the Corporation: Barton as "God's Fiddle"

One might presume that during the prosperous and expansive 1920s, large corporations in the United States did not need the services of a Bruce Barton to provide them with public legitimacy and a sense of self-righteous purposefulness. But business executives of the new era saw as their role not only to build profit-making industrial empires but also to take on broader responsibilities for human welfare. They envisioned themselves, as GE's Owen D. Young put it, as the "trustees" of great institutions, partaking in a public trust. Barton proposed strategies for inducing the public to confirm their flattering self-images. In his recurrent talk of "soul," Barton insisted that big business, having earlier solved its "production problems," had now tackled its legitimacy problems. It had done so, in the case of General Motors and General Electric, through well-conceived advertising campaigns that had infused charisma into the organization, both for the public and for its own employees.

Industrial responses to the problems of production, Barton observed, had led to the "creation of great aggregations of capital, big operating companies, and bigger holding companies." Such entities initially seemed menacing; by long-standing republican tenets their power was suspect. But Barton supplied a formula to address these apprehensions: identify size with service. Viewing no corporate aspiration as too lofty, Barton suggested that giant corporations not confine themselves to the quest for a guarded popular acceptance; they should earn, through proper publicity, accolades of public "love."[88]

While accepting the rhetoric of the Barton formula, companies such as General Motors did not depart from their well-known hardheadedness (the primary object of the corporation was not to make cars but to make money, Sloan had averred).[89] But as their highly publicized corporate images suggest, they recognized the wisdom of Barton's insistence that people in modern society needed to be given ways to relate to bigness. With vast corporations under the control of professional managers, such relations had to be both more stable and less personal than mere identification with an individual. People needed to be shown the connection between bigness itself and service. Barton concluded in 1929 that the complexity of modern society and the "tremendous mass of advertising" had reduced American consumers to a condition in which—"subconsciously, perhaps"—they said to themselves, "'We shan't try to read and assimilate everything; it's impossible. We'll pin our faith and our buying habits to a few big names that we know and can trust.'" His agency's work with GM and GE, Barton added, had made them the biggest and most trustworthy names in automobiles and in electricity. Thus, like the protagonist of a 1924 ad by BDO, the consumer would decide, "'I'm going to let General Motors do my worrying from now on.'"[90]

If such an attitude did not quite meet Barton's rhetorical aspirations for expressions of public love, it was still satisfactory to General Motors and General Electric. After an intensive study of public attitudes toward big business, the historian Louis Galambos has concluded that by 1929 "most middle-class Americans had come to accept the giant corporation as a permanent feature of their society. For the most part, they had not learned to love big business but they had decided they could live with it." That acceptance, along with the increased demand for company stocks, convinced many corporate leaders that they had obtained sufficient external benefit from their institutional advertising.[91]

Barton and the GM and GE executives concurred in seeing the institutional campaigns as tools for achieving corporate integration. In all large companies, Barton observed, a struggle took place between "a headquarters point-of-view and a division point-of-view." Barton always saw himself as the spokesman for headquarters.[92] He sought to foster headquarters ascendancy with messages that would hearten and unify all levels in the corporation. The company magazine of General Electric's National Lamp Works reproduced a speech in which Barton characterized all those in the GE family as "engaged in the great profession of lighting the world." They operated, he said, under a charter from "the beginning of time . . . recorded in the four words, 'Let there be light.'" The magazine editorialized: "None of us can read his [Barton's] message, without gaining a loftier conception of our privileges and duties as 'Trustees of Light.'" At General Motors, Barton also served as an internal morale builder, a shaper of corporate culture. In 1925 he had urged Sloan to move further with his corporate image efforts and "take the leadership among corporations" by demonstrating that General Motors not only "has great wealth, great stability . . . [but] also has a soul."[93]

Internal corporate propaganda sometimes implausibly exaggerated and romanticized the "corporation consciousness" created by the institutional campaigns. Supposedly even "the sweating giants who labor in the flame-shot murk of automobile foundries" could wish for "no finer reward" than the opportunity to identify with GM's country doctor ad, in which a life is saved "through the instrumentality of the automobile." But in actuality the main targets—and major beneficiaries—of internal image advertising were not blue-collar workers but the headquarters staff, local dealers, and above all the top executives and middle managers in the various divisions. By presenting an idealized portrait of a cohesive, powerful, and benevolent corporation to the public, Barton afforded the crucial managerial cadres an energizing vision of the corporation "as a whole."[94]

Barton had always fixed his sights on goals beyond higher sales and successful new products. Current profits were fine, and no advertising agency could retain even an institutional account without holding out the promise of some impact on sales. But Barton dedicated himself to a nobler purpose. His early work in the General Motors and General Electric institutional campaigns provided an outlet for his desire to midwife new ideals in business leadership and service, to literally capitalize both these qualities and give them a hallowed aura. It also fueled his ambition to usher in a managers' millennium, to guide a new managerial elite that aspired to serve and be recognized as the public's trustees. Responding with becoming modesty to President Swope's praises after three years of the GE campaign, Barton turned, characteristically, to a spiritual comparison. "You remember what John Bunyan said when the lady congratulated him on his sermon," he wrote Swope. "'Madam, I am only God's fiddle.'" Barton, too, had merely carried out a higher mission. "I am the fiddle of the GE Advertising Department."[95]

The campaigns that Barton masterminded for General Motors and General Electric, with their attention to internal cohesion, charted the course for the sophisticated endeavors in image creation that ultimately would follow. When the industrial giants Du Pont and United States Steel experienced dramatic "conversions" to multifaceted public relations and institutional advertising campaigns in the mid-1930s, Barton, the veteran evangelist of business statesmanship, supplied the direct inspiration (see Chapter 6). As one cynic later reflected, Barton possessed "the knack of shedding light-rays of goodness upon the companies, the men and the institutions he glorified."[96] No one else seemed to imbue the quest for enhanced corporate legitimacy, both externally and internally, with quite so much "soul."

5 TO BE AN INSTITUTION: THE SERVICE IDEAL AND THE INSTITUTIONAL STYLE

The decade of the 1920s favored America's largest corporations with bountiful financial success and increased popular acceptance.[1] It also ushered in, for corporations of national scope, unprecedented perceptions of broad public responsibilities. "Today, business formally assumes the obligations of a profession," proclaimed Owen D. Young, chairman of the board of the General Electric Company, in 1927. Like the "ministers of our churches," Young avowed, the "ministers of our businesses" should acquire the skills, the "moral and religious training," and the "broad outlook in history, politics, and economics" that would enable them to assume the "trusteeship" of society now thrust upon them. Other corporate executives chose such phrases as "stewardship," "industrial statesmanship," "public service," and "public trust" to describe the company's role in society.[2]

These sentiments were certainly not new among corporate leaders. Andrew Carnegie had forcefully promoted the idea of personal stewardship; such early practitioners of welfare capitalism as John Wanamaker, John Patterson, and George W. Perkins had advanced more corporation-centered models of stewardship (see Chapter 1); and many a local business proprietor had assumed a role as civic leader. But not until the 1920s did many large, national corporations so deliberately and self-consciously launch major publicity campaigns to define themselves as public trustees. The aspiration to be not merely a business but an institution now obsessed many a major corporation (Fig. 5.1).

The word "institution" had acquired a variety of meanings and nuances by the twentieth century. This made it all the more useful in corporate rhetoric. By one definition an institution was simply any practice, association, custom, or relationship that had become "a material and persistent element in the life or culture of an organized social group." This status was exactly what the big business corporation needed to attain to overcome any lingering resistance to its popular legitimacy. It conformed with the legal condition of the corporation as unbound by the mortality of individual entrepreneurs and investors; the longevity of the corporation

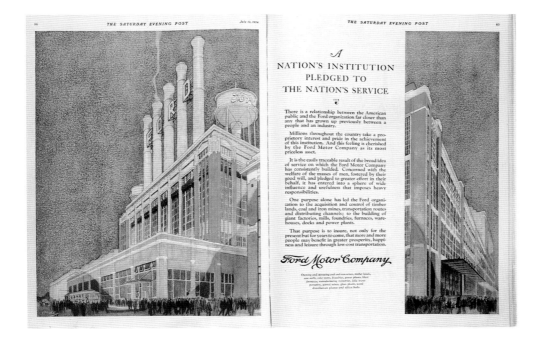

FIGURE 5.1

Enthralled, like many corporations of the era, with a self-image as a great social institution, Ford fused images of service and power to validate its claim. It had amassed tremendous economic power only to carry out its "responsibilities."

itself would endow institutional status. But by this definition virtually any business corporation could, after some span of existence, style itself "an institution."

By contrast, many corporate image campaigns of the 1920s summoned a grander, more stately sense of the term. Defined by its "charitable or educational character," an institution—such as a university, a court of law, a hospital, a patriotic or religious organization, or a philanthropic foundation—was an entity viewed as exemplary for society. Used in this spirit, the word "institution" drew on its legacy of association with civic beneficence or the establishment of a religious sacrament.[3] To warrant the designation of "institution" in this sense, a corporation could not simply lay claim to qualities of permanence and indispensability in the everyday life of society. It needed to rise above the status of "mere business," to become "something more than a mere money-making machine."[4]

Following the pattern that Bruce Barton had set for General Motors and General Electric, one major corporation after another stepped forward in the 1920s to proclaim that its allegiance to goals above mere profit entitled it to the status of institution. Several examples of such proclamations suggest the dominant rhetorical mode:[5]

Metropolitan desires that it shall not be considered by the public a money-making institution, which is doing work for profit. . . . What we are trying to do is to use that business as a public institution for the purpose of serving the American people. (Haley Fiske, president, Metropolitan Life Insurance Company, 1922)

It is not enough to advertise a product. The public ought to be acquainted with the honesty and high character of the institution back of the product. (Colonel Robert Stewart, Standard Oil Company of Indiana, 1922)

Bauer & Black is more than a business house; . . . it is an institution of the highest ideals. (Bauer & Black, 1923)

Founded on the principle that a business earns the right to exist only as it serves, the Ford organization has grown to be more than a business. It is an institution that serves its millions. (Ford Motor Company, 1924)

My conception of industry is not primarily for profit but it is for service. (Gerard Swope, president, General Electric Company, 1927)

A National Institution: In an industrial country such as ours, certain privately owned and privately managed institutions because of the service they are called upon to render are national in their scope. (Armour and Company, 1927)

What excited this institutional itch within so many corporations during the 1920s? Clearly their experiences during World War I played a part. Through these many business leaders had come to know the satisfaction of tying their economic interests to larger, more exalted purposes; some executives had also discovered their skills in political policy-making and in exercising influence in the public arena. From a narrower, more practical standpoint, mergers and new merchandising opportunities had made it increasingly desirable in some industries to market individual brands by identifying them with a quickly recognized, favorably viewed corporate image. Finally, the need to cultivate public favor as political protection had certainly not vanished in the post-muckraking era, particularly for firms with elements of monopoly control. In fact, the rapid proliferation of new media and recollections of the impact of wartime propaganda had made everyone more conscious of public opinion and the power of imagery.

Even the long-standing tradition of philanthropic benevolence had taken on a new style among the leaders of great corporations. During the nineteenth century individual entrepreneurs had most frequently satisfied their aspirations to be well thought of, as well as economically successful, through acts of personal philanthropy. Usually they scrupulously distinguished their indulgences in charity and cultural patronage from the narrow economic rationality of their business operations. But many of the corporate managerial elite of the 1920s, lacking extensive fortunes or renown within a specific local community, could not enjoy a reputation for philanthropic service apart from their role in the corporation. Even some of the most prominent and wealthy corporation owners recognized the potential gains in public goodwill and political protection to be had through the company's reputation for public service. To present themselves as more than profit-seekers, corporate executives increasingly associated themselves with their corporation's acts of public beneficence and "statesmanship." In so doing they adopted what had become, by the mid-1920s, a dominant institutional style in advertising and publicity—one calculated to win regard for a corporation as an esteemed national institution.

"Suitable for Framing": High Art and Class Imagery

Perhaps the most distinctive characteristic of the images—verbal, graphic, and architectural—that major corporations put forth in their bid for institutional status was their self-conscious creation as works of art. The designers of corporate imagery did not necessarily strive to make it "beautiful" in some conventional sense, nor did they always insist on being au courant with contemporary artistic trends. But they sought to give it the social and cultural status of art. If artists and illustrators who accepted commissions from advertisers might fear the "taint of commercialism" on their reputations, as art historian Michele Bogart observes, business corporations, conversely, looked to escape the stigma of mere profit-seeking through their association with art.[6] Embracing a variety of artistic styles, they aimed in their institutional ads at an elusive quality, dependent not so much on the status of high art as on the suggestion of high social class—a look that was "suitable for framing."

In their selection of layouts for corporate image ads, agency art directors favored ample white space—the "conspicuous waste" of expensive space implying the status and power of the advertiser (Figs. 5.2 and 5.3).[7] Convinced that dignity and stature were most effectively conveyed by clean lines and an uncluttered look, the crafters of institutional ads usually opted for "a large rectangular picture, a headline and a copy block ending with a signature." These balanced layouts connoted stability. They also conformed to the notion that a "portrait in oils" of the corporation's ideals should have its integrity protected. The illustrations were thus exempt from the devices then in vogue in product advertising to capture readers' attention, such as angled, overprinted headlines and the fragmentation of illustrations into "queer and outlandish shapes."[8]

Just in case the public might fail to recognize the corporation's association with uplift and high culture, the sponsors of such ads sometimes prompted readers to hold institutional advertisements in proper regard. The Vacuum Oil Company introduced a 1927 campaign by announcing: "We are privileged to reproduce here one of a series of drawings of industrial subjects by the late Joseph Pennell, one of America's great artists." Similarly, *Advertising and Selling* noted that Hugh Ferriss's charcoal drawings had produced a "truly institutional and inspiring advertising campaign" for the Lehigh Portland Cement Company. His visionary architectural renderings, an ad for the Walker Engraving Company observed, transformed the "very brutality" of the "enormous wealth and industry of the age of Mammon" into the exalted beauty of "a cathedral" (Fig. 5.4). General Motors bluntly prefaced an ad in its 1927 institutional campaign with the message, "This is a famous drawing by a famous artist." A few institutional ads even carried invitations to send for copies. E. R. Squibb & Sons took pleasure in revealing that one of its

Running errands for the nation's butcher shops

Your juicy steak, national in its popularity, is far from being national in its origin.

Ten Mississippi valley states raise and feed much of the beef which you like so well.

The big herds of quality cattle are fattened in an even smaller area, know as the "corn belt." No feed has yet been discovered that is as cheap and fattening as this yellow grain.

This meat must be dressed, chilled and shipped many miles to the other 38 states. Whose job is it? Your local butcher cannot do it. If each butcher built a packing plant, there would be endless duplication

and expense—making meat too high priced.

Time has proved that the dressing and distribution of meats on a large scale through centrally located plants is economical to the consumer and has given him a wider choice as to quality.

Local butchers have found that they can order any grade and weight, without waste, and suited exactly to their customer's desires.

Swift & Company is running this errand for the nation at a surprisingly small rate of pay. We receive only a fraction of a cent per pound profit on the meat we sell. The public saves money by such service.

Swift & Company, U. S. A.
Founded 1868
A nation-wide organization owned by more than 30,000 shareholders

Western Electric in 1877

Part of the Western Electric of today. The great telephone factory at Chicago.

Grown Great Through Service

THE men of history grew great according to the measure of their service. So with institutions.

Western Electric is an industrial institution whose growth is no miracle, but the result of greater service. Nearly half a century ago it started on a simple idea—to make the best telephones and telephone equipment that human skill could build.

In our work for the Bell Telephone System, our ideals today are the same as those that have guided us for nearly fifty years—to grow greater by serving more.

Western Electric
SINCE 1882 MANUFACTURERS FOR THE BELL SYSTEM

FIGURES 5.2 & 5.3
In contrast to the eye-catching imbalance and sense of movement in many contemporary product ads, the institutional style favored decorous gentility and the implied power of a willingness to "waste" expensive white space.

campaigns had brought "innumerable requests for reproductions of the illustrations for framing."[9]

Corporations also drew on classical allegories or historical and literary allusions in their effort to convey an air of high art and civic responsibility. Raymond Rubicam, a copy supervisor at N. W. Ayer in the early 1920s and later a partner in his own agency, gained prominence in the trade from his ability to create such an ambience in ads for E. R. Squibb and Steinway pianos. His famous "Hakeem of Bagdad" ad for Squibb (see Fig. 5.8), linking the corporation with ancient wisdom, helped establish his credentials. Bruce Barton regularly adapted biblical tales and historical anecdotes to his institutional texts. The virtues and sayings of noted historical figures appeared so frequently in corporate advertising that one exasperated critic of the institutional style expressed relief in discovering any ad "that does not mention Hannibal, Napoleon, Cleopatra, Julius Caesar or the Statue of Liberty."[10]

Copywriters assumed that, particularly in institutional advertising, readers needed to be lured into the substance of the text by a good story or a tantalizing anecdote. And if that anecdote or story could spin a web of prestige around the company by associating it with ancient wisdom, literary and artistic masterpieces, or heroic figures and epochs, so much the better. Some institutional ads, such as *Sine Cera* for N. W. Ayer and *ὁ Οἰκονομικός* for *McCalls,* even carried headlines in

FIGURE 5.4
Hugh Ferriss's renderings of "inspirational," cathedral-like skyscrapers gave visual expression to the idealization of business as service.

Latin or Greek to further elevate the atmosphere. Even if readers were ignorant of Joshua or Achilles, as well as of Greek and Latin, one agency president observed, such ads would still enable them to "enjoy a sort of illumination, as if they were learning something." Meanwhile, the advertisements would place the corporate message within a setting "full of the dignity of literary or historical association."[11] Moreover, conspicuous association with the humanities might counteract stereotypes of the large business corporation as narrowly preoccupied with profit-making and as soulless in its pursuit of gain. Surely a company that seemed so highly educated, so knowledgeable about the words and actions of past sages and heroes, would carry out its social responsibilities with honor.

In a further attempt to distinguish corporate image advertisement from the less elevated product advertising, a few companies explicitly identified their institutional ads as part of a series. For internal purposes, of course, advertisers and agencies regularly designated ads of all kinds as elements in a series or campaign. On their proof sheets they so marked and numbered them. But only in institutional campaigns would an advertiser occasionally include in the ad copy a label such as

"Number 1 in a Series." These designations appeared on the Swift & Company ads of the mid-1920s, as well as on the ads of the Du Pont "chemical engineer" campaign in 1922. In 1920, and again in 1922 and 1924, Western Electric numbered each of its institutional advertisements as installments in a series. In 1928 the pharmaceutical firm Parke, Davis & Company specifically identified each ad as "one of a series of messages" in a campaign entitled "Building the Fortresses of Health." Concerned with maintaining its ethical standing with the medical profession while aggressively advertising its household preparations, the company wanted to make sure that a doctor or pharmacist who read any one of the ads would see that it was sponsoring a health education service through an entire series of institutional ads.[12]

The explicit identification of certain institutional ads as linked in a series disclosed the didactic impetus that lay behind many an institutional campaign. Product advertisements aimed to give sufficient information in an individual ad, so as not to offend the reader by prevailing upon him or her to read yet another ad about a soap or a toothpaste. But corporate leaders believed that the public ought to be grateful to receive the broader civic edification of institutional ads. Furthermore, designation as a series often coincided with a strategic plan to package the series in some impressive folder or brochure to distribute to clients and stockholders. These were to be works of art both individually and as a collection. In sequence they would constitute a company epic.[13]

Mundane Analogies: The Simple Grandeur of the Humanized Corporation

The genteel splendor of much corporate imagery during the 1920s, as faithfully as it reflected aspirations to the stately status of public institution, still failed to dispel the charge of soullessness in one respect. Even the most exalted claims to benevolent service might not allay fears of the giant corporation as cold, impersonal, and unfathomable in the complexity and obscurity of its operations. Companies whose very size suggested the potential exercise of monopoly control or oligopolistic power had reason to devise corporate images that would humanize as well as exalt the corporation. By familiarizing the public with them and their operations, usually by analogy to the mundane activities of common citizens, a number of companies hoped to fuse their claims to awe-inspiring public leadership with a perception of comfortable, everyday indispensability.

Thus the giant meatpackers Swift and Armour purported to act as "good neighbors" to fellow Americans by "running errands" or providing an "ice box" just like theirs, only larger—thus seeking to defuse potential political antagonism by making themselves seem less distant and mysterious to the average citizen. The H. J. Heinz Company managed to employ this tactic of familiar scale for marketing as well as humanizing purposes. In an ad entitled "The Homelike Kitchens of Heinz," the company cast an air of homemade quality over all its products. "Big and efficient as the kitchens of a nation must be," Heinz explained, "we have escaped the factory atmosphere. We do not manufacture. We cook and bake as nearly as we can like a capable hostess preparing delicious meals for favored guests." A visiting housewife, used to her own cozy kitchen, would feel a "thrill

The
HOMELIKE
KITCHENS
OF
HEINZ

HOMELIKE! That's the word. That just describes them. Thousands and thousands of housewives have inspected them, and all have felt this thrill of recognition. They look like places where good things to eat are being made. They are full of tempting odors. They are white and clean and well cared for. The sunshine lies across the floors. The Heinz girls are busy and neat and cheerful. It is a domestic picture that warms the heart of every woman with a spark of housekeeping instinct.

And that is one thing we have striven for—these homelike surroundings, this domestic spirit. Big and efficient as the kitchens of a nation must be, we have escaped the factory atmosphere. We do not manufacture. We cook and bake as nearly as we can like a capable hostess preparing delicious meals for favored guests. Such is the attitude of all our employees—they too feel this friendly obligation to dispense good cheer.

FIGURE 5.5

While the institutional style generally favored dignified refinement, corporations also sought to humanize themselves by portraying their vast operations as efficient versions of such everyday tasks as "running errands" (see Fig. 5.2) and home cooking.

of recognition" when she experienced the "domestic spirit" of the great Heinz factory (Fig. 5.5).[14]

Unsurprisingly, Bruce Barton was the most enterprising in his use of the "good neighbor" and familiarization ploys. Looking to link the corporation emotionally to the lives and experiences of "plain folks," Barton had identified the corporation's vast resources with the essential work of the familiar postman, doctor, and minister in his 1924 institutional ads for General Motors (see Chapter 4). During

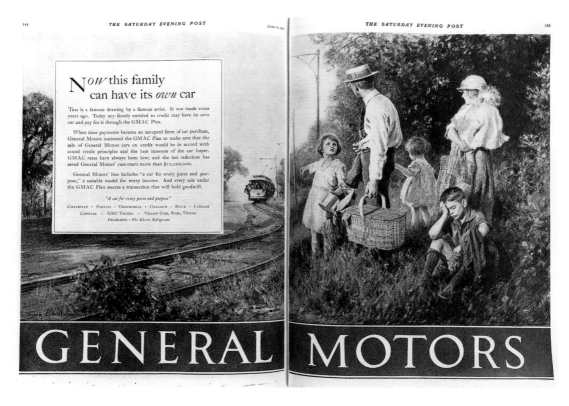

FIGURE 5.6

Barton's agency developed this poignant, humanizing tribute to GM's compassionate installment plan. Proclaiming the image "a famous drawing by a famous artist,"

GM proffered a modernized, consumption-oriented, optimistic version of Jean-François Millet's *Man with the Hoe.*

the next several years Barton's advertising agency had employed noted illustrators to fashion panoramic scenes of the plight of average families without cars. One such family sat forlornly on the front porch watching the neighbors pull out of their driveway for a refreshing weekend spin, while another saw a Sunday picnic come to a dismal end as an overcrowded trolley left them tired and stranded far from home (Fig. 5.6).[15] In 1929 Barton and BBDO again won accolades within the trade for creating a "distinctive and human" institutional atmosphere for GM, in which each picture in the series seemed "to be a cross section of an episode out of the reader's own experience." Depicting "just folks without pose or primp," this GM series promoted the virtues of a second car through images of a young mother romping with her children in a field of flowers and another with her daughter being helped to their car by a friendly neighborhood grocer.[16]

Barton attained new heights in the fusion of the sublime with the prosaic in the ads of a 1927 "anniversary" institutional series for Marshall Field & Company. In "The Man Behind the Counter at the Crossroads," he personalized this giant

The above Poem
was written by Irvin Clay Lambert,
for thirty years an employe
of Marshall Field & Company

FIGURE 5.7
Frequently recycled during the
1920s, the poem in this Marshall
Field ad epitomized the elevated
language of one strain of institutional
advertising. Its refrain, "Builded for
service," completed the effect of the
monumental architecture in evoking
a time-honored institution.

wholesale mart and department store as just one of those thousands of familiar
merchants who shopped for goods by considering "whether this article or that
would appeal to his neighbors at home." In "Fidelia Field" and "Principally Behind the Scenes," Barton and BDO copywriter Tom Cronyn both ennobled and
humanized the Marshall Field store through a tribute to the moral guidance of
mothers everywhere and the reassurance that the American dream lived on at
Marshall Field, where "today's newest delivery boy may be tomorrow's president."[17] But surely the masterstroke in Barton's work to clothe Marshall Field in
the mantle of a national institution was an ad in the series entitled "The Things
Unseen."

Marshall Field had long prided itself on its elevated taste and ornate decor; its
famous stained-glass Tiffany Dome prompted the store to appoint itself "Cathedral of All the Stores" (see Fig. 1.2). As early as 1917 it had incorporated a poem
with that title into its advertising (Fig. 5.7).[18] Now Barton and Cronyn seized on
one of the store's customary practices to confirm its qualifications for both the
title of cathedral and that of national institution. Marshall Field's owners had come
from an "old fashioned background," this ad revealed. Like most folks, they liked
to hold on to some of their devout family traditions. That was why Marshall Field
executives not only insisted that the store remain closed on Sundays, but they even
pulled down the shades to mask the allure of its valuable show windows. This
selfless act, a deliberate sacrifice of commercial advantage, ensured that passersby
would not be distracted from Sunday thoughts of home and church by the emotions that the sensuous materialism of Field's window displays would stimulate.[19]

The store distributed some six thousand proofs of this ad to churches and other religious organizations; it was pleased to learn of the many sermons the ad had inspired. In addition to "widespread favorable comment . . . including requests of proofs from many retail merchants who dealt with Field's Wholesale business," the ad had produced "a noticeably good effect on the personnel" of Marshall Field. Moreover, through the "inspirational editorials" that its institutional ads represented, the company ensured that its name would not simply denote "a department store in Chicago, Illinois." Rather, it would be "known as a national institution."[20]

The Marshall Field ads, although homey in appeal, maintained an elevated tone, a dignified format, and sufficient white space to achieve a "suitable for framing" ambience. Through the rhetorical negotiation of a simple human interest story or an analogy to everyday life, Barton had again displayed how companies ranging from General Motors to giant wholesalers and retailers could both humanize themselves and convey their status as powerful public benefactors. Marshall Field's spiritual sensitivity to "the things unseen," and its work as a neighborly merchant to unite the nation by breaking down geographic barriers, were just the qualities, Barton's agency pointed out, that had enabled this institution to rise not merely to the pinnacle of commercial success but above mere commercialism—to become the "Cathedral of All the Stores."[21]

Equilibrium in the House of Squibb

In November 1921 the pharmaceutical firm of E. R. Squibb & Sons, in the text of a lengthy advertisement adorned only with an ornate border, recounted a tale passed down from ancient Persia (Fig. 5.8). "Hakeem, the Wise One," venerated and respected for his astute counsel, had once been approached by a young man who had spent his money freely but unwisely. Hakeem advised him, somewhat cryptically, "'A thing that is bought or sold has no value unless it contain that which cannot be bought or sold. Look for the Priceless Ingredient.'" In the archaic language of legend the text then related the sage's reply to the young man's inevitable inquiry as to the nature of this Priceless Ingredient: "Spoke then the Wise One: 'My son, the Priceless Ingredient of every product in the market-place is the Honor and Integrity of him who makes it.'"[22]

Here was institutional advertising of the most elevated tone. Yet it embodied a veiled merchandising strategy as well as a parade of ego-enhancing company aphorisms. Squibb was trying to sell exactly what "cannot be bought and sold"—its corporate reputation, or corporate image. Up to the 1920s Squibb had advertised only in medical journals, never in general magazines or newspapers. It had marketed 90 percent of its products directly to hospitals or through doctors' prescriptions. But now it was rapidly expanding its line of nonprescription drugs and household products—from talcum powder and cold cream to cod-liver oil and vitamin supplements—and packaging them for over-the-counter sales.[23]

Even with this aggressive move into consumer products, the heart of Squibb's business remained prescription, or "ethical," drugs. This meant that its fortunes lay largely in the hands of doctors and pharmacists. Squibb wished to expand its over-the-counter sales without sacrificing its standing among these professionals. In short, it sought broader commercial success without incurring any "taint of commercialism" and without arousing the wrath of doctors for luring customers into

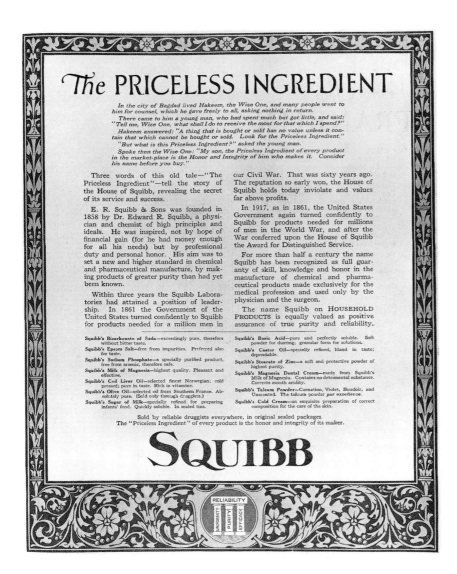

FIGURE 5.8

An all-print ad, if sufficiently ornate in design and profound in message, could convey the image of a leading social institution. The "Priceless Ingredient" in every Squibb product was "the honor and integrity of its maker."

FIGURE 5.9
Neglect and carelessness had met
their match in the figure of the
dentist, Squibb augustly proclaimed.
While eulogizing its professional
customers, the company also
advertised its institutional stature
by evoking classical civilizations
and the notion of the "masterpiece."

habits of "self-medication." In its effort to enshrine all its products under the single halo of its standing with the medical and dental professions, Squibb chose scientific authority and purity as the qualities guaranteed by its "priceless ingredient" of corporate integrity.[24]

The Squibb corporation embarked on a deliberate image-building campaign in 1921 for reasons only superficially parallel to those that would soon motivate General Motors and General Electric. Like GM and GE, Squibb was expanding the line of goods it marketed directly to the consumer. Unlike either of these emerging industrial giants, however, Squibb was also avidly seeking to safeguard its image among a narrow group of professional customers. Moreover, Squibb was not struggling with major problems of internal cohesion. Nor was it a Wall Street firm that needed to personalize itself to compensate for such origins. Although no longer managed by the Squibb family, the firm was still privately held. It retained the family name and used it to identify all products sold directly to consumers. Many of its "priceless ingredient" ads helped sustain the aura of the founder's righteous devotion to purity through stories of Dr. Squibb's indignant rejection of all inferior ingredients. Because of these unique circumstances, Squibb exemplifies yet another of the varied motives that inspired the construction of widely publicized corporate images.[25]

The elevated aura that generally characterized institutional advertising in the 1920s found its consummate expression in the sequence of Squibb campaigns. As part of its studied contempt for lowly commercial aspirations, the company took to calling itself the "House of Squibb," apparently to connote both a long aristocratic heritage and a gentlemanly concern for personal reputation. The elegant yet refined borders of its ads accentuated the tone set by the stately cadences of their headlines and the solemn profundity of their maxims.[26] Lofty adages such as "The Master Formula of every worthy business is honor, integrity and trustworthiness" and "Pride of product is greater than . . . pride of profit" reinforced the unrelenting high-mindedness of the campaign.[27]

The subsequent institutional campaigns of 1924 and 1925 paired such moralizing with theatrical settings. In "Decay and the Masterpiece" the crumbling ruins of a Greek temple provided a suitably elevated backdrop for a tribute to the "men who fight with the ardor of idealists for the preservation of beauty"—the nation's dentists (Fig. 5.9). More mundane but equally dramatic were ads such as "Emergencies Often Arise at Night" and "A Mother's Responsibility," which praised the woman who avoided "uncertain medicinal products" and declined to use anything "that is not approved by her physician." In a message aimed at two prime audiences, consumers seeking the security of expert authority and the doctors themselves, Squibb presented a responsible housewife proudly displaying her medicine cabinet (visibly packed with Squibb products) to her family physician. The headline read: "I *knew* you would approve, Doctor" (Fig. 5.10).[28]

In the late 1920s Squibb concluded that radio was a sufficiently dignified medium for the promotion of its image of scientific reliability. While a "purely entertainment program" would have been "quite out of keeping" with Squibb's public image, it could properly and altruistically sponsor a series of talks on "preventative medical subjects." The twenty-three prominent doctors who delivered these "Priceless Ingredient Talks," Squibb disclosed, did so "without compensation, just because of public spirit." Squibb did not mention any specific products on these programs, but it concurrently promoted its over-the-counter products in print ads that emphasized Squibb's tradition of "close and constant co-operation with the medical profession."[29]

Just in case any doctors or dentists had failed to appreciate its efforts, Squibb clearly revealed its strategy in its house organs and in its ads in the *Journal of the American Medical Association.* Addressing members of the AMA, Squibb pointed out that its ads for cod-liver oil "do not tell the reader when or how to use it . . . because that is the unquestioned province of the physician." In one 1929 ad in the AMA journal, Squibb assured doctors that it was actually "telling the layman how completely his physician is equipped to guard him from disease." Thus, by recounting the advances of medical science, its ads served "to draw closer the bond of confidence between physician and patient."[30]

In its trade publication, the *Squibb Message,* Squibb assured its audience of professional druggists that pharmacy was "primarily a profession" and, like the House of Squibb itself, "only secondarily a business." Squibb ads were devised to "help increase the prestige of pharmacists" and to emphasize "the difference between professional and commercial service." Such an appeal to "the druggist's pride in his

"I *knew* you would approve, Doctor"

MEDICINE CABINETS that are "100 per cent Squibb" are replacing the proprietary medicine Noah's arks in the homes of thinking people everywhere. And the family physician nods in approbation.

For the medicine cabinet is tremendously important. It is the little apothecary-shop-in-the-home; the instant-available source of household products for emergency needs. Certainly no place for products of unknown origin or doubtful value.

Physicians know Squibb Products. Prescribe them daily in their own practice. And they know the House behind those products. They know that since the inception of the business in 1858, E. R. Squibb & Sons have never compromised with quality.

Little wonder, therefore, that physicians and pharmacists alike are always glad to say a good word for any product bearing the

Squibb label. Extreme purity and correct strength are essentials of every product of the House of Squibb. The "priceless ingredient" presupposes that!

Put your house in order. Begin with the medicine cabinet. Reject the worthless, the nondescript. Restock with products that are above suspicion — those bearing the purity-mark, "Squibb." To be doubly sure, insist upon the original Squibb packages.

Then you may open the door of your medicine cabinet, with everything to reveal and nothing to conceal. Then you may say, and be sure of your ground: "I *knew* you would approve, Doctor."

Squibb's Bicarbonate of Soda—Free from all impurities; without bitter taste. Will not irritate the stomach.
Squibb's Epsom Salt—More agreeable to take than the ordinary unpurified market product.
Squibb's Castor Oil—Purified by special process. It is remarkably free from that nauseating taste.
Squibb's Boric Acid—Granular for solutions, or soft powder for dusting. A soothing, mild antiseptic.
Squibb's Milk of Magnesia—A superior corrective for acid mouth and stomach. For children and adults.
Squibb's Dental Cream—Made with Squibb's Milk of Magnesia. Protects the teeth from Acid Decay. Heals tender gums.
Squibb's Cold Cream—An exquisite preparation of correct composition for the care of the skin. Will not become rancid. Does not grow hair.

E. R. Squibb & Sons, 80 Beekman Street, New York, Manufacturing Chemists to the Medical and Dental Professions since 1858.

SQUIBB

THE "PRICELESS INGREDIENT" OF EVERY PRODUCT IS THE HONOR AND INTEGRITY OF ITS MAKER

FIGURE 5.10
In a less exalted style, Squibb implied to consumers the endorsement of its products by expert authority, at the same time ingratiating itself with doctors by suggesting that users should seek their advice.

status as a professional man," noted the agency leader William Benton, reflected the fact that the average druggist had actually "drifted so far away from the professional point of view, and is keenly aware of this drifting, that he likes to be complimented, to boost up his falling prestige." Regarding the slogan of National Pharmacy Week, "Your Druggist Is More Than a Merchant," Benton explained: "We do not think he is, but he likes to think he is, and upon this desire of his we can base a very strong appeal for his cooperation." Although Squibb was not quite so caustic in its outlook, it neglected no opportunity to flatter the drugstore proprietors.[31]

Squibb's commitment to the ideal of pharmacy as "primarily a profession and only secondarily a business" also complemented its well-publicized battle against the proliferating chain stores on behalf of the "old-time professional drug-store." Squibb counted on its corporate image to support the high prices of its products. The chains might damage its market in two ways: by selling lower-priced competing products and by advertising Squibb household products at low prices as "loss leaders," thus undermining the company's profits and prestige. Squibb saw its fortunes tied to traditional retailing by druggists who appreciated quality and made their recommendations count among their customers. For a period Squibb even encouraged druggists to unite with Squibb as its "partners" in a profit-sharing and stockholding plan. As Squibb explained to the trade, its institutional advertising educated the public about the need for purity and thus helped pharmacists build a business on the foundation of a full line of superior products. It would stand to reason that an emphasis on quality, integrity, and scientific expertise should also appeal to pharmacists and doctors whose own status was based on public perceptions of, and respect for, those same features.[32]

For all the high-mindedness of its ads and for all its emphasis on cooperation with doctors and pharmacists, Squibb never ignored the sales dimension of its institutional campaign. The Squibb sales force, like most of their colleagues in other businesses, very likely doubted the efficacy of institutional advertising. Certainly Squibb executives expended considerable energy to counteract a skepticism they suspected within their sales force and among their customers. "Druggists Gain by Squibb Plan of Publicity," it assured the drugstore proprietors after only six months of the campaign. "Bring the *Advertising Portfolio* into play," it goaded its salesmen. "Show the striking illustration of the magnificent Squibb Laboratories. Your customers will marvel at their magnitude. Let them see the new Squibb Building on Fifth Avenue. There is a last monument to 'The Priceless Ingredient.'" The company's most successful salesmen, it insisted, were those who had "sold the Institution of Squibb."[33]

From the outset the Squibb institutional advertisements carried a full list of Squibb household products at the bottom of the page or sometimes a panoramic "family picture" of the line of products. Although the campaign emphasized Squibb's philanthropic commitment to service through quality, the company itself characterized the effort as "a selling plan for quality." When it embarked on its series of institutional radio programs, Squibb unsubtly reminded its sales force of the "value to your customers and to you of this new Squibb service." The *Squibb Sales Bulletin* admonished its readers: "This service is costing the House of Squibb a large amount of money and while in providing it we are rendering a service of inestimable value to humanity, you should never lose sight of the fact that any money spent for advertising must bring direct or indirect returns in the way of profits on increased business."[34]

With profits thus fused with philanthropy, Squibb institutional advertising reached a zenith by the early 1930s in the portrayal of the corporation as an agent of public service. In "That People May Live and Be Happy" (1931), Squibb announced that it was "more a professional institution than a commercial business." The ad further explained that "those who serve medicine also serve humanity. Theirs can never be an ordinary business. Nor can their success be measured by commercial standards. The conscientious maker of medicinal products must combine the ideas of the scientist with the pride of the artist . . . forgetting profit, remembering only quality of product."[35]

Notwithstanding the spuriousness of its claims to an indifference to profit, Squibb's ongoing image campaign did actually influence company policy. Public relations advisors had often piously asserted that public statements of high purpose could virtually compel a corporation to live up to its image. More realistically, a recent comparative study of corporate cultures asserts that "when people publicly espouse a particular point of view, they become much more likely to behave consistent with that point of view *even if they did not previously hold that point of view.*" In the case of Squibb the campaign simply gave broad dissemination to a self-image long steeped in company tradition, that of cooperation with the medical profession. But new opportunities in the 1920s to market nonprescription products had

THEY SHALL SERVE MANKIND FOREVER

These are the mighty dead who gave man victory over death. Because of them, we can control diseases that sap and destroy the lives of mankind—smallpox and diphtheria, tuberculosis and typhoid, and many hazards of surgery and childbirth.

Millions who are alive today owe life and health to these discoverers, and to the great army of medical science, of yesterday and today; the army of which these, are but a few of the shining leaders.

Their work shall never be forgotten

humanity, to whom they brought inestimable gifts. The torch of knowledge they pass on will never dim, but burn on brighter.

The greatest advances achieved by medical science have been made in the past seventy-

five years. During this three-quarters of a century the House of Squibb has worked in constant service to the medical profession.

E. R. SQUIBB & SONS
Manufacturing Chemists to the Medical Profession since 1858

FIGURE 5.11

Even in the depression years, Squibb continued to devote a significant part of its advertising budget to preserving its image as a distinguished institution, one whose service paid homage to those memorialized here.

made it tempting for Squibb to adopt a more overtly commercial posture. George Flanagan surmises that Squibb turned to institutional advertising in 1921 primarily to "counteract a negative image once induced by its own over-enthusiastic tooth-paste advertising." In 1928, still struggling to bridge the gap between ethical drugs and household products, Squibb even split its sales force so that one segment could promote prescription drugs to doctors and pharmacists while another could more aggressively merchandise products ranging from perfume to "Vitavose."[36]

In 1931, during an internal power struggle, Vice President Theodore Weicker lamented that in recent years the original Squibb ideals had "at times been crowded out of their true position" in the rush for larger profits. The time had come, Weicker insisted, to take a stand against those who asked, "'Why shouldn't our salesmen carry anything that's sold in the drug store?'" Urging the company to recommit itself to "the field of medicinal specialties created by scientific research and introduced . . . through professional use," Weicker called successfully for renewed fidelity to a corporate image upheld by nearly a decade of institutional advertising.[37]

In fact, the effusive claims to high-minded service and noncommercialism in the 1931 ads may have directly reflected Weicker's struggle to hold the company to a central concentration on products marketed to doctors and pharmacists. In a report to company executives in September, Weicker vigorously warned that "home-doctoring with products launched primarily for commercial exploitation" would surely decline in the face of further scientific and medical advance. The firm had only to consult its own carefully constructed corporate image to recognize that it could best position itself within the drug market by adhering to its declared status as a "professional institution" (Fig. 5.11).[38]

A Tower of Service: The Metropolitan Life Insurance Company

Squibb's institutional advertising, although it offered moral and intellectual edification, could not make the paramount claim of having provided a great public service in the very process of disseminating a corporate image. That distinction was reserved for the Metropolitan Life Insurance Company, which had launched its own prestige-minded, yet uniquely "altruistic," institutional campaign in the early 1920s.

Beginning in August 1922 with advertisements in twenty-nine national magazines, from *Women's Home Companion* to *Detective Story,* Metropolitan Life displayed nearly every mode and motive of the emerging lexicon of institutional advertising. Metropolitan ads sought to influence political opinion, build employee morale and corporate consciousness, establish a reputation for community service, and promote the ideals of welfare capitalism. Moreover, while the company basked in warm praise for the "unselfishness" of its institutional advertising, its executives alerted Metropolitan's local agents to the uses of the campaign in stimulating insurance sales. Widespread acclaim for the campaign from the public and from the advertising profession seemed to confirm that Metropolitan Life could accomplish all these goals while reaping the psychological rewards of recognition for its indisputable service of educating the public.[39]

The "social conscience" tenor of the Metropolitan Life campaign arose logically from the company's particular position within the American insurance industry. Metropolitan Life had originated as a company devoted almost exclusively to the sale of "industrial" insurance—very small policies offered to working-class families. The premiums, assessed weekly to keep them small, were collected by a multitude of Metropolitan agents who made constant rounds of their policyholders' homes and tenements. This mode of collection accommodated the economic circumstances of Metropolitan's primary customers, who could not save ahead for larger payments. It also reflected the company's sense of a need to maintain a frequent presence to prevent an unacceptable rate of lapses by those living so close to the margin.

If Metropolitan agents sometimes prodded their clients to invest in a degree of security they could ill afford—Metropolitan was accused of "robbing the poor" because of the exorbitant costs of its insurance—the company also took a special interest in the health and work conditions of its policyholders. The continual face-to-face contact of its agents with the immigrant urban masses ensured that the company would at least remain conscious of their afflictions and the insecurities of their everyday environment. Before the end of the nineteenth century, Metropolitan Life had begun to distribute pamphlets on health in industrial areas. In its own interests, as well as those of its policyholders, it promoted incipient forms of workmen's compensation.[40]

This particular sensitivity to conditions that threatened good health, together with the introduction of a large female workforce in clerical positions in its home office, may have led Metropolitan to institute a variety of employee welfare programs at an early date. It created a lunchroom for clerks in 1893 and built a gymnasium in the home office in 1894. A staff savings program, a glee club, employee locker rooms, a vacation savings fund, and noon-hour dancing were introduced over the next decade and a half. "Mother Metropolitan," as the company sometimes called itself, provided women clerks with a sewing room and expert advice if they wished to stay after working hours to make their own clothes. Its early welfare measures also encompassed workplace regulations that seem harshly restrictive in retrospect—separate building entrances, hallways, and elevators for women, a ban on women leaving the building during lunchtime without special permission, and a policy that "women clerks [were] not allowed to take down their hair in the office nor in the lavatories." By the conventions of the era, however, such paternalistic constraints were seen to protect young women during working hours, when their reputations were unguarded by family.[41]

Amid this attention to employee welfare, and with its agents instructed to act not only as premium collector but also as "counselor and friend" to each policyholder, Metropolitan Life took a decisive step in 1909 to define its corporate image: it created a "Welfare Division," hiring social worker Lee K. Frankel away from the Russell Sage Foundation to head the program. More than a decade before it would begin to disseminate its corporate image through advertising, the company already sought to confirm a "modern popular conception" that insurance companies were "no longer business enterprises but social institutions."[42]

Metropolitan president Haley Fiske's interest in workmen's compensation had initially brought him into contact with Frankel. As a former director of the United Hebrew Charities in New York City, Frankel was well known as a social worker and reformer. The Russell Sage Foundation had sponsored his trip to Europe in 1908 to study workers' insurance. Frankel and other social reformers toyed briefly with the idea of involving the Sage Foundation in the insurance business as an experiment in social amelioration.[43] Fiske was quick to recognize both a threat and an opportunity. He had watched apprehensively the advance of state involvement in various forms of insurance in Europe. During an era of reform enthusiasm private insurers were likely to sense that the preoccupation of leading American social workers with European models did not bode well for their firms.

But European trends might be averted in the United States, Fiske concluded, if private enterprise tackled social insurance with enlightened activism. He approached Frankel and managed to persuade him that his social reform objectives might be accomplished most rapidly through Metropolitan Life. Here was an institution, Fiske argued, that already served the underprivileged and had thus earned the right to employ, in its very limited advertising, the slogan "the company OF the people, BY the people, FOR the people." With the proper guidance it could promptly transform itself into an effective agency for their social betterment. In his message to policyholders on Frankel's appointment, Fiske solemnly proclaimed: "Insurance, not merely as a business proposition but as a social programme, will be the future policy of the Company."[44]

With this move in 1909 Metropolitan Life had already taken a large step toward institutional status. Like AT&T before it, and like General Motors, General Electric, and Squibb during the 1920s, Metropolitan Life was advancing a claim to represent something beyond the merely commercial. The company's in-house historian suggested as much when he noted how Frankel and the Welfare Division helped transform Metropolitan "from a typical business organization into an institution for social progress." By the time it launched its institutional advertising campaign in 1922, Metropolitan Life had grown used to sweet accolades for service that the other corporations longed to hear. That year *Printers' Ink* matter-of-factly referred to Metropolitan Life as "this business institution — or 'public institution' as it has been described." [45]

Under Frankel's influence Metropolitan quickly expanded its public service activities. On the advice of Lillian Wald, the founder of the Henry Street Settlement House in New York City, Frankel established a Metropolitan brigade of visiting nurses to provide health care and advice to the company's clients. This corps soon became the pride of the company, amassing a record of nearly five million visits to policyholders by the end of the 1920s. Metropolitan launched a campaign to lower infant mortality rates, offered home financing for workers, announced a "war on consumption," and built a sanitarium for its employees. It also expanded its publication and distribution of health pamphlets. The most popular, issued in 1912 as *The Child,* was later reissued as *Your Baby.* Frankel's Welfare Division threw itself into community clean-up campaigns and health demonstrations. It even launched a major experimental program in preventive medicine through community-wide health examinations in Framingham, Massachusetts, in 1916. [46]

As early as 1913, after only four years of work by the Welfare Division, dozens of clergymen were commending Metropolitan Life for the "greatness and grandeur" of its work. Some did not hesitate to characterize the company's service to humanity as "sacred" or "divine." The Right Reverend David H. Greer, Episcopal Bishop of New York, noted the similarity between Metropolitan Life Insurance and the "company" that he represented; both had placed themselves in the service of "a life deeper than the physical . . . 'the soul.'" [47] By 1920 the noted settlement-house worker and director of Chicago Commons, Graham Taylor, could enthusiastically contrast Metropolitan Life with those corporations that people had rightly seen as "soulless." This company, Taylor proclaimed, had been a "principal pivotal corporation" in the movement from "a purely materialistic . . . to a more social and democratic . . . procedure in industrial relations." [48]

The Metropolitan as Social Servant

Metropolitan Life had initiated a dramatic expansion of its social welfare activities during a period in which its competitive position in the industry and its potential markets were changing drastically. At the beginning of the century Metropolitan had ranked far below the "big three" insurance companies: New York Life, Mutual Life, and Equitable. It had begun to write a few "ordinary" policies — the larger policies purchased by those in the middle class and above — but the bulk of its business remained in small industrial policies for the working class. Then, in 1905–6, the Armstrong Committee investigations revealed scandalous misconduct by the "big three" insurance companies, prompting temporary legal restrictions on their acquisition of new business.[49]

Metropolitan Life seized upon these restrictions as a "veritable springboard" to the ordinary life insurance field. George Gaston, second vice president, regaled the company's agents with "good and sufficient reasons why the choicest quality of Ordinary for large sums should come to the Metropolitan." "It belongs as much to us," he proclaimed in 1908, "as to any other company." Between 1906 and 1913 Metropolitan agents more than doubled the company's ordinary business, surpassing Equitable's gains by a sixfold margin and more than doubling the concurrent record of New York Life. Soon Metropolitan had outdistanced all the others to become the largest insurance company in the world in terms of total insurance in force. By the beginning of the 1920s it had become number one in ordinary life insurance alone. The space in the home office devoted to ordinary insurance had expanded from "less than a single room" in the mid-1890s to "twenty-three whole floors" in 1923.[50]

As Metropolitan achieved this transformation it prided itself on retaining the social conscience of its proletarian origins. But it now served, and sought further new business from, a "class audience" as well. The company's nursing service and health campaigns had put its agents "on a distinctly higher and better plane," Frankel concluded. The result was "a better agency force," one "equipped to handle life insurance as a social proposition rather than as a purely sordid business enterprise."[51] In its early years Metropolitan had shunned advertising and reached its industrial insurance customers mainly through door-to-door contact by its horde of field agents. But President Fiske did not hesitate to use other means of image building.

The company's many health pamphlets celebrated the power, prosperity, and stability connoted by Metropolitan's palatial headquarters on Madison Avenue, completed in 1909. Crowning this monster of an office building (which had briefly given the company bragging rights as the creator and premier occupant of the world's tallest inhabitable structure) soared the famous Metropolitan Tower. Here Fiske installed a beacon light, visible from all directions, which he christened "The Light That Never Fails." For years the tower, its light beams, and the slogan served as the logo on all Metropolitan publications. That tower, along with the company's health pamphlets and social work, insisted Vice President Gaston, made the Metropolitan "the best-advertised company in the world." President Fiske put it another way. Although the tower had not been built as an advertisement, still it served that purpose well. "We do not have to advertise," he concluded, "for the tower advertises itself." During the era preceding its institutional advertising campaign the Metropolitan's tower proclaimed, in iconic idiom, what the company most wished to have said about itself: "This is a public institution" (Fig. 5.12).[52]

Still, for all the company's social dedication—evident in its elaborate Welfare Division and extensive nursing service—top executives were distressed "to find out how small a proportion of the general public really knows anything about it." In 1922, taking for its text the words "Let your light so shine before men that they may see your good works," the company finally packaged its social programs as the content of a corporate image campaign. Although Frankel had argued that its welfare work should not be viewed as a form of advertising, the company could hardly feel obliged to keep its good deeds a secret! Besides, advertising might advance

An Adventure in Advertising

It Closes the Big Men

"CAN I write him for $50,000?" That was still the question, after Manager TISCHBEIN had worked on his prospect for a month. Then he closed the case in twenty minutes by using *An Adventure in Advertising.* He tells you on page 5 how he did it.

Can you do what he did?

Manager TISCHBEIN thinks you can. He realizes, now, that the book makes the big man believe in you and in your Company.

The messages in the book have reached the public heart. Page after page has been reprinted by other organizations, by newspapers, and by magazines. Health Departments have quoted them; editors have written about them; clergymen have preached from them.

The size of the volume, its character, and its contents make a deep impression; and it is now proving that it has the power to close the big men.

Get a copy from your Manager and give it a thorough trial. See what it will do for you.

METROPOLITAN LIFE INSURANCE COMPANY
NEW YORK

FIGURE 5.12
Here Metropolitan Life merchandised its "tower power" in a magazine directed to its agents. A prestigious stature, symbolized in the big, beautiful skyscraper, could command the patronage of those able to afford larger, more expensive insurance policies.

Metropolitan's welfare services by promoting wider distribution of its health and safety booklets.

In one of its earliest institutional ads, "The Lady with the Lamp," Metropolitan Life placed its service directly within a lineage of social benevolence. Florence Nightingale's lamp, for which wounded soldiers had thankfully watched, symbolized her spirit. This spirit had "illumined the way for the first training school for nurses" and then evoked the "Great Light" that inspired Metropolitan to found the visiting nurse program. Then the lamp's symbol had been re-created in "the great lantern atop the Metropolitan Tower—The Light That Never Fails."[53]

Metropolitan executives heavily stressed the "unselfish" spirit of the ensuing campaign, which was to run for decades, and rightfully claimed credit for disseminating up-to-date health information. Like many other institutional ads, the Metropolitan's adhered to a standard format. During the early years all included the Metropolitan tower light and the signature of President Fiske. Looking back at this series in the 1980s, George Flanagan noted that their "smartly starched typogra-

FIGURE 5.13
Ennobled by the public service of its informative institutional ads, Metropolitan Life could forgo dignified appearances, opting instead for an unpretentious, utilitarian look. Use of the common touch to expand knowledge would generate its own prestige.

phy and their deep seriousness of purpose, combined . . . with a reassuring air of friendly cheerfulness, rather strongly suggested the mood of a well-appointed doctor's office."[54] Metropolitan Life even called attention to the contrast between the simple utilitarianism of its black-and-white institutional ads and the decadent materialism of the "highly colored" consumer goods ads among which they appeared (Fig. 5.13). Although the campaign was "*not* intended to sell insurance—directly," the home office executives informed the field force, still agents could find many ways to employ it in their sales pitches. Metropolitan executives may also have hoped for the benefits that John B. Watson, a noted behaviorist and academic psychologist who had become vice president of the J. Walter Thompson advertising agency, was predicting from the linkage of institutional advertising with insurance company recruitment. Watson observed that insurance companies had great difficulty persuading good men to take positions as agents. Prestige for such companies, he suggested, would mean prestige for those in the selling force and thus would reduce turnover among agents.[55]

Certainly Metropolitan spared no effort in persuading its agents of the benefits the campaign was bestowing on them. Despite the "gatherings of the clan" that the company sponsored to promote corporate "family" cohesion, turnover among agents had been excessive, and executives deplored its cost. To augment its institutional campaign the company launched a new employee publication in 1923, *Tower Talks*. The first issue trumpeted the "lowest ever" turnover of agents while declaring its aim to become "the guide, philosopher and friend of Mother Metropolitan's 15,000 field men." Each issue of *Tower Talks* carried one of the company's institutional ads on its back cover. The high ideals of the advertisements, *Tower Talks* assured the agents, were paving the way in each prospect's mind for "the agent's welcome."[56] Metropolitan vice president Robert Cox explained patiently to the field agents that the ads were not intended to produce immediate orders but to let the public know "what Metropolitan's ideals and aspirations really are." With this repute behind him the agent would find his prospects ready to listen. Moreover, the high tone of the campaign would facilitate his approach to the more lucrative, middle-class prospects. By 1927 the company's sales manager was giving agents step-by-step instructions on how to use the national ads in sales interviews.[57]

The Metropolitan "health and welfare" ads rarely contained any ostensible sales message. In *Printers' Ink*, Vice President Cox noted that the Metropolitan, "as a business institution that has been favored with public patronage," was simply recognizing that it owed the public the wider dissemination of its knowledge of preventive health measures, "without exacting in exchange therefore any sort of trade or business dealings from readers of its advertisements." Indeed, the ads were both informative and socially beneficial. Metropolitan campaigned for vaccinations and boldly explored such diseases as cancer and syphilis in a straightforward way virtually unknown in articles in the family magazines of the day. In less dramatic ads it attacked illiteracy and child labor and promoted regular physical examinations, correct diet, exercise, thrift, and general health consciousness.[58]

In its early use of radio for institutional advertising Metropolitan Life made a very explicit statement about itself by taking a practical approach to public health and associating itself with advances in medical knowledge. Beginning in 1925, when radio was still widely considered inappropriate for direct advertising and effective only in promoting goodwill for the corporate sponsors of programs, Metropolitan Life initiated a program of morning calisthenics. Exploiting the most visible symbol of its benevolent guardianship, Metropolitan built a broadcasting studio in its headquarters tower and entitled its series *Tower Health Exercises*. Each class opened with the sound of a bugle and chimes from the tower. The host, Arthur Bagley, took his audience through their paces with "friendly wisecracks and philosophy." The program distributed exercise pamphlets (crowned with pictures of the tower, of course) and promoted the company's health and welfare booklets (Fig. 5.14). After ten years, *Advertising Age* noted, this "oldest daily feature on the air" had still never made a single commercial announcement.[59]

The clear public service provided by these ads and programs, particularly the many that promoted preventive health care, won Metropolitan Life a reputation as the most philanthropic advertiser of the era. One agency president, Earnest Elmo Calkins, argued that Metropolitan's advertising was "of such public importance that the Government could well afford to carry it on." While publicizing its welfare activities, Metropolitan also pressured other corporations to undertake their own programs of welfare capitalism. In an ad entitled "He's a Great Boss" the company recapitulated the familiar lament about the loss of contact with employees that came with the scale of big business. It then offered a solution. "Some of

FIGURE 5.14
Broadcasts from its tower reinforced
Metropolitan Life's image as a benevolent patriarch—and eventually
matriarch, in the rhetoric of "Mother
Metropolitan"—attending from
above to the health and security
of millions.

the great bosses in America" still earned the trust and affection of workers—even those they had never met—through their programs of group insurance.[60]

The merchandising of Metropolitan's group insurance programs as part of its public service campaign exemplified its subtle fusing of business strategies and political sensibilities. In a positive vein, President Fiske liked to think of group insurance as the ultimate answer to the conflicts between workers and employers. Through such programs Metropolitan could "go to the employers and tell them how to treat their employees" and also "teach the men in the factory that their employer has a heart and cares for them." Where better could businessmen learn what it meant for a company to have a heart and a soul than from "Mother Metropolitan"?[61] But programs to insure employees against disabilities and even against job loss also appealed to Metropolitan as a defensive strategy. Government would soon take over responsibility for unemployment insurance, warned Metro-politan vice president Leroy Lincoln, if private companies did not demonstrate "progressive leadership." In the words of the company historian, Marquis James, Lincoln believed that "humane action by private enterprise was a great dike against socialism."[62]

In 1931, in an attempt to counteract the effects of the depression, Metropolitan Life finally embarked on an advertising campaign aimed directly at sales. But it did so only after a careful study of "the kinds of business advertising which shall be appropriate to the eminence and standing of the Metropolitan," and it segregated the two kinds of copy so that the "dignified" new business ads would not taint the celebrated institutional series by appearing in the same issue of any publication.[63] In late 1932, during the depth of the depression, Metropolitan found another paternalistic mission for its institutional campaign. It would promote "confidence"—a confidence "that will reach into every home and loosen the purse strings that the insidious forces of doubt and depression have tightened."[64]

Such confidence-inspiring ads as "Look Ahead" and "Get Readjusted," Vice President Lincoln pointed out, while "purely altruistic," were "bound to yield added prestige and good will toward this company of ours." They would also boost the morale of the Metropolitan sales force. Lincoln ordered five copies of the proof of "Get Readjusted" sent to each of the company's field agents. He admonished them to memorize it so that they would "find themselves automatically repeating [it]" to themselves and their clients. So completely had the elevated style and public service content of institutional advertising seemed to coincide with the success of Metropolitan business during the 1920s that even during the depression, Metropolitan executives did not hesitate to credit this long campaign for their company's "preeminent position."[65]

The "Fearsome Dignity" of N. W. Ayer

Nothing so underscored the mounting conviction that any business might aspire to be an institution than the claim to that status by one of the leading designers of corporate imagery, the N. W. Ayer & Son advertising agency. Advertising agencies, quite logically, did not attempt to publicize themselves to the public at large. What corporate client would wish for the public to become aware of the "hired gun" it had acquired to shape consumer preferences? Moreover, few businesses had such a reputation for sham and trickery as did advertising agencies. But Ayer found reasons to aspire to the status of an institution, at least within a select circle. After all, why should not an advertising agency—one already engaged in corporate image creation for so august a corporation as AT&T—practice what it preached by fashioning its own corporate image?

Beginning in 1912, on the strength of its three-year association with AT&T, Ayer had begun publicizing its particular expertise in serving companies that sold "service of a public or semi-public nature." As the nation's "oldest, largest and most highly organized" agency, Ayer suggested, it could best offer counsel to corporations faced with "pernicious molestation" from muckrakers and politicians. Ayer prided itself, as its president later affirmed, on "the high character of our customers." The agency often referred to itself as the House of Ayer, serving other "conservative houses" of business. ("'House,' by the way, is spelled with a capital H," sneered an unimpressed critic from a rival agency.)[66]

Given its highly visible, genteel presence, its consummate faith in uplift, and its orientation toward clients who wished to think of themselves as institutions, Ayer concluded in 1919 that institutional advertising in its own name was the obvious

BEAUTY

THE compelling power of beauty has put the civilization of centuries in debt to ancient Greece. Her art and architecture have inspired our proudest creations.

So complete is the influence of beauty over our lives that we can trace our progress by its expression. Beauty has many forms; the perfectly balanced machine and the perfectly sculptured marble each carries the charm of harmony.

The sway of beauty is of greater economic importance today than ever before. Prior to the coming of mass production and standardization the craftsman could cast about until he hit upon a design that pleased the greater number of his little group of consumers.

Now appearance often dictates success or failure, for the whole equipment of a plant may be based on the value of a design; and the value of that design depends upon its ability to please the public.

This meeting of public approval is the severest test to which the manufactured article is subjected. And not the least of it comes through advertising, the great distributor of the evidence of beauty.

Beauty in advertising, and beauty in the thing advertised, are both potential agents in securing consumption. Advertising has capitalized the beauty of the wares of commerce through publishing proof of their desirability.

N. W. AYER & SON, *ADVERTISING HEADQUARTERS*
PHILADELPHIA
NEW YORK   BOSTON   CLEVELAND   CHICAGO

FIGURES 5.15 & 5.16
Here, in the balanced, dignified, squared-off style of "Ayer No. 1," the agency's own institutional ads imparted the high-minded profundity that rival agencies sometimes ridiculed as stilted and pretentious.

next step. By putting itself on the line for the new genre as it financed a long-running institutional campaign on its own behalf, Ayer sought to position itself as the mouthpiece for all advertising, and thus its very epitome. Just as General Motors and General Electric would soon identify themselves with all the contributions their industries made to civilization, Ayer reinforced the reputation it had already gained as the agency for AT&T (and would soon amplify through its institutional ads for Squibb) by stepping forth immodestly as the champion of the entire advertising industry.

In its campaign to "advertise advertising," Ayer employed sage maxims to tout the service that advertising offered the public. In magazines, farm papers, and a total of 1,187 newspapers, large and small, the Ayer ads appeared anonymously. Within the trade, however, Ayer did not neglect to remind "leaders in industry, finance and commercial activities generally" of its contributions to building a "national consumer-consciousness." The agency assembled proofs of these "anonymous" ads in lavish folders and binders to distribute to prospective clients. "There

IMAGINATION

THE spirit of advancement is un- loosed in imagination. Many of the castles built in the air have be- come wonderful realities for the profit of the people.

A man dreamed of a world that was round, and America was discov- ered. A man caught a vision of vast power from a tea kettle, and steam came to our aid.

Men saw through the eyes of their minds great carriers racing across continents and oceans, speech con- veyed thousands of miles, ships fly- ing through space and surging under water. They imagined machines that would write, add, sew, weave, print, picture motion, cut steel, talk; and the things they imagined came to life.

Then men with other imaginations took these creations and multiplied them, by scores, by hundreds, by thousands, by millions; so that it required a nation to consume them.

Yet other men of imagination saw these multiplied products made known to all who read; they saw imagination developed in the many, along with desire to possess. And advertising came to create this desire.

So from the minds of the inventor, the producer, the distributor, along to the creative makers of advertising, there is an unbroken chain of achieve- ment. And not the least important link is advertising, for production is a liability until consumption is as- sured. That is why the experienced imagination of advertising has been so instrumental in making dreams of great industries come true.

That is why advertising is the pro- vider of economic independence to production.

N. W. AYER & SON, *ADVERTISING HEADQUARTERS*
NEW YORK   PHILADELPHIA   CLEVELAND
BOSTON   CHICAGO

are many commercial institutions gaining . . . in opportunity and growth through ideals of service," Ayer noted. These were "of the class we wish to serve." Ayer also published signed advertisements, in a similarly elevated, institutional style, in the trade journals and in such magazines as the *Saturday Evening Post.* Inviting vex- ation, envy, and eventually bemusement by the other agencies, Ayer haughtily dubbed itself "Advertising Headquarters."[67]

Taking the AT&T style to an even higher level, the typical Ayer institutional ad carried a lofty headline such as "Character" or "The Philosopher's Stone" or "Ser- vice." It then explicated the concept through an extended conceit (Figs. 5.15 and 5.16).[68] Critics of Ayer found inviting targets in the pretentiousness and archaic language of these ads. Such passages as "A year is passing. Spent and impotent here, it goes—to be reborn, the infant of the ages" or "Down the sea of the centuries man sails the ship of his dreams, seeking the harbor of happiness" spurred a recip- rocal creativity in parodies.[69] One junior copywriter who defected from Ayer to the J. Walter Thompson agency graphically defined the mystique of the former for the amused edification of his new colleagues: "You will not find any smelly under-wear, bad breath, skin eruptions, discolored teeth, violent coughing, streaming eyes or odoriferous armpits in Ayer copy and art." Such ridicule did not unsettle Ayer. The agency earnestly aspired to have others recognize that contact with Ayer "meant uplift," its president avowed. Did rivals mock N. W. Ayer & Son as too conservative? "Our answer to this," replied the agency, "is that we have much to conserve. . . . Great interests are intrusted to us."[70]

Ayer could legitimately claim, moreover, that many of the corporate image ads it crafted for others—if not those in which it lionized itself—had humanized its clients by describing their complex operations and services in familiar terms. The agency had made a neighbor and small-town democrat out of AT&T; it had dis-tinguished Armour and Company from distant and alienating corporations by hav-ing the giant meatpacker declare simply to the public, "We are your delivery man." In "Even the *Hairs* Are Numbered," it had alluded to the old charge of using all of the hog but the squeal as a folksy way to underscore the company's efficient use of by-products.[71] If Armour and Company warranted the status of national insti-tution because its immense size enabled it to carry out efficiently such everyday, indispensable services, then who could deny the same stature to the advertising agency that interpreted for the public that noble mission?

Radio and the Institutional Style

Just as certain advertising agencies became associated with institutional campaigns, so did certain media. Radio emerged as an advertising medium in the mid-1920s, precisely when an institutional style of advertising came to maturity. Here was a coincidence with consequences. Because of its inherent "intrusiveness" into the midst of home and family, radio was at first regarded as a perilous medium for ad-vertisers, one in which they might easily forfeit their welcome.[72] But when radio manufacturers found it too expensive to continue to finance programming, and when no substantial constituency for government support came forth, the broad-casting stations turned to commercial sponsors.

Almost everyone agreed, at the outset, that such sponsors would have to limit themselves to a short, formal identification on the air and reap their only reward in the public's gratitude for the entertainment they provided. In other words, radio advertising would be institutional advertising in its most pristine form. A com-pany would merely "keep its name before the public" and benefit from whatever pleasing associations the program content afforded.[73] From the standpoint of cor-porate imagery, however, these apparent limitations of radio could still be viewed as advantages. Advertisers had generally turned to magazines rather than news-papers for their institutional advertising—partly for easier access to national cov-erage but also, as an AT&T executive noted, because magazines provided the appropriate setting for the "substantial and dignified" style of an institutional mes-sage. Radio, especially on Sunday evenings, was presumed to offer a similarly re-fined atmosphere. A properly designed program, one advocate of radio advertis-ing observed, could convey the same "suggestion of quality" as did "a beautiful oil painting." As late as 1936 the trade journal *Tide* still stereotyped the institutional style in terms of high art. "Generally, when anybody thinks about institutional ad-vertising," the journal confidently asserted, "he visions impressive color pages, big fine photographs, graceful, high-sounding copy on slick magazine pages. Or he hears a symphony over the radio."[74]

A number of institutional advertisers also looked to radio as a forum in which they could associate themselves with the spread of scientific information. Squibb sponsored professional talks about medical research and dramatic accounts of "medical and surgical achievements"—a conspicuous public service, NBC executives remarked, that Squibb was "extremely anxious to merchandise to the medical profession." General Electric offered talks on "adventures in science" to popularize the work of its research laboratory.[75] Du Pont, while featuring a different product on each broadcast, still adhered to the institutional style by presenting, with "orchestral accompaniment," such talks as "The Many Unusual Ways in Which Chemistry Enters Our Daily Lives." Other institutional advertisers, less concerned with claims to cutting-edge scientific contributions, disseminated "middlebrow culture" or talks on health or food preparation to demonstrate their role as providers of education and practical public service.[76]

Above all, however, the institutional advertisers on radio cultivated the public with "good music." More often than not, classical or semiclassical music provided the suitable atmosphere, just as had elevated prose and white space on the printed page.[77] Usually such programs carried a long "intermission" message from the sponsor in the form of a statement of corporate ideals. Although a corporation might seek a wider audience through more popular symphonic music, the institutional aura had to be respected. As the General Motors sales manager put it in the mid-1930s, a clear cultural "line of demarcation" distinguished GM's institutional program from those of its car divisions. A publicist for GM warned NBC in 1937 that the GM symphonic program "has gone as popular as we dare go" and that "any further bending in the direction of so-called popular music would seriously interfere with the future consideration of such a program as an institutional one."[78]

Significantly, institutional advertising over the radio often seemed to exert its most evident effects indirectly—by fostering internal corporate cohesion. NBC dubbed broadcast advertising "the great coordinator." It cited the General Motors and General Electric musical programs as prime examples of the way that radio, by speaking in a single voice on behalf of both the parent company and its dealers or affiliated organizations, could nurture the corporation's "family ties." Similarly, the network described how the *Cities Service Concert Orchestra* and *Cities Service Cavaliers* had helped "weld the minds of such a vast assemblage into a real unity, conscious of its mass power." Letters from Cities Service employees in "distant outposts" confirmed that the company's radio programs made them "feel as much a part of their great entity as the workers at Wall Street Headquarters." Daniel Starch, in a survey publicized by Metropolitan Life Insurance, observed that nearly all radio advertisers were impressed by the extent to which their ads inspired cooperation by the company's dealers. Once again corporate leaders found a way to use external public relations to promote a "corporation consciousness" within.[79]

Some Stratagems through Science: Du Pont and Ford

Whereas allusions to high culture defined the institutional style in its early years, eventually scientific themes would predominate in these ads. Even a corporation such as Du Pont, which had remained skeptical about the need to spend large sums for image creation, could speculate that by associating itself with the publicly anointed term "science," it might reinforce claims of high quality in its products, attract talented young scientists and engineers, and create a corporate image of future-mindedness. One way to cultivate this association was to reject the old "founder and factory" mode of corporate fanfare and publicize something just as tangible, yet more expressive of long-range vision and public service: the company's research laboratory. By making known its devotion to research and testing, a corporation could inspire confidence in products that the consumer could not evaluate directly before purchase. By promoting its research laboratory it could implant in the public mind the impression that any new product developed there would represent state-of-the-art technology and a contribution to public welfare.

Companies like AT&T, Western Electric, and General Electric had something to brag about in basic research, even though their laboratories gave primary attention to practical applications. General Motors initially publicized its proving grounds more than its research laboratories, saying less about science than about the rigors of its testing procedures.[80] Of all of the technology-intensive companies, however, Du Pont—a corporation that still considered its main business to be selling its products to other manufacturers and thus saw little need to craft a public image of itself for either political or marketing purposes—was the first to scout the possibilities of making the laboratory the centerpiece of its corporate image.

During 1921 and 1922 Du Pont briefly suspended its disbelief in the usefulness of institutional advertising and mounted a national campaign to enshrine the figure of the chemical engineer. Each selection in this explicitly numbered series of ads carried an idealized representation of the aproned scientist. "This is today's Prometheus," the first ad in the series announced. Anchored like a statue to a nondescript sculpted base, the chemical engineer, sleeves rolled up in testimony to his commitment to practical experiment, gazed upward in heroic profile at the test tube in his hand (Fig. 5.17). Du Pont eschewed any subtleties, bluntly associating the heroic chemical engineer with its own "extensive chemical staff." The ads unblushingly claimed: "His visions have crowded the highways of commerce!" and "In little more than a Century, He has advanced Civilization by Ten Centuries!"[81]

Du Pont's short-lived campaign aimed mainly to promote the company's image in the eyes of potential employees among young college graduates. It further sought to allay public suspicions that Du Pont was using its war profits to expand threateningly into "unrelated fields of effort"; the figure of the chemical engineer showed how chemical research united everything in its emerging "family of products." Thus, the series not only served to cultivate "the nation's goodwill," the company advised its employees. It also, by linking Du Pont's "many products, so different in appearance and in use," enhanced the "sales value" of the "Du Pont Oval, the company's unifying logo."[82]

Before the end of the 1920s other corporations, with wider goals, would enshrine their laboratories as corporate icons. Both General Electric and Western Electric increasingly centered their corporate images around their laboratories, generating an aura of forward-looking, scientific adeptness. When critics complained of the vagueness of this institutional style, the advertisers linked their claims to public service to a specific element in the corporation's activities.[83] The obvious contribution of an image of scientific expertise to the marketing of new products deflected

"Came Prometheus, the Fire-Bringer, he who matched
from the sun's glowing chariot thrice-precious fire
and brought it, hidden in a fennel-stalk, to earth,
that men might live like gods in its pleasant warmth."
(Transl. Greek Myth)

THIS is today's Prometheus . . . . . Bringer
of comforts . . . . The Chemical Engineer!

One of civilization's pioneers, it is he who has
brought to mankind comforts and conveniences
that a century ago were only wishes.

It is he who, searching in the hidden depths of
Nature, has bared her secrets and laid at the feet
of the world's industries new substances, new uses
for them, new ways of using the present materials of commerce in the satisfying of man's wants.

It is he who, watching on the frontiers of science,
has seen in his test-tubes visions of industries yet
unborn that are to drive commerce to the far corners of the earth in the service of man's needs.

The world's debt to The Chemical Engineer is
one that can never be paid.

This is one of a series of advertisements published
that the public may have a clearer understanding
of E. I. du Pont de Nemours & Co. and its products.

E. I. DU PONT DE NEMOURS & COMPANY, Inc. *Wilmington, Del.*
TRADE (DUPONT) MARK

FIGURE 5.17
Calling attention to this ad as "one of a series," Du Pont moved to unite its increasing variety of products in the public's understanding. Amid elevating white space, it constructed an all-embracing corporate persona as "today's Prometheus"—the chemical engineer.

other criticism. Soon this tactical merger of science, corporate image, and practical merchandising found even more sophisticated expression in a campaign by the
Ford Motor Company. Once again the architect of corporate uplift was the Ayer
agency.

In 1927, in response to General Motors' massive inroads on its market share in
the lower-price automotive field, Ford undertook a retooling and redesigning effort to launch the new Model-A. At the same time, basically for defensive purposes, the company began to familiarize the public with its visions for the future
of commercial aviation through an award-winning series of institutional advertisements. Subsequently heralded as "rich and visionary" ads that had served as "a
major factor in popularizing flying among the reading public," they were strikingly illustrated and bore such typically exalted or alliterated N. W. Ayer titles as
"Lift Up Your Eyes" and "When Fledglings Fly" (Fig. 5.18).[84]

Since Ford was the world's largest manufacturer of commercial airplanes in 1928,
the promotion of air transportation seemed sufficient reason for such a campaign.
But an internal document at N. W. Ayer suggests a more intriguing objective. Dur-

LIFT UP YOUR EYES !

How long ago did Wilbur Wright circle the drill field at Fort Myer while a few score of astonished witnesses stared open-mouthed at the sight of this first man to fly with wings for more than an hour? . . . confidently over the sands of Sahara and the Great Arabian Desert, where only the camel had dared venture before. . . . He has skimmed the terrible dark jungles of the Amazon, and scaled high above the silent places of Alaska. . . . He has flown *the first outstanding example of a generation that is born air-conscious!* Just as the past generation was born to steam, accepting railway transportation as an accomplished fact—and just as the present generation has accepted the aut~

FIGURE 5.18

As in its earlier choice of a balanced layout for the institutional ads of AT&T, the Ayer agency adopted a dignified format and exalted headlines as it associated Ford with cutting-edge technological vision and competence.

ing 1926, the Ayer memo notes, rumors abounded, "evidently started and circulated by the competition," that the Ford Motor Company "had lost its engineering ability." Perhaps this was why General Motors was forging ahead. Suspicions of a lack of engineering expertise at Ford might cripple sales of the new Model-A. Charles Lindbergh's dramatic solo flight across the Atlantic in May 1927, according to the Ayer memo, gave Ford a chance to rebound and squelch the rumors.[85]

Ford had been quietly developing a capacity in aviation. Now it was decided, probably sooner than the company would otherwise have intended, to parade this activity before the public. Ayer reported that the impressive series of aviation ads had the "indirect effect of definitely answering the stories." Although they never explicitly discussed engineering expertise, "subconsciously" these institutional ads, by proclaiming the future of aviation, reassured the public that Ford was still technologically adept. As the Ayer memo summarized the strategy, "How could he [Ford] be in the forefront of such a new and outstanding development in motor transportation unless he had the engineering ability in his organization to develop it?"[86]

Although I have found no other evidence about the campaign strategy to corroborate the Ayer memo, the notion of "effect through indirection" (or even misdirection) also characterized such experiments in institutional advertising as the Pennsylvania Railroad campaign of 1927 (discussed in Chapter 3) and the Bruce Barton strategy at General Motors in the early 1920s (discussed in Chapter 4). But less sophisticated approaches would lead, by the beginning of the 1930s, to a crescendo of noisy attacks on the vagueness and pomposity of the institutional style in corporate image creation.

"Elegant Inanities" and "Rhetorical Piffle"

No attempt to characterize the main elements of an institutional style in the 1920s can do justice to the multitude of motives and strategies that inspired the decade's flourishing campaigns of corporate image creation. By the end of the 1920s, participation in the deliberate quest to reshape corporate identities extended from the great national and international monopolies such as AT&T and Alcoa to such relatively provincial "institutions" as local department stores. Even such business-is-business, manufacturing-oriented companies as Republic Steel were buying full-color pages in the *Saturday Evening Post* to dramatize their "new spirit of service" (Fig. 5.19).[87] In fact, by the late 1920s corporations had begun to employ so many venues and media to trumpet their ideals and service, as one AT&T executive observed, that the seasoned practitioners in the field found themselves hard-pressed to hold attention for their now-conventional messages. "Our Institutional copy stood out in the old days," one AT&T publicity officer reflected at the end of the 1920s, "first because it was so very excellently done, and second, because no one else was doing it." Another AT&T officer lamented that "most readers no longer linger over a favorite magazine as they did when magazines were few in number and advertisers were few and small." To make an impact, greater ingenuity or more intensive repetition was now required.[88]

The dominant institutional style of the 1920s was one of uplift. It reflected the pride that agency copywriters, art directors, and executives took in their emerging profession, one that associated them with the aspirations of the great corporations for recognition as high-minded, service-oriented institutions. But for the down-to-earth, self-defined realists in the agencies, this style was stilted and ineffectual. All agreed that institutional advertising afforded copywriters the greatest latitude in demonstrating their virtuosity. But advertising professionals debated whether this freedom was a good thing for the reputation of advertising. An institutional campaign, the trade journal *Tide* reflected wistfully, represented "the last refuge of the copywriter." Commenting on the colorful and literary "prologues" so common in institutional ads, a writer in *Printers' Ink* observed: "It is here . . . that the copywriter may spread his rhetorical wings, as it were. . . . He can engage in unaccustomed extravaganzas of speech, with no one to criticize."[89]

No one to criticize? Not quite. In 1933 an agency president defined the particular vulnerability of institutional advertising to hard-nosed skepticism when he described it as "a form of presentation that is singularly attractive to any advertising writer because it does not involve the acid test of profitable turn-over." In the course of the many denunciations of the pompousness and ineffectuality of 1920s

Part of the Youngstown plant of the Republic Steel Corporation. Other Republic plants are located in Cleveland, Warren, Niles, Canton and Massillon, Ohio; Chicago and Moline, Ill.; Pittsburgh; Birmingham, Ala.; Buffalo and Brooklyn, N. Y.; Gary and Muncie, Ind.; Detroit; Hamilton, Ont.

... A NEW SPIRIT OF SERVICE

When a group of leading steel producers united to form the Republic Steel Corporation, they created one of America's most important industrial units—a new giant in steel. ∤ ∤ Assets exceed $335,000,000. ∤ ∤ Properties include rich iron ore deposits, coal mines, limestone and dolomite reserves, thirteen blast furnaces, ten modern steel plants, six tremendous batteries of coke ovens, rolling mills, finishing and manufacturing departments. ∤ ∤ Already Republic is the world's largest producer of alloy steels. It has the greatest capacity for the

production of Enduro Nirosta KA2, the perfected stainless steel. Its new electric welding process is revolutionizing the making of steel pipe. ∤ ∤ Its highly specialized metallurgical research division has been incorporated as a separate unit to foster the development of new steels and new uses for steel with a constant aim toward greater values and improved products. ∤ ∤ These tremendous facilities, vitalized by a spirit of service and progress, are destined to bring far-reaching benefits both to industry and to the public at large.

REPUBLIC STEEL CORPORATION
HEADQUARTERS: YOUNGSTOWN, OHIO

FIGURE 5.19

To gain attention while professing statesmanlike service, Republic Steel recognized the power of what John Stilgoe has termed the "industrial zone aesthetic." U.S. Steel would later exploit such imagery in technicolor institutional films.

institutional advertising from the vantage point of the hard-bitten 1930s, one trade critic touched on both the most enticing and the most berated aspects of the institutional style. "It chirped like a canary and invited the 'bird,'" he recalled. "We copy-writers loved it, because it gave us a chance to write a lyrical vegetable-platter from which no direct sales were expected. . . . We wrote 'builded' when we mean 'built' and poured into it generally the chiseled perfection and suave insincerity of a high-school valedictory." [90]

Compared to product advertising, whose effects could be gauged, however imprecisely, by sales, institutional advertising had a less measurable impact. This seeming unaccountability of the institutional ad, as well as its frequent pretentiousness, stirred the ire of those who styled themselves advertising realists. To them institutional advertising provided a haven for copywriters who indulged in a taste for poetry and literature rather than accepting advertising as a selling force. As John Caples, a mail-order advertising specialist, charged at the end of the 1920s, "In institutional advertising you can be as absurd as you want to and nobody can ever prove that the advertising isn't any good." The result, wrote another critic in *Advertising and Selling,* was "elegant inanities" and "rhetorical piffle." Yet another adversary of the institutional style tried to imagine the revenge that the much-abused and, as a result, now-impoverished word "service" would seek in the "next world":

"'You made me,' it would say to Institutional Advertising, 'you with your fearsome dignity and artistic typography at any price. You made me what I am today.'"[91]

With the advent of the Great Depression the institutional style came under renewed attack as the epitome of all that had been weak, ineffective, and misbegotten in previous advertising styles. Those in the practical camp had already put it bluntly in the late 1920s. One accused copywriters of "thinking soulfully of the aesthetic value of an advertisement, instead of its supply of two-fisted salesmanship-in-print," while another put it more metaphorically, in prose that even the creator of an institutional campaign would have found sufficiently elevated: "Words are the building stones with which are constructed the Cities of the Mind. With words, a master may fabricate a beautiful cathedral, its lacy Gothic towers mounting to the skies. Using those words as building stones another master may erect a highly efficient business structure. . . . Advertisement writers, sometimes, try to build Cathedrals. They forget that an advertisement is a business building."[92]

To Be an Institution

Could institutional advertising credibly refute the "cathedral" charge? Did it even wish to? We might well imagine a Bruce Barton or one of his admirers finding the audacity to respond: "Why is it that you *insist* on making a distinction between business structures and cathedrals?"

I have discovered no such explicit defense, and I would be surprised to find one that directly espoused the religious metaphor. Still, many corporate leaders of the 1920s aspired to a nobler status than that of mere businessmen and to a recognition of their firms as more than mere companies. William Allen White, the celebrated editor and champion of Progressivism, told the executives of electrical manufacturing firms and utility companies in 1926 that "you and all like you who sell service to humanity are priests of a new order, torch-bearers for a new era." And advertising agents constantly encouraged corporate leaders to "uncover in the industry something which has in it the quality of service to mankind and which . . . will yield spiritual as well as monetary rewards."[93] Certainly the rhetoric that entreated the public to recognize authentic "souls" in these monumental entities seemed archaic by the end of the 1920s. But a more secular apotheosis of the corporation—public acknowledgment of its standing as an institution—still seemed a fitting aspiration.

As the size and scope of major corporations expanded, it was hardly surprising that their own executives became impressed with the magnitude of their operations and their seeming indispensability to the nation. Many felt they were more qualified to solve the country's basic social and political problems than were the elected politicians. Executives of Westinghouse, for instance, almost instinctively saw themselves as "employed today in the public service." Other corporations, ranging from automakers to pharmaceutical firms, deemed their role in modern American life so vital that they deserved to be acknowledged as central institutions. As the Western Electric Company expressed the sentiment in an ad depicting both its factory and Abraham Lincoln, "The men of history grew great according to the measure of their service. So with institutions."[94]

Becoming an institution had once required some act of investiture. Although

FIGURE 5.20

The corporate craving for "soul"—manifested in the aspiration to be recognized for "something besides ambition, or pride, or wish for gain"—found expression in the headline, prose, and visual imagery of this 1927 exercise in self-congratulation.

American society provided no such formal ritual, institutional advertising afforded many corporations with the sense of having purged themselves of lower, commercial motives. In this vein the "House of Squibb" proclaimed its commitment to the tenet that "pride of product is greater than . . . pride of profit." Standard Oil of Indiana even more righteously proclaimed: "This Company has put service first and profits last." The Goodyear Rubber Company avowed that "an unalterable purpose," not the "wish for gain," had enabled it to establish itself as "a city that is set on an hill" (Fig. 5.20). In another institutional ad Goodyear remarked with apparent diffidence: "We like to think of the Goodyear business as something more than a successful enterprise. We like to look upon it, in all its magnitude and variety, as the creation of a grateful public for its own service."[95]

But did self-investitures through institutional advertising actually secure the legitimacy that the corporate giants were seeking? Institutional advertisers with predominantly political goals usually claimed results in terms of acceptable legislation or the avoidance of government investigations and suits. At various points Swift expressed relief that "the law as finally passed is much less drastic than laws that had been previously proposed" and concluded that its campaign had been "well worth the effort and expense" because of the understanding and goodwill it had produced. In 1928 *Printers' Ink* praised the institutional advertising of AT&T under the subheading "Stopping Government Ownership Talk." Even in mounting "bul-wark[s] against the possibility of adverse legislation," however, the precise effect of institutional advertising campaigns was difficult to estimate.[96]

Beginning in 1929, Arthur Page of AT&T started contracting with professional pollsters to carry out surveys of the readership of institutional ads (see p. 84). By 1937 both the Psychological Corporation and the Curtis Publishing Company had instituted surveys of public attitudes toward large corporations that provided quan-tifiable data for judging the overall results of public relations and institutional ad-vertising efforts.[97] But in the 1920s, during the first flood tide of corporate image advertising, these somewhat more sophisticated forms of assessment had not yet been developed. Expenditures on institutional advertising, particularly of the more purely boastful or abstract kind, found their warrant more in the intensity of aspi-ration than in proof of results.

Without the same opportunities enjoyed by their entrepreneurial forebears for pioneering accomplishment, transcendence of the profit motive through individ-ual charity, or the acquisition of local civic stature through community booster-ism, the executives of the more bureaucratic corporations of the early twentieth century sought their higher calling in a more collective, institutionalized sense of service. They reminded themselves of the vast scope of their operations and their great burdens of public responsibility as a way of confirming their role as leaders of true institutions.[98] And indeed, by 1929 the business writer Whiting Williams would declare that "certain of our huge commercial units are now generally re-garded no longer as mere companies, but, instead, as institutions, nothing less!"[99]

But such "feel-good" motives could not sustain any significant investment in in-stitutional advertising during the early years of the Great Depression. The collapse of many welfare capitalism programs in the early 1930s and the wide acceptance of unions, in spite of the efforts of some employers to spread the work and provide relief for their employees, raised daunting questions.[100] Was it really wise, as "in-stitutions" such as Metropolitan Life professed to believe, for business corporations to transform the relationship between the employer and its workers or clients into "something more than a contractual one"?[101] How much of that responsibility over aspects of the worker's life previously governed by other social institutions did the business corporation really wish to embrace?

In the chilling atmosphere of the early 1930s, with major corporations and their leaders the objects more of public suspicion than of adulation, business leaders continued to value the effects of image campaigns on internal morale.[102] But with-out ever surrendering the notions of their proper public stature and leadership, they shifted their focus from the institution as an agent of civic beneficence to a more modest sense of that word. They wanted the giant corporation to be seen as occupying a legitimate, unquestioned place among society's accepted, integral or-ganizations. As the 1930s progressed, a more compelling motive than either inter-nal morale or public stature would spur a new wave of corporate image campaigns: the urgent need to save the system of free enterprise itself.

6

THE 1930s:

SAVE THE SYSTEM

Anyone might well have predicted that one speech would gain the spotlight at the December 1935 convention of the National Association of Manufacturers (NAM)—that of Bruce Barton. By now legendary as the mellifluous corporate voice for some of the nation's largest companies, Barton arrived at the convention trailing clouds of advertising glory. During the previous six months he had captured for his agency the prestigious new institutional advertising accounts of both Du Pont and United States Steel. These coups, comparable to his astonishing performance in late 1922, when he had landed the General Motors and General Electric accounts, gave him the status of potential savior in the eyes of businessmen who increasingly deplored the havoc of the New Deal.

Barton placed the dominant issue before the convention with dramatic clarity. "Industry and politics, at the moment, are competitors for the confidence and favor of the same patron"—namely, "the public." "Politics knows it," Barton chided his audience; "industry, for three years, has acted as if it did not." Before concluding, Barton further jarred his audience with a blow to their most vulnerable spot—business leaders' sense of their own social and political isolation. If executives were to travel around the country and talk to people, he admonished them, they would be surprised "to discover how little we are liked, how much our incomes are resented and our motives misunderstood." Instead of pouting and sulking, however, they ought to persuade people that "we are more reliable than the politicians [and] . . . will work for them more cheaply and with more satisfaction." The business world needed to tell this story "with all the imagination and art of which modern advertising is capable." [1]

Although Barton emphasized advertising, major corporations soon turned to the whole range of public relations activities to respond to the challenge. Ironically, the crisis conditions that seemed to call for maintaining a low profile and "sticking to business" incited many corporations to claim a wider civic role. While launching a counterattack against the New Deal, major corporations institutionalized the public relations function within their managerial structures. Many afforded their PR officers an internal stature they had rarely enjoyed before. By the end of the 1930s the head of public relations at General Motors could express satisfaction in the rising status of "a type of work once regarded almost with disrespect." Wherever businessmen now congregated, he observed, public relations was "very nearly the No. 1 topic of conversation."[2]

Barton was certainly not the first to call for business to "find its voice" in the contest for public opinion. At the 1935 NAM convention, just prior to Barton's speech, Alfred P. Sloan Jr. of General Motors had declared that it was time to face up to the ultimate battle between "political management" and "private enterprise" and to protect the "very foundation of the American System." And the NAM itself had announced that it would expand its budget threefold in 1936 to counteract the pernicious influence of Franklin Roosevelt. It planned to mount a massive campaign to "sell the 'American way of life' to the American people." The organization's president, from the same podium at which Barton would later speak, proclaimed that business, "in sheer self-defense," would enter the political arena to avoid being destroyed.[3]

But Barton upstaged all the others, not through more intense demonization of Roosevelt and the New Deal but rather by turning the glare of criticism on business leaders themselves. It was true that recent initiatives by the New Dealers and their use of effective sales techniques had threatened corporate autonomy and the free enterprise system, but laggards in manning the corporate battlements bore their own moral responsibility. "If any manufacturer says, 'I do not care what the common mass of people think about my business, whether it be popular or unpopular with them,'" Barton warned, "that man is a liability to all industry. No major industry has any moral right to allow itself to be unexplained, misunderstood or publicly distrusted, for by its unpopularity it poisons the pond in which we all must fish."[4]

By precept and example, Barton suggested that the great battle on behalf of free enterprise had to be fought through individual initiatives by the major corporations themselves. Although he did not criticize the efforts of the NAM, Barton obviously considered them only complementary to broad-spirited public relations campaigns by the great "flagship" corporations, such as those he had recently converted to the cause. Unattuned to public relations subtleties, the NAM lacked Barton's modulated voice and his flair for the dramatic but positive, generous corporate gesture. In Richard Tedlow's phrase the NAM "sought to sell free enterprise the way Procter & Gamble sold soap."[5] And while many conservatives in the business community looked to immediate political action, through the American Liberty League or the Republican Party, to overthrow Roosevelt in the election of 1936, Barton was not at all sanguine about such prospects. Roosevelt had proved himself exceptionally capable as a salesman. Businessmen, who prided themselves on their salesmanship, should blush for shame. Their narrow, negative attacks on the New Deal had failed to sell the public; more significantly, these leaders had utterly failed to recognize the need to expand their corporate responsibilities to meet threats posed to the entire business system.

The Confession

Barton's eloquent appeals, both at the NAM convention and at other business gatherings over the subsequent six months, helped underwrite a wondrously self-vindicating stance by business leaders, one that justified a new emphasis on public relations. So widely and uniformly was this posture adopted that it warrants a categorical label: "the Confession." Executive after executive confessed that he and his peers had unwisely ignored the need to explain and defend the greater mission of his own company and of the capitalist system. The reason for this failure, each piously protested, had been his single-minded devotion to the production ethic.

Business leaders, in Alfred Sloan's words, had been "preoccupied in exploring the secrets of nature and creating a continuous flow of new products." They had viewed the public simply as consumers and had concentrated all their efforts on producing cheaper products of high quality to improve the consumers' standard of living. In the process of such righteous service, however, they had neglected to keep the public informed about the workings of the system, and thus the public came to misunderstand the motives of business leaders. Barton seized on just this point. "Business says to *itself*," he told members of the Illinois Manufacturers Association in May 1936, "'We have created most of the comforts and satisfactions of modern life'—but it does not say this to the 130,000,000 in language they can understand. My plea is that we should be as diligent, as ingenious, and as resourceful in our approach to them as voters as we have proved ourselves to be in our approach to them as buyers."[6]

From 1935 to 1939 countless corporate executives reiterated the Confession in hundreds of public forums.[7] Several years later a General Motors public relations executive, looking back on the previous decade, summarized the essence of the Confession so definitively that his narrative deserves quoting at length:

> The producer figured that he had a big job in producing alone. He thought that if he produced a good product and sold it to the public in large quantities, that as he got out more and better things for more people in more places at generally lower costs, he was doing all that was necessary. But suddenly he was struck with something which put him in a daze. He had been unaware of something which had been gradually developing for years. Knowledge of the product and interest in it on the part of the public had been so great that it practically obscured the process by which it was produced. . . .
>
> The public did not understand the producer. . . . He was accused of making too much profit, of making any profit. . . . Here obviously was something the producer did not understand. The producer was geared to producing and not to talking. Polemics might be meat for a politician but it was poison for the producer. . . . This was something new and he was an amateur.[8]

For any corporate leaders too bewildered or too mute to articulate the Confession for themselves, a host of trade journalists, advertising agents, and emerging public relations professionals proved eager to rehearse it for them. One implication of the Confession, after all, was its suggestion that expert assistance was needed by corporate executives so inexperienced in this unique form of "conversation" with the public. "Business has a story to tell," reiterated those who offered their PR expertise. Once a corporation acknowledged its failure to tell its own story and to

FIGURE 6.1
The National Broadcasting Company conveyed to businessmen, through the dramatic urgency of this photograph, their need to "tell their story" to the people. Through radio they could emulate FDR and "do the next best thing to visiting them personally."

"educate the public toward what business is really doing in our economic scheme of things," the need to hire the expert storytellers of the public relations firms and advertising agencies seemed evident. Throughout the last half of the 1930s, business leaders would never escape constant heckling from the trade press to "tell their story."[9] Radio networks, periodicals, and advertising agencies steadily and ingratiatingly offered to help business "find its voice" (Fig. 6.1).[10]

Finding the proper voice, however, was no small undertaking. As William Bird has argued, it involved both the acquisition of a "new vocabulary" of colloquial speech and the greater use of nonbookish media, such as cartoons, radio, and film.[11] Above all, it demanded that corporate leaders speak about the most serious matters in the rhetorical styles of political demagogues and mass entertainers. Having proffered their service to the public in the 1920s as "business statesmen," they were now being pressed to renounce their noble (if politically blind), stick-to-business insensibility to public opinion and to confess to impotence in a central quality of business performance—salesmanship. Bruce Barton played on this potential sense of embarrassment, goading the great producers of consumer goods to action by telling them flatly that they had been beaten at their own game. The best advertiser of the previous three years had not been any of the great manufacturers or prominent advertising agencies, Barton taunted. It had been Franklin D. Roosevelt and his federal bureaucracy.

Again and again Barton tortured his business colleagues with this distasteful truth. "The present occupant of the White House is preeminent among all men in public life in his ability to think in selling terms and speak in advertising language," Barton reminded Illinois manufacturers. To another audience he described FDR as "the only man who is talking to the consumer in terms of his own interest." To drive home the point more dramatically Barton mimicked FDR's exasperatingly effective "fireside chats": "My friends, you are feeling better, and I am going to tell you some of the things that are going to make you feel still better." If it was political snake oil that Roosevelt was selling, Barton implied, advertisers should be even more chagrined. They were the ones who were supposed to know the selling game. Yet business executives still clung "to the fatuous notion that we can hold conventions and *tell* them, when we ought to be thinking all the time how, by sincere personal effort, we can *sell* them," Barton insisted.[12]

Barton was far from alone in stressing the necessity of seeing Roosevelt as a tutor as well as an adversary. Since the first fireside chat, contributors to the advertising press had been praising the president's instincts as a "copywriter" and urging his techniques upon each other. In trade journals and around the conference tables of individual corporations, advertising and public relations executives spoke of FDR and his advisors as "an example of proper public relations" and as "an advertising-minded" administration. The more they thought about Roosevelt, and the more often they suffered defeats at his hands, the more corporate leaders concluded that the New Deal had outstripped them in effective use of radio and films for "institutional" and image-creating purposes and the more they resolved to apply their skills to the use of these media in public relations. Recognizing that the secret of Roosevelt's success lay in his capacity to speak the "language of the common man," they urgently pursued their own quest for a popular idiom in which to translate their corporate messages and enlighten the economically illiterate.[13]

Business leaders—and particularly advertising agents—had long held a low opinion of popular intellect. Their experience in observing consumer tastes, evaluating the relative success of various advertising appeals, studying the content of popular media and other amusements, and appraising the results of consumer surveys had convinced them that a majority of the public was emotional, irrational, and fickle.[14] This impression of the people's capacities helped explain how the public could have fallen for demagogic antibusiness propaganda. But the more constructive conclusion was that "these people," as an ad agency magazine put it, "often don't understand business or how it operates."[15] This kind of illiteracy, while dismaying, still allowed for faith in the results of a great literacy campaign directed toward those who were uninformed and therefore easily misled. Designed to educate the masses, this campaign would rely on messages of stark simplicity that carried an aura of folk wisdom.

Ford's Answer: "One Foot on the Land"

While many corporate leaders were making their confessions and ardently seeking the right vernacular in which to tutor the average citizen, one highly independent yet significant business leader approached the same objective from a quite different direction. At the beginning of the 1930s Henry Ford, despite his slippage in the competitive struggle against General Motors and the emerging Chrysler Corporation, still enjoyed an immense popular reputation as the friend of the common man. Even at the depth of the Great Depression, according to the newspaper columnist Arthur Brisbane, Ford remained the most trusted public figure in the United States. Ford's sustained popularity stemmed partly from his successful early fight "on behalf of the people" against the Selden patent. It then gained momentum from his major role in expanding car ownership through a no-frills, reliable, and ever-cheaper product; his development of the farm market for both the Model-T and the Fordson tractor; and as David Lewis has carefully documented, his self-publicity as the champion and friend of the masses. His announcement of the five-dollar day for his workers in 1915 won him an enduring reputation among the public as the big-business leader most sympathetic to workers.[16]

The historian John Staudenmaier has aptly characterized Henry Ford as an exemplar of an outlook of "technological ambiguity"—the fusion of "exultation with anxiety" in contemplating new technologies. Ford revealed the evasive, anxious facet of this ambiguity during the 1920s in his creation of the Ford Museum and his idyllic nineteenth-century town, Greenfield Village.[17] Much of his success had derived from his effective molding of products and merchandising to the needs and values of the rural market. And he deeply mistrusted urban life. "The city," in Lewis's pithy digest of Ford's views, "had been a mistake." In his preindustrial Greenfield Village at Dearborn, Ford proclaimed the superiority of small-town culture through such monuments to an arcadian past as a one-room country schoolhouse and the supposed birthplace of that master of sentimental nostalgia, songwriter Stephen Foster.[18]

Even before he conceived Greenfield Village, Ford had embarked on a project establishing small "village industries" as an operating part of his giant manufacturing enterprise. These took the form of water-powered factories in rural areas intended to employ farmers during their slack winter months. With their economic support not entirely dependent on either farming or manufacturing, the farmer/operatives would enjoy an extra degree of security. Ford created several such plants in the 1920s and widely publicized this scheme as social reform.[19]

With the onset of the Great Depression, Ford further promoted the seemingly anachronistic concept of village industries as a crucial element in his company's public image. In 1931 he began rather circuitously to link the Ford Motor Company's image to ideas of a return to the land. He published such semi-institutional advertisements as "Two Boys Will Go Adventuring This Summer," which fantasized about a plan by parents to reward their sons for good grades in high school by enabling them to embark on an auto tour that combined pleasure and adventure with didactic ordeal. Following a rigid schedule, the boys would tour factories and mines, "get back to the sources of raw materials," and—by being "thrown a great deal on their own resources"—move beyond book learning to develop practical knowledge and self-reliance.[20]

Having thus implicitly suggested how America should regain its bearings through "first-hand contact" with nature and industry, Ford stepped forward "in person" to deliver sermons on social and industrial policy. In June 1932, through the conspicuous seriousness of all-print advertisements in newspapers and magazines, Ford informed the nation's citizens of his personal solution for the depression. Charity and relief were futile, he argued. The answer was to situate workers where they could labor on the land as well as in the factory and thus supplement their incomes with food for their families. "The Basis of All Is the Earth: It Has Never Failed," he moralized to his employees in the *Ford News*. So intent was Ford on forging operating models for the nation through his village industries that he required each worker at his factory in Iron Mountain, Michigan, to plant a garden "of sufficient size to supply his family with at least part of its winter vegetables." Those who failed to comply would be fired.[21]

By the end of the 1930s Ford claimed credit for establishing some fifteen village industries, each of which enabled its workers to enjoy a "more natural tempo of life" and a "higher level of neighborhood character" than in a city. The *Ford News* celebrated the efforts of Ford "thrift gardeners" at various plants. By closing the gap between farm and factory, Ford had made these workers residents of "an American village . . . the best place on earth to live."[22] Still, although Ford argued that the village industries were efficient elements in his manufacturing network, he refused to hold them to the profit standards of his major plants. In a telling disclosure of their role as a gesture to public relations, one of Ford's lieutenants observed that "you couldn't talk money to him in regards to these plants."[23]

Ford was far from alone in romanticizing the image of "one foot in industry, one foot on the land." Many corporations had developed "community gardens" during the depression, setting aside plots near their factories where workers could grow vegetables for their families. In 1932, for instance, the B. F. Goodrich Company created the "Akron Community Gardens, Inc.," as a "cooperative farm operated on mass production principles." Noting that some good employees were now out of work and others had been cut back to three days or less each week, the company hoped to enable these families to resist charity "to the last" by providing a source of subsistence (Fig. 6.2). By 1934 United States Steel was claiming to have sixteen thousand acres under cultivation in over eighty thousand employee garden plots. This arrangement was saving the company a considerable sum in "relief expenditures" to its employees.[24] Recognizing the dangers of a pattern of business cycles in which severe intermittent unemployment fostered industrial unrest, employers of large labor forces were understandably attracted to visions of the stability that might be gained if workers could look beyond the company's factories to other means of survival during such crises. Even as corporations were eliminating or reevaluating their welfare programs, employee gardens remained a form of corporate "soul" that many companies were still pleased to publicize.[25]

Ford also emphasized his vision of rural, human-scale applications of technology in his "industrialized barn" exhibit at the Century of Progress Exposition in 1934. Almost by chance he came up with another means of maintaining his public im-

FIGURE 6.2
A number of corporations found factory gardens an acceptable way to fulfill a sense of benevolent responsibility toward their unemployed or partially employed workers without engaging in inappropriate charity. Even in this romanticized depiction, the corporate presence loomed ominously.

age as a down-to-earth, homey benefactor of the people. As a relaxing interval for visitors viewing the extensive photomurals and dioramas that glorified the technology of Ford production processes, Ford offered performances of popular music by the Detroit Symphony Orchestra. These were also broadcast live from the fairgrounds. When radio listeners expressed widespread appreciation, the exhibit director, Fred Black, and Henry's son, Edsel Ford, a connoisseur and patron of the arts, pressed for the continuation of orchestral broadcasts as an institutional advertising program. Although Edsel proclaimed at the first broadcast of the new series, in October 1934, that "we wish to assure you that our program will not be interrupted by irritating sales talks," an orchestral program did lend itself to an intermission. The company decided to fill this time with a series of serious yet down-to-earth talks that would make "a modest contribution to straight thinking and common sense." [26]

Here, as in his audacious purchase of expensive institutional ads to preach his gospel of "one foot on the land," Ford again drew on his long-standing reputation for commonsensical popular wisdom. Anyone who could fight off the patent hold-

SEPTEMBER 9, 1937

Advertising & Selling

Now's the
Time to Talk
it Over!

Tell the millions—*in
their own homes*—your
aims and ideals

NEVER before has so great
an opportunity arisen for
closer cooperation between
management and worker, between industry and the public.
For *inside* the plant, man-to-
man discussions and frank explanations have succeeded the
curt command. And *outside* the
plant, Public Opinion—the ultimate force in a democracy—is
keenly alert. Eager for the facts

which will mould its judgment.
The most direct and intimate
way of presenting your industry's aims to the public and to
your own workers is through
Radio—*the one medium* which is
invited into 24,500,000 American homes. The surprising
records of NBC Network Programs on such missions are available to business through NBC
representatives—*everywhere*.

*RCA presents the "Magic Key of RCA" every Sunday,
2 to 3 P. M., E. D. S. T., on the NBC Blue Network*

NATIONAL BROADCASTING COMPANY
A Radio Corporation of America Service

FIGURE 6.3
A radio talk, NBC advised corporate leaders, offered "the most direct and intimate way" of restoring a personal, man-to-man relationship with workers, while also garnering public approval.

ers, make a cheap, dependable car for the common man through mass-production methods, and sympathize with the needs of the farmer, many people assumed, could surely offer wise solutions for social and economic problems. If other corporate heads had commanded such a popular following, they would have been sorely tempted to deliver institutional radio talks themselves. But Ford had been stung by ridicule during his court appearance in a famous libel suit in 1919 and decided for the future to "hire someone to talk for me that knows how."

William J. Cameron, a former newspaperman and family intimate, assumed that role. Cameron enjoyed "constant and trusted contact" with Henry and Edsel Ford. He lunched with them daily in their private dining room, discussed his future scripts alone with Henry Ford, and learned to anticipate Henry's response to any issue. Cameron created a "'plain folks' atmosphere" on the program, delivering his six-minute intermission talks in what David Lewis describes as "a folksy style remi-niscent of an earnest village parson."[27] In his commentaries during the 1934–35 radio season on such topics as "American individualism," "wages versus pater-nalism," and "a day at Greenfield School," Cameron reflected both the rural, production-ethic nostalgia that Henry had embodied in Greenfield Village and the down-home defenses of free enterprise that would soon come to characterize many corporate public relations campaigns. Cameron provided highly personalized portraits of Henry Ford, describing the manufacturer as "rising at 6 in the morning" to join others as simply "one of the tens of thousands of Ford men going to work"; he observed that Ford "issues no orders," but "if he wants something done, he goes to the man concerned and talks it over with him." Such vignettes implied that Henry Ford had surmounted the much-lamented loss of employer-employee contact, rejuvenating morale through face-to-face relationships.[28]

Although themes centering on Henry's philosophies or Ford company policies dominated the first season of talks, Cameron worked in fourteen thinly veiled attacks on the New Deal before the end of the second season. He also continued to relate homey stories that revealed Ford as a "common, ordinary, kindly, generous, democratic man, just like us." Contemporary critics, as well as later ones, characterized Cameron's talks as "gems of propaganda," which created misleading impressions through a "plain folks device." Some of those same qualities attracted the favorable attention of other corporate leaders, who, noting the apparent popularity of the talks (Cameron received nearly 150,000 requests for transcripts during the 1937–38 season), would look to the same format for their own nascent institutional campaigns (Fig. 6.3).[29]

Communing with the Common Folk

If Henry Ford, whom many Americans already saw as "believably like themselves, an accessible friend," still needed a William Cameron to help him speak to ordinary citizens in their own language, most corporate leaders would need considerably more than that. Dismayed by their sudden loss of popular esteem, and constantly harangued by advertising agents about their incompetence in familiarizing the public with their companies and with the free enterprise system, they grasped eagerly at a variety of tactics for getting "reacquainted" with average citizens. Explaining an economic system and providing an understanding of a corporation's entire operations in a popular vernacular seemed a much more formidable task than simply advertising products. At least the trade press made it seem so. No matter how plain and folksy the company executives tried to make their communications, fresh voices always emerged to berate business leaders for their stuffy approach and call for a new idiom that would be even simpler and more dramatic.

Critics of the corporate failure to communicate across the gulf of vast differences in class and in economic literacy pointed to one prime example: the 1920s style of institutional advertising. By boasting pompously, in elevated, multisyllabic terms, about something so abstract as their "service," corporations in the 1920s had isolated themselves from the public. Get rid of that "dignity complex," advisors urged. Big business should "take its hair down" and stop using "big words or abstract concepts." It should adopt the language of the waitress and the truck driver; it should attain "human interest" by paying less attention to the corporation's interests and more to the hopes, fears, and illusions of "the great masses of plain common folks." Could those entrusted with shaping corporate images make such a leap? An advertising man taunted his peers in 1937 with the model most likely to provoke them: "If Mr. Roosevelt learned to talk their language, starting as he did, you and I can, too."[30]

This is a Cow

The cow is the mother of capitalism.

In fact, cattle and capitalism are the same word.

Capital means "head." Capitalism is a count of heads of cattle. Such it was at the dawn of history, and such it is, with modifications, today.

Capitalism might almost be called cattleism.

FIGURES 6.4 & 6.5
In *A Primer of Capitalism—Illustrated,*
one advertising agency demonstrated
to corporate leaders its talent for
simplifying business's message.
Economic illiteracy among voters
revealed a need to "keep it simple"
and to brand the politician as the
consumer's real enemy.

Initiatives in translating corporate imagery into the vernacular took many forms. One was the quest for some elemental, lowest common denominator of simplicity. An article in *Advertising and Selling* in 1937 counseled, "For the Mass Mind— Put Your Copy in Low Gear." Early the next year, reflecting on the great success of Disney's *Snow White and the Seven Dwarfs, Advertising Age* editorialized, "They Like It Simple."[31] When the Aluminum Company of America (Alcoa) found itself in a public relations crisis in 1937, facing the Department of Justice's "sweeping bill of complaint" that charged it with monopolistic practices and demanded its dissolution, it responded with advertising that "banished every intricate word" in favor of "the most elementary terms." Alcoa reaped great praise in the trade press for corporate image ads of calculated naïveté. *Advertising Age* admired the "simple, easy-to-understand stories" through which the company was "striving mightily to prove that it is not a monopoly." *Advertising and Selling* honored the Alcoa ads for putting forth simple explanations of economic complexities.[32]

The J. Walter Thompson advertising agency chose to take literally the admonitions against complexity. It responded with a booklet entitled *A Primer of Capitalism* to demonstrate its mastery of the new institutional style. On pages dominated by cartoon illustrations, the agency presented lessons such as "This is a Cow. . . . The cow is the mother of capitalism" and "Under private capitalism, the *Consumer,* the *Citizen,* is boss. . . . In state capitalism, the *Politician* is the boss. . . . He tells consumers what they can buy" (Figs. 6.4 and 6.5).[33] A number of corporations interpreted the language of ordinary people not only as simple but specifically as breezy, slang-filled conversation. In Johns-Manville's communications to em-

ployees the factory itself burst into folksy discourse. "The conventionally cold, staid pile of bricks and smokestacks" spoke in comic-strip balloons to explain to "George A. Citizen" why "I'm no good to anybody unless I'm busy." Standard Oil conveyed its institutional messages in "informal chit-chat between neighbors," and General Electric brought home the story of America's rising standard of living through a conversation between "Mom" and "Bobby."[34]

To speak in the idiom of average citizens meant also to place the topic in the context of everyday experiences. Many corporations and advertising agencies considered this strategy an apt response to the constantly repeated warnings about the need to humanize the corporation. In a folksy setting the corporation could carry on friendly "conversations" that placed great economic principles and institutions within a scale that simple neighbor folk could grasp (Fig. 6.6). *Advertising Age* praised ads that combined local references with colloquial speech. It noted how *Nation's Business,* the organ of the national Chamber of Commerce, had managed "to separate the word 'big' from the word 'business' in the public mind." The magazine had done this by depicting business as composed not of "a mysteriously intangible something" but "simply of such men as the corner grocer and the man who sells shoes." The president of N. W. Ayer & Son fantasized that the ideal public relations approach would be to have the corporation executive "drop in after dinner from time to time in every home in America" and express his company's concern for service, good citizenship, and neighborliness.[35]

Going beyond the quest for vernacular language and a neighborly manner, corporations gave the common folk themselves a conspicuous presence in their im-

"Fine thing, the Telephone"

"HELPS TO KEEP PEOPLE CLOSE AND FRIENDLY

FIGURE 6.6

AT&T turned to a short text, folksy characters, and vernacular voices to associate itself with the common people. This colloquial style diverged sharply from the more formal prose of its earlier ads (see Chapter 2).

age ads. Whereas images of the consumer in product ads typically came to a halt at the lower boundaries of the prosperous middle class, images of the citizen now went further to depict a "salt of the earth," grassroots constituency. General Motors' advertisements in 1937 teemed with stereotypical common folk, as did those of the new Du Pont campaign that Bruce Barton's agency devised in 1936 (see Fig. 6.11). The Association of American Railroads turned to a homey, grandmotherly type to publicize the friendliness and safety of railroad service, and AT&T picked an unfashionably stout farm woman, prosaically shelling peas at a kitchen table, to represent a typical AT&T "partner" (see Fig. 2.19). For United States Steel, Barton's agency turned to youngsters to suggest a folksy, classless persona for the giant corporation. The late 1930s did not mark the first use of prototypical common folk in ads, but the era did witness their first prominent appearance as elements of the corporation's image.[36]

The radical change that these efforts represented in corporate imagery is perhaps best exemplified by the title of an article in the J. Walter Thompson house organ in 1937. With an apparent sense of astonished discovery, the magazine declared: "Workers Are People" (Figs. 6.7 and 6.8). Confessing earlier sins of omission, the author of this feature article noted that "to many of us a factory is a building full of machinery and populated by a strange variety of human being who borrows many of his characteristics from the machine." But a resurgence of concern for worker morale (inspired by an unprecedented, mounting level of unionization and massive strikes) had now led the agencies to discover the "employe of almost any large corporation" as the true "forgotten man" of the age. *Forbes* magazine offered

JULY 1937

PEOPLE
Monthly Bulletin of the J. Walter Thompson Company

WORKERS ARE PEOPLE
by William D. Kennedy

FIGURES 6.7 & 6.8
The transformation in corporate perceptions and parlance necessary for reaching the common man, the J. Walter Thompson advertising agency implied in its monthly bulletin, was colossal. A major step was simply to get used to viewing workers as people!

Aim of a labor-education program: A fair week's work for a fair week's pay . . . mutual respect born of understanding of each other's problems.

businessmen its assistance in their efforts to visualize the common man. It carried a series of twenty photographs of "typical American workmen" on its covers during 1937 and 1938.[37]

With many of the old programs of welfare capitalism in disarray and company unions increasingly ineffective in forestalling inroads by the CIO and AFL, convincing internal propaganda seemed more essential than ever. Here again, the need for a new language, as well as solicitous attention to workers, was inescapable. Employee magazines, many of which had folded during the stringent times of the early 1930s, once again proliferated. In the first nine months of 1937 more than four hundred company magazines were launched or revived—an increase of 45 percent over the previous year. In conformity with the drive toward simplification, editors of these magazines eagerly adopted the verbal and visual language of the commercial mass media. Photographs often dominated the formats. General Motors very self-consciously modeled its employee magazine after the sensationally successful new *Life* magazine (see Fig. 6.21).[38] In a more remarkable transformation, a bevy of major corporations suddenly recast their staid annual reports in 1937 and 1938 as vernacular "reports to employees." The trade press celebrated the new political awareness of companies that had forsworn their long columns of figures and their austere, pictureless blocks of impenetrable prose for drastically simplified statements, often replete with pictographs, photographs, and charts. Some executives, dismayed by the connotations that such previously noble words as "profit" and "dividend" now held with the public, even searched for new words to substitute.[39] Nearly every account of a company's conversion to a "report to employees" mentioned that the traditional annual report had been "re-written in simple language" or phrased "in words which employees can understand." The Johns-Manville Company, whose president had admonished fellow business leaders to "personalize and humanize business . . . keep it as simple as an old shoe and as small-town as a Cape Cod or Iowa village," used big print and numerous pictures to adapt its 1937 *Annual Report* to its employees, while the Swift company's "readable" report gained accolades from *Advertising Age* in an item titled "Swift Tells All." For the same year General Foods replaced its "conventional, sedate" report with a quarterly "tabloid newspaper . . . copiously illustrated."[40]

From the standpoint of social history, one of the most striking aspects of the quest for a common-folk style in corporate public relations was the way it eventually brought ethnic names and faces into visibility on the advertising pages. Prior to 1935 one could have searched endlessly in national advertising for a single protagonist with other than an Anglo-Saxon or vaguely Scandinavian name. Consumers were never identified as Polish, Czech, Hungarian, Slovakian, Italian, Greek, or Russian. In some special instances a company seeking a "craftsmanship" image might include Swiss or Dutch "masters," but the presence of eastern and southern European immigrants either as citizens or consumers was not acknowledged. Even in the employee magazines families of distinct ethnic backgrounds never gained featured status.[41]

During 1936 and 1937 the first signs of a breakthrough emerged. In its new company magazine United States Steel gave recognition to Stephen Yablanki for his skills both in music and in the hardening and tempering of tools. Westinghouse turned to the family of Mike Slzechinski to sell the system by demonstrating the

The Slzechinskis
are buying
A NEW CAR

America builds more and buys more — thanks to electrically-driven machines

WHEN Mike Slzechinski's relatives in the "old country" hear he has bought an automobile, they'll conclude he is either crazy or rich. Of course, he is neither. He is just an average American workman, enjoying the benefits of a production system that turns luxuries into commodities by creating an abundance of them.

Working under this system, the automobile industry is making it pos-sible every year for more Americans to enjoy better cars. Its purchases stimulate business and employment all along the line. It employs directly a vast army of workers who earn enough themselves to be good customers for the products they make.

Westinghouse engineers have had no small part in building this system, which is founded largely upon the ability of machines to multiply the productive powers of men. Wherever you see machines and men at work, you are likely to see Westinghouse electric motors and control apparatus. Through the intelligent application of electricity to modern production prob-lems, Westinghouse is helping the automobile industry — and every in-dustry — to make America the con-stant envy of the entire world as a place to live and enjoy life.

Westinghouse
The name that means everything in electricity

FIGURE 6.9

Boasting in 1937 of an American system that made car owners of workers, Westinghouse foreshadowed an emerging strategy in corporate populism. It chose to highlight as an "average American workman" a man of eastern European origins.

capacity of "an average American workman" to purchase a new car (Fig. 6.9). Studebaker, which had turned recently—"in the midst of reorganization and la-bor turmoil"—to ads that linked a merchandising strategy to cultivation of em-ployee loyalty, now publicly celebrated Joseph Szuba, metal finisher, Scoutmaster, American Legionnaire, and member of South Boston's Kosciuszko Civic Club, as an exemplary Studebaker employee. In 1938 and 1939 the *Chrysler Motors Maga-zine* ran stories on such workers as Sigmund Borkowski, member of the Polish So-ciety of America, and Evangelos Hodjis from Macedonia. In 1940 Alcoa boasted of the life trajectories of Joseph Triska, "the Bohemian immigrant boy of 1902," and Frank Gecsy, of evident eastern European origins, in its national advertising (Fig. 6.10).[42]

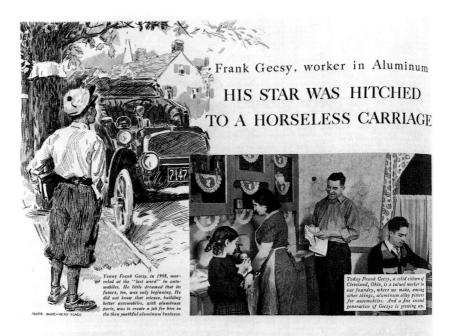

Frank Gecsy, worker in Aluminum

HIS STAR WAS HITCHED
TO A HORSELESS CARRIAGE

Young Frank Gecsy, in 1908, marveled at the "last word" in automobiles. He little dreamed that its future, too, was only beginning. He did not know that science, building better automobiles, with aluminum parts, was to create a job for him in the then youthful aluminum business.

Today Frank Gecsy, a solid citizen of Cleveland, Ohio, is a valued worker in our foundry, where we make, among other things, aluminum alloy pistons for automobiles. And a fine second generation of Gecsys is growing up.

Every job in the aluminum industry is a made job, and Frank's was no exception. It was created just in time to be ready when he was ready to go to work. ... works in ... the plants where

practical. And science had to discover many more alloys before the making of aluminum castings became enough of a business to create jobs for young fellows like Frank Gecsy

equipment, and pooling their daily findings, are likely to multiply their results many fold. They look, so to speak, with many eyes through the same microscope; they peer into ...

FIGURE 6.10
Frank Gecsy was among the immigrant protagonists of Alcoa's all-American stories of mobility and success. The illustrator James Montgomery Flagg, of the World War I "I WANT YOU" poster fame, supplied the drawing.

Reluctant Convert: Du Pont and *The Cavalcade of America*

Up to 1933 the Du Pont Company would have seemed one of the least likely of major corporations to adopt a common-folk vernacular and join the public relations craze. Lammot du Pont, the company's chief executive after 1926, was adamant on two points: first, that Du Pont should waste no funds on institutional advertising or publicity that did not directly promote the sale of its products, and second, that since most Du Pont products were refabricated by another manufacturer into consumer goods in which the Du Pont material was no longer identifiable, Du Pont should not concern itself much with the ultimate consumers. It was in this spirit that Lammot, as late as November 1932, had tersely rejected the notion of a campaign to advertise the "deeper significance" of the Du Pont logo.[43] The company's disinterest in corporate imagery was further epitomized by its brusque refusal, in contrast to most of the nation's largest corporations, to create its own exhibit for the 1933 Century of Progress Exposition in Chicago. Moreover, Du Pont remained a family-controlled firm, and the du Ponts resolutely shunned personal publicity. Lammot frequently turned down invitations to speak in public, noting that the preparation of speeches took too much time from his attention to the business.[44]

The Du Pont penchant for obscurity and narrow attention to business was shattered in 1934 by the publication of H. C. Engelbrecht's *Merchants of Death,* an exposé of the immense profits reaped by munitions traders during World War I. A Senate committee, headed by Gerald Nye of North Dakota, soon commenced hearings on the same subject. The company's officers did not enjoy their moment in the limelight of the Senate hearings. Contentious, ineffective, and hardly forthcoming, they quickly found themselves and their company identified in the public mind with the "merchants of death" epithet.[45] At the end of this ordeal the Ivy Lee and T. J. Ross public relations firm, which Du Pont had retained for advice during the hearings, sought to spur the company to recognize that its problems stemmed from its insensitivity to public opinion and its unwillingness to counteract the spread of negative impressions. The result, admonished T. J. Ross, was that Du Pont had become synonymous "with munitions making generally" and should therefore be "prepared for the worst" in future legislation. Given "the temper of the times," Ross advised, Du Pont should find a way to persuade the public of "its function as a great industrial corporation" and explain that its business was "almost entirely a peacetime business."[46]

At the beginning of 1935 pressure for some active response to its public stigmatization was also building within Du Pont. Chaplin Tyler, an engineer who prepared technical articles for the company, submitted a twenty-six-page report in January that urged an extensive publicity campaign. Perhaps with an eye to the prejudices of Lammot du Pont, or simply in deference to the company's customary skepticism about institutional advertising,[47] Tyler couched his proposal in terms of "technical publicity." He emphasized that such an effort would contribute to employee morale and to the marketing of new products as well as encourage the public to see the company as "an essential part of the local and national community."[48]

Apparently Tyler struck the right note. Lammot du Pont observed that "if there were such a thing as 'technical company advertising' it would meet my criticism of the suggested plan." That a public relations campaign would ensue was not yet certain, however. As Vice President Walter Carpenter fumed privately to another executive in early February, "While we bellyache about the other fellows using us as an example of all that is iniquitous, when we get a chance to step up and do something to present our side we find a thousand reasons to shy off. . . . It costs too much—it might be misunderstood . . .—it isn't simon pure product advertising, etc., etc., etc. . . . Why in hell don't we do something."[49]

Within a few months Bruce Barton, whose agency handled Du Pont product advertising, had interjected himself into the discussion with a typically astute proposal. While reminding Lammot du Pont that college students, women's club members, and church congregations—groups that were "all against war"—were both voters and customers, Barton took pains to explain that his expensive proposed campaign (costing between $500,000 and $650,000) would be just as much a tool for merchandising and internal morale as an investment in political protection. "You are going to be more and more a maker of products which go to the public under your own name," he pointed out to du Pont. "By the end of the first year of the campaign," he promised, "your whole sales organization will vote for its continuance." Moreover, Du Pont employees would be influenced both by the new image and by "the attitude of their friends, their relatives, their neighbors," which "is part of their morale." Still, after reviewing all these positive incentives, Barton did not neglect to play the "fear card." Pointing to a community survey that revealed that 80 percent of the people interviewed had "a friendly attitude" toward General Motors and General Electric but only 20 percent did for Du Pont, Barton chided his client: "Any business that lives in an atmosphere of unpopularity is living dangerously—like a man in an atmosphere of plague."[50]

In September 1935 Du Pont announced the launching of a massive new public relations and merchandising campaign. It would include a series of institutional magazine ads, a network radio program—*The Cavalcade of America*—and a positive-image slogan: "Better Things for Better Living . . . through Chemistry." Not mentioned in the bulletins and news releases, but clearly part of Du Pont's conversion to public relations, was the company's sudden emergence as a major independent exhibitor in the great expositions. For the 1935 National Cotton Show at Memphis it created "by far the most comprehensive exhibit . . . the Du Pont Company ever prepared for such a purpose," and it made even more ambitious plans for the 1936 Texas Centennial.[51]

Through such exhibits Du Pont strove to create regional goodwill by demonstrating its contributions to the economies of these areas. While the company thoroughly instructed the sales force in how to tie its marketing efforts to the public relations campaign, it made it clear that the objective of the ads, the exhibits, and *The Cavalcade of America* was "not to directly sell Du Pont products" but to explain the company's goals and activities and "foster the confidence, respect and goodwill of the public." *Tide,* noting the relationship of the campaign to the "nasty cracks" about big business and munitions heard recently "in Washington and elsewhere," characterized the Du Pont initiatives as a "humanizing campaign."[52]

Chaplin Tyler had warned Du Pont executives that "the willingness or capacity of the majority of the public to wade through discussions is surprisingly limited." Thus, with the aid and encouragement of Barton's agency, Du Pont searched for a new language in which to talk chemistry, progress, and free enterprise to the common man. In the 1936 magazine campaign, for instance, Du Pont conspicuously selected rustic types to carry its message. Photographed in natural, "human interest" poses, figures like spry old "Grandma Perkins" and the salty whittler "Captain Ezra Whittaker" opened their conversations with readers with folksy expressions such as "Men folks . . . Humph!" or ". . . and allus spit to loo'ard!" (Fig. 6.11). The ads aimed to highlight the usually unnoticed ways in which chemistry touched the everyday activities of people "in various walks of life."[53]

Du Pont's new radio program, *The Cavalcade of America,* sought affinity with average Americans through dramatic re-creations of "little-known but authentic episodes in the lives of American people through the years." The *Du Pont Magazine* noted that "the designers of this program have dipped into the common mass for their instances of heroism, virtue, ingenuity and public service." Not surprisingly, Du Pont found a large number of scientists among the "common mass," enough to suggest that the growth of a science-based company like Du Pont had "closely paralleled the progress of the nation." During the intermissions of these weekly

**"Men folks . . .
Humph!"**

GRANDMA PERKINS' knitting
needles clicked viciously. Humph! Men
folks! Always trying to show how
much they know!

Well—she gave them a lesson or two
about chicken raising. In spite of Zeke
and the boys she put some of that
new-fangled Cel-O-Glass on the chick
pens, just like she read in the paper,
and the springers were doing better
than they ever did before. Men folks
—Humph!

It was the same way with her favorite chair—the old roll-seat rocker. Zeke
wanted to throw it out on the wood-
pile. But Grandma got some Duco
Cement, and put the spindles back as
good as new. Then she got a can of
Duco and brightened it up slick as a
whistle.

ᵈma Perkins ᵈ‾ ‾ᵗʰ ‾w any-

FIGURE 6.11

Plain and folksy was clearly "in" by
1936. Du Pont enlisted salt-of-the-
earth figures like "Grandma Perkins"
to testify to the company's capacity
to make life "more complete for
people everywhere."

dramas of historical incidents, a Du Pont representative told human interest stories that revealed "the importance of chemical research to the average person."[54]

In *The Cavalcade of America* Du Pont found a highly satisfying way to combine
popularized history and chemistry with an image of prestige. The company characterized its broadcasts as "inspirational in type" and as "vivid and thrilling without
being over-sensationalized." The historical episodes presented a classless, largely
conflict-free view of how Americans had achieved progress by exercising the conventional virtues and carrying out scientific research. By omission these narratives
helped Du Pont erase its old image as a munitions company. One writer characterized the show's departure from the usual war-and-politics emphasis of popular
history by observing that "four years of episodes of American history were broadcast before a shot was heard." Du Pont employed such well-known academic his-

torians as Dixon Ryan Fox, Arthur Schlesinger Sr., and James Truslow Adams at $100 to $150 per script to check the programs for factual accuracy. It eventually counted Maxwell Anderson, Stephen Vincent Benet, and Robert Sherwood among its scriptwriters. The program's high standards—and informative, low-key talks on science—brought it accolades from educators and awards for high quality as family entertainment from women's groups.[55]

Thus Du Pont secured, if nothing else, the goodwill of those who were thankful for anything that raised the standard of radio entertainment. Dixon Ryan Fox, the historian who supervised the professional advisory committee, assured Lammot du Pont after more than a year of broadcasts that the program had largely erased the "ugliness" in the average undergraduate's picture of Du Pont and was reinforcing its image as "an American institution."[56]

Whether Du Pont had mastered the vernacular of the common folk was another matter. The intermission talks sought to impart a human interest flavor with such introductory ploys as a humorous story about an old lady who liked Du Pont's rayon yarn but assumed the company "must feed the rayon worm good things to eat to get such nice results" or a description of the puzzle presented to chemistry by the need of missionaries on a South Seas island to find a way to keep tropical insects from devouring their Bibles. Still, one Du Pont executive described the shows in retrospect as "ponderous," and a historian of Du Pont public relations has noted the distinctly high-culture tastes of William Hart, the Du Pont advertising director in charge of the program. Radio ratings did not indicate any vast popularity for the *Cavalcade* (the Hooper Ratings for the third week of May 1937, for instance, list it at 13.2, while the shows of the rival networks, *One Man's Family* and *Broadway Merry-Go-Round,* scored 36.6 and 18.0, respectively).[57]

Just as Du Pont's *Cavalcade* conveyed more an atmosphere of education and uplift than of colloquial conversation with ordinary folks, so too the company's executives staunchly resisted any complete capitulation to the public relations rage. Even as the company mounted an extensive exhibit at the Texas Centennial Exposition and the national advertising campaign presented its "jes' folks" figures, President Lammot du Pont commented that "personally, I do not see that business needs 'public relations' particularly." The next year he reaffirmed privately to Vice President Walter Carpenter that he placed far more importance on manufacturing excellent products at low cost than on "any meeting of the public interest."[58] Early in 1938, when one employee suggested that the heads of large corporations make "trips throughout the country to become acquainted with people" and thus create a "common bond" between people in the hinterlands and large industrial organizations, Lammot rejected the notion with the curt reply that his responsibilities were too great for him to find time "to indulge in such trips."[59] A stick-to-business executive, Lammot would have agreed enthusiastically with the comment by a contributor to *Advertising and Selling* that it was "a shame that business has to take time out" from real business activities for public relations.[60]

Still, despite such truculent resistance, by the time of the 1939–40 World's Fair Du Pont had come remarkably far in recognizing the need to speak the people's language. It had incorporated crowd-pleasing forms of entertainment into its now-elaborate fair exhibits and had pioneered the successful use of nonconcert radio for enhancing its corporate image. Polls indicated that the company had improved its standing with the public. As Carpenter pointed out, however, it still evoked twice as much unfavorable opinion as other corporate giants like General Motors and United States Steel. Although he warned against the "dangerous attitude" of those who would ignore the importance of public goodwill, he was unsuccessful in several attempts to shape company policy to meet public relations goals. In 1937 and 1939, for instance, he could not persuade the Executive Committee to stop all its international trading in munitions—even though such operations, he insisted, accounted for far less than 1 percent of company profits.[61]

The Cavalcade of America endured through the early 1940s only by surviving temporary cancellations and regular, less-than-enthusiastic internal reappraisals. Thus, Du Pont, notwithstanding its new image and concern for a popular idiom, serves as a reminder of the strength of the business traditionalism that had to be overcome as the managerial emphasis shifted in the 1930s to broader corporate horizons and extensive public relations. Only when Carpenter, with what Charles Cheape describes as his awareness of the need to factor external issues more fully into corporate decision making, became president of the company in 1940 would Du Pont move beyond the defensive impulse that had momentarily propelled it into shaping a corporate image and begin to enter the "modern era of public relations."[62]

Bruce Barton and the "Conversion" of United States Steel

Amid all the agonizing over the need for business to mount a public relations counteroffensive against the New Deal, no single event evoked such admiration or so rekindled hopes within the advertising trade as did a dramatic announcement by United States Steel Corporation in December 1935. For the first time in its history, the company declared, it would carry its corporate message directly to the American public through institutional advertising. The trade press reacted as though the exhortations of a revival minister had finally brought the town atheist to the sinner's bench. Among the prominent industrial giants, U.S. Steel had stood as the last holdout against advertising in the popular media. Now stiff-necked resistance had yielded. Moreover, compared to Du Pont, U.S. Steel embarked on the courtship of the common man with far fewer reservations. Appropriately, it was that familiar evangelist of business statesmanship, Bruce Barton, who had inspired U.S. Steel's dramatic conversion. In fact, the recent news of his successful proselytization of U.S. Steel was what gave him the leverage to challenge giant industry, at the 1935 NAM convention, to take up the righteous defense of the faith. U.S. Steel's conversion had made "the Confession" seem obligatory for others in the business community.

Barton had set his sights on U.S. Steel as early as 1930, when he noted in a letter that some of its younger executives were thinking about a broader advertising program. Myron C. Taylor had taken over the leadership of the corporation after the death of Elbert Gary in 1927 and had begun a massive reorganization. During the first decade of the century, U.S. Steel had enjoyed a reputation for good public relations, one based partly on Gary's own assurances that he would keep the public fully informed and partly on the new giant's cautiousness not to inflame antitrust sentiments. But the corporation's public relations had slumped into desuetude in the early 1920s. The financier Thomas Lamont, a member of the board of directors and an enthusiast for good PR, confided privately to correspondents that the corporation "had been gradually filling up with dry rot" in the last ten years of Gary's regime. During this period, when "the whole outfit . . . had been steadily running down hill," its problems ranged from antiquated equipment and "hide bound" management to the lack of a vivid, humanized corporate image.[63]

Myron Taylor did not find it easy to change things in an overgrown giant like U.S. Steel. In 1934, to facilitate structural reform and centralization, he commissioned the engineering firm of Ford, Bacon and Davis to make a thorough analysis of virtually every aspect of the operations of U.S. Steel and its many subsidiaries. Barton, in his quest of the greatest prize in the world of advertising—the U.S. Steel account—astutely emphasized the role of the corporate image in consolidating morale behind the new, integrative changes. Moreover, by 1935 the challenge of the New Deal and the activism of the CIO had created a need for political protection and antiunion suasion that seemed to justify a deliberate and costly effort to humanize the industrial giant. In this context Barton sold the corporation on a major institutional advertising campaign.[64]

Barton's "conquest" of U.S. Steel immediately assumed epic proportions in the company-culture narratives of his agency, Batten, Barton, Durstine, and Osborn. The BBDO newsletter announced his triumph under the headline "Veni, Vidi, Vici." Barton had "made a lot of important presentations that have influenced the history of great corporations like General Electric and General Motors," the newsletter reverently declared, "but he hit a high spot of his career when he went to work on U.S. Steel." Like a knight of old, but armed with "a huge easel and a taxiload of 30 × 40 charts," Barton had "invaded" U.S. Steel headquarters. He had exercised such mastery that President Myron Taylor joined forces with him and scheduled a repeat performance before the entire board of directors on the following day. By the third day of this blitzkrieg, according to the newsletter, Barton and other BBDO executives had gained so sweeping a mandate that they met with the presidents and vice presidents of the U.S. Steel subsidiaries to "acquaint them with the new order of things in the Corporation."[65]

Barton had swayed U.S. Steel with the same argument he was to present two months later before the NAM convention—that in an era of government activism, no great corporation dared ignore the public. With business "in the doghouse," U.S. Steel would make a fundamental mistake by hanging back in conservative silence, meaning nothing more to the public than "a symbol on brokers' boards and ticker tapes." To emphasize these broad political purposes of U.S. Steel's new public relations campaign, however, would be to neglect the most astute aspect of Barton's salesmanship—his ability to frame his proposals to elicit support from divergent interests within the corporation. Barton recognized the existence in U.S. Steel, as in other large corporations he had advised, of powerful subsidiary and division executives who distrusted all forms of public relations that would not result in product sales. These men viewed institutional advertising as a raid on their divisional budgets; they had to be convinced of its concrete benefits for their own operations.[66]

Barton had the perfect formula to offer—one that combined public visibility with the same attention to merchandising and internal integration that he had successfully proposed to General Electric and General Motors in the 1920s. Part of that integration and greater efficiency would result from uniting the previous "little trickles" of trade journal advertising by the various subsidiaries into "one mighty river" of national publicity that "every one will see and talk about." His agency advocated national advertising for U.S. Steel, Barton told the corporation's directors in his legendary presentation,

> not only because it will be a dramatic gesture of leadership to the whole business world, not only because it is the cheapest and most effective way of creating pride in the institution in the minds of its people, but also because its effect will be to make the entire membership of the organization, from top to bottom, more sales minded. It is not an exaggeration to say that if the whole organization of the Corporation, from top to bottom, can become five per cent or ten per cent less production minded and more sales minded that change will mean a difference of millions of dollars in the pockets of the stockholders.[67]

In vintage argumentation, Barton thus offered both an expansive vision of industrial leadership and a means of invigorating sales within each corporate division. With its emphasis on corporate cohesion, morale, and greater sales-mindedness, Barton's proposal coincided perfectly with the reorganization plans of Taylor and his public relations—minded right-hand man, Edward R. Stettinius Jr., formerly a coordinator of PR at General Motors.

From the outset the U.S. Steel advertisements employed typical Barton qualities of subtlety and indirection. They familiarized the public with U.S. Steel by glamorizing its big customers—a tactic that avoided direct self-praise while revealing how both the steel corporation and those it wished to flatter (and to whom it wished to sell its products) had contributed to the progress of the nation.[68] The first ad praised the automobile industry for moving its annual auto show from January to November, thus stimulating demand and creating more work during the winter months. Personalizing this contribution to economic recovery with the headline "Bob Miller will have a job *this* winter," BBDO and U.S. Steel won praise from *Time* magazine and the appreciation of the car manufacturers. Intense internal merchandising, a classic element in Barton's formula and the key to his expectations of creating "pride in the institution" through gestures of leadership, inspired enthusiastic feedback about the impact of the campaign on executive morale.[69]

One of the most dramatic ads in the series, a celebration of Andrew Carnegie entitled "He Came to a Land of Wooden Towns and Left a Nation of Steel," did provoke some negative reactions. Lumbermen decried it as "a blow below the belt" to their industry for insinuating "that wood is a symbol of backwardness and primitive civilization." But lumbermen were not a major customer of U.S. Steel, and the ad's sweeping vision of the transformation of a nation very effectively associated U.S. Steel with conventional notions of progress. The tribute also unfolded artlessly into a political message. Having lauded Carnegie as a "master builder," U.S. Steel then asked rhetorically, "Does our country no longer need great builders? Have we no frontiers left, as some would assert?" Without mentioning the New Deal, U.S. Steel took a stand with Andrew Carnegie in favor of new economic frontiers and against any "counsel of despair."[70]

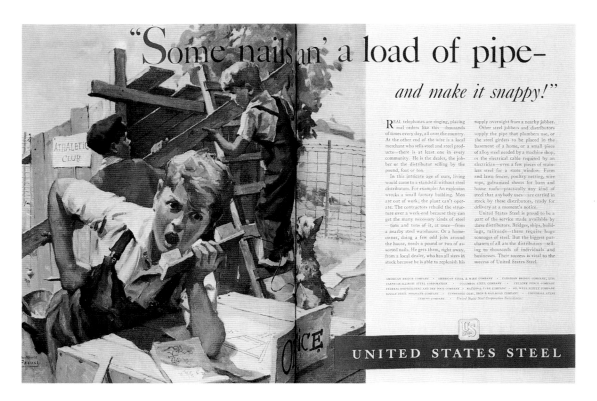

The ad shows the headline: "Some nails an' a load of pipe— and make it snappy!"

REAL telephones are ringing, placing real orders like this—thousands of times every day, all over the country. At the other end of the wire is a local merchant who sells steel and steel products—there is at least one in every community. He is the dealer, the jobber or the distributor selling by the pound, foot or ton.

In this intricate age of ours, living would come to a standstill without steel distributors. For example: An explosion wrecks a small factory building. Men are out of work; the plant can't operate. The contractors rebuild the structure over a week-end because they can get the many necessary kinds of steel—tons and tons of it, at once—from a nearby steel warehouse. Or a home-owner, doing a few odd jobs around the house, needs a pound or two of assorted nails. He gets them, right away, from a local dealer, who has all sizes in stock because he is able to replenish his

supply overnight from a nearby jobber. Other steel jobbers and distributors supply the pipe that plumbers use, or the steel girders to be placed in the basement of a home, or a small piece of alloy steel needed by a machine shop, or the electrical cable required by an electrician—even a few pieces of stainless steel for a store window. Farm and lawn fences, poultry netting, wire rope, galvanized sheets for barn and house roofs—practically any kind of steel that anybody uses—are carried in stock by these distributors, ready for delivery at a moment's notice.

United States Steel is proud to be a part of the service made available by these distributors. Bridges, ships, buildings, railroads—these require huge tonnages of steel. But the biggest purchasers of all are the distributors—selling to thousands of individuals and businesses. Their success is vital to the success of United States Steel.

AMERICAN BRIDGE COMPANY • AMERICAN STEEL & WIRE COMPANY • CANADIAN BRIDGE COMPANY, LTD.
CARNEGIE-ILLINOIS STEEL CORPORATION • COLUMBIA STEEL COMPANY • CYCLONE FENCE COMPANY
FEDERAL SHIPBUILDING AND DRY DOCK COMPANY • NATIONAL TUBE COMPANY • OIL WELL SUPPLY COMPANY
SCULLY STEEL PRODUCTS COMPANY • TENNESSEE COAL, IRON & RAILROAD COMPANY • UNIVERSAL ATLAS
CEMENT COMPANY • United States Steel Corporation Subsidiaries

UNITED STATES STEEL

FIGURE 6.12
When United States Steel, the largest of manufacturing corporations, finally recognized the need to humanize its image, one tactic it chose was to personify itself as a familiar gang of energetic, industrious boys.

As U.S. Steel moved on to sing the praises of the oil companies, hardware dealers, and streamlined trains, it proved itself the equal of any in the quest for a popular idiom and imagery. Turning to a Norman Rockwell style, it depicted young boys in rumble seats quizzing gas station attendants and found a metaphor for itself in the vital transactions carried out by other youngsters in building their clubhouse. U.S. Steel, in these colorful double-spread advertisements, interjected itself into the small-town atmosphere that was being celebrated by the regional painters of the era and that attracted even leftist intellectuals searching for a vision of community. At heart U.S. Steel was just a bunch of hometown boys, and the economic system no more mysterious than their "few cents' worth of nails" (Fig. 6.12).[71]

U.S. Steel's sudden venture into institutional advertising was far from a single gesture or a half-hearted commitment. By 1936 the corporation had recruited an experienced publicist, J. Carlisle MacDonald, as its public relations officer, had established a Public Relations Department, and had launched a company magazine, the *U.S. Steel News.* In the magazine, and soon in its annual reports as well, the company strove to communicate in a popular vernacular, both visually and verbally. It began, in the words of *Advertising Age,* to "humanize itself"—not only by running special features on President Myron Taylor and conveying his wish to "keep in close touch" with all employees of the corporation, but also by explaining to its employees, as the headlines put it, "Why We Have Stockholders" and "How We Earned Our Living." Its accounts, U.S. Steel insisted, were no more complicated than those of a family household, and the corporation itself, "in spite of its size," was "just a corner store for steel, iron and other products."[72]

While U.S. Steel, like many other corporations of the era, gave its workers a new visibility, especially in the pages of *U.S. Steel News* (Fig. 6.13), it quickly discovered that another, more traditional, genre of corporate visual imagery could be adapted to its urgent needs for simplicity and emotional impact. Beginning in 1936, the cover illustrations of the company magazine romanticized U.S. Steel with dramatic depictions of fiery furnaces (Fig. 6.14).[73] These, in turn, suggested another medium through which the company might also convey an impressive corporate image to the public—namely, film. U.S. Steel had presented films of its operations many times before, but now it undertook a full-scale production. Between 1937 and 1938, it developed three versions of a glorious story of steel, two of these in technicolor. Heralding the premiere of the first film, *U.S. Steel News* promised that viewers would "witness for the first time the drama of industry presented in the identical manner in which Hollywood offers its most appealing attractions." With a musical score "inspired by the rhythm of the mills," the U.S. Steel films presented, this reviewer avowed, "a spectacle of such gorgeous splendor as I have never dreamed of."[74]

The four-reel version, *Men Make Steel*—which carried no advertising beyond the notice that it was made on the properties of U.S. Steel and its subsidiaries—gained showings at major urban theaters, including Radio City Music Hall. Pare Lorentz, famous for his own film documentaries (in black and white), called it the most exciting film he had seen in months and "the most beautiful color picture ever made." But U.S. Steel did not rely solely on the stark beauty of what John Stilgoe has called an "industrial zone aesthetic" in the factory scenes. It also humanized steelmaking—and, by extension, itself—by incorporating scenes of workers stopping to chew tobacco or enjoy soft drinks.[75]

U.S. Steel further extended the range of its public relations activities when it commissioned a leading industrial designer, Walter Dorwin Teague, to create a striking exhibit building for the corporation at the New York World's Fair of 1939–40. At about this time it also joined other major corporations in finding workers of modest circumstances and even of immigrant backgrounds to celebrate as exemplary employees. In early 1941 the *U.S. Steel News* featured George Giley Jr., "first helper at no. 52 furnace of no. 4 open hearth," as "Mr. America at Gary" and electrician Adam Kendzia, a Polish immigrant and the head of an "ideal family of five," as "Mr. America of Cleveland."[76]

Once Bruce Barton had led U.S. Steel to recognize the importance of its public image, the corporation did not backslide. Perhaps because it found itself immediately overwhelmed with problems arising from the challenge of the CIO and the antagonism of some other steel companies that reacted bitterly to its 1937 accommodation with CIO chief John L. Lewis, U.S. Steel could not afford the sporadic complacency of the family executives at Du Pont, who faced little effec-

US STEEL NEWS

JULY 1940

SAFETY NUMBER

FIGURES 6.13 & 6.14
On the covers of its new company
magazine, U.S. Steel exhibited its
corporate culture in two distinct
ways: domestic affirmations of
worker satisfaction and dramatic
industrial scenarios (cf. Fig. 5.19).

tive labor agitation during the late 1930s. U.S. Steel's new public relations director preached the gospel of public relations consciousness and humanization for every element of the company's operations.[77] Although he and the BBDO agency did encounter some internal resistance—especially by sales and divisional managers who were inclined to impede centralization and begrudge PR expenditures—U.S. Steel created a network of public relations managers at major subsidiaries. Executives in this network began actively to promote plant visits, variously labeled as open houses, community days, or family days.[78] That U.S. Steel had taken to heart Barton's homilies can be seen from the text of one of its internal bulletins, quoted in 1938 by *Advertising Age:*

> The most important thing that faces a big corporation today is what the American people will think and what the American people will do about big business.
>
> If advertising makes people realize that the subsidiaries of the United States Steel Corporation contribute to their comfort and well-being, if it helps to make people proud of our organization rather than critical, if it helps build a

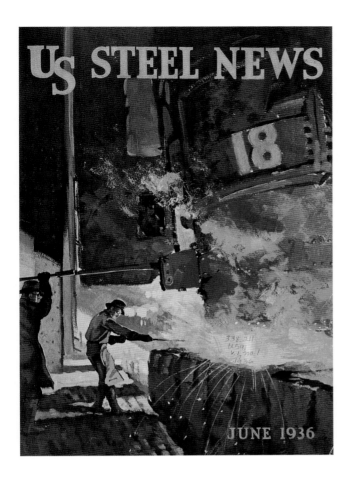

US STEEL NEWS

18

JUNE 1936

better sense of loyalty among all the far-flung employees of United States Steel Corporation subsidiaries, and if it makes your customers feel more friendly toward your company, then it will have paid its way.[79]

GM's Customer Research:
Mass-Producing the Personal Touch

Of the major corporations that became converts to the public relations persuasion in the 1930s, General Motors explored the array of possible initiatives most vigorously, rivaling even such traditional advocates as AT&T in the breadth of its activities. GM executives were as sensitive as any others to what the president of the Ayer agency characterized as "this constant black rain of vilification and abuse" cascading down on the leaders of all large companies. But like much of corporate America, even after a period of dismay at its sudden denigration and a season of inglorious failure in battling FDR on the electoral front in 1936, GM cast off a "hunker-down and stick-to-business" mentality and embraced constructive forms of public relations as a response. Thus, conditions that seemed likely at first to constrict the social role of large corporations ultimately spurred them to broaden their reach as they contested the federal government's claims of competence to act for the best interests of the people. As the most successful of the great corporations in retaining profitability in the wake of the depression, General Motors was best positioned to make ample investments in the institutionalization of corporate public relations.

Much of the impetus for expanded public relations at GM stemmed from the concerns and initiatives of its president, Alfred P. Sloan Jr. During 1931 and 1932 Sloan was searching for new structures and a new rallying cry to help pull the company out of a malaise that had deepened with the depression. In both 1930 and 1931 the corporation had brought together its executives for national conferences at White Sulphur Springs, West Virginia. Such meetings were crucial for GM, Sloan told the assembled managers, because of the barriers that pure size and distance had erected against the flow of energizing ideas. He wanted their proposals for "a bigger and better General Motors." Although in comparison with other automakers and most other industries GM was prospering, it was not doing a good job of responding to customer complaints and to revelations of chronic defects in some models. The chairman of the board, Lammot du Pont, worried that GM was not making enough of an effort to find out "what the public really wants."[80]

When Paul Garrett, the financial columnist for the *New York Post,* joined the company as its first full-fledged public relations director in May of 1931, he noted another internal defect. For all Barton's earlier efforts to promote internal cooperation, especially in advertising, many of the divisions had now fallen back into traveling their separate ways. At the White Sulphur Springs conference in October 1931 Garrett pointed out the startling lack of consistency in GM publicity. Sometimes the ads of the individual divisions stressed the GM connection; at other times they ignored it completely. Seizing on an approach that would address the concerns of Alfred Sloan and Lammot du Pont, as well as his own dissatisfaction with the lack of corporate unity, Garrett proposed to enhance GM's public relations by working "from the inside out," starting with General Motors' own personnel, its stockholders, and its customers.[81]

Garrett began this "inside out" process by soliciting the views of stockholders who had recently sold part or all of their GM stock. Many small stockholders expressed amazement and delight that the giant corporation had taken a personal interest in their views. Garrett mimeographed large selections from the flood of responses and distributed them to GM executives. Among those that Garrett chose to disseminate, several embraced the concept of the General Motors "family." Miss Florence Wilkinson of Philadelphia replied that although she had sold her GM stock, she had also bought a Pontiac, "so I am really still in the family"; Miss Minnie Richards, a schoolteacher, avowed that although she had "slipped out of the 'family' under the pressure of necessity," her "respect for the integrity and administrative ability" of GM was "unabated."[82]

At the same time the company was also receiving volumes of mail regarding another public relations effort—a radio program of orchestral music with a local theme. Each week GM's *Parade of the States* was dedicated to one of the states, and the orchestra played selections associated in some way with that state. The centerpiece of each program was the reading of a tribute to the state composed by Barton. General Motors circulated advance copies of each florid tribute to the honored state to its political leaders, newspaper editors, school superintendents, clubs and fraternal orders, and chambers of commerce. The response to Barton's idealized verbal portraits was overwhelming, reflecting the continuing pull of identification with geographic localities. By the end of 1931, Garrett reported, the company was receiving more than five thousand letters of appreciation a week. He distributed multipage anthologies of "typical excerpts" from these letters to a long list of executives.[83]

The warming reassurance of this flood of positive letters suggested a tactic to address individual complaints while providing a "conversation piece" for use in public relations. General Motors had intermittently been sending questionnaires to GM car owners to inquire about "what people really want in the way of a car." This operation, carried out by Henry ("Buck") Weaver as a function of the central Sales Division, was dramatically elevated to the status of an independent unit in 1933. Sloan gave it the new designation of "GM Customer Research Staff" and featured it in a publicly divulged letter to GM stockholders.[84] Customer research, Sloan announced, was now an "*operating philosophy*" within General Motors that "must extend through all phases" of the business.[85]

By mid-1934 about 300,000 people had responded to Weaver's customer questionnaires. Many of them offered unsolicited comments in addition to their answers to the list of queries about style, price range, and engineering features. By 1938 GM had distributed some 1,500,000 such questionnaires. People were greatly flattered to have their advice solicited, Weaver observed, especially by a large and prominent corporation. *Fortune* would later compliment Weaver for the "ingratiating, arresting and informal" tone of voice he achieved in the questionnaires, both through folksy phrasing and "deliberately careless typography" (Figs. 6.15 and 6.16). They sounded, *Fortune* remarked, "as though GM thought its customers were individually as well as collectively important." Thus, the questionnaires not only made GM more secure in its alertness to public tastes, but they also offered, as *Fortune* would later note, considerable "propaganda value."[86]

All these qualities answered to a concern that Paul Garrett had voiced very soon after assuming the leadership of Public Relations at GM. "No big corporation in the world," he had admonished fellow executives, "must rise or fall so completely on its reputation with Mr. and Mrs. Jones, their small boy and the daughter at school, as General Motors."[87] Customer research cultivated just that kind of close relationship. Significantly, as Weaver's surveys acquired a larger public relations mission in 1933, GM authorized him to make one critical change in his operations. Instead of sending out questionnaires with no GM identification, as had been Weaver's practice in the past, they would now go out "in the name of the General Motors Corporation." If people liked "to have their advice sought," as the previous surveys indicated, GM should fully "capitalize on the tremendous by-product of goodwill and sales influence." With its name prominently displayed, GM would then glean the goodwill evoked by the "touch of judicious flattery" incorporated into the questionnaire booklet.[88]

In a pamphlet titled *The Philosophy of Customer Research,* Buck Weaver amplified this theme of attention to the individual into a full-fledged prescription for the ills

20

GENERAL CHARACTERISTICS

Of course you want ALL these things – but which will influence you most when it comes to choosing your next car?

☑ CHECK 3 OR 4 ITEMS

☐ Appearance?

☐ Comfort?

☐ Dependability?

☐ Ease of Control?

☐ First Cost?

☐ Operating Economy?

☐ Pick-up?

☐ Safety?

☐ Smoothness?

☐ Speed?

☐ . . . . ?

R
E
M
A
R
K
S

Thanks for your cooperation

While it is the primary purpose of this little book to GATHER information, it has been the aim to make it interesting and informative – and we sincerely hope that the time and effort that you have devoted to filling it out may prove helpful to you when it comes to selecting your next car.

"The motor car has become intimately woven into our social and economic fabric. It has enriched the lives of our people. It has transformed a nation into a neighborhood."

– Bruce Barton

FIGURES 6.15 & 6.16

These pages from GM's customer questionnaires exemplify the visual embellishments and deliberately informal tone that their author,

Henry "Buck" Weaver, believed would foster customer interest and participation.

of mass society. Customer research, he proclaimed, was nothing less than a tool for "human understanding." As a business grew larger, he argued, its need "for reckoning with the tastes of the individual" grew greater because of the widening gap between customer and business executive. This was particularly true in what Sloan had portrayed to stockholders as an increasingly complex, "kaleidoscopic era characterized by swift movements—social as well as economic." And if GM gave ostensible recognition to the individual by reaching out through questionnaires, the exercise also established the company—as a 1934 GM ad proclaimed—as the epitome of "PROGRESS— out of the common sense of the common people." [89]

Surely here was a concept of the operations of a large business corporation that was worthy of being termed a "philosophy." Conducted "on a highly scientific basis," customer research would provide the corporation with a "correct interpretation of what the public actually thinks." In 1934 GM made prominent use of the slogan "An Eye to the Future—An Ear to the Ground" in its nationwide institutional advertising campaign. The "ear to the ground" was Weaver's consumer research operation. It ensured, GM claimed, that its cars reflected the de-

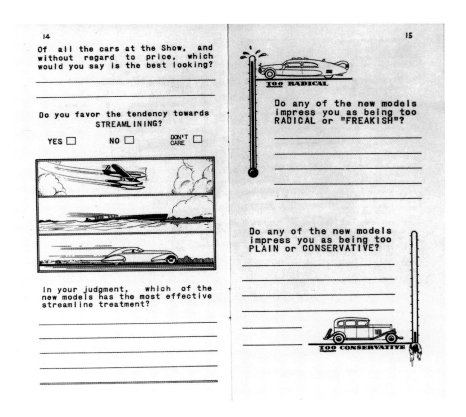

14

Of all the cars at the Show, and without regard to price, which would you say is the best looking?

_____

Do you favor the tendency towards STREAMLINING?

YES ☐   NO ☐   DON'T CARE ☐

In your judgment, which of the new models has the most effective streamline treatment?

_____
_____
_____
_____
_____

TOO RADICAL

Do any of the new models impress you as being too RADICAL or "FREAKISH"?

_____
_____
_____
_____
_____

Do any of the new models impress you as being too PLAIN or CONSERVATIVE?

_____
_____
_____
_____

TOO CONSERVATIVE

sires of the public. GM's effort was a perfect example of the workings of free enterprise within a business system conceived on what Charles McGovern calls an "electoral model."[90] That the corporation, like the ideal elected representative, operated entirely in the service of its consumer constituents was clear from its active solicitation of their ideas and choices. Weaver, with his penchant for dramatic visual explications, made customer research the crucial link to complete the chain that started with the company's engineering department and moved next to production, sales, the dealer, the consumer, and finally, thanks to customer research, back to engineering again (Fig. 6.17).[91] With a giant corporation displaying such sensitivity to the needs and desires of its mass of customers, no government intervention could make the relationship any more "democratic."

Customer research thus gained a place in GM's anti–New Deal propaganda. Increasingly alarmed by the government's inroads on the autonomy of business executives, Sloan (who would later refer back to his "tirades" against the New Deal) and other GM leaders emphasized the democratic aspects of customer research in their efforts to advance the economic education of the American people.[92] In

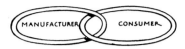

100 YEARS AGO

Under the conditions of the one man shop, with the head of the business serving as designer, manufacturer, purchasing agent, salesman and service expert,- an intimate understanding of customer tastes and desires was automatically assured.

MODERN INDUSTRY

By the very nature of things, the bigger an institution grows, the wider becomes the breach between the customer and those responsible for guiding the destiny of the institution.

With producer and consumer so widely separated it becomes increasingly difficult to keep the business sensitively attuned to the requirements of the customer.

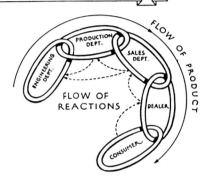

GENERAL MOTORS

There is a need for some kind of a liaison which would serve as a substitute for the close personal contact which existed automatically in the days of the small shop.·

CONSUMER RESEARCH
- aims to fill this need by providing an auxiliary and more direct line of communication between producer and consumer.

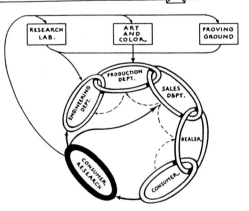

H. G. W.   —   SALES SECTION   —   GENERAL MOTORS   —   DETROIT, MICHIGAN.

FIGURE 6.17
In these diagrams Weaver reenacted a process of estrangement between producer and customer that paralleled the isolation of manager from worker that corporate executives so lamented (see Chapter 3). Customer research would restore the bond between producer and customer.

1936, for instance, a GM institutional ad featured a story on the customer research operation during an election season campaign to persuade Americans to look to the business corporation, rather than to perpetuation of the New Deal, for the nation's well-being.[93] The ad series "Who Serves Progress Serves America" sought, according to a Harvard Business School analysis, "to teach fundamental economic truths in terms of specific examples chosen from General Motors experience." While Roosevelt's New Deal might claim to serve the people, the argument in the ads implied, corporations such as GM, by sending out "more than a million letters to car owners" assessing their "tastes and desires," had in fact made themselves the people's faithful representatives. A culminating ad within the series, appearing only two weeks before the November 1936 election, juxtaposed a historical vignette of an election scene with a photograph of members of the GM Customer Research Staff reviewing questionnaire responses. This operation, the caption pointed out, constituted "the 'ballot box' of a great business." In what amounted to an election editorial, General Motors asked whether the nation should proceed toward "restriction and regimentation" or whether it should allow the true creators of wealth to serve their constituencies.[94]

Customer research had emerged at GM as one answer to converging corporate concerns about internal morale, the political environment, customer dissatisfaction, and the development of a long-range strategy. General Motors sought to expand the circle of those impressed with its personal touch by giving its customer questionnaires a central role in its advertising. As part of its "An Eye to the Future—An Ear to the Ground" campaign, it devised an attention-grabbing scene that neatly dramatized Paul Garrett's vision of intimate contact with the Joneses. An elated young boy shared with the audience of readers his thrill at seeing his father recognized by a great corporation. "Look dad," he exclaimed, "a letter from General Motors!" (Fig. 6.18).[95]

The Many Agendas of a "Public-Minded Institution"

General Motors' venture in customer research, which soon made it the leading corporation in that field, represented only part of the company's expanding public relations program in 1933 and 1934. Under Garrett's influence GM's *Annual Report* for 1932 mentioned public relations for the first time—as a "vital relationship." The next year's *Annual Report* called for all employees and dealers to "build goodwill for GM by being public-minded members of a public-minded institution."[96] The company had commissioned a history of GM that shunned "unnecessary superlatives" and emphasized "the enlightened social as well as economic contribution" of the corporation. GM expanded its budget for "institutional talking pictures" and began the publication and widespread distribution of popularly slanted technical booklets by the Research Division. Garrett moved to impose the unity of a "common approach" on the public relations of the various GM divisions and to devise a formula for consistent contributions to local charities.[97] As preparations went forward for the GM exhibit at the 1933–34 Century of Progress Exposition, Garrett assembled a prestigious group of leaders in government, business, religion, and education at an elaborate banquet to open the GM display, thus providing President Sloan with a suitable audience for a major public relations address. Sloan highlighted GM research but also took pains to counteract political interference

FIGURE 6.18

By 1934, with public relations now its central objective in customer research, GM dramatized the thrill it expected average folk to experience upon receiving a questionnaire from an immense and famous corporation.

and popular pessimism by demonstrating that business was eager to lead the way into the technological future.[98]

By 1935 GM's public relations offensive was moving forward on multiple fronts. The company had resumed its institutional radio campaign with the *General Motors Symphony Orchestra Concerts,* performed "under the batons of the greatest conductors in the world." During the "intermissions" GM delivered traffic safety messages and—following up on its Century of Progress emphasis—publicized its engineering research. It also initiated plans to put its displays of science and technology on the road in a traveling public relations campaign known as the "Parade of Progress."[99]

Over the next three years General Motors repeatedly reassessed the extent to which, and the means by which, it should shoulder responsibility for "selling the system." In the *Annual Report* at the end of 1935 Sloan had avowed GM's responsibility, not only to its stockholders but also to "the community at large," to promote a "better understanding not only of . . . our increasingly complicated national economy but also of the economic consequences of the things that are done . . . if our country is to remain a democracy." Yet GM executives remained unsure how conspicuously they should enter the public debate. They recognized a new degree of power in public opinion but confessed their distance from many popular attitudes. "Note how many things happening today get their interest *not from any intrinsic worth as you and I reckon,*" Garrett mused to his fellow officials, "but from a wide public feeling." Such a recognition of elite insularity might seem to dictate a prudent silence. Yet a company as large as GM, one so involved in the "home town[s] of the American Public" as to see its own interests and those of the public as "really coterminous," could hardly sit back and passively absorb the impact of changes in opinion.[100]

How to go about selling the system was the next problem. In 1935 a tentative decision by GM to take up the defense of bigness, out of a sense of duty to itself and to the economic system, precipitated a prolonged internal debate. Sloan believed that the auto industry enjoyed sufficient public goodwill that it could afford to champion—by "fearlessly putting forth the facts"—the cause of big business generally. He envisioned another great "publicity dinner" with a radio hookup, at which distinguished guests would offer testimonials on behalf of the constructive value of bigness. Lammot du Pont, an influential member of the GM board, was inclined to agree that since Americans were "notoriously in favor of everything 'bigger and better,'" the positive virtues of bigness could be "put across." But the phrase "business bigness" seemed sufficiently risky, even in a proposed letter to GM stockholders, that other GM leaders nervously proposed changes in emphasis and wording.[101]

In considering the content of the intermission talks during its radio concerts in 1936—a presidential election year—GM officials noted that "never before" had the vital interests of business been so linked to political events and that never had it been so crucial to develop "prudent means of opposing and offsetting unfriendly interests." Some of the GM institutional advertising in mid-1936 took on the flavor of an electoral campaign, lashing out against those (unnamed) persons who advocated "regimentation" and who proposed to divide the wealth rather than multiply it.[102] But as GM further planned its campaign in defense of bigness, more restrained views prevailed. Initially, Garrett was inclined to take up cudgels for the system; he even contemplated such possible slogans as "bigness serves best" or "bigness is as bigness does." "Everyone knows we are big," he noted, "and it should be our job to make a virtue of bigness as we practice it." But he also acknowledged the prudent judgment of several executives who questioned "whether we should deliberately stick our necks out."[103]

Ultimately, the campaign went forward under a far less defiant slogan: "Who Serves Progress Serves America." Garrett granted that this was "not quite so striking a defense of bigness." But he also observed that "nowadays . . . the psychology of a subtle public approach assumes an importance never known before to industry." Internally, GM exercised less caution. Two weeks before the November 1936 election Sloan warned in letters to employees that the company could be gravely damaged by anything that could lead to "class strife" or "economic shackles." And publicly, the company boldly purchased space in the *American Federationist,* the official journal of the AFL, for ads that presumed to speak from the laborer's standpoint, inviting workers to conclude that "what happens to General Motors happens to me" (Fig. 6.19).[104]

Against this background of effort, one might expect Franklin Roosevelt's overwhelming victory in November and the sitdown strikes in GM plants early the next year to have crushed the GM public relations onslaught. But General Motors

"WHAT HAPPENS TO GENERAL MOTORS HAPPENS TO ME!"

Here in Detroit we who work in the automobile industry see train after train of raw materials rolling constantly through the factory gates and think of them only as the stuff from which cars are made.

They are not only that. They represent the work of hundreds of thousands of men and women in all sorts of industry in every state of the union. Farmers, steel puddlers, glass makers, leatherworkers, miners, lumbermen—a whole cross-section of working America shares in the creation of a General Motors car.

When business is good for this corporation, business is good for them. When

cars stream off the assembly lines, orders stream forth for more raw materials to keep them busy earning good money.

What happens to General Motors happens to more people than you can call to mind. For General Motors is a symbol of America at work, and of the American system whereby the co-operation of all promotes the welfare and prosperity of the whole nation. Think of General Motors—and you must think in terms of many hundreds of thousands of Americans who find occupation in supplying raw materials, building General Motors products, and servicing those products after sale.

FIGURE 6.19
In 1936 General Motors ran a series of ads in the AFL's official journal urging workers to recognize how their interests coincided with those of a company crucial to the prosperity of the whole nation.

was a corporation, not a candidate. Its public relations activities were by then bureaucratically institutionalized, and the company's relative prosperity persisted. Far from losing faith in its public relations ventures, GM concluded that it now needed to focus on the long haul. Moreover, the failure of narrowly conceived confrontations with the New Deal inspired some GM executives to look to a wider sociopolitical arena of activity. President Sloan called for the leaders of big business to develop "an enlightened and militant statesmanship," since industry's responsibilities had "broadened" to include "the direction America shall take," and the corporation's astute managerial theorist, Donaldson Brown, proposed a major structural modification to adapt to the new political environment in which big business operated.[105]

In May 1938, in a long letter to Sloan, Brown tacitly suggested that the corporation move beyond its proclivity to sit and curse the New Deal. Rather, it should come to terms organizationally with the new, more complex terrain of business operations. General Motors should recognize and keep in step with "the handwriting on the wall," Brown argued, by creating a new internal group, a "Research Organization in Political, Social and Economic Trends." With the aid of expert assessments, filtered through a managerial group cognizant of operational realities, GM's leaders could operate from a timely and perceptive understanding of such trends. The conventional economics of business, which corporate leaders had understood so well, Brown added, had now reverted to something better described by that antique term, "political economy." Corporate policy could "no longer be formulated independently of political considerations." A company's officers should draw on the best of current knowledge in the areas of "economic and public psychology." If corporate leaders wished to regain the mantle of industrial statesmanship that they had donned so easily in the 1920s, they would have to sell themselves to the public by demonstrating that they were better prepared to deal with broad social and economic issues than were either labor leaders or politicians.[106]

Although it obtained only the briefest of trials in GM structural experiments, Brown's scheme reveals how expansive big business's defensive responses to the New Deal could become. Visions of the corporation developing competence in all fields of political economy, social policy, and public psychology would eventually meld with the seemingly disparate corporate endeavor to identify the company with the common man—and strategically to do so in the setting of "home town" America. In the late 1930s, and even more resolutely in the next decade, GM would attempt to attain this fusion, in accordance with Garrett's program for public relations "from the inside out." The crucial arena lay within its own plant communities. Every day, Garrett reminded his fellow executives in a vivid use of the election analogy, more than 28 million GM employees, dealers, stockholders, suppliers, and car owners were "casting a vote for or against us in a sort of informal nation-wide poll with their friends." They, like the company that linked them together, were "neighbors to the nation" and should be turned into a host of local public relations emissaries.[107]

As it turned from the failures of 1936 to the further institutionalization of its public relations activities, General Motors revived and intensified its efforts to speak in a popular vernacular. Even the General Motors Symphony Orchestra was not immune to this resolution. An NBC official reported in the spring of 1937 that GM executives had made it clear "in no uncertain terms" that the concerts would be "a whole lot more popular in theme." Of the GM sales manager the NBC representative reported, "I feel that he is thinking in terms of THE MASSES." Buck Weaver declared himself "more and more obsessed with the idea that there is a vast neglected area for effective propaganda in behalf of the capitalistic system—along the lines of something low-brow instead of high-brow." To provide "enough entertainment value to offset the natural human prejudice against anything that's too logical," he proposed that the company look for a newspaper columnist "with the showmanship of a Will Rogers." In its 1937 institutional ads GM featured the most distinctively folkish characters yet adopted for a corporate image. In pictures that rivaled the contemporary exposé photographs of Dorothea Lange and Margaret Bourke-White, GM presented wizened old carpenters and plain-as-a-mud-fence grannies to testify to GM's folk instinct for true value (Fig. 6.20).[108]

This intensified quest for the popular idiom reached its zenith in 1938 with the founding of a General Motors employee magazine entitled *GM Folks*. The corporation had developed ideas for a companywide house organ soon after Garrett became public relations director in 1931, but the plan had never materialized.[109] Very likely Garrett and other headquarters people had hesitated to push the centralization of public relations too precipitously and to seem to duplicate or usurp the work of the divisional and plant publications already in existence. But the labor struggles of 1937 dictated that no stone be left unturned in exploiting available channels of communication to the workers.

Had a GM employee magazine appeared in the early 1930s, it would surely have been quite different from *GM Folks*. The new publication was blatantly modeled

Test the VALUE

Make sure the next car you buy has these important features:

UNISTEEL BODY
—fused solidly together top, bottom and sides, without a bolt or nut or rivet—providing in Body by Fisher strength and safety with new style and comfort which glorify steel construction.

KNEE-ACTION
—the true gliding ride—makes every mile you travel more comfortable and assures better control of steering in emergency.

HYDRAULIC BRAKES
—improved in design to match the flashing performance of the new cars with the safety of smooth and powerfully sure straight-line stops.

TURRET TOP
—puts the safety of solid steel over your head in every closed car of the General Motors family.

NO DRAFT VENTILATION
—keeps the air you breathe healthfully free from drafts and makes driving safer by keeping the inside of windshield and windows fog-free.

Remember how your Mother tested the Cake with a broom-straw?

PROGRESS calling for close to a hundred million dollars — set aside for plant modernization and new tools, dies and machinery—distinguishes the new General Motors cars offered for 1937. Each of these cars has its own individuality—but all are strikingly representative of General Motors value—and all offer these outstanding GM features listed here.

FIGURE 6.20 *(above)*
Less politically preoccupied than in 1936, GM's institutional ads for 1937 delivered their messages through the personas of unmistakably plain and simple folk.

FIGURE 6.21 *(right)*
GM Folks unblushingly mimicked that instant success, *Life* magazine. In its ubiquitous photographs GM aimed to reveal that its workers and executives alike were just folks.

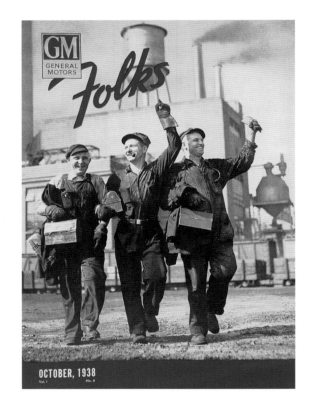

FIGURES 6.22, 6.23, & 6.24

Three scenes, the second two reprised for each Chevrolet plant city, imparted the message of the short film *From Dawn to Sunset*. Workers trekked happily to work along pleasant streets, picked up paychecks, and enjoyed sufficient affluence as consumers to boost local economies.

on the recently launched and hugely successful *Life* magazine (Fig. 6.21). Photographs, often in the style of *Life*'s human interest features, dominated virtually every page. These pictures, Garrett observed, "say in effect that we are wholesome, normal people all working together to our mutual benefit."[110] With sections devoted to employee hobbies, personal profiles, company clubs, and sports teams and with occasional features on welfare benefits, *GM Folks* did not differ significantly in content from hundreds of previous employee magazines. But in style and tone it clearly reflected the breezy intimacy and informality that the 1930s had fostered. The role of each of the close-ups of individual employees was to contribute to one, central conclusion—that, "all told," the company was made up of ordinary American folks. General Motors families lived in "neat, well-tended, typically American homes"; they liked to go fishing, listen to the radio, work in their gardens, go to movies and concerts, and play baseball with the kids. They worked hard on the job, and at home they were "no slouches at raising radishes, and redheads, and now and then an All-American fullback or two." Above all, they lived well, much better than their grandparents and in a style that was "downright luxurious" by the standards of other lands.[111]

In evoking the everyday lives of its employees as its corporate image, *GM Folks* was furthering the approach it had taken the year before in one of the triumphs of the GM film program, a twenty-five-minute documentary on the Chevrolet plants. Entitled *From Dawn to Sunset,* this fast-paced, crisply edited film recounted the daily lives of Chevrolet assembly-line and office workers. Viewers first followed the prosaic routines of men rising, shaving, and eating breakfast. As they emerged from the doors of their substantial small-town and suburban houses, they quickly formed a larger and larger phalanx of eager, energetic men parading down the tree-lined streets toward the factory (Fig. 6.22). A swelling chorus of voices expressed in song their joyous anticipation of the workday ahead. An undefiant viewer could not credibly have associated this company with the sitdown strikes of only a few months before.[112]

The message of *From Dawn to Sunset* was most emphatically conveyed through the recurrent images of workers receiving paychecks and then shopping with their families (Figs. 6.23 and 6.24). By providing short vignettes of each of a number of

Chevrolet plant cities, the film managed to repeat the themes of payday and consumption nearly a dozen times. In fact, those scenes occupied over thirteen minutes of the twenty-five-minute film, while depictions of workers on the factory assembly line totaled less than three minutes. In this light the image of the company went beyond that of fulfilled workers to encompass everyday Americans who conscientiously, but almost effortlessly, obtained their tickets to the good life as consumers. The abrupt cuts from payline to department store situated the company and its plant as the economic provider for the entire community. The narrator confidently assured viewers that the process they were observing constituted "the American way."

How General Motors Became "Home Folks"

The plant city focus of *From Dawn to Sunset* exemplified one of the most basic of all the General Motors public relations projects of the 1930s, one that also involved a major strategic decision in corporate deployment and structure. In the mid-1930s GM had adopted a definite policy of plant decentralization. As new factories were built, they would go to new communities, giving GM a much wider geographical range. While this policy was shaped to reduce distribution costs, it also reflected the company's political and public relations agenda. GM executives did not make a public issue of their idea, as Henry Ford had done with his village factories, but Sloan and other GM leaders shared a reaction to the depression that was prevalent among New Deal reformers as well as corporate leaders—a disillusionment with the concentration of people in large cities and a vision of an industrial population relocated so that it would not be totally dependent on urban factories. In a 1937 pamphlet for workers GM touted the "available garden plots" and "easy access to the country" in such smaller population centers. "Workers are closer to nature, so to speak," the company observed, and "in times of depression . . . the problem of taking care of the unemployed is greatly simplified."[113]

This program of localized manufacture would distribute buying power more widely, GM explained, and help create a "more balanced national economy." As a 1938 article in *Harper's Magazine* pointed out, the policy also represented a strategic move in labor relations. Factories in smaller communities would seem "more like home-grown local industries." The willingness of GM to relocate to new areas would make plant cities fearful of losing their GM factories to other sites. Assuming that business cycles would recur, the more widely dispersed workers might be better able to fend for themselves during periods of unemployment. From the standpoint of national politics, decentralization would ensure more "neighbors" for General Motors and give more localities a visible stake in the well-being of the corporation.[114]

A major project in public relations accompanied the decentralization program. Already in 1935 and 1936 Garrett was giving strong corporate support to local factory open houses and publicizing a new "good neighbor" approach to plant communities. In some communities, he observed, "General Motors was regarded as a pretty cold proposition, headed by men in Detroit and New York, interested only in getting what they could out [of the place]." Garrett called for a "better understanding of our philosophy of decentralized operations" and fostered the creation of local public relations committees, composed of leading officers of each GM

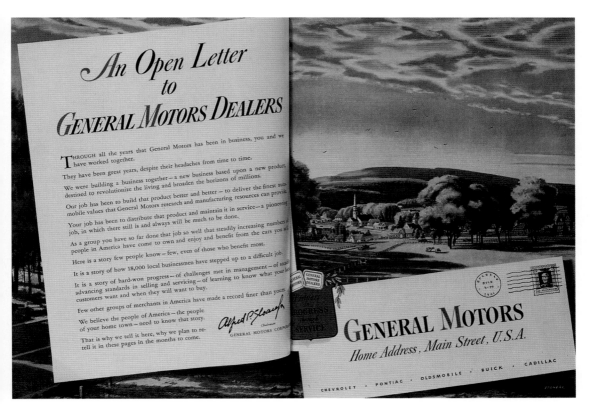

FIGURE 6.25

Its scope of influence, its goals, and
its extensive network of dealers,
suppliers, and plants, General
Motors' leaders concluded, made
it virtually indistinguishable from
the nation and its people. Thus,
GM's home address was "Main
Street, U.S.A."

plant. These committees should seek to identify GM as "the right kind of folks in
the community" and encourage a wide range of employee activities to "keep the
family happy after work." General Motors spurred its local executives to get involved in community activities; it urged its local public relations committees to
cultivate friendly contacts with the town's editors and opinion leaders and to take
out small ads in club, church, and voluntary association publications as "goodwill
contributions." As Garrett's assistant put it in a telegram of suggestions for a forthcoming speech, "Our whole plant city philosophy is pointed towards the principle
that we are a local industry in the cities in which we operate."[115]

By 1938 General Motors was operating plants in forty cities and towns, having
added ten new communities since 1934. The corporation publicized its local presence in ads that featured an open letter to its dealers and a large envelope prominently addressed to "General Motors, Home Address, Main Street, U.S.A." (Fig.
6.25). In a newspaper ad, above a list of all the plant cities, GM inserted the prominent headline "Home Folks to All These Towns." (In *GM Folks* an ad with a similar list carried the title "We're 'Home Folks' in All These Communities.") The
General Motors *Annual Report* for 1938 featured a map depicting GM's role as

FIGURE 6.26
As General Motors decentralized its operations, it paved the way for its entrance into each new community with ads that personalized the corporation as a new neighbor, reaching out with a friendly handshake.

"neighbor and customer in every community." Garrett's continuing dedication to an "inside out" program, along with the spur provided by lack of community support for the company during the sitdown strikes, had intensified GM's commitment to a significantly localized, "neighborhood" approach to public relations.[116]

Although the search for a "common man's language" persisted in public relations departments at GM and elsewhere, the plant city activities proved the most successful tactic in reaching average Americans in their everyday lives. To borrow the slang of the 1960s, corporate PR executives in the 1930s were straining to "rap" with average Americans by discovering "where they're at." The "where" in that formulation, General Motors gradually perceived, lay less in language than in physical locality. For example, after a three-year effort in Dayton, Ohio, Garrett was able to report in 1938 that the corporation had "entirely reversed" its former status as a little-liked "outside concern." Simultaneous open houses at the five Dayton plants had attracted an impressive, gratifying turnout of sixty-seven thousand people. Within their first year of operations, local PR committees had organized some twenty-one open houses. Such events evoked "neighborly editorials" in the local press. "Family parties," publicity about "friendly items of local interest," and open houses where "Jim Jones, the machinist," and his coworkers, "not the bosses," played host—all these demonstrated, Garrett concluded, that "it is likely to be the simple, the homely things by which industry becomes well thought of at home."[117]

As General Motors continued to decentralize manufacturing after 1938, the company devoted increasing attention toward cultivating local goodwill in each new community it entered. Not only did it develop close ties with civic leaders and local "influentials," but it also publicized its neighborly intentions through local advertisements explaining its economic contributions to the community and vowing to do its part as a good citizen (Fig. 6.26). The company also seized every opportunity to cultivate the "good neighbors" rhetoric of the plant community campaigns for its national image. As in *From Dawn to Sunset,* the persistent casting of those communities in the image of small-town "Main Street, U.S.A." represented GM's increasingly sophisticated response to "the curse of bigness." General Motors' theme—that "there is no real difference between the folks that live in the community and the folks that work in the plant"—when transposed to the national level, intimated that General Motors, with its geographical reach and its "typical folks" employees, was virtually synonymous with America as a whole. "In an important way," declared one ad, "General Motors has identified itself with American life everywhere."[118]

"Not . . . a Sissified Perfume": Corporate America and the Public Relations Turn

Toward the end of World War II, in speaking to a group of corporate executives, Paul Garrett observed that the problems facing management were not at all those that faced a previous generation of businessmen. Their predecessors could never have envisioned "the winding chambers in the labyrinth of public attitudes through which the men of management must successfully pass" to obtain their fundamental goal of profit. That perception jibed with Donaldson Brown's assertion, in defense of his proposal for a new cadre of corporate experts in public psychology and political economy, that in the past GM executives had been selected "because they were outstanding operators, not philosophers," and they had rightly refused to spend time and effort trying to understand "the new forces of mob psychology and political pressures."[119]

These observations paid homage to the "strictly business" mentality of corporate leaders who resented the way the events of the 1930s had forced them to divert their attention from the proper concerns of businessmen. At the same time these reflections showed how the new, broader dimensions of business activity and responsibility had carved out a place for the once-denigrated public relations officer, a figure who as recently as 1930, even in so PR-conscious a corporation as AT&T, might find himself viewed by executives in other departments of the company as merely "a sounding brass and a tinkling cymbal."[120] Whereas the specific marketing and financial needs of individual companies still prompted some corporate image advertising in the 1930s, as it had in previous periods, businessmen's dismay at the inexplicable public denigration of the economic system, and their fear that it faced an hour of extreme danger, were the main impetus for the new public relations craze. The perceived need to save the system reshaped the search for "soul" among large corporations in the 1930s and led to more sophisticated ways of suggesting such soul through populist rhetoric and imagery.

By the mid-1930s perceptions of the new business environment seemed to validate Bruce Barton's precept that every large corporation owed a responsibility to all others to defend itself and the economic system. In a manner quite distinct from their endeavors during the 1920s, a number of corporate leaders now discovered a crucial wider purpose through which to evade the taint of mere commercialism. An executive from the American Rolling Mill Company urged every advertiser to "resell the American system" by devoting an inch at the bottom of every ad to "selling industry to its workers and others." The American Federation of Advertising resolved that the obligation "to interpret what industry has done for the well-being of America" amounted to a "higher responsibility than private trading." One advertising manager, frustrated by the lack of results, demanded of the National Industrial Advertisers Association in 1937 that it "quit puttering with the problem of reselling the capitalistic system" and raise $5 million for the purpose. At the convention of the Association of National Advertisers in 1937, the president of the Johns-Manville Company reinforced the moral demand on the entire business community with an apocalyptic warning: "Every company that fails to do its part in public relations for business contributes [not only] to possible destruction . . . of its own business but also to the scuttling of our whole system of private enterprise as well as our democratic system of government."[121]

The corporate pursuit of soul through public relations in the late 1930s did not want for encouragement. Leaders of advertising agencies, lured by potential commissions from new institutional advertising campaigns and the opportunity to play a more prominent role in guiding corporate leadership, gave full voice to the cry for industry to carry its case to the public—to "sell the system." Publishers of trade journals and national magazines, glimpsing larger advertising revenues from an expansion of corporate PR, jumped at the chance to impress business with their helpfulness and patriotic support for the cause. Together these groups prodded corporate leaders to recognize that they had not made adequate use of the true voice of business, namely, advertising.[122]

The major advertising agencies engaged in intense competition to demonstrate their alertness to the public relations issue and their capacity to present the industry's case. The BBDO agency began publishing eloquent defenses of business in its house organ (circulated to present and prospective clients) as early as 1934. Under such provocative titles as "The DEVIL—11 Wall" and "No-Man's Land," the agency upbraided the railroads, utilities, financial houses, and the steel industry for their "policy of silence" in the face of attacks. As the public relations tide began to rise in 1936, N. W. Ayer & Son courted potential institutional advertising accounts with a series of twelve pamphlets to "promote a better understanding of the service which is being rendered by industry to the American public." The series included such blunt titles as *Why Business Is Big* and *What Is a Capitalist?*[123]

Having promoted the new consciousness of public relations so strenuously, the advertising agencies then sought to organize themselves to accommodate the new corporate needs. Some agencies, such as Young & Rubicam and Erwin, Wasey, created distinct public relations or publicity departments. Young & Rubicam went so far as to incorporate the department separately as a wholly owned subsidiary— partly to avoid use of the agency name when it pressed magazines and newspapers for free publicity. Other agencies, although eager for the commissions from institutional advertising campaigns, complained about the constant pressure from corporate clients to write press releases and carry out publicity programs without extra compensation. Some agencies developed publicity staffs of up to thirty employees; others encouraged their clients to contract separately with specialized public relations firms.[124]

The rise of professional polling services in the 1930s offered considerable reinforcement for this emphasis on public relations. One of the leading merchandisers of the more sophisticated of such studies was the Psychological Corporation, an organization first launched in 1921 by applied psychologists in an effort to widen the market for their services and free themselves from the academic domination of their field.[125] In early 1937 the Psychological Corporation made the first of its semiannual surveys of popular attitudes toward large manufacturers (known informally as the "Business Barometer" or the "Link Audit"—after the director of the Psychological Corporation, Henry C. Link). Enlisting major corporations as clients (including, at various times, General Motors, Du Pont, Ford, General Electric, Bethlehem Steel, U.S. Steel, Westinghouse, U.S. Rubber, Alcoa, Eastman Kodak, Johns-Manville, Standard Oil, and AT&T), the Link Audit provided them with confidential, detailed breakdowns of various aspects of its studies. Meanwhile, such other pollsters as the Curtis Publishing Company, the Opinion Research Corporation (Gallup), *Fortune* magazine, and Elmo Roper began publishing or privately distributing their own studies of public attitudes—both toward big business in general and toward selected corporations in particular.[126]

These studies provided a more certain foundation for the shaky business of estimating the returns from PR expenditures; moreover, the surveyors themselves promoted greater attention to public relations. The Psychological Corporation, for instance, might pat a company on the back for its fine increase in the percentage of favorable comments since the previous survey or admonish big business in general that the public was not buying the current truisms about free enterprise and that companies needed "a new and more realistic vocabulary for expressing these permanent values."[127] Since the inception of marketing surveys in the early 1920s, corporate chief executives had been able both to compare their total sales with those of their competitors and to measure their market shares within various regions, outlets, and segments of the population. The resulting concrete sense of "how we're doing" had been absent, however, from calculations of the effects of corporate image campaigns. Now, by the end of the 1930s, company leaders could indulge in the fascinating game of comparing the status of their public images with those of all of the other corporate giants.[128] With company image measured, like production and sales, in studies that carried all the implied authority of exact statistics, it was small wonder that the public relations director gained more stature within most corporations and more regular access to the CEO.

Evidence of the possibilities of such stature appeared most vividly within the company that set the standard for the expansion and institutionalization of corporate public relations during the 1930s: General Motors. By 1939 the GM Public Relations staff numbered more than fifty people and operated on a $2 million annual budget. It had directed the corporation's massive road show, the "Parade of Progress" (see Chapter 7), and had reinforced the neighborliness of *GM Folks* through employee newspapers edited locally at twenty-five of the GM plants. Thirty-nine GM plants boasted local public relations committees composed of plant managers and personnel directors. A "Plant City Bulletin" familiarized each local committee with the ideas for community activities and contacts being pursued at other plants. In 1940, after less than a decade at GM, Garrett became the first public relations director to acquire the status of corporate vice president.[129]

Although General Motors, with its multiplicity of public relations projects, stood foremost among those companies that had taken the new gospel to heart, scores of other corporations had undertaken major initiatives and had institutionalized the public relations function within their headquarters and divisional bureaucracies.[130] Large corporations may not have taken literally Barton's admonition to place public relations above all else in their priorities, but PR had, in a very short period of time, won unprecedented prominence in corporate thinking. *Forbes* magazine reflected widespread convictions when it predicted that the impending 1939 New York World's Fair would be "keyed to public relations." AT&T's remarkable success in deflecting criticisms during the Federal Communications Commission investigations of 1935 and 1936 (see Chapter 2) further supported the long-term efficacy of attention to the political dimensions of a corporation's public image.[131]

Fortune undoubtedly oversimplified these developments in declaring 1938 "the season in which the concept of public relations suddenly struck home to the hearts of a whole generation of businessmen," but it was right in recognizing that by the end of the 1930s the design of corporate imagery had taken on new dimensions. Recalling the reluctance of "virile" producers to take into account the sentiments of the (feminine) masses, the magazine harked back to businessmen's disparagement of public relations through gender associations. But it went on to affirm the new need for attention to corporate imagery. It crowned PR as the "New Goddess" of business and insisted that businessmen no longer regard public relations as a "sissified perfume." Rather, they now had to recognize it as an "elixir . . . they most urgently needed."[132]

THE CORPORATIONS COME TO THE FAIR: THE VISIT TO THE FACTORY TRANSFORMED

7

The great world's fairs, from their debut in the 1850s, had been "largely occupied with the exhibits of industry," as the designer Walter Dorwin Teague observed.[1] But during the half century from the Columbian Exposition in Chicago in 1893 to the New York World's Fair of 1939–40, major American corporations both intensified their participation and decisively altered the content and style of their displays. These transformed exhibits showed how significantly the deliberate fashioning of corporate images had matured.[2] We can best analyze the nature of this change by asking four simple questions. When the corporation came to the fair, during each phase of this era,

- What did it bring?
- Where did it display what it brought?
- How did it display what it brought? and
- What assumptions about its audience did its style of display suggest?

A quick, elementary answer to the first of these questions foreshadows the transformations in corporate display that this chapter will explore: first (during most of the nineteenth century) the corporation primarily brought its products to the fair; then (beginning roughly with the Panama-Pacific Exposition of 1915), it tried to bring its factory to the fair; finally, with increasing self-consciousness throughout the 1930s, it sought to display its corporate image.

To postulate such a tidy progression—from product to factory to image—is, of course, to obscure the typical disorderliness of the historical process. Even at the end of the 1930s, few corporations neglected to put some of their products on exhibit in their fair displays. And one might argue that the massive engines of the Pennsylvania Railroad or the elaborate towers of Heinz's pickle bottles at late nineteenth-century expositions did not simply publicize specific products; they dramatized the corporation's image as well. Still, American corporations pursued new display strategies as they came to see the great expositions more as public relations projects than as arenas for technical exchange and sales promotion.

Increasingly in the 1930s, major corporations staged their displays in their own separate buildings. They also searched for ways to involve audiences in a more participatory mode. A Chrysler Corporation press release on its exhibit at the New York World's Fair in 1939 suggested just how far many companies had departed from older conceptions of fair exhibits as exercises in technical education and expressions of producer values. Its display, Chrysler avowed, "dramatizes a newer concept of what an industrial exhibit should do. It puts the whole emphasis on what the product does for the consumer—and not on the complicated processes by which that product is produced." Assessing his company's strategy at the recent Texas Centennial Exposition, a newly minted expert on industrial display at Du Pont observed in 1936 that the object of an exhibit was no longer narrow merchandising or technical edification; it was "to educate the public regarding the company as an institution."[3]

Corporate Display and the Operational Aesthetic

The transformation from product to factory to image in corporate fair exhibits began between 1893 and 1915, when the United States experienced a veritable eruption of fairs and exhibits—regional, national, and international. Close on the heels of Chicago's momentous Columbian Exposition of 1893 came the Cotton States and International Exposition in Atlanta in 1895, the Tennessee Centennial Exposition in Nashville in 1897, the Trans-Mississippi and International Exposition in Omaha in 1898, and the Pan-American Exposition in Buffalo in 1901. The surge then continued with the World's Fair and Louisiana Purchase Exposition in St. Louis in 1904 and regional fairs in Portland (Oregon), Jamestown (Virginia), and Seattle from 1905 through 1909. After only a brief pause, this intense phase of regional promotions culminated in the Panama-Pacific and Panama-California expositions in San Francisco and San Diego in 1915.

Since the 1870s at least, companies that wished to market new technologies had looked to local and national exhibits as prime marketing venues. At such sites as the Franklin Institute in Philadelphia and Mechanics Hall in Boston, companies and individual inventors drew large, enthusiastic audiences to displays that, even as they served the merchandising needs of manufacturers and utility companies, won praise for their educational contributions and their "democratic" diffusion of technical information. Almost invariably, the trade and scientific journals depicted the audiences as studious in their attention to the exhibits and—by their dress and deportment—largely representative of the city's social elite (Fig. 7.1). In effect, these exhibits attracted a "targeted audience" for the promotion of new technologies. Promoters assumed that this self-selected group consisted mainly of those whose technical curiosity made them serious students of new devices and those whose class position made them likely consumers of the most advanced products.[4]

An earnestly republican organization, the Franklin Institute boasted that its electrical exhibits were "distinctly educational in character" and that the "thousands of people, young and old," who visited the displays had acquired "a thirst that they

FIGURE 7.1

Depictions of visitors at early
expositions, like this 1884 drawing
in the *Electrical World,* incorporated
women to convey gentility while
recognizing men, like the one
examining his guidebook here, as the
serious students of new technologies.

will never lose for knowledge on the subject." But the Institute also observed that the exhibits had served effectively to "bring producers and consumers together." Thus, already in the 1880s the prescribed and actual audience responses to such displays revealed the divergent propensities of the corporate exhibit. A George Eastman or a Henry Ford might recall how he had drawn inspiration for his own work from careful attention to technical details or had systematically planned to "traverse every aisle" of such exhibits. But corporate promoters also strove, with apparent success, to dazzle and awe less studious visitors with lavish, spectacular displays that, in the words of David Sicilia, "blended pedagogy with performance."[5]

In tracing the history of the Boston Edison Company, Sicilia observes that during the 1880s and 1890s utility companies looked to industrial exhibits both to promote their services to consumers and to forge marketing links with appliance manufacturers. So useful for both merchandising and public relations was Boston Edison's 1898 exhibit at Mechanics Hall that the company set up its own permanent display at its headquarters building. Within a decade Boston Edison was also employing a mobile exhibit, the "House of Light," to market its services and to project its corporate image beyond the confines of central office and exhibition hall. The Eastman Kodak Company, with its vital stake in displaying the simplicity of a new technology, had already pioneered the moving corporate exhibit. It

FIGURE 7.2

A typical early twentieth-century Heinz fair exhibit stressed the products, their availability for sale, and their prize-worthy qualities. At the same time the aesthetics and order of the display, as well as the small pictures of Heinz girls at work, conveyed a corporate image.

first staged publicity stunts, followed by lectures and lantern slides, in a number of communities in Great Britain. Then it launched "a spectacular traveling photographic show" in the United States.[6]

Local exhibits might answer many of the marketing and public relations needs of some businesses, and traveling exhibits would prove feasible in a variety of industries. But the emerging giant manufacturers, as they eyed national markets, increasingly considered displays at the broadly visible national and regional fairs the best opportunities to gain prestige and national exposure. Here they expected to reach a large segment of the public in more arresting ways than those afforded by the various print media. National, mass-circulation magazines had only begun to appear in the 1890s. The great fairs and expositions still came closest to providing a national stage on which a corporation could dramatize its presence. Those companies not initially attracted by the opportunities for showmanship might still fear to be absent if a major competitor seemed likely to make a splash at the fair. And some companies recognized possible ancillary effects from corporate exposition displays. A grand image-enhancing exhibit at the fair, they perceived, could powerfully stimulate the morale of their own employees.[7]

FIGURE 7.3

As late as the 1915 Panama-Pacific Exposition many exhibitors still considered row upon row of machines a suitably impressive display technique.

Two modes of presentation dominated the corporate exhibits of this era. In the first, impressive quantities of products or equipment were amassed in the most eye-catching, awe-inspiring, or thematically evocative way. Here spectators confronted pyramids of bottled pickles, knights on horseback constructed of prunes, towers of a thousand incandescent lamps, massive stacks of steel ingots, and rows upon rows of lathes or motors (Figs. 7.2 and 7.3).[8] In the second, visitors were instructed in the company's complex methods of manufacture or its impressive technologies of service in the hopes of stimulating empathy with the corporation. AT&T organized its corporate "temple" in the Electricity Building at the 1893 Columbian Exposition to display "an elaborate switchboard of the latest design." It also instructed visitors in its technological expertise with sectional drawings of various instruments. Spurred by its need to promote a service more than a product, AT&T was one of the first corporations to involve visitors in some form of participation. At certain hours guests could speak from a long-distance booth to an AT&T operator in New York or hear their own voices amplified by a delicate transmitter. AT&T's switchboard display supplemented the opportunity to witness the operators at work with "brief and concise" lectures on its method of operation. In an unrelentingly didactic style, AT&T's official fair brochures exhorted visitors: "Let us see how this is done. . . ."[9]

Agglomerations of products and instructional lectures were not, of course, the only forms of corporate presence at the 1893 fair or its immediate sequels. General Electric and Westinghouse both hoped to astonish the multitudes by converting buildings into "fairy-like palaces" with the "most stupendous" lighting effects "ever conceived." General Electric's eighty-two-foot Edison Tower of Light stirred much popular enthusiasm in 1893. As David Nye has observed, the opportunities for theatricality afforded by night lighting inspired the rapid growth of a subprofession of "illuminating engineers" who combined talents in engineering with those in showmanship. Significantly, however, the displays within these attention-commanding towers of light were oriented toward promulgating technical know-how (GE assured visitors in 1893 that it had filled its space "with thousands of object lessons to the electrical investigator").[10] Corporations drew on the tradition of late nineteenth-century electrical exhibits at the Franklin Institute, where little primers gave the unlearned "a thirst for deeper draughts of electrical knowledge." Corporate exhibitors remained highly conscious of an audience that would likely wish to make "careful notes and observations" of apparatus. These were people, as Robert Rydell observes of the fair visitors at the St. Louis Exposition in 1904, who "took notes as they walked."[11]

Such industrial exhibits appealed to the "operational aesthetic"—a term coined by Neil Harris to characterize the popularity and effectiveness of P. T. Barnum's many exhibits and hoaxes. Barnum, Harris argues, took advantage of the widespread penchant of nineteenth-century Americans for understanding processes. By inviting the public to test its powers of observation and evaluation, Barnum both exploited the credulity of the public and catered to its pride in "the common sense of the average citizen." Of course, the industrialists considered their exhibits explicitly educational and far from hoaxes. But like Barnum, they assumed that their audiences would experience "a delight in observing process." Relying on the persistence of republican values in American society, the industrial exhibitors of the turn of the century still sought to give visual pleasure through displays that would enable the layperson to enjoy a sense of technical competence.[12]

What major corporations hoped to gain most from their fair exhibits, especially in the wake of the muckraking attacks of the first decade of the twentieth century, was not immediate sales but rather public respect and understanding. And when they asked themselves what would best foster that attitude, they almost instinctively focused on their processes of production. If only people could know about the many complicated, coordinated steps involved in the manufacture of their products, the intense effort and sophisticated expertise it required, and their seemingly miraculous transformation of "useless" raw materials into functional consumer goods, then they would appreciate the immense service that the corporation provided to the public. Those who clearly understood these processes of production would recognize the link between bigness and production efficiencies; they would perceive the wisdom of defending business autonomy from debilitating interference.

If some members of the public were attracted to antimonopoly agitation and unfair regulatory legislation, many business leaders concluded, that was because the scale of modern life and the complexities of manufacture had prevented the average person from knowing about these marvelous processes of production. Assuming that what they found most salient in their firm's success was also what the exposition visitor would find most entrancing, businessmen devised creative display formats, from scale models to dioramas, to demonstrate their operating processes. The most modern displays at the 1893 Columbian Exposition featured working demonstrations of the manufacture of such products as matches, carpets, and newspapers. The Pennsylvania Railroad constructed scale models of tunnels and terminal yards, with miniature trains, to show "the methods employed to increase the capacity of a yard" and how ever-greater volumes of traffic were handled with safety. Among the many "operative exhibits" at the 1904 St. Louis Exposition was a demonstration in which "hides were converted into leather and then made into shoes by a model factory, turning out 300 pairs a day."[13]

The Best Way to Show Off: The Factory Tour

The strategy of operational-aesthetic displays enticed many production-oriented executives to do what they liked to do best: show off their factories. Corporate presidents of the era took great pride in the size and extent of their manufacturing works as vivid testimonies to their entrepreneurial prowess. Many had founded their firms and fostered their growth from small operations to large factories. Some, like John Patterson of National Cash Register (see Chapter 1) and C. W. Post of the Postum Company, liberally funded tours for factory visitors, hoping not only to cultivate customers but also to inspire public admiration for their paternalistic efforts to imbue industry with beauty and benevolence.[14]

While anticipating that visitors would wish to be well educated in the technical details of their complex manufacturing operations, the corporations that most aggressively promoted factory tours were often those that also sought to impress a "class audience" of the social elite, including women. The souvenir booklets that such companies distributed to factory visitors often merged a vaunting pride in extensive factory grounds and buildings with either or both of two Victorian claims to the possession of a corporate soul—a beneficence toward workers, as evidenced through employee welfare programs, and a humanized outlook, as revealed through the beautification of the factory or the company's appreciation of uplifting art.[15]

At the Postum Company, during the first two decades of the twentieth century, visitors were ushered into the elegant lobby of an administration building, "a wonderfully designed example of English architecture, with its quaint beauty and its settings of flowers and greenery in the midst of humming factories" (Fig. 7.4).[16] They then spent a half hour viewing proprietor C. W. Post's extensive art collection in an upstairs gallery before continuing on to the "numerous manufacturing departments where, under the most sanitary and modern methods," the company's cereals were produced and packed. The company's souvenir booklets, didactic in their guide to manufacturing operations ("Let us first see how Grape-Nuts is made . . ."; "Now please attend to the exact facts, which a journey through the works will make plain . . ."), aimed both to impress visitors with the company's prodigies of production ("Day and night the great factories run") and to convey a corporate image of scrupulous cleanliness and resolute uplift and refinement. Postum provided visitors with picture postcards of the plant and stamps for mailing them. The frontispiece of several successive editions of the souvenir booklet read: "Here let Art be used to soften Commerce."[17]

Several other corporations, including Eastman Kodak, National Cash Register, Shredded Wheat, and Hershey, conspicuously utilized the factory tour for public relations (Fig. 7.5). But few early twentieth-century corporations so effectively

"THERE'S A REASON"

ONE OF THE OFFICE BUILDINGS
OF THE POSTUM CEREAL CO. LTD.
BATTLE CREEK, MICH.

used the tour to project a favorable corporate image as did the H. J. Heinz Company. The paternalistic Henry Heinz had made something of a fetish of cleanliness, the careful and aesthetic packing of jars, and benevolent oversight of his (largely female) throng of workers. All these elements of the company image were showcased in the plant tour. In his story of the Heinz Company, Robert C. Alberts maintains that Heinz "was the first industrialist to invite the public to call and inspect the full range of his plant operations." He estimates that by 1900 an average of twenty thousand people were taking the plant tour each year.[18]

At the Heinz plant a company guide led visitors through the perfectly ventilated stables, the box factory, the Time Office (where employees punched in and out), the girls' dining room, the Baked Bean Building, and the Bottling Department, "where several hundreds of spotlessly clean girls packed, inspected, corked, capped and labeled various sizes of pickles" (Fig. 7.6). Visitors could also admire the various outward signs of the "inward spiritual grace" embodied in the company. These ranged from the female workers' "neat uniforms with dainty white caps" to the flower boxes on the separate roof gardens for men and women and the didactic stained glass windows of the company auditorium (Fig. 7.7). They could appreciate the extent to which Heinz workers were, "even as they work[ed], . . . surrounded by appeals to their good taste and finer sensibilities" in the form of paintings, statuary, and inspirational mottoes. The visitors, steadily recruited by continual ads in the Pittsburgh newspapers, were treated to frequent taste samples,

You Are Welcome

If we could induce every
one of the hundred million
persons in this country and
Canada to visit "The Home
of Shredded Wheat" and witness the process of making
Shredded Wheat Biscuit and
Triscuit we would not need to
print this advertisement—or any other advertisement. Nearly one hundred thousand visitors from every habitable portion
of the globe pass through this factory every
year. They are impressed with the beauty
and cleanliness of the factory. They are
convinced of the wholesomeness, purity
and nutritive value of

Shredded Wheat

FIGURE 7.4 *(opposite)*
True to its motto of using art
"to soften commerce," the Postum
Company's elegant visitors' guide
presented a homelike, genteel image
of its factory—which in 1900 was
already staffed by more than twenty-
five hundred workers.

FIGURE 7.5 *(left)*
Having viewed the "beauty and
cleanliness of the factory," the well-
dressed visitors to "The Home of
Shredded Wheat" were expected
to come away "convinced of the
wholesomeness, purity, and nutritive
value" of the product.

FIGURE 7.6
Not only were the pickles carefully
arranged in patterns, but the women
workers at Heinz were socialized
into patterns of middle-class behavior, cultural tastes, and work
routines. Visitors could witness both
sanitary work conditions and welfare
capitalism in action.

FIGURE 7.7
Visitors to the auditorium at Heinz's Pittsburgh factory would note the company's efforts to uplift as they read the adages on its stained glass windows.

a farewell lecture, one of the famous "pickle pins" for scarf or lapel, and—after 1905—a visit to the "House Where We Began." The plain two-story house in Sharpsburg, Pennsylvania, where Henry Heinz had first prepared horseradish sauce in 1860 had arduously been lifted from its foundations and floated down the Allegheny River to nestle in the courtyard of the huge Heinz plant in Pittsburgh. It served to narrate, architecturally, an edifying story of success through diligence and morality (see Figs. 1.13 and 1.14).[19]

Capitalizing on the popularity of his factory tours, Heinz devised a way to give his company's soul a wider visibility. At the "iron pier" at Atlantic City, which Heinz purchased and rechristened the Heinz Pier in 1898, he constructed a pavilion with an assembly hall and provided exhibits and entertainments to attract visitors (Fig. 7.8). Among these was a large map of the various Heinz plants and an "industrial and sociological" exhibit of the Heinz welfare programs. There, as Robert Alberts relates, "a member of the company's Sociological Department delivered a lecture with seventy-six stereopticon slides, providing to this wider audience a vicarious equivalent of the tour through the Allegheny plant."[20]

It was not mere happenstance, of course, that many of the entrepreneurs who chose the visitor tour to express pride in their factories were in the food industry. Virtually every producer of brand-name foods recognized a need to publicize its attention to cleanliness and otherwise allay public fears about the safety of foods processed and packaged far from the home and local community.[21] The giant Chi-

FIGURE 7.8

At Heinz Pier in Atlantic City, Heinz in effect brought its factory to the public. Blazoning the company name, it cultivated an image of uplift through concerts, an art gallery, and "sociological exhibits" of its factory welfare programs.

cago meatpackers, for instance, quickly saw the value of factory tours in countering rumors and exposés about diseased animals and unsanitary products. They also perceived that demonstrations of the vastness and complexity of their operations, including their efficient use of by-products, might counteract charges of collusion and profiteering.

The packers had first formalized their factory tours in 1893, as a supplement to their fairground exhibits at the World's Columbian Exposition. For four months, according to the historian Louise Wade, approximately ten thousand visitors per day were guided through Packingtown by "a trained corps of uniformed guides."[22] Although the practice had been initiated for reasons of civic pride as well as corporate promotion, the packers came to realize that the power of their plants to awe tourists could serve public relations purposes. By early in the twentieth century both Swift and Armour were bestowing elaborate souvenir booklets on their thousands of visitors. Invariably, the booklets reiterated the main themes of the tour. Armour called attention to the "scrupulous cleanliness" of its Sausage Room while avowing, a bit defensively, that the "origin" of its sausage was "beyond all doubt or suspicion." It also boasted of its worldwide "commanding position" in sales and production volume as evidence of its efficiencies (Fig. 7.9).[23]

By the second decade of the twentieth century both Swift and Armour were attempting to use their tours to refute public suspicions of anticompetitive collusion as well. In a "personal" message in his company's 1917 booklet, J. Ogden Armour assured visitors that "although people do not always appreciate it, this is the most competitive of all industries." Armour's vast size, he added, should be seen as a testimony to its record of efficiency. Swift confined itself to the observation that its business was "conducted on the lines of a public service corporation." Armour provided tourists with awe-inspiring views of the stockyards on a postcard that they could send to friends and relatives back home. Swift, by 1918, was offering a special pamphlet, *Swift & Company: A Visitor's Impressions,* with "a detachable stamp" and instructions to "use this stamp for sealing and mail this book to a friend." As early as 1910, Swift reported 142,000 visitors for the year; by 1916, Armour claimed over 200,000.[24]

While the meatpackers, perhaps through their place on standard visitors' tours of Chicago, counted the greatest number of factory visitors before 1920, the Ford Motor Company could claim to have attracted the most fervent and enthralled spectators. They came to Ford's factories, in John Staudenmaier's phrase, on "industrial pilgrimages." Henry Ford had begun to set up plant tours very soon after he introduced the Model-T in 1908. By 1912 and 1913 his corps of twenty-five to thirty guides was leading "thousands of persons" along the assembly line in the "largest single manufacturing institution in the world," at Highland Park, just outside Detroit.[25]

When Ford instituted the five-dollar day in 1914, David Lewis observes, the Highland Park plant became "'a national landmark' . . . , a place to be seen by every visitor to Detroit." By 1917 over two hundred thousand people a year were viewing Ford's assembly line in operation. People came from around the world to pay homage to Ford's seemingly perfect integration of men and machines. For

FIGURE 7.9

Armour complemented the
company-as-colossal-factory image
on the cover of a visitors' guidebook
with station-by-station drawings that

emphasized the company's service
and attention to cleanliness (see
Fig. 7.10). It invested heavily in
visitors' reactions.

those unable to make the pilgrimage to Detroit, Henry Ford captured the experience in newsreels of the assembly line in operation, presumably the first such films to document factory production.[26]

The confidence of many early twentieth-century businessmen in the factory tour as the best possible instrument of public relations was nowhere so fervently expressed as in their efforts, through films, exhibits, and written testimonials, to extend their tours to the public at large. In 1919 General Electric's "engineer-author," Charles Ripley, invited readers to witness the wonders of production at the GE plant at Schenectady. Such a "factory tour," made mobile through the printed page in his *Romance of a Great Factory,* may have lacked the immediacy of firsthand experience, but Ripley strove to replicate the factory tour by including photographs on nearly every page. He repeatedly coaxed readers to join vicariously in the tour with such phrases as "here it is that you touch elbows with men who are second to none in their respective trades" and "as you walk up the main avenue of the Schenectady works—surrounded by throbbing workshops—you will see. . . ." In some instances, he simply let his own wonderment pour out in apparent spontaneity, implicitly inviting readers to interpret the factory through his emotional responses: "I walked, amazed, between long rows of ponderous punch presses, some of them pounding as fast as a machine gun." As a climax Ripley took his Ediphone with him on a tour by crane across the top of one of the major buildings, vividly narrating an experience that even an actual factory tour would not have offered.[27]

Live Hog Pens

THE hogs are not dressed the same day they are brought from the yards, but are allowed to rest until the day after their arrival. Swift & Company have yardage capacity for 5,000 live hogs.

In its various forms the factory tour, so cherished by many early business leaders for shaping and projecting a corporate image, could claim a host of virtues as a vehicle of public relations. A tour could present the company at its best. It could make particularly salient some quality essential to marketing or public relations—such as the cleanliness of the plant, the difficulty or precision of the work, or the scientific sophistication of the production processes. Tours could impress the public with the scope, complexity, and physical immensity of a company's operations; they could also suggest openness and frankness. Visitors usually toured in small groups, thus acquiring a depth of experience rarely approached through other media (Fig. 7.10). Perhaps most attractive of all, to production-minded managers as well as to many visitors, guided tours promised to provide a real "understanding" of the operations of the enterprise.

Ford's film of the factory tour, Ripley's attempt to convey the wonders of the factory through prose, and the many souvenir booklets for visitors nonetheless remind us of some major limitations in the actual factory tour as a vehicle for projecting the corporate image. The factory was fixed in place. Its on-site tours could never reach those who did not visit a particular city or region. The factory tour not only demanded that the audience be mobile; it also required a very active preestablished interest to attract tourists to the plant. Brochures and films might attempt to spread the message of the tour, but the greatest potential for attracting a larger, more nationally representative audience lay in the major expositions. What marvelous venues they might prove for disseminating a corporate image—if only the factory tour could somehow be made the company's exhibit!

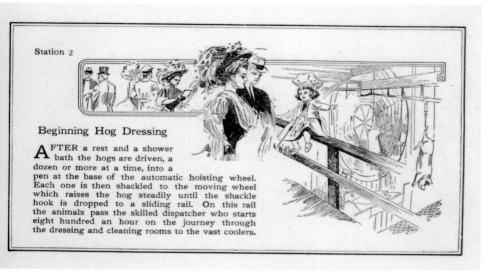

Station 2

Beginning Hog Dressing

AFTER a rest and a shower bath the hogs are driven, a dozen or more at a time, into a pen at the base of the automatic hoisting wheel. Each one is then shackled to the moving wheel which raises the hog steadily until the shackle hook is dropped to a sliding rail. On this rail the animals pass the skilled dispatcher who starts eight hundred an hour on the journey through the dressing and cleaning rooms to the vast coolers.

FIGURE 7.10

These scenes, similar to many in Armour's didactic tour guide (see Fig. 7.9), portrayed the factory visit as a genteel educational occasion for well-dressed people in small groups.

The Factory Comes to the Fair

Henry Ford was only the most celebrated of the many business leaders who gloried in the massive scale, systems of coordination, and production efficiencies of their modern factories. In fact, so narrowly production-minded were some executives, and so compulsively did they seek ego satisfaction by "showing off" their impressive buildings, that advertising experts had to wage a persistent campaign during the first quarter of the twentieth century to convince advertisers that a picture of the factory at the top of an advertisement was not the best way to spur consumer interest in the product.[28] Since an exposition display offered far greater possibilities for showing the factory and its operations than an advertisement, it is not surprising that corporate leaders pondered how they might take advantage of them.

By the time of the Panama-Pacific Exposition of 1915, the yearning of business leaders to bring their factories, as well as their products, to the fair had intensified. In one building on the exposition grounds, General Electric created a "miniature lamp factory" to show MAZDA lamps being assembled; elsewhere factory machinery created Shredded Wheat biscuits for the edification of fair visitors. The Western Electric Company presented a "complete No. 1 type switchboard circuit, equipped with the new automatic ringing . . . features . . . and . . . arranged to show every step in the operation." If the Heinz exhibit still relied on an immense "pyramid of canned and bottled condiments" for dramatic effect, it also used the inside of its tower to show a film of its processes of production.[29]

The United States Steel Corporation brought its factories to the fair both through

models and through film. Operating scale models of a blast furnace, a Bessemer converter, and an open-hearth furnace demonstrated "the process of the actual manufacture of steel from the raw material to the most highly finished products." The company's six-and-a-half-hour series of silent films, entitled *The Story of Steel from Mines to Finished Products,* guided visitors through all U.S. Steel's factories, pointing out every detail of production. These films, U.S. Steel emphasized, had been created "at great labor and expense" in order to demonstrate factory operations "in a clear, concise, yet comprehensive manner, and in logical sequence." Although visitors were not compelled to sit through the entire series of films, all were shown once each day. Lecturers gave simultaneous detailed explanations "so that the audience may clearly understand the processes being shown upon the screen." Supremely conscious of an educational mission, U.S. Steel hoped that a "careful study" of its exhibit would "commend itself to all observant and investigative minds."[30]

Of all the corporate displays in San Francisco in 1915, however, the unchallenged champion was the Ford Motor Company exhibit. Henry Ford, the epitome of the production-oriented entrepreneur, gave form to the manufacturer's instinct to bring the factory to the fair. By constructing an operating Ford assembly line that turned out between eighteen and twenty-five Model-T Fords a day as the centerpiece of his 1915 exhibit, Ford seemed to prove that demonstrations of manufacturing processes were exactly what the public wanted to see, as well as what businessmen most wanted to show. Frank Vivian, the Ford exhibit manager for that fair, recalled the strenuous efforts required to keep the surging crowds at a safe distance from the machines and the workers. On opening day the mob of visitors had simply crushed the railing in its eagerness to get close to the conveyor belt. People would line up more than two hours early to gain a position near the rail (Fig. 7.11).[31]

As considerations of public relations began increasingly to shape the strategies of exposition displays, the notion of bringing the factory to the fair—thus enabling the public to "understand what we do"—seemed at this point the optimum way to promote a favorable corporate image. Although both Ford and United States Steel brought their factories to the fair in another sense in 1915, responding to continuing public suspicions of the giant manufacturer as soulless corporation by devoting portions of their displays to their welfare programs for factory workers,[32] it was Ford's coup (and considerable investment) in manufacturing a complex product before the public's eyes that reinforced that company's claim to the most dominant, positive corporate image of the era. Henry Ford, who visited the fair himself for several weeks, would go down to the exhibit each day before it opened to tinker with the machinery. He was as enraptured by his display of actual production processes as any fairgoer. Its success attested to the continued survival of republican values within business and of a "serious" public, one eager to know about the processes of manufacture.

A Century of Progress: Modernism and Movement as Responses to the Depression and the New Deal

Planning for the great exposition to celebrate Chicago's one hundredth anniversary began amid the economic boom of the late 1920s. By 1933, however, the onset of a severe economic depression had transformed the event, in the words of *Collier's*, into "a symbol of the trial by ordeal of a whole nation's morale." The Century of Progress Exposition was now entrusted with the task of arousing the nation from the depression. Walter Chrysler, according to a Century of Progress press release, even characterized the exposition as crucial to the "struggle for survival" of "our own system of private enterprise." Other corporate participants, led by General Motors, also viewed the fair as a stage from which to launch a defense of corporate ideology and the economic system. Harvey S. Firestone Sr. put it bluntly: "I see in the Fair a great opportunity for private enterprise to show its achievements to millions of people." A "crescendo of social criticism and reform," in John Cawelti's words, "had made business leaders increasingly conscious of the need for public understanding and support. They responded by carrying the newest techniques of institutional advertising and corporate image-making into the erection of individual corporate buildings at the 1933 fair."[33]

With the public reputation of big business at a low ebb and corporate hopes for a dramatic economic revival through boosterism still springing eternal, corporate leaders seized on a modernist style that would project confidence in the future. The angular, upthrusting, hard-edged elements of modernist architecture had initially epitomized the optimistic business mood of the late 1920s in the United States. In 1932 and 1933 corporate leaders and their architects and designers still prized this

FIGURE 7.12

By 1933 major corporations were insisting on individual buildings to project their image through striking architecture and thorough control of their exhibit environment. The General Motors building at Chicago's Century of Progress Exposition was one example of this trend.

imagery. For the 1933 fair they envisioned modernism as an appropriately daunt-less and inspiriting response to a depression that had persisted, in their view, as a consequence more of popular mood than of economic logic. Investing their hopes in the fusion of science and industry, they designed their fair buildings and the in-ternal decor of their exhibits as architectural statements of an unwavering belief in the recuperative thrust of science and technology.[34]

Although a number of major corporations still wished to bring their factories to the fair in 1933, they would no longer allow these simulated factories to be housed in composite buildings of classical design. An early proposal for the fair, in 1928, called for the firms in various industries to cooperate in composite exhibits, but this idea failed miserably; corporations insisted on exercising total control over their own exhibit environments so as to impress the public with their unique images. Whereas only 9 of the 137 buildings at the 1893 Chicago Exposition had been built by individual business corporations (mostly by small companies, with their build-ings located in the amusement section), twenty major corporations—including General Motors, Chrysler, Firestone, Goodyear, and Sears—erected their own structures in 1933. Many of these (including, by 1934, the Ford building) were among the largest and most architecturally innovative on the grounds (Fig. 7.12).[35]

The architectural contrasts between the Century of Progress Exposition and San Francisco's Panama–Pacific Exposition of 1915 were staggering. Gone were the potted palms calculated to lend gentility to 1915 exhibits such as that of the Westinghouse Company. Gone, also, were the assumptions that had led Westinghouse to measure its success at that fair by the number of awards and medals its products received. By the 1930s a more sophisticated consciousness of public relations had relegated medals to the category of tributes garnered by giant pumpkins, not giant corporations. Now, as the *Architectural Forum* observed, corporations strove "to exemplify in the building design, as well as in the display, the spirit and force of the company."[36]

Even more strikingly absent in 1933 were the classical facades, like the Greek Temple with large columns and sphinxes behind which the Bell exhibit was entombed in 1893 or the Italian villa with Pompeian decor that enveloped the AT&T exhibit in 1915. As one of its own publications observed with some astonishment, the conservative Bell System, always so intent on wrapping itself in the visual symbolism of a great and dignified institution of public service, even resorted in 1933 to such modernist details as sans serif lettering in its exhibit. Chrysler topped its dramatic building with "four pillars of neon light." Attempting, as Cawelti observes, to "take their cue from science and the machine," the architects and designers of the 1933 fair sought to achieve "effective traffic flow" through functional design and to symbolize the inevitability and beneficence of technological change.[37]

Inside the fair's machine-inspired architecture, many of the corporate exhibitors displayed new drama and inventiveness in their efforts to bring their factories to the fair. Feeling the need for popular understanding even more intensely in the midst of the depression than they did during the earlier era of muckraking, many continued to pursue public empathy by displaying the energy, the expertise, and the technological virtuosity that went into their work of manufacture and service. Everywhere, in animated models, dioramas, and full-scale operations, the processes of manufacture took place before the visitors' eyes. Not only could visitors view the making of Chevrolet cars on the assembly line in the General Motors exhibit; they could also witness a quite different assembly line in operation, carrying out the mixing and packaging of mayonnaise, at the Kraft-Phenix exhibit (Fig. 7.13). The National Biscuit Company created a miniature factory, Coca-Cola gave visitors a view of its bottling operations, and Owens-Illinois Glass exhibited a working model of a glassmaking plant.[38] Although some corporate leaders still presumed that audiences wanted to school themselves in the techniques of production, many design-minded observers now attributed the success of such exhibits mainly to the power of motion to command popular attention.

Corporate exhibitors not only employed strikingly novel architectural styles at the Century of Progress, but they also made a massive financial commitment to public relations through technological display, adopting budgets of unprecedented size for their buildings and exhibits. General Motors put over $3 million into its 1933–34 display; the Ford Motor Company, in 1934 alone, invested over $2.5 million, nearly a third as much as its entire annual advertising budget for newspapers, magazines, and radio.[39] Even more significantly, with so much riding on the suc-

FIGURE 7.13
By the time of the 1933–34 Century of Progress, experts now considered some form of motion indispensable to attract and hold spectator attention. Exhibits of factory processes, such as Kraft's mayonnaise assembly line, could satisfy that requirement. This postcard enlisted spectators to further publicize their experience.

cess of these dramatizations of corporate identity, major companies now hired professional industrial designers to infuse showmanship and stylistic unity into their exhibits.

Rising costs and expensive expertise brought increasing pressures for accountability. As the industrial designer emerged as a prominent figure in corporate display, so did the survey expert, who claimed an ability to measure audience responses and calculate an exhibit's impact. By the time of the 1939 World's Fair, the advanced "production qualities" and audience awareness of the major corporations' industrial exhibits made them the "hit shows" of the fair, overshadowing both the amusement zone attractions and the official thematic exhibits.[40] To the dismay of some businessmen, the boundaries between business and show business were becoming increasingly indistinct.

Exhibiting Technology: Modernism and the Photomural

Nothing drew more attention to the new significance of the industrial designer in corporate displays than the acclaim reaped by the Ford Motor Company for its exhibit at the Century of Progress in 1934. The organizers of that exposition, recalling the tremendous success of Henry Ford's operating assembly line at the 1915 Panama-Pacific Exposition, counted heavily on Ford's participation. And Ford fully intended to rejuvenate his assembly line for a triumphant 1933 encore. But he was preoccupied with other things in 1930 and 1931, including his own

FIGURE 7.14

The gear motif inscribed into the very architecture of the 1934 Ford building at the Century of Progress unmistakably manifested the stylistic unity that the designer Walter Dorwin Teague sought in every aspect of the Ford exhibits.

programs for ending the depression and enabling industrial workers to regain security through partial subsistence on the land. By the time he made up his mind to submit a proposal to the exposition's board of directors, General Motors had already won approval for a Chevrolet assembly line exhibit. "Ford was furious," reports David Lewis, a historian of Ford's public relations. In a fit of moral outrage at the theft of his idea, he walked out on the fair and launched his own highly successful event, the Ford Exposition of Progress, during 1933 in Detroit and New York City.[41]

When the Century of Progress Exposition reopened for a second year, in 1934, the grand entrance of the Ford Motor Company marked a significant moment in the transformation of the corporate industrial exhibit. In place of an operating assembly line, Ford now introduced a massive "fair within a fair" of diverse features. The Ford display became the biggest news story of the fair's second year. The critics agreed that Ford "stole the show" in 1934, attracting 76.9 percent of all fair visitors to his exhibit and outdrawing the previous attendance leader, General Motors, by a two-to-one margin.[42]

The industrial designer Walter Dorwin Teague was generally credited with the impact of the Ford exhibit. He injected a modernistic, machine-aesthetic motif—heralded by the striking and symbolic gear shape of the exhibit's main building—into each aspect of the Ford displays (Fig. 7.14). Upon entering the building's mammoth rotunda, visitors found themselves surrounded by an immense photomural of production activities at the River Rouge plant, intended as a vicarious and powerfully impressionistic version of the tour through the factory. Of "astounding size and technical perfection," this two-story-high, six-hundred-foot-long selective representation of the dynamism and modernistic beauty of the Ford plant,

FIGURE 7.15
Ford brought his River Rouge
factory to the fair at the Century
of Progress through the immense
photomurals of the entrance rotunda.

Moved later to Dearborn, the
rotunda became the visitor's center
for the factory itself.

as well as the dedication of its workers, established the context for all the subsidiary
exhibits. Beneath the mural's stunning photomontages, in huge chromium letters,
a series of maxims ("The recovery we need is of our American spirit of independence"; "With one foot on the land and one in industry, America is safe"; and the
like) gave visitors authoritative counsel for troubled times. The combined effect of
the "greatest photographic panorama ever built" and these "ringing aphorisms, below which no signature appears and for which none is needed," according to one
observer, was "that of Gibraltar giving voice to a battery of guns" (Fig. 7.15).[43]

In the rotunda photomural, as in much of the rest of the Ford exhibit, Teague
strove to meld the stylistic motifs of modernist design with the prescriptions of
Henry Ford, a man little attuned to the currents of artistic modernism. Considering himself a model for, and educator of, the mechanically minded common man—
and increasingly obsessed with restoring the worker's links to the land as a way to
alleviate the ills of economic depressions—Henry had decreed that the central precept of his 1934 exhibit should be "Man must go to the earth for all materials" (see
Fig. 7.20).[44] This lesson would be driven home through the display, among other
things, of an "industrial barn" illustrating the promise of soybeans as a crop through
which farmers could prosper by supplying materials for auto production. Teague
found a viable solution to the apparent disjuncture between Henry's preoccupa-

MONUMENTAL ENTERPRISE

A trip through the River Rouge Plant, where the process of Ford car manufacture is begun, is a revelation in scientifically guided human endeavor.

The methods, alone, are of startling interest. One does not merely marvel at *what* is being done—one thrills at *how* it is done.

Here it is evident that Man has conquered machinery. Science has supplanted muscle with mechanical power, and brain has conquered brawn!

Everywhere materials are on the move and men standing still at their work. Yet

the engineering skill, with which this vast and complex enterprise has been organized to function perfectly as a unit, is amazing.

Among the varied activities of the Rouge are blast furnaces, the largest foundry in the world, glass and cement plants, tractor and body factories, a paper mill, power plants, conveyor systems, salvaging and by-products divisions.

For all its size, this remarkable industrial unit is but the expression of an idea—service to mankind. Yet the River Rouge Plant is but half completed today—its work only begun.

Ford Motor Company

Owning and operating coal and iron mines, timber lands,
saw mills, coke ovens, foundries, power plants, blast
furnaces, manufacturing industries, lake transportation, parcel mines, glass plants, wood
distillation plants and silica beds

FIGURE 7.16

Widely viewed as the champion of the common man, Henry Ford worried little about attacks on the size of his business. In romanticized ads like this, he exulted in the massive power of his new River Rouge plant.

tions and his own sense of "good design" by seizing on another of Ford's obsessions—his enchantment with his massive River Rouge factory. Teague also benefited from the opportunity to work directly with Ford's son, Edsel Ford, who was far more aesthetically inclined than his father and more sympathetic to artistic modernism.

In other exhibits at Chicago in 1933 and 1934, Teague and other designers combined elegance, monumentality, and modernistic motifs to bestow an image of high-toned technological progressiveness on companies such as the Norge Corporation and Bausch & Lomb. And the machine aesthetic, along with a passion for monumentality, had already characterized Ford's earlier publicity of his River Rouge plant. The photographers Margaret Bourke-White and Charles Sheeler, commissioned by Ford in the 1920s, had produced striking images of the plant that found a place in the emerging canons of the machine aesthetic.[45] Moreover, hoping to impress a wider audience than that of plant visitors with the massiveness, "preternatural power," and perfect integration of his new industrial colossus, Ford had launched a major advertising campaign in 1924 to disseminate magnificent, idealized images of the River Rouge plant (Fig. 7.16). He also had a model of the Rouge created for the company's New York office and invited "every man, woman and child in New York" to tour the "Ford works in miniature" (Fig. 7.17).[46]

FIGURE 7.17
In a 1924 exhibit in New York City,
Ford adopted the scale model as one
way of taking his cherished factory
on the road.

At the Century of Progress, Teague re-created something of the image and aura of the River Rouge plant in the massive Industrial Hall that opened out in one direction from the motif-setting rotunda. Here, in a wing of exhibits estimated by one reporter to be "the size of two football fields," visitors witnessed exhibits of the production processes of scores of Ford suppliers. Teague selected only those processes of each that could be displayed most dramatically through dioramas, photographic scenes, miniature models, and above all, full-scale working models. Photographs that ostensibly instructed viewers in "how we do things" also dramatized and aestheticized factory production through the modernistic visual resonance of endlessly repeated images (Fig. 7.18).[47]

Although Henry Ford's rustic and eclectic interests constrained Teague to find room among the Ford displays for a soybean processing display and a Ford Museum, which included Ford's original Bagley Avenue workshop, Teague labored to infuse dramatic impact and an air of modernity into every aspect of the exhibit. He had authority over all elements of Ford's presence at the fair, down to the design of uniforms for scores of attendants and the creation of a streamlined lounge for Ford executives. Teague lectured Edsel Ford that unity was central to "all good design." Through patterns of spatial organization, graphic and visual consistency, and color coordination, he claimed to have brought "a great number of varied elements . . . into harmony."[48] By insisting not only that the individual corporate buildings at the fair be architecturally distinctive but also that the "industrial ex-

FIGURE 7.18
Photographers with a penchant for the modern used repeated images to captivate the eye and derived elements of design from machinery and products. The resulting aesthetic brought something like the reverberations of a jackhammer into the visual field.

hibits themselves . . . be works of art," Teague and other industrial designers devised a major role for themselves in the creation of corporate images.[49]

Ford's assembly line was not on display. But the photomural in the rotunda and the various other photomontages, dioramas, and working displays gave visitors a romanticized version of the traditional factory tour. The mode of the mural, with its communal, public service air and its evocation (through the influence of Thomas Hart Benton and other "regionalist" painters) of heartland, plain-folks Americanism, had already been discovered by a few corporations during the previous decade as a way of associating the narratives of their businesses with those of the nation at large. Through such murals they also celebrated their own brand of the "producerist" ideology that Erika Doss defines as particularly characteristic of the early 1930s murals by Benton. The epic narratives, in mural or diorama form, that embellished the exhibits of General Electric, General Motors (which included a Diego Rivera mural), and several other corporations at the Century of Progress in 1933 aimed to encompass those qualities of "monumental solemnity," "simplifications and compressions of form," and "technological optimism" that Karal Ann Marling discerns in the broader mural movement that culminated in the WPA and post office murals of the New Deal era.[50]

But the photographic mural, with its montages of abstracted details chosen for their evocative symbolic value (smokestacks, conveyor belts, and interlocking gears), was even better suited than the painted mural to project the corporate im-

FIGURE 7.19

From such photographic images as these, who could deduce any trace of worker alienation or dissatisfaction? Here the assembly line worker regains the aura of a craftsman immersed in the task.

age of a technologically sophisticated company.[51] As Sheeler and Bourke-White had demonstrated, the photograph could aestheticize the machine and the factory setting. "Mural-photographs were not new [in 1933–34]," Vicki Goldberg, the biographer of Margaret Bourke-White points out. But they "suddenly seemed so and caused a brief flurry of excitement . . . when the technique for sensitizing paper in large sheets was perfected." Within three years of the close of the Century of Progress Exposition, corporations would more than double their commissions for industrial photomurals. Displayed in immense size, photomurals conveyed the monumentality of industrial operations. They glamorized the machine. Photographic attention to repetitive forms and contrasting textures imparted a modernistic sensibility. In 1934 Bourke-White created murals with these qualities to illustrate Alcoa's processes in producing and casting aluminum parts for Ford cars. In the form of "huge picture books," these reinforced the modernism of the Ford display.[52] Teague's choices of photographically frozen moments for the impressionistic representation of certain processes of production added the element of the engaged worker, who, although aesthetically subordinated to machine forms, still refuted, by his obvious absorption in his task, any notion of soulless alienation within the corporation (Fig. 7.19).[53]

Sensing, as did an increasing number of other large corporations, that exhibits at major fairs might better serve as broad public relations tools than as magnified selling booths, Ford created an atmosphere in which, according to the *New Outlook,* "the usual ballyhoo of salesmanship is strangely and satisfyingly missing."

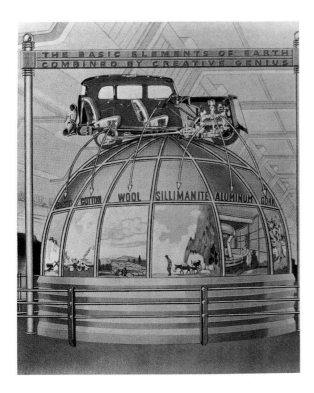

THE BASIC ELEMENTS OF EARTH
COMBINED BY CREATIVE GENIUS

COTTON WOOL SILLIMANITE ALUMINUM CORK

FIGURE 7.20
The notion of the industrial exhibit
as medium of education persisted in
1934 in such dramatic visual lessons
as Ford's demonstration, with
stylized vignettes, of the relation
of the motorcar to the earth.

Visitors were expected to take in the lessons of the production-oriented theme of "going to the earth for all materials" by observing a vivid pictorial representation of how basic materials were incorporated into the Ford car (Fig. 7.20).[54] In such an exhibit, graphic artists like Teague carried out the crucial task of simplifying and romanticizing the process of manufacture. The power and virtuosity of their artistic design aimed at enfolding the company image in a high-toned aura of quality and service. As consultants to the corporations, the new professional designers almost invariably found themselves on the side of the head office and its interests in a unified corporate image, as against the more diffuse concerns of the company's product and geographical divisions. The designers also lined up on the side of public relations departments, with their concerns for long-range corporate reputation, as against sales departments, with their concerns for quick results. The appearance of a professional design consultant at Ford amid the general deemphasis on sales pressure at the fair was no coincidence.

Many of these exhibits, with their persistent allusions to educational values, exemplified the continuing appeal to manufacturers of the operational aesthetic. They wanted public approval on their own terms—an admiration, based on a practical understanding, for the ingenuity and efficiency of their processes of manufacture. What the fair exhibit could accomplish for corporate public relations, more than any other medium, Teague explained, was "to give the public a feeling of intimacy with industry's methods."[55] But another, quite different, strategy of display was increasingly found in many exhibits, including even those that focused on the factory. More attuned to the limits of the public's attention and more tolerant of visitors' expectations to be entertained (as well as—or instead of—instructed), many public relations strategists began to give priority to the audience's apparent preference for animation and participation. Designers, including Teague, now claimed a dimension of indispensable expertise that had little to do with aesthetic judgments as traditionally understood. Like advertising agents, they asserted a special insight into the public's desires, preoccupations, and competence. Their conclusions would lead to the demise of the model of the factory tour and the ascent of displays that would communicate less technical, but more humanizing and reassuring, qualities of the corporate image.

The new corporate-exhibit showmanship that blossomed at the Century of Progress encompassed a variety of techniques beyond the modernistic design and vast, dramatic photomurals of the Ford display. At least a half-dozen companies included mechanical mannequins or talking robots in their displays to convey an image of technological sophistication. Visitors, by listening in on headsets, could imagine themselves in the place of Oscar, a papier-mâché dummy at the AT&T exhibit. They could be entertained by radio-controlled tractors or the mechanical cow at the International Harvester exhibit or listen at the GM building while Chief Pontiac joked with the crowd.[56] Linking the company image to scientific advances, such popular elements even found their way into the exhibits of a number of science-based corporations that had concluded that they could best promise a prosperous future in the midst of depression by attempting to bring their research laboratories, rather than their factories, to the fair.

In defiance of conventional logic, the cultivation of science as a corporate image tended to favor the trend toward showmanship rather than reinforce the operational aesthetic. Since much of the work of the research laboratories outstripped the layperson's understanding—far more so than the mechanisms of the assembly line—exhibitors heeded a mounting chorus of admonitions about spectator incompetence. Exhibits based on the work of corporate research laboratories were often intended more to evoke awe and mystery than to promote systematic education. Thus General Electric dubbed its display the House of Magic, a characterization that Westinghouse mimicked with its House of Wonders. Although General Electric spoke of making "educational features . . . easily available to the mass of people," it unflinchingly adopted the language of showmanship to describe what went on within the House of Magic. There "Maestro" W. A. Gluesing, a former professional magician, served as a "scientist-magician," operating various devices with "a wave of his wand" and using a revolving demonstration platform "to keep the show moving at a fast pace." The *GE Monogram* characterized the company's exhibit as "a thrilling presentation of electrical wonders."[57]

General Motors most conspicuously reflected the evolution of the industrial exhibit by attempting to bring both its factory (in the form of an operating Chevrolet assembly line) and its research laboratory (in the form of a special "research exhibit" room) to the Century of Progress. During 1933 GM's research laboratory display was only a minor aspect of its presence at the fair. In the appraisal of one GM executive, it distinctly lacked showmanship; its features ranked a "very bad second" to those of General Electric's display. Too many people approached the GM research displays "with a type of embarrassed reverence like the average person at the

Art Gallery viewing a Gainsborough."[58] In 1934 GM made amends for this failure to realize the full public relations potential of its research laboratory. It built an entirely new, air-conditioned room, the Hall of Research, to showcase an exhibit that now included eight "action displays" of GM's "pioneering achievements." The laboratory chief, Charles Kettering, worked to simplify and dramatize the demonstrations, giving them such folksy names as "frozen motion" and labeling them with such challenges as "Can you bend a railroad rail?"[59]

Now convinced that celebrating technological expertise was the best way both to build GM's own reputation and to restore confidence in the economic system, President Alfred Sloan highlighted the new research exhibit when the fair reopened in 1934. He staged an impressive dinner, to which he invited hundreds of scientists, businessmen, and civic leaders, and solicited from each guest a statement on the prospects for science and industry during the coming decades. Sloan exulted that it was "tremendously encouraging" to hear from men who could speak with authority that science (not the New Deal) was "ready to show the way to greater industrial progress." A GM press release reported that the dinner speakers "foresaw progress so sweeping and irresistible" stemming from the cooperation of science and industry that "it will hurdle the current ills of the depression era." The GM exhibit still had an educational mission, but one quite different from the popular explanations of manufacturing processes. Its central purpose was to lead visitors to associate General Motors with scientific progress and to teach them to rely on corporate technological innovation, not New Deal "regimentation," as the proper response to the depression.[60]

If manufacturers like General Motors, General Electric, and Westinghouse felt the need to cultivate admiration for their technological expertise through simplified "action displays" of their scientific and technical virtuosity, a politically sensitive service corporation was likely to seek customer sympathy and involvement with even more of a popular touch. In a review of the AT&T exhibit a company official noted that all its demonstrations, "in so far as possible, were personalized, and . . . were designed for active public participation." AT&T aimed to do more than simply display technological advances; it wanted to convey a message about the "institutional character and policy of the Bell System" and to stress "the human element in the business."[61]

As it demonstrated its operations, AT&T looked particularly to educating visitors not in the techniques of manufacture but in how to use various AT&T services. The "hit" of its show was the free long-distance telephone call. Those whose names were drawn by lottery or who were patient enough to wait in a long line could place a free call to any one of fifty-five American cities. Over the duration of the exhibit some thirty-five thousand visitors made such calls. Nearly a million others participated by listening in on the calls through headsets that AT&T foresightedly provided. So popular was "listening in" (one observer reported men and women "three and four deep" crowding around the "listen-in" receivers) that AT&T quickly supplemented its initial eighteen headsets with an additional forty-nine to meet the demand.[62]

For many, AT&T noted, this was their first experience with long-distance service. The callers seemed not to mind having their conversations overheard; furthermore, the spontaneous character of the calls, with the opportunities for wide

FIGURE 7.21
Eager public participation was
nowhere so successfully mobilized at
the 1933–34 Chicago exposition as
at the AT&T display, where people
thronged to eavesdrop on long-
distance calls by other visitors.

visitor participation in eavesdropping, ensured that the exhibit was "crammed with
the drama, the pathos, and the humor of everyday life" (Fig. 7.21). One AT&T
researcher, according to Robert Rydell, declared that the entire exhibit was based
on the drawing power of a single element—"emotional thrill." "Finding a way to
sustain that thrill," Rydell concludes, "became one of the chief concerns of phone
company public relations experts."[63]

Facing Up to the Feminized Masses

Whatever the public may have learned at the 1933–34 Century of Progress, the
most intensive educational experience at that fair—and at the several large regional
expositions during the next three years—was the schooling of a new group of specialists in the techniques and psychology of corporate displays. On the heels of the
sudden escalation of corporate financial investments in fair displays (one observer
estimated that 650 manufacturers had spent over $25 million on exhibits and build-
ings) came an increased pressure for accountability. Through a host of evaluative
tactics, public relations officers, designers, and advertising agencies soon laid claim
to a new expertise in appraising exposition audiences.[64]

Straightforward calculations of the cost per visitor of fair exhibits were easy and
popular; they could be contrasted directly with the cost per reader or listener for
institutional messages in magazines or on the radio. But it was difficult to assess the
relative quality of contacts made through advertising and those arising from personal involvement at the expositions. In the search for more qualitative appraisals

of the effects of fair exhibits, corporations now embarked on a multitude of both structured and informal surveys.

Arthur Page, the head of public relations at AT&T, requested an exhaustive analysis of the company's 1933 exhibit from AT&T's chief statistician. The resulting report included not only figures on costs, attendance, and participation but also information on the sex, age, and hometown of the long-distance callers and the content of their calls. The Ford staff compiled a forty-two-page analysis of all corporate exhibits in 1934. Ford also contracted with an independent company, Ross Federal Service, to count attendance at its exhibits at Chicago in 1934 and Dallas in 1936. It even asked the head-counters to record all "overheard comments" from visitors at the displays. Du Pont required its lecturers at Dallas to report every two weeks on the effectiveness of its various displays and the receptivity of the audience. Nearly everybody kept detailed records on attendance, closely monitored the attendance figures for other exhibits, and designed some form of survey or self-assessment.[65]

The exhibitors were not alone in treating the Century of Progress Exposition and its immediate successors as learning experiences. Marketing and audience research, especially for radio, had quickly acquired new levels of sophistication in the early 1930s. Advertising agencies were paying close attention to the new flood of what by previous standards seemed to be more rigorous and scientific data about audiences. In 1933 and 1934 advertising trade journals offered careful analyses of what was "working" at the Chicago fair. Advertising agencies, like their corporate clients, mused over private reports from their representatives on successes and failures in the art of exposition displays. Describing the Chicago fair as "a great human-nature laboratory," a speaker at a forum at the J. Walter Thompson agency observed that the visitors, as much as the exhibits, had been on display. He entitled his analysis "Twenty-Two Million Gold Fish." Never before had the responses of audiences come under such intense—and occasionally systematic—scrutiny.[66]

Several vivid lessons emerged from this welter of information and speculation. Again and again, observers pointed to animation and participation as the keys to success in a display. A *Printers' Ink* observer characterized the Chicago fair as a triumph for motion. "Exhibits which involve some moving element," he commented, "are seldom lonely." Even dioramas worked best when they involved "a spot of motion, if it be only a tiny flashing light." Another admiring critic noted that "every exhibit which can possibly induce motion of some sort is presented dynamically. . . . Instead of long rows of idle machinery . . . the exhibits of the Fair comprise a whole series of mechanically motivated demonstrations, almost theatric in effect."[67] So quickly was this lesson being learned at Chicago that General Electric, in revising its display for 1934, announced that "not a spot is to be left without action of some kind."[68]

In advice to clients Walter Dorwin Teague repeatedly drove home this same point. When Du Pont began its plans for a 1936 exhibit at Dallas, Teague's office warned the Du Pont advertising manager that the public simply would not look at a static exhibit. A lecturer at the eventual Du Pont display confirmed this view, observing that "they like to see something moving—something that can be understood at a glance." Although Du Pont had tried to use its lectures and moving displays to tell a serious story about its development of varied products from agricultural raw materials, one of its fledgling public relations experts, Chaplin Tyler, noted that "the thing that is getting all the attention—as usual—is the motion part of the exhibit." When the Ford Motor Company moved its 1934 Chicago display to Dearborn as a permanent exhibit, Teague later explained, his role as industrial designer was to transform elements with a "static conventional character" into "compelling displays." Motion was his method. For the Ford exhibit at the 1936 Great Lakes Exposition, Teague insisted on a "revolving motor on a pedestal facing the main entrance." The crowds would be attracted by "something in action for the visitor to see as soon as he comes in."[69]

Experts stressed the desirability of audience participation as the second great lesson to be drawn from exhibits at the Century of Progress. Linked together, animation and participation worked effectively to ensure that acme of all objectives: holding the attention of the masses. Ford's retrospective report on the Century of Progress made particular note of such display features as the Libby-Owens-Ford pitching cage, in which visitors were invited to try to shatter a small circle of safety glass with their best baseball pitch, and General Motors' "push-button maps," in which visitors could learn the answers to questions by activating lights. In dozens of other exhibits, visitors could speak into microphones to see their voice profiles on oscilloscopes, push buttons to light up sections of dioramas, or turn on fans that revealed the decreased air resistance of streamlined forms. AT&T surpassed all other exhibitors in 1933 in its variety of participatory displays. Those not eavesdropping on long-distance calls could listen to their voices amplified in the Hall of Electrical Echoes or dial telephone numbers and watch colored lights trace the paths of the calls. An AT&T retrospective evaluation remarked on the effectiveness of these "personalized" demonstrations in "attracting and maintaining the interest of large groups of individuals." The exhibits that demonstrated the greatest "pulling power," a Ford report concluded, simply underlined "a truism of industrial showmanship: make the public do something."[70]

As corporations and their new design experts applied the lessons of animation and participation to their exhibits in the late 1930s, they also incorporated a third lesson: the need for simplicity. Over the previous decade, advertising agents had increasingly lectured corporations on the urgency of addressing the masses in simple, readily understood terms.[71] Observations about visitors to the 1933–34 Century of Progress Exposition and during regional fairs in 1935 through 1937 reinforced that message. "An exhibit had to be clearly interpreted for the public," one advertising agency representative noted in Chicago in 1934, since "the public resents the necessity of making its own interpretation." The AT&T exhibit was successful, a company evaluator concluded, because it told a story of scientific discovery in "simple and living terms" and was thus fully accessible to a visitor with no technical background. The Ford report on the fair praised exhibits that made their points simply and dramatically, rather than providing a "technical discussion" that would "mystify the layman."[72]

Observations by exhibit managers and lecturers contributed to such lessons. At the 1936 Du Pont exhibit in Dallas, the lecturer Wilburn McKee reported to company officials that many visitors took the attitude, "Oh, well, this is chemistry and I don't understand it." People were impressed by the "magic of chemistry," he added, but they confessed that it was "hard for the ordinary person to understand"

FIGURE 7.22

By 1936, at this exhibit at the Texas Centennial at Dallas, Du Pont was requiring its lecturers, here shown standing stiffly at attention, to file weekly reports on visitor responses. Scrutiny of the audience seemed invariably to teach one lesson: simplify—and then simplify further.

(Fig. 7.22). Another Du Pont lecturer, Harvey Watts, noticed that visitors were drawn to demonstrations with a "magical touch" and seemed to recognize that the chemicals being demonstrated were "useful to them in some way." But they were "not especially interested in knowing how." Teague drew on these impressions to urge Du Pont to "carry the process of simplification still further" as it prepared for the 1939 fairs. In consonance with this outlook, Du Pont lecturers in San Francisco in 1939 reported back proudly that while some other exhibits were still too technical, Du Pont had conveyed its story "to the general public with no strain on their mental processes."[73]

The nature of the fair, with its numerous exhibits posing "great demands on the public's time and attention," also argued for a simple and dramatic presentation. A study of previous expositions, carried out for the directors of the forthcoming 1939 New York World's Fair, concluded that exposition visitors "prefer attractions in tabloid doses at tabloid prices." Most visitors hoped to gratify their curiosity by taking in as many of the sights and shows as possible. The same motives that led some designers to plan ways to ensure the "continuous flow of movement by the vast crowds" and speed their passage with "ramps and free-flowing interior designs" led others to consider how to hold those crowds long enough to make a favorable impression on them, or—as Teague put it—to "magnetize" them. In the face of the new complexities of industrial production, a few designers sympathized with the plight of the intelligent and interested layman and even with that of the puzzled visitor, usually presented as "she."[74] But most of the planners of corporate exhibits, in their assessments of fair visitors, retraced the same trajectory of disillusionment and contempt that a majority of advertising copywriters had traversed over the previous decade.

Throughout the 1920s, advertising experts continuously harangued their colleagues on the necessity of "short words—short sentences, simply-expressed ideas."

Copywriters had to recognize that "average intelligence is surprisingly low." Some of the most successful agencies and advertisers in the early 1930s were those that took the most pessimistic view of audience intelligence, aimed the lowest, and turned to tabloid and comic-strip formats. New, more scientific, studies of audiences failed to restore stature to this hypothesized public. At the Young & Rubicam agency, where George Gallup was pursuing his studies of readership, an agency memorandum observed: "Invariably our interviewers are amazed at the low level of taste—most of them call it stupidity—of the typical woman newspaper reader." Having discussed one sample, the memorandum succinctly fashioned a transition to the next community study with the sentence: "Stupid women are by no means typical [only] of Pittsburgh."[75]

The specification of gender in these observations was far from mere happenstance. A disdain for the ignorant, emotional, and frivolous masses and a habitual identification of consumers as female were inextricably linked in the minds of most advertising leaders. In the 1930s these attitudes began to spread to appraisals of fair visitors. Earlier, although the predominance of women among the purchasers of consumer goods had encouraged advertisers to take a low view of their audience's reasoning capacities, corporate exhibitors had usually held to a more respectful vision of fairgoers. The assumption that they could speak man-to-man through their industrial displays had enabled many corporate leaders to cling to their preference for the operational aesthetic, telling their story of production in considerable detail. Simple reflex determined the use of masculine noun and pronoun when the monumental 1893 *History of the World's Fair* pontificated, "No man ever leaves the Machinery Building a bit disappointed. If he surveys all that is to be seen carefully and intelligently he has obtained an amount of information concerning mechanic arts that he had never dreamed of." At the very least, visitors at an exposition would segregate themselves by gender; most industrial exhibits could anticipate an audience composed primarily of men. As Frank Vivian recollected from the Panama-Pacific Exposition of 1915, "They always said at the fair, 'If you're looking for a woman on the fair grounds, go up to the Food Building, but if you want a man, you've got to go down to Ford's.'"[76]

Some corporate leaders struggled to retain this image of the exhibit as a man-to-man communication. As late as 1939, although it now openly acknowledged that the "Fairs of 39 are Family Affairs," United States Steel still hopefully suggested that "other members of the family" would find entertainment elsewhere on the grounds "while the 'lord and master' loses himself in a maze of industrial exhibits." In its 1939 promotional film, *The Middleton Family at the New York World's Fair,* Westinghouse also continued to assume a gender-segregated audience. Immediately upon reaching the Westinghouse displays, members of this typical "Middleton" family parted ways; young Bud and his father headed for the scientific part of the exhibit after reminding Babs and her mother that they would want to go off on their own to see the display of Westinghouse consumer goods.[77]

But companies such as U.S. Steel, Westinghouse, General Electric, and Du Pont could not ignore the fact that they were increasingly selling goods directly to consumers, many of whom were women. Moreover, as they came to envision their exhibits as public relations activities, they focused on the entire potential audience of citizens, not merely on that segment that might be curious about technical processes. The corporate PR officers and design specialists who now were responsible for the displays measured their success ever more rigorously through calculations of total attendance, average duration of fairgoer visits, and costs per visitor. These results, and the inevitable comparisons with figures for the exhibits of major competitors, fixed their attention on the totals generated by the fair audience as a whole. Defined as a mass audience for displays of the corporate image, visitors at fairs now seemed little different from the heterogeneous mass audiences for magazine, newspaper, and radio advertising. Moreover, the newer, more comprehensive audience surveys increasingly described the majority of male visitors as just as distracted, uncomprehending, and inattentive as their female counterparts.[78] At the end of the 1930s, as fair audiences seemed more and more to take on the feminine qualities of the prototypical consumer and as the operational aesthetic continued to attenuate, the drive toward greater simplification and more showmanship in industrial exhibits proceeded apace.

The Research Laboratory on Parade

On 29 January 1936 it was fourteen degrees and snowy in Detroit. That was something of a relief from the below-zero temperatures of two days before, but hardly weather for a "parade." Nevertheless, a parade did set forth from the Motor City that morning that was to continue for three years, visit 146 cities, appear before more than three million people, and spawn yet another parade as an offshoot.[79] Christened the General Motors Parade of Progress, this caravan of scientific exhibits represented one of the most extensive of all efforts to put a corporate image on the road. It owed its origins directly to the vastly increased corporate investments in industrial displays at the 1933–34 Century of Progress Exposition. And it showed how the lessons the new experts had learned about audiences at that fair were increasingly taken to heart by business leaders during the interval leading up to the greatest of all the early twentieth-century fairs, the New York World's Fair of 1939–40.

One consequence of the large financial investments in Century of Progress corporate displays was the impulse to recycle these exhibits in some way. Many companies retained and remodeled portions of their 1933–34 exhibits to use again at Dallas, Cleveland, and other regional expositions between 1935 and 1938. Ford moved the entire rotunda of its 1934 fair building to a site next to the River Rouge plant in Dearborn, creating the largest permanent display building in the nation. Some of those who found themselves saddled with expensive, space-occupying apparatuses decided that Atlantic City, with its claim to center stage as the nation's premier convention center and tourist attraction, would make a good site for exhibits already carefully developed to give mobility to a corporate image.[80] General Motors sought to capitalize further on its investment, and preserve its image of progress through science and free enterprise, by putting the research laboratory component of its 1934 exhibit on the road.

The GM Research Division exhibit had been completely remodeled for the second year of the fair and was now housed, "at heavy expense," in its own separate, air-conditioned room. Here the division showed off its "exacting methods" and precision instruments. Allen Orth, the exhibit manager and one of the lieutenants

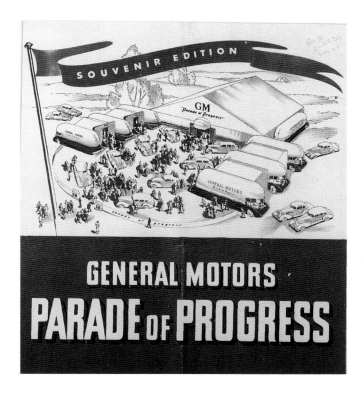

FIGURE 7.23
This attractive cover graced the booklet that General Motors distributed to visitors to its Parade of Progress—the tent show that figuratively put the company's research laboratory on the road. The Parade could dominate the consciousness of a city of fifty thousand during a three-day visit.

of the division's "Boss," Charles Kettering, recalled later the Parade of Progress's precise moment of conception. He and "the Boss" were standing in "the so-called Hall of Progress" just before the closing of the exhibition, he reminisced, when "I happened to remark that it was a shame that all of these exhibits had to be destroyed and thrown away."[81]

Between January and March of 1935 Orth and Kettering developed a "caravan" idea that would spare the exhibit, transforming it into a road show that fused showmanship, public relations, and popular edification into a "Circus of Science." By March GM's public relations director, Paul Garrett, had "finally caught the fire of the caravan suggestions" and had even adopted a five-year plan for the road show, instead of a onetime tour in 1936. If General Motors' expertise in science and technology could be made as interesting as a circus, why shouldn't it copy the circus in other respects and keep its tent show on the road year after year?[82]

In an ideological sense, the Parade of Progress was also founded on GM initiatives at the Century of Progress Exposition. At his well-publicized dinner for scientists, businessmen, and civic leaders at the reopening of that fair in 1934, GM president Alfred Sloan had aimed to give his company "a priceless identification with scientific progress." General Motors conceived of this identification as an important political stratagem as well as a long-range marketing device. The nation was turning a sympathetic ear to Roosevelt's New Deal programs of restrictions, security, and "regimentation," Sloan and other GM executives concluded, because people had lost their faith in progress and in the future. Americans, Sloan

lamented, were being encouraged by New Deal policies to give up trying to produce a greater abundance and to turn instead to government to "divid[e] up what
we already have." To counter this deplorable drift in sentiment, it was crucial to
remind people of new worlds still to be conquered. This could best be done, urged
Kettering, by showing "how large industries grow out of simple scientific facts
properly applied." The Parade of Progress that took to the road in 1936 figuratively translated the words of Sloan's dinner speech into the vernacular of Kettering's simplified displays of technological feats. It put these displays on wheels and
entertainingly merchandised them to local citizens under a circus tent (Fig. 7.23).[83]

The ensemble charged with this missionary tour of instruction and publicity
consisted of a crew of fifty men and a caravan of thirty-three vehicles. Eighteen
jumbo, streamlined trucks carried the scientific displays and opened out into exhibit halls when parked on the local grounds (Fig. 7.24). Fifteen new GM cars
accompanied the trucks to represent the models produced by the various manufacturing divisions. On the road the thirty-three vehicles, organized "on a semi-
military basis with the same precision and efficiency which giant circuses utilize"
and "spaced at 200-foot intervals as a courtesy to other motorists," stretched out
impressively over a distance of nearly two miles.[84]

While the Parade of Progress drew on the experience and popularity of a number of recent automotive road shows—including the Goodrich Silver Fleet cross-
country expedition of 1929 and several Ford Motor Company "tent shows" in
1930 and 1931—GM's version concentrated much less on promoting products
than on cultivating goodwill for the company and promoting confidence in big
business.[85] Previous nationwide "road shows" had been devised by corporate sales
departments; the Parade of Progress was a Research Division project, sponsored
by the Public Relations Department at GM headquarters. Beyond its naive educational intentions, it shouldered the burdens of ideological suasion.

The Parade of Progress would begin a typical visit to a small city with a highly
publicized procession of the caravan down Main Street, accompanied by the local
mayor, GM dealers, and chamber of commerce leaders. After this circus-style arrival, the Parade would park its exhibit trucks on some well-situated empty lot or
central park and pitch a large tent capable of holding an audience of five hundred
(see Fig. 7.23). The tent housed the "big-show" performances—popular demonstrations of the wonders of science by increasingly professional GM lecturers. Canvas awnings linked six of the large vans into a continuous walk-through exhibit
of GM technical apparatuses, many adapted to spectator participation. Normally
the Parade would remain in town for at least two days, sometimes as many as four.
Visitors were invited to attend from midmorning until evening; admission was
free. In Southern cities special hours were set aside for segregated black visitors, in
deference to local customs. Within the first few months, crowds of more than one
thousand at a time often overtaxed the capacities of the tent.[86]

Like any other theatrical show, the Parade of Progress staged a premiere. On 17
February 1936 it played to a capacity audience in Miami, Florida. Like the circus,
the Parade had chosen Lakeland, Florida, as its winter training grounds; Miami was
the closest city large enough to generate substantial publicity and warm enough
to accommodate a tent show in February. The premiere brought "amazement on
every hand," the *Miami Herald* reported. Sloan deemed the event significant enough

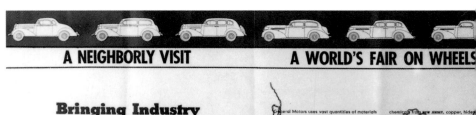

By ALFRED P. SLOAN, JR.
President, General Motors Corporation

Progress in living conditions and transportation has been rapid since the turn of the century. And this progress is largely due to industrial ingenuity. ● Modern industry is not something apart and remote from the life of the average man. Few people realize the community of interest which exists, and must exist, between great businesses and the millions who constitute their markets. Only those developments which are good for the people as a whole are good for industry, since industry both depends upon and contributes to the prosperity and buying power of the millions who buy its products. ● Industry therefore has steadily worked with its eyes on the future, striving through the medium of research to improve its products, to make those products available at lower prices, and thus to provide more employment and a higher standard of living for all. The General Motors Parade of Progress is undertaking to "bring industry to the people," and by showing the individual citizen in his home community what the contributions of industry mean to him and his family, to establish a basis of mutual understanding and friendliness, and at the same time to increase confidence in the future progress of America.

General Motors uses vast quantities of materials and manufactured products from every state in the Union. A partial list follows:

Asbestos and cotton come from ALABAMA, copper and hides from ARIZONA, lumber and manganese from ARKANSAS, gold, lumber, oil, and pumice from CALIFORNIA, gold, silver and tungsten from COLORADO, machinery from CONNECTICUT, and lacquers and paints from DELAWARE.

Sugar cane products from FLORIDA, pigskin and textiles from GEORGIA, lumber and wool from IDAHO, glass from ILLINOIS, limestone and steel from INDIANA, zinc from IOWA, grain and its by-products from KANSAS, and coal, oil, and porcelain from KENTUCKY.

Lumber, oil, and sulphur from LOUISIANA, paper and wood pulp from MAINE, textiles from MARYLAND and MASSACHUSETTS, copper and lumber from MICHIGAN, and iron and lumber from MINNESOTA.

Cotton from MISSISSIPPI, aluminum, lead and zinc from MISSOURI copper and oil from MONTANA, hides from NEBRASKA, borax, copper, and silver from NEVADA, textiles and chemicals from NEW HAMPSHIRE.

chemicals from NEW JERSEY, copper, hides ver from NEW MEXICO, and manufactured ...

Turpentine ... NORTH CAROLINA, ... hid ... NORTH DAKOTA, lamps, machinery, ... ber, and steel from OHIO, oil and lumber ... OKLAHOMA, lumber and wood produc ... OREGON, steel from PENNSYLVANIA, and m ... from RHODE ISLAND.

Textiles from SOUTH CAROLINA, silver fro DAKOTA, coal and oil from TENNESSEE, cott mercury, mohair, oil, and wool from TEXAS ... from UTAH, paper and machinery from ... coal and lumber from VIRGINIA, lumber fro INGTON, coal from WEST VIRGINIA, lead or from WISCONSIN, and hair, oil, and wo WYOMING.

This exchange of materials from mine and farms for manufactured products mal jobs for more people and more widely di the better things of life. It has been ap —"What happens to General Motors to me."

---

to warrant a trip to Miami in his yacht. Boss Kettering came south to make the opening address, setting forth a challenge to the nation and, implicitly, to the New Deal's alleged loss of faith in the future. "During the depression," Kettering lamented, "people got the idea that the world was finished." General Motors, however, offered a characteristically American response to such social pessimism. Kettering promised that "we, in this show, are going to try to prove that it is not."[87]

Several days later Sloan reiterated Kettering's pledge. He proudly announced that attendance had already "exceeded our most optimistic hopes" and predicted that "scientific industrial research," which had been mainly responsible for the progress of the first third of the twentieth century, would now move forward even more swiftly. Emphasizing the themes that dominated the corporation's concurrent institutional advertising, Sloan asserted, in his address and his comments in the visitors' brochure, that the Parade of Progress would show "the individual citizen in his home community what the contributions of industry mean to him and his family." The Parade's dramatic scientific demonstrations would impress upon hometown folks their dependence on big business and on its capacities, through research, to ensure progress. Thus, the Parade took on the defense of large industry and united the interests of "great businesses" (particularly those that, like GM, assumed the role of "large public-minded institutions") with those of "the individual citizen in his home community." The Parade would literally bring that image of General Motors and big business home by making it tangible in scores of midsized American cities.[88]

General Motors Comes to Hometown America

Although the Parade of Progress held its premiere in Miami, the itinerary on which it then embarked was strongly biased toward cities too small to have hosted major auto shows or to have featured educational exhibits comparable to those aboard

THE SILVER-TOPPED STREAMLINERS   28 UNITS IN MOBILE EXPOSITION

World's Largest Highway Leviathans
33 Feet from Stem to Stern

TWO MILES LONG ON THE ROAD

light huge streamliners, specially built in the leetwood plant of Fisher Body, transport this mobile world's fair from town to town. The caravan trucks are piloted by a group of carefully selected and rigidly trained young men.
The 233-inch chassis and the engines which are encased in insulated steel are built by General Motors Truck Company.

Six of the great carriers form public exhibition space at show locations. The other two transports carry the vast tent and various show properties.
Every precaution is taken for safe driving. Navigation lights, dual rear-vision mirrors, and directional arrows are auxiliary aids to highway safety. In traveling, the units are spaced at 200-foot intervals as a courtesy to other motorists.

Heading the parade in transit is the specially built and equipped 185-inch chassis Chevrolet sedan, fitted with public address system for safe driving announcements, and for the broadcasting of music.
It is fully equipped as an office on wheels and is air-conditioned, one of the first vehicles in the country to be so fitted.
Three Chevrolet tractor-and-trailer units, measuring 28 feet from end to end, have specific use in the caravan.

One houses the 35 KW Winton-Diesel engine that generates electricity to light the exposition and run the research devices. The second is a rest and locker room for the caravan crew and the third is a motion-picture projection room, with space for the development and printing of film.
The complete caravan includes 1936 models of all General Motors cars—Chevrolet, Pontiac, Oldsmobile, Buick, LaSalle and Cadillac.

FIGURE 7.24

On the road, and especially parading into a city of modest size, the streamlined trucks of General Motors' Parade of Progress connoted the cutting-edge modernity that the company established as the motif of its traveling show.

the GM caravan. As *Tide* described the strategy, the Parade would "touch mostly on small towns where it should for the time it stays be all the rage." In North Carolina, in the spring of 1936, it targeted such cities as Greensboro (population 54,000), Durham (52,000), and Raleigh (33,000). Although it did pay visits to Los Angeles and San Francisco during its swing through California the following year, the Parade also lavished its attention on Eureka, Ukiah, Stockton, Bakersfield, Santa Ana, and Riverside—all cities of less than 50,000 people.[89] As one of the Parade organizers put it, "The big towns would obscure us. We wouldn't be much good in New York City or Chicago." But in cities of 10,000 to 75,000, the GM Parade could dominate the consciousness of the community during a three-day visit. During 1937, in fifty-six communities, it attracted audiences that averaged 34 percent of the population of the cities visited.[90]

The small cities provided a gratifying response beyond mere attendance figures. One organizer reported back to the company that cooperation from state and local officials had been "nothing short of amazing." They genuinely appreciated the visits; they often made a special effort to get on the Parade's itinerary, participated in the motorcades, and helped the Parade gain exemptions, on educational grounds, from certain local taxes and fees. Manchester, New Hampshire, invited the Parade of Progress to set up its tent and exhibits on the village green, authorizing use of the area by outsiders for the first time since 1861, when it had served as a recruiting station for the army. Orlando met the Parade of Progress with a brass band and a police escort; San Antonio successfully pleaded not to be left off the itinerary.

General Motors responded to such "neighborly" enthusiasm by carrying a "Book of Good Neighbors" from city to city, to allow mayors and other dignitaries to express their warm wishes "for their sister cities and for GM."[91]

Learning from experience, the Parade steadily looked for new ways to win public favor. It spun off a "portable show," which could easily be brought to schools, luncheon clubs, and the like, stimulating attendance at the big show in the late afternoon or evening. At hospitals for veterans or for crippled children these portable shows promoted the good neighbor image of GM. Early in 1937 GM expanded the feeder show into a "Midget Caravan." Instead of rejecting invitations from communities too small to justify a Parade of Progress visit, General Motors could now provide a scaled-down show carried in a single "super-streamlined truck." First tested in Moscow, Idaho, the Midget Caravan, soon renamed "Previews of Progress," visited towns with populations of 5,000 or less.[92]

This abbreviated display also served well for "family parties" of GM employees. A local plant showing, in the view of GM public relations head Paul Garrett, served to bring "thousands of GM people . . . out in the open, so to speak, where they could look each other over" and find that "other members of the family were pretty much like themselves—with about the same ambitions, about the same responsibilities, and about the same troubles, too." Such "family parties" brought home to the people "that General Motors is not merely a name in the newspapers, not simply a listing on the stock exchange." Rather, it was "made up of people—of folks—just folks."[93]

Just as General Motors had eagerly termed the caravan a "Circus of Science," so its lessons in science aimed to inspire amazement more than erudition. The company prided itself on the way its "wonders of science" demonstrations had been "charged with powerful popular appeal." This appeal generally took the form of "magic" tricks and such Barnumesque challenges as "See the law of gravity defied!" and "See your voice turned into light!" From beginning to end, the road show was Kettering's "baby." Years earlier, the well-publicized and widely known head of General Motors' research laboratories had developed lectures, complete with both amusing and astounding demonstrations, to popularize scientific principles. He joined his enthusiastic lieutenants in the Research Division in creating dramatic demonstrations for the auto shows, the Century of Progress Exposition, and the Parade of Progress. Kettering had a particular knack, as his colleagues have recalled, for expressing "even technical things . . . in simple and unforgettable ways." It was "Boss Ket," related Allen Orth, who had come up with such "believe-it-or-not" signs as "Fry an egg on ice!" "Frozen motion," one of Kettering's verbal inventions, translated for the masses an exhibit in which a stroboscope with synchronized neon lights made moving machinery appear to stand still (Fig. 7.25).[94]

Throughout the tour of the Parade of Progress, General Motors committed substantial resources to advance work in each community to build up enthusiasm and curiosity by the time of the Parade's arrival. Furthermore, in 1938, with the help of copywriter Charles Lewis of the Arthur Kudner advertising agency, it discovered a post-visit technique for "crystallizing the imprint of General Motors on the community." A day or two after the caravan left town, General Motors would insert a reminder advertisement in local newspapers. For this purpose Lewis created

FIGURE 7.25

The message of such "magic tricks" of science as "frozen motion" and "gravity defied" was that GM's research promised future wonders. New technologies, not the New Deal, would surmount the depression.

what was immediately recognized as an advertising masterpiece. Entitled "We Hope We Set a Boy to Dreaming," the ad captured the sincere missionary instinct that inspired many of Boss Kettering's protégés among the Parade's technicians and lecturers. They had savored each instance in which a young boy left the demonstrations to go try his own experiments. (If any girls did so, the Parade leaders did not officially recognize it; current conventions associated science and technology exclusively with males.) Now their sense of mission was incorporated into an institutional creed that tied huge General Motors to a hallowed image of the hometown boy as curious explorer and aspiring inventor.[95]

In the powerful illustration for this ad, a boy of about twelve, surrounded by a microscope, test tubes, and beakers, gazes upward, his cheek against his hand, into an unseen, consecrating source of light (Fig. 7.26). His "dream" is obviously one of idealism and aspiration, one that will carry him, the text affirms, "on a road of

FIGURE 7.26

In this inspiring ad, GM sought to embed a human-scale image of itself in each town as its Parade departed. The bright, enthusiastic, individualistic boy who dreamed of discovery and invention stood for the corporation.

usefulness and service to himself, his country and his fellow men." In a subtle ideological pitch that translated the large industrial laboratory into an endearing image of boys pursuing their visions by "turning to their home chemistry sets . . . , tool kits and workbenches," General Motors reminded hometown America that "the real hope for continued progress lies in the spirit of individual initiative." Thus, the promise of the nation's future would be realized only if the boy—and by extension, the corporation—could pursue his visions without impediment.[96]

The Parade of Progress left the road late in 1938, having set up camp in nearly 150 communities and having drawn over three million visitors. When it had first set forth as "a world's fair on wheels," *Advertising Age* characterized it as representing "the conviction of Alfred P. Sloan, Jr. that a new type of institutional advertising is required to meet the problems of 1936." Through the Parade, GM had projected an image of itself as both a civic-minded neighbor of local communities and their prophet of a brighter, technological future.[97] The exhibits of the Parade and of the Previews of Science (rejuvenated and renamed the "Casino of Science") would be seen again at the 1939–40 New York World's Fair. There, however, they would become a secondary attraction within GM's Futurama show, with its even more dramatic and participatory form.[98]

Industrial Showmanship and Impression
Management at the 1939–40 World's Fair

With few exceptions, the association between business and show business never occurred to leaders of major industrial corporations of the late nineteenth and early twentieth centuries. Indeed, most manufacturers would have rejected the notion with contempt. The advance of national advertising during the early twentieth century, however, began to encroach on the air of seriousness that pervaded the leadership of giant corporations. The advent of radio, which linked entertainment and advertising so intimately, gave particular impetus to this trend. Curiously, though, despite considerations of showmanship that fairs demanded of exhibitors, company exhibits at major fairs remained something of a preserve for public displays of corporate seriousness. As late as 1933, companies that had already associated themselves on radio with comedians, popular singers, or even soap operas were still trying to induce fairgoers to understand their manufacturing operations and respect their dignity.

By the late 1930s, however, as corporations feverishly prepared for what they expected to be the biggest of all the world's fairs, resistance to a complete capitulation to show business faced a formidable challenge. Some corporate leaders found stimulating diversion in the new show-business activities of their companies. Others, who were less enthusiastic, safeguarded their seriousness by delegating to the experts all responsibility for this necessary submission to the public's demand to be entertained. None could avoid the rising tide of warnings, from the new experts in design and in audience response, that only increased showmanship would save their displays from obscurity at the great New York and San Francisco fairs of 1939. In the mid-1930s Teague had cautioned both Du Pont and U.S. Steel that in the coming years, "highly skilled and experienced specialists in visual dramatization will be more essential than ever."[99] Those who still clung to a sense of educational responsibility could only comfort themselves with the thought that the masses would learn the most from the best show.

Planning for the 1939 corporate exhibits began early. Teague started design work for Du Pont in mid-1937; General Electric implied that its plans were already well advanced when it declined to consider a proposal submitted by Peter Michelson and V. E. Scott in August 1937. The intense drive to improve public relations and repair corporate imagery between 1936 and 1939 ensured that major businesses would regard this fair as important; their fears of popular "misunderstanding" of the economic system meant that concerns about ideology and imagery would shape their exhibits far more than endeavors to sell products or provide technical education. *Forbes* magazine identified public relations as central to corporate strategies for the fair, and Bernard Lichtenberg, a PR professional, frankly titled a 1938 article "Business Backs New York World Fair to Meet New Deal Propaganda." Nearly every major corporation acted as if it had taken to heart the admonition in Michelson and Scott's proposal: this fair, "unlike other world expositions of the past," would be no mere "showroom for the display of goods" but rather "a *World Stage* upon which to dramatize the advantages of the American system of free enterprise."[100]

As we have seen in Chapter 6, the defense of the economic system had gained priority on the corporate public relations agenda of the late 1930s. Du Pont made explicit its purpose in 1939 to make "a case for free enterprise showing its fruits and indicating what might come"; Westinghouse vowed to "show the public that all this development has been the result of private enterprise and initiative." Teague explained to advertising experts that they would see an "almost complete abandonment of direct selling"; instead, the "entire emphasis of shows" would shift to "the social and economic services they [the corporations] perform for the country."[101]

The major corporations also acted as though they were responding to another exhortation in the plan that Michelson and Scott had submitted to GE: the call for "a new kind of interpretive showmanship" that would "present the story of industry in terms that the masses can understand." Moreover, the fair management's designation of the New York exposition as an "everyman's fair" echoed the corporations' search in the late 1930s for a language in which to reach ordinary people.[102] Designers and corporate PR officers concluded that the complexities of production had become too great for "the masses" to comprehend and that the short attention span of most visitors precluded any complicated message. Therefore, they would have to construct their exhibits not to provide technical education but merely to implant a single impression. As Teague had already admonished Du Pont in 1935, the company should be happy if each visitor went away "gratified by the entertainment and with a mental picture of the broad range of Du Pont activities and their importance to himself." To that end, he later explained, the company should look to "complete elimination of technical details not familiar to the public, with the whole complex process reduced to a few dramatic steps."[103]

One tactic in this endeavor, adopted by Teague and other designers, was to emphasize a "key statement" at the entrance to the corporation's exhibit. For the 1939 Du Pont exhibit Teague articulated such a statement through a hundred-foot-tall "Tower of Research." Fashioned of abstracted shapes of the apparatuses used in

FIGURE 7.27
Du Pont's Tower of Research, its
building's entrance statement at the
New York World's Fair, exemplified
the new corporate showmanship.
Rather than technical edification,
the exhibits promoted empathetic
understanding of the big institution.

chemical reduction, the tower emitted rising bubbles to incorporate the crucial
element of motion (Fig. 7.27). For Ford, Teague proposed a striking symbolic figure illuminated by flashing electric lights, "the object being to create an impression of . . . invincible action."[104] These display gestures were little more than dramatic corporate signatures. Corporate leaders still talked about the educational
value of their fair exhibits, but now the central goal of that "education" was clearly
to promote an appreciation of the company as an institution, not a systematic understanding of its processes of production.

With such broad objectives now foremost in their minds, corporate exhibitors
in 1939 gave full rein to the impulses of showmanship, earnestly applying the lessons of animation, participation, and simplification. Chrysler Motors, adopting
"the newer concept of what an industrial exhibit should do," rejected demonstrations of assembly lines in favor of an exhibit entitled "60 Minutes of Magic"
and billed as a "5-Star Show." Visitors made their way past a "frozen forest" (a
demonstration of the powers of air conditioning) to gaze curiously at "engineering wonders" and experience a simulated rocket ride to London. In 1940 *Chrysler
Motors Magazine* exulted about the "central carnival theme" that had superseded
"the old formula of product and manufacturing demonstrations and displays."[105]

General Electric astonished 1939 visitors with ever more spectacular "tricks" in
its House of Magic. *Business Week* called the GE show "pure science . . . served
to the public as unalloyed entertainment." Most visitors did not understand the
"tricks they saw performed with thyratrons and stroboscopes," the article pointed

FIGURES 7.28 & 7.29
In 1939 and 1940 Du Pont conveyed
messages about its scientific prowess
through such diverting but instructive amusements as a marionette
show and a magic trick that had a
company chemist pluck a woman
in nylons out of a test tube.

out. "But they came away thrilled, mystified, and soundly sold on the company."
AT&T aimed, first, "to enlist participation by visitors in doing something of interest to themselves" through Bell equipment and, second, "to employ scientific
novelty of such a nature as to be easily understood by the general public." Observing how visitors clamored to make long-distance calls, with 270 "listening-in
receivers" in nearly constant use, the *Bell Telephone Quarterly* declared that the key
to the success of its exhibit could be captured in a single word: *"entertain."* Du
Pont enabled a scientist to conjure out of a giant test tube a woman modeling ny-
lon hosiery; it closed its 1939 presentation with a marionette show (Figs. 7.28 and
7.29). The company boasted that its exhibit would not include any of the "mysterious, too-deep-for-me science of the textbooks."[106]

Westinghouse devised one of the most elaborate scenarios to reaffirm the free
enterprise system through its display of technology. The company energetically
promoted showings of its movie, *The Middleton Family at the New York World's Fair.*
The eighteen-minute-long film dramatically recounted a visit to the Westinghouse displays by a typical American family that, before this visit, had faced troubling prospects. Fourteen-year-old Bud, discouraged by the depression, was convinced that no new frontiers or opportunities existed and had dourly reconciled
himself to the motto of his high school's most recent graduating class, "WPA, Here

FIGURE 7.30

Westinghouse translated a movie about its 1939 display into comic-strip ads, encouraging Americans to view the fair through the eyes of "a family of folks you know—friends who live just around the corner from everyone." Sure enough, the Middletons find Westinghouse represented by a local boy, who instructs them in the research exhibit.

we come!" His older sister, Babs, had been so swayed by her dubious romance with Nicholas Makaroff, an art teacher with Marxist proclivities, that she haughtily informed her grandmother that calendar pictures weren't "Art."[107]

But Dad Middleton wisely looked to the fair's corporate displays to counteract such notions. Almost instantly the Westinghouse exhibit persuaded Bud that corporate science and engineering offered bright new challenges worthy of his dedication. The surly Makaroff, a devotee of abstract painting and a poseur who said "au revoir" instead of "goodbye," tried in vain to expose the propaganda in this "temple of capitalism." But the contrast of his negativism only highlighted the upbeat feeling conveyed by the men at the fair exhibit from the Westinghouse labs. They operated "on the principle that nothing is impossible"; their research had created hundreds of new jobs because they had recognized that "the company can't stand still under the American system of private enterprise." Meanwhile, Grandma Middleton employed a clever ruse to discredit Makaroff by exposing him as a fraud. Fortunately, Jim Treadway, a young Westinghouse engineer from the Middletons' hometown and a host at the Westinghouse Junior Science Laboratories at the fair, entered the scene to provide Babs with a new romantic interest, to show Bud how to operate the hands-on exhibits, and to explain the fair's inspiring technological

FIGURE 7.31

Electro—the Moto-Man, in these cartoon vignettes, exemplified "the gift . . . Westinghouse engineers have given to . . . women." Now, relieved of housekeeping burdens, women could "do so many more things with you men—like coming to the fair."

visions, as well as the links between research and free enterprise, to the Middleton family.[108]

Westinghouse also brought the Middleton's story to the public through a series of cartoon sequences in single- and double-page magazine advertisements (Fig. 7.30). Although the Makaroff subplot was too complicated for inclusion, the new format publicized Westinghouse's "Elektro—the Moto-Man" and the many other features of the Hall of Electrical Living and the Playground of Science (Fig. 7.31). In the studied style of folksy discourse so avidly contrived by corpo-

FIGURE 7.32

Between 1915 and 1939, Ford
displays moved from the operating
assembly line to the animated
"cyclorama." Its intention still
"educational," Ford now sought

primarily to elucidate the economic
system and portray Ford's contribution to a "widening circle" of
employment.

rate advertisers and public relations experts in the late 1930s, Westinghouse introduced its All-American family with a breezy, "Here's a family of folks you know —
friends who live just around the corner from everyone . . . the Middleton Family,
from Everywhere, U.S.A.!"[109]

The Ford Motor Company had already abandoned the assembly line in 1934 for
module demonstrations of selected production processes against context-setting
photomural backdrops. Now, in 1939, it sought to convey an overall impression
of the company and the economic system by means of a massive, thirty-foot-high
rotating "cyclorama" with animated figures (Fig. 7.32). Entitled "The Ford Cycle
of Production," the cyclorama comprised eighty-seven groups of carved figures of
men, women, and animals demonstrating how twenty-seven raw materials were
transformed into Ford cars. With their appeal enhanced by "humorous details . . .
added through plastic noses, eyes, horns and tails," the animated figures portrayed
typical production activities while a recorded "turntable lecture" intoned a message about the "widening circle" of employment created by Ford's vision of an automobile for the masses (Figs. 7.33 and 7.34).[110]

Fair visitors to the Ford exhibit in 1939 could next view a film, *Symphony in F,*
in which the animated figures from the Ford Cycle of Production were "brought

COTTON PICKING

FIGURES 7.33 & 7.34
With racist stereotypes and humorous Disney-like animals, Ford
aimed to explain the production of
sophisticated machinery from basic
raw materials in a way so simple
that anyone could understand.

FIGURE 7.35
A giant "altarpiece" that projected
an impressionistic image of the
company, Ford's three-dimensional,
animated mural sought to dramatize
the sounds and motions of mass
production. Never had the factory
"come to the fair" in so abstract an
incarnation.

to life as actors and actresses" in a cartoon feature. In 1940 *Symphony in F* was superseded in the Ford exhibit by a musical comedy and ballet called *A Thousand Times Neigh*. As Teague proposed it to the Ford Company, this dramatization of history would "have a fantastic, Walt Disney quality" and would be done "entirely in verse." His allusion to Disney echoed an earlier, private comment by the Ford publicity director, who had characterized *Symphony in F* as "a puzzling combination of 'Snow White' and an educational, industrial reel."[111]

Through a much-ballyhooed "activated mural," Ford made a dubious effort to retain the educational tenor of the operational aesthetic while adhering to Teague's admonitions about the need to provide visitors with a quick, impressionistic vision of the company. Seizing on Edsel Ford's partiality for modern art, the muralist Henry Billings persuaded the company to dramatize its story with an immense "animated" mural in its entrance lobby. As a "general prologue" to Ford's exhibit of the Cycle of Production, the mural incorporated a cross-section of a V-8 motor and a maze of "whirling gears and pistons . . . thus dynamically reproducing certain phases of the Ford plant at Dearborn." Shafts, gears, and connecting rods protruded into the third dimension to present viewers with a highly abstract, kinetic vision of "the increased accuracy and precision of modern mass production (as achieved by the Ford Motor Co.)." As the animated parts moved faster and faster, during each repetition of the cycle of action, hidden floodlights glanced off the moving pistons to spray beams of light around the hall. This awesome, forty-foot-high spectacle, as Alice Marquis has described it, "stood against a curved wall resembling the apse of a church. It suggested a gigantic altarpiece whose central figure was a V-8 engine." A member of the fair's theme committee called it "an altar piece for science," which radiated "high ideals" and "a tremendous sense of power" (Fig. 7.35).[112]

Billings frankly explained that his "activated" mural was conceived "not to instruct but to impress." A visitor could "stop and read the story if he wants to," Billings observed, but the symbolism was "intended to excite the imagination rather than define." Ford executives, however, were reluctant to forsake the educational dimension. A Ford press release insisted that Billings had shaped the mural to play "the dual role of gratifying the eye and of satisfying the mind by dramatizing for the world the complex story of the making of automobiles." The working Model-T assembly line at the 1915 Panama-Pacific exposition likewise dramatized the process of production and thus satisfied the mind, but the Billings mural, another Ford press release suggested, interpreted those processes in a more modern way, "achiev[ing] an authenticity that only actual glass and steel can give." This "authenticity" resembled that sought by Teague in his design for the hundred-foot Tower of Research in front of the Du Pont exhibit—the capacity to implant a certain impression through a "key statement" conveyed by abstract symbolism.[113]

Conveyor Belt to the Future: GM's Futurama

The impression-creating gesture had come to dominate corporate exhibits by the time of the 1939 World's Fair, and there General Motors made the grandest gesture of all. Its Futurama ride won virtually everyone's vote as the "hit show" of the fair. Even the head of the Ford Motor Company's Press Department acknowledged privately, "There is unfortunately no question but that the GM exhibit is decidedly more popular than ours."[114] One neutral survey of a thousand departing fairgoers—perhaps the nation's first "exit poll"—awarded the GM exhibit 39.4 points, versus only 8.5 points for second-place Ford, as the most interesting exhibit. When asked which fair exhibit they would most like to visit again, 47.5 percent of these respondents picked General Motors, as compared to 7.3 percent for second-place General Electric and only 3.8 percent for Ford.[115] Even the showman Billy Rose's spectacular Aquacade, the best-attended show in the fair's amusement section, could hardly match the popularity of the GM Futurama. People stood in line for hours to gain a place among the twenty-eight thousand visitors who could enter the Futurama each day. Even during the "chill drizzle" of an unseasonably cold June day in 1939, the *New York Journal American* reported, a queue of more than nine thousand "snaked back from the building more than a mile at one time."[116]

Like most of the major corporations, General Motors had now turned to a professional for the design of its exhibit. Norman Bel Geddes, unique among industrial designers for his background as an expert in theatrical staging and lighting, supplied both the concept for Futurama and the technique.[117] Through his design Bel Geddes involved visitors experientially with the corporation—not by urging them to witness the difficulties and triumphs of its processes of production but by offering them a chance to share its wider social and technological vision. Guests at Futurama found themselves thoroughly entertained even as they took a serious look at the nation's future—through General Motors' eyes. Bel Geddes's Futurama transformed that time-honored invitation to "come visit our company." Corporations would henceforth entice fairgoers not to "tour our factory" but to "share our world."

The impetus for Bel Geddes's grandiose project stemmed from his earlier work for the J. Walter Thompson advertising agency. In 1936 he had provided a number of sketches of solutions to traffic congestion for use in a prospective advertising campaign by the Shell Oil Company.[118] Sensing the dramatic possibilities of conveying his vision through photographs rather than sketches, Bel Geddes expanded the project, constructing an elaborate scale model of a futuristic city of super-skyscrapers, expressways, and elevated sidewalks to separate pedestrians from motor traffic. He used lighting so effectively that Bruce Bliven, who reviewed the project for *New Republic,* marveled at the striking illusion of depth and distance obtained through "masterful photography" of the model.[119]

In the process Bel Geddes gained a glimpse of himself as a designer and planner of cities and transportation on a grand scale. He denounced the irrationalities, inefficiencies, and dangers of present conventions in highway building and championed rational engineering and mistake-proof technologies. He planned to expand his futuristic model as an exhibit for the Goodyear Rubber Company at the 1939 World's Fair. When Goodyear suddenly canceled its exhibit in February 1938, Bel Geddes instantly mounted a desperate siege of General Motors, which had previously dismissed his proposal, to salvage his wondrous idea.[120]

It was now less than fifteen months before the fair would open. General Motors had already decided on an updated model of the Chevrolet assembly line that it had used in Chicago in 1933–34 as its focal exhibit, supplemented by an expanded research display from the Parade of Progress road show. In his struggle to supplant an already approved plan at GM, Bel Geddes first gained reconsideration by persuading Paul Garrett, GM public relations director, and Alfred P. Sloan Jr., past president of GM and chairman of the board, of the virtues of his venturesome concept. According to Bel Geddes's account, Sloan liked the idea of "something to catch the public's imagination beyond mere merchandising." Then, during a dramatic, hours-long meeting with forty GM executives, Bel Geddes won over the corporation to his project primarily though a negative argument: did General Motors dare to spend $2 million on its planned re-creation of the 1933–34 assembly line exhibit, only to "admit that they haven't had a new idea in five years"?[121]

Bel Geddes easily aligned his conception for Futurama with General Motors' interests. An animated model of a scientific motorway system of the future, he assured GM, could demonstrate the need for vastly expanded highway facilities, encourage automobile ownership, and display GM's concern for highway safety. It could convey the corporation's optimism about the capacity of private industry to promote prosperity and create new jobs, thus expressing, in a positive way, the bitter antagonism of GM leaders toward FDR and the New Deal. And it would suggest the modernity, benevolence, and forward-looking social vision of the corporation.[122]

With his own vision thus comfortably fused with General Motors' public relations needs, Bel Geddes proceeded with the detailed design and construction of his future world. His venturesome plan called for an immense model, on a scale of 1 inch to 200 feet, of a major segment of the nation as of 1960. The model would cover 35,738 square feet and contain several million structures.[123] Bel Geddes strove for verisimilitude in every last detail. He even contracted with Eddie Rickenbacker, a famed World War I pilot, to fly a dozen of his staff members over a portion of western Pennsylvania (where, incidentally, construction was beginning on an innovative turnpike) so that they could observe exactly how certain features appeared and what level of detail was visible at various heights. When staff members noted that from five hundred feet they could see cows "lashing and swinging their tails" and a farmer throwing feed to chickens, Bel Geddes insisted on including animations of such "human interest" details in his Futurama design. He simulated the spray of waterfalls by combining tiny water sprays with air jets, showed airplanes in flight with their moving shadows visible on the ground, and used chemical vapors to create low clouds that would "cling to mountain sides."[124]

In 1937 an advertising agency newsletter, seeking to comment knowingly on current trends, noted that industrial designers rather than architects had suddenly gained control over the design of fair buildings. "The industrial designer," it explained, "first plans the exhibit and then clothes it in an appropriate building." Bel Geddes did just that. With his central exhibit clearly in mind, he designed the GM building with imposing, unembellished, curved surfaces that loomed up to convey "a sense of power" yet concealed the actual shape of the massive Futurama model.[125] The "stark simplicity and mystery of the building" and the lure of the winding ramps leading up to it would "intrigue" visitors into entering the exhibit, Bel Geddes predicted (a writer in *Architectural Record* later characterized the GM building as a "vast carburetor, sucking in the crowds"). As one of his staff observed, there was no way of guessing from the exterior of the building what it might contain. But it reached out with a giant curved "hook" to scoop in the passing throngs (Fig. 7.36).[126]

Once the visitors crossed from the bright outdoors through the almost hidden entrance, they descended (like "pilgrims . . . bound for some magic shrine") on

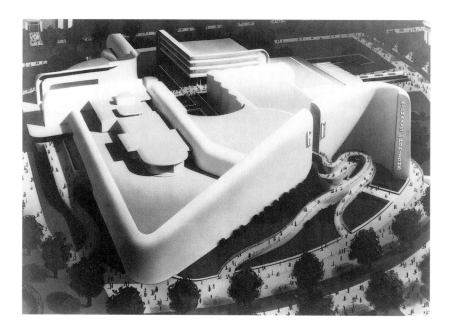

FIGURE 7.36

The streamlined design of the 1939 GM fair building suggested both "a sense of power" and an orientation toward the future. Its curving ramps and dark, mysterious entrance embodied the use of mass psychology to entice visitors.

sloping ramps that were dimly lit, to accustom their eyes to darkness. Soon they found themselves immersed in the "subdued twilight" of a seemingly boundless "Map Lobby." Here an immense map (sixty by one hundred feet) curved high over their heads against the backdrop of diverging walls and a misty "gray blue tone" of illumination, making the viewers feel they were not in a room at all but rather were gazing out into limitless space at a map suspended in the sky (Fig. 7.37).[127] As each visitor experienced the solemnity of this setting, a "quiet, intimate voice—as though of a friend walking at his shoulder"—explained the meaning of the changing lights on the huge map. Superimposed over the illuminated map of the nation's main cities and waterways, the first projection, in "red electric bands," highlighted the highway system of 1939. The lights then switched to reveal the projected traffic congestion by 1960 and changed colors and configurations again to outline the solution—a future network of superhighways. In the theory of Bel Geddes's design, visitors had now acquired both the proper mood and the necessary information for the next phase of the exhibit, a dramatic opening curtain on a pageant in which they would ultimately participate.[128]

Ushered into chairs on a moving conveyor, the visitors embarked on a relaxed, fifteen-minute serpentine ride. Each chair, a GM press release noted, held "individual, synchronized sound equipment which in a quiet voice serves as a private guide to the spectator as he travels through the wonderlike miniature world of the future."[129] This "soft-speaking," "intimate," but also "authoritative" voice rein-

FIGURE 7.37

Just beyond the entrance to Futurama, dimly lit ramps and an immense
map, seemingly suspended in space,
cast an aura of seriousness and
prepared visitors for the momentous
passage into a future world.

forced the visitor's sense of having been allowed to share the exciting world of a
friendly and benevolent sovereign.[130] As the unseen voice invited each visitor to
"come tour the future with General Motors," one reporter recounted, "you glide
into a black tunnel, swing miraculously around a corner, and the World of 1960 is
spread before you . . . in dazzling light" (Fig. 7.38).[131] Even the truculent critic
Stuart Chase was enthralled by the spectacle that Bel Geddes had designed to greet
his audience at this "opening curtain" to Futurama:

> Suddenly the world of 1960 opens before you, reaching over hill and dale,
> field and village, to a far horizon. You know that it is all a model . . . but the
> effect is very real. Cows are grazing in the pastures. Blossoming fruit trees in
> immaculate patterns cover whole hillsides. Crop lands are plowed on the
> contours. . . . Barns and silos are streamlined.

Meanwhile, the voice of the visitor's "private guide" coached the appropriate response by intoning, "The world of tomorrow is a world of beauty."[132]

The world that unfolded was a scale model of a segment of the United States,
over which the spectators cruised as if in a low-flying airplane. The "quiet authoritative voice" at their ear interpreted the scene beneath them as a world that
could soon be theirs, a planned world of superhighways, idyllic cities, and cozy,
village-like suburban communities. The essayist E. B. White wrote that this "soft
electric assurance of a better life" had infected his blood with "such a strong sweet
poison" that he did not want to wake up. Futurama's vision of the future not only
associated General Motors with foresightedness, technological sophistication, and
a concern for highway safety; it also promoted the larger GM ideology. The

FIGURE 7.38

The conveyor-belt chairs on which visitors to GM's Futurama voyaged into the future were fitted with side blinders that controlled their angle of vision and synchronized speakers that emitted the quiet voice of a seemingly private guide.

soundtrack reminded visitors that the exciting future they were experiencing had been "enriched . . . by a new understanding of the true function of industry as an integral part of the nation's social and economic life." If that tribute to free enterprise was vague and muted, the "Press Guide" proudly quoted the statement of GM chairman Alfred Sloan that for industry to move forward toward this future it was necessary to "destroy the economic barriers that now prevent the essential expansion of enterprise . . . and that repress the spirit of individual initiative."[133]

But the success of Futurama had far less to do with ideology than with Bel Geddes's inventive display tactics and his attention to both detail and theatricality. Bel Geddes relied heavily on animation, from moving water in the waterfalls to the whirling of a ferris wheel in an amusement park (Fig. 7.39). He also brought his experience in innovative stage lighting to play, backlighting most areas to conceal any flaws in the model and elsewhere deflecting and diffusing small rays so that "afternoon sunlight floods the pink and white orchards." A reporter from the *Charlotte (N.C.) Observer* exclaimed that the "scenery is so startlingly real, the cars and the planes so life-like, that you are unconsciously projected into a new world." Another newspaper reported that some visitors found this experiential trip into the future so vivid that they burst into tears.[134] Above all else, Bel Geddes drew his audience *into* his future world, emotionally and physically. Nowhere was this more

Bel Geddes reveled in opportunities
to convey authenticity through
detail. Here he demonstrated his flair
by incorporating in his animated
model the sounds and sights of
an amusement park over which
Futurama visitors seemed to fly.

dramatically accomplished than in the "surprise ending," which propelled visitors
onto a whole new plane of experience.

After gliding over a massive city (modeled on St. Louis), divided to contrast the
"old city" of 1939 with the spectacularly futuristic architecture and open space of
the city of 1960, the spectators were brought down closer to one small segment of
the new city, a particular intersection toward which the narrator directed their attention (Fig. 7.40). Here they could admire from on high, yet in full and explicit
detail, a rational new mode of urban planning in which pedestrians and auto traffic
were segregated onto different levels. "On the elevated sidewalks," as Bel Geddes
described the visitors' entrancing vision at this moment, "the city crowds are walking, gazing in the shop windows, lounging on the building roof gardens. Children
are playing in the parks. Cars are moving in the streets" (Fig. 7.41).

Then came the climax of the ride. As Bel Geddes described it:

> Suddenly the spectator, in his chair, is swung about! He can scarcely believe
> his eyes. He is confronted with the full-sized street intersection he was just
> looking down on. He gets out of his chair and becomes part of the crowd.[135]

No longer "a spectator looking at an animated scale model," the visitor now
viewed "the city intersection again, this time as the real thing," and entered an actual full-scale intersection as "a pedestrian projected twenty years forward into the
heart of a great city" (Fig. 7.42). The intersection had become, in Folke Kihlstedt's

The Corporations Come to the Fair   **3 0 7**

FIGURE 7.40 (above)
Bel Geddes's future city of 1960
included skyscrapers of dramatic
height, open space, and friction-free,
elevated superhighways with lanes
designed for fifty, seventy, and a
hundred miles per hour. People
would live in the surrounding small
communities and commute for
work and pleasure.

FIGURES 7.41 & 7.42 (opposite)
After hovering over this modern
intersection—with separate levels for
pedestrian and auto traffic—Bel
Geddes's visitors suddenly found
themselves thrust into GM's future,
leaving their chairs to walk about the
intersection in full-scale prototype.

words, "an embryonic cell for a yet unborn world." Visitors could walk across the elevated sidewalks, look down on a plethora of GM cars and trucks simulating traffic on the streets below, gaze into the shop windows, and enter any of the large buildings on the four corners of the intersection to see such additional General Motors' exhibits as a magician's show that provided "a homespun idea of research." To commemorate this time-warp experience, all visitors received pins proclaiming, "I have seen the future."[136]

The phrase was effective but clearly too modest in its claim. Not only had they seen General Motors' future, they had seen it "come to life" and had actually walked around in it! The exhilaration of that participatory experience seems to have shielded visitors from recognizing a singular irony: as comfortable passengers on GM's trip to the future, they had been emancipated from the relative tediousness of the old "tour-of-the-factory" display, only to find *themselves* being carried along on an assembly line (the moving-chair conveyor belt), while General Motors constructed their vision of the future.[137]

"Come Experience Our World"

The qualities that most strikingly set Futurama apart from competing exhibits lay in Bel Geddes's dramatic new techniques for inducing an experiential mode of visitor participation. These began with the sound system, where the individual speakers, synchronized with the progress of each chair, enabled General Motors to tell its story in a conversational tone and avoid negative reactions that surveyors had noted at earlier fairs, where visitors complained of "being talked at through loudspeakers." As a Bel Geddes lieutenant explained to Richard Grant of GM, it was crucial to perfect the sound system, since "the speaker's voice should be very soft with excellent quality and with the sound source apparently close to each individual," to give the effect of "talking individually to each spectator." In many of his descriptions of the ride, Bel Geddes used the word "whispers" to suggest the intimate quality he believed he had achieved in the voice of his mass-produced "private guide." But the voice was not only intimate; it was also, in E. B. White's recollection, "a voice of utmost respect, of complete religious faith in the eternal benefaction of faster travel."[138]

The conveyor-belt "easy chairs," fitted with "wings" on each side to severely limit the visitors' peripheral vision, were also crucial to an enhanced sense of participation. They ensured that visitors would direct their attention at each moment to just what Bel Geddes wanted them to see. This system also solved the problem of maintaining extensive control over the visitors' path and rate of movement. As one of Bel Geddes's staff members later emphasized, "You will remember that these were very comfortable moving chairs that not only permitted, but *necessitated,* the viewing of the model in the correct sequence and timing."[139]

Bel Geddes had not merely created an exhibit. He had created a "world," or what David Nye has more recently termed a "total environment." Other exhibits had increasingly aimed at audience participation. AT&T had exulted in the way "the crowd made the show its own," as some visitors made long distance calls and hundreds of others listened in on them. But Bel Geddes's Futurama, by having the visitor physically enter a world created by and for the corporation, made audience participation even more engaging.[140] And if all these devices—from the winged chairs to the unseen voice to the ingenious lighting effects—did not fully create an encompassing "total environment" for the visitor/participant, the theatrical emergence into the full-scale city intersection of the future ultimately induced Bel Geddes's audience "not merely [to] see the events, . . . [but to] *experience* them."[141] Walt Disney would expand on these insights and devices in Disneyland, as would the corporate exhibitors who thereafter increasingly turned both to Disney and to "enter our world" rides to cultivate public understanding and empathy.

Beyond Bel Geddes's enhanced techniques, the most significant impact of Futurama was the decisive shift from the concept of "tour our factory" to that of "share our vision." It is difficult to imagine that Bel Geddes's exhibit would have enjoyed such popularity had it transported visitors on an entertaining and educational tour through a model of a General Motors factory. And what of the surprise ending, which not only transported Futurama visitors into a life-sized segment of a world of the future but also placed them alongside showroom windows, where they could comfortably imagine themselves in the role of consumer? A moving-chair exhibit of a model of GM production lines would hardly have been so compelling if it had suddenly deposited visitors on a full-scale factory floor, with no evident role for them to play in such an uncomfortably alien, albeit contemporary, world.[142]

Through the exercise of pondering the solution to traffic problems, Bel Geddes seized on an idea that had been percolating among the creators of industrial exhibits—namely that, especially for public relations purposes, the future (rather than products, company history, or production processes) might provide the best theme for a successful, image-building exhibit.[143] In shifting from the factory to the future, Bel Geddes and General Motors managed to introduce many qualities of theatrical entertainment while retaining a prestige-enhancing air of seriousness. Futurama constituted a major public relations success not so much for the effectiveness of any of its specific messages[144]—although Paul Hoffman, the president of Studebaker, praised Bel Geddes for "blasting open the minds of men as to our highway needs"—but because the great corporation had benevolently offered the public an entrancing "free show" without crossing over the indistinct boundary to pure entertainment.[145] General Motors did not flinch from the implication that it had not had a new idea in twenty-five years when it re-created a "Futurama" for the 1964–65 World's Fair. To this day the corporate exhibitors at EPCOT have departed little from Bel Geddes's paradigm of the state-of-the-art public relations exhibit, either in concept or in basic technique.

8

LITTLE TOWNS AND
BIG CORPORATIONS:
THE WARTIME IMAGERY
OF A NATION UNITED

Every Friday and Saturday evening for fourteen weeks, from June through August of 1942, tens of thousands of General Motors workers and other local citizens of Dayton, Ohio, jam-packed a huge exhibit tent at the Dayton fairgrounds to witness the company's patriotic spectacle. A cross between a stage revue and the community pageants so popular during the first decade and a half of the twentieth century, this theatrical rendition of company and community mobilization for war initially carried the title *Plowshares*. Among its "cast of over 100" the pageant boasted "figures from Hollywood and New York" in several leading roles. But most of the chorus members and bit players were GM employees. Dayton was the "plant city" for six General Motors factories, including its major Frigidaire works. In offering its employees, their families, and other local residents a dramatization of the "first hand evidence" of what General Motors was doing for the nation's war effort, *Plowshares* fused the company's image with that of the "hometown" of its factories and, by extension, with all of "Main Street, U.S.A."[1]

This pageant of war production, according to surviving drafts of the script, interspersed stage scenes with newsreel footage of war action and filmed images of current Dayton production lines to create "a masterpiece of enlightenment and a thriller from start to finish." As a venue for this wartime dramatic production, GM recalled from retirement its famed Silver Dome, the elaborate exhibit tent and auditorium for its traveling show of the late 1930s, the Parade of Progress. As one *Plowshares* brochure explained, the three separately curtained stages of the Silver Dome allowed for rapid pacing as the story unfolded through thirty-eight "thrill-packed scenes." Just as the manufacturing facilities of GM plants had been converted to war production, the printed program noted, so the corporation's sales expertise had been mobilized for war service to make possible such engrossing pageantry.[2]

The narrative of *Plowshares* focused on a typical American family. Music of a "pastoral-like character" set the mood for the opening "Our Town" tableau of a serene family gathering, suddenly interrupted by the "offstage roar of a bomb." In responding to the menace of war, the community turned spontaneously to the technical expertise and productive capacity of General Motors. In one draft of the revue an authoritative historian stepped forward to explain that although GM "didn't know guns . . . it did know machines." Thus, it was GM's "know-how" that had made possible "the task of beating plowshares into swords." Subsequent revisions in the script gave these lines to a narrator and finally ousted both historian and narrator, placing this commentary in the mouth of the local common man and hero, "John Doe."[3]

The most important scene in *Plowshares,* according to the General Motors employee magazine, was that in the local barbershop (replete with barbershop harmony). This folksy backdrop offered a spokesman for American business, Mr. Jones, just the right milieu in which to explain "the problems of plant conversion" to John Doe.[4] When the strident voice of an agitator demanded to know "Why weren't we ready? . . . Why haven't our great factories been turning out war materials during the months . . . that have passed?" the curtain on another of the three stages opened to reveal a figure of authority ("the voice of fact") and to display the photographic evidence of GM's productive feats in Dayton. These displays made it clear that General Motors had, "in fact," outdone itself in war production. Moreover, since the corporation encompassed a "huge family of plants" and stood as "a symbol . . . of organized production power," it provided the community and nation an essential resource in winning the war while giving local citizens the means to express their patriotism. "It makes one very proud," one viewer exclaimed of the pageant, "to be a 'Daytonian' as well as an American."[5]

Since virtually every family in the nation had a relative or friend in military service, GM's public relations staff reasoned in mid-1942, the corporation could expand its role in local morale boosting by serving "as an emotional liaison between the camps and the homes." In a weekly radio broadcast called *Cheers from the Camps,* GM linked the folks on Main Street with the "human" aspects of war mobilization by broadcasting directly from the training camps (Fig. 8.1). Servicemen provided the main talent for the programs, at no cost to the company. Each week's show featured a different camp, to which a mother or father or a wife or sweetheart of one of the men was brought to be interviewed on the program; selected soldiers could also speak directly to the folks back home (Fig. 8.2). Interspersed musical numbers embodied the down-home qualities of the barbershop quartet, the camp glee club, and the community sing ("hymns with the whole camp joining in"). This vehicle for corporate imagery would "touch the emotional heartstrings of ordinary American families," GM calculated. Thus establishing itself as a mediator between average Americans and the new recruits, GM created the perfect context for its "reassuring" reports from the GM production line.[6]

Eventually, General Motors broadened and institutionalized its local-citizen, plant-city persona by transforming its early Dayton pageant into a traveling revue entitled *Arms for Victory* (Fig. 8.3). This revue, which again featured GM employees, played before workers and the public in some 144 performances in twenty-eight plant cities. General Motors also adapted the concept to radio; it broadcast *Victory Is Our Business* weekly in twenty-five of the cities in which GM operated war production plants. This program dramatized news from both the fighting front and the home production front. It localized its appeal through interviews

FIGURES 8.1 & 8.2
General Motors seized the opportunity to devote a radio program
to local wartime morale. In 1942
most American soldiers were still in
training camps. GM associated itself
with intimate human contact (via
a mass medium) by promising to
restore family ties.

"CHEERS FROM THE CAMPS"

A Radio Program
in which General Motors
will

"Hello, Mother – Hello, Dad"

Boys will talk to their folks over the air.
A number of such messages will be
broadcast by the boys themselves on
each program.

FIGURE 8.3

Originally titled *Plowshares,* GM's plant city–based revue of its wartime mobilization included "38 Thrill-Packed Scenes." In one of these, set in a hometown barbershop, GM's common man–hero refuted critics by extolling GM's "know-how."

with war workers in each of the plant cities. By early 1943 some version of the GM revue had been viewed by about 650,000 employees, and the locally oriented radio shows had reached millions. At these pageants "GM folks with boys in the branches of the armed forces and even returning war heroes" made "impromptu" appearances to "tremendous ovations."[7] Assuming functions that unified communities during wartime, GM's revues came to represent a kind of Main Street on which local patriotic "parades" took place.

General Motors was not alone in reviving the tradition of the local pageant, a ritual that David Glassberg describes as serving, at the height of its popularity in the early twentieth century, to "retain the intimacies of community" while joining in the progress promised by technology and mass society. Bausch & Lomb combined a "scientific story and patriotism" in employee-produced "stage spectacles" that claimed audiences of eighteen to twenty thousand. Such "colorful events" aimed at the "inspiration, education and indoctrination" of employees and their families. Westinghouse "induced" its employees to put on a show with local plant talent that was performed "over and over again, and eagerly attended." United States Steel, "recognizing the importance of plant town and community goodwill," organized a "home talent show" as part of a program of "intensified field work." Eastman Kodak contributed a marching Choral Society and two elaborate floats to Rochester's "War Week Parade" in June 1942. A year later, upon receiving an army and navy "E" award for excellence in production, it staged a performance that attracted a record crowd of employees and Rochester residents to Red Wing stadium.[8] A significant transformation marked the momentary revival of local pageantry and mass-participation community rituals during World War II: these "community" events were now almost entirely organized by "outside" corporations.

The corporation increasingly presented itself as the community in several other ways during the war. Companies promoted the sale of war bonds, facilitating their purchase through payroll deductions and encouraging employees to take pride in surpassing figures that they had defined as company goals. They expanded their company recreational programs substantially, a move that, as Elizabeth Fones-Wolf points out, "helped restore legitimacy to management's involvement in their employees' leisure-time activities." As a patriotic service and employee welfare initiative, Westinghouse transformed its Home Economics Institute into a participatory, rally-inspiring "Health for Victory Club." Far more than in World War I (partly because of the duration of this war and its level of casualties), corporations actively identified themselves with their "boys overseas," publicizing the war service of their workers and fostering familial support for them among current employees. Company magazines carried regular features on "our boys" in the service, displaying their names and photographs and encouraging employees to write to these members of the company's family. Some corporations sent their own letters or even batches of cookies to servicemen. Memorials to those employees who had made the final sacrifice and pledges of continued employment for veterans defined the company to its workers as perhaps their most significant community.[9]

Such affirmations of responsibility betokened a large role for major corporations in both national and local morale. If it was "showmanship" that kept the workers happy, as *Life* reported, then impresarios the corporations would be. The corporate effort expended on staging the various pageants, revues, and more prototypical E-award ceremonies found ample justification not only in a sense of patriotic service but also in labor relations. The old lament about lost personal relationships could be viewed as particularly appropriate to the conditions of World War II, with the dramatic increase in the size of plant workforces, extensive geographical mobility of workers, enormous employee turnover, round-the-clock shifts, frozen wages, and larger contingents of women workers (whom many employers considered temporary). But the vision of a necessary, joint effort for a higher purpose enticed employers to meld loyalty to the corporation with war patriotism. Particularly during a war in which large companies played so vital a role, it became harder for corporate executives to recognize any difference, as Alfred Sloan had already remarked in 1939, between the interests of the corporation and the interest of the people and the nation.[10]

War as Doom; War as Deliverance

By the end of 1942 hundreds of corporation-sponsored community events, like *Plowshares* in Dayton, had exemplified the wartime serviceability of the new public relations emphasis on plant cities. On the national level as well, through vastly expanded forms of institutional advertising, one large corporation after another had seized the opportunity to fuse its own image with that of a virtuous people engaged in a hallowed common cause. Following nearly a decade of confinement in "the dog house of public opinion" during the 1930s, and after an interlude as public "whipping boy" while early war production fell short of the sudden demands for quick mobilization in a two-front war, the managers of American industry now regained public favor. Recollections such as one reprinted in *GM Folks* captured their exhilarating sense of vindication. "For too long," the author recalled, it had been "fashionable, among the malicious and ignorant," to attack big business and the free enterprise system. But the war had "forced the demagogues to shut their mealy mouths," as big business had been "called out of the doghouse to save the life of the nation—even the lives of the demagogues themselves." Paul Garrett, vice president of public relations at General Motors, more temperately characterized the moment as an "auspicious time" for big business when the National Association of Public Relations Counsel met in September 1944. As a result of its achievements in war production, through "sheer hard work and ingenuity," Garrett asserted, the management of private industry had won a place on "the pedestal of public approval."[11]

World War II, thanks not only to the extensive exertions of major corporations but also to the promotional activities of the military forces, was to acquire the character of a public relations war.[12] But the approach of war during the years between 1939 and 1941 had not seemed so favorable an omen in the eyes of most corporate executives. In fact many had feared the worst as war threatened to envelop the United States. Businessmen found themselves torn between pressures to convert rapidly to all-out defense production and their eagerness to exploit improving markets for domestic goods. They suspected that unless the nation was actually called upon to defend itself, they might not receive appropriate credit for their contributions to preparedness. Moreover, if war should not come or should it be very brief, those companies that best maintained their domestic production, and the attendant sales, service, and dealer networks, would enjoy an immediate advantage in the ensuing peacetime economy.[13]

Two specters haunted business leaders during the year before the bombing of Pearl Harbor. One was the fear that a vast expansion of the nation's industrial plant might saddle companies with a dangerous capacity for the overproduction that many associated with the recent depression. The other apprehension, in the wake of FDR's 1940 election victory, was that centralized planning, a proclivity for trust-busting, and the regulatory "regimentation" that characterized the New Deal in the eyes of many corporate leaders would accelerate under war conditions. War would certainly bring the additional economic controls of a "war socialism," which might then prove permanent. These tendencies, President Charles E. Wilson of the General Electric Company observed in November 1941, meant that in the immediate aftermath of war the free enterprise system would "face the greatest challenge in its history." [14]

For these reasons many corporations preferred to bet on peace. Du Pont's chief economist, in a confidential five-year forecast in early 1940, proposed that the company assume "that the U.S. will not become involved in any serious war during the next five years." [15] Such forecasts made conversion to war production, although politically correct, seem perilous economically. "Corporation prestige and proper public relations," GM president Charles E. Wilson remarked to the board chairman Alfred P. Sloan in September 1940, required that the company live up to public expectations that it "cooperate actively with the Government and make a good showing in the manufacture of needed defense materials." Thus, GM should obtain some defense business for each of its plant cities. But it should allot such work to plants where war supplies "can be produced with the greatest efficiency and least disturbance to our normal business." Making wise decisions during this interlude of competing pressures would most likely involve weighing each problem from three standpoints, according to Walter Carpenter Jr., the president of Du Pont and chair of the Finance Committee of General Motors: "first, from the commercial, second, the patriotic standpoint and, third, the public relations standpoint." [16]

An internal document, circulated in May 1941 at General Motors, reflected some predictable resentments against the interference with good business decision making that the war crisis was engendering. The report called for "balanced judgment" amid the current pressures, while acknowledging that auto production might have to be cut back as "a sop to public 'morale'" and that "a deliberate course of appeasement" to labor demands might have to be taken to avoid alienating government agencies that called for all-out defense production. Despite these painful accommodations to the needs of public relations, General Motors relinquished domestic production only with great apprehension. Not until January 1942 did it remove the new car models from the showroom windows of its Detroit headquarters and replace them with defense products. [17]

This wary, measured response to pressures for all-out defense mobilization would soon exacerbate the public relations problems of the automobile and other industries. "Not in recent memory," Paul Garrett of GM reported in the fall of 1942, "has this industry been so criticized as [it was in early 1942] for its alleged slow rate of conversion to war." The company's sensitivity to this blot on its image would be revealed in the spirited defense of its mobilization record in the barbershop scene in *Plowshares*. [18] Standard Oil of New Jersey, under fire from Harry Truman and his Senate committee investigating the defense program for its agreements with Germany's I. G. Farbenindustrie, suffered what the historians Bennett Wall and George Gibb have called "a siege of adverse publicity so great in volume and so abusive in character, it far overshadowed all previous attacks." In 1941 Standard backed away from contesting a major government suit because of the "hostile climate toward big business" and immediately hired a professional public relations consultant. When the Aluminum Company of America failed in 1941 to live up to its war production promises, thus seeming to confirm the dangers of national reliance on a monopoly, it felt the lash of public censure almost as intensely.[19]

Advertising agencies and trade journals, fearing a sharp decline in their own business as major corporations withdrew from domestic production and thus had little to sell to the public, further stimulated corporate anxieties. A prominent advertising journalist warned companies as early as October 1939 not to contribute to a war psychology. "If we permit our country to be drawn into another world war," he predicted, "we can be certain that private enterprise will all but vanish. It will become public business, completely regimented and regulated by government and finished off by ruinous taxation."[20] In an editorial entitled "Keep Out of War-Time Dog House," *Advertising and Selling* encouraged major corporations to cultivate goodwill by explaining, through institutional advertising, why they stood to gain far more from peace than from war. The journal's implied objective was to help companies avoid a postwar stigma, suffered by some of them during the 1930s for having led the nation into World War I.[21]

In 1941 big business perceived the specter of further regimentation by the government at every turn. Many corporate executives, deeply offended by the withdrawal of public esteem during the 1930s, were still licking their wounds. The successes of organized labor in the late 1930s, as Howell Harris observes, had not only affected businessmen's economic interests. They had also struck a devastating blow to business leaders' sense of their legitimate authority and had challenged their vision of the economic system.[22]

A mood approaching self-pity emerged in such public commentaries as that of Charles Wilson of General Electric in "Can We Save Free Enterprise?"[23] Bruce Barton, now an ad agency "elder" as well as a former congressman, shared his own gloomy predictions with his agency's client, the Du Pont Company. At a private "advertising clinic" in mid-1941, the agency executives passed along Barton's observation that "any American company" had to be viewed as a citizen beleaguered once again, who would "do well to come out of this present mess with both his shirt and his reputation." Later in 1941, drawing on his instinct for the commonplace touch, Barton described "all of American industry" as sharing "a mental state like anticipating a trip to the dentist." Even after the United States had entered the war, the trade journal *Advertising and Selling* still talked about the impending "doom of capitalism." Citing a recent survey by the Psychological Corporation, the journal reported that "a large majority of business men" believe that "the jig is up . . . that free enterprise is doomed."[24]

Those already troubled by such fears could hardly find reassurance in the details of the Psychological Corporation's survey. Entitled "The Perils of Peace," this confidential report on a study carried out for the General Electric Company (and eventually circulated to several of the largest American corporations) noted that the American public was dangerously undismayed by trends toward a socialist state. Moreover, efforts to alert them to this grave danger and to argue for the merits of free enterprise seemed to "leave the people cold." Unless big business could finally devise the "new vocabulary" it had been seeking since the mid-1930s— one that would enable it to reach the common people through the mass media— it faced a much greater peril than war in the years just ahead, the Psychological Corporation warned.[25]

Once the United States entered the war, however, corporate public relations executives and advertising agents quickly discerned and exploited the positive opportunities of the new situation. Those corporations now fully engaged in war production incessantly proclaimed their patriotism and the indispensability of their huge productive capacities. Others, even if they still produced consumer goods, found ways of touting their own sacrifices as they preached wartime sacrifice to the public. If the war could be seen as a perilous threat to big business, it could also be interpreted as an energizing challenge. After so wrenching a period of public disfavor, corporations were easily attracted to the idea of advancing their moral legitimacy through identification with the nation's war effort. In a 1942 pamphlet George Romney of the Automotive Council for War seemed actually to quote with relish the lamentations of a fellow business spokesman who recalled how thoroughly American industry had been "maligned, mauled, mishandled and mayhemmed by politicians, reformers, labor leaders, left-wingers and mud slingers until the average manufacturer felt like an outcast of society."[26] Their deeply felt need for vindication led corporate leaders zealously to seize wartime opportunities for "service."

Fortuitously, but only after agonizing delay, federal officials divulged a wartime tax policy that made publicizing the corporations' war service economically attractive as well. In May 1942, Secretary of the Treasury Henry Morgenthau announced that the federal government would consider "ordinary and necessary" advertising costs—those that bore "a reasonable relation to the business activities in which the enterprise is engaged"—as deductible for corporations before calculating their profits.[27] This deduction was of great importance, since an excess profits tax of 90 percent was in effect. Rather than allow money to be siphoned off into the federal treasury at that rate, companies could spend these funds on advertising at minimal cost. In effect, the government was heavily subsidizing forms of advertising that were "essential" only in that they kept established corporate brands and images before the public and secured whatever contributions these corporate messages might make to wartime morale. Institutional or public relations advertising rapidly escalated from only $1 million in 1939 to $17 million by 1943.[28]

Another boost to the prospects for favorable corporate public relations in wartime came in the form of the War Advertising Council—a voluntary organization, staffed largely by agency executives, that sought to recruit advertisers to image-enhancing war service. The War Advertising Council arose from a November 1941 meeting of seven hundred corporate executives sponsored by the Association of National Advertisers and the American Association of Advertising Agencies. Convened, as Robert Griffith has related, to "consider the dangers posed by 'those who would do away with the American system of free enterprise' or 'modify the economic system of which advertising is an integral part,'" the group endorsed a major campaign to publicize the benefits of advertising and heighten its prestige by promoting its use "in the public interest." Less than a month later, with the American entrance into the war, an uncontested public interest was suddenly established.[29]

Formally organized early in 1942, the War Advertising Council strove initially to coordinate the diffuse and often misdirected early efforts by advertisers to prove their patriotism through war service. It organized campaigns for manpower recruitment, the salvage of fats, and the purchase of war bonds. By 1943 the Council had adopted the slogan "A War Message in Every Ad." It set about persuading unconverted advertisers that they could do good business for themselves, and strike a blow for the prestige of business and advertising, by incorporating "a vital government message" into each of their ads. One method was the "double-barrelled" ad, with "one barrel for the war theme, one barrel for the product." Companies not amenable to that approach had other options: "You can sell your head off and still include a plug for a war theme," the Council promised, through tactics that it labeled "the sneak punch" and the "plug with a slug."[30] By 1946 the Council was receiving accolades within the advertising profession for having accomplished its mission of public service and ideological guidance so well that "neither any private group nor Government itself can charge that advertising lacks a sense of social responsibility." At the end of the war the Council also boasted of its role in the extensive networking of business and advertising executives with government officials. It continued its work into the postwar decades under the abridged title of the Advertising Council. Throughout its career the Council took the high road, aiming for an image of helpfulness on noncontroversial causes.[31]

Beyond expanding their institutional advertising and reinforcing the morale-building aspects of their plant city activities, many major companies pursued other wartime avenues for the long-range molding of their corporate image. Before the first year of American participation in the war had passed, most top executives had assigned staff to compile a full record of the company's wartime activities. Liberal allowances for publicity in war contracts made possible lavish publications, flattering to employees and useful in promoting noncommercial images of the corporations. By 1943 AT&T had a full-time information manager and former journalist on the road gathering material for such a war history and Standard Oil of New Jersey had commissioned leading artists and photographers to develop a visual record of that company's wartime service.[32] General Motors, seeking "more fully [to] capitaliz[e] the war history data," decided to document, in separate albums, the contributions of each division of the corporation. This effort resulted in more than thirty handsome, self-congratulatory tomes, each issued in thousands of copies for distribution to division employees, within this one corporation alone. Many of these war albums appeared in glossy pictorial editions.[33] Apart from architectural expressions, and a smattering of company-financed histories over the previous decade, these war albums constituted the most elaborate visual testimonies that corporations had yet dedicated to their sense of their own significance in the nation's history and their status as major national institutions.

Fighting for the "Fifth Freedom"

Even as they publicized their impressive contributions to the war effort, corporate leaders kept a vigilant eye on just what they were fighting for. When the "Four Freedoms," as set forward by Roosevelt in his 1941 annual message to Congress, gained immense national exposure and popularity through Norman Rockwell's sentimental illustrations in the *Saturday Evening Post* (and later, on war bond posters), corporate PR officials promptly joined in promoting these shared notions of war goals. Not only did Rockwell's use of warm, small-town and family imagery correspond with the "jes' folks" ambience that corporate publicity had desperately sought in the late 1930s, but certain specific messages of the "Four Freedoms" lent themselves well to corporate purposes. The ideal of Freedom of Speech could be harnessed to the argument for continued advertising as an indispensable financial prop for a press independent of government control or subsidy. Freedom from Want could be expansively translated into the particular capacity of big business, under free enterprise, to produce more and better things for all citizens.[34]

But a number of business leaders, judging Roosevelt's list of essential freedoms inadequate, preferred to champion a "fifth freedom"—the freedom of enterprise. Here what Frank Fox has called "Madison Avenue's private war"—or the war within the war—became explicit in conversations among business leaders, as they identified the New Deal and its potential legacies as an enemy at least equal to the Axis powers. Although he did not use the phrase "freedom of enterprise," Alfred Sloan of General Motors had outlined this interpretation of war purposes several months before Roosevelt's "Four Freedoms" address. To "defend the American way of living," he had urged late in 1940, meant to defend "against aggression from within as well as from without." The greatest of the dangers and the most difficult to counter, he asserted, were the "attacks from within."[35]

Various business leaders applied slightly different labels to the fifth freedom (Fig. 8.4). While most favored "freedom of enterprise," others opted for "freedom of choice" or "freedom of individual enterprise." The shipbuilder Henry Kaiser, seeking a stance more cognizant of the need for "social justice" and less critical of the New Deal, used the term "freedom to produce." James Webb Young, in a November 1941 speech that sparked the creation of the War Advertising Council, warned ad agents to make sure they would not wake up after the war "and find that we have lost the freedoms we thought we were fighting for—not only the four freedoms of our President, but the fifth freedom of a dynamic economy."[36]

Other business leaders easily drifted from the notion of a fifth freedom to the perception that, as the chairman of the board of directors of Monsanto Chemical Company put it, the nation was "engaged in two wars." Beyond the military war against the Axis powers, another war required ideological mobilization against those who proposed "salvation . . . in exalting the state and having it plan our lives and our economy." In early 1945, although buoyed by the enhanced wartime stature of business, Paul West, the president of the Association of National Advertisers, still identified the "greatest challenge—and opportunity—ever to confront us" not as that of gaining victory abroad but of winning the "war of ideologies" at home.[37]

While most corporations gave first priority in their wartime advertising to the narrow enhancement of their own corporate images, many found ways to unite this objective with self-sacrificing deeds in defense of the fifth freedom. Some, having described their own prodigious efforts and achievements in war production, simply inserted a line about the indispensability of "America's system of free enterprise" to this accomplishment.[38] Others stated the case more directly. The editor of the trade journal of wholesale grocers called upon his readers to recognize that "the preservation of Free Enterprise is as much a food distributor's business as selling canned peas." For several months in 1944 Armour and Company conspicuously split its advertising pages into two parts, devoting the larger, heavily illustrated segment to the promotion of products while regularly allocating a full adjacent column to a free enterprise editorial. Under such headlines as "Modern Business as a National Resource" and "Spiritual Dividends," Armour explained that the "mod-

FIGURE 8.4
In this cartoon, available free to
businesses in poster form, the "fifth
freedom" stood simply for the
beneficence of free enterprise.

ern corporation works for the nation as a whole—not merely for its own stockholders" and asserted that free enterprise epitomized the freedom of choice that
"exalts the individual, recognizes that he is created in the image of God, and gives
spiritual tone to the American system." In the course of these moral lessons Armour and Company merged imperceptibly with "the individual citizen, no matter how humble," who was fighting to uphold the "American way" and reject any
"pushing around" or "regimentation."[39]

As the nation's wartime attention focused on the evils of the political systems of
the enemy nations, corporate executives found it increasingly plausible to frame
their defense of the fifth freedom as a fight against "regimentation." That term
came to serve as a code word for the New Deal, signaling the dangers of the federal government's programs to individual freedoms while suggesting their similarity to the policies of dictatorial regimes. Forced to acknowledge the temporary need
for extensive government controls, corporate executives were anxious to "make
sure that the restrictions and regulation that are now necessary to win the war shall
not be permanently imposed upon us."[40] Alfred Sloan expressed the hope that

Americans would learn from experiences with "a regimented economy" during the war to adopt a "changed attitude" in the postwar years and work to "deflate" the bloated federal bureaucracy. Other rhetorical ploys attacked the New Deal's affinity for planning by identifying Adolf Hitler as the greatest of all government "planners." The GI protagonist of a Republic Steel ad, writing home to his father from overseas, attributed the "mess" in Europe to three things: dictatorship, regimentation, and bureaucrats. He recounted how his wartime service had alerted him to the chilling similarities between New Deal policies and "Axis tyrannies."[41]

The theme of encroaching regimentation also neatly linked the fifth freedom with the other of FDR's freedoms most celebrated by corporate leaders—the Freedom from Want. Those same elements of the free enterprise system that had afforded Americans the steadily advancing standard of living synonymous with the American way had also, the Chrysler Corporation averred, given Americans "the will and heart to grow big, strong . . . until we were ready to out-produce the regimented Axis nations at their own game of war." Thus, the enemy's way of life stood in stark contrast to the American way in two inseparable respects: material impoverishment and a lack of freedom. Regimentation had deprived their people of opportunity and of the good life by forcing their submission to "slave wages." By contrast, through the inevitable postwar "rebirth of free enterprise," Americans could look forward to "the more abundant life to come." Drawing on this connection between political rights and the standard of living, many companies found it tactically astute to infuse a free enterprise message into their ads by conflating familiar products with the everyday "simple things" for which, in their precept, Americans were fighting.[42]

The Wartime Corporation as Common Man

A focus on simple things, in turn, afforded advertisers the opportunity to feature common folks as protagonists in their institutional ads. And obviously, the most felicitous figure to recruit as a corporate persona during wartime was the soldier. In fact, the military uniform defined and homogenized a whole contingent of supremely meritorious common men—the enlisted men, or GI Joes—of all the services. Paul Fussell has astutely observed that the majority of military men depicted in wartime advertisements were officers.[43] That was certainly true of the product ads, especially those that promised women a good "catch" for a husband if they used the right brand. In institutional advertisements, however, corporations almost never identified themselves with military officers. Rather, they preferred the "average" GI—"Private Bill Jones" or "Leatherneck Joe," the marine (Fig. 8.5).[44]

The Nash-Kelvinator Company, in an extended series of ads in popular magazines, entrusted its free enterprise messages to heroic but homesick airmen and infantrymen. These guys just wanted to get back to their hometowns, where they wanted "*everything* just the way I left it." In their yearning for the simple things, they recognized in the small local shop or business a model for their relationship to the values embedded in free enterprise. Nash-Kelvinator's individualistic servicemen fought to return to those small-town opportunities to get ahead (to go back to "that old roll-top desk of mine at the electric company" or to reopen "my little garage"); they also yearned to recapture the pristine innocence and auton-

"LEATHERNECK" JOE ...MECHANIC

Sure I'm a Marine—and proud of it.

But someday, we'll finish this fight over here—and I'll be coming home. I can hardly wait to step back into my overalls and my job at the shop—working for old Bill.

He's really gone places—Bill, I mean—starting from scratch with nothing but his two hands and a mind of his own. It took a lot of work—but his shop is something to be mighty proud of—why, all the cars and trucks in town used to show up there for repairs.

No bureaucrat told Bill what to do or how to do it. He just went ahead on his own—and got results.

I figure that we're fighting to hang onto just that sort of OPPORTUNITY—the right to work out our own futures, in our own way, without a lot of unnecessary interference and regulation.

I can't understand the folks who feel that if the government took over everybody and everything, all our problems would be solved.

That's sniping at the very things that make our country great. That's playing right into the hands of the gents who say the American way of life is out of date and doesn't work.

Sure, there is always room for improvement, but I can't swallow that radical stuff. It always hits us little guys the hardest.

Back home the summer's just starting. The folks around the old shop are pitching in just as they've always done. There's a shortage of materials, probably—and machinery —and not enough help. But I'll bet they're keeping a lot of vital cars and trucks on the road these days.

Nobody could *make* them work like that. They do it because they're free Americans. And they value that freedom.

Someday I aim to have my own shop. And I want to run it my own way. I don't want to be coddled—and I don't want *anything* I'm not entitled to.

I want a fair price for the jobs I do. I want good tools and machinery to make my work faster, better and easier. I want a comfortable home for my family. I want to go to the church I choose. I want to live as a free American.

Meanwhile, I've got fighting to do. And believe me I'm going to do my best to make a good job of it. But I can't help worrying about those who are trying to regiment America while I'm away.

The folks at home must stop 'em—by never forgetting for a second, the wonderful freedoms and opportunities that have made our country what it is.

They must keep America American. *I pray to God they will.*

REPUBLIC STEEL

BUY WAR BONDS AND STAMPS —AND KEEP THEM!

The Army-Navy E Flag waves over seven Republic plants and the Maritime M floats over the Cleveland District plant.

GENERAL OFFICES: REPUBLIC BUILDING, CLEVELAND 1, OHIO
Export Department: Chrysler Building, New York 17, New York

ALLOY, CARBON, STAINLESS STEELS · COLD FINISHED STEELS · PLATES · BARS · SHAPES · STRIP · SHEETS · PIPE · TUBING
TIN PLATE · NUTS · BOLTS · RIVETS · NAILS · PIG IRON · FARM FENCE · WIRE · FABRICATED STEEL PRODUCTS

FIGURE 8.5

Republic Steel spoke through the voice of an enlisted man who realized that "radical stuff . . . always hits us little guys the hardest." Joe looked forward to returning to work for "old Bill"—the local repairman whose business flourished without help or interference from any "bureaucrat."

omy of small-town life, now threatened by the bureaucratic inroads of the New Deal. In several cases Nash-Kelvinator ads assigned servicemen's dutiful wives the task of assuring their men that "when you come back to me, you will find nothing changed." As one Nash-Kelvinator airplane gunner reflected, "There's only one decent way to live in this world—the way my folks lived." Without specifically identifying New Dealers as dangerous tinkerers with the system, he warned the home folks, "When you find a thing that works . . . be careful with that monkey-wrench."[45]

Republic Steel found a way to link the mature wisdom of a common man of the older generation with the moral authority of his soldier son. In "Old Joe said to Young Joe," a parental graduate from the school of hard knocks urged his son to be vigilant that "nothing stops . . . progress—neither enemies from the outside, nor from the inside." When Young Joe got out there in the thick of the action, Old Joe explained to him, he would be fighting "to protect the opportunity that all Americans have of starting at the bottom and getting to the top" and defending "your right to live your own life in your own way without being pushed around by some bright young bureaucrat who wants to do all your planning for you."[46]

At home, corporate imagery favored "John Smith, Family Man," a figure redolent of Norman Rockwell's "Freedom of Speech" illustration. It was this ordinary citizen, United States Steel averred, "whose labor and living have established what we know as 'The American Way.'" At General Motors the PR director Paul Garrett dubbed this archetypal figure "John Peters," assigned him a wife and two children, and situated him as a mechanic in Muncie, Indiana—the site both of the Lynds' famous sociological studies of "Middletown" and of a major GM plant. This all-American, common-man figure, in Garrett's typification and in General Motors' publicity, was buying a home, had faith that the United States was "a pretty good country," and liked "to think for himself." General Electric's model workers in its York, Pennsylvania, plant were "neighborly folk"—"home-loving, hard-working." Like the typical Americans that U.S. Rubber honored in an October 1942 ad entitled "What Are We Fighting For?" they were best characterized through the "homely fragments of their daily life." Such down-to-earth Americans deserved reassurances, Garrett urged, from "those who know the simple economics of our American way of life." Big business could best convey its spirit of service to them, a BBDO agency man noted, through the earthy and the humble, the "intimate and personal."[47]

In this vein, and with the addition of nostalgia as a powerful component, General Motors characterized its wartime production program as the efforts of "blacksmiths by the millions." Designed to showcase the technology of "shot-blasting," the GM ad by this title observed that such "highly developed techniques" were possible because "in our land, men receive just rewards for their enterprise." In a film dramatizing its war production program, U.S. Steel presented itself to the public in the persona of a veteran steelworker, played in a folksy, salt-of-the-earth manner by the actor Walter Brennan. Alcoa capitalized on the frequent wartime portrayals of Uncle Sam in overalls to convey an image of company executives and assembly workers united in common labor. Overalls "never have gone out of fashion in the Alcoa family," it proclaimed.[48]

The peculiar exigencies and opportunities of wartime advertising led several large corporations to address different messages to different segments of the population, a strategy that often reinforced a folksy, rural-oriented, common-man imagery. The Kraft Company entrusted its National Dairy Products advertising with the task of "strengthening farmer morale" by telling "the story of farmers' efforts and sacrifices to the American people." These ads appeared not only in prestigious national magazines but also in country newspapers in Kraft production areas, so that farmers could see Kraft's testimonies to their heroic service. With tax provisions making a normal amount of advertising almost costless, major corporations

FIGURE 8.6
Every American farmer ran a business, General Motors claimed, pretty much the same way that corporations did. Both succeeded within a system that let them apply their own "management know-how."

that had few consumer products to sell also cultivated the long-range goodwill of rural folk. Some companies gave special attention to small entrepreneurs in the rural sector, a group that had been relatively neglected in consumer advertising yet might be enlisted as a sympathetic political constituency for the future. General Electric undertook a campaign to persuade them that GE's interests and problems were very similar to their own. As "the real backbone of the nation," General Electric pointed out to farmers, ranchers, miners, and lumbermen, they had much in common with "a great corporation such as GE." In a sense they were all common men, all engaged in the common enterprise of management. On that basis farmers and other rural businessmen might empathize with the problems involved in managing factories.[49]

General Motors made almost a fivefold increase—from $69,700 to $320,900—in its advertising appropriation for farm publications in 1944, devoting 12 percent of its expanded budget for institutional advertising to that area. In these publications GM observed that "the American farmer's job is a good deal like a manufacturer's. His farm is his factory." If farmers had once been among the greatest adversaries of business bigness, perhaps they could now be encouraged to recognize how closely the elements of autonomy and "management know-how" linked their enterprises with those of companies like General Motors (Fig. 8.6). The "partnership" between farming and manufacturing, GM avowed, "goes as deep as freedom—that old-time American freedom to tackle your job your way—To give it all you've got—and to get the reward you earn."[50]

In an approach less slanted toward the cultivation of immediate political and economic sympathies, Du Pont reached out through the most stirring of modern media to link itself emotionally with the farming community. No one, a Du Pont advertising executive pointed out, was "giving the farmer Army-Navy 'E's' for efficiency in production. Nobody was making speeches about what a great guy he was and what a good job he was doing." Du Pont sought to do just that through a forty-minute movie, produced "by a Hollywood cast under a Hollywood director." Entitled *Soldiers of the Soil,* the melodramatic story focused on the anxieties of the hero, John Landis, one of three adult sons of an established farm family. As the film opened, one of John's brothers returned blinded from war service with the marines while the other brother enlisted. Remaining at home to run the farm, John asked—in an agony of guilt over his brothers' sacrifices—"Is the job I'm doing the biggest I can do?"[51]

John's brother David, the blind veteran, carried Du Pont's message of reassurance to American farmers. In a fervent address to the local church congregation, during which he recalled his family's history on the farm in a narration "laced with poignant flashback photography," David convinced John and the other farmers that their work as "soldiers of the soil" was, in fact, the greatest contribution they could make to victory. Through a film "free from commercialism," one that recounted a farm family's "sorrows and joys . . . tears and laughter," Du Pont looked to gain stature in farm communities. With this "tribute to farmers" it aimed to "sell the farmer on himself" while letting him know that he "was not alone in this fight for more food" (Fig. 8.7).[52]

In depicting farm families in such films, companies like Du Pont, General Electric, and General Motors found it only natural to recapitulate the simple, wholesome images of the regionalist painters. Perhaps still influenced by their earlier perceptions of a populist countryside as politically antagonistic to the legitimacy of mammoth corporations, these wartime advertisers did not hesitate to employ virtual clones of Norman Rockwell figures as a way of associating themselves with "the American scene." Whether through explicit mention of the role of their products and services in ameliorating both the work and the leisure of farm families or simply through their highly visible sponsorship of an ingratiatingly noble image of the farmer, they sought to further legitimize their massive power by linking it with the nation's traditional common man.[53]

Even the War Advertising Council, with its ambition to restore lost prestige to advertising, assumed a down-to-earth tone of voice to reinforce its claims to civic service. In "We're Just Little People" it called for civilians to help prevent inflation by not seeking higher wages. The protagonists of the ad, a Rockwellesque "plain folks" couple, the husband with his pipe and newspaper and the wife in her apron, observed colloquially that the sacrifices they were making amounted to no more than "chicken feed compared to the ones our sons are making." In "Let Freedom Ring," an all-purpose inspirational ad, the Council chose a one-room country schoolhouse scene that fused Rockwellesque figures with the style of Paul Sample or Grant Wood.[54]

FIGURE 8.7

In *Soldiers of the Soil,* Du Pont let farmers know that it empathized with those who made great sacrifices for the war without public recognition and heroic stature. This was no mere industrial film; it was a "Hollywood" production.

Even more than in the late 1930s, everyday folks—enlisted men, folksy storekeepers and country doctors, salt-of-the-earth grandparents, and assembly-line employees (including both women and distinct ethnic representatives)—had gained a central role in corporate imagery. Furthermore, corporate publicists did not hesitate to cast such characters simultaneously as the voice of the people and the voice of the corporation. The advertising manager for Hart, Schaffner & Marx noted that military induction centers were a good place for advertisers to "meet Joe America" and learn to use his language. General Electric, speaking through the persona of a puzzled housewife whose husband had just shipped out for overseas service, talked about the postwar possibilities for "ordinary people like us." Standard Oil confidently spoke for "Private Bill Jones, and the Rest of Us," while Republic Steel had its soldier spokesman converse on behalf of "[us] ordinary folks at home."[55]

Good Taste and Ethnic Inclusiveness

On 8 December 1941 the *Telephone Hour* claimed the status of "the first major program on the air after the beginning of hostilities . . . specifically designed to meet the public's need for patriotic inspiration at such a time." AT&T's advertising agency, N. W. Ayer & Son, took great pride in its preparedness, having helped AT&T enhance its image at this crucial moment through a message that had been carefully thought out and preapproved for use when the occasion demanded. Ayer congratulated itself on the tact and tone of the program as well as on its own foresight:

> The *Telephone Hour* moved with dignity toward its purpose, omitting nothing that would add to the client's stature in the mind of an excited people, and including nothing that might be taken as a mawkish perversion of the patriotic theme. Criticisms have been numerous to the effect that other programs which had not been prepared for the change, or which were put together on the spur of the moment, either overflowed with patriotic emotion, neglected to mention the war at all, or confused patriotism with advertising in such a way that it offended rather than inspired.[56]

That final allusion to the issue of good taste in patriotic advertising reflected the anxious concerns that continued to beset PR and advertising professionals even as big business seized on its wartime opportunities and expanded its institutional advertising. It was far from certain, even a year or more into the war, that corporate America would find the right voice, one that would enable it to take maximum advantage of its wartime opportunity to regain its status and fuse its image with the central aspirations of the public.

In fact, some companies made significant missteps. In their eagerness to display their patriotism, they romanticized the war in their institutional advertising; in their product advertising they claimed credit for contributions to victory that minor products or those only tenuously connected with war operations had supposedly made. But several influences brought greater restraint, especially among the largest corporations. Letters from servicemen and surveys of combat veterans revealed a deep resentment of ads that exploited the suffering of soldiers or that made winning the war seem easy. Servicemen were also contemptuous of ads that glorified "a particular piece of equipment out of all proportion to its part in the war effort."[57]

When Raymond Rubicam, president of the Young & Rubicam advertising agency, wrote to former agency men who were serving in the military, he garnered many biting critiques of war advertising. Among the varied responses the most common were complaints of "phoniness" and "sloppy, second-rate sentimentalizing." One navy officer quoted a sample of typical "emotional copy" and then interjected, "Excuse me while I vomit." A navy lieutenant observed that servicemen did not welcome "being told that someone's microphone or roller bearing is winning the war."[58] Anticipating a backlash against self-glorifying corporate war ads, some top executives expressed revulsion at the idea of "boasting" about "these great deeds of us who are fighting the war so gallantly on the home front."[59]

To many business and advertising leaders, including the heads of the War Advertising Council, the likely boomerang effects of ads that offended servicemen and invited public incredulity stood in the way of their cultivating long-term corporate advantages through responsible wartime advertising. Provided with an opportunity to shut up those critics and "crackpots" who had mounted a decade-long smoldering, erosive campaign against the alleged "abuses of advertising," these leaders warned that the whole enterprise of advertising was now "on trial." The war crisis had given it an ultimate chance "to redeem itself." But the clock already stood at "two minutes to twelve." This opportunity "must never be lost," added the agency executive Walter Weir, if the advertising industry was to rise to the necessary stature to perform its most crucial function, the safeguarding of free enterprise in the postwar world.[60]

For most major corporations, as Ayer's self-congratulatory observations about the *Telephone Hour* suggested, the central concerns were to find just the right tone for wartime public relations and to reach a suitably broad audience. After nearly a decade of trying to master a vernacular in which to address ordinary folks, corporate publicists welcomed the war-bred impression of a more unified nation, one in which even those previously considered most disparate in class position and economic literacy might be reached through the same vocabulary and stirred by the same imagery that mainstream Americans responded to. Although corporate image advertising still sought to speak in the vernacular, it no longer reflected quite the same compulsion to "go slumming" in search of some proletarian dialect. Instead, corporations now ventured to find the right tone and offer the right representations to encompass the uncommon as well as the common man.

For instance, in a war that they sometimes characterized as "a little man's war" or a "people's war," corporate publicists broadened the Rockwellesque image of the ordinary citizen through ethnic diversity. By early 1942 General Motors was praising the wartime commitment to freedom of "Patasky, Koehler, Olsen, McKay, Steining, Spicuzza, Wojciechowski, Finklebaum, Lopez, O'Brien, Cartier, Van Duesen and plain Sam Jones—Americans all."[61] When the *Ford Times* wanted to celebrate the family cooperation that had gone into its employees' victory gardens, it selected for attention the Pliska family, of which nine members worked for Ford. Studebaker, in its continuing focus on second-generation employees, featured the Lukavich and Kowalski families.[62] In 1943 Kodak's employee magazine carried a "This Is America" series, with sympathetic profiles of a different immigrant group each issue. In this respect the corporation was endorsing an ideology of cultural pluralism that the federal government promoted to encourage all citizens to identify with the nation's war efforts. The increasing prominence of first- and second-generation immigrants in the successful union drives of the mid and late 1930s had already inspired some corporate leaders to provide ethnic workers with a fuller image of themselves within the corporate family. Now, anxious to display their responsibility and leadership as partners to the "little man" in winning this war, they were inclined to respond to any clear signals about how to establish their affinities with workers, whatever their ethnic origins (Fig. 8.8). Thus, the ethnic diversity that was deliberately incorporated into wartime movies also won recognition in corporate publications and news releases.[63]

When the Marines got Lukavich they took a good man

But his team-mate father still builds
Cyclone engines at Studebaker

TWENTY-ONE years ago last January, a mechanic named Paul Lukavich signed his first pay voucher as a Studebaker employee. His son Steve, now in the Marine was th——'ubby ba'

Studebaker craftsmanship endure. The huge quantities of Wright Cyclone engines that Studebaker builds for the Boeing Flying Fortress—the tens of thousands of —debaker mili———' in the

FIGURE 8.8
The acceptance — even the embrace — of newer immigrant groups as full-fledged Americans, capable of serving as prototypes of the common man, gained headline status in this worker-recognition ad by Studebaker.

High Culture and Corporate Legitimacy

In a quite different assertion of social and cultural leadership, a number of corporations reached out to establish more visible links with high culture or, at least, with high-middlebrow culture. Although they did so partly out of the confidence in the institutional stature that their war service provided them, they also often hedged their bets by attempting to make their sponsorship compatible with a populist orientation. Some even went so far as to argue that their sponsorship of art or classical music might rescue high art from elite bondage as "something precious and reserved for the few." NBC's blue network hailed Texaco's sponsorship of the Metropolitan Opera broadcasts, beginning in 1943–44, with the pronouncement: "Once for the privileged Few." Thanks to Texaco, it avowed, "the lustre of the Diamond horseshoe now casts a radiant glow in every home which owns a radio."[64]

Between 1940 and 1945 first AT&T and then General Motors and United States Steel began to sponsor high culture through the nation's most concentrated media, radio. An even broader move toward corporate patronage of the arts can be seen in the changing sponsorship of radio programs designated as "concert music." During the 1939–40 season all but five out of seventeen such programs were provided by the networks as noncommercial "sustaining" programs. But by the 1944–45 season, twenty out of twenty-two such programs could claim major corporations as their commercial sponsors. As a radio critic described the strategy in the early 1930s, the corporation's recognition of quality in one field—the arts—was presumed to remind the public of its excellence in every other respect. Thus, the "inspiring and elevating music of our great masters"—or, by the same token, the display of refined taste in painting and sculpture—would "forcibly bring before the public mind the high standards of service" of the company. General Motors sought just such an association in "bring[ing] together a great orchestra . . . and a great industrial organization." By sponsoring the NBC Symphony Orchestra under Arturo Toscanini, it could "tell the facts of its wartime production" to the public "in accompaniment of this great music."[65] Certainly no charge of crass wartime advertising or the failure to display civic service would be leveled here.

For some corporations, wartime sponsorship of high culture was more defensive and precisely targeted. Standard Oil of New Jersey (SONJ; later EXXON) became the patron of prominent artists and photographers while struggling to overcome a negative image. Widely denounced for impeding the development of synthetic rubber in the United States—out of fealty to patent agreements with I. G. Farbenindustrie, the huge German petrochemical company—Standard squirmed as Senator Harry Truman, then the head of a respected Senate investigating committee, remarked: "I think this approaches treason." With no established public relations department and no trained PR executives, Standard belatedly took to heart the ubiquitous warnings of the trade press and generated a strategy that evolved from defensive damage control to positive image building.[66]

In one sense SONJ looked backward to the proclivity of major corporations before 1930 to seek prestige through association with high culture. But it did so with an eye to the populist language and imagery that corporate public relations had adopted during the late 1930s. And it found a new, more studied justification for targeting an elite audience than had big business leaders of the 1920s. To appeal to a select audience was no mere indulgence; it now reflected a shrewd attention to the findings of pollsters and to new academic theories on the role of persuasion through mass media. An Elmo Roper poll had revealed that a particular segment of American society was "proportionately more critical" of Standard Oil and of its prewar cartel agreements. Roper pointed out that these professional, erudite, discerning citizens, branded by sociological theorists as the "influentials" or "thought leaders" of society, also constituted a sophisticated cultural elite, one apt to pay attention to high art. Since this group was crucial in Standard Oil's drive for image rehabilitation, sponsorship of the nation's most innovative artists and prestigious photographers seemed an astute focus for its wartime public relations.[67]

Early in 1943 SONJ created a formal public relations department and took on the sponsorship of a massive project documenting the company's wartime operations through photographs. As director of the photography project it chose Roy Stryker, who was known for his work with Walker Evans, Margaret Bourke-White, and John Vachon on the noted Farm Security Administration project. This choice reflected the corporation's desire to assign high culture to the task of establishing its social legitimacy within the nexus of familiar American institutions. The Standard Oil project included no prints of top company officers or of cor-

FIGURE 8.9

Roy Stryker, who had directed
the FSA photography project
documenting American poverty,
managed the photographing of
Standard Oil's wartime operations.

Common folk, like those in
Sol Libsohn's "Lunch Counter
in a Diner," now included S.O.
employees, who "were people
too."

porate headquarters. Its photographers focused on the everyday lives of average
Americans in the communities in which many Standard Oil Company workers
lived. The series told the story of oil, in the words of one critic, "always with the
accent of the man on the job."[68] From this perspective Standard Oil's wartime self-
portrait seemed hardly distinguishable from a sympathetic portrayal of small-town
America (Fig. 8.9).

In 1945 Standard further commissioned sixteen of the nation's leading painters
to document "the five crucial years [1940–1945] in which petroleum was called
upon to help preserve the civilization which it had done so much to create." This
was a "prestige" campaign, as the trade journal *Tide* put it, one aimed at providing
a "class" and quality image for company and product (Fig. 8.10).[69] Of course, SONJ
was no pioneer in seeking to link high art and corporate image; nor was AT&T or
any of the other wartime sponsors of concerts and artists. Many leading American
businessmen of the late nineteenth and early twentieth centuries had prided themselves on their roles as patrons of the arts. But whether sponsoring the opera or
simply hauling home art treasures from Europe, they generally patronized the arts
as individuals, looking more to legitimate their personal wealth through this association than to frame a corporate image.[70] During the 1920s, however, several corporations turned to high art to give their product or corporate persona a refined

FIGURE 8.10

Aiming to mollify its critics, who it presumed would appreciate its sponsorship of high art, Standard Oil commissioned prestigious painters to portray its wartime operations. Here, Thomas Hart Benton seemed to mimic the industrial aesthetic of Charles Sheeler's earlier paintings of Ford's River Rouge plants. People were dwarfed, while the company acquired magnitude and majesty.

aura. And in 1935, in what has often been highlighted as the most significant episode in a progression toward an eventual nexus between modernist high art and the large corporation, President Walter Paepcke of the Container Corporation began to commission paintings for his advertisements from such established figures in the international art world as A. M. Cassandre, Herbert Bayer, Fernand Léger, and Gyorgy Kepes. Before the end of the 1930s, fueled by new tax provisions for charitable and educational contributions, corporations like IBM were creating corporate art collections. The war's legitimizing effects on big business soon encouraged a still more expansive cultural reach.[71]

The wartime linkage between industry and the arts also embodied an institutional itch to assume cultural responsibility. As Alfred Sloan observed in introducing the GM-sponsored NBC Orchestra in 1943, General Motors was stepping forward to meet that great public need, in time of war, to "retain in so far as possible those educational and cultural activities which have so enriched Americans in all walks of life."[72] In the same spirit in which major companies had aspired to the status of civic institutions in the 1920s, giant corporations in the 1940s also hoped such sponsorship would remove the taint of "mere commercialism" from their public images. But these forays into cultural leadership were taken with the resolve that common folk should not be left behind. AT&T opted for a program of "music for everyone," consisting of "familiar melodies from the classics, light opera and musical comedy," and consciously "lightened up the music somewhat" as the war approached. Although as an "institution" General Motors required a "high-class, dignified program," Sloan suggested that the corporation replace Toscanini and the NBC Symphony with "a more popular type of music"; short of so drastic a step, he wondered if the NBC Symphony couldn't reach out to ordinary listeners by sticking to "reasonably tuneful" selections with "just a little bit of melody."[73]

All these cultural endeavors owed part of their inspiration to a widespread sense among major corporations of the historical significance of their wartime roles. They also reflected the corporations' increasingly sophisticated consciousness of the range of their constituencies, as their realms of interests and activities seemed now to coincide almost perfectly with those of the nation at large. Corporations that aspired to an ascribed role of national leadership were recognizing the value of "covering all the bases," culturally as well as socially, politically, and economically, as they looked toward the postwar world.

The Corporation and "American Know-how"

As corporations turned to common-folk protagonists and imagery to associate the "fifth freedom" of free enterprise with the wartime goals and values of average Americans, many also claimed for themselves a virtue often vaunted as an intrinsic aspect of national character. This was the trait known in familiar, Main Street vernacular as "American know-how"—a shrewdness of judgment based on experience and a quick capacity to master technical apparatus. The term carried strong democratic connotations. Clearly distinct from book learning, know-how was the kind of expertise available to all through everyday experience. Historically, it recalled the tests of frontier life. Suggesting the mastery of skills essential for personal independence, know-how attained the moral authority of an association with traditional republican values.[74]

The know-how motif in wartime corporate imagery derived both from the search for a tasteful way to brag about corporate accomplishments in war production and from a very specific managerial concern. Vignettes of corporate self-congratulation that emphasized the application of know-how to war production highlighted the importance of the fifth freedom (Fig. 8.11). The opportunities for risk and reward under free enterprise, they asserted, underlay the particularly American attribute of know-how. By stressing know-how more than size, the industrial giants positioned themselves as simply the nation's handymen and tinkerers writ large. The initiative and inventiveness that stemmed from America's pioneer past, and which had long been lodged in the technical ingenuity of small-town mechanics, was thus defined as a quality that linked the industrial corporation with the Main Streets of America and united both for inevitable victory in war.[75]

A more specific motive for the wartime celebration of corporate know-how lay in the reaction by automakers to union initiatives—like that of the United Auto

FIGURE 8.11

Addressing the reader of this newspaper ad as "a 'stockholder' in Fighting America," General Motors explained that free enterprise had stimulated businessmen to acquire the "Know-How" that was "getting the [wartime] job done."

Workers in the immediate prewar period—that challenged traditional management prerogatives. Walter Reuther's bold proposal in 1941 for the creation of a tripartite industrial council of managers, unionists, and government representatives to accelerate the auto industry's production of planes had shocked and embarrassed company executives. In proposing an unprecedented sharing of managerial power and promising production efficiencies in the process, Reuther had challenged the notion of management's monopoly on significant know-how. Although GM executives sought to refute Reuther's charges of inadequate mobilization by the manufacturers, an internal GM report in February 1942 suggests that the Reuther plan did have an impact on company policies. The author argued that the corporation should carefully distribute war projects among GM plants in order to please the authorities in Washington. He concluded that this would be the best way to get "the 'monkey off our back' in this matter of joint labor and management control." Reuther's scheme had threatened the corporation so gravely only a month earlier, he recalled, that he was "glad that many of you don't know how close a squeak we've had on that one."[76]

What was more, a recent surge of union organization among foremen in the auto plants, especially at Chrysler and Ford, had alarmed all the auto manufacturers and seemed likely to reemerge as a major issue at the end of the war. Top executives, as Howell Harris relates, "could see an awful possibility of being effectively isolated at the pinnacles of their organizations, without any remaining subordinates over whom they had unchallenged unilateral authority." Nelson Lichtenstein points out that "the stakes were high in the battle over foreman unionization because this fight was central to the large conflict over the legitimacy and limits of corporate power. . . . Foreman organization . . . eroded the vitality of corporate ideology in society at large by shattering the unitary facade of management."[77]

Such concerns led to what Lichtenstein has called "a passionately held axiom of corporate spokesmen" during the 1940s "that foremen were part of management." Executives at General Motors undertook special efforts to ensure that foremen were included on the distribution list for inspirational messages from top executives. They were made part of "supervisory executive groups," units designed to create a unifying "divisional atmosphere" as well as to trumpet company production accomplishments to the press.[78] In wartime ads that claimed credit for managerial expertise, both GM and Ford included foremen, by implication, within management while downplaying, through disregard, the role of skilled and unskilled workers. Although they associated know-how with the traits of common Americans who gained success in a free enterprise economy, they implied that the crucial know-how in the modern corporation came almost entirely from above— in the form of managerial expertise.[79]

At General Motors, the company's Public Relations Policy Group agreed that its "major task in 1943" was to "tell the production story but with increased emphasis upon the managerial 'know-how' aspect." Already in 1942 a series of ads "in hundreds of newspapers" had begun relating GM's "Good News from the Production Front." These accounts placed particular emphasis on "the part that management planning and know-how" had played in achieving production records. It was vital, in the company's strategy, to convince the public that "supervisory 'know-how'" was irreplaceable.[80] Several months earlier, as he began to work on a war history of General Motors, Henry Weaver had observed that too little effort had been devoted to telling the "story of the brain work, the planning, the creative effort, the engineering skills and inventive genius . . . which are really the essence of the mass production idea." More emphasis on these critical elements of managerial efficiency in war production and less emphasis on the assembly line, he argued, would "correct the impression that labor is entitled to an ever-increasing share of the industry's earnings."[81]

The upshot of these considerations was the constant use of the phrase "know-how" in the ongoing "Good News from the Production Front" publicity campaign, both in the print media and on radio. General Motors' sponsorship of the NBC Symphony Orchestra in 1943 afforded the company a generous intermission slot for institutional messages. For these cameo appearances GM recruited Charles Kettering, its most famous public figure. Drawing on his stature as an applied scientist and his skill as a folksy popularizer, Kettering told story after story of the corporation's contribution of technical and managerial genius to the war effort. Even in its expanded wartime institutional campaign in the farm press, GM made sure to stipulate "management know-how" as one of the common elements that made "partners" of farmers and manufacturers.[82]

In such magazine advertisements as "Pulling a Smoothie" (Fig. 8.12), GM cast its engineers in the role of boy tinkerers to explain how the very thing that had made "prewar America a fine place in which to live" had fostered the development of know-how. By allowing GM and its technical experts to "earn fair rewards by accomplishing useful things," the American system had made its companies rich in the experience needed for war production. In "The Truck That Took to

Pulling a smoothie

GENERAL MOTORS
"VICTORY IS OUR BUSINESS"

FIGURE 8.12
Naturally she adores the young
tinkerer with the know-how to
perfect his home-built vehicle.
General Motors was this boy writ
large, its know-how the product of
the free enterprise system.

Water," a GM engineer explained to a young boy how the "traditional American
practice of a just reward for good and useful work" had stimulated the "know-
how" that had enabled GM to produce such a flexible war vehicle in record time.
America's enemies had miscalculated, GM declared elsewhere, because they had
"overlooked our 'secret weapon,'—industrial 'know-how.'"[83]

The Ford Motor Company recurrently returned to the know-how theme in the
midprogram commercials on its news commentary show, *Watch the World Go By*.
Although generally disinclined to brag about its war service, Ford enthusiastically
reviewed various instances in which "industrial brains, fostered through the system
of free enterprise," had enabled American industry to shorten the war. Constantly
alluding to "engineering genius," "brainpower," and "industrial 'know-how,'"
Ford concluded that no other factor so clearly distinguished the "American system of free enterprise" from the "Nazi 'slave system'" as did the sharing of "know-
how" in America.[84] Not to be outdone, the Chrysler Corporation mounted its
own tribute to managerial know-how in 1944 with a series of advertisements in
large-circulation magazines on the theme of "imagination and teamwork." While
including workers and small business suppliers as part of the team, Chrysler clearly
identified management as providing the crucial element—that of imagination
(Fig. 8.13).[85]

The auto manufacturers, while they surpassed all others in their resort to the
rhetoric of corporate know-how, certainly held no exclusive rights to this tactic.

Imagination is a factory whistle you never hear . . . it's a call to action for people who like their work.

Management at Chrysler Corporation is "men in their shirt sleeves." They keep the spark of imagination active throughout the entire producing and operating Chrysler organization. They stimulate the exchange of ideas and experience among its divisions to strengthen *each* with the resource~

FIGURE 8.13

Chrysler defined "imagination" as strictly an attribute of management—a management of "men in their shirt sleeves." Given that group's apparent monopoly on know-how, none remained for blue-collar workers to claim.

John Benson, president of the American Association of Advertising Agencies, had proposed early in the war that the advertising profession "should plead the cause of management in American business as the real source of all material progress." Arthur Page, vice president for public relations at AT&T, expressed pride in the "know-how and organization" that his company was able to apply immediately to the nation's war needs. Walter Gifford, the company's president, felt satisfied that corporate management, which had been "not only the 'forgotten man' but the much-abused man" during the prewar years, could now, through its contribution of skill and leadership to the building of America as the "Arsenal of the United Nations" at war, claim its proper credit. It was now clear that America led the world in many ways, but "in none perhaps more than in the art of management."[86]

Visions of Tomorrow: Futurama Realized

"Tomorrow is going to be a thrilling experience," the Aluminum Company of America promised American women in October 1942, just ten months into the war. The thrill would come from the "fascinating new products" that wartime technology had inspired and that were "already planned for the day when."[87] Glimpses of a technologically wondrous future, as a reward for wartime sacrifices and faith in the free enterprise system, emerged very early during World War II as a central element in corporate imagery. As an alternative to boasting about their war production, corporations quite logically seized on this strategy for asserting their know-how and keeping their names before the public. It allowed them to allude to their war contributions while putting forth an image of creativity and technical expertise, even if, for the time being, they were unable to offer consumer goods. Here the images so vividly promoted at the 1939–40 New York World's Fair, with its "world of tomorrow" theme, found incessant reinforcement. With the public still worried that the country might revert to depression after the war, the "visionary copy" that featured postwar technology "stated precisely what Americans wanted to hear."[88]

Even before the United States entered the war, Alcoa had promised that "industry is already learning 'To Beat Swords into Plowshares for Tomorrow's Aluminized America.'" Drawing on Futurama's vision of the "city of the future," Alcoa conveyed its own dream of the technological revolutions in transportation, house building, and packaging that would soon make "your sons and daughters . . . the pilots of an Aluminized America." Alcoa's pilot metaphor was hardly unique. Aviation, as Frank Fox points out, was to become "a topic for the most rhapsodic excursions of the imagination" during the war. "The airplane had revolutionized war; it would revolutionize the peace as well."[89] Already in 1941 the BBDO advertising agency had prodded clients to think ahead toward the technology of a "golden future" by asking themselves, "What kind of car will a bomber pilot want?" BBDO went on to observe that "people are beginning to have vague, rose-tinted visions of wonderful things to follow the fighting. They love electrons. Family planes are catching on." Many visions of the future featured the personal helicopter (Fig. 8.14).[90]

Few corporations anticipated the delights of revolutionary postwar technology so persistently as did General Electric. With virtually no consumer products on the market, the company looked to reinforce its already-prominent reputation for research. GE reminded its stockholders and employees of "the importance of a constant report of stewardship," which it could best accomplish by interpreting its work to the public as "a means to a better life." Its scientists and engineers, GE promised, were "learning much about new materials like plastics, new developments like television, new sciences like electronics, that will help to make . . . victory worthwhile."[91] *Advertising and Selling* endorsed this method of making victory seem worthwhile; it praised "Jules-Verne Advertising" for keeping the public's "hopes and spirits high." Seeking to promote war bonds as "advance payments" on appliances and cars that would become available soon after the war, companies such as Alcoa, Kaiser Steel, Minneapolis-Honeywell, General Electric, and U.S. Steel used world-of-tomorrow images to make victory worthwhile for

FIGURE 8.14
An obsession with the personal helicopter as the promise of tomorrow found one expression in Seagram's vision of the business executive who commuted from office to hunting lodge. Note the Futurama-like urban scene in the inset image.

themselves as well. *Family Circle* magazine, aligning itself with this strategy, featured a gleaming new refrigerator in a war bond ad headlined, "This is what victory looks like." [92]

As General Electric's world-of-tomorrow campaign unfolded, its copywriters inspired fabulous expectations. In one ad the company addressed the woman who regretted that she could not serve patriotically "beyond this shore," as did the men in the military. But she could aid the cause equally well, GE assured her, by undertaking to "keep our dreams alive." To do so, the ad counseled, "When you try to imagine the future, after he returns, be sure your imaginings are full of bright and cheerful hues, for that world of tomorrow will be resplendent in things you don't know—never even imagined." Other GE ads took the initiative in compensating for the consumer's lack of imagination. GE was fighting for "that better world" in which the housewife would become "Princess Mary White," who, "instead of a pumpkin coach," would "drive a car such as you have never dreamed of, and fly a plane as readily as you would drive a car." A young girl might well look forward not only to "a big shiny automobile" but also to her own airplane, "or even something like a magic carpet—who knows." As for "Junior," although many of the wonders in which he might be interested had to remain secret at present, he should look forward confidently. The world of tomorrow, "the world you dream of," GE emphasized, was "being made right now" in the General Electric laboratories.[93]

General Electric owned no patent on world-of-tomorrow visions. Virtually every manufacturer with a relevant product urged the American housewife and the bride-to-be to save through war bonds for her "dream kitchen" of the future.[94] Lest that sphere seem too confining, others coaxed her imagination to soar out through the kitchen window, beyond the driveway, to the family's own aerodrome. The B. F. Goodrich Company, in a pioneering television broadcast in 1943, prophesied that "the plane of tomorrow will be a family plane. One that hubby may go off to work in every morning. And perhaps, on Saturdays, you'll take the children on a picnic . . . up in the blue. For this little job can stop in mid-air . . . and it will land on a dime—or a rooftop for that matter." Already in its 1942 advertising, Goodrich had suggested that even during wartime, it was "not hard to imagine a family plane" as part of "the shape of things to come" (Figs. 8.15 and 8.16).[95]

As a strategy of corporate image building during an era when advertising was virtually costless and consumer products were lacking, this emphasis on technological "miracles" possessed its own persuasive logic. But a number of companies put such advertisements to double service by incorporating free enterprise doctrine. Whether American families would replace the automobile with the helicopter, one advertiser emphasized, would be determined by the right of free choice guaranteed by the American economic system. A spokesman for the Ford Motor Company reminded radio listeners that "night after night . . . I've told you about the way the folks in industry have learned new and better ways of doing things . . . of the production miracles that have been achieved at Ford plants." After the war, he promised, this new "know-how" would be translated into the higher standard of living made possible by "free men working in free industry." General Electric likewise occasionally used world-of-tomorrow ads to plug the advantages of free enterprise. In the process of promising "Junior" his future "free choice of the climate" through air conditioning, GE reminded him that he would also receive those precious "hand-me-downs" of prewar American liberty and democracy, with "no alterations needed." Asserting that "no one can improve on freedom," GE proffered television and air conditioning as ways that the company could "improve some of the things that let us express it."[96]

While associations between new technologies and the freedoms provided under free enterprise carried the main burden of ideological guidance in most corporate world-of-tomorrow ads, General Motors also ventured to champion the further mechanization of industry, noting privately that this stance no longer involved the slight public relations risk that it had during the 1930s. Although people back then, GM's public relations chief noted, had "lived by the machine," they had "still derived some sense of threat from it." But now, "at this grave hour," he exulted in 1942, "the machine becomes the protector of their right to work and live in a free America."[97]

For all the tactical advantages in using world-of-tomorrow imagery, corporations soon became uneasy with this approach. Many worried that the postwar public would grow cynical as the unrealistic expectations were dashed. Prompted by this concern, the plastics industry even launched an antifuturist campaign in 1943,

FIGURES 8.15 & 8.16
B. F. Goodrich steadily projected an airplane-dominated future. "Will ordinary folks own a family plane?" it asked. "No question about it!" was the immediate answer. It also imagined family planes awaiting buyers in Main Street showrooms.

seeking to "neutralize" the "plastics utopianism" of "too many Sunday supplement features" that had depicted plastic "as a 'miracle whip' material with which anything can be done." For the auto industry in particular, sanguine assumptions about a wondrously transformed postwar world proved downright disconcerting. As early as November of 1942, President Charles Erwin Wilson of General Motors wrote to Lammot du Pont decrying "the great deal of harm . . . being done by men who are talking too loosely about the post-war cars that will be produced by the automotive industry." One of Du Pont's most celebrated and visible scientists, he complained, seemed to have gone out of his way to make "sensational statements" about postwar technology. Particularly distressing had been his assertion that the immediate prewar auto models had already "aged, technically, at least two decades" as a result of wartime advances.[98]

The reality for General Motors, Wilson protested, was quite different. Whenever the war ended GM would have to resume production quickly on "substantially the same products we were producing when the war started." Chairman Alfred Sloan had earlier expressed the same concern about public expectations that the "immediate post-war car will be radically different from the 1942 car." This was a dangerous fantasy, Sloan argued, when the truth of the situation was that "the initial post-war car will of necessity be the 1942 car."[99] By 1944 Ford management was also lamenting the public's belief that the postwar car would be "revolutionary in design" and "something like Buck Rogers space patrol." Besides creating unwanted pressures, an internal Ford report suggested, the "fantastic predictions of the postwar era" annoyed combat soldiers who wondered if efforts were

going into such dreams and designs that could better be applied to winning the war. Meanwhile Kettering was trying to demolish some of the postwar fantasies during his intermission talks for GM's symphony broadcasts. He "blasted as myth" the notion that Americans would soon find available cars with "transparent, plastic tops shaped like an egg, or detachable helicopter blades to permit the car to take to the air."[100]

Ironically, at almost the same time, tire companies like Goodrich were promoting just such images in their ads, and the erstwhile designer of GM's Futurama exhibit, Norman Bel Geddes, was busy "dreamlining tomorrow" with images of family "air flivvers" carrying housewives to parking lots on the roofs of the department stores of the future.[101] Henry Kaiser was calling for a radically redesigned lightweight car while freely speculating that "the family plane and helicopter are nearer than we think." These expansive visions finally provoked Sloan to go public in the fall of 1944 in another attempt to dampen overheated imaginations. Postwar cars would, of course, be better, Sloan wrote reassuringly. But there would be "nothing radically new," nothing to approach the "wonderful pictures appearing in our magazines, drawn by artists whose imaginations have an unlimited ceiling."[102] General Motors was already worried about retooling quickly enough after the war to meet pent-up postwar demand, a crucial requirement if it was to continue to anchor its broader legitimacy (and thus a significant degree of autonomy) in customer satisfaction. It did not need additional worries over public dissatisfaction with styling as well as with availability.

Although the public would prove far more willing than Sloan imagined to dis-

count the futuristic imagery of the ads after the war, the publicly expressed trepi-
dations of the auto manufacturers reflected some deep concerns in corporate board-
rooms. Corporate leaders saw a need to win this war in more ways than one. They
conjured up the specter of vast economic planning by the government in the postwar era, particularly if corporations failed to quickly absorb returning veterans into
the labor force and foster vibrant consumer activity. Donaldson Brown warned
GM's postwar planning committee at the outset of 1943 that it was "common talk
in Washington" that if private industry was not sufficiently prepared with its own
plan for the postwar world, government would do the planning, in line with "theories of collectivism in some form." Major corporations wished to start working
to avert this crisis as soon as possible, yet—wary of accusations that they were not
devoting all their energies to the war effort—they feared to do so publicly.[103]

The appropriate alternative to government planning, most agreed, was vigorous
individual planning by thousands of business corporations—a form of planning,
as a leading Kodak executive put it, that came "from the bottom up rather than
from the top down." New engineering and styling advances had to be accomplished as quickly as possible, so that, as Sloan commented of GM's products, "cars
pass more rapidly from the first owner to the scrap pile." World-of-tomorrow advertising posed a dilemma in that it was needed to "agitate the imaginations and
desires of post-war customers" and thus stimulate a "radical reversal" of popular
thinking—away from the wartime "emphasis on self-sacrifice and absolute needs."
But by creating a "false glamor," such imagery might provoke eventual disillusionment, setting the stage for government intervention to revitalize the economy.[104]

Another potential dilemma inherent in the world-of-tomorrow style of corporate image advertising arose from the profound resistance of corporate publicists to
one of the major visual legacies of the 1939–40 New York World's Fair—the association of stylistic modernity with images of the gleaming, streamlined city. Immense futuristic metropolises, like the one to which visitors were conveyed in the
Bel Geddes/General Motors Futurama, had been portrayed as the locus of technology's triumph. Yet the molders of wartime corporate images, seeking to identify their companies with heartland American values, cultivated the aura and imagery of that conventional and hallowed habitat of the prototypical citizen, the
American small town. After all, was not Norman Rockwell, the nation's premier
visual interpreter of the common folk, situating virtually all his wartime images in
rural areas and small towns? Thus, a major quandary loomed for those who wished
to exalt the imagery of modernity.

If this dilemma ever vexed the creators of wartime corporate imagery, they certainly revealed little hesitancy or confusion. Without any debates or conversations
that I can discover, either public or private, they simply banished the concept of
the future as modernistic city. Instead, they found ways to bring home the imagery
of technological utopia to small-town and domestic settings. Advertising illustrations showed streamlined houses, barns, and garages—almost all in small-town,
suburban, or rural scenes.[105] Du Pont even brought the favored imagery of personal air transport right down to the Main Streets of America's "Lambert Hollows." It depicted the helicopters of two everywoman figures, "Mrs. Kimball" and
"Mrs. Brown," in a parking lot right outside the window of the "village market"
in "Anyplace, U.S.A." (Fig. 8.17). A subsequent Du Pont Cellophane ad conveyed

FIGURES 8.17 & 8.18
Du Pont's Cellophane Division joined the ranks of technological utopianism but located this futurism in towns that could be "Anyplace, U.S.A." After the war, "almost all the shopping housewives" would use the plane parking lot or benefit from helicopter deliveries.

the small-town feel of personal interactions and service by depicting the delivery man from the bakery hovering over "Mrs. Brown's" modernistic house in his helicopter and calling down in a neighborly fashion, "Need any bread today?" (Fig. 8.18).[106]

While Bel Geddes's 1939 Futurama had provided futuristic superhighways for commuters that allowed suburban small towns to survive, the wartime world-of-tomorrow advertisers more commonly turned to the family plane or helicopter as a way of uniting technological progress with the preservation of small-town America. The Stewart-Warner Corporation had its typical couple in their family airplane decide to "drop down at Middletown for gas and a bite of lunch" (Fig. 8.19).[107] And in the model vignette of the "Home Sweet Home" of the future, a helicopter or an airplane wing was likely to be in view from the living room window. Despite the powerful legacy from the 1920s and 1930s of the resplendent city as a visual cliché for the future, this symbol of national aspiration and technological advance receded almost to the vanishing point during World War II. AT&T's "Rainbow in the Sky," replete with assurances of new technological "conveniences and luxuries" from the laboratories of its war-occupied scientists, cast its glimmering promise not over some skyscraper metropolis but over a rural farm scene.[108]

"Let's Drop Down at Middletown
For Gas and A Bite of Lunch"

THAT'S YOU in the driver's seat of your 194X family airplane. You're off for the week end with the wife and kids. There are ... to go and ... says

Speed Indicator will tell your air speed in miles per hour.

What Direction? . . . The Stewart-Warner ... will keep ... your cou...

ment panels by which you can travel in complete confidence. Each will be the result of years of experience in producing instruments f... ... of cars. To

FIGURE 8.19
Except for the creation of an airfield adjacent to every small town, little would change in Main Street America as a result of the anticipated feats of postwar technology.

A Sense of Place: The Corporation Moves to Main Street

Wartime corporate imagery, a psychologically minded critic might well have concluded, disclosed a collective fixation on "Main Street." Corporation after corporation turned to idyllic scenes of small towns to convey what the nation was fighting for and those values the company stood for. In depicting American homes protected by planes built with Alcoa aluminum, the giant monopoly chose a traditional village Main Street, with the spire of a town hall or church visible in the background, as the site for its archetypal "Mr. Smith's Home," in "Your Town, U.S.A." When Mack Trucks displayed the fire-fighting uses of the domestic part of its production, it likewise chose a Main Street scene, with the modest town hall prominently featured in the background. And the United States Rubber Company seemed reflexively to turn to images of small-town Main Streets (Figs. 8.20 and 8.21).[109]

Institutional ads calling for faith in "the American way of life" or in "the Land of the Free" invariably evoked rural or small-town scenes to represent those sentiments.[110] Faith in "our institutions" seemed to call for an illustration of a small-town setting with a headline like "Moving Mountains on Elm Street" or "The Battle of Elm Street" (Fig. 8.22). Frank Fox has selected "American Pastoral" as an apt label for this mystique of lost innocence. Its imagery appeared everywhere in the early 1940s, but nowhere more strikingly than in the institutional ads of major corporations. In a war with goals perceived less idealistically than in World War I, yet a war that was still, in its own way, in defense of American innocence, big business seemed determined to link itself with the most favored images of that innocence. It was no mere chance when, casting about for a likely place of origin for a typical GI on the battlefront, a copywriter for a Nash-Kelvinator institutional ad settled on a "little Iowa town."[111]

In similar fashion Chrysler Corporation told its story of "America's traditional freedom of competitive individual enterprise" against the backdrop of a local car dealership, with the top of the town hall visible. Ford apparently did not worry about the architectural incongruities of placing the art deco wall of its modern local dealer's store against the background of a nineteenth-century town hall and the classical columns and bas-relief of an unidentified building—all symbolically sheltered by an immense village tree. For its message on "why victory must be won," Dundee Mills picked a public square with a town hall and village green where "men in shirt sleeves—farmers, business men, salesmen—chat together, bench on bench." When the text of a wartime institutional message described the values shared by a village in Kansas, a "rocky shoulder of Maine," and "a foreign quarter of New York City," the choice for a single illustration predictably fell to the Kansas village. Even when a headline such as "From Hill and Vale to City Street" alluded to the whole range of locales in 1940s America, one could be certain that it would not be the "city street" but something more like a small-town setting that would appear in the illustration.[112]

Although there was no grand conspiracy among major corporations to plant their symbolic roots in the terrain of small-town America, still the pervasive fusion of corporate image with Main Street did not lack a basic logic, conscious or unconscious. Given that one long-standing barrier to greater moral legitimacy for the giant corporation had been its immense size and seeming aloofness, no better counterimage could be offered than that of a friendly neighbor and civic contributor located right nearby on Main Street. AT&T had long been aware of this goal (see Figs. 2.21 and 2.22), which it thoroughly infused into the "neighborliness" of its 1941 advertising campaign. Eagerly, AT&T quoted an unnamed Vermont newspaper editor (epitomizing the civic conscience of a small town) who observed that although he didn't "know how big the telephone company is," he could judge the company simply by recognizing its identity with the people who worked for it locally, his own neighbors and friends.[113]

Beyond its usefulness in finessing the issue of bigness, the stereotyped imagery of small-town Main Street clearly resonated for corporate leaders with conservative values in politics and economics. Here was the embodiment of homogeneity and unity, of an assumed lack of class differences and conflicts. When advertisers talked about the "thrilling sight" during the war of a *completely united nation* that,

FIGURES 8.20 & 8.21
In ad after ad during 1944, the
United States Rubber Company
choose to interpret its wartime
service against Main Street backgrounds so stylized they resembled
Grant Wood paintings.

they hoped, would "remain so after victory," they conjured the vision of a rural or small-town scene. Thus, Republic Steel's "jes' folks" champions of free enterprise were shown clustered in a rustic barbershop or grouped around the pot-bellied stove of a general store (Fig. 8.23). The *American Legion Magazine* seized on the "Great American Cracker Barrel" as a symbol to rally its readers behind traditional values. The Hearst chain offered businesses free use of an advertisement, "with or without a credit line to Hearst Newspapers," that would enable them to take on the persona of the suspendered keeper of a country store. It implied that the words of this folksy provincial could most effectively convey the war accomplishments of free enterprise. The J. Walter Thompson advertising agency even directly appropriated Grant Wood's *American Gothic* for a blistering anti–New Deal message about American freedoms. As the advertising executive Thomas Brophy commented to a corporate client in 1943, smaller communities were "simon-pure American," not "union-ridden nor plagued with class dissensions, racial hatreds." They represented "the conservative backbone of the country."[114]

One of the favored elements in conservative philosophies of free enterprise had invariably been the story of occupational and social mobility, based on merit, under conditions of equal opportunity. Those who spoke for the giant corporations bore the burden of demonstrating that opportunities for young men in America

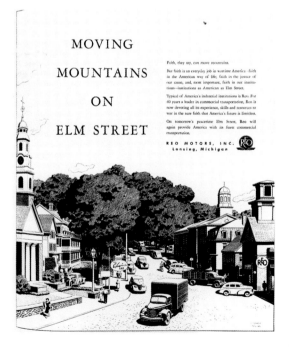

FIGURE 8.22 (left)
Automobile manufacturers like itself, according to Reo Motors, represented "institutions as American as Elm Street." As the images in an array of other corporate ads made clear, "Elm Street" denoted the long-established, prosperous residential avenue next to "Main Street."

"Boys, I'll tell you what Free Enterprise really is!"

"It's a lot of little things—and some mighty big things, too.

"But in a nutshell, it's our right to live our own lives, run our own jobs and our own businesses in our own way—without needless interference.

"It's our right to criticize the government, bawl out the umpire, or make a speech on the public square. It's our right to travel when and where we choose—to work or not, as we please.

"It offers *opportunity* to anyone who really wants it. It rewards thrift, hard work and ingenuity. It thrives on competition and raises our standard of living. It encourages invention, stimulates research and promotes progress.

"It offers us a chance to save and invest and build and grow.

"Under Free Enterprise men who have faith in an idea can take risks to develop it. Our railways started that way. So did the motor car industry—and oil and steel and aviation and scientific mechanized farming.

"Free Enterprise made small shops and factories into big ones—and then started more small ones. And now, fighting a desperate war in which production will turn the scale, America is out-producing every other country in the world, hands down—and is doing it faster and better.

"Yet in spite of all this, some folks would like to change our American way of doing things —and rebuild our whole country under a *new* and *different* system.

"If they had their way, Tom here, wouldn't own this store. He'd be regimented with a lot of other storekeepers and told how to run his business by some bureaucrat who probably never tended store in his life.

"Ed's farm would belong to the state, and Ed would be told how to run it and what to raise by someone he wouldn't even know.

"Jim would be working for a state-owned factory—with his job and wages frozen. And I don't know *where* we country doctors would be.

"We fellows aren't rich—and probably never will be. But we've got a lot of self-respect and religion and decency and common sense. We own our own homes and farms, send our kids to college, have cars, radios, and a lot more of the luxuries of life than millions of people living under fancy political systems and 'planned economies' in other countries.

"Sure, we're willing to put up with a lot of irritating things right now—in order to win the war—but I don't believe we'll stand for being pushed around much after it's over.

"Frankly, I don't like the name Free Enterprise for the system under which this country has grown great. I'd rather call it *American* Enterprise, because it's the most American thing we have. It really *is* America. Let's *keep* it."

REPUBLIC STEEL

GENERAL OFFICES: CLEVELAND 1, OHIO
Export Department: Chrysler Building, New York 17, New York

ALLOY, CARBON, STAINLESS STEELS • COLD FINISHED STEELS • PLATES • BARS • SHAPES • STRIP • SHEETS • PIPE • TUBING
TIN PLATE • NUTS • BOLTS • RIVETS • NAILS • PIG IRON • FARM FENCE • WIRE • FABRICATED STEEL PRODUCTS

FIGURE 8.23
Defining free enterprise as "the American way of doing things," Republic Steel adopted the persona of a hometown doctor and a setting suggestive of common folks and commonsense philosophizing to warn against bureaucrats and regimentation.

When Whistle Stops Become Ocean Ports...

Thousands of Americans reared in small towns and villages, will remember their boyhood thrill when "The Limited" made one of its rare stops—on signal—at their town. In the lexicon of railroading, such places—too small to warrant regular scheduled service—were called "whistle stops."

But in tomorrow's peacetime world, hundreds of remote and isolated points—the whistle stops of yesterday—can become ports in the ocean of the air.

For with air travel there are no "inland" towns. Some midwestern communities are

actually closer by air to foreign countries than are some coastal cities. And the development of feeder line helicopter transportation, can bring nearby towns within minutes of great airports serving transoceanic airlines.

In addition to its use for short haul feeder line service, the helicopter can be useful for "shuttle" transportation from

metropolitan centers to airports, and its ultimate development will make possible its use as a private, home-based aircraft.

At McDonnell, we are devoting full-time efforts to the production of planes, parts, and plastics for Allied war use. But our engineers and designers are working too, toward the development of better aircraft —better adapted to the needs of the future.

McDONNELL *Aircraft Corporation*

Manufacturers of PLANES · PARTS · PLASTICS · SAINT LOUIS - MEMPHIS ·

FIGURE 8.24
Although progress has brought modern air travel to this "whistle stop," the village's postwar role as a port "in the ocean of the air" seems hardly to have disturbed its small-town scale, the source of its imputed qualities of neighborliness and simplicity.

had not vanished with the coming of the industrial behemoths. Their solution was to argue both that mobility was just as possible within the large corporation as it had been without and that the needs of large corporations stimulated the prosperity of many small businesses. In the face of increasing evidence to the contrary, they continued in the 1930s and 1940s to assert, to the applause of other corporate leaders, that virtually all their top executives had come "up from the ranks."[115] And, pictorially and verbally, they tended to situate the smaller businesses created by their myriad needs in small towns, presenting themselves as products of those rural communities that had retained their traditional values while succeeding in the urban world of industry and advanced technology.

As if patting a child on the head to betoken their role as protector, patron, and promoter of its innocence and promise, giant corporations cherished the local community for the purity and simplicity of its values and praised its every demonstration, through the adoption of current technology, that it was "up-to-date." Their expectation that time-honored social values could (and should) be coupled with the latest technological advance was a steady theme of their Main Street imagery. McDonnell Aircraft Corporation expressed it most strikingly in an ad that predicted that tiny towns, formerly mere "whistle stops," would retain their old qualities while being linked by air into a network that would transform them into significant economic "ports" of the postwar world (Fig. 8.24).[116]

Ever since the largest corporations had confronted public relations problems, they had sought to associate themselves as closely as possible with small business as one of their major strategies. AT&T had persistently cultivated the image of the telephone monopoly as "a local business," one that "belongs to Main Street," in the years before the war. Presuming that size made no difference (except when they wished to assert superior service through the efficiencies that the magnitude of their operations allowed), they set forth the case against government regulation through the example of the struggling small-business proprietor, the little guy on the make. Republic Steel turned to "old Bill," the owner of the little repair shop, to explain the potential evils of "unnecessary interference and regulation." Bill epitomized every business that had started "from scratch"; he had succeeded because "no bureaucrat told Bill what to do or how to do it."[117] An identification with "Main Street," especially when almost everyone was using that phrase to evoke an America under attack, served well the corporations' desire to be unobtrusive.

Main Street imagery could also be fused with emerging corporate strategies for purposes beyond finessing the issue of size. It complemented strategies of decentralization and dispersion; it could help corporations contend with local reactions to the menace of "outside" control. It was thus not entirely a coincidence that Main Street imagery intensified as the plant city orientation developed into a top priority in many a corporate public relations program.

On Main Street in Plant City

The context of wartime emergency provided optimum conditions for employing rhetoric about small-town America to merge the images of company and community in many a plant city. A suggestive example of this process can be observed in Dayton, Ohio, the city where General Motors had already strenuously pursued a plant city campaign to overcome a particularly strained situation. Factory open houses and a variety of efforts by local GM public relations officials in the late 1930s had brought the big corporation into a more congenial relationship with "Main Street" in Dayton. With the coming of the war, GM went a step further. While advancing the plant city strategy, it simultaneously attempted to boost morale among its new wartime workers to surmount national resentments over its tardy conversion to full war production. First, in mid-1941, the corporation encouraged its employees to join with the city in producing a great historical pageant, *Frontiers of Freedom,* to celebrate the centennial of Dayton's city charter. Less than a year later, the dramatization of GM war contributions and free enterprise ideology in *Plowshares,* the pageant of GM war production, further fused the company image with Main Street America.

General Motors, according to its PR director, carefully distributed its war production so as to avoid setting up "war boom" towns that would eventually become ghost towns. By spreading its plants geographically (as had been its conscious policy since the late 1930s, principally for antiunion reasons), GM had "created a minimum of community problems." The factory in one of GM's new wartime "hometowns," Bedford, Indiana, was depicted in the company's employee magazine as surrounded by a white picket fence, perhaps to suggest the company's neighborliness. GM did not always succeed in its neighborly approaches to prospective plant cities. In Cincinnati, in 1944, tactlessness and a lack of coordination between corporate headquarters and GM's Fisher Body Division gave a group of residents near the planned "Duck Creek" site an opportunity to organize effective protests to the city council and thwart the project. GM's leaders took this setback as a salutary warning; thereafter they reminded themselves frequently of the need for excellent plant city PR to avoid "another Duck Creek." To emphasize its local presence GM allocated most of its funds for participation in war bond purchases to its various plant cities. Like several other major corporations, it continued after the war to look to geographic dispersion of manufacture and concomitant decentralization of public relations to local communities.[118]

In its own claim to eminence in plant city consciousness, the Ford Motor Company found latitude for plugs for the free enterprise system as it boasted of the war achievements of its 1920s and 1930s "village industry" plants (see Chapter 6). Still championing the drastic decentralization of industry while retaining mass production methods, Ford continued to advance his idea of village industries even after the United States had entered the war. During 1941 the *Ford News* characterized the war-born Willow Run plant as the latest of the company's experiments in "industrial decentralization." The essay emphasized the "rural setting" of Willow Run, the way in which its plants, although ultramodern in equipment, "fit with complete harmony into carefully landscaped grounds," and its "striking contrast" to the huge Rouge River plant. Ironically, Willow Run—as the nation's largest bomber production plant by 1943—would come to epitomize the problems of wartime boom towns.[119]

Of course, actual plant cities, even those much smaller than the war-bloated Willow Run encampments, did not look or act like the towns of the corporations' Main Street vignettes. No community with a major industrial plant was going to retain either the small size or simple social structure implied by such illustrations. Nor were the politics and economies of such communities going to reflect the interplay of interests among a limited number of relatively equal shopkeepers, farmers, local professionals, and small businessmen that the image of Main Street conventionally symbolized.[120] But the shared conviction that communities were well served by all morale-building activities enabled companies engaged in war production to easily assume roles of conspicuous leadership in the common cause. The many local ceremonies for the government's awarding of E flags to war plants (awards that, Paul Fussell suggests, were passed out "with notable lack of discrimination" in the interest of good morale) and the local war bond rallies and parades enabled the branches of major corporations to participate visibly in community events.[121]

For all the contradictions implicit in the corporate penchant for collapsing the rhetorical and visual images of the plant city into those of Main Street, the rationale seems clear enough. Modern plant cities needed to display the social and political harmony that the idyll of small-town unity and cohesion evoked. The corporation wished to be recognized not as a cold absentee employer but simply as one local citizen among many, albeit a citizen capable of stepping forward on occasion as patron and benefactor. Embedded within this Main Street nexus of neighborly folks and familiar businesses of comprehensible and comfortable size, the corporation would find full acceptance of its social legitimacy.

Of all the wartime initiatives for plant cities on the part of corporate leaders, the ones that most closely linked this PR strategy with the prevailing small-town

America imagery harked back to that popular company welfare program of World War I and the depression: the employee garden. Dozens of large corporations created garden plots during World War II to help alleviate food shortages, link workers to the company, improve morale, and identify the corporation with the most prosaic and pastoral of war efforts. Ford, drawing on its "one foot in industry and one foot on the land" legacy of programs of industrial dispersion, offered such plots to its workers in Dearborn who did not have backyards. The company loaned Ford tractors to prepare community grounds and appointed a director for its "Garden Educational Service." As early as August of 1941 the company newsletter reported that "thrift gardens" could be found "at most of the fourteen Ford assembly branches." In the *Ford Times,* Henry Ford observed that the British had "learned that they can maintain war production while to a great extent maintaining themselves on the soil." Given Ford's long-standing preoccupation with such a social balance, it is hardly surprising that he concluded, "There is a great feeling of satisfaction in that."[122]

Like Ford, General Motors found the promotion of victory gardens an agreeable activity for local public relations; they embodied the kind of community cooperation that made excellent content for employee magazines. Father, mother, and child formed a "planning committee" that echoed, in miniature, the industrial one shaped by GM's corporate know-how. Not to be outdone, Chrysler Motors announced a plan to create "a simple Victory garden" at every plant. These would not be "big production" gardens but small plots that workers could replicate in their own backyards. Alcoa celebrated the feats of the "Alcoa Family's Victory Gardeners." Just as it gladly accepted local leadership in organizing war bond rallies, meeting workers' needs for wartime recreation, and honoring the service of "our boys" at the front, the company seized on the sponsorship of victory gardens, viewing them as one more local site in which to display its deep involvement with the community as a whole.[123] Company victory gardens symbolized once again the way in which the corporation—as the organizer and motivator of its employees for war service, and in its increasingly visible solicitousness for its "boys" who risked their lives for family, community, and nation—demonstrated a social and moral legitimacy never so easily conceded as now, in the face of the external threats of war.

CONCLUSION:
LIKE A GOOD NEIGHBOR

In 1938, buoyed by seven years of rising influence within General Motors, Public Relations Director Paul Garrett had summoned sufficient bravado to prophesy that, within his lifetime, "the time will come . . . when the big jobs in industry will be bossed not by the technicians of production, engineering or merchandising but by the generalissimo of public relations." Only half a decade later he could matter-of-factly categorize the major problems with which management had contended in recent years—government relations, unions, community relations—as all falling within the province of public relations. Too discreet to proclaim himself the heralded generalissimo, he seemed almost to apologize to traditional corporate managers for the extent to which public relations issues had come to dominate, and even seemingly distort, their business lives.[1]

Wartime opportunities, together with fears of a loss of business autonomy in the postwar era, had greatly augmented the emphasis on public relations within corporate management. While their prodigious war production achievements were crucial to their companies' rise in public stature, corporate executives could hardly overlook the importance of their public relations activities in publicizing their exploits and in ameliorating their plant city relations. Corporate public relations officers, Garrett observed, had recognized the signs of a new public confidence in industry and had resolved to maintain this trust by making "production *plus* interpretation" their defense mission. Affirming that the giant corporations were still "in competition with the government for the greatest prize of all—the good will of the public," the PR director at United States Steel had summoned his fellow executives to wartime battle stations. It was not enough, he warned them, for the corporation to "do its best to help win the war." The American people had to *know* that it was doing its best.[2]

Few companies failed to impart such knowledge. Corporate PR divisions proliferated during the war; their personnel and expenditures mushroomed. Hundreds of elaborate albums documenting company war service appeared as new cadres of local PR officers cultivated community feeling in plant cities. Never had the giant corporations sponsored so many rallies, pageants, open houses, and recreational activities; rarely since the nineteenth century had they so fervently played the role of local good citizen. During the 1930s a few major corporations had discovered the virtues of a plant city focus as the core of a program that fused good PR with efforts to improve labor relations. Many more seized on this strategy during the war years. The postwar era would witness the cresting of a veritable wave of corporate neighborliness in plant cities across the nation (Fig. C.1).[3]

Many individual corporations prided themselves on the healthy recuperation of their corporate images through wartime service. Opinion polls provided them with the satisfaction of ostensibly exact measurements of their gains. The Psychological Corporation reported in the fall of 1944 that General Motors had obtained an "all-time high" in favorable public perceptions.[4] Du Pont, which had not even been able to claim a 50 percent positive rating from the public in 1937, had won the favor of 69 percent of women by 1944 and 76 percent of men. General Electric, according to surveys at the beginning of 1945, stood "higher than ever with the public," enjoying favorable views of 86 percent of those interviewed. When Alcoa commissioned the Opinion Research Corporation to make an extensive study of the attitudes of the "aware" public in 1946, it was reassured that the company had "enter[ed] the postwar years with a minimum of public ill-feeling toward it." Although more than half of those surveyed still believed "that Alcoa has a monopoly of the aluminum business," the great majority nonetheless gave the company credit for "a wartime job well done." By a ratio of four to one, they held favorable views of the company.[5]

Another development of the early 1940s that could be measured in more tangible terms was the relative position and power of big business in the American economy. Small business had been losing ground in relation to large corporations since early in the century, but World War II brought an additional impetus to this trend. Companies with over ten thousand workers increased their share of industrial employment from 13 to 30 percent of the nation's total between 1939 and 1944, while those with a hundred employees or fewer dropped from 26 to 19 percent. War production contracts favored the giant manufacturers, as did the processes of postwar reconversion. Beyond such measurable shifts in dominance within the economy, as Mansel Blackford perceptively observes, their pure persistence also enhanced the legitimacy of the great corporations. "The fact that big business had been part of the American scene for 40 years," Blackford points out, "led most Americans to accept its permanence."[6]

On the ideological front success also seemed evident, although never fully secure. Social and moral legitimacy would always be subject to renegotiation, and as Garrett cautioned his fellow executives at GM, a giant manufacturer would "not always be a war production 'hero.'" Nonetheless, in the contest for public favor against the New Deal administration—a struggle that Bruce Barton had so vividly delineated back in 1935 (see Chapter 6)—the large corporations had quickly achieved wartime victories. Even at the outset of American war participation, polls indicated that the public blamed labor leadership and the government to a much greater degree than industrial management for delays in war production. Less than a year after the bombing of Pearl Harbor, Garrett observed that "devotion to a cause close to people's hearts" through defense production had already enabled big business to win a "high regard . . . beyond its own public relations dreams." Industry, so of-

FIGURE C.1

An emphasis on public relations in plant cities reinforced the emphasis on the corporation as neighbor during the postwar years. The General Motors division that "lived" in Muncie, Indiana—America's designated "Middletown"— presented itself not as a corporation but as a suburban family.

ten known in the 1930s by what it opposed, had fused itself with the nation, as "a part of the community and as a part of the great war effort." Leaders of big business, Thomas Cochran concludes, had gained the status "both at home and abroad as spokesmen for the American social system."[7]

Victory on the ideological front was also cautiously proclaimed by the War Advertising Council, which sought to persuade advertisers and agencies to support its continuation as a peacetime promoter of noncontroversial civic causes. The

Council pointed to the wartime public service advertising that it had induced from corporations as the best form of public relations they had ever carried out. Its role in enhancing "the prestige of business in general" and in convincing the public of "the worth of the system of free enterprise," the WAC argued, would be equally necessary during peacetime, to ensure public recognition of the social responsibility that business had so magnificently learned to display during the war.[8]

Whatever challenges still faced them in the postwar era, corporate leaders seemed not to dread, or even to expect, a renewal of the most significant charge they had combatted for the previous four decades—that of business "bigness." "With the coming of World War II," one corporate executive later recalled, "the bigness so recently deplored was suddenly perceived as fundamental to the nation's strength." The largest corporations were now, in Richard Eells's phrase, "among the institutional bulwarks of society." Thus, the mantle of "institution," which they had donned with such pretentious yet anxious bluster in the 1920s, now seemed theirs without dispute. "Less than ten years ago," the management theorist Peter Drucker observed in 1946, "it still seemed to be a vital issue of American politics whether to have Big Business or not." But in the wake of World War II it was "nothing but sentimental nostalgia" not to recognize the large corporation as "America's representative social institution."[9]

Did this new outlook mean that the great corporations had solved the problem of "soul"? Had they finally succeeded, during a battle for national survival, in convincing the public of their humanity, their civic responsibility, and their moral legitimacy? Or had they merely achieved the unquestioned status of institutions in the less venerable meaning of that term—simply as entities that had become "material and persistent elements . . . in the culture"? After all, two generations of Americans had come to maturity since these terrifying leviathans of disproportionate power had arisen. Few Americans now had lived in a society in which the names of AT&T, United States Steel, Standard Oil, General Motors, General Electric, Ford, and Armour were not as familiar to them as those of their neighbors down the block. Not just in their functional roles but also through their persistent media presence, those bewilderingly powerful new corporate giants of the 1880–1910 era had become ordinary, ubiquitous components of everyday life.

These questions about corporate soul and the status of corporations as institutions must be conceived differently at this point, because the terms of the debate, and their rhetorical context, had changed. The word "soul" by the mid-1940s had come to seem archaic, both to assailants and to defenders of the giant corporation. Not only was the word used less often, even in the context of religion and individual salvation, but it had also framed the whole issue of the giant corporation's social and moral legitimacy too much as an either/or question. An evangelical summons, in the noble phraseology of a Bruce Barton peroration, had stirred many a corporation to new awareness of the potential power of its image, both external and internal. But the welter of practical public relations activities, particularly within what was now seen as the crucial domain—that of the plant city—suggested a less spiritual, more social, substitute for the quest for a soul. J. Carlisle MacDonald of United States Steel conveyed this new orientation in the title of his recollections as director of public relations for United States Steel, *And Be Neighborly.*

Few metaphors better suited the giant corporation in its mature 1940s bid for

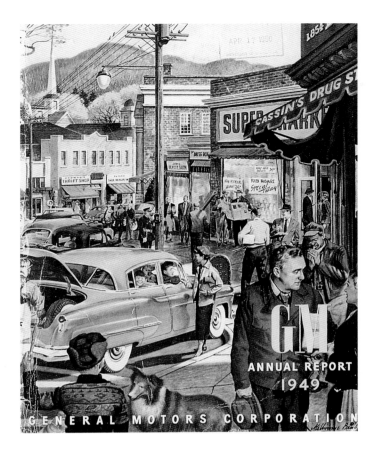

greater legitimacy. Rhetorically, the good neighbor metaphor reduced the giant corporation, as had the famous court opinion of 1886, to the stature of just another person. It placed the company (or at least its local plant) within the ambience of that social formation most redolent of comfortable, friendly, and agreeable relationships among individuals and groups—the local community (Fig. C.2). And while it certainly required the corporation to acknowledge its responsibility for the cooperation and goodwill conventionally associated with the notion of neighborliness, it did not specify the extent of that obligation or define it in legal terms.

Thus, the image of neighborliness seemed a very desirable one to promote on both the local and the national level. In the less innocent world of the postwar era, it humanized the corporation as much as it could expect. Bruce Barton, ever the shrewd analyst of popular imagery, made the point most persuasively. Five years after the war he was trying to sell U.S. Steel on yet another corporate image campaign, urging it to present itself to the public in explicit language as a "good neighbor." Of all the possible compliments that could be offered to a person in American society, he concluded, this was "one of the simplest, and yet one of the most profound."[10]

Of course, the good neighbor metaphor was hardly new. Western Electric had made it a central theme in its early 1920s efforts to persuade Chicagoans of the virtues of its huge Hawthorne plant; AT&T had long stressed the telephone's power to create "neighborhood" relationships over long distances. As many of the largest corporations expanded their geographical reach through acquisitions and new plants, especially after the thrust toward decentralization in the late 1930s, the theme of neighbors seemed ever more appropriate. It cast an aura of familiarity over ever-more-complex economic and spatial relationships, taking advantage of a slackening in public distrust of business bigness to finesse ever-increasing discrepancies in scale.[11]

In the early 1940s AT&T vigorously renewed the campaign it had initiated in the 1930s to demonstrate its role as a local "good neighbor." Within the popular imagery of Main Street it found a congenial atmosphere in which to suggest that the local telephone exchange was "just like the grocery, the drug store or the shoe dealer" and that its employees were "often your friends and neighbors" who "share community life with you." If AT&T stretched the idea of neighborhood in order to cast a comfortable, folksy image, other corporations (such as General Motors, in its ads "Making a Neighborhood Out of a Nation" and "Neighbor and Customer in Every Community") further drained it of meaning in the interests of humanizing the corporation.[12]

American culture has long nurtured a tolerance for, even a partiality toward, the booster, the teller of tall tales, the self-promoter. Individuals and organizations alike are thus entitled to put their best foot forward. But the giant corporation, arising after the mid-nineteenth century, demolished all balance in size and power between the framers of the new corporate images and their audiences. Over time a cadre of those most talented in devising verbal and visual imagery came to dominate such discourse on behalf of the largest, richest organizations. Although individuals, and occasionally those united in voluntary groups, did not lack all capacity to counter or even undercut the flood of imagery from the corporations, the encounters became increasingly disproportionate as the twentieth century wore on. The citizen incessantly addressed as favorite, friend, neighbor, and even family member of the corporation had to develop a prickly, discriminatory wariness in order to resist acquiescence and maintain a realistic sense of conflicting interests. Corporate publicity was hardly the only agent in the distortion of meanings in popular discourse, but its omnipresence and political thrust have ensured corporate imagery a prominent role in public dialogues on family, class, community, and politics.

Earlier aspirations to gain a corporate soul had often been expansive, pious, unfocused, and quixotic. Now, with their public relations responsibilities allocated among a number of specific programs, often on the local level, corporate spokesmen sought, through the metaphor of the good neighbor, less to claim some inner spirit than to make the appropriate outward gesture—a neighborly handshake. That was the perfect gesture for collective "persons" no longer quite so anxious about proving their legitimacy to themselves but still wishing to voice their penchant for civic service and cooperation rather than crass commercialism.

Although its image as good neighbor might seem to preclude the corporation's need for a further search for soul, we must not forget that the mission and meaning of corporate imagery was not limited to its external effects. Corporate executives had long recognized the impact of external communications on internal morale. Even so, in focusing on the effects of corporate imagery on the rank and file of employees, they seem to have remained only vaguely aware of one of the most significant roles of the corporate image—that of fostering morale and shaping company culture on their own, executive, level. One wonders how plausibly they could have acknowledged that godlike role—not of creating a soul but simply of creating themselves in their own image. Although in recent decades business advisors and theorists have underscored the importance of self-conscious organization building and the infusion of a "core ideology" for long-term corporate success, they have given little attention to the use of external public relations to this end.[13]

Executive morale was greatly enhanced by the large corporation's hard-won status as "America's representative social institution," in Peter Drucker's phrase, or as Edward Littlejohn would later term it, "the guiding institution of American life." Certainly this status provided business leaders the secure confidence they needed to exert Cold War leadership on the home front as well as act as the "spokesmen for the American social system" abroad.[14] But did corporate leaders really wish to assume the responsibilities that might accrue to a social institution so "representative" that it seemed to encompass many of the functions previously exercised by such long-established institutions as family, church, and community? Did it really want to become the guardian of the nation's Main Streets and Lambert Hollows?[15]

Corporate America, by the mid-1940s, was certainly addicted to the rhetoric of paternal neighborliness and democratic modes. But the giant corporations were willing to fulfill that rhetoric only through certain limited gestures; they were ill-suited to set social priorities or govern people's lives. Moreover, they lacked any democratically sanctioned responsibility to do so. The corporation had attained a prominent place within the nexus of society's institutions—much as it had envisioned in its quest for a corporate soul—but this status only raised new questions about its future social and political station.

ABBREVIATIONS OF ARCHIVAL SOURCES

AC	Advertising Council Papers, University of Illinois, Champaign-Urbana
AL	Aluminum Company of America (Alcoa) Archives, Pittsburgh
ALD	Alderson Library, University of Virginia, Charlottesville
ATT	AT&T Corporate Archives, Warren, New Jersey
AWP	Arthur W. Page Papers, State Historical Society of Wisconsin, Madison
BB	Bruce Barton Papers, State Historical Society of Wisconsin, Madison
BBDO	BBDO Library and Archives, New York
BFG	B. F. Goodrich Company Papers, University of Akron, Akron, Ohio
BL	Baker Library, Graduate School of Business, Harvard University
BPL	Broadcast Pioneers Library, University of Maryland, College Park
BS	Bethlehem Steel Company Papers, Hagley Museum and Library, Wilmington, Delaware
CFK	Charles F. Kettering Papers, GMI Alumni Collection of Industrial History, GMI Institute, Flint, Michigan
CHS	Chicago Historical Society
CMc	Cyrus McCormick Papers, State Historical Society of Wisconsin, Madison
CP	Century of Progress Papers, University of Illinois, Chicago
CPL	Century of Progress Collection, Chicago Public Library
CSM	Charles Steward Mott Papers, GMI Alumni Collection of Industrial History, GMI Institute, Flint, Michigan
DM	Dennison Manufacturing Company Papers, Baker Library, Graduate School of Business, Harvard University
DP	E. I. Du Pont de Nemours & Company Papers, Hagley Museum and Library, Wilmington, Delaware
DPL	Detroit Public Library

DPP	Du Pont Photographic Collection, Hagley Museum and Library, Wilmington, Delaware
EK	Eastman Kodak Company Archives, Rochester, New York
ELB	Edward L. Bernays Papers, Library of Congress
EPHJ	E. P. H. James Papers, State Historical Society of Wisconsin, Madison
ERS	Edward R. Stettinius Jr. Papers, University of Virginia, Charlottesville
FC	Fairfax Cone Papers, University of Chicago
FL	Firestone Library, Princeton University
FM	Ford Motor Company Papers, Edison Institute, Dearborn, Michigan
FR	Frigidaire Papers, GMI Alumni Collection of Industrial History, GMI Institute, Flint, Michigan
GCC	Gordon C. Cole Collection, National Museum of American History, Smithsonian Institution
GEC	George Eastman Manuscript Collection, International Museum of Photography, George Eastman House, Rochester, New York
GEF	General Electric Company, Public Relations Archives, Corporate Library, Fairfield, Connecticut
GES	General Electric Company Library, Schenectady, New York
GM	General Motors Public Relations Collection, GM Corporate Library, Detroit
GMB	General Motors Collection, Baker Library, Graduate School of Business, Harvard University
GMI	GMI Almuni Collection of Industrial History, GMI Institute, Flint, Michigan
GS	Gerard Swope Files, General Electric Archives, Schenectady, New York
GWP	George W. Perkins Papers, Columbia University
HBSA	Harvard Business School Archives
HC	Hooper Ratings Collection, State Historical Society of Wisconsin, Madison
HCR	Historical Corporate Reports Collection, Baker Library, Graduate School of Business, Harvard University
HHC	Hal Higgins Collection, University of California, Davis
HHP	H. J. Heinz Company, Photographic Collection, Pittsburgh
HJH	H. J. Heinz Company Papers, Edison Institute, Dearborn, Michigan
HJK	Henry J. Kaiser Papers, Bancroft Library, University of California, Berkeley
HML	Hagley Museum and Library, Wilmington, Delaware
IH	International Harvester Company Papers, Navistar Archives, Chicago
ILL	Ivy L. Lee Papers, Princeton University
JDE	J. D. Ellsworth Papers, State Historical Society of Wisconsin, Madison
JMS	John M. Shaw Papers, State Historical Society of Wisconsin, Madison
JR	Julius Rosenwald Papers, Regenstein Library, University of Chicago
JWH	John W. Hill Papers, State Historical Society of Wisconsin, Madison
JWT	J. Walter Thompson Company Papers, John W. Hartman Center for Sales, Advertising, and Marketing History, Duke University
KGF	Kraft General Foods Archives, Morton Grove, Illinois

LKF	Lee K. Frankel Papers, Metropolitan Life Insurance Company Archives, New York
LL	Lenox Lohr Papers, University of Illinois, Chicago
MLIC	Metropolitan Life Insurance Company Archives, New York
NBC	National Broadcast Company Papers, State Historical Society of Wisconsin, Madison
NBG	Norman Bel Geddes Papers, Harry Ransom Humanities Research Center, University of Texas, Austin
NCF	National Civic Federation Papers, New York Public Library
NMc	Nettie McCormick Papers, State Historical Society of Wisconsin, Madison
NWA	N. W. Ayer Company Archives, New York
NWAS	N. W. Ayer Collection, National Museum of American History, Smithsonian Institution
NYPL	New York Public Library
NYWF	New York World's Fair (1939) Papers, New York Public Library
ODY	Owen D. Young Papers, St. Lawrence University, Canton, New York
OHRO	Oral Historical Research Office, Butler Library, Columbia University
OYGE	Owen D. Young Files, General Electric Archives, Schenectady, New York
PCC	Penn Central Collection, Pennsylvania State Historical Society, Harrisburg
PRR	Pennsylvania Railroad Archives, Hagley Museum and Library, Wilmington, Delaware
RF	Rockefeller Family Papers, Rockefeller Archive Center, North Tarrytown, New York
RH	Ralph Hower Papers, Baker Library, Graduate School of Business, Harvard University
RP	Richard Prelinger Archive of Industrial Films, Prelinger Associates, New York
S&C	Swift & Company Archives, Chicago
SQS	E. R. Squibb & Sons Archives, Princeton
TDB	Thomas D'Arcy Brophy Papers, State Historical Society of Wisconsin, Madison
TL	Thomas Lamont Papers, Baker Library, Graduate School of Business, Harvard University
USX	U.S.X. Archives, Pittsburgh
WDT	Walter Dorwin Teague Papers, Geroge Arents Research Library, Syracuse University
WF	World's Fair Collection, Edison Institute, Dearborn, Michigan
WLA	Westinghouse Company Library and Archives, Pittsburgh
WLB	William L. Benton Papers, University of Chicago
WWA	Atterbury Papers, Penn Central Collection, Pennsylvania State Historical Society, Harrisburg
Y&R	Young & Rubicam Archives, New York

Introduction

1. *The Story of the Day's Work,* pamphlet, n.d., Pennsylvania Railroad folder, JWT; *Saturday Evening Post,* 18 June 1927, 180.

2. Pennsylvania Railroad Company, *Leaders of the Largest Fleet of Trains in America,* pamphlet, 1927, box 17, WWA. According to the trade journal *Tide* (2 [Dec. 1928]: 3), the Pennsylvania Railroad "created the . . . typical, small town of Lambert Hollow." Presumably the railroad would have chosen its home state as the site of its ideal village, actual or imagined, but Abraham Howry Espenshade made no mention of Lambert Hollow among the 1,218 "counties, cities, towns, villages, townships, and streams" reviewed in his *Pennsylvania Place Names* (1925; reprint, Detroit, 1969).

3. The giant meatpacking firms Swift & Company and Morris Company used similar village metaphors in their advertising; see *Saturday Evening Post,* 31 Jan. 1925, 31; 3 Mar. 1928, 164. Henry Ford sought to give a somewhat more independent aura to the small towns that housed his "village industry" plants in the 1920s and 1930s (see Chapter 6).

4. *Tide,* 15 July 1942, 56; *GM Folks* 6 (Sept. 1943): 10; General Motors Corporation, press release, 30 July 1943, CFK.

5. N. C. Kingsbury, "Results from American Telephone's National Campaign," *Printers' Ink,* 29 June 1916, 182; *Saturday Evening Post,* 27 Mar. 1926, 46–47; ibid., 23 July 1927, 54–55; ibid., 28 June 1924, 56–57; ibid., 12 July 1924, 88–89; *Literary Digest,* 9 Apr. 1927, 85; *Intelligencer,* 4 Mar. 1922, 15, 26; Armour and Company, "A National Institution," ad proof, 8 Dec. 1927, NWAS. For a more extensive discussion of the implications of becoming an institution, see Chapter 5.

6. Neil J. Mitchell, *The Generous Corporation: A Political Analysis of Economic Power* (New Haven, Conn., 1989), 6–7, 55, 70, 143.

7. James Willard Hurst, *The Legitimacy of the Business Corporation in the Law of the United States, 1780–1970* (Charlottesville, Va., 1970).

8. Norman Cooley Angell, *The Integration of American Society: A Study of Groups and Institutions* (New York, 1941), 212.

9. Robert H. Wiebe, *The Search for Order, 1877–1920* (New York, 1967), 12, 2–4, 12, 44. Particularly perceptive in exploring both geographical and broader meanings of community is Thomas Bender, *Community and Social Change in America* (New Brunswick, N.J., 1978).

10. Mitchell, *Generous Corporation,* 110–11.

11. David E. Nye, *Image Worlds: Corporate Identities at General Electric, 1890–1930* (Cambridge, Mass., 1985), esp. 5, 15–16, 28–29, 95, 133–34, 155–60.

12. Oliver E. Williamson, "The Firm as a Nexus of Treaties: An Introduction," in *The Firm as a Nexus of Treaties,* ed. Masahiko Aoki, Bo Gustafson, and Oliver E. Williamson (London, 1990), 2–4, 11–15.

13. *Printers' Ink,* 24 Apr. 1924, 12.

14. National Electric Light Association, *Proceedings of the 49th National Convention* (New York, 1926), 44.

15. American Telephone and Telegraph Company, proceedings of publicity conference, 1921, pp. 4, 12, box 1310, ATT.

16. On the long-standing close association of the morally charged concept of "community" with the small town in America, see Bender, *Community and Social Change.*

17. Kenneth Lipartito, *The Bell System and Regional Business: The Telephone in the South, 1877–1920* (Baltimore, 1989), 4–5, 209.

Chapter 1

1. Morton J. Horowitz, "Santa Clara Revisited: The Development of Corporate Theory," *West Virginia Law Review* 88 (1985): 181–83, 190, 198, 218–21. On the issue of legal legitimacy, see also Charles W. McCurdy, "The Knight Sugar Decision of 1895 and the Modernization of American Corporation Law, 1869–1903," in *Managing Big Business,* ed. Richard S. Tedlow and Richard R. John Jr. (Boston, 1986), 341, 361, 364–65.

2. Naomi R. Lamoreaux, *The Great Merger Movement in American Business, 1895–1904* (New York, 1985), 1–2.

3. John Kimberly Mumford, "This Land of Opportunity: The Heart of a 'Soulless Corporation,'" *Harper's Weekly,* 11 July 1908, 22–23, and 18 July 1908, 21–22; "Corporations and Souls," *Marion (Ohio) Star,* [1912], clipping, carton 30, PCC; Arundel Cotter, *United States Steel: A Corporation with a Soul* (New York, 1921); "Puts Flesh and Blood into 'Soulless Corporation,'" *Printers' Ink,* 6 Apr. 1922, 121–22; "Refuting the Old Idea of the Soulless Corporations," *Corn Exchange* 12 (Nov. 1926), as cited in W. Atterbury to Charles S. Caldwell, 10 Nov. 1926, carton 16, PCC; Norton E. Long, "Public Relations Policies of the Bell System," *Public Opinion Quarterly* 1 (Oct. 1937): 19.

4. Edward K. Hall, "A Plea for the Man in the Ranks," speech ms., 22 Mar. 1932, p. 22, box 23, ATT.

5. *General Motors World* 2 (Mar. 1923): 8.

6. H. A. Batten, *Public Relations,* pamphlet, 28 Apr. 1937, NWA; Edward K. Hall, *Public Relations,* pamphlet, 14 Dec. 1909, p. 6, BL.

7. Vanderbilt and Morgan are quoted in Matthew Josephson, *The Robber Barons* (New York, 1962), 187, 441; Rockefeller is quoted in Edward Chase Kirkland, *Dream and Thought in the Business Community, 1860–1900* (Ithaca, N.Y., 1956), 2–3. See also John Tebbel, *The Marshall Fields: A Study in Wealth* (New York, 1947), 44, 70–71, 78, 92–93; Ray Eldon Hiebert, *Courtier to the Crowd: The Story of Ivy Lee and the Development of Public Relations* (Ames, Iowa, 1966), 109–113; Richard Tedlow, *Keeping the Corporate Image: Public Relations and Business, 1900–1950* (Greenwich, Conn., 1979), 1–2; John A. Garraty, *Right-Hand Man: The Life of George W. Perkins* (New York, 1960), 91.

8. I use the term "legitimacy" not as an attribute that an entity either possesses or entirely lacks but rather as an unstable, shifting, and contested quality—always susceptible to enhancement or depletion. At issue was the social and moral legitimacy of the large corporation (that of smaller business corporations was hardly ever challenged) in its relation—in size, power, scope of responsibility, and freedom of action—to such other institutions as the family, the community, and the state. The question is the extent of legitimacy that the giant corporation enjoyed *within the nexus of social institutions.*

9. Mansel G. Blackford, *A History of Small Business in America* (New York, 1991), 28; Lamoreaux, *Great Merger Movement,* 159.

10. Susan Porter Benson, *Counter Cultures: Saleswomen, Managers, and Customers in American Department Stores, 1890–1940* (Urbana, Ill., 1986), 31; John Wanamaker Company, *The Golden Book of*

the *Wanamaker Stores* (Philadelphia, 1911), 58, 61, 162; Ralph M. Hower, *History of Macy's of New York, 1858–1919* (Cambridge, Mass., 1943), 155–56. On the struggle of the small urban retailers against the department stores in Chicago and New York in the 1890s, see William Leach, *Land of Desire: Merchants, Power, and the Rise of a New American Culture* (New York, 1993), 27–30; Lloyd Wendt and Herman Kogan, *Give the Lady What She Wants! The Story of Marshall Field and Company* (New York, 1952), 245.

11. Tebbel, *Marshall Fields,* 31–32, 60; John Dennis Jr., "Marshall Field: A Great Mercantile Genius," *Everybody's Magazine* 14 (Mar. 1906): 297. On the early "civic" status of the Field, Leiter & Company Store, see the comments from the *Chicago Tribune* quoted in Wendt and Kogan, *Give the Lady What She Wants!* 167.

12. Wanamaker, *Golden Book,* 63, 90; Leach, *Land of Desire,* 112–14; 118–22. Incursions into other cities were rare, but even when Wanamaker acquired the old A. T. Stewart emporium in New York City in 1896, competition there only increased.

13. Ivy Lee, "Building Prestige for a Store," speech ms., 1925, enclosed in Burnham Carter to William Hotchkin, 13 Feb. 1925, box 27, ILL; *Printers' Ink,* 14 Dec. 1922, 42, 44, 48; *Advertising and Selling,* 5 Mar. 1930, 31; *Printers' Ink,* 14 Dec. 1922, 41–44; Joseph H. Appel, *The Business Biography of John Wanamaker: Founder and Builder* (New York, 1930), 31–38; Wanamaker, *Golden Book,* 73–74, 176, 239–40, 249, 261, 264, 267; Leach, *Land of Desire,* 101, 120–21, 199–201, 209–12; Benson, *Counter Cultures,* 18. "There are few charitable or commercial movements in the Quaker city with which [Wanamaker's] name is not associated," observed the *Ladies' Home Journal* 6 (Aug. 1889): 19.

14. Tebbel, *Marshall Fields,* 21, 33, 63, 144. See also Dennis, "Marshall Field," 299, 302; Wendt and Kogan, *Give the Lady What She Wants!* 181, 185, 221. Dennis (298–99) tellingly links this atmosphere to the store's business practices: "The arrangements for the comfort of the sales-people coupled with the extreme respectability and high standing of the house have enabled it to maintain a lower wage scale than any of its competitors. Young men and women are glad to work for Marshall Field & Co. at less than the usual rate of wages because connection with that house means a better regard by the world, it sounds better, it is something of a distinction, it classes them as the aristocrats of their trade."

15. Tebbel, *Marshall Fields,* 140–43; Benson, *Counter Cultures,* 18–20; *Chicago Tribune,* 27 Sept. 1907, 18. On the aesthetic aura of the store, see the pamphlet by Hamilton Hull, *Marshall Field & Company: The World's Greatest Merchandisers* (Chicago, 1907), 2–3, 23–24, 35.

16. Wanamaker, *Golden Book,* 74, 87, 247–49, 261, 264; Leach, *Land of Desire,* 136–37.

17. Wanamaker, *Golden Book,* 88, 102–3, 229, 232–33; Appel, *Business Biography,* 108–14, 431. By 1908, Wanamaker's boasted a company glee club, a "Girls' Military Band," a concert series, and summer outings for women sales clerks.

18. Benson, *Counter Cultures,* 142, 145–46; Hower, *History of Macy's,* 305; Alfred Lief, *Family Business,* vol. 1, *A Century in the Life and Times of Strawbridge and Clothier, 1868–1968* (New York, 1968), 104, 125–26; Morrell Heald, *The Social Responsibilities of American Business: Company and Community, 1900–1960* (Cleveland, 1970), 7; Kim McQuaid, *A Response to Industrialism: Liberal Businessmen and the Evolving Spectrum of Capitalist Reform, 1886–1960* (New York, 1986), 55, 61–62; *National Civic Federation Review* 3 (July 1909): 20; Institute of Social Service, "Association Cottage," July 17, 1904, box 41, CMc.

19. Hower, *History of Macy's,* 121; Tebbel, *Marshall Fields,* 58, 77–78; Thomas W. Goodspeed, "Marshall Field," *University Record* 8 (Jan. 1922): 4–44, 47, 49.

20. For an excellent discussion of the gender issues in relations between managers, saleswomen, and customers, see Benson, *Counter Cultures.* On the psychological effects of such service roles, especially as assigned to women, see Arlie Russell Hochschild, *The Managed Heart: Commercialization of Human Feeling* (Berkeley, 1983).

21. Charles Dellheim, "The Creation of a Company Culture: Cadburys, 1861–1931," *American Historical Review* 92 (Feb. 1987): 14–15, 19, 30; Michael B. Miller, *The Bon Marché: Bourgeois Culture and the Department Store* (Princeton, 1981), 9, 11, 237–38.

22. Dellheim, "Creation," 35; Miller, *Bon Marché,* 9, 14, 116, 126, 142, 221, 228, 237–38.

23. On American attention to such English models as Cadburys, see Unsigned [Gertrude Beeks] to J. C. Hale, 30 Apr. 1913, box 80, NCF; *National Civic Federation Review* 2 (June 1905): 12–13. The best account of Pullman, Illinois, is Stanley Buder, *Pullman: An Experiment in Industrial Order*

and Community Planning: 1880–1930 (New York, 1967). See also Stuart D. Brandes, *American Welfare Capitalism, 1880–1940* (Chicago, 1976), 16–20.

24. Marlene Hunt Rikard, "An Experiment in Welfare Capitalism: The Health Care Services of the Tennessee Coal, Iron, and Railroad Company" (Ph.D. diss., University of Alabama, 1983), 2–3, 17, 21, 28, 30–32, 37, 77, 80. On U.S. Steel's early welfare programs at its Duquesne plant, see James Rose, "The United States Steel Duquesne Works, 1886–1941: The Rise of Steel Unionism" (Ph.D. diss., University of California, Davis, 1997), 15–19.

25. H. Lee Scamehorn, *Pioneer Steelmaker in the West: The Colorado Fuel and Iron Company, 1872– 1903* (Boulder, Colo., 1976), 139–43, 149; Brandes, *American Welfare Capitalism,* 55.

26. C. R. Carter, "How Young Rockefeller Is Making American Citizens by Trust Methods," *Chicago Sunday Tribune Workers' Magazine,* 27 November 1904, 3; Scamehorn, *Pioneer Steelmaker,* 153.

27. Scamehorn, *Pioneer Steelmaker,* 150–55; Carter, "Young Rockefeller," 3; R. W. Corwin, "A Vast Field of Endeavor," *National Civic Federation Review,* 1 Feb. 1905.

28. Carter, "Young Rockefeller," 3.

29. Scamehorn, *Pioneer Steelmaker,* 172–73; Alan R. Raucher, *Public Relations and Business, 1900– 1929* (Baltimore, 1968), 24–31; Hiebert, *Courtier,* 97–109, 116–17.

30. John G. Wood to G. F. Steele, 6 Mar. 1905, Welfare file, 1905–6, box 42, CMc.

31. Samuel Crowther, *John H. Patterson: Pioneer in Industrial Welfare* (Garden City, N.Y., 1923), 206; Lena Harvey Tracy, *How My Heart Sang: The Story of Pioneer Industrial Welfare Work* (New York, 1950), 154; "Report," enclosed in Gertrude Beeks to Stanley McCormick, 3 Nov. 1902, p. 4, NMc. Susan Porter Benson (*Counter Cultures,* 146) reports the same concern of department store entrepreneurs to stress the self-interest factor in welfare work: "Like workers in other industries," she observes, "retail workers resented welfare work when it was too obviously tinted with noblesse oblige or paternalism. Canny observers realized that the best way to circumvent employee resentment was to acknowledge frankly the employer's self-interest in the welfare work."

32. *NCR,* 15 July 1899, 347–48.

33. National Cash Register Company, *The Human Side of Industry,* pamphlet, n.d., BL; "National Cash Register Company Welfare Work: Abstract of Memorandum by Gen. Thomas," 19 Jan. 1905, box 80, NCF.

34. National Cash Register Company, "Factory Lecture," n.d., pp. 12, 14, 26–27, and passim, box 80, NCF; *NCR* 18 (May 1905): 106, 131–32; *Printers' Ink,* 28 Sept. 1911, 32; Tracy, *How My Heart Sang,* 108; Issac F. Marcosson, *Wherever Men Trade: The Romance of the Cash Register* (New York, 1948), 196–97; Paul de Kruif, "Boss Kettering," *Saturday Evening Post,* 12 Aug. 1933, 49.

35. Daniel T. Rodgers, *The Work Ethic in Industrial America, 1850–1920* (Chicago, 1978), 87; *NCR* 18 (May 1905): 137; Frank Crane, *Business and Kingdom Come* (Chicago, 1912), 14, 79.

36. Henry Dennison, "Notes 1900, Dayton, Ohio, on Ideas from NCR to Apply to Our Factory," 1900–1915 folder, case 1, DM; Gertrude Beeks, "Notes on Investigation Trip, 1901" and "Notes of Trip," enclosed in Beeks to McCormick, 3 Nov. 1902, file 3B, box 27, NMc; Henry Bruere, "Report of National Cash Register Company, Dayton, Ohio, July 4, 1903," box 80, NCF; *Cassier's Magazine* 28 (July 1905): 219–22.

37. National Cash Register Company, *The Beginning of a New Era in Manufacturing,* pamphlet, 1899, n.p.; idem, *Art, Nature, and the Factory,* pamphlet, 1904, n.p.; idem, *Human Side,* n.p.; *Cassier's Magazine* 28 (Sept. 1905): 340–42; Stanley C. Allyn, *My Half Century with NCR* (New York, 1967), 34, 146; Marcosson, *Wherever Men Trade,* 227–29, 232–33, 246; *NCR,* 1 July 1899, 334–35; ibid., 15 July 1899, 341, 352; ibid. 18 (June 1905): 143.

38. Marcosson, *Wherever Men Trade,* 30; de Kruif, "Boss Kettering," 45; Roy W. Johnson and Russell W. Lynch, *The Sales Strategy of John H. Patterson* (New York, 1932), 15.

39. Allyn, *Half Century,* 21, 40, 146; Marcosson, *Wherever Men Trade,* 28, 30; Crowther, *Patterson,* 229, 236.

40. De Kruif, "Boss Kettering," 49–50, 58; Allyn, *Half Century,* 20–21; Johnson and Lynch, *Sales Strategy,* 34, 300; Crowther, *Patterson,* 220–21.

41.   Marcosson, *Wherever Men Trade,* 56; Tracy, *How My Heart Sang,* 97–117. Patterson was known, said one of his successors as company president, "to discharge an employee merely through dislike of the way the man combed his hair"; Allyn, *Half Century,* 40.

42.   Crowther, *Patterson,* 190, 196–98; Tracy, *How My Heart Sang,* 110; Allyn, *Half Century,* 33.

43.   Terence E. Deal and Allen A. Kennedy, *Corporate Cultures: The Rites and Rituals of Corporate Life* (Reading, Mass., 1982), 4. For details on the boys' gardens, see Tracy, *How My Heart Sang,* 99–101, 108–9; National Cash Register Company, *Art, Nature, and the Factory; Cassier's Magazine* 28 (Sept. 1905): 341–42; Marcosson, *Wherever Men Trade,* 47–48, 226–27; Crowther, *Patterson,* 200; Crane, *Business and Kingdom,* 24–26.

44.   Crowther, *Patterson,* 5–6; Marcosson, *Wherever Men Trade,* 29, 40; H. P. Judson to the Members of the Faculties, 19 Oct. 1905, folder on Welfare Reports, 1905–6, box 42, CMc; Johnson and Lynch, *Sales Strategy,* 116–17; Beeks, "Notes on Investigation Trip, 1901," 26.

45.   Beeks, "Notes on Investigation Trip, 1901," 1, 9, 11–12, 25.

46.   Beeks, "Notes on Investigation Trip, 1901," 9, 25–30; "Interview with Miss Ella M. Hass," 3 Aug. 1901, box 80, NCF; Unsigned to Beeks, 29 Apr. 1904, box 80, NCF. One observer, referring to the "ridicule" heaped upon welfare work, proposed that the central rule had to be an absence of philanthropy. In Patterson's defense, he noted that the president of the NCR had always done such work as "pure business" and had told his employees from the outset that he expected "re-payment in your greater efficiency." A. A. Thomas to Beeks, 7 Dec. 1908, box 80, NCF.

47.   Untitled manuscript, p. 2, Recollections folder, case 1, DM; McQuaid, *Response,* 80.

48.   Marcosson, *Wherever Men Trade,* 127–29; Crowther, *Patterson,* 231–32; Thomas J. Watson Jr. and Peter Petre, *Father, Son & Co.: My Life at IBM and Beyond* (New York, 1990), 10–13.

49.   Garraty, *Right-Hand Man,* 91–92, 95–97, 100; Robert Ozanne, *A Century of Labor-Management Relations at McCormick and International Harvester* (Madison, Wisc., 1967), xv–xvi.

50.   Brandes, *American Welfare Capitalism,* 28–29, 113–14; Charles S. Close, *Welfare Work in the Steel Industry,* pamphlet, 1920, BL.

51.   Garraty, *Right-Hand Man,* 87, 91–92, 95, 100; Ozanne, *Century,* 63; George W. Perkins to Theodore Roosevelt, 31 Jan. 1902, box 5, GWP. See also Perkins to J. P. Morgan, 26 June 1902, box 5, GWP.

52.   Perkins to Morgan, 31 Dec. 1902, letterbook 6, box 5, p. 290, GWP. Also David Grotta to Perkins, 1 Jan. 1903; H. H. Porter to Perkins, 2 Jan. 1903; W. L. Saunders to Perkins, 3 Jan. 1903; Samuel Untermyer to Perkins, 5 Jan. 1903; P. S. Grosscup to Perkins, 9 Jan. 1903; William Barrett Ridgely to Perkins, 9 Jan. 1903: all box 27, GWP.

53.   Brandes, *American Welfare Capitalism,* 90; Ozanne, *Century,* 63, 71–74, 80, 82; Heald, *Social Responsibilities,* 32–33; Perkins to Stuyvesant Fish, 3 Jan. 1903, letterbook 6, box 3, GWP.

54.   "Transcript of a Meeting with Mr. P," 17 July 1902, file 3B, box 30, NMc; Helen M. Kramer, "Harvesters and High Finance: Formation of the International Harvester Company," *Business History Review* 38 (autumn 1964): 292; Brandes, *American Welfare Capitalism,* 90; Garraty, *Right-Hand Man,* 142, 219.

55.   Brandes, *American Welfare Capitalism,* 111–12.

56.   Ozanne, *Century,* 29, 31–32. See also Nikki Mandell, "'A Human Contact Mechanism': The Corporate Welfare System and the Gendering of Labor Management, 1890–1930" (Ph.D. diss., University of California, Davis, 1997), 79–80.

57.   Ozanne, *Century,* 31–32; Sanford M. Jacoby, *Employing Bureaucracy: Managers, Unions, and the Transformation of Work in American Industry, 1900–1945* (New York, 1985), 59.

58.   Beeks, "Notes on Investigation Trip, 1901"; idem, "Report on Entertainment," file 3B, box 27, NMc; Beeks to Stanley McCormick, 2 Dec. 1902, file 3B, box 30, NMc; Gertrude Beeks, "Proposed Budget, Sociological Department, One Year," enclosed in Beeks to John G. Wood, 2 Dec. 1902, file 3B, box 30, NMc; idem, "Report on First Annual Outing," [1901], box 39, CMc; John R. Commons, "Welfare Work in a Great Industrial Plant," *American Monthly Review of Reviews* 28 (July 1903): 79–81; Ozanne, *Century,* 32–35, 50–54.

59.   S. M. Darling to C. S. Conner, 11, 18 July 1904, box 40, CMc; Darling to Maud Kendall,

22 Apr. 1904, box 40, CMc; Darling to Cyrus H. McCormick, 22 Oct. 1903, Welfare folder, 1903, box 39, CMc; Ozanne, *Century,* 164–65. The quote is from Darling to McCormick, 31 Oct. 1903, box 39, NMc.

60.   Ozanne, *Century,* 36–37, 82–83, 86–88; Stella Virginia Roderick, *Nettie Fowler McCormick* (Rindge, N.H., 1956), 189–90, 193–94, 200; Henry Bruere to John G. Wood, 27 Jan. 1904, box 41, CMc.

61.   Owen W. Jones, "Factory Employes Welfare," [1904], box 42, CMc; Beeks to McCormick, 13 Apr. 1907, box 40, CMc; M. L. Goss to B. A. Kennedy, 13 May 1907, box 40, CMc; Bruce Barton, "The Welfare of the Laborer," *Home Herald* 14 (Apr. 1909): 5; *Harper's Weekly,* 18 July 1908, 22.

62.   Brandes, *American Welfare Capitalism,* 32. On the absence of strikes as proof of the effectiveness of a corporate "social secretary," see also *Chicago Tribune,* 24 Sept. 1902, 5.

63.   *Chicago Tribune,* 24 Sept. 1902, 1; ibid., 25 Sept. 1902, 12; *Chicago Evening Post,* 24 Sept. 1902, clipping, box 42, CMc.

64.   Ozanne, *Century,* 86; George W. Perkins to Cardinal Gibbons, 7 Jan. 1907, box 27, GWP; *National Civic Federation Review,* 1 Mar. 1910, 20; Beeks to G. F. Steele, 21 Feb. 1905, box 42, CMc.

65.   *Harper's Weekly,* 11 July 1908, 23. Although Bruce Barton depicted Cyrus McCormick Jr. as kindly and sympathetic, he managed to shield International Harvester against suspicions of non-businesslike, philanthropic indulgence. The company, he observed, was acting "in the right way" by promoting self-help rather than dependence; it thus managed to "keep the corporation heart warm and yet restrain its beatings until they are tuned more or less closely to the rise and fall in the interest rate." Barton, "Welfare of the Laborer," 5.

66.   International Harvester's emphasis on Beeks's success with mirrors for female workers reinforced the notion that work amenities were particularly feminine and perhaps even frivolous.

67.   Charles M. Ripley, *Life in a Large Manufacturing Plant* (Schenectady, N.Y., 1919), 7.

68.   Swift & Company, *Year Book, 1916* (Chicago, 1916), 26–27; Clarence J. Hicks, *My Life in Industrial Relations: Fifty Years in the Growth of a Profession* (New York, 1941), 43; Conferences on Welfare Work at Chicago Commons, "Minutes of Second Meeting, Apr. 10, 1906," box 87, NCF; Kathleen McCarthy, *Noblesse Oblige: Charity and Philanthropy in Chicago, 1849–1929* (Chicago, 1982) 18, 72. Like other employers, International Harvester regularly confronted the likelihood that, if its welfare programs seemed too costly, its employees would resent being "bought off" with trivial favors instead of having those funds added to their wages. While boasting, on the one hand, of the hundreds of thousands of dollars the company devoted to welfare programs each year, its executives also surveyed the NCR and other firms as to what percentage of their payrolls they had dared to expend on welfare; those estimates ranged from 1 to 3 percent. The labor expert John R. Commons, in a favorable review of International Harvester welfare work in 1903, came to the company's rescue with the assurance that "the sums expended in betterment work are so slight compared with the sums at stake in increased wages or shorter hours that their redistribution would raise wages almost inappreciably." John H. Wood to Harold F. McCormick, 18 Sept. 1905, box 42, CMc; "Memo—Welfare Work," [20 Sept. 1905], box 42, CMc; Commons, "Welfare Work," 80; Beeks, "Notes on Investigation Trip, 1901," 29.

69.   E. A. S. Clarke to Harold McCormick, 6 Apr. 1904, box 39, CMc; G. F. Steele to McCormick, 17 Jan. 1907, box 42, CMc.

70.   Welfare workers were often known as "social secretaries," "house mothers," and "company matrons." See Mandell, "'A Human Control Mechanism'"; Angel Kwolek-Folland, "Gender, Self, and Work in the Life Insurance Industry, 1880–1930," in *Work Engendered: Toward a New History of American Labor,* ed. Ava Baron (Ithaca, N.Y., 1991), 173. In 1908 the National Civic Federation supplemented its Welfare Department, whose membership was restricted to employers, with a "Woman's Department." This new group would draw on "woman's intuition" and exert the special influence of "those who are normally and naturally interested" in welfare issues. *National Civic Federation Review* 3 (Sept. 1908): 12, 17, 20–23; (Mar. 1909): 22–23; (July 1909): 23.

71.   *Harvester World* 5 (Sept. 1914): 30.

72.   *New York Times,* 22 Aug. 1912, 6. On Perkins's aspirations for a "good trust" image for Harvester and United States Steel, see Daniel Nelson, *Managers and Workers: Origins of the Twentieth-*

Century Factory System in the United States, 1880–1920, 2d ed. (Madison, Wisc., 1995), 114, 116; Heald, *Social Responsibilities,* 32; Garraty, *Right-Hand Man,* 277–78.

73. Ozanne, *Century,* 49–50, 57, 246, 252.

74. Daniel J. Boorstin, "A. Montgomery Ward's Mail-Order Business," *Chicago History* 2 (spring–summer 1973): 148–49; *System* 11 (Apr. 1907): 340–41; Philip J. Kelly, *The Making of a Salesman* (New York, 1965), 33–34; Cecil C. Hoge Sr., *The First Hundred Years Are the Toughest* (Berkeley, 1988), 21, 35; Benson, *Counter Cultures,* 18, 103. John Wanamaker, whose ads addressed customers in a personal tone, with his signature below, also prided himself on sending personal handwritten replies to their letters; Appel, *Business Biography,* 67, 220–24, 296, 303–4.

75. *Printers' Ink Monthly* 2 (Jan. 1921): 25, 99–100.

76. David L. Lewis, *The Public Image of Henry Ford: An American Folk Hero and His Company* (Detroit, 1976), 15–24, 211–34, and passim.

77. Gregory W. Bush, *Lord of Attention: Gerald Stanley Lee and the Crowd Metaphor in Industrializing America* (Amherst, Mass., 1991), 101; Gerald Stanley Lee, "Advertising Goodness," *Everybody's Magazine* 28 (Feb. 1913): 149; *Printers' Ink,* 20 Mar. 1913, 3–4, 6; ibid., 28 June 1917, 82, 84; ibid., 13 Dec. 1923, 58, 60; *Literary Digest,* 9 Sept. 1922, 68; Kenneth Goode and M. Zenn Kaufman, *Showmanship in Business* (New York, 1936), 83.

78. Charles Francis McGovern, "Sold American: Inventing the Consumer, 1890–1940" (Ph.D. diss., Harvard University, 1993), 97; Susan Strasser, *Satisfaction Guaranteed: The Making of the American Mass Market* (New York, 1989), 218; *Printers' Ink,* 20 Mar. 1913, 4; Elinor Selame and Joe Selame, *The Company Image: Building Your Identity and Influence in the Marketplace* (New York, 1988), 56; *Judicious Advertising* 1 (Sept. 1903): 56; ibid. 2 (Aug. 1904): inside front cover; *Printers' Ink,* 20 Mar. 1913, 4, 6. On the early effectiveness of photos of the manufacturer, see also Ralph F. Bogardus, "Tea Wars: Advertising Photography and Ideology in the *Ladies' Home Journal* in the 1890s," *Prospects* 16 (1991): 302.

79. Sarah Stage, *Female Complaints: Lydia Pinkham and the Business of Women's Medicine* (New York, 1979), 9, 40–42, 141, 145; Robert Jay, *The Trade Card in Nineteenth-Century America* (Columbia, Mo., 1987), 87.

80. Hopkins is quoted in James Sloan Allen, *The Romance of Commerce and Culture: Capitalism, Modernism, and the Chicago-Aspen Crusade for Cultural Reform* (Chicago, 1983), 14–15. On this point, see the discussion of Bethlehem Steel and Armour and Company in Chapter 3.

81. *System* 15 (Jan. 1909): 79–81; ibid. 23 (Mar. 1913): 237; ibid. 28 (Sept. 1915): 258; *Printers' Ink,* 29 June 1916, 125; Wanamaker, *Golden Book,* 213. In a similar manner, John Dennis Jr. ("Marshall Field," 299) described the Marshall Field store as inseparable from the personality of Field himself: "The very soul and inspiration of it, the life and engine of its being, was the man that crafted it as surely as if with his own hands he had carved all, the man in whose dreams all had birth, of whose character all is but a reflection."

82. *Printers' Ink,* 8 July 1915, 79.

83. *Printers' Ink,* 25 Sept. 1907, 4–6; Benson, *Counter Cultures,* 81; Stephen Potter, *The Magic Number: The Story of "57"* (London, 1957), 61, 84; Robert C. Alberts, *The Good Provider: H. J. Heinz and His 57 Varieties* (Boston, 1973), 122–23, 133, 151. On the development of the pickle pin into one of the earliest spectacular electrical signs in New York City, see David E. Nye, *American Technological Sublime* (Cambridge, Mass., 1994), 188.

84. Helena E. Wright, "Selling an Image: Views of Lowell, 1825–1876," in *The Popular Perception of Industrial History: Essays from the Lowell Conference on Industrial History, 1985,* ed. Robert Weible and Francis R. Walsh (Lanham, Md., 1989), 142, 144, 146, 152, 156.

85. Jay, *Trade Card,* 19, 79–80; *American Heritage* 18 (Feb. 1967): 52–53; Strasser, *Satisfaction Guaranteed,* 100–101. For other examples of trade cards, see *Harper's Bazar,* 11 Dec. 1897, 1045; *Argosy* 24 (May 1897): 3 (ad section); *Western Electric News* 1 (May 1912): cover.

86. *Printers' Ink Monthly* 1 (Feb. 1920): 66. See also *System* 24 (July 1913): 56; Pamela Walker Lurito, "Advertising's Smoky Past: Themes of Progress in Nineteenth-Century American Advertisements," in Weible and Walsh, eds., *Popular Perception of Industrial History,* 184.

87.   Roy S. Durstine, *This Advertising Business* (New York, 1928), 99. See also Helen Woodward, *Through Many Windows* (New York, 1926), 298–99; Charlie Brower, *Me and Other Advertising Geniuses* (Garden City, N.Y., 1974), 169.

88.   *Printers' Ink,* 15 Sept. 1910, 30; *Printers' Ink Monthly* 1 (Feb. 1920), 63–65, 351; *System* 24 (Nov. 1913): 559.

89.   *System* 24 (Nov. 1913): 558–59; *Printers' Ink Monthly* 2 (May, 1921): 81; Lurito, "Advertising's Smoky Past," 184–85; Jay, *Trade Card,* 19, 79–80; Frank Fox, "Advertisements as Documents in Social and Cultural History" (M.A. thesis, University of Utah, 1969), 175. See, for example, the ads in *U.S. Steel News* 1 (Oct. 1936): inside front cover and p. 29; trade cards reproduced in *American Heritage* 18 (Feb. 1967): 52–53.

90.   John R. Stilgoe, *Metropolitan Corridor: Railroads and the American Scene* (New Haven, 1983), 85, 87. Presidential candidates William McKinley and Theodore Roosevelt had put black smoke imagery to effective use in the campaigns of 1896 and 1904, associating their party and platforms with the coming of prosperity in the wake of the depression of the mid-1890s; see American Heritage, ed., *The American Heritage Pictorial History of the Presidents of the United States* (New York, 1968), 2:605; Irwin Shapiro, ed., *The Golden Book of America: Stories from Our Country's Past* (New York, 1957), 147.

91.   Hall, "Public Relations," 6.

92.   Jay, *Trade Card,* 79; *Saturday Evening Post,* 31 Oct. 1908, 28–29; ibid., 3 Apr. 1915, 75; ibid., 15 May 1915, 63; *Ladies' Home Journal* 36 (July 1919): 60; ibid. (Sept. 1919): 101; *American Heritage* 18 (Feb. 1967): 52–53; *Advertising and Selling* 33 (Nov. 1923): 10; *National Geographic* 28 (Nov. 1915): n.p.

93.   *Literary Digest,* 16 Oct. 1920, 45; ibid., 29 May 1926, 55; *Nation's Business* 12 (Apr. 1924): 85; *Saturday Evening Post,* 19 July 1924, 103; Armour and Company, "Meat Selection . . . a Souvenir of Your Visit to the Armour Building, 'A Century of Progress,'" 1934, n.p., CHS; *Power Notes,* July 1920, n.p., clipping, box 34, GEC. For a discussion of the use of such narratives by management, see Ian I. Mitroff and Ralph H. Kilmann, "On Organization Stories: An Approach to Design and Analysis of Organizations through Myths and Stories," in *The Management of Organization Design: Strategies and Implementation,* ed. Ralph H. Kilmann et al. (New York, 1976), 190.

94.   *Advertising and Selling* 32 (Apr. 1922): 6; *Printers' Ink,* 31 Jan. 1924, 61–62; Postum Company, *A Door Unbolted,* pamphlet, 1906, p. 3, KGF; *Judicious Advertising* 2 (Nov. 1903): 65; *System* 27 (March 1915): 303–5; ibid. (May 1915): 490–91; ibid. (Aug. 1915): 154–56.

95.   Alberts, *Good Provider,* 153–56; *Pittsburgh Telegraph,* 31 Mar. 1904, clipping, box 50, HJH; "The Home of the 57," [ca. 1910], HHP; *Ladies' Home Journal* 39 (May 1922): 127. The house is now part of Greenfield Village, Dearborn, Michigan.

96.   Nelson, *Managers and Workers,* 14; Wright, "Selling an Image."

97.   Procter & Gamble, *The Story of a Great Industry,* pamphlet, n.d., p. 6, BL; Alfred Lief, *"It Floats": The Story of Procter & Gamble* (New York, 1958), 64–67; idem, *The Moon and the Stars: The Story of Procter & Gamble and Its People* (Cincinnati, 1963), 13; Tracy, *How My Heart Sang,* 142; James A. Cox, *A Century of Light* (New York, 1979), 46, 207, 210; Leroy Fairman, *The Growth of a Great Industry,* pamphlet, [1910], pp. 30–32, HHP; *American Magazine* 86 (July 1918): 67; Henry Dennison, "Notes on Ideas from NCR," [1900], 1900–1915 folder, case 1, DM; Douglas Collins, *The Story of Kodak* (New York, 1990): 107–8; Eastman Kodak Company, press release, 11 Oct. 1933, EK; *New York Herald,* 20 Nov. 1914, clipping, scrapbook 2, GEC; *American Photographer and Photography,* 31 Jan. 1923, 91, clipping, GEC; *Hoboken Observer,* 3 Dec. 1920, clipping, GEC; Elizabeth Ann Lewis, "A Lesson in Industrial Geography: A Visit to Kodak Park," [1922], scrapbook 3, GEC.

98.   Reyner Banham, *Theory and Design in the First Machine Age* (New York, 1967), 83; Alan Windsor, *Peter Behrens: Architect and Designer* (London, 1981), 91; Grant Hildebrand, *Designing for Industry: The Architecture of Albert Kahn* (Cambridge, Mass., 1974), 62–66, 213, 220, 222.

99.   William R. Taylor, *In Pursuit of Gotham: Culture and Commerce in New York* (New York, 1992), 52, 58–59; Gail Fenske and Deryck Holdsworth, "Corporate Identity and the New York Office Building," in *The Landscape of Modernity: Essays on New York City, 1900–1940,* ed. David Ward and Olivier Zunz (New York, 1992), 142.

100. Kenneth Turney Gibbs, *Business Architectural Imagery in America: 1870–1920* (Ann Arbor, 1984), 24–28, 90; Arnold L. Lehman, "The New York Skyscraper: A History of Its Development, 1870–

1939" (Ph.D. diss., Yale University, 1974), 33–36; Thomas A. P. van Leeuwen, *The Skyward Trend of Thought: The Metaphysics of the American Skyscraper* (Cambridge, Mass., 1988), 7, 71. As van Leeuwen points out, many deplored this "dwarfing" of a spire that had been the pride of the city. Henry James, in *The American Scene*, laments seeing Trinity's steeple reduced to "abject, helpless humility" (quoted in van Leeuwen, *Skyward Trend*, 7).

101. The *Tribune* made additions to its building in 1883, and the *Herald* and *Times* erected new and taller skyscrapers in 1886 and 1888. In 1890, Joseph Pulitzer outdid the competition with his 309-foot *New York World* building.

102. S. Parkes Cadman, "Foreword," in Edwin C. Cochran, *The Cathedral of Commerce: The Highest Building in the World* (New York, 1916), n.p. David Nye (*American Technological Sublime*, 180) emphasizes the exquisite illumination of such skyscrapers as the Woolworth building in explaining their "sublime" qualities. See also Montgomery Schuyler, *American Architecture and Other Writings*, ed. William H. Jordy and Ralph Coe (Cambridge, Mass., 1961), 2:425n; John K. Winkler, *Five and Ten: The Fabulous Life of F. W. Woolworth* (New York, 1940), 186, 193, 195; Lehman, "New York Skyscraper," 92–95.

103. Mona Domosh, "The Symbolism of the Skyscraper: Case Studies of New York's First Tall Buildings," *Journal of Urban History* 14 (May 1988): 329–33; van Leeuwen, *Skyward Trend*, 103.

104. Gibbs, *Business Architectural Imagery*, 26–28, 37–39, 90; *Harper's Weekly*, 19 Dec. 1896, 1256.

105. Gibbs, *Business Architectural Imagery*, 37, 39, 93; Domosh, "Symbolism," 337, 339.

106. "Advertising Value of a Tall Tower," *Printers' Ink*, 29 Apr. 1908, 12; *Metropolitan* 26 (historical number, 1912): n.p.; Domosh, "Symbolism," 337, 339. See also Gibbs, *Business Architectural Imagery*, 138.

107. Gibbs, *Business Architectural Imagery*, 104, 138; Morton Keller, *The Life Insurance Enterprise, 1885–1910: A Study in the Limits of Corporate Power* (Cambridge, Mass., 1963), 26–30; Michele H. Bogart, *Public Sculpture and the Civic Ideal in New York City, 1890–1930* (Chicago, 1989), 307.

108. *Saturday Evening Post*, 14 Oct. 1922, 38; Tebbel, *Marshall Fields*, 150–51; Wendt and Kogan, *Give the Lady What She Wants!* 263, 271, 273; S. R. Ditchett, *Marshall Field and Company: The Life Story of a Great Concern* (New York, 1922), 59; Wanamaker, *Golden Book*, 103; Appel, *Business Biography*, 417.

109. Quoted in Gibbs, *Business Architectural Imagery*, 102, 104. See also Keller, *Life Insurance*, 39.

110. Lee, "Advertising Goodness," 158. For a perceptive account of the sources of Gerald Stanley Lee's exaltation of business and his search for a higher moral authority to inspire and discipline "the crowd," see Bush, *Lord of Attention*. Metropolitan Life made ample use of the religious implications of the tower, observing that it pointed to heaven, that its tower chimes were received as a "blessing" by the working men of the city, and that a scale model of the building and tower had inspired a sermon on "The Greatest Clock in the World." See *Intelligencer* (New England Territory), 18 Nov. 1911, 5; Haley Fiske, "Address, 1910–1911 Annual Banquet," in Metropolitan Life Insurance Company, *Addresses Delivered at the Triennial Convention and Managers' Annual Banquet of the Metropolitan Life Insurance Company* (New York, 1923), 1:25; W. O. Washburn to Lee K. Frankel, 16 Oct. 1911, LKF.

111. Louis J. Horowitz and Boyden Sparks, *The Towers of New York: The Memoirs of a Master Builder* (New York, 1937), 109; Nye, *American Technological Sublime*, 93–94, 100. Mona Domosh ("Symbolism," 333) suggests another aspect of the quest for legitimacy through skyscraper architecture, noting that Joseph Pulitzer and others wished to enhance themselves and their businesses in the eyes of the cultural elite by seeking (without conclusive success) to "impress . . . the arbiters of good taste."

112. Taylor, *Gotham*, 47–48; the phrase "super billboard" is taken from Earl Schultz and Walter Simmons, *Offices in the Sky* (Indianapolis, 1959), 63–66. See also Fenske and Holdsworth, "Corporate Identity," 146, 154; Hugh McAtamney & Company, *The Master Builders: A Record of the Construction of the World's Highest Commercial Structure* (New York, 1913), 26, 36; Montgomery Schuyler, "The Towers of Manhattan and Notes on the Woolworth Building," *Architectural Record* 33 (Feb. 1913): 104, 108; Gibbs, *Business Architectural Imagery*, 143–46.

113. Daniel Bluestone, *Constructing Chicago* (New Haven, 1991), 5, 128, 143–44, 150; Gibbs, *Business Architectural Imagery*, 15, 39, 67, 133; David Milne, "Architecture, Politics, and the Public Realm," *Canadian Journal of Political and Social Theory* 5 (winter–spring 1981): 132–34.

114. Winkler, *Five and Ten,* 66. On the anthropomorphic qualities and egoistic expressions of self-made manliness in the skyscraper, see van Leeuwen, *Skyward Trend,* 62, 64–65, 67, 69.

115. Lamoreaux, *Great Merger Movement,* 159, 172, 190.

116. Hiebert, *Courtier,* 40–41, 47; Raucher, *Public Relations,* 20–21; *Printers' Ink,* 27 June 1906, 3–4.

117. Hiebert, *Courtier,* 48–49; Raucher, *Public Relations,* 19–20; Ivy L. Lee, "An Open and Above-Board 'Trust,'" *Moody's Magazine* 4 (July 1907): 158–64. On George Parker's background in politics and public relations, see Scott M. Cutlip, *Public Relations History: From the Seventeenth to the Twentieth Century— The Antecedents* (Hillsdale, N.J., 1995), 212–14.

118. No single year, perhaps no single decade, can be said to mark definitively the rise of organized corporate public relations. As early as the 1880s, as Alan Raucher points out, George Westinghouse had hired a press agent to counter scare-inducing attacks on his system of alternating current. On some of the early ventures in corporate public relations, see Scott M. Cutlip, *The Unseen Power: Public Relations—A History* (Hillsdale, N.J., 1994), 1–98; Raucher, *Public Relations,* 8–13; Tedlow, *Keeping the Corporate Image,* 12.

119. Charles Edward Russell, "The Greatest Trust in the World," pt. 1, *Everybody's Magazine* 12 (Feb. 1905): 147–56; ibid. 14 (Jan. 1906): 73–75; ibid. (Feb. 1906): 250–57; ibid. (Mar. 1906): 407–13; ibid. (Apr. 1906): 435–44, 545–49; ibid. (May 1906): 608–16, 640–49; ibid. 15 (Oct. 1906): 549–53; Thomas W. Lawson, "Frenzied Finance—The Story of Amalgamated," pt. 3, *Everybody's Magazine* 14 (Feb. 1906): 73–86; Ray Stannard Baker, "Railroads on Trial," *McClure's* 26 (Jan. 1906): 318–31; Samuel Hopkins Adams, "The Great American Fraud," *Collier's,* 7 Oct. 1905, 14–15, 29; C. C. Regier, *The Era of the Muckrakers* (Gloucester, Mass., 1957), 127–38.

120. *Everybody's Magazine* 14 (Jan. 1906): 130; *McClure's* 27 (May 1906): 36–49; Keller, *Life Insurance,* 250–51, 262.

121. H. Roger Grant, *Insurance Reform: Consumer Action in the Progressive Era* (Ames, Iowa, 1979), 29, 41, 43; Garraty, *Right-Hand Man,* 161–64, 179; Keller, *Life Insurance,* 253–54, 266–68, 289–90.

122. Thomas DeWitt Cuyler to A. J. Cassatt, 4 June 1906, box 46, PCC.

123. *New York Times,* 6 June 1906, 7; *New York Herald,* 13 June 1906, 8; *Literary Digest,* 2 June 1906, n.p.; ibid., 18 Aug. 1906, n.p.; ibid., 13 Oct. 1906, 517; *Saturday Evening Post,* 1 Sept. 1906, 22; ibid., 20 Oct. 1906, 29; *Printers' Ink,* 27 June 1906, 31; Ralph M. Hower, *The History of an Advertising Agency: N. W. Ayer & Son at Work, 1869–1939* (Cambridge, Mass., 1939), 117.

124. Both Parker and other advisors to Cassatt stressed the effectiveness of the work that Parker & Lee had done for Baer and the mine operators and for Equitable Life. Parker proposed a "steady, methodical, sober and persistent campaign" to counteract the current "mania for exposure." Samuel Rea to A. J. Cassatt, 12 July 1906, box 44, PCC; Cuyler to Cassatt, 4 June 1906, PCC; [George Parker], memorandum, [May–June 1906], attached to Parker to Cuyler, 2 June 1904, box 46, PCC; Raucher, *Public Relations,* 34–35.

125. *Printers' Ink,* 27 June 1906, 6; Raucher, *Public Relations,* 49–51.

126. David E. Nye, *Image Worlds: Corporate Identities at General Electric, 1890–1930* (Cambridge, Mass., 1985).

127. Marion Pinsdorf, *Communicating When Your Company Is under Siege: Surviving Public Crisis* (Lexington, Mass., 1987), x, 135.

128. Dennis, "Marshall Field," 299. For a few examples among thousands, see *System* 24 (July 1913): 83, 88, 104; ibid. (Oct. 1913): 398, 400–401; ibid. (Nov. 1913): 512, 536; *Saturday Evening Post,* 12 Nov. 1921, 86; ibid., 19 Nov. 1921, 31; ibid., 26 Nov. 1921, 63.

129. National Cash Register Company, *Beginning of a New Era.* Stanley Allyn, a president of the NCR in the post-Patterson era, described the breadth of the company's involvement in its employees' lives under Patterson as follows: "Mr. Patterson was concerned with every employee's health, his diet, his hobbies, recreation and community service, his wife's social schedule, his children's education. By a torrent of memoranda and lectures, Patterson 'suggested' how his workers should dress, act and organize their time. . . . Working at NCR was not a job, it was a way of life" (*Half Century,* 17).

130. *Harvester World* 2 (Jan. 1911): inside front cover; Wanamaker, *Golden Book,* 300–301; Joseph F. Kett, *Rites of Passage: Adolescence in America, 1790 to the Present* (New York, 1977), 181.

131. On these issues, see Bernard Barber, *The Logic and Limits of Trust* (New Brunswick, N.J., 1983), 119–21; Francis X. Sutton et al., *The American Business Creed* (Cambridge, Mass., 1956), 62–63, 163.

Chapter 2

1. J. D. Ellsworth, "The Start of General Magazine Advertising," Jan. 1931, p. 4, box 1066, ATT; Joseph C. Goulden, *Monopoly* (New York, 1968), 71–72.

2. *Fortune* 19 (Mar. 1939): 86, 88; *Advertising Age*, 13 Dec. 1937, 12; ibid., 25 Apr. 1938, 1; Arthur W. Page, "Public Relations Today and the Outlook for the Future," 13 Dec. 1937, p. 4, vol. 5, AWP; Norton E. Long, "Public Relations Policies of the Bell System," *Public Opinion Quarterly* 1 (Oct. 1937): 7, 19–20.

3. L. L. L. Golden, *Only by Public Consent: American Corporations Search for Favorable Opinion* (New York, 1968), 25.

4. AT&T vice president N. C. Kingsbury defined the company's campaign as one to "make known to the American people that as a corporation we seek to be absolutely fair and honest . . . that we have before us a lofty ideal of civic service." It was necessary, he insisted, "to keep reiterating it over and over again in thousands of different ways, through thousands of different mediums." *Printers' Ink,* 9 Dec. 1915, 39.

5. For an account of how AT&T's 1907 strategy revolved around the building of a national network, with emphasis on long-distance service and technological innovation, see Louis Galambos, "Theodore N. Vail and the Role of Innovation in the Modern Bell System," *Business History Review* 66 (spring 1992): 95–116.

6. *Printers' Ink Monthly* 22 (June 1931): 54; Claude S. Fischer, "The Revolution in Rural Telephony, 1900–1920," *Journal of Social History* 21 (fall 1987): 6–7; idem, *America Calling: A Social History of the Telephone to 1940* (Berkeley, 1992), 42, 72; Goulden, *Monopoly,* 66, 71. The lawyer, James J. Storrow, is quoted in Leonard S. Reich, *The Making of American Industrial Research: Science and Business at GE and Bell, 1876–1926* (New York, 1985), 137, 282.

7. *Printers' Ink Monthly* 22 (June 1931): 54; Fischer, "Revolution in Rural Telephony," 6; Goulden, *Monopoly,* 66, 71; Galambos, "Theodore Vail," 101. For a detailed account of some of the competitions with local independents, see Kenneth Lipartito, *The Bell System and Regional Business: The Telephone in the South, 1877–1920* (Baltimore, 1989), 83–96, 113–37.

8. Lipartito, *Bell System,* 113–14; Fischer, *America Calling,* 43–46; Robert W. Garnet, *The Telephone Enterprise: The Evolution of the Bell System's Horizonal Structure, 1876–1909* (Baltimore, 1985), 128; Goulden, *Monopoly,* 53; Golden, *Only by Public Consent,* 29.

9. Albert Bigelow Paine, *In One Man's Life: Being Chapters from the Personal and Business Career of Theodore N. Vail* (New York, 1921), 66–68, 80, 112–13; Horace Coon, *American Tel & Tel: The Story of a Great Monopoly* (New York, 1939), 103. In 1900, AT&T had replaced American Bell as the parent company of the entire system, including the Western Electric manufacturing arm, the long lines, and the regional operating companies.

10. Noel F. Griese, "AT&T: 1908 Origins of the Nation's Oldest Continuous Institutional Advertising Campaign," *Journal of Advertising* 6 (summer 1977): 18; Comptroller to Theodore N. Vail, 26 July 1909, box 1377, ATT; "An Interview with Theodore N. Vail . . . for *N.Y. World,* 8/11/12," box 1080, ATT; Connie Jean Conway, "The Public Relations Philosophy of Theodore N. Vail" (M.S. thesis, University of Wisconsin, 1958), 133; Reich, *Making of American Industrial Research,* 139–40; Fischer, *America Calling,* 45–46.

11. *American Telephone Journal,* 13 July 1907, 21; ibid., 17 Aug. 1907, 107; Fischer, *America Calling,* 38–45.

12. Christopher Armstrong and N. V. Nelles, *Monopoly's Moment: The Organization and Regulation of Canadian Utilities, 1830–1930* (Philadelphia, 1986), 141–42, 146, 151, 157.

13. Ibid., 175, 181, 184, 188.

14. Long, "Public Relations," 11–12; R. T. Barrett, "Bell System Advertising and Publicity," 1931, p. 30, box 1066, ATT; J. D. Ellsworth, "The Twisting Trail," [ca. 1936], JDE.

15. Fischer, *America Calling,* 63, 72–73; Ellsworth, "Twisting Trail," 123–24.

16. [McCullough], "Publicity and Advertising," p. 2, enclosed in B. C. Brooks to J. D. Ellsworth, 21 May 1907, box 1317, ATT; *Printers' Ink,* 6 June 1906, 9; ibid., 20 June 1906, 28; *New York Tribune,* 2 May 1906, 2; ibid., 10 May 1906, 4; ibid., 11 May 1906, 4. See also Commerce and Industry Association of New York, *Telephone Competition in Various American Cities from the Standpoint of the Public,* pamphlet, 1906, 5; Ellsworth, "Twisting Trail," 123–24.

17. Alan R. Raucher, *Public Relations and Business, 1900–1929* (Baltimore, 1968), 48–49; [McCullough], "Publicity," 4–6.

18. J. D. Ellsworth, untitled ms., n.d., box 1066, ATT; Ellsworth to E. K. Hall, 18 Feb. 1908, box 1317, ATT; W. H. Campbell to Ellsworth, 29 Oct. 1908, box 1317, ATT; Ellsworth, "Twisting Trail," 135–38.

19. *Printers' Ink Monthly* 22 (June 1931): 56.

20. Long, "Public Relations," 6–7, 20. AT&T vice president E. K. Hall expressed the sentiment in its classic form: "We start out in our dealings with the public under a heavy handicap; they do not know us, they misunderstand us, they mistrust us, and there is a continued tendency to believe that our intentions toward them are unfair"; Hall, *Public Relations,* pamphlet, 1909, pp. 6–7, BL.

21. Ellsworth, "Twisting Trail," 144.

22. Ibid., 144–45; Golden, *Only by Public Consent,* 33; *Judicious Advertising* 14 (Jan. 1916): 91; Theodore Vail, address at opening of annual conference of the Bell System, Oct. 1913, box 1081, ATT; Northwestern School of Business, "Public Relations: From the Annual Report of Mr. Vail as President of AT&T, 1908," pp. 7, 12, box 1081, ATT.

23. Ellsworth, "Start," 3; *Saturday Evening Post,* 27 June 1908, 2; ibid., 17 Oct. 1908, 36; *Ladies' Home Journal* 25 (Dec. 1908): 66; ibid. 26 (Feb. 1909): 54; "Institutional Advertisements," vol. 1, pp. 1–5, box 1251, ATT.

24. "Institutional Advertisements," vol. 1, pp. 1–5; *Saturday Evening Post,* 17 June 1908, 2; ibid., 15 Aug. 1908, 32; *Country Life in America* 14 (July 1908): 323; ibid. (Sept. 1908): 491.

25. *Printers' Ink,* 29 June 1916, 182; Thomas F. Garbett, *Corporate Advertising: The What, the Why, and the How* (New York, 1981), 4; George David Smith, *The Anatomy of a Business Strategy: Bell, Western Electric, and the Origins of the American Telephone Industry* (Baltimore, 1985) xx; John A. Howland, "Corporate Communications: Which Alternatives?" speech ms., 29 Nov. 1977, p. 1, in possession of author. The resort to metaphor and allegory was particularly dominant in the years 1911 through 1914.

26. For justifications of a campaign thus based "on faith," see J. D. Ellsworth, "Notes on Publicity," 1923, box 1066, ATT; comments of P. L. Schauble in proceedings of publicity conference, 1929, p. 83, box 1310, ATT. On the difficulties in assessment, see *Printers' Ink,* 29 June 1916, 183.

27. Ellsworth, "Twisting Trail," 140; Illegible [S. Conover] to AT&T, 19 Feb. 1909, 14 Mar. 1910, box 1317, ATT.

28. J. D. Ellsworth, memorandum for Mr. Vail, 20 Feb. 1909, box 1317, ATT; *Printers' Ink,* 29 June 1916, 182; Reich, *Making of American Industrial Research,* 152; Garnet, *Telephone Enterprise,* 137, 139, 144. Louis Galambos notes the importance of "intensified communications throughout the System" in Vail's promotion of "a lasting corporate culture." AT&T institutional advertising, although manifestly directed outward to the public, also came to play a role in this internal cultivation of a certain corporate culture. Galambos, "Theodore Vail," 119, 123, 125.

29. *Printers' Ink Monthly* 22 (June 1931): 56; minutes of advertising conference, 28 June 1916, p. 3, box 1310, ATT; Edward K. Hall to A. Burg, 23 Sept. 1909, box 1317, ATT; enclosure to Walter S. Allen to J. D. Ellsworth, 8 Oct. 1909, box 1317, ATT; Allen to N. C. Kingsbury, 12 Sept. 1912, folder 125.07.02-1, ATT. I am indebted to Sheldon Hochheiser for insights into the role of such specific-function conferences as a means of system coordination within AT&T.

30. Hall, "Public Relations," 12–13.

31. Armstrong and Nelles, *Monopoly's Moment,* 156, 184, 188; John Brooks, *Telephone: The First Hundred Years* (New York, 1975), 148; David E. Nye, *Electrifying America: Social Meanings of a New Technology* (Cambridge, Mass., 1990), 176–77; David B. Sicilia, "Selling Power: Marketing and Monopoly at Boston Edison, 1886–1929" (Ph.D. diss., Brandeis University, 1991), 394–95, 426.

32. Vail, address at annual conference, 1913, 22; Armstrong and Nelles, *Monopoly's Moment,* 156,

184, 326; Neil J. Mitchell, *The Generous Corporation: A Political Analysis of Economic Power* (New Haven, 1989), 128−29; Morton Keller, *Regulating a New Economy: Public Policy and Economic Change in America, 1900−1930* (Cambridge, Mass., 1990), 79; Brooks, *Telephone,* 148−49.

33. *Printers' Ink,* 26 Mar. 1914, 96; Goulden, *Monopoly,* 297; S. L. Andrews to C. A. Heiss, 26 Mar. 1926, folder 125.03.03-13, ATT; Garnet, *Telephone Enterprise,* 131, 153, 156−57; Fischer, "Revolution in Rural Telephony," 7; Reich, *Making of American Industrial Research,* 179. The Kingsbury Commitment set the terms for government policy toward AT&T for more than half a century.

34. *Bell Telephone News* 4 (Aug. 1914): 7−8; Garnet, *Telephone Enterprise,* 130, 152; Theodore Vail to Edward J. Sill, 21 Jan. 1908, 21 Jan. 1909, roll 47, presidential letterbooks, ATT. See also "Excerpts from Annual Report of March, 1911," p. 13, box 1081, ATT; Long, "Public Relations," 16−17; Lipartito, *Bell System,* 185−86, 202.

35. J. D. Ellsworth to N. C. Kingsbury, 23 Oct. 1912, folder 125.08.02-1, box 23, ATT; proceedings of publicity conference, 26 June 1914, p. 23, box 1310, ATT; minutes of advertising conference, 1916, 3. See also *Bell Telephone News* 4 (Oct. 1914): 4; ibid. (Nov. 1914): 3; ibid. 5 (Jan. 1915): 15.

36. Theodore Vail, "Some Observations on Modern Tendencies," address to National Association of Railway Commissions, 13 Oct. 1915, p. 2, box 1081, ATT; proceedings of publicity conference, 1914, 4, 24; minutes of advertising conference, 1916, 3−4, 6−8, 19, 28, 31; *Printers' Ink,* 4 Jan. 1917, 17−18.

37. Minutes of advertising conference, 1916, 36; Arthur W. Page, "Special Talk," General Commercial Conference, June 1927, pp. 3−4, vol. 5, AWP; Fischer, "Revolution in Rural Telephony," 9−11.

38. For an example of how another company used AT&T's advertising schedule, minus the farm papers, see F. H. Gale to G. Swope, 15 Feb. 1923, folder 201.2, GS. For Ellsworth's statement, see Ellsworth to E. K. Hall, 18 Feb. 1908, box 1317, ATT. Despite the new emphasis on direct messages to the public through paid advertising after 1908, publicity agents from the Bell companies still bragged about their access to influence and free publicity. In 1914, one Bell representative was praised for his success in becoming "intimately acquainted" with 98 percent of the newspaper owners and editors in his state. "That friendship is played up in different ways," an AT&T executive observed. Others remarked how eagerly some editors accepted and printed the Bell company handouts, and one local representative rather cynically wondered why the companies should worry about the details of advertising copy when the whole purpose was simply to gain the publisher's goodwill through advertising expenditures. "Meeting of Publicity Men, 1914," pp. 14, 16−17, 23, box 1310, ATT.

39. J. D. Ellsworth, "Public Utility Advertising," in *Advertising and Selling Digest,* ed. William G. Lownds (New York, 1926), 183.

40. For this analysis, I have evaluated all the texts and images of the AT&T series of institutional advertisements over the first twenty years, from their origins in 1908. The seven ads between 1908 and 1912 that I refer to were July 1908, Jan. and Mar. 1909, June and Nov. 1910, and Jan. and Oct. 1911. The 1914 ads cited appeared in *Literary Digest,* 18 Apr. 1914, 919; ibid., 15 Aug. 1914, 281.

41. Vail felt a need to compensate for the public's lack of appreciation for the challenges and complexities of AT&T's work. "Who realizes the work and thought of which it is the product?" he observed of AT&T service. Yet what "outsider" who was given a tour of a telephone central office was "not almost overwhelmed by the immensity and complexity that he saw for the first time"? Vail, address at annual conference, 1913, 13.

42. See especially *Saturday Evening Post,* 10 Dec. 1910, 34; 11 Feb. 1911, 34; 8 Apr. 1911, 58; 13 May 1911, 46.

43. *Saturday Evening Post,* 12 June 1909, 47; ibid., 10 Dec. 1910, 34; ibid., 14 Jan. 1911, 44; ibid., 8 July 1911, 30; ibid., 9 Sept. 1911, 62; *North American Review* 190 (Dec. 1909): inside front cover.

44. "Attended Pay Station," Panama-Pacific Exposition, box 1061, ATT; *Western Electric News* 4 (May 1915): 1, 9.

45. On the more practical elements in this resistance, see Sally Clarke, "Negotiating between the Firm and the Consumer: Bell Labs and the Development of the Modern Telephone" (paper presented at the Shelby Cullom Davis Center, Princeton University, 8 April 1995).

46. Proceedings of publicity conference, 1921, p. 12, box 1310, ATT.

47. For an example of early AT&T brochures lauding its operators, see *On Telephone Duty: True Stories of the Intelligence and Heroism of the Girl at the Switchboard,* n.d, BL.

48. *Literary Digest,* 21 Mar. 1914, 649; Alvin von Auw, *Heritage and Destiny: Reflections of the Bell System in Transition* (New York, 1983), 363. Also, in a 1914 magazine article, AT&T "related instances of heroic devotion to duty by Bell linemen"; see Conway, "Vail," 76.

49. *Saturday Evening Post,* 11 Dec. 1915, 56; enclosure to R. T. Barrett to Eugene L. Barron, 11 Feb. 1944, box 1079, ATT; enclosure to J. B. Hunter to P. Ullaney, 5 Mar. 1943, box 1079, ATT; "Weavers of Speech: 1915−1947," box 1079, ATT; "Recollection of Mr. Lewis Seaber," n.d., box 1079, ATT. For later adaptations of *Weavers of Speech,* see AT&T, *Telephone Almanac* (1928), n.p.; ibid. (1934), n.p.

50. Kenneth Lipartito, "When Women Were Switches: Technology, Work, and Gender in the Telephone Industry, 1890−1920," *American Historical Review* 99 (Oct. 1994): 1084−85. Lipartito observes that managers sought women of a background sufficiently genteel to enable them to interact with subscribers, as one manager put it, "on an equal plane." Michele Martin notes that the early upper-middle-class subscribers often viewed the operators as their "servants," acting in a capacity comparable to that of (well-cultivated) household maids; Martin, *"Hello, Central?": Gender, Technology, and Culture in the Formation of Telephone Systems* (Montreal, 1991), 50−61, 99, 144. See also R. T. Barrett, "The Changing Years as Seen from the Switchboard," *Bell Telephone Quarterly* 14 (Jan. 1935): 44−52. For many years during the 1920s and 1930s, the operator and the lineman represented AT&T on the covers of its annual *Telephone Almanac.*

51. Richard S. Tedlow, *Keeping the Corporate Image: Public Relations and Business, 1900−1950* (Greenwich, Conn., 1979), 28; Hall, "Public Relations," 12−13, 20, 23−24.

52. *Literary Digest,* 26 Mar. 1921, 47; ibid., 15 Apr. 1922, 72; ibid., 19 June 1924, 42; ibid., 11 Oct. 1924, 54; *American Magazine* 88 (Mar. 1923): 149; AT&T, *Telephone Almanac* (1942), n.p.; AT&T, *A Bridge of Voices: A Selection from More than 900 Messages on the Telephone Hour, 1940 to 1958* [Philadelphia, 1958], 5.

53. *Long Lines* 4 (Oct. 1924), back cover; *Printer's Ink,* 6 Apr. 1922, 121.

54. *Literary Digest,* 19 Jan. 1924, 42; AT&T, *Telephone Almanac* (1928), n.p; John N. Schact, *The Making of Telephone Unionism, 1920−1947* (New Brunswick, N.J., 1985), 32, 35. See also Brenda Maddox, "Women and the Switchboard," in *The Social Impact of the Telephone,* ed. Ithiel de Sola Pool (Cambridge, Mass., 1977), 272; Martin, *"Hello Central?"* 64.

55. "A Visit to the Bell System's Exhibit at the World's Fair," *Bell Telephone News* 23 (June 1933): 2; C. T. Smith, "Exhibiting Telephone Progress at the World's Fair," *Bell Telephone Quarterly* 13 (Jan. 1934): 15−16; New York Telephone Company, press release, n.d. [1939], p. 6, box 1004, NYWF.

56. *Western Electric News* 4 (Nov. 1915): 16ff.; *Telephone Review* 6 (Jan. 1915 suppl.): inside front cover, box 1063, ATT; *Bell Telephone News* 4 (Feb. 1915): 2−6, 25; AT&T, *The Story of a Great Achievement,* pamphlet, 1915, BL.

57. According to the former AT&T executive Alvin von Auw, who winced at the use of this image to characterize "a high technology business applying advanced marketing strategies," the origins of the "Ma Bell" label are obscure. It may have stemmed from the company's retention of its $9 dividend on behalf of its purported widow and orphan stockholders during the Great Depression, or from the "character of the old-time chief operator who always took care of 'her girls,'" or simply from the corporate maternalism of a company that "knew what was best for its consumers." Von Auw, *Heritage,* 360. I have found no use of the phrase before the mid-1930s, and no subsequent recollections suggest an earlier date.

58. Fischer, *America Calling,* 75, 81−82, 231−36; Claude S. Fischer, "Touch Someone: The Telephone Industry Discovers Sociability," *Technology and Culture* 29 (Jan. 1988): 32−36, 39−41, 44−45, 48−49; Martin, *"Hello Central?"* 125, 147, 163−64, 171; Lana F. Rakow, *Gender on the Line: Women, the Telephone, and Community Life* (Urbana, Ill., 1992), 34, 42−43, 64, 72.

59. Fischer, *America Calling,* 234−36.

60. Wm. Ray Gardiner to J. D. Ellsworth, 27 May 1909, box 1317, ATT. The agency man ac-

knowledged that he did not dare to rank this ad above the two others; but he did feel obliged, he said, to "take up the cudgels in the ladies' behalf because I am afraid you will not favor it."

61. *Saturday Evening Post,* 29 May 1909, cover; 13 Nov. 1909, 64.

62. Ibid., 3 Feb. 1934, 49. In its September 1925 institutional ad, AT&T showed a woman placing a telephone call as her maid greeted a woman caller at the door. While some readers might have assumed that the lady of the house was calling another woman, the text of the ad, which referred to making "important agreements or appointments" on the telephone, suggested that she was tending to household management. An August 1928 ad featured a woman as a representative of "the public" using the telephone for what might have been a social conversation, but it did not reveal the partner to her conversation. *Literary Digest,* 15 Aug. 1925, 49; 11 Aug. 1928, 53. In the late 1920s, as the company became more sales-oriented, and in the 1930s, when the depression and anti-business sentiments made it particularly conscious of the need to further "humanize" itself, AT&T finally moved decisively to emphasize not only women but even children as telephone users. See *Saturday Evening Post,* 1 Feb. 1930, 103; ibid., 30 July 1932, 31; ibid., 22 Oct. 1938, 3; *Tide* 10 (Oct. 1936): 4–5.

63. *Saturday Evening Post,* 12 Oct. 1912, 44; 14 Dec. 1912, 40; 13 Sept. 1913, 54; see also 8 May 1915, 59; 9 Oct. 1915, 54.

64. *Literary Digest,* 18 June 1921, 45; ibid., 12 Feb. 1927, 58; ibid., 9 Apr. 1927, 60; *American Magazine* 104 (Mar. 1927): 185; AT&T, "Institutional Advertisements," vol. 2, pp. 195, 221, 223, 253, 265.

65. *Saturday Evening Post,* 10 Dec. 1910, 34; 11 May 1912, 50; 12 Apr. 1913, 58; 13 Sept. 1913, 54; 13 Feb. 1915, 52; 10 Apr. 1915, 58; 9 Oct. 1915, 54; 8 July 1916, 54.

66. Fischer, *America Calling,* 265–67; Constance Perrin, *Belonging in America: Reading between the Lines* (Madison, Wisc., 1988), 4, 45, 49.

67. It is hardly surprising that Ayer should have seized on the dramatic overcoming of distance to illustrate AT&T's beneficent service to the nation. But the neighborhood metaphor offered a comforting image that went beyond the telephone's actual capacity to triumph over scale. Through the telephone, people *could* make "neighbors" of those at some distance—but only one at a time, and only in those attributes of neighborliness attainable by verbal interchange. They could not overcome the aspects of scale—of extent of population—that made a neighborhood quite different from a nation, and they were highly unlikely to use the telephone to bridge those racial, ethnic, and class differences that were conventionally seen as nonexistent in the comfortable, ideal "neighborhood." AT&T found no reason to suggest these reservations. At a time when they were becoming aware of some of the negative consequences of large scale—in distant and problematic relations with employees and customers—people in the world of big business could find real satisfaction in the belief that they were fostering the return of neighborhood qualities.

68. *Saturday Evening Post,* 10 Dec. 1910, 34; 8 May 1915, 59; 14 Apr. 1917, 114. This theme occasionally reemerged through the mid-1920s; see *Independent,* 9 Apr. 1921, 387; *Literary Digest,* 13 Dec. 1924, 50; ibid., 14 Aug. 1926, 52.

69. Vail to L. C. Royce, 28 Oct. 1908, roll 47, presidential letterbooks, ATT; W. R. Gardiner to J. D. Ellsworth, 27 May 1909, box 1317, ATT; *Western Electric News* 16 (May 1927): 1.

70. Arthur W. Page, speech at publicity conference, April 1927, p. 5, vol. 5, AWP; proceedings of publicity conference, 1929, pp. 7–8, box 1310, ATT; *Good Housekeeping* 86 (June 1928): 198; *Los Angeles Times,* 20 July 1929, pt. 2, p. 2; *American Magazine* 122 (June 1936): 134; *Saturday Evening Post,* 29 Mar. 1930, 59; ibid., 5 Mar. 1938, 103; AT&T, *Bridge of Voices,* 7, 10 (broadcasts of 2 Apr. 1940 and 12 May 1941).

71. Schact, *Making of Telephone Unionism,* 20.

72. *Literary Digest,* 19 Nov. 1921, 47.

73. *Saturday Evening Post,* 11 Feb. 1911, 34; 11 Nov. 1911, 48; 10 Aug. 1912, 36; 8 Mar. 1913, 57.

74. Ibid., 11 Nov. 1911, 48.

75. Ibid., 12 June 1915, 52; 10 July 1915, 30; 13 May 1916, 84; 10 Mar. 1917, 110.

76. *American Magazine* 87 (May 1919): 172. I characterize the young woman as a widow because

if she were married she would not be shown opening her dividend check in the presence of her sons but in the absence of her husband. A divorced mother was certainly a possibility in the real America of 1919, but not in the advertiser's ideal society of favorable associations. This image anticipated the ultimate reputation of AT&T stock as the favored investment of widows and orphans.

77. *American Magazine* 90 (Dec. 1920): 105; *Literary Digest,* 19 Nov. 1921, 47; ibid., 14 Oct. 1922, 60; ibid., 13 June 1925, 48; *Saturday Evening Post,* 22 Nov. 1924, 154; *Printers' Ink,* 8 Dec. 1927, 215.

78. "Public Relations Course, December 18, 1933," p. 3, vol. 5, AWP.

79. *American Magazine* 104 (Nov. 1927): 159; ibid. (Dec. 1927): 134; *Advertising and Selling,* 11 July 1928, 71; *Saturday Evening Post,* 30 Aug. 1930, 68; ibid., 20 Jan. 1932, 27; illustrative material, publicity conference, 1934, p. 12, box 1310, ATT.

80. *Literary Digest,* 20 Nov. 1920, 116. In group portraits of AT&T investors women remained a minority, but they enjoyed a better ratio to men than they did in depictions of telephone users during the same period. In some instances, the women portrayed in a group scene of investors even included a maid. See *Literary Digest,* 19 Nov. 1921, 47; 10 Dec. 1927, 57.

81. *Saturday Evening Post,* 8 Feb. 1936, 83; illustrative material, publicity conference, 1934, 12–13. See also *American Magazine* 119 (May 1935): 3; *Saturday Evening Post,* 30 Jan 1932, 27; Alan M. Kantrow, *The Constraints of Corporate Tradition* (New York, 1984), 183; Raucher, *Public Relations,* 55.

82. *Saturday Evening Post,* 22 Nov. 1924, 154. Such phrases as "in every state of the Union," "in every section of the United States," "in nearly every town and city in the country," and even "it belongs to Main Street" stressed the notion of democracy fulfilled by an unspecified degree of regional and small-town or rural representation among the investors. *Saturday Evening Post,* 30 Aug. 1930, 68; ibid., 30 Jan. 1932, 27; ibid., 16 Oct. 1937, 119; *Literary Digest,* 8 Oct. 1927, 56; ibid., 12 Nov. 1927, 52; ibid., 10 Dec. 1927, 57.

83. Noobar R. Danielian, *AT&T: The Story of Industrial Conquest* (New York, 1939), 188; Raucher, *Public Relations,* 55. Raucher characterizes AT&T's use of numbers to support the democracy theme as "statistical legerdemain."

84. *Printers' Ink,* 7 Sept. 1911, 89; ibid., 16 Apr. 1914, 100; ibid., 28 Apr. 1932, 20; ibid., 1 Aug. 1935, 15; Raucher, *Public Relations,* 37, 100; *Literary Digest,* 6 May 1922, 50; *Saturday Evening Post,* 29 Oct. 1921, 92; ibid., 11 June 1927, 35; *Chicago Tribune,* 16 Nov. 1926, 18; Roger William Riis and Charles W. Bonner Jr., *Publicity: A Study of the Development of Industrial News* (New York, 1926), 162.

85. Untitled memorandum [BBDO to Niagara Hudson Co.], [1933], box 79, BB; emphasis mine. The term "blurred ownership" is from Richard Ohmann, comp., "Doublespeak and Ideology in Ads: A Kit for Teachers," in *Teaching about Doublespeak,* ed. Daniel Dieterich (Urbana, Ill., 1976), 47.

86. Ellsworth, memorandum for Mr. Vail, 20 Feb. 1909, box 1317, ATT; Danielian, *AT&T,* 272–73; *Advertising Age,* 25 Apr. 1938, 1.

87. George A. Flanagan, *Modern Institutional Advertising* (New York, 1967), 34.

88. Ibid.

89. Ellsworth, "Public Utility Advertising," 188–89.

90. Proceedings of publicity conference, 1921, 7; ibid., 1923, pp. 2, 4–5, 15, box 1310, ATT.

91. Paul H. Woodruff to J. D. Ellsworth, 20 Mar. 1909, box 1317, ATT; Federal Communications Commission, *Telephone Investigation, Exhibit 2096E* (Washington, D.C., 1938), 4:4, 23–29, 191–92, and passim; Danielian, *AT&T,* 272–73, 277–79, 292–95, 397–14; *Advertising Age,* 25 Apr. 1938, 1–2; Conway, "Vail," 69–71.

92. Conway, "Vail," 69–71; *Fortune* 19 (Mar. 1939): 86; Morrell Heald, *The Social Responsibilities of Business: Company and Community* (Cleveland, 1970), 112; *Advertising Age,* 25 Apr. 1938, 1–2; Danielian, *AT&T,* 284–86; Roy Carleton, "Boy's and Girl's Book of the Telephone," [1928], box 1022, ATT; "On Telephone Duty—Heroism of Operators," [1910], box 1131, ATT; Theodore Vail to E. C. Bradley, 1 June 1909, presidential letterbooks, reel 48, ATT. For an example of the replication of national themes in local Bell advertising, see *Chicago Tribune,* 2 Feb. 1925, 17.

93. Proceedings of publicity conference, 1921, 3–4, 9–10.

94. Ibid.

95. Ibid., 3–4, 12–13.

96. Illegible [S. Conover] to Ellsworth, 15 June 1909, box 1317, ATT; *Judicious Advertising* 7 (July 1909): 18–19; Ellsworth, "Twisting Trail," 124; *Printers' Ink,* 29 June 1916, 182.

97. See, for instance, the comments on the initiation of an institutional advertising campaign by the Pullman Company in 1916 (*Printers' Ink,* 24 Aug. 1916, 12).

98. Proceedings of publicity conference, 1929, 47, 83.

99. Ellsworth, "Start," 7; unsigned, "Confidential to the Directors," n.d., box 1, ATT; Barrett, "Bell System Advertising"; Danielian, *AT&T,* 243, 254.

100. "Publicity and Advertising," p. 8, enclosed in G. C. Brooks to J. D. Ellsworth, 21 May 1907, box 1317, ATT; Ellsworth, memorandum for Mr. Vail; Schact, *Making of Telephone Unionism,* 34; Raucher, *Public Relations,* 52.

101. *Advertising Age,* 2 May 1938, 26; anonymous comment by President, Oil Company, in "Elmo Roper Report," [ca. 1945], p. A156, box 2, folder 2, FC. For examples of these "modeling" ads, see *Saturday Evening Post,* 11 Dec. 1915, 56; 12 Feb. 1916, 58; 14 Oct. 1916, 105; 9 Dec. 1916, 70.

102. Proceedings of publicity conference, 1929, 43, 56, 58–59; *Printers' Ink,* 24 Apr. 1924, 12. See also *Printers' Ink,* 3 June 1915, 81. On the deleterious working conditions and the "continual tension" between operators and management that such morale building sought to surmount, see Lipartito, "When Women Were Switches," 1088–90, 1096–1100.

103. *Bell Telephone Magazine* 1 (July 1922): 39, 42; proceedings of publicity conference, 1923, 5; ibid., 1927, pp. 20–21, box 1310, ATT; ibid., 1928, p. 20, box 1310, ATT; ibid., 1929, 45; H. B. Thayer to B. L. Kilgour et al., 4 Jan. 1922, box 9, ATT; W. B. T. Bell to Thayer, 13 Jan. 1922, box 9, ATT. See also the quote from Vice President Hall in General Commercial Conference, 1921, in Federal Communications Commission, *Telephone Investigation,* 4 : 12.

104. Tedlow, *Keeping the Corporate Image,* 92; Page, speech at publicity conference, 1927, 3; "Philosophy of the Business," General Plant Conference, Oct. 1928, box 2034, ATT; Bruce Barton to Paul S. Clapp, 17 Sept. 1930, box 78, BB. For the slogan, see, for instance, *Saturday Evening Post,* 5 Jan. 1929, 141; 7 Dec. 1929, 69. The "no standing still" slogan testified to a deliberate consciousness among the new leaders, whom Vail had fostered, to perpetuate a culture of innovation. See Galambos, "Theodore Vail," 123, 125, and passim on the legacy of that corporate culture.

105. Proceedings of publicity conference, 1928, 61; Barton to Clapp, 17 Sept. 1930. For examples of the new style, see *Literary Digest,* 21 Jan. 1928, 60; 11 Aug. 1928, 53. In 1931, Page stressed the linkage between public relations and "selling" by affirming that "we need to sell . . . because it keeps our people public relations minded . . . we need to sell to remove the suspicions that still flourish against monopoly"; Page, "Public Relations," speech at General Operating Conference, May 1931, box 2034, ATT.

106. Tedlow, *Keeping the Corporate Image,* 93; Danielian, *AT&T,* 315; Arthur W. Page, "Public Relations," speech at General Operating Conference, May 1930, p. 4, box 2034, ATT; Preston C. Mabon, "The Art of Arthur Page," *Public Relations Journal* 27 (Mar. 1971): 6.

107. Mabon, "Art of Arthur Page," 6. Several years later, a nationwide survey by another professional firm showed that over 66 percent of the respondents had singled out one company (its name was not revealed by the surveying firm) when asked, "What Utility Company . . . is the best managed and fairest in its dealings with the public?" N. W. Ayer & Son proclaimed proudly that there could "be little question" that the unnamed utility was Ayer's client, AT&T, and that "this attitude should effectively block any attempt to needlessly hamper the operations of this company through legislative action." Sigurd Larmon, address, 1936, p. 12, file S-216, Y&R.

108. Arthur C. Richardson and C. Theodore Smith, "Finding Out What People Think of Us," *Bell Telephone Magazine* 25 (spring 1946): 5–7; Mabon, "Art of Arthur Page," 6; Leonard W. Doob, "An 'Experimental' Study of the Psychological Corporation," *Psychological Bulletin* 35 (Apr. 1938): 220–21; Smith, "Exhibiting Telephone Progress," 3–22.

109. Danielian, *AT&T,* 205–7; Goulden, *Monopoly,* 26; Arthur W. Page, *The Bell Telephone System* (New York, 1941), 69–71, 76–77; "Bell System Public Relations as Indicated by Conference of March, 1932," 1932, pp. 1–2, 6, box 1310, ATT.

110. On the need to emphasize cheapness, see Arthur W. Page to All Presidents, 8 Nov. 1930, box 2, JMS; Page, "Public Relations," 1931, 2. The "Main Street" ad appeared in *Saturday Evening Post,* 16 Oct. 1937, 119. See also *American Magazine* 121 (June 1936): 134.

111. *Saturday Evening Post,* 26 Aug. 1933, 54. For other examples, see ibid., 28 Nov. 1936, 45; 16 Oct. 1937, 119; 5 Mar. 1938, 103.

112. Page, "Public Relations Today and the Outlook for the Future," 13 Dec. 1937, p. 4, vol. 5, AWP; Federal Communications Commission, *Telephone Investigation,* 4:5; *Advertising Age,* 25 Apr. 1938, 1–2; Danielian, *AT&T,* 243, 254; *Fortune* 19 (Mar. 1939): 88. The quoted characterization of the FCC staff is from Brooks, *Telephone,* 196–99.

113. "Mr. Page on Public Relations," *Long Lines* 19 (Apr. 1940): 1; *Printers' Ink,* 24 Apr. 1924, 147; Market Research Corporation of America, *Industrial Relations, Public Relations, Economic Research, Market Research,* pamphlet, [1938], p. 17, box 53, ERS; "Chemical Memorandum," n.d., n.p., box 64, DP. For AT&T's own censure of those who waited to mount a defense at the last moment, see minutes of advertising conference, 28 June 1916, pp. 26–27, box 1310, ATT.

114. Conway, "Vail," 55; *Judicious Advertising* 14 (Jan. 1916): 93; Ellsworth, memorandum for Mr. Vail; Federal Communications Commission, *Telephone Investigation,* 4:10; Danielian, *AT&T,* 272–73; *Advertising Age,* 25 Apr. 1938, 1; *Printers' Ink,* 9 Dec. 1915, 39. President Vail had observed in 1913 that "only constant repetition and frequent seeing" would leave a lasting impression on the public. Moreover, as Louis Galambos ("Theodore Vail," 119) suggests, in fostering an enduring internal corporate culture, Vail demonstrated the same belief in the efficacy of "learning by repetition." As late as 1967, George Flanagan was still praising the AT&T series for having, "with a relentless continuity, year after year," served well as the "building bricks in a towering structure"; Flanagan, *Modern Institutional Advertising,* 34.

115. *Printers' Ink,* 9 Dec. 1915, 39; ibid., 26 June 1916, 182; Ellsworth, memorandum for Mr. Vail.

116. *Printers' Ink,* 9 Dec. 1915, 39; Long, "Public Relations," 19; proceedings of publicity conference, 1921, 9; ibid., 1923, 2; ibid., 1928, 60.

Chapter 3

1. Ellis W. Hawley, *The Great War and the Search for a Modern Order: A History of the American People and Their Institutions, 1917–1933* (New York, 1979), 23–24, 100–101. In "Herbert Hoover, the Commerce Secretariat, and the Vision of an 'Associative State,' 1921–1928," *Journal of American History* 61 (June 1974): 117–19, Hawley describes the "associative state" as one "tied to, cooperating with, and helping to develop and guide" a new socioeconomic order based on "the development and proper use of cooperative institutions, particularly trade associations [and] professional societies." By means of "promotional conferences, expert inquiries, and cooperating committees," the government would foster the emergence of a kind of "private government" based on service and efficiency, one that "would theoretically serve as midwife to a new, non-statist commonwealth."

2. Morton Keller, *Regulating a New Society: Public Policy and Social Change in America, 1900–1933* (Cambridge, Mass., 1994), 5; Hawley, *Great War,* 23–24, 36; Louis Galambos, *The Public Image of Big Business in America, 1880–1940: A Quantitative Study in Social Change* (Baltimore, 1975), 158–59, 181, 183, 186; Alan Brinkley, *The End of Reform: New Deal Liberalism in Recession and War* (New York, 1995), 35; Robert D. Cuff, *The War Industries Board: Business-Government Relations during World War I* (Baltimore, 1973), 273–74.

3. Cuff, *War Industries Board,* 1, 39; David M. Kennedy, *Over Here: The First World War and American Society* (New York, 1980), 114–15, 131–32; Warner & Swasey Company, *The Warner & Swasey Company, 1880–1930* (Cleveland, 1930), 43; L. L. L. Golden, *Only by Public Consent: American Corporations Search for Favorable Opinion* (New York, 1968), 98.

4. Cuff, *War Industries Board,* 5, 47, 266, 272–74; Ida M. Tarbell, *Owen D. Young: A New Type of Industrial Leader* (New York, 1932), 135; H. M. Gitelman, *Legacy of the Ludlow Massacre: A Chapter in American Industrial Relations* (Philadelphia, 1988), 223. On the expected ease of simultaneously carrying out national service and corporate work, see L. B. Jones to George Eastman, 28 Nov. 1917, box 29, GEC.

5. Otis Pease, *The Responsibilities of American Advertising* (New Haven, 1958), 11–13; *Literary Digest,* 29 Oct. 1921, 44–45.

6. Printers' Ink, *Fifty Years: 1888–1938* (New York, 1938), 288–90, 294; Pease, *Responsibilities,* 17. See also *Printers' Ink,* 2 Aug. 1917, 98; 11 Apr. 1918, 160.

7.   *Judicious Advertising* 16 (Mar. 1918): 69–93; ibid. (Apr. 1918): 32; Printers' Ink, *Fifty Years,* 290, 308–9, 320, 340; Frank W. Fox, *Madison Avenue Goes to War: The Strange Military Career of American Advertising* (Provo, Utah, 1975), 11; Frank Arnold, "Reminiscences," pp. 5–6, OHRO; *Advertising and Selling* 36 (Feb. 1943): 114; Roger William Riis and Charles W. Bonner Jr., *Publicity: A Study in the Development of Industrial News* (New York, 1926), 105–7.

8.   Stephen Vaughn, *Holding Fast the Inner Lines: Democracy, Nationalism, and the Committee on Public Information* (Chapel Hill, 1980), 148, 155; George Creel, *How We Advertised America* (1920; reprint, New York, 1972), 156–59, 165. For examples, see *Literary Digest,* 13 Apr. 1918, 143; ibid., 19 May 1918, 78; *Saturday Evening Post,* 6 Apr. 1918, 51.

9.   *Printers' Ink,* 21 Mar. 1918, 126, 128; James R. Mock and Cedric Larson, *Words That Won the War: The Story of the Committee on Public Information, 1917–1919* (Princeton, 1939), 99.

10.   *Printers' Ink,* 21 Mar. 1918, 126, 128; Mock and Larson, *Words,* 99.

11.   Ivy L. Lee, "Notes for Mss. on War," box 3, ILL; *Advertising and Selling* 32 (Nov. 1939): 24; Mock and Larson, *Words,* 96–97; Vaughn, *Holding Fast,* 141, 143; *J. W. T. News Bulletin,* 5 Aug. 1918, 2, JWT.

12.   Pease, *Responsibilities,* 17; Vaughn, *Holding Fast,* 142, 191–92; Creel, *How We Advertised,* 157, 165. The J. Walter Thompson agency declared that "no one can read the accounts of this war service performed by advertising men without feeling that it brings with it a great opportunity for the advertising profession." Here was the chance to "reveal to a wide circle of influential men . . . the real character of advertising and the important function which it performs." *J.W.T. News Bulletin,* 5 Aug. 1918, 2. Ivy Lee later claimed that through the war period advertising advanced from being looked on as a business (and the advertising agent "frankly viewed as a plausible pirate") to being acknowledged as a profession; Lee, "Notes for Mss. on War."

13.   Ivy L. Lee, "Ministers of Propaganda," [1918], in Notes and Clippings, vol. 27, box 2, ILL; idem, "Editing Public Opinion," n.d., chap. 1, p. 4, box 2, ILL. See also idem, *Publicity for Public Service Corporations,* pamphlet, 10 Oct. 1916, p. 44, HML.

14.   *Judicious Advertising* 17 (Oct. 1919): 65–66. Teagle is quoted in Bennett H. Wall and George S. Gibb, *Teagle of Jersey Standard* (New Orleans, 1974), 126.

15.   *Saturday Evening Post,* 4 Jan. 1919, 82–83. The businessman in *Forbes* is quoted in Morrell Heald, *The Social Responsibilities of American Business: Company and Community, 1900–1960* (Cleveland, 1976), 49. The elevated sentiments and overblown rhetoric that arose in linking companies and their products with the war cause would permeate the style of one major strain of postwar institutional advertising, replete with glittering generalities about "honor," "dedication," and "service." As an ad agency executive later recalled, "It didn't seem possible for an advertiser to get out an advertisement without displaying some such blasting headline as 'Integrity,' or 'Fidelity'"; BBDO, *Newsletter,* 15 July 1931, p. 14, BBDO.

16.   *Printers' Ink,* 1 June 1916, 25.

17.   Bethlehem Steel Company, *The Bethlehem Steel Company Appeals to the People . . . ,* pamphlet, n.d., box 25, BS; *New York Times,* 31 May 1916, 8; Ray Eldon Hiebert, *Courtier to the Crowd: The Story of Ivy Lee and the Development of Public Relations* (Ames, Iowa, 1966), 161; *Advertising and Selling,* June 1916, clipping, box 9, ILL.

18.   *New York Times,* 22 May 1916, 6; ibid., 26 May 1916, 22; *Chicago Tribune,* 17 July 1916, 8.

19.   The *Miami Herald* called the company's bid "a pathetic request"; the *Miami Metropolis* termed it a "damnable outrage." The *New York Times* thought the company had made "at least a tactical mistake" in suggesting, through its offer to lower prices, that it had previously been overcharging the government, while the *Buffalo Enquirer* recalled that the sweet reasonableness of the armor makers had suddenly emerged only after the rival government plant "seemed to be a sure thing." Clippings, vols. 9 and 13, ILL. See also quotes from the *Milwaukee Leader* in Paul Tiffany, "Corporate Management of the 'External Environment': Bethlehem Steel, Ivy Lee, and the Origins of Public Relations in the American Steel Industry," *Essays in Economic and Business History* 5 (1987): 5.

20.   Minutes of advertising conference, June 1916, pp. 26–27, box 1310, ATT; *J. Walter Thompson News Bulletin,* 6 June 1916, 2, JWT; Ivy L. Lee, *Human Nature and Railroads* (Philadelphia, 1915), 9; idem, "Constructive Publicity," n.d., p. 37, box 2, ILL.

21.   Lee's biographer insists that Bethlehem gained such a reputation for "honesty, forthrightness

and efficiency" through the advocacy campaign that it won a large share of subsequent war contracts. Hiebert, *Courtier,* 156–62; see also Lee, "Constructive Publicity," 6; Tiffany, "Corporate Management," 6; *Editor and Publisher,* 19 Aug. 1916, 23.

22. The packers had so persistently alienated the public that even such a radical proposal did not lack influential supporters. Among them was Herbert Hoover, President Wilson's wartime food administrator, who urged the president to move toward government operation or ownership of the stockyards. See U.S. Federal Trade Commission, *Summary of the Report of the Federal Trade Commission on the Meat-Packing Industry* (Washington, D.C., 1918), 3–5, 11, 40–44; *Chicago Tribune,* 2 Apr. 1918, 1, 4.

23. Mary Yeager, *Competition and Regulation: The Development of Oligopoly in the Meat Packing Industry* (Greenwich, Conn., 1981), 220; Lewis Corey, *Meat and Men: A Study of Monopoly, Unionism, and Food Policy* (New York, 1950), 49, 52.

24. The series of ads appeared regularly in the *Saturday Evening Post:* 13 July 1918, 96; 17 Aug. 1918, 92; 7 Sept. 1918, 132; 25 Jan. 1919, 128; 5 Apr. 1919, 164; 12 July 1919, 152; 6 Sept. 1919, 184; 4 Oct. 1919, 188. By 1919 these two leading meatpacking firms had adopted distinct yet complementary styles, almost as if their advertising aimed to replicate that same mastery of "the arts of cooperation and oligopolistic competition" that, the infuriated FTC charged, had enabled them to "maintain price agreements without overt collusion"; Yeager, *Competition,* 137.

25. *Literary Digest,* 8 Feb. 1919, 35; 8 Mar. 1919, 35; 19 Apr. 1919, 45. Even before the FTC published its report, Armour had launched a counterattack through ads that presented the company "in the light of a public utility." It explained, for instance, how its own "Bureau of Agricultural Research" had developed meat by-products, thus reducing its production costs and its prices to the consumer. Voluntarily putting such facts "frankly before the thinking public," it noted, would surely "result in a better and more friendly understanding on the part of the public." See *Judicious Advertising* 15 (July 1917): 37–39; *Printers' Ink,* 1 March 1917, 3–4; Armour and Company, *Containing Facts about the Business and Organization,* pamphlet, 1917, pp. 24–25, 33, 39, CHS.

26. Although Philip Armour had initiated a public defense of the "family name and business" in 1906 and both companies had offered factory tours to foster public favor, neither had adopted any sustained campaign of institutional advertising; see Yeager, *Competition,* 119.

27. Swift & Company, *Year Book, 1919* (Chicago, 1919), 5, 11, 56, CHS; Armour and Company, *Year Book, 1918* (Chicago, 1918), n.p., CHS; idem, *Year Book, 1921* (Chicago, 1921), 2, 14–15, S&C. After describing the merits of large size for almost two years, Swift finally put the case bluntly in 1920 in an ad that explained "why Swift & Company has to be 'big'"; *Saturday Evening Post,* 17 Apr. 1920, 200.

28. Swift's emphasis on its twenty thousand stockholders, the FTC charged, was simply a smoke screen to obscure the fact that it "is now and has always been completely under the control of the Swift family"; U.S. Federal Trade Commission, *Summary,* 21, 44–45; Corey, *Meat and Men,* 79. On Swift's early claims to have "deliberately cast aside a small family business reaping a large percentage of profit for a larger business with its problematical but surely smaller profits," see Swift & Company, *Year Book, 1912* (Chicago, 1912), 20–21, CHS.

29. *Saturday Evening Post,* 9 Aug. 1919, 160; ibid., 3 Sept. 1921, 88; ibid., 28 May 1925, 37; Swift & Company, *Year Book, 1924* (Chicago, 1924), 55, S&C.

30. Corey, *Meat and Men,* 86–87; Robert M. Aduddell and Louis P. Cain, "Public Policy toward 'The Greatest Trust in the World,'" *Business History Review* 55 (summer 1981): 239–40; idem, "The Consent Decree in the Meatpacking Industry, 1920–1956," *Business History Review* 55 (fall 1981): 362, 371.

31. *Advertising and Selling,* 4 Sept. 1920, 12, 14; *Printers' Ink,* 10 July 1919, 93–94; ibid., 7 Dec. 1922, 127; Swift & Company, *Year Book, 1919,* 11; idem, *Year Book, 1921* (Chicago, 1921), 11, S&C.

32. Joseph A. McCartin, "'An American Feeling': Workers, Managers, and the Struggle over Industrial Democracy during the World War I Era," in *Industrial Democracy in America: The Ambiguous Promise,* ed. Howell John Harris and Nelson Lichtenstein (New York, 1993), 68–69, 71–77, 79–83.

33. Gitelman, *Legacy of Ludlow,* 158–59, 200, 215, 217–18; Clarence Hicks, *My Life in Industrial Relations: Fifty Years in the Growth of a Profession* (New York, 1941); John D. Rockefeller to Frank P. Walsh, 9 Feb. 1915, box 23, RF.

34. George Frank Lord, *Advertising in War Time,* pamphlet, Oct. 1918, pp. 12–13, HML: David Brody, *Workers in Industrial America: Essays on the Twentieth-Century Struggle* (New York, 1980), 52–54; Sanford M. Jacoby, "Employee Attitude Surveys in Historical Perspective," *Industrial Relations* 27 (winter 1988): 74; Howell John Harris, "Industrial Democracy and Liberal Capitalism, 1890–1925," in Harris and Lichtenstein, eds., *Industrial Democracy,* 60; Daniel T. Rodgers, *The Work Ethic in Industrial America, 1850–1920* (Chicago, 1978), 57–59; Stuart D. Brandes, *American Welfare Capitalism, 1880–1940* (Chicago, 1976), 26.

35. *Literary Digest,* 25 Jan. 1919, 43.

36. *Saturday Evening Post,* 25 Jan. 1919, 63; ibid., 22 Mar. 1919, 53; ibid., 19 Apr. 1919, 55; *Literary Digest,* 18 Jan. 1919, 43; ibid., 15 Feb. 1919, 69; ibid., 15 Mar. 1919, 65; ibid., 13 Dec. 1919, 85. Hydraulic's ostensible motive had been to promote corporate liberalism as an immediate necessity for "the preservation of our industrial life," but its vice president was not surprised that the campaign "had rebounded to Hydraulic's benefit from a purely product sales standpoint." Not only had it "created for Hydraulic a corporate character in the public mind," but by seizing on an issue that troubled many business leaders, it won attention for this relatively small company and appreciation for its "statesmanlike" posture. *Judicious Advertising* 17 (Oct. 1919): 51; *Printers' Ink,* 31 July 1919, 3–4, 6, 154; ibid., 1 Feb. 1920, 24.

37. *Literary Digest,* 2 Feb. 1918, 48–49; Brandes, *American Welfare Capitalism,* 123.

38. *Printers' Ink,* 13 Dec. 1917, 146; ibid., 24 Jan. 1918, 25–28; ibid., 26 June 1919, 37, 39; *Judicious Advertising* 17 (June 1919): 11–12; ibid. (Oct. 1919): 45; *Literary Digest,* 7 Dec. 1918, 75. See also *Saturday Evening Post,* 26 July 1919, 156.

39. E. K. Hall, "A Plea for the Man in the Ranks," speech ms., 22 Mar. 1923, pp. 3, 11, box 23, ATT; Theodore Roosevelt, *Theodore Roosevelt: An Autobiography* (New York, 1913), 510; W. E. C. Nazro, "Welfare Manager in a Large Manufacturing Community," *National Civic Federation Review,* 1 Feb. 1905.

40. Swift & Company, *Year Book, 1926* (Chicago, 1926), 53, S&C; W. W. Atterbury, "The Railroad Outlook," in *Information for Employes and the Public* (monthly bulletin of the Pennsylvania Railroad Co.; hereafter cited as *Information*), Nov. 1925, 2; *Saturday Evening Post,* 3 Apr. 1920, 191.

41. H. A. Batten, *Public Relations,* pamphlet, 28 Apr. 1937, pp. 8–9, 15, NWA; Procter & Gamble, *The Story of a Great Industry,* pamphlet, n.d., pp. 8–9, BL. For other versions of the Lament, see *Information,* Oct. 1926, 2; John D. Rockefeller Jr., "Labor and Capital—Partners," *Atlantic Monthly* 117 (Jan. 1916): 14; John W. Hill, "Industry's Job in Public Relations," speech ms., 17 June 1938, box 39, JWH. General Robert E. Wood, chief executive officer of Sears, Roebuck & Company, held out until the eve of World War II before confessing that it had become "humanly impossible" for him and his officers to retain the "element of personal knowledge and acquaintanceship" that had been "such a vital element in the strength of Sears"; James C. Worthy, *Shaping an American Institution: Robert E. Wood and Sears, Roebuck* (Urbana, Ill., 1984), 124. Similar messages at this late date include Edward R. Stettinius, speech ms., 27 Jan. 1938, pp. 4–5, box 52, ERS; *Kraftsman* (Kraft Foods) 1 (Mar.–Apr. 1943): 2. The pharmaceutical executive Eli Lilly did not fully perceive the need to overcome "the personnel problems of bigness" until just after World War II; see James H. Madison, *Eli Lilly: A Life, 1885–1977* (Indianapolis, 1989): 114–16.

42. *Information,* Oct. 1926, 1–2, 7.

43. Hall, "Plea," 5.

44. "Proposal for a General Motors Magazine," [11 Nov. 1932], General Motors, New York, 1932 file, CFK; George J. Yundt, *Telephone Companies and Corner Grocery Stores: A Comparison,* pamphlet, July 1919, p. 3, BL.

45. J. Carlisle MacDonald, "Public Relations at the Employee Level," *Public Relations Journal* 48 (Sept. 1948): 5; John D. Rockefeller Jr., *The Personal Relation in Industry,* pamphlet, 11 Jan. 1917, p. 12, box 23, RG 2, RF; "Speech for Bayard Colgate for Radio," [1934], box 216, folder 5, WLB. Even the heads of much smaller companies, such as Henry Dennison of the Dennison Manufacturing Company, could be heard calling for restoration of "a human contact in industrial concerns that has been lost through growth in size"; Dennison, "What the Employment Department Should Be in Industry," speech ms., Apr. 1917, case 1, DM.

46. Hall, "Plea," 6–7, 22. See also E. K. Hall, "Working toward Employer-Employee Cooperation," *Service Letter on Industrial Relations,* 5 Feb. 1929, p. 2, box 549, acc. 2723, ERS. Recounting

how one worker had "always felt until about a year ago that [he] was kind of a servant of the family" but now was "beginning to feel like . . . a honest-to-God member of the family, just a real member," Hall concluded: "There is the story in a nutshell." President Walter Teagle of Standard Oil of New Jersey expressed the same hope of making the employee feel like "a member of the family rather than a servant of the family," a statement that was disseminated to employees in the company magazine; *The Lamp* 3 (Feb. 1921): 20.

47. Report on internal house organ, 7 Jan. 1922, p. 6, Hawkins 1922 file, CFK.

48. In fact, the merging of these symbols set a significant precedent in the business world of the late nineteenth century. John Wanamaker, the most effusive of all the department store entrepreneurs in employing company-as-family rhetoric, was flattered to have his immense new store compared to an army. When Ulysses S. Grant came there to buy a military uniform for a postpresidential world tour, he lauded the complexity and scale of Wanamaker's operations in a phrase that Wanamaker treasured. "It takes as much generalship to organize a business like this as to organize an army," Grant observed. Wanamaker himself could comfortably address his employees as his "store family" and, in the next breath, speak of being "in the ranks with you." Joseph H. Appel, *The Business Biography of John Wanamaker: Founder and Builder* (New York, 1930), 177–78. On the cultivation of the "store family" idea by Wanamaker and other mass retailers, see William Leach, *Land of Desire: Merchants, Power, and the Rise of a New American Culture* (New York, 1993), 118–21.

49. Alfred D. Chandler Jr., *Strategy and Structure: Chapters in the History of the Industrial Enterprise* (Cambridge, Mass., 1962), 21–23, 38–39; idem, *The Visible Hand: The Managerial Revolution in American Business* (Cambridge, Mass., 1977), 79–121; JoAnne Yates, *Control through Communication: The Rise of System in American Management* (Baltimore, 1989), 77.

50. Peter F. Drucker, *The Concept of the Corporation*, 2d ed. (New York, 1972), xv; Alfred P. Sloan Jr., *Adventures of a White-Collar Man* (New York, 1941), 136; George David Smith, *From Monopoly to Competition: The Transformations of Alcoa, 1888–1986* (New York, 1988), 19; *Cheesekraft* 1 (Nov. 1920): 5.

51. Drucker, *Concept of the Corporation*, xv; AT&T, *The Story of a Great Achievement*, pamphlet, 1915, p. 12, ATT; Elbert Hubbard, *Our Telephone Service*, pamphlet, 1913, p. 28, BL; John Dennis Jr., "Marshall Field: A Great Mercantile Genius," *Everybody's Magazine* 14 (Mar. 1906): 297–98.

52. *Saturday Evening Post*, 9 Jan. 1915, 34; ibid., 12 Feb. 1916, 58; ibid., 9 Sept. 1916, 66; Charles M. Ripley, *Life in a Large Manufacturing Plant* (Schenectady, N.Y., 1919), 9, 64. On the use of the metaphor of "army" mainly to evoke size, see *Schenectady Works News*, 1 June 1923, 2; W. W. Atterbury, *He Profits Most Who Serves Best*, pamphlet, 18 Sept. 1923, p. 5, ALD; *Kodak Magazine* 1 (June 1920): n.p. For examples of "army" applied to clients, subscribers, stockholders, and customers, see *Du Pont Magazine* 1 (July 1913): 1; *Metropolitan* 23 [1904]: n.p., MLIC; William Banning, "Advertising Technique and Copy," 1921, p. 10, box 1310, ATT; report, 7 Jan. 1922, p. 9, Hawkins 1922 file, CFK; *Nation's Business* 12 (Mar. 1924): 85; *America Calling*, pamphlet, 1936, box 34–31, NWA.

53. Yates, *Control through Communication*, 15, 97. In her discussion of the applications of sophisticated information systems, Yates gives particular attention to the Metropolitan Life Insurance Company—one of the corporations that indulged most thoroughly in the use of the family metaphor.

54. Alfred D. Chandler Jr. and Stephen Salsbury, *Pierre S. du Pont and the Making of the Modern Corporation* (New York, 1971), 591; *The Lamp* 3 (Feb. 1921): 20.

55. *Alcoa News*, 28 May 1934, 1; ibid., 15 Apr. 1935, 1; ibid., 30 Sept. 1935, 1; *The Next Step* (N. W. Ayer & Son employee newsletter) 1 (Dec. 1920): 10–12; Swift & Company, *Year Book, 1916* (Chicago, 1916), 15, CHS; *Western Electric News* 8 (Dec. 1919): 18; H. J. Heinz Co., *Sixty-one Years of Friendly Industrial Relationships*, pamphlet, 8 Nov. 1930, pp. 9, 13, BL; *Carnation* 14 (Jan.–Feb. 1934): 33; ibid. 15 (July–Aug. 1935): 11; ibid. (Sept.–Oct. 1935): 2–3; *Welcome to "Caterpillar,"* pamphlet, [1942–43], box 27, folder 51, HHC; Haley Fiske, "The Metropolitan: A Solvent of Discord," 1924, in Metropolitan Life Insurance Company, *Addresses by the President of the MLIC and the Guests of the Company at the President's Triennial Conventions, 1910–1928* (New York, 1923–28), 3:337; *Home Office* 3 (Mar. 1922): 4; ibid. 5 (Mar. 1924): 14.

56. Angel Kwolek-Folland, *Engendering Business: Men and Women in the Corporate Office, 1870–1930* (Baltimore, 1994), 129–35; idem, "Gender, Self, and Work in the Life Insurance Industry, 1880–1930," in *Work Engendered: Toward a New History of American Labor*, ed. Ava Baron (Ithaca, N.Y., 1991), 171–72.

57.   Lee Frankel, "The Metropolitan Agent," speech ms., 1916, p. 6, box 13-05-03, LKF; *Intelligencer* (New England Territory), 12 June 1909, 2; *Metropolitan* 26 (historical number, 1912): n.p.; ibid. 23 [ca. 1905]: n.p., MLIC; *Home Office* 1 (May 1920): 3; ibid. 3 (Mar. 1922): 3–4; ibid. 5 (Mar. 1924): 14. See also Kwolek-Folland, *Engendering*, 129. On John Wanamaker's similar view of himself as serving "in relation of father" to his employees (with store matrons as meddling mothers), see Leach, *Land of Desire,* 119.

58.   Metropolitan Life Insurance Company, *The Welfare Work Conducted by the MLIC for the Benefit of Its Employes,* pamphlet, 1912, p. 5, BL; idem, *Welfare Work for Employees,* pamphlet, 1915, BL.

59.   *Ford Man,* 20 Sept. 1917, 1. See also *Wellville Post* 2 (Aug. 1926): 24. The journalist's quote is taken from Yates, *Control through Communication,* 17.

60.   *Home Office* 1 (May 1920): 2; *Information,* 19 Jan. 1917, 2; *Bethlehem Review* 7 (22 Apr. 1925), 1; *Oil-Power* 2 (Dec. 1917): 163; Heinz, *Sixty-one Years,* 9; *NCR,* 15 July 1899, 351. The very term "esprit de corps" carried strong military connotations. Corporations that most often used the imagery of army and family interchangeably, such as AT&T and the Pennsylvania Railroad, steadily sought the same quality in their employees—the *spirit* of service.

61.   *Pullman News* 1 (June 1922): 48; ibid. (Aug. 1922): 98; F. W. Lovejoy et al. to George Eastman, 15 Nov. 1918, pp. 1–2, box 31, GEC; *Printers' Ink,* 10 Jan. 1912, 124; ibid., 9 May 1912, 62; *Fort Wayne Works News* 1 (July 1917): 1. See also Brandes, *American Welfare Capitalism,* 1; *The Lamp* 3 (Feb. 1921): 20.

62.   For further examples of such portraits, see *Fort Wayne Works News* 2 (June 1918): 4–5; *Saturday Evening Post,* 15 Nov. 1925, 108–9; *Ford News,* 15 Dec. 1923, 3; *Literary Digest,* 18 Sept. 1915, 625.

63.   Another problem with these panoramas was that they afforded no comfortable place for the company president to appear, as either troop commander or paterfamilias. The scale would dwarf him no matter where he was stationed in relation to the massed workers. The only conventional solution would have been his cameo portrait as an inset, but that would clearly separate him physically and psychologically from his family/legion.

64.   *Saturday Evening Post,* 14 Nov. 1925, 108–9; ibid., 2 July 1927, 56; *Pullman News* 5 (May 1926): 10–11; *Schenectady Works News,* 1 June 1923, cover and p. 2; *Ford News,* 15 Dec. 1923, 3; *Literary Digest,* 18 Sept. 1915, 625.

65.   For the World War II era, see *Life,* 13 Nov. 1944, 21; *GM Folks* 6 (Mar. 1943): 27; ibid. (Dec. 1943): 25; Westinghouse Electric and Manufacturing Company, "Fifty-ninth Annual Report," 31 Dec. 1944, p. 32, HCR.

66.   Howell John Harris, *The Right to Manage: Industrial Relations Policies of American Business in the 1940s* (Madison, Wisc., 1982), 102n.32; *Carnation* 14 (Jan.–Feb. 1934): 13. Sometimes the concepts of team and family were conflated within the same statement, or even the same sentence; see *System* 25 (Jan. 1914): 15; *The Lamp* 21 (Apr. 1939): 15.

67.   *Printers' Ink,* 13 Jan. 1916, 104; *The Lamp* 21 (June 1938): 28. What corporate leaders sought above all was the sentiment expressed in an unsigned testimonial by an employee of the Western Electric Company in 1927. Although he harbored "an inherent distrust of large corporations," this "anonymous fledgling" confessed, he had found in AT&T "not a ravenous monster . . . but a family helpful, firm, and resourceful," a truly "exceptional family." "There is hardly a day," he reflected, "in which I am not rather surprised at the positive attitude I find myself holding toward the Company and my work. It may be that I have found something transcendental about the Bell System." This employee's exceptional family included "my boss who knows me" and who also "has *his* business father, and so on . . . up the pyramid." Ultimately, the concept of family, even in a modernizing age, did not seem to business leaders to disrupt patriarchy. *Western Electric News* 16 (June 1927): 16–17.

68.   Leo Spitzer, *A Method of Interpreting Literature* (Northampton, Mass., 1949), 117–21; Smith, *From Monopoly to Competition,* 162; Madison, *Lilly,* 99; Jeanette White, oral history, interview by E. Adkins, 10 Feb. 1988, p. 19, KGF; Marge Pshea, oral history, interview by E. Adkins, 26 Feb. 1991, pp. 3, 11, KGF.

69.   Association of Industrial Editors, *Industrial Editorship on Economic Understanding* (New York, 1949), 7; *Printers' Ink Monthly* 18 (Apr. 1929): 95. Those who stood to gain from the proliferation of employee magazines, such as the Addressograph-Multigraph Corporation and individual public relations officers, gladly contributed to expectations of "close harmony" that would result as the

magazine made the company welcome into the employee's home and family. Addressograph-Multigraph Co., *Close Harmony,* pamphlet, 1939, box 1002, NYWF.

70.   Howard Elliott to W. W. Atterbury, 8 May 1920, box 18, ILL; Ivy Lee to Elisha Lee, 10 June 1930, box 18, ILL; Lee, "Editing Public Opinion," chap. 4, p. 4; *Western Electric News* 1 (Mar. 1912): 1; "Proposal for a General Motors Magazine" (emphasis mine). See also *Kraftsman* 1 (Mar.–Apr. 1943): 2; Stanley C. Allyn, *The Employee Publication: The Voice of Industry,* pamphlet, [1947], BL.

71.   Stuart Brandes (*American Welfare Capitalism,* 62) identifies the "first company publication directed primarily at employees" as the *Factory News,* initiated by the National Cash Register Company in 1890. That company's previous house organ was the *NCR,* first published in 1886 for the company's sales agents and "later expanded to cover the doings of all personnel at home and abroad"; Isaac Marcosson, *Wherever Men Trade: The Romance of the Cash Register* (New York, 1948), 41.

72.   Julien Elfenbein, *Business Journalism,* 2d ed. (New York, 1969), 157; C.A.R. to "Betty," undated typed memo, attached to first volume of *Westinghouse News,* WLA; Hiebert, *Courtier,* 97–101; *Industrial Bulletin* (Colorado Fuel and Iron Company) 1 (Oct. 1915): 4, 9. The first issue of the CF&I employees' magazine carried an open letter from Rockefeller in which he spoke of his "pleasant consciousness that I have a host of friends in this large company family, many of whom I have spoken with personally, others whom I shall hope to take by the hand when I am here again."

73.   David E. Nye, *Image Worlds: Corporate Identities at General Electric, 1890–1930* (Cambridge, Mass., 1985), 71, 92. A study in 1921 reported that 91 percent of the 334 employee publications then in existence had been started in 1917 or later; see Willis Wissler, *Study of Content and Arrangement of Employe Magazines,* pamphlet, Nov. 1930, pp. 1–2, BL. On the extent of turnover, see Daniel Nelson, *Managers and Workers: Origins of the New Factory System in the United States, 1880–1920,* 2d ed. (Madison, Wisc., 1995), 84–86, 156, 161–62; Lizabeth Cohen, *Making a New Deal: Industrial Workers in Chicago, 1919–1939* (New York, 1990), 170–71, 179, 197–99; Henry Dennison, "Recollections," p. 4, case 1, DM.

74.   Sanford M. Jacoby, *Employing Bureaucracy: Managers, Unions, and the Transformation of Work in American Industry, 1900–1945* (New York, 1985), 6, 96; *The Lamp* 3 (Feb. 1921): 20; *Western Electric News* 1 (Mar. 1912), 1; ibid. 4 (Jan. 1915), 25.

75.   *Pullman News* 1 (May 1922): 3; ibid. (Nov. 1922): 207; ibid. 5 (July 1926): 87; ibid. 6 (Feb. 1927): 339; *Ford Man,* 15 Oct. 1917, 2; *Wellville Post* 2 (Mar. 1926): 14. *Du Pont Magazine* took a more subtle approach, printing a speech of gratitude offered by a company office boy, Guy Davis. The editor advised readers that Davis had shown "an appreciation of his duties and his importance as a link in the machinery of the organization that may well be studied by all of us"; *Du Pont Magazine* 4 (July 1915): 7. *Alcoa News* similarly found room for a letter from a plant worker who asked other employees whether "we are doing all we can to help ourselves" and urged them to support the company and themselves during economic depression by evangelizing their friends and neighbors with "the gospel of aluminum"; *Alcoa News,* 2 May 1932, 2.

76.   *Ford Man,* 15 Oct. 1917, 2–3; *Westinghouse Electric News* 1 (June 1915): 1; ibid. (Aug. 1915): 9; ibid. 2 (Nov. 1915): 13. See also *Bethlehem Review,* no. 1 (24 Apr. 1924): 4.

77.   *The Lamp* 2 (Jan. 1920): 25–26; *Swift Arrow* 1 (20 May 1921): 1, 3; Yates, *Control through Communication,* 195; *Printers' Ink,* 13 Jan. 1916, 104. For examples of editorial claims and exhortations, see *Pullman News* 1 (Nov. 1922): 194; *Fort Wayne Works News* 3 (Apr.–May 1919): 6–7; *Main Wheel* 1 (Apr. 1920): 3; *Information,* 5 Apr. 1917, 2; *Ford Man,* 20 Sept. 1917, 1; *Westinghouse Electric News* 1 (Nov. 1914): 1; ibid. 2 (June 1915): 8; ibid. 13 (Mar. 1927): 31; *Western Electric News* 1 (Mar. 1912): 1; *General Foods Quarterly* 1 (1938): inside front cover; *Kraftsman* 1 (Mar.–Apr. 1943): 2; Wissler, "Employe Magazines," 3; AT&T, proceedings of publicity conference, 1923, p. 12, box 1310, ATT. The Ford advertising manager argued that *Ford Man* should be a "personal" paper in which "the employees in the Ford family could express . . . their candid opinions." The very title, he suggested, "carried a psychological significance. 'The Ford Man': me, you, him, them; my paper, your paper, his paper, their paper." C. Brownell to E. G. Liebold, 2 Nov. 1920, box 22, acc. 572, FM. The editors and public relations executives frequently found it necessary to remind themselves that "the magazines are not produced for executives" and that they must "humanize the publications and . . . guard . . . against snobbishness and dogmatism." Even by 1936, when United States Steel belatedly inaugurated a corporation-wide employee magazine, these lessons still failed to counteract the impulse of the editor to please top management. Advisors to the corporation noted that the first issue of *U.S. Steel News* contained "nothing for the mass of employees and their families to get excited

about" and seemed to have been "prepared to please the head officers of a corporation." Bruce Barton to Edward R. Stettinius Jr., 23 Apr. 1936, box 64, ERS; Samuel Crowther to Stettinius, 18 Apr. 1936, box 64, ERS.

78. *Printers' Ink,* 13 Jan. 1916, 109; *Western Electric News* 8 (Dec. 1919): 19; Yates, *Control through Communication,* 76; *Bell Telephone News* 4 (Mar. 1915): 20−30; Lee, "Editing Public Opinion," chap. 5, p. 3; David B. Sicilia, "Selling Power: Marketing and Monopoly at Boston Edison, 1886−1929" (Ph.D. diss., Brandeis University, 1991), 438; William Von Phul to Stettinius, 6 May 1936, box 64, ERS; Cohen, *Making a New Deal,* 179; see also *Printers' Ink,* 8 Nov. 1928, 150. According to Brandes (*American Welfare Capitalism,* 63), one editor defined the ideal company magazine as one that published some "two thousand names a month so that each employee would see his name in print at least once a year."

79. Brandes, *American Welfare Capitalism,* 64−65; *Alcoa News,* 15 Apr. 1935, 1; *Wellville Post* 1 (9 May 1925): 1; ibid. (25 June 1925): 15; ibid. 2 (Mar 1926): 14, 17; ibid. (Apr. 1926): 3; *RCA Family Circle* 1 (July 1935): 2−3; *Hawthorne Microphone,* 13 Apr. 1925, 2−3; Jacoby, *Employing Bureaucracy,* 50; *Printers' Ink,* 13 Jan. 1916, 104; "The Family Circle," *BBDO News Letter,* 2 Mar. 1935, n.p.; *Printers' Ink Monthly* 7 (Dec. 1923): 43; Gerald Zahavi, "Negotiated Loyalty: Welfare Capitalism and the Shoeworkers of Endicott Johnson, 1920−1940," *Journal of American History* 71 (Dec. 1983): 605−7. Early on, many house organs, such as the *Westinghouse Electric News, Pullman News, Mutual Magazine* (Pennsylvania Railroad), and *Western Electric News,* incorporated special sections for wives, with cooking and style hints, and for children, with stories and puzzles. *Mutual Magazine* entitled its section of recipes and household hints "Our Home Circle." Gerald Zahavi ("Negotiated Loyalty," 607) notes that "photographs of families, children, babies, and homes filled the pages of the *E-J Workers' Review.*"

80. *Fort Wayne Works News* 4 (Nov. 1920): 5; *Printers' Ink Monthly* 8 (Jan. 1924): 112. See also *Main Wheel* 1 (Feb. 1920): 2; *Mutual Magazine* 11 (Sept. 1925): 27; ibid. 12 (June 1927): 33; ibid. 13 (Feb. 1928): 10−11; *Ford Man,* 15 Dec. 1917, 1; ibid., 18 Mar. 1918, 1. On the very similar role and content of employee magazines in Germany during the same era, see Mary Nolan, *Visions of Modernity: American Business and the Modernization of Germany* (New York, 1994), 197−98.

81. *Pullman News* 1 (May 1922): 3; *Printed Salesmanship* 49 (Mar. 1927): 73; Chaplin Tyler, *Public Relations and Your Company,* pamphlet, 16 Jan. 1936, pp. 1, 4, HML; Harris, *Right to Manage,* 191.

82. *Erpigram,* 20 Dec. 1928, 2; *GE Monogram* 2 (Oct. 1924): 16; *Wellville Post,* 9 May 1925, 1; *Fort Wayne Works News* 1 (July 1917): 1; *Printers' Ink,* 20 Sept. 1928, 179−80. On the need for corporations with geographically extended operations to unite their salesmen, dealers, factory workers, and other employees through the company magazine, see Norval A. Hawkins, report to Operations Committee, 7 Jan. 1922, pp. 2, 5−6, Hawkins 1922 file, CFK; Ivy Lee, "Some Suggestions Concerning Anaconda Publicity," 18 Jan. 1924, box 4, folder 5, ILL; Ivy Lee to John D. Ryan, 18 Jan. 1924, box 4, folder 5, ILL; A. W. Page to All Publicity Managers, 19 May 1932, F. B. Jewett files, series 1, box 11, ATT; Thomas Logan to Gerard Swope, 15 Mar. 1924, folder 201.2, GS; "Ink Spots and Sole Leather," n.d., pp. 58, 63, IH; A. H. Young to W. A. Irvin, 23 Dec. 1935, box 64, ERS.

83. *Harvester World* 3 (Jan. 1912): 26−27; Wadsworth W. Mount to Alfred P. Sloan Jr., 7 Aug. 1937, enclosed in Mount to Lammot du Pont, 21 Dec. 1937, box 48, acc. 1662, DP; Mount to Lammot du Pont, 10 Dec. 1937, 21 Dec. 1937, box 48, acc. 1662, DP; R. C. B. May to Gerard Swope, 27 Oct. 1938, GS.

84. *Saturday Evening Post,* 12 Aug. 1922, 63; "Western Electric Advertising, 1920−1922," scrapbook, ATT; *Western Electric News* 11 (Aug. 1922): back cover; *Intelligencer,* 24 Feb. 1923, 24; Heinz Co., *Sixty-one Years,* 17, 19, BL; "Allis-Chalmers Family Party," radio script, 16 Apr. 1938, box 3, folder 5, HHC.

85. *Printers' Ink Monthly* 1 (May 1920): 32, 34; *Erpigram,* 1 Nov. 1929, 1. See also *Time,* 16 June 1930, 65.

86. Pennsylvania Railroad, press release, 28 Dec. 1925; A. J. County, "Christmas Message," 29 Dec. 1925; Elisha Lee, address, 29 Dec. 1925; W. W. Atterbury, "Address at Christmas Party," 29 Dec. 1925: scrapbook 139, ILL.

87. *Western Electric News* 1 (July 1912): 7; Metropolitan Life Insurance Company, Policyholders Service Bureau, *Institutional Company Magazines,* pamphlet, 1932, p. 24, BL. At United States Steel, the editor recognized the desirability of home distribution of the new employees' magazine in

1936, because "home influence may well prove decisive in an industrial crisis" and the worker's wife or mother could be expected to be "more conservative in her attitude toward any move that would interrupt family income." The problem of identifying home addresses for all employees, however, seemed insurmountable. G. L. Lacher to A. H. Young, 11 Feb. 1936, box 64, ERS. On this issue, see also Elizabeth Fones-Wolf, *Selling Free Enterprise: The Business Assault on Labor and Liberalism, 1945– 1960* (Urbana, Ill. 1994), 81; F. R. Henderer, *A Comparative Study of the Public Relations Practices in Six Industrial Corporations* (Pittsburgh, 1956), 177.

88. Zahavi, "Negotiated Loyalty," 607.

89. For a review of the relative significance of various motivations, which ultimately emphasizes the predominance of profit-maximizing judgments, see H. M. Gitelman, "Welfare Capitalism Reconsidered," *Labor History* 33 (winter 1992): 5–31.

90. *Pullman News* 1 (June 1922): 48; ibid. (Oct. 1922): 171; ibid. 5 (June 1926): 56. All employees, the company averred, "from the humblest helper to the president," shared a bond of mutuality.

91. Heald, *Social Responsibilities*, 102, 111–12; Whiting Williams, "Business Statesmanship: A New Force in Business," *Magazine of Business* 55 (Apr. 1929): 388, 460.

92. For this more nostalgic view of welfare and employee representation programs, see John D. Rockefeller Jr. to J. F. Welborn, 11 Aug. 1914, box 23, RG 2, RF; Edward R. Stettinius, "The Value and Cultivation of Good Will in American Industry," speech ms., Jan. 1939, box 51, ERS.

93. Elisha Lee, *Supervision and Discipline: A Plan for Closer Industrial Relations,* pamphlet, 1923, 3–6, ILL; Rockefeller, *Personal Relation,* 16–17, 30, 32; Hall, "Plea," 11–12; *The Lamp* 2 (Jan. 1920): 27–28. See also Jacoby, *Employing Bureaucracy,* 50, 62. On German envy of the reputed capacities of American managers and engineers for openness, lack of pretense, and informality in shop floor leadership, see Nolan, *Visions of Modernity,* 193.

94. Nelson, *Managers and Workers,* 100, 114–17; Daniel Nelson, "The Company Union Movement: A Reexamination, 1900–1937," *Business History Review* 56 (autumn 1982): 339; Michael B. Miller, *The Bon Marché: Bourgeois Culture and the Department Store, 1869–1920* (Princeton, 1981), 90– 94, 194–97, 220; Charles Dellheim, "The Creation of a Company Culture: Cadburys, 1861– 1931," *American Historical Review* 92 (Feb. 1987): 13–44.

95. U.S. Steel even devoted a major segment of its corporate exhibit at the Panama-Pacific Exposition to its improvements in safety and sanitary conditions for workers, its development of employee lockers and showers, and its sponsorship of vegetable and flower gardens for its employees. It boasted of a welfare program that encompassed model houses, visiting nurses, classes in practical housekeeping ("for the foreign-born women"), schools, plant restaurants, and employee stock-purchase plans. United States Steel Corporation, *Description of Exhibits, U.S. Steel Corporation, 1915 Fair, San Francisco* (Pittsburgh, 1915), 47, 49, 51; Charles L. Close, *Welfare Work in the Steel Industry,* pamphlet, 1920, pp. 16, 23–24, 36–37, BL.

96. On the increased consciousness of the extent and costs of labor turnover, see David F. Noble, *America by Design: Science, Technology, and the Rise of Corporate Capitalism* (New York, 1977), 262, 294; Kim McQuaid, *A Response to Industrialism: Liberal Businessmen and the Revolving Spectrum of Capitalist Reform, 1886–1960* (New York, 1986), 85–86; *The Lamp* 3 (Feb. 1921): 1. Kenneth Lipartito emphasizes the importance of comforts and conveniences, from free lunches to reading circles and tasteful restrooms, in AT&T's efforts to attract the "best class of operators"; Lipartito, "When Women Were Switches: Technology, Work, and Gender in the Telephone Industry, 1890–1920," *American Historical Review* 99 (Oct. 1994): 1090, 1098. A local newspaper hailed the lunchrooms maintained in Rochester by Bausch & Lomb and Kodak under the celebratory title "Factory Restaurant Ousts Dinner Pail"; *Democrat and Chronicle,* 6 Mar. 1921, clipping, scrapbook 3, GEC.

97. *Western Electric News* 1 (Aug. 1912): 12; ibid. 2 (July 1913): front cover; *Mutual Magazine* 11 (Dec. 1925): 17; *Alcoa News,* 30 Nov. 1936, 2; Alvin Von Auw, *Heritage and Destiny: Reflections on the Bell System in Transition* (New York, 1983), 354. On employee participation in vacation camps, see also Susan Porter Benson, *Counter Cultures: Saleswomen, Managers, and Customers in American Department Stores, 1890–1940* (Urbana, Ill., 1986), 195. On workers' response to corporate welfare programs, see Cohen, *Making a New Deal,* 72–75, 183–84, 193–96, 206–11.

98. *Saturday Evening Post,* 3 Mar. 1928, 102–3; *Pennsylvania News,* 15 Aug. 1928, 10–12; ibid., 15 Sept. 1938, 6.

99. McQuaid, *Response to Industrialism*, 129; Robert F. Burk, *The Corporate State and the Broker State: The Du Ponts and American National Politics, 1925–1940* (Cambridge, Mass., 1990), 12; Hicks, *My Life*, 55, 58; Standard Oil Company of New Jersey, *Announcement to Employees*, pamphlet, 1918, n.p., BL.

100. "Minutes of Meeting of Officers, Division Managers, Works Managers and Superintendents to Consider Plan of Harvester Industrial Council," 25–26 Feb. 1919, pp. 3, 7–8; A. H. Young to H. F. Perkins, 16 Jan. 1919: folder 213, IH. See also Kim McQuaid, "Corporate Liberalism in the American Business Community, 1920–1940," *Business History Review* 52 (autumn 1978): 345; Brody, *Workers in Industrial America*, 55–59.

101. Hall, "A Plea for the Man in the Ranks," speech ms., 22 Mar. 1923, p. 12, box 23, ATT; *Information*, Nov. 1925, 2; *The Lamp* 3 (Feb. 1921): 20. On the interlinkage of company magazine and employee representation, see G. L. Lacher, "U.S. Steel News," 1936, p. 7, box 64, ERS.

102. Employee representation plans also operated more generally to facilitate the expansion of managerial control. Daniel Nelson ("Company Union Movement," 336–37, 339, 352) describes company unionism, in its "most advanced form," as part of a larger "managerial thrust" that "extended the managerial hierarchy to the shop floor, enlarging the realm of the personnel officials, curtailing the prerogatives of the line supervisors and enlisting lower echelon employees in the operation of the firm." In effect, as Lizabeth Cohen puts it, management used representation plans to "invad[e] 'the foreman's empire'" and ally itself with workers against foremen, thus helping the employer not only to ward off union organizers but also to "accomplish other goals close to his heart: the restriction of the foreman's authority and the individualization of employee-employer relations"; Cohen, *Making a New Deal*, 168–69, 172–74, 187–90. See also Jacoby, *Employing Bureaucracy*, 186–89.

103. AT&T, proceedings of publicity conference, 1928, pp. 20, 40, 42, 49, 53, 55, 57, box 1310, ATT.

104. Nelson, "Company Union Movement," 346, 348; Cyrus McCormick Jr., *Employee Representation*, pamphlet, 30 Nov. 1925, pp. 6–7, 13, file 213, IH; "Harvester Industrial Council Report of an Inquiry Conducted under the Direction of the Special Conference Committee," 10 Aug. 1928, pp. 30–42, file 213, IH. At Du Pont, a 1919 staff report assured executives that the Standard Oil Company's experiment with employee representation had demonstrated that the "scheme is entirely innocuous insofar as danger to the Company's established labor policies is concerned." Standard Oil's plan did not cost much, the report observed, and it enabled the company to use "clever humbug" in justifying its wages. The system induced the employee representatives "to look at most matters from the Company's viewpoint." Lammot du Pont to Harry McGowan, 9 Aug. 1933, box 72, acc. 1662, DP; L. du Pont to Executive Committee, 28 May 1934, box 72, acc. 1662, DP; T. C. Schwenke to T. W. Ervin, [Jan. 1935], box 20, acc. 1813, DP; W. S. Carpenter Jr., speech at Dye Works Managers' Dinner, 22 May 1935, box 20, acc. 1813, DP; Wm. L. Allen to C. A. Patterson, 17 May 1918, box 26, acc. 1662, DP. Such results led some large corporations to form or maintain employee associations when they faced no threat of unionization; see John Schact, *The Making of Telephone Unionism, 1920–1947* (New Brunswick, N.J., 1985), 43–45.

105. Zahavi, "Negotiated Loyalty," 609–12, 616; Nelson, "Company Union Movement," 352, 357; Schact, *Making of Telephone Unionism*, 2, 14, 43–44; John T. Broderick, *Forty Years with General Electric* (Albany, N.Y., 1929), 137, 142–43; Cohen, *Making a New Deal*, 206–10. For contemporary reservations about the effects of employee representation on workers, see Cyrus McCormick to Thomas Lamont, 13 Dec. 1918, box 221, TL. For the warning of one industrial figure that employee representation would make employees "organization-conscious," see Worthy, *Shaping an American Institution*, 161.

106. Hiebert, *Courtier*, 49, 75, 81–82; Lee, "Constructive Publicity," n.d., box 2, ILL; Ivy Lee to George D. Dixon, 21 June 1912, box 18, ILL; W. W. Atterbury to Samuel Rea, 8 Oct. 1920, box 1153, acc. 1819, PRR; Atterbury to Ivy Lee, 25 Oct. 1920, box 165, acc. 1810, PRR; Atterbury to Elisha Lee et al., 27 Oct. 1920, box 165, acc. 1810, PRR.

107. On Atterbury's sponsorship of, and reliance on, Ivy Lee, see Atterbury to Samuel Rea, 8 Oct. 1920, box 1153, acc. 1819, PRR; Atterbury to Ivy Lee, 12 May 1920, box 18, ILL; Howard Elliott to Atterbury, 8 May 1920, box 18, ILL.

108. George H. Burgess and Miles C. Kennedy, *Centennial History of the Pennsylvania Railroad* (Philadelphia, 1949), 589–90; *Mutual Magazine* 11 (May 1926): 6; John F. Stover, *The Life and Decline of*

the *American Railroad* (New York, 1970), 201–2; Chandler, *Strategy and Structure,* 38–39. The Pennsylvania Railroad had been the most prominent corporation in adopting the line-and-staff structure of the army. Chandler suggests, however, that this choice arose more from the internal needs of extended railroad operations than from any imitation of military organization.

109. Robert H. Zieger, *Republicans and Labor, 1919–1929* (Lexington, Ky., 1969), 192; Leonard Painter, *Through Fifty Years with the Brotherhood of Railway Carmen of America* (Kansas City, Mo., 1941), 171. On the issue of discipline, see R. M. Patterson to W. W. Atterbury, 18 Feb. 1908, Pennsylvania Railroad Corporation Papers, HML.

110. Burgess and Kennedy, *Centennial History,* 591; Peter Lyon, *To Hell in a Day Coach: An Exasperating Look at American Railroads* (Philadelphia, 1968), 153.

111. *Mutual Magazine* 12 (May 1926): 6; Lyon, *To Hell,* 15; Ivy L. Lee, "What Is to Become of Our Railroads?" speech ms., Jan. 1923, p. 15, box 16, ILL; *Information,* 22 Mar. 1922, 7–8.

112. W. W. Atterbury, "Railroad Outlook"; *Information,* Nov. 1925, 2; W. W. Atterbury, *Let Railroad Men Run the Railroad Business,* pamphlet, Dec. 1921, pp. 5–6, BL; Pennsylvania Railroad [PRR], *Speaking for 8,000,* pamphlet, 22 Aug. 1921, HML; PRR, *Pennsylvania Railroad Employe Representation, 1925,* pamphlet, 1925, pp. 26–27, 30, HML.

113. Zieger, *Republicans and Labor,* 132–33; Lyon, *To Hell,* 154; *Mutual Magazine* 12 (May 1926): 9; Elisha Lee, "Cooperation Instead of Conflict in Railroad Service," speech ms., 26 Oct. 1925, p. 3, vol. 139, ILL.

114. By 1926, Atterbury and other Pennsylvania officers had thrown their influence behind the Watson-Parker bill, which abolished the Railroad Labor Board and substituted a system of mediation and arbitration. The 1926 legislation, which Robert Zieger credits with ushering in a period of "relative peace and stability" in railroad labor relations, endorsed in principle the rights of workers to bargain collectively through agents of their own choosing. Although it represented a defeat for those who wished to combat all labor organization, it sustained the role of company unions. As an internal PRR memo put it, "We do not understand that the Watson-Parker bill will in any way change the relations of the Pennsylvania Railroad to its employees." The PRR board of directors congratulated Atterbury on his work behind the scenes to secure passage of the bill in this favorable form. Zieger, *Republicans and Labor,* 195, 205–6, 210–12, 215; Ivy Lee to John D. Rockefeller, 3 May 1926, box 20, ILL; *Pennsylvania Standard* 1 (Feb. 1926): n.p., vol. 144, ILL; E.L. [Elisha Lee] and W.W.A. [W. W. Atterbury], memo, 23 Apr. 1926, MG-286, box 3, folder 8/12, WWA; minutes of the board of directors, 12 May 1926, p. 73, PRR.

115. H. W. Schotter, *The Growth and Development of the Pennsylvania Railroad Company* (Philadelphia, 1927), 418; *Printers' Ink,* 17 Mar. 1927, 93; minutes of the board of directors, 20 June 1926, 153, PRR; Ivy Lee and J. L. Eysmans to W. W. Atterbury, 27 Apr. 1926, box 16, WWA.

116. The J. Walter Thompson agency made this survey in the quick-and-cheap method typical of agency practice in that era. It simply polled executives in its New York, Chicago, and Cincinnati offices, asking them also to forward copies of the survey to their friends and clients who traveled extensively by train. Thus, the survey focused on agency officers, who may have realized that negative feedback would help make the case for an extensive institutional campaign. Still, the criticisms were widespread and specific enough to suggest real problems. I have not been able to discover whether the agency presented the entire survey, with all its damning observations, to the PRR executives or simply conveyed the general results. See "Pennsylvania Railroad, June 26, 1926, Investigation," reel 52, JWT.

117. For at least a decade, Lee had cajoled leaders of the Pennsylvania Railroad to shed their image of soullessness by displaying less haughtiness in their operation of a "mechanically perfect institution" and more sensitivity to the needs and inclinations of human nature. Railroad executives, in particular, Lee observed, had been so content with emphasizing the machines they operated that the public had come to see *them* as machines. Through the human interest story, he proposed to portray the railroads (and their executives) as "composites of human nature." Ivy L. Lee, "Address on 'Courtesy,'" typescript with penciled editing, 24 Nov. 1914, box 421, acc. 1810, PRR; Lee, *Human Nature and Railroads,* 2, 4–5, 9, 14.

118. "Ivy Lee: New York's Door Opener," clipping, [ca. 1921], box 12, ILL; Lee, "Editing Public Opinion," chap. 5, p. 2; Ivy L. Lee and J. L. Eysmans to W. W. Atterbury, 27 Apr. 1926, box 16, folder 42/25, vol. 1, WWA; memo, 2 Nov. 1925, box 16, folder 42/25, vol. 1, WWA.

119. *Advertising Age,* 17 Nov. 1934, 8; *Advertising and Selling Fortnightly,* 24 Feb. 1926, 29; *J. Walter Thompson News,* 29 Apr. 1926, 108–9; *Printers' Ink,* 11 Feb. 1926, 197.

120. *The Limiteds of the Freight Service* (n.d.), *Stories of the Day's Work* (1929), and *Your Name—What Does It Mean?* (n.d.), pamphlets, Pennsylvania Railroad folder, inactive file, JWT; *Pennsylvania News,* 15 Aug. 1927, 12; *Saturday Evening Post,* 9 Apr. 1927, 85; ibid., 16 June 1928, 56; *Information,* 5 Apr. 1925, 1–2; ibid., 1 Nov. 1925, 1.

121. *Pennsylvania News,* 15 Aug. 1927, 12; J. Walter Thompson Company, *News Letter,* 15 Nov. 1928, 1; *Printers' Ink,* 17 Nov. 1927, 44; *Information,* 16 Sept. 1928, 1.

122. Ivy L. Lee to Editor, *Pennsylvania News,* 13 Oct. 1926; Lee to Atterbury, 13 Oct. 1926; Lee to G. B. Harley, 13 Oct. 1926: box 59A/60, WWA.

123. Ads in the Statler series appeared in the *Saturday Evening Post:* 15 Jan. 1921, 52; 20 Aug. 1921, 88; 7 Jan. 1922, 37, 1 Apr. 1922, 88; 24 June 1922, 94; 19 Aug. 1922, 55; 18 Nov. 1922, 120. See also *Printers' Ink,* 9 Feb. 1922, 25–26.

124. Lee, "Editing Public Opinion," chap. 4, pp. 5–6; Ivy Lee, "Advertising," speech ms., Oct. 1930, p. 7, box 4, ILL.

125. *The Story of the Day's Work,* pamphlet, 1928, and *Stories of the Day's Work,* pamphlet, 1929, Pennsylvania Railroad folder, inactive file, JWT. The series ran in the *Saturday Evening Post:* 11 Dec. 1926, 81; 20 Apr. 1927, 111; 1 Oct. 1927, 73; 12 Nov. 1927, 53; 26 Nov. 1927, 124; 7 Apr. 1928, 99. The praise garnered by the redcap ad occasioned a minor embarrassment. When one admirer inquired as to the name of the heroic porter, the Pennsylvania discovered it could not identify him, although his service had provided the content for a prize-winning national ad. *Literary Digest,* 18 Dec. 1926, 45; G. B. Harley to W. W. Atterbury, 3 Sept. 1926, box 16, folder 42/25, WWA; Blanche Eisenrath to Atterbury, 28 Dec. 1926, box 16, folder 42/25, WWA; Ivy Lee to Atterbury, 17 Jan. 1927, box 16, folder 42/25, WWA; Atterbury to R. C. Tallmadge, 28 Dec. 1926, box 16, folder 42/25, WWA; Steward L. Mims to Lee, 6 May 1928, box 17, folder 42/25, WWA; *Your Name—What Does It Mean?*

126. *Saturday Evening Post,* 11 Aug. 1928, 94; ibid., 15 Dec. 1928, 43; *Stories of the Day's Work,* n.p.; *Literary Digest,* 2 Oct. 1926, 47; ibid., 30 Oct. 1926, 51.

127. *Saturday Evening Post,* 14 Jan. 1928, 112. On the combination of paternalistic and instrumental motives that had given rise to the PRR pension plans and their perceived advantages in excluding "any voice on the part of the employees," see Brian Grattan, "'A Triumph in Modern Philanthropy': Age Criteria in Labor Management at the Pennsylvania Railroad," *Business History Review* 64 (winter 1990): 645–47, 651, 654–55.

128. *Limiteds of the Freight Service,* n.p.; *Stories of the Day's Work,* n.p.; *Pennsylvania News,* 1 Jan. 1927, 6; ibid., 1 Feb. 1927, 6; ibid., 1 Oct. 1927, 6; ibid., 1 Dec. 1927, 6; *Mutual Magazine* 13 (Jan. 1928): 4.

129. "Report on Pennsylvania Railroad," 26 June 1926, reel 52, JWT; "Memorandum of Discussion," 26 May 1927, memo no. 513.1, box 1169, PRR; memo, L.E. to M.W.C., n.d., box 1169, PRR; *Printers' Ink,* 24 Nov. 1927, 120–21.

130. William Kennedy, "Workers Are People," *People* 1 (July 1937): 27, JWT; J. Walter Thompson Company, *News Letter,* 31 Jan. 1929, 4; *Tide* 2 (Dec. 1928): 3.

131. Lee, "Editing Public Opinion," chap. 4, p. 7; minutes of representatives meeting, 11 June 1929, p. 14, JWT; "A Columnist's Sidelights on the Pennsylvania Railroad," n.d., n.p., Pennsylvania Railroad folder, inactive file, JWT.

132. Minutes of representatives meeting, 16 May 1928, pp. 1–2, JWT; *Mutual Magazine* 13 (Jan. 1928): 4; *Printers' Ink,* 25 Apr. 1929, 181–82.

133. Lee, "Advertising," 8; *Baltimore & Ohio Magazine* 17 (Jan. 1930): 5; ibid. (Mar. 1930): 10–11, 17; *Tide* 4 (Aug. 1930): 1–2; *Saturday Evening Post,* 26 July 1930, 101; ibid., 13 Dec. 1930, 60.

134. W. A. Atterbury to C. M. Sheaffer, 22 Mar. 1932, box 58A, WWA; Atterbury to Henry Tatnall, 5 Apr. 1932, box 58A, WWA; Atterbury to W. T. Brown, 6 Apr. 1932, box 58A, WWA; Lyon, *To Hell,* 171.

135. Minutes of representatives meeting, 21 Feb. 1928 and 11 June 1929, JWT; J. Walter Thompson Company, *News Letter,* 31 Jan. 1929, 4. For plaudits from the trade press, see *Tide* 2 (Dec. 1928):

3; *Printers' Ink,* 9 May 1929, 130, 132. Even the N. W. Ayer & Son agency offered an indirect compliment to its competitor in *Saturday Evening Post,* 1 Feb. 1930, 89.

136. Lee, "Editing Public Opinion," chap. 4, pp. 3–4; Elisha Lee, address, in *Information,* 26 Oct. 1928, 6; J. George Frederick, *For Top-Executives Only: A Symposium* (New York, 1936), 173.

137. Hall, "Plea," 18; AT&T, proceedings of publicity conference, 1928, 112.

138. *Information,* 15 July 1926; *Pennsylvania News,* 1 Jan. 1927, 1–4; County, "Christmas Message," 29 Dec. 1925, scrapbook 139, ILL. Alvin von Auw of AT&T commented on how that company's employees had taken its public image to heart over the years and found satisfaction in merging their own roles with the company's wider image of service, but his most plausible examples were of executives climbing the managerial ladder; von Auw, *Heritage,* 354, 361–62.

139. Nye, *Image Worlds,* 95–102, 108–9; Owen D. Young, "General Electric Dinner, April 16, 1914," speeches file, ODY; memorandum (Association Island address), 1 July 1926, speeches file, ODY; "Association Island Address," 14 July 1929, speeches file, ODY; "Advertising Conference Address," 25 July 1922, speeches file, ODY; *Printers' Ink,* 6 Mar. 1913, 43–44, 46.

Chapter 4

1. General Motors Corporation, *A Famous Family,* pamphlet, [1923], GM; Verne Burnett to Charles F. Kettering, 2 May 1924, CFK; *Literary Digest,* 21 June 1924, 55; ibid., 20 Sept. 1924, 78; *Saturday Evening Post,* 18 Aug. 1923, 88–89; ibid., 26 Feb. 1924, 94–95; ibid., 12 Apr. 1924, 118–19; Alfred H. Swayne, "Making Friends for the Family," *Judicious Advertising* 22 (Jan. 1924): 25–26.

2. For statistics on GM's workforce, assets, and components, see Moody's Investor Service, *Moody's Analysis of Investments and Security Rating Books,* part 2: *Industrial Investments* (1924), 2011; U.S. Federal Trade Commission, *Report on Motor Vehicle Industry* (Washington D.C., 1939), 546.

3. Bruce Barton, *The Man Nobody Knows* (Indianapolis, 1925); Alice Payne Hackett and James Henry Burke, *Eighty Years of Best Sellers* (New York, 1977), 101; *Advertising Age,* 7 July 1934, 1; James Rorty, *Our Master's Voice* (New York, 1934), 313, 318–20.

4. Ed Roberts, "BBDO Short History," n.d., p. 3, BBDO. In his enthusiasm for the dramatic, Roberts may have collapsed the events slightly. A 1923 listing of "first billing" dates on active BDO accounts indicates 1 Dec. 1922 for GM and Jan. 1923 for GE; memorandum for Mr. Powell, 19 Apr. 1923, BBDO. (Note that Barton, Durstine, and Osborn merged with the Batten Company in 1928; references in the text and notes to BDO versus BBDO reflect this change.)

5. Thomas K. McCraw and Forrest Reinhardt, "Losing to Win: U.S. Steel's Pricing, Investment Decisions, and Market Share, 1901–1938," *Journal of Economic History* 49 (Sept. 1989): 593, 611, 618–19.

6. Alfred P. Sloan Jr., *My Years with General Motors* (New York, 1964), 27; Sloan to Charles F. Kettering, 12 Apr. 1924, CFK; Swayne, "Making Friends," 25.

7. Alfred D. Chandler Jr. and Stephen Salsbury, *Pierre S. du Pont and the Making of the Modern Corporation* (New York, 1971), 473, 512, 597; Donaldson Brown, *Some Reminiscences of an Industrialist* (Easton, N.J., 1977), xi; *Printers' Ink,* 13 Dec. 1923, 17; Sloan, *My Years,* 27; Arthur Pound, *The Turning Wheel: The Story of General Motors through Twenty-five Years, 1908–1933* (Garden City, N.Y., 1934), 197.

8. The production percentages are derived from Lawrence H. Seltzer, *A Financial History of the American Automobile Industry* (Boston, 1928), 84, 135. See also Ed Cray, *Chrome Colossus: General Motors and Its Times* (New York, 1980), 208; Alfred D. Chandler Jr., *Strategy and Structure: Chapters in the History of Industrial Enterprise* (Cambridge, Mass., 1962), 143.

9. Cray, *Chrome Colossus,* 189–90; Chandler and Salsbury, *Du Pont,* 524–25, 535; Chandler, *Strategy and Structure,* 154; Louis Galambos and Joseph Pratt, *The Rise of the Corporate Commonwealth: U.S. Business and Public Policy in the Twentieth Century* (New York, 1988), 73; *Printers' Ink,* 29 Sept. 1921, 3, 6. On centralization, see also Robert F. Burk, *The Corporate State and the Broker State: The du Ponts and American Politics, 1925–1940* (Cambridge, Mass., 1990), 10–11.

10. Donaldson Brown, "Centralized Control with Decentralized Responsibilities," in *American Management Association Annual Convention,* ser. 57 (New York, 1927), 12, reprinted in *Managerial In-*

novation at General Motors, ed. Alfred D. Chandler Jr. (New York, 1979). It may have taken several months for Sloan to gain approval of the General Purchasing Committee proposal; see Sloan to G. B. McCann, 29 Nov. 1922, A. P. Sloan Jr. 1922 file, CFK.

11. Chandler, *Strategy and Structure,* 155; Chandler and Salsbury, *Du Pont,* 547; Arthur J. Kuhn, *GM Passes Ford, 1918–1938: Designing the General Motors Performance-Control System* (University Park, Penn., 1986), 21, 127; Brown, *Some Reminiscences,* 53; T. K. Quinn, *Giant Business: Threat to Democracy—the Autobiography of an Insider* (New York, 1953), 100; Sloan to A. H. Swayne, 11 Feb. 1924, documents II folder, case 1, GMB. Donaldson Brown recalled that he and Sloan had always sought, rather than to cram a policy "down the throats of those depended upon to carry [it] out," to "have the men feel they had invented the course of policy themselves"; "Rough Notes of Meetings with Donaldson Brown," 3 June 1957, pp. 13–15, carton 2, GMB.

12. Sloan, "Memo on Institutional Advertising," 19 Sept. 1922, n.p., separate reports, 1920–1924 folder, case 1, GMB; BBDO, "Report on Sales and Advertising Policies for the U.S. Steel Corporation," enclosed in M. L. MacLeod to E. R. Stettinius, 25 Oct. 1935, box 558, ERS.

13. Sloan, "Memo on Institutional Advertising," n.p.; Sloan, *My Years,* 105.

14. C. S. Mott, "Organizing a Great Industrial," *Management and Administration* 7 (May 1924): 526, reprinted in Chandler, *Managerial Innovation.*

15. Roberts, "BBDO Short History," 3; BDO, "General Motors," 1928, p. 13, account status binder, BBDO; Charles Brower, *Me and Other Advertising Geniuses* (Garden City, N.Y., 1974), 73–74; idem, "The Man Everybody Knew," July 1967, BBDO; Sloan, *My Years,* 104. Although his agency colleagues remarked that Barton's enthusiasms for wider spheres of activity had kept him from ever being "in the business with both feet," they readily acknowledged his exertions and prowess on the "big jobs" of shaping the image of an industrial giant.

16. "Meeting of General Motors House Organ Editors," 8 Feb. 1923, attached to H. G. Weaver to C. F. Kettering, 2 Mar. 1923, CFK; BDO, "General Motors," 13. On Barton's role at GE, see Barton to Gerard Swope, 27 Sept. 1922, 23 Dec. 1922, 4 Oct. 1923; Swope to Barton, 14 Nov. 1922: GS. On the scope of the GE campaign, see David E. Nye, *Electrifying America: Social Meanings of a New Technology* (Cambridge, Mass., 1990), 268, 274.

17. *Advertising and Selling,* 29 Aug. 1935, 36; Gordon Eugene White, "John Caples and His Contributions to Advertising and Communications Research" (Ph.D. diss., University of Illinois at Champaign-Urbana, 1971), 69–70; Rorty, *Our Master's Voice,* 321. Barton's facile flair for sincerity of expression, though an attribute to any corporation concerned with its public image, may also have helped spawn the "quiet desperation" and doubt about the worth of his own vocation that Jackson Lears has discerned in Barton's career and writings. See T. J. Jackson Lears, "From Salvation to Self-Realization: Advertising and the Therapeutic Roots of the Consumer Culture, 1880–1930," in *The Culture of Consumption: Critical Essays in American History, 1880–1980,* ed. Richard Wightman Fox and T. J. Jackson Lears (New York, 1983), 30, 34–37.

18. William Alfred Corey to Bruce Barton, 11 Nov. 1917, box 88, BB; Harvey S. Lamp to Barton, 27 Nov. 1917, box 88, BB; M. E. Voorhies to Barton, 28 Nov. 1917, box 88, BB; *Every Week,* 2 Feb. 1918, 19; ibid., 27 Apr. 1918, 22; ibid., 22 June 1918, 3; memo, unsigned [F. R. Davis] to Gerard Swope, 28 July 1922, GS; F. H. Gale to Swope, 9 Aug. 1922, GS.

19. United War Work Campaign, "Memorandum of Agreement between the Cooperating Organizations," 4 Sept. 1918, box 144, BB; "Letter of President Wilson, Sept. 3, 1918," box 144, BB; Barton to M. E. Carr, 7 Oct. 1918, box 70, BB; *Every Week,* 26 Nov. 1917, 2.

20. Bruce Barton, *I Am New York and This Is My Creed,* pamphlet, n.d.; M. McLeod to Hugh H. Gray, 20 June 1934: Bankers Trust file, box 3, BB. In the late 1920s, Barton recycled the "Creed" in an ad for the Bankers Trust Company.

21. "BBDO History" (labeled "return to Gouge"), [ca. 1924], p. 11, BBDO; Eldon R. Ernst, *Moment of Truth for Protestant America: Interchurch Campaigns following World War I* (Missoula, Mont., 1974), 96–98.

22. Ernst, *Moment of Truth,* 96–97, 106; *Nation,* 5 June 1920, 746; *Saturday Evening Post,* 10 Apr. 1920, 130–31.

23. Pierre du Pont to Stockholders, 1 Feb. 1923, CFK.

24. BDO, "General Motors," 13; Alfred P. Sloan Jr. to Charles Kettering, 8 Nov. 1922, 12 Apr.

1924, CFK. On Sloan's low-key bureaucratic style, see Donald Finlay Davis, *Conspicuous Production: Automobiles and Elites in Detroit, 1899–1933* (Philadelphia, 1988), 150–51. Just as it inaugurated the institutional advertising campaign, the corporation abandoned a proposal for a General Motors house organ, offering instead to supply news items to the editors of the various division publications to "use . . . in your own house organs to whatever extent you and your management may determine." Perhaps this move was intended to assuage any feelings of lost autonomy on the part of the operating divisions. "Meeting of General Motors House Organ Editors," 2.

25. "Meeting of General Motors House Organ Editors," 4; Graduate School of Business Administration, Harvard University [GSBH], *First Five Years: Harvard Advertising Awards, 1924–1928* (New York, 1930), 76; C. F. Kettering, *Can Engineering Principles Be Applied to Advertising?* pamphlet, 1927, p. 25, box 35, BB; H. G. Weaver to Owen D. Young, 16 Jan. 1923, file 87.2.43, folder 2-145, ODY; General Motors Corporation, memo beginning "The following articles . . . ," mimeo, n.d., CFK; Kettering to H. G. Weaver, 5 Jan. 1923, 14 Feb. 1923, CFK; Kettering to Verne Burnett, 11 Apr. 1924, CFK; Burnett to Kettering, 2 May 1924, CFK; Sloan to Kettering, 12 Apr. 1924, CFK.

26. Kettering to Sloan, 29 June 1923; Sloan to Kettering, 29 June, 3 July, 24 Aug., 1 Dec. 1923: CFK.

27. Sloan to Swayne, 11 Feb. 1924, documents II folder, case 1, GMB; Chandler, *Strategy and Structure*, 156; Chandler and Salsbury, *Du Pont*, 547–48; Kuhn, *GM Passes Ford*, 35–43, 104, 109, 127; Richard S. Tedlow, *New and Improved: The Story of Mass Marketing in America* (New York, 1990), 167; Sloan to Kettering, 3 July, 24 Aug., 1 Dec. 1923, CFK.

28. Chandler and Salsbury, *Du Pont*, 547.

29. GSBH, "General Motors Corporation, Institutional Advertising," 1957, adv. 759, p. 3, pamphlet file A-167, GM.

30. BDO, "Report on General Motors Campaign for Harvard Awards," [1924], p. 3, BBDO.

31. Chandler and Salsbury, *Du Pont*, 517; BDO, "Report," 8–10; GSBH, *First Five Years*, 75.

32. Brower, "The Man Everybody Knew"; idem, *Me and Other Advertising Geniuses*, 73; Barton to C. E. Patterson, 22 July 1930, GS; Davis, *Conspicuous Production*, 3–4, 98, 146, 151, 156, 158.

33. General Motors, *Famous Family;* idem, *Institutional Advertising by General Motors,* pamphlet, Feb. 1923, pamphlet file A-204, GM. See also GSBH, "General Motors Corporation," 9–12.

34. Swayne, "Making Friends," 28; Cray, *Chrome Colossus*, 320; Chandler and Salsbury, *Du Pont*, 499; Peter F. Drucker, *Adventures of a Bystander* (New York, 1979), 284.

35. *Saturday Evening Post*, 19 Nov. 1927, 144–45; Alfred P. Sloan Jr., *How Members of the General Motors Family Are Made Partners in General Motors,* pamphlet, 12 Mar. 1927, pp. 1–2, box 20, ERS; BDO, "Report," 14–15.

36. BDO, "Report," 14–15; *Literary Digest,* 14 May 1924, 68; *American Magazine* 98 (Oct. 1924): 90.

37. *Literary Digest,* 22 May 1926, 56; ibid., 26 June 1926, 53; press release, 5 Feb. 1924, GM.

38. Press release, 5 Feb. 1924, GM; BDO, "Report," 11, 17, 19; GSBH, *First Five Years,* 75.

39. Swayne, "Making Friends," 27; BDO, "Report," 14, 19; Neil H. Borden and Martin V. Marshall, *Advertising Management: Text and Cases,* rev. ed. (Homewood, Ill., 1959), 393.

40. BDO, "Report," 6; Swayne to Kettering, 19 May 1924, CFK; Seltzer, *Financial History,* 65.

41. Swayne, "Making Friends," 27; advertising case 521 (GM), p. 10, reel 12, case studies, HBSA; BDO, "Report," 6–7.

42. Swayne to Kettering, 19 May 1924, CFK; Swayne, "Making Friends," 27; *General Motors World* 3 (Mar. 1924): 1; Bruce Barton, speech at University of Buffalo, 1929, box 145, BB; *Printers' Ink,* 14 May 1925, 106.

43. Barton to Kettering, 13 Jan. 1923, CFK; Swayne to Kettering, 29 May 1923, CFK; Kettering to Swayne, 29 May 1923, CFK; Lockwood Barr to C. W. Adams, 17 Jan. 1923, CFK; Walter C. Boynton to C. W. Adams, 17 Jan. 1923, CFK; R. K. Evans, "Oral Interview," n.d., GMI.

44. Lears, "From Salvation to Self-Realization," 33; Barton to Gerard Swope, 27 Sept. 1922, 31 May 1924, GS; Barton to J. D. Danforth et al., 2 Aug. 1951, box 76, BB. For the conventional notion of emphasizing an individual personality, see Roger William Riis and Charles W. Bonner Jr.,

Publicity: A Study in the Development of Industrial News (New York, 1926), 163–64. For a contemporary dissenting view, see "Sell the Organization," *Printers' Ink,* 26 Jan. 1928, 176.

45. Barton to Sloan, 1 July 1925, enclosed in Barton to Swope, 17 Aug. 1925, GS.

46. BDO, "Report," 16; Verne Burnett to Kettering, 2 May 1924, CFK; General Motors Corporation, memo beginning "The following articles . . . ," mimeo, n.d., CFK; minutes of General Motors Personnel Association, semiannual meeting, 20 Sept. 1923, CFK; H. G. Weaver to Owen D. Young, 16 Jan. 1923, file 87.2.43, folder 2-145, ODY.

47. "Meeting of General Motors House Organ Editors," 5; minutes of GM Personnel Association; *Saturday Evening Post,* 12 July 1924, 104–5.

48. BDO, "Report," 8, 14, 16; "Meeting of General Motors House Organ Editors," 5; Barton to C. W. Adams, 31 Jan. 1923, CFK.

49. "Meeting of General Motors House Organ Editors," 4–5; *General Motors Institutional Advertising Campaign,* pamphlet, [1923], CFK; "May Institutional Ad," enclosed in Verne Burnett to Kettering, 2 May 1924, CFK; Swayne to Kettering, 19 May 1924, CFK; "Osborn Report on Dealers," enclosed in Swayne to Kettering, 19 May 1924, CFK; Swayne to Owen D. Young, 19 May 1924, ODY; BDO, "General Motors Good-Will as Indicated by a Survey of 40 GM Dealers," file 87.2.43, folder 2-145, ODY.

50. These were General Motors' calculations; BDO's differ. A 1928 BDO memorandum declared that the budget for the first year of the institutional campaign had been $500,000 and that by 1927–28 it had stabilized at $1 million. A 1950s retrospective summary by General Motors, in contrast, set the actual expenditures for 1923 and 1924 in the $300,000–360,000 range and for 1925 and 1926 at approximately $648,000 and $622,000, respectively. Although total advertising appropriations for all divisions of the corporation for the 1923–28 period are not available, it appears that expenditures on the institutional campaigns amounted to at least 10 percent of the total advertising budget for these years, at times perhaps as much as 20 percent. GSBH, "General Motors Corporation," 3; minutes of Executive Committee, 29 June 1922, 20 Oct. 1922, case 2, GMB; BDO, "General Motors," 1928, account status binder, BBDO.

51. Seltzer, *Financial History,* 220; Sloan to Swayne, 11 Feb. 1924, documents II folder, case 1, GMB; Cray, *Chrome Colossus,* 216.

52. *Saturday Evening Post,* 24 Oct. 1925, 90; ibid., 7 Nov. 1925, 125; *Printers' Ink,* 19 Aug. 1926, 166; ibid., 9 Dec. 1926, 189–90; ibid., 2 June 1927, 33.

53. The figures are taken from a confidential compilation in the Frigidaire archives that relies on statistics from *Refrigeration and Air Conditioning News,* 6 Jan. 1937, and from the Frigidaire Market Research and Order departments. A table showing more extended trends appears in Tedlow, *New and Improved,* 313. There are large, unexplained discrepancies between the figures from the two Frigidaire departments from 1926 through 1928, but the massive increase in production and market share is clear in any case. I am indebted to Richard Tedlow for calling this document to my attention. See Frigidaire Market Research Department, "Mechanical Refrigerator Units," 9 Mar. 1949, file 79-10.4-352, box 43, FR.

54. *Good Housekeeping* 84 (Mar. 1927): 113; *Printed Salesmanship* 49 (July 1927): 427; *Literary Digest,* 16 Oct. 1926, 63.

55. *Saturday Evening Post,* 16 July 1927, 94–95; ibid., 2 July 1928, 82–83; *Printers' Ink,* 10 Nov. 1927, 86–87.

56. As GM's experience with its Frigidaire demonstrates, the creation of an impressive corporate image did not assure the success of all new products marketed under the aegis of a giant corporation. Richard Tedlow's account of the role of "scope economies" in distribution in the marketing of GE refrigerators reminds us that the power of the corporate image was only one element among many in the "merchandising mix"; see Tedlow, *New and Improved,* 311–13.

57. Martin P. Rice to Owen D. Young, 16 Aug. 1921, GS; Rice to Gerard Swope, 9 June 1922, GS; Thomas Logan to Swope, 20 July 1922, GS; W. O. Batchelder to H. L. Monroe, 9 Aug. 1922, GS; Barton to F. H. Gale, 20 Oct. 1922, GS; Barton, "A Memo for Mr. Swope," n.d., enclosed in Barton to Swope, 27 Sept. 1922, GS; Hubert M. Snider, "GE Advertising: 30 Minutes of the First 75 Years," 15 Sept. 1977, p. 8, GEF.

58. Barton to J. S. Smith and D. W. Burke, 16 Jan. 1917, box 76, BB; Thomas Logan to Swope, 13 July 1922, GS; Atherton Brownell to Swope, 7 Sept. 1922, GS; Barton, "Memo for Mr. Swope"; David Loth, *Swope of GE: The Story of Gerard Swope and General Electric in American Business* (New York, 1958), 102–3, 109–11.

59. For examples of the Westinghouse ads, see *Saturday Evening Post,* 18 Nov. 1916, 55; 2 Dec. 1916, 60; 9 Dec. 1916, 88. Although seven of the nine members on the Sales Committee were persuaded to spend at least $500,000 on an institutional campaign, the two dissenting votes and disagreement among the other members about an optimum budget resulted in a decision to defer any action. See Snider, "GE Advertising," 3; Sales Committee minutes, 1898–1920, extracts, Neil B. Reynolds Historical File, GEF; F. R. Davis to F. H. Gale, 31 July 1918, GEF; Josephine Young Case and Everett Needham Case, *Owen D. Young and American Enterprise: A Biography* (Boston, 1982), 147, 162.

60. Leonard S. Reich, *The Making of American Industrial Research: Science and Business at GE and Bell, 1876–1926* (New York, 1985), 74, 81; idem, "Lighting the Path to Profit: GE's Control of the Electric Lamp Industry, 1892–1941," *Business History Review* 66 (summer 1992): 307–8, 314–17; John Winthrop Hammond, *Men and Volts: The Story of General Electric* (Philadelphia, 1941), 340; David E. Nye, *Image Worlds: Corporate Identities at General Electric* (Cambridge, Mass., 1985), 115; James A. Cox, *A Century of Light* (New York, 1979), 38; Owen D. Young, Association Island speech, 19 July 1936, file 87.2.591, ODY; attachment to Young and Swope to Board of Directors, 17 Nov. 1939, file 87.2.287, ODY.

61. Ronald R. Kline, *Steinmetz: Engineer and Socialist* (Baltimore, 1992), 196–97, 233, 274. Kline (272) provides an arresting account of the quandaries and benefits that GE encountered in employing an outspoken socialist, through pastoral and picturesque images, to "humanize the corporation" and represent a "consistent paradoxical reality—an individual genius granted freedom by a 'progressive' corporation to help bring about an electrical utopia"; see also pp. 192–309 passim. For an example of GE's celebration of the immigrant-to-wizard story, see *Saturday Evening Post,* 28 Mar. 1925, 82.

62. Fred M. Kimball, "Advertising Policy of General Electric Company . . . ," 18 Aug. 1922, p. 7; Thomas Logan, "Remarks at Conference," 26 July 1922, p. 6: GS.

63. Reich, "Lighting the Path to Profit," 309, 317, 321. Coffin is quoted in Hammond, *Men and Volts,* 387. Coffin's reticence, Hammond remarks, allowed GE to remain in the minds of many simply "an 'interest' controlled by 'Wall Street.'"

64. On the "enlightened managerial capitalism" of the new team of Young and Swope, see Kim McQuaid, *A Response to Industrialism: Liberal Businessmen and the Evolving Spectrum of Capitalist Reform, 1886–1960* (New York, 1986), 115–17; idem, "Young, Swope, and General Electric's 'New Capitalism': A Study in Corporate Liberalism," *American Journal of Economics and Sociology* 36 (July 1977): 323–34.

65. Wolfgang Schivelbusch, *Disenchanted Night: The Industrialization of Light in the Nineteenth Century,* trans. Angela Davies (Berkeley, 1988), 166–67, 178–79.

66. BDO, "Edison Lamp Works of General Electric Company," 1928, account status binder, BBDO. The Edison ads appeared regularly in *Saturday Evening Post:* 2 Mar. 1920, 73; 17 Apr. 1920, 77; 10 July 1920, 68; 2 Oct. 1920, 59; 30 Oct. 1920, 47; 5 Feb. 1921, 39; 5 Mar. 1921, 2; 2 Apr. 1921, 25; 30 Apr. 1921, 32; 3 Sept. 1921, 33. See also *Ladies' Home Journal* 39 (June 1922): 8.

67. Logan, "Remarks at Conference," 33; Thomas Logan, "Memo for Mr. Young," 13 July 1922, GS; J. G. Barry to Department, District, and Local Office Managers, 1 Aug. 1922, GS; Barton, "Memo for Mr. Swope," 5–6.

68. Loth, *Swope of GE,* 74, 117, 133; BDO, "General Electric," 1926, p. 14, account status binder, BBDO; E. O. Shreve, "Management—Its Application to Sales," speech ms., 1930, file 87.2.590, GS; Case and Case, *Owen D. Young,* 255; Nye, *Electrifying America,* 265, 267–68.

69. Gerard Swope to G. C. Osborne, 17 Feb. 1923; Swope to T. F. McManus, 28 Feb. 1923; Thomas Logan to Swope, 11 Sept. 1923; Swope to P. S. Zimmerman, 3 Dec. 1923, 2 May 1934; Swope to Bruce Barton, 26 Mar. 1925; Swope to Logan, 5 Dec. 1927; Swope to Martin P. Rice, 28 Apr. 1930: GS.

70. Bruce Barton to F. H. Gale, 30 Oct. 1933, GS; Barton to Swope, 23 Nov. 1923, GS; Swope to

H. L. Monroe, 26 Nov. 1923, GS; *Schenectady Works News,* 20 July 1923, 16; General Electric Company, *General Electric Publicity, 1924* (Schenectady, N.Y., 1924), 9.

71.   Quinn, *Giant Business,* 62–63, 70, 80; Cox, *Century of Light,* 211; Paul W. Keating, *Lamps for a Brighter America* (New York, 1954), 138; J. Handly Wright and Byron H. Christian, *Public Relations in Management* (New York, 1949), 140; Barton, "Memo for Mr. Swope"; Logan, "Remarks at Conference"; Martin P. Rice to Owen D. Young, 16 Aug. 1921, GS; Barton to Gale, n.d., enclosed in Barton to Swope, 23 Dec. 1922, GS; Young to E. W. Rice Jr., 14 Mar. 1923, file 87.2.11, ODY; Young and Swope to Board of Directors, 17 Nov. 1939, file 87.2.287, ODY; BBDO, "History of General Electric," [Oct. 1929], client binder II, BBDO.

72.   Martin P. Rice to Young, 16 Aug. 1921, GS; Rice to Swope, 9 June 1922, GS; Thomas Logan to Swope, 20 July 1922, GS; W. O. Batchelder to H. L. Monroe, 9 Aug. 1922, GS; Snider, "GE Advertising," 8.

73.   *Schenectady Works News,* 15 June 1923, 16; ibid., 6 July 1923, back cover; Barton to Swope, 4 Oct. 1923, 23 Nov. 1923, 19 Nov. 1925, GS; Barton to F. H. Gale, 30 Oct. 1923, GS; Swope to H. L. Monroe, 26 Nov. 1923, GS; G. P. Baldwin to Swope, 29 July 1922, GS; Barton, "Memo for Mr. Swope"; GE, *General Electric Publicity, 1924,* 9; BDO, "General Electric," 1926, pp. 13–14, awards file, BBDO; BDO, "General Electric," 1928, pp. 2, 4, account status binder, BBDO. Emphasis in the final quote is mine.

74.   Barton to F. H. Gale, 20 Oct. 1922, GS; Barton, "Memo for Mr. Swope"; GE, *General Electric Publicity, 1924,* 5, 13.

75.   Barton to Swope, 20 Nov. 1922, 21 Feb. 1923, GS; Owen D. Young, "Good Will: Association Island, 1925," file 87.2.591, ODY; Young, Association Island speech. For Barton's much later recollection of the importance of Young's warning about the impact of pure size on the public's sense of corporate illegitimacy, see Barton to Chester Lang, 21 Jan. 1954, box 76, BB.

76.   Barton to Swope, 20 Nov. 1922, 21 Feb. 1923; [Swope] to Barton, 19 Nov. 1923: GS.

77.   Barton to F. H. Gale, 22 Dec. 1922, GS; Barton to Swope, 27 Sept. 1922, 4 Oct. 1923, GS; Barton to Gale, 30 Oct. 1922, GS; *Electricity and the American Public: Developing an Electrical Consciousness,* pamphlet, n.d., GS; Hubert Snider, address, [1977], GEF; *GE Monogram* 4 (Apr. 1927): 25. On GE's awareness of the variety of audiences it addressed through its several forms of publicity, see Nye, *Image Worlds,* 5, 15–16, 28–30, 124–33.

78.   *Saturday Evening Post,* 15 Mar. 1924, 205; ibid., 17 Apr. 1926, 91; ibid., 7 Aug. 1926, 90; *Printers' Ink,* 17 Sept. 1925, 28; *GE Monogram* 1 (Dec. 1923): back cover; ibid. 4 (Apr. 1927): 25. For a good comparative view of the ad formats, see GE, *General Electric Publicity, 1924.*

79.   "General Advertising for 1923—Progress Report," 3 March 1923, GS; Barton to F. H. Gale, 23 Dec. 1922, GS.

80.   T. J. McManus to Swope, 21 Apr. 1926, GS; "Knowing More about GE," [1932], Hammond Files, I-5147, GES; *Saturday Evening Post,* 7 Aug. 1926, 90; ibid., 11 June 1927, 83; "General Electric," 1926, pp. 1–3, awards file, BBDO; Nye, *Image Worlds,* 132; idem, *Electrifying America,* 270–72.

81.   For examples of GE and GM ads that promoted refrigerators on the basis of corporate research prestige, see *Saturday Evening Post,* 10 Dec. 1925, 106; ibid., 4 June 1927, 140–41; ibid., 16 July 1927, 94–95; *Ladies' Home Journal* 44 (July 1927): 96.

82.   Frigidaire Market Research Department, "Mechanical Refrigerator Units," box 43, FR; minutes of representatives meeting, 24 Feb. 1931, pp. 4–5, JWT; ibid., 4 Oct. 1932, pp. 3–4, JWT.

83.   W. W. Trench to Young, 16 July 1933, GS; Swope to C. Weaver, 19 June 1922, GS; *Silent Hostess* 1, no. 1 (Jan. 1928): 18–19; ibid. 1, no. 2 (1929): 16–17; BDO, "Report and Recommendations, 1926," p. 16, GEF.

84.   Had they been privy only to the private discussions and correspondence of Ford Motor Company executives, Barton and BDO might have made even greater claims for the success of the General Motors campaign. In July 1924, a year and a half after the onset of the extensive GM campaign, Ford suddenly departed from its tradition of relying on free publicity to enhance its corporate image. In large-circulation magazines and farm publications, Ford outdid General Motors in claims for benevolent service through vast control. Ads carrying such headlines as "Monumental Enterprise" and "Prodigies of Power" presented dramatic views of Ford's new River Rouge plant as tes-

timony to its leadership in "an industrial epic." But behind the scenes, Edsel Ford's friends had beseeched him, to no avail, to consult with BDO before embarking on a size-oriented campaign that might "boomerang." See "Advertising, Ford-1924-Institutional," acc. 19, FM; Wetmore Hodges to Edsel Ford, 12 Apr. 1924, box 10, acc. 572, FM; *Saturday Evening Post,* 28 June 1924, 52–53; ibid., 12 July 1924, 88–89; ibid., 26 July 1924, 52–53.

85.   Alex Osborn to George S. Anderson, 27 Sept. 1926, box 79, BB; Bruce Barton to John McKinlay, 15 Feb. 1929, box 77, BB; GSBH, "General Motors Corporation"; Borden and Marshall, *Advertising Management,* 396.

86.   BDO, "Report and Recommendations, 1926," 16; Barton to Swope, 26 May 1927, GS; Barton to C. E. Patterson, 22 July 1930, GS.

87.   Minutes of representatives meeting, 24 Feb. 1931, 4–5; ibid., 4 Oct. 1932, 3–4; minutes of creative staff meeting, 5 Oct. 1932, p. 11, JWT.

88.   National Electric Light Association, *Proceedings of the 49th National Convention* (New York, 1926), 44. On Sloan's rhetorical rebuttal of charges of soullessness, see *Printers' Ink,* 31 Mar. 1927, 77.

89.   Chandler and Salsbury, *Du Pont,* 517; Case and Case, *Owen D. Young,* 367.

90.   Barton to McKinlay, 15 Feb. 1929, box 77, BB.

91.   Louis Galambos, *The Public Image of Big Business in America, 1880–1940: A Quantitative Study in Social Change* (Baltimore, 1975), 221.

92.   Barton spoke specifically of the success of GM management in winning "ascendancy over the once independent divisions." Several years later he assured the president of Du Pont that he could devise an institutional campaign to influence employee morale, offering to demonstrate his claim with "plenty of evidence from the history of other 'institutional campaigns.'" Without doubt he had the General Motors and General Electric cases in mind. BDO, "General Motors," Sept. 1928, account status binder, BBDO; Barton to C. E. Patterson, 22 July 1930, GS; Barton to Lammot du Pont, 18 May 1935, box 20, acc. 1813, DP.

93.   Brower, "The Man Everybody Knew"; *Light* 1 (May 1923): 3–5; ibid. (Aug. 1923): 19; Barton to Sloan, 1 July 1925, GS.

94.   Barton to C. E. Patterson, 22 July 1930, GS; BDO, "National Campaign, General Motors," p. 4, awards file, BBDO; *General Motors World* 3 (Mar. 1924): 1. For a flattering assessment of the success of GM and GE in promoting "pride in the company," see "Presentation to General Foods Corporation of Radio Program 'General Foods Hour,'" [ca. 1931], box 216, folder 9, WLB.

95.   Barton to Swope, 28 Dec. 1925, GS. For an insightful analysis of Barton's idealism and ambivalence, see Lears, "From Salvation to Self-Realization," 30–38. The best discussion of the vision of trusteeship of the professionally trained managerial elite of the 1920s is Richard Tedlow, *Keeping the Corporate Image: Public Relations and Business, 1900–1950* (Greenwich, Conn., 1979), 68.

96.   GSBH, "General Motors Corporation," 25; *Space and Time,* 12 Apr. 1939, n.p., Durstine file, box 18, BB.

Chapter 5

1.   According to Louis Galambos's exhaustive study of public opinion, there had been an interval of "sharply critical" attitudes toward large corporations after 1918, but the situation had "stabilized by 1922"; Galambos, *The Public Image of Big Business in America, 1880–1940: A Quantitative Study in Social Change* (Baltimore, 1975), 193–95, 213, 220–21.

2.   "Owen D. Young Peers into the Future of Capital and Labor," *Printers' Ink,* 9 June 1927, 100, 104. On the emerging sense of trusteeship on the part of many leaders of large businesses, see Kim McQuaid, *A Response to Industrialism: Liberal Businessmen and the Evolving Spectrum of Capitalist Reform, 1886–1960* (New York, 1986), 150; Morrell Heald, *The Social Responsibilities of Business: Company and Community, 1900–1960* (Cleveland, 1970), 61, 95, 97. Striking contemporary expressions of this view appear in Whiting Williams, "Business Statesmanship: A New Force in Business," *Magazine of Business* 55 (Apr. 1929): 460; Arthur Page to Ellery Sedgewick, 31 Jan. 1928, box 1, AWP. On the changing legal ramifications of the notion of trusteeship, see Allen Kaufman and Lawrence

Zacharias, "From Trust to Contract: The Legal Language of Managerial Ideology, 1920–1980," *Business History Review* 66 (summer 1992): 526–27.

3. *Webster's New International Dictionary of the English Language,* 2d ed., unabridged (Springfield, Mass., 1961), s.v. "institution."

4. Earnest Elmo Calkins, *Business the Civilizer* (Boston, 1928), 287.

5. *Intelligencer,* 4 Mar. 1922, 15, 26 (Fiske quote; see also *Printers' Ink,* 3 Aug. 1922, 25); Edward L. Bernays, *Biography of an Idea: Memoirs of Public Relations Counsel Edward L. Bernays* (New York, 1965), 290 (Stewart quote); *Literary Digest,* 6 Jan. 1923, 41 (Bauer & Black ad); "Servant of the Millions," proof sheet, No. F 36, acc. 19, FM (Ford ad); Gerard Swope, "The Responsibilities of Modern Industry," *J. Walter Thompson News Bulletin,* Jan. 1927, 13; "A National Institution," proof sheet, 8 Dec. 1927, box 495, NWAS.

6. Michele H. Bogart, *Advertising, Artists, and the Borders of Art* (Chicago, 1995), 17, 161.

7. For examples of the dramatic use of white space, see *Saturday Evening Post,* 7 Sept. 1918, 132 (Swift); ibid., 25 Apr. 1925, 48 (General Electric); *Literary Digest,* 15 July 1922, 40 (Du Pont); ibid., 19 Aug. 1922, 58 (Western Electric); ibid., 16 Sept. 1922, 49 (AT&T).

8. George A. Flanagan, *Modern Institutional Advertising* (New York, 1967), 112, 114; *Printers' Ink,* 2 Sept. 1926, 80; Roland Marchand, *Advertising the American Dream: Making Way for Modernity, 1920–1940* (Berkeley, 1985), 142–45.

9. *Saturday Evening Post,* 11 June 1927, 144–45; ibid., 6 Aug. 1927, 36; *Advertising and Selling,* 20 Apr. 1927, 26; *Printed Salesmanship* 49 (Aug. 1927): n.p.; *Tide* 2 (Dec. 1928): 2. See also *Printers' Ink,* 2 Sept. 1926, 76; *Squibb Message* 6 (Dec. 1934): 2.

10. *Saturday Evening Post,* 11 Oct. 1919, 135; *Tide* 3 (July 1929): 3; *Advertising and Selling* 32 (Aug. 1922): 17, 37. In the early 1920s advertising trade journals recognized the popularity of this style, printing articles with titles such as "History Supplies Costume Copy," "Teaching History through Advertising," "History as a Factor in Good-Will Advertising," and "Making an Advertising Ally Out of History." *Printers' Ink,* 29 June 1922, 69, 72; ibid., 3 Apr. 1923, 142; *Printers' Ink Monthly* 4 (May 1922): 66; ibid. 12 (Jan. 1926): 44; *Advertising and Selling Magazine,* 25 June 1921, 12. In his text *Advertising Copy* ([New York, 1924], 176), George Burton Hotchkiss observed that "associations with men of the past are most suitable for institutional copy. A manufacturer cannot, with very good grace, boast of his character and ideals. He can, however, tell of the struggles and triumphs of men of the past. . . . His praise of their . . . moral qualities implies that he also has high ideals."

11. *Printers' Ink,* 5 Apr. 1923, 143; 4 Feb. 1926, 65–66; 22 Nov. 1928, 4, 6. 5. See also Bruce Barton to R. H. Gale, 30 Oct. 1922, GS; *Literary Digest,* 20 Oct. 1917, 52; *Tide* 2 (Feb. 1928): 6–7; ibid. 4 (June 1930): 1; Bruce Barton, "Radio Speech," 4 Mar. 1924, box 75, BB; N. W. Ayer & Son, Inc., *In Behalf of Advertising: A Series of Essays Published in National Periodicals from 1919 to 1928* (Philadelphia, 1929), 17; *Saturday Evening Post,* 28 Jan. 1928, 45; ibid., 28 Sept. 1928, 108–9; *Literary Digest,* 27 May 1922, 39; *Printers' Ink,* 29 Dec. 1927, 1.

12. *Printers' Ink,* 9 Aug. 1928, 108, 113; *Tide* 5 (Sept. 1931): 8; *Saturday Evening Post,* 23 Sept. 1922, 76; ibid., 6 Dec. 1924, 41; ibid., 18 Aug. 1928, 69; *Literary Digest,* 15 July 1922, 40; ibid., 19 Aug. 1922, 58; ibid., 26 Aug. 1922, 51; ibid., 27 Jan. 1923, 55; *Western Electric News* 8 (Jan. 1920): inside front cover; ibid. 10 (Jan. 1922): inside back cover; Helen Woodward, *It's an Art* (New York, 1938), 283; *Advertising and Selling,* 25 Dec. 1929, 24. Even regional and local institutional campaigns, such as that of Mandel Brothers in Chicago in 1926, sometimes adopted this device; *Chicago Tribune,* 23 Nov. 1926, 15.

13. *Literary Digest,* 6 Nov. 1920, 111; ibid., 19 Aug. 1922, 58; ibid., 26 Aug. 1922, 51; *Saturday Evening Post,* 18 Sept. 1920, 187; ibid., 7 Jan. 1928, 89; ibid., 7 July 1928, 35; ibid., 18 May 1929, 101.

14. *Saturday Evening Post,* 22 Mar. 1924, 112.

15. *Printers' Ink,* 25 July 1929, 109. The series appeared in the *Saturday Evening Post:* 12 July 1924, 104–5; 11 July 1925, 130–31; 15 May 1926, 118–19; 11 June 1927, 144–45.

16. These examples are found in *American Magazine* 107 (Mar. 1929): 113; (Apr. 1929): 121; (June 1929): 115.

17. "The Man behind the Counter at the Crossroads," 21 Sept. 1927; "Principally behind the Scenes," 2 May 1927; T. C[ronyn] to G. Ray Schaeffer, 7 Feb. 1928: box 77, BB.

18. *Judicious Advertising* 15 (Nov. 1917): 35, 39–40; *Advertising and Selling* 33 (Jan. 1923): 19; S. H. Ditchett, *Marshall Field and Company: The Life Story of a Great Concern* (New York, 1922), 78–79.

19. "The Things Unseen," 14 July 1927, box 77, BB. For a persuasive account of the powerful effects achieved by window displays, even by the end of the nineteenth century, see William Leach, *Land of Desire: Merchants, Power, and the Rise of a New American Culture* (New York, 1993), 39–70. Leach (70) points out that the Sunday curtaining of Marshall Field windows also had the theatrical effect of "building up anticipation" for the new displays that would be revealed the next day.

20. Louis C. Pedlar to G. Ray Schaeffer, 5 Nov. 1924, box 77, BB.

21. *Chicago Tribune,* 26 Dec. 1927, 11; "Man behind the Counter"; "Things Unseen"; James S. [illegible] to "Dear Sir," 16 Dec. 1927, box 77, BB.

22. *Saturday Evening Post,* 5 Nov. 1921, 31; 4 Feb. 1922, 41.

23. *Printers' Ink,* 20 Mar. 1924, 73.

24. Ibid., 73–74; Wilfred W. Fry, "Remarks at N. W. Ayer Conference, Fall 1924," p. 2, box 34-33, NWA.

25. *Saturday Evening Post,* 3 Dec. 1921, 35; ibid., 4 Feb. 1922, 41; Fry, "Remarks at N. W. Ayer Conference," 2.

26. *Saturday Evening Post,* 4 Feb. 1922, 41; *Squibb Sales Bulletin,* 19 Jan. 1929, 17–18; ibid., 11 Jan. 1930, 13; *Squibb Message* 1 (Jan. 1923): n.p.

27. F. W. Nitardy, "Memorandum with Reference to Priceless Ingredient Story," 13 May 1931, file 1.520, SQS; J. E. Aurelius to Paul Westphal, 7 June 1971, SQS; *Advertising and Selling,* 12 Apr. 1934, 50; *Good Housekeeping* 74 (Jan. 1922): 5; ibid. (Mar. 1922): 7; ibid. (May 1922): 7; *Saturday Evening Post,* 3 Dec. 1921, 35; ibid., 7 Jan. 1922, 63.

28. Book 240 (Squibb), NWAS; *Ladies' Home Journal* 41 (June 1924): 106; *Saturday Evening Post,* 9 Feb. 1924, 72; ibid., 5 Apr. 1924, 85; ibid., 4 May 1924, 79.

29. Minutes of representatives meeting, 3 Apr. 1929, p. 8, JWT; "Experience Story: E. R. Squibb," in NBC Sales Manual, 1928, folder 4, box 5, EPHJ; *Squibb Sales Bulletin,* 19 Jan. 1929, 17–18; ibid., 11 Jan. 1930, 13.

30. Books 239 and 260 (Squibb), NWAS; *Literary Digest,* 7 June 1924, 49.

31. *Squibb Message* 1 (Jan. 1923): 1–2; ibid. 2 (Jan. 1924): 1; William Benton to [unknown], 8 Dec. 1925, box 214, folder 1, WLB. Benton was commenting not on Squibb but on the promotion of a product by another pharmaceutical firm.

32. *Squibb Message* 1 (May 1922): 1–2; ibid. 2 (June 1925): 8; ibid. 4 (Oct. 1929): 5; *Squibb Sales Bulletin,* 14 Dec. 1929, 427; ibid., 1 Mar. 1930, 61; *Printers' Ink,* 2 Dec. 1926, 93, 97; ibid., 14 Sept. 1927, 208; ibid., 22 May 1930, 89.

33. *Squibb Message* 1 (May 1922): 1–2; ibid. 4 (Oct. 1929): 5. The prestige-building ads might seem like "old stuff" to the sales force, Squibb acknowledged, but druggists would "be interested in seeing the high type of institutional advertising that the House of Squibb is doing, for them as well as for itself." *Squibb Sales Bulletin,* 11 Jan. 1930, 13; ibid., 18 Jan. 1930, 22–23.

34. *Squibb Message* 1 (Jan. 1923): 1; *Squibb Sales Bulletin,* 16 Feb. 1929, 49.

35. *Ladies' Home Journal* 48 (Feb. 1931): 154. Another advertisement that same year, "The Power to Affect Human Welfare," avowed that as "an institution of professional men," Squibb had spent vast sums on research "without considering the effect on profits." Even so, the 1931 annual report indicated that the company had increased its net profit in that depression year by 5 percent, to a total of $1,651,234, and had spent more than ten times as much money on advertising and promotion as on research. *Ladies' Home Journal* 48 (Apr. 1931): 98; E. R. Squibb & Sons, *Annual Report, 1931,* SQS. (See also the similar ratio of expenditures in the *Annual Report, 1928*).

36. James C. Collins and Jerry I. Porras, *Built to Last: Successful Habits of Visionary Companies* (New York, 1994), 71; Flanagan, *Modern Institutional Advertising,* 99. On the claims by public relations advisors and executives to shape corporate behavior by setting up public expectations, see Richard S. Tedlow, *Keeping the Corporate Image: Public Relations and Business, 1900–1950* (Greenwich, Conn., 1979), 37, 44, 48.

37. Theodore Weicker to Carleton H. Palmer, 4 Sept. 1931, pp. 2–7, SQS.

38. Ibid. The continuing bias of the institutional campaign is apparent in a 1934 survey, which revealed that the public knew "the name of Squibb as a symbol of quality" but was not aware of the "extensive line of Squibb products covering all the needs of the average American home"; *Squibb Message* 6 (Dec. 1934): 1. For an earlier analysis of the impact of the institutional advertising, see "Market Trends Involving Squibb Products," [1925], pp. 10–14, file 1.42, SQS.

39. *Tower Talks* 1 (Apr. 1923): back cover; ibid. (Nov–Dec. 1923): 3; *Milestones in Metropolitan Advertising,* pamphlet, 1938, MLIC; *Printers' Ink,* 10 Aug. 1922, 267; ibid., 16 Dec. 1926, 108; ibid., 27 Apr. 1933, 18; *Tide* 3 (Sept. 1929): 1.

40. Marquis James, *The Metropolitan Life: A Study in Business Growth* (New York, 1947), 73–74, 188; Louis I. Dublin, *A Family of Thirty Million: The Story of the Metropolitan Life Insurance Company* (New York, 1943), 428; President, Metropolitan Life Insurance, to P. J. Kraus, 17 Feb. 1894, box 35-172-17, MLIC; Lee K. Frankel, *Industrial Insurance,* pamphlet, 11 June 1909, p. 11, box 13-05-02, folder 7, LKF. Metropolitan executives cited two justifications for the significantly higher cost of insurance to working-class policyholders: the higher mortality rate in this group and the extra expense for weekly collection of premiums. President Haley Fiske even repeated the phrase "robbing the poor" in order to refute that accusation; Fiske, "1909–1910 Address," in Metropolitan Life Insurance Company, *Addresses Delivered at the Triennial Conventions and Managers' Annual Banquet of the Metropolitan Life Insurance Company,* vol. 1 (New York, 1923), 8.

41. Haley Fiske and Raymond V. Carpenter, *An Epoch in Life Insurance: Twenty-five Years of Administration at the Metropolitan Life Insurance Company* (New York, 1917), 89, 101–5; *Rules and Regulations Governing Office Employes of the Metropolitan Life Insurance Company,* pamphlet, 1895, pp. 54–56, employee manuals, subject file 19-04-03, MLIC; *Rules Governing Home Office Clerical Employees,* pamphlet, 1914, pp. 13, 20, employee manuals, subject file 19-04-03, MLIC; Olivier Zunz, *Making America Corporate, 1870–1920* (Chicago, 1990), 117–20; Angel Kwolek-Folland, "Gender, Self, and Work in the Life Insurance Industry, 1880–1930," in *Work Engendered: Toward a New History of American Labor,* ed. Ava Baron (Ithaca, N.Y., 1991), 169.

42. Frankel, *Industrial Insurance;* Lee K. Frankel, *Corporate Welfare Work,* pamphlet, 1913, p. 4, box 13-05-01, folder 1, LKF.

43. James, *Metropolitan Life,* 184–88; Dublin, *Family,* 423. The results of Frankel's study in Europe appeared in Lee K. Frankel and Miles M. Dawson, *Workingmen's Insurance in Europe* (New York, 1911).

44. James, *Metropolitan Life,* 183–86; Dublin, *Family,* 423. Championing insurance as a social program did not imply support for compulsory health insurance, as one might expect it to. Metropolitan joined other segments of the private sector in staunchly opposing the idea in 1917. See *Compulsory Health Insurance: Statement Issued by Social Insurance Department, the National Civic Federation,* pamphlet, May 1917, box 13-05-01, LKF.

45. *Printers' Ink,* 3 Aug. 1922, 25, 167; Dublin, *Family,* 440.

46. James, *Metropolitan Life,* 187–89, 205–6, 214–19; Dublin, *Family,* 89–90, 430; Frankel, *Industrial Insurance,* 10; Frankel, *Corporate Welfare Work,* 4; Fiske and Carpenter, *Epoch,* 90–91.

47. Metropolitan Life, *Addresses,* 1:50–51, 78–79, 82.

48. Taylor is quoted in James, *Metropolitan Life,* 215.

49. James, *Metropolitan Life,* 117, 119, 163, 166–68.

50. Ibid., 117, 120, 131, 139, 163, 168–69; *Intelligencer,* 5 Dec. 1908, 1–2; *Intelligencer* (Keystone Territory), 1 May 1909, 2; *The Metropolitan Life Insurance Company: Its History,* pamphlet, 1914, pp. 19–21, 24, MLIC; *Home Office* 2 (Mar. 1921): 1; ibid. 5 (Dec. 1923): 1.

51. Lee K. Frankel, *Popularizing Health Conservation,* pamphlet, 1913, pp. 11, 13, box 13-05-03, folder 9, LKF.

52. *Metropolitan* 22 (1903): n.p., Advertising 1900–1921 folder, MLIC; James, *Metropolitan Life,* 116, 174; *Intelligencer,* 31 July 1909, 1; Fiske, "1909–1910 Address," 9.

53. *Printers' Ink,* 8 Mar. 1917, 12, 18; ibid., 3 Aug. 1922, 25; *Saturday Evening Post,* 7 Oct. 1922, 88; *Intelligencer,* 24 Feb. 1923, 24; Advertising 1922 folder, MLIC.

54. Flanagan, *Modern Institutional Advertising,* 176. For examples, see *Saturday Evening Post,* 25 Aug. 1923, 119; 28 Nov. 1925, 100.

55. *Printers' Ink,* 3 Aug. 1922, 25; ibid., 10 Aug. 1922, 167; ibid., 5 Apr. 1923, 125–26, 133, 136; *Tower Talks* 1 (Feb. 1923): 15.

56. *Tower Talks* 1 (Feb. 1923): 12, 15, 24; *Metropolitan Life Insurance Company: Its History,* 86–87, 210–11. On the gender issues in the "Mother Metropolitan" appellation, see page 105 above; Angel Kwolek-Folland, *Engendering Business: Men and Women in the Corporate Office, 1870–1930* (Baltimore, 1994), 131, 134.

57. *Intelligencer,* 24 Feb. 1923, 23–24; *Tower Talks* 1 (Apr. 1923): back cover; ibid. 5 (Nov. 1927): 2–3.

58. *Printers' Ink,* 3 Aug. 1922, 26, 28; ibid., 7 June 1923, 179; Advertising 1922 folder, MLIC. These ads ran regularly in the *Saturday Evening Post;* representative examples include 25 Aug. 1923, 119; 31 May 1924, 106; 28 June 1924, 103; 28 Nov. 1925, 100; 29 June 1928, 101; 26 Oct. 1929, 28; 28 June 1930, 99. See also *Ladies' Home Journal* 46 (Sept. 1929): 149; *Tower Talks* 6 (Oct. 1928): back cover.

59. *Metropolitan Life Health Exercises,* pamphlet, [1925], box 1, EPHJ; E. P. H. James to D. S. Tuthill, 25 Nov. 1927, box 4, NBC; Paul Wing to William S. Rainey, 3 Jan. 1935, box 39, NBC; N. W. Ayer & Son, *What about Radio?* pamphlet, [May 1931], p. 66, NWA; *Advertising Age,* 2 Mar. 1935, 30; Otis A. Pease, *The Responsibilities of American Advertising* (New Haven, Conn., 1958), 37–38.

60. *Printers' Ink,* 3 June 1926, 4, 6; Calkins, *Business the Civilizer,* 291; *Saturday Evening Post,* 29 Sept. 1928, 118; *Delineator* 116 (Oct. 1930): 43.

61. Dublin, *Family,* 80, 87–88; *Saturday Evening Post,* 29 Sept. 1928, 118; *Delineator* 116 (Oct. 1930): 43; *Home Office* 5 (Mar. 1924): 13; Haley Fiske, "The Metropolitan—A Mother's Care for the Missions That Own It" (21 Nov. 1927), in Metropolitan Life, *Addresses,* vol. 3 (New York, 1927–28), 543, 558.

62. James, *Metropolitan Life,* 201, 228. In 1924, when the Metropolitan's institutional series won an industry trophy for "best advertising," its officers were praised for "disclosing the highest type of practical American idealism in business" and "making the most effective answer to the radical who appeals to class hatred"; *Home Office* 5 (Nov. 1924): 1, 3.

63. *Metropolitan Underwriter* (1931 convention supplement), 64; *Printers' Ink,* 20 Aug. 1931, 44.

64. Leroy A. Lincoln to Managers, Superintendents, and Detached Assistant Managers, 22 July 1931, 23 Aug. 1932, circular letters file, MLIC.

65. Ibid.; Reginald R. Lawrence to Managers and Superintendents, 23 Aug. 1932, circular letters file, MLIC; *American Magazine* 114 (Sept. 1932): 69.

66. "Minutes of Meeting after Dinner," 5 Jan. 1905, p. 4, NWA; F. Wayland Ayer, "Speech for Business Getting Conference," 19 June 1922, p. 32, NWA; *The Next Step* 1 (Aug. 1920): 16; ibid. 2 (Feb. 1921): n.p.; N. W. Ayer & Son, *Better Business,* pamphlet, 1914, p. 41, NWA. As late as 1933, Ayer was still referring to itself as a "House" and capitalizing the word in its correspondence. See Wilfred Fry to Ivy Lee, 27 Sept. 1933, folder 42/25, carton 17, WWA.

67. Alan R. Raucher, *Public Relations and Business, 1900–1929* (Baltimore, 1968), 4; *The Next Step* 2 (Feb. 1921): 3, 29; ibid. (Aug. 1921): 8; Ayer, *Better Business,* 4; "The Dawn of a Better Day," in *The Ayer Idea,* pamphlet, p. 41, NWA; "Minutes of Meeting after Dinner," 1–5, 8–10; F. Wayland Ayer, "Talk by Mr. Ayer," 9 Sept. 1908, pp. 1–2, NWA; N. W. Ayer & Son, *Medals and Markets,* pamphlet, 1934, n.p., NWA; "Twelve More Advertisements," 1921 folder, box 15-51, NWA; Fry, "Remarks at N. W. Ayer Conference," 1–2; "Re N. W. Ayer & Son House Advertising," enclosed in H. A. Batten to Ralph Hower, 1 Feb. 1939, folder C1, RH; minutes of creative staff meeting, 4 May 1932, p. 3, JWT. This implicit assertion of leadership was hardly new for the Ayer agency. Since its founding in 1869, N. W. Ayer & Son had vociferously, albeit genteelly, laid claim to a higher standard of ethics than all other agencies, along with a more professional mode of charging for its services. See Ralph M. Hower, *The History of an Advertising Agency: N. W. Ayer and Son at Work, 1869–1939* (Cambridge, Mass., 1939), 203–4, 357.

68. *Literary Digest,* 14 June 1919, 47; ibid., 16 July 1921, 35; *Saturday Evening Post,* 1 Oct. 1921, 69.

69. *Literary Digest,* 14 June 1919, 47; ibid., 6 Nov. 1920, 112; ibid., 4 Dec. 1920, 122; ibid., 27 May 1922, 39; *Saturday Evening Post,* 4 Oct. 1919, 63; *Printers' Ink,* 27 Dec. 1927, 1; "Twelve Advertisements," box 15-15, NWA; Ayer, *In Behalf of Advertising,* 14. This scorn for pretentiousness in institutional advertisements gained impetus from Ayer's boasts about its awards and about the num-

ber of its copywriters who were also novelists, poets, and essayists. Ayer talked freely about "great writing" and "use of the tools of literature." Even Ayer's top copywriters, a former agency copywriter claimed, could not "escape the Ayer point of view that a piece of copy—an advertisement—is first of all a literary production bearing sweetness and light to the world." Ayer, "Medals and Markets," n.p.; Stanley Burnshaw, interview with author, 13 Feb. 1980; minutes of creative staff meeting, 4 May 1932, 5–6.

70. "Minutes of Meeting after Dinner," 4; Ayer, "Speech for Business Getting Conference," 32; *The Next Step* 1 (Aug. 1920): 16; ibid. 2 (Feb. 1921): n.p.; Ayer, *Better Business,* 41; penciled note on H. A. Batten, "Notes on Chapters 12–19," enclosed in Alice Kimberline to Ralph Hower, 1 May 1939, RH; minutes of creative staff meeting, 4 May 1932, 7.

71. "We Are Your Delivery Man," box 495, Armour and Company proof sheets; "Even the *Hairs* Are Numbered," box 494, Armour and Company proof sheets: NWAS.

72. Marchand, *Advertising,* 89–94. On the tenor of such "goodwill" broadcasting and advertising, see the text of the Boston Edison announcement of 1924 in David B. Sicilia, "Selling Power: Marketing and Monopoly at Boston Edison, 1886–1929" (Ph.D. diss., Brandeis University, 1991), 545.

73. Marchand, *Advertising,* 88–92; BDO, "General Motors," account status binder, 1928, BBDO; G. F. McClelland, "Radio Broadcasting as an Advertising Medium," in *Advertising and Selling Digest,* ed. William G. Lownds (New York, 1926), 147–50.

74. *Tide* 10 (July 1936): 35; Marchand, *Advertising,* 90–92; J. D. Ellsworth, "Public Utility Advertising," in *Advertising and Selling Digest,* 186; Orrin E. Dunlap Jr., *Radio in Advertising* (New York, 1931), 115–16, 170.

75. R. C. Witmer to D. S. Shaw, 14 Dec. 1932, box 14, NBC; Lowell P. Weicker to M. H. Aylesworth, 12 Dec. 1932, box 14, NBC; Morris Fishbein to John Royal, 2 Dec. 1932, box 14, NBC; *Saturday Evening Post,* 6 Sept. 1930, 62–63; ibid., 20 Sept. 1930, 74–75; ibid., 4 Oct. 1930, 34–35.

76. Metropolitan Life Insurance used its morning exercise program to publicize and distribute its booklets on health, thus "building good will." Swift & Company not only offered talks on food preparation for the homemaker but also sponsored William Lyon ("Billy") Phelps, a former Yale professor of English, in a book review format that sought to popularize great literature. See Metropolitan Life Insurance Company, *Radio as an Advertising Medium,* pamphlet, 1930, pp. 2, 9–10, 24, MLIC; Metropolitan Life Insurance Company, *All in the Day's Work,* employee manuals file, box 19-04-03, folder 2, p. 40, MLIC; *Public Service through Advertising,* pamphlet, n.d., company scrapbook, MLIC; Dunlap, *Radio in Advertising,* 106; Joan Shelley Rubin, "Swift's Premium Ham: William Lyon Phelps and the Redefinition of Culture," in *Mass Media between the Wars,* ed. Catherine L. Covert and John D. Stevens (Syracuse, N.Y., 1984), 3, 6–13.

77. His symphony program for Philco "did not pay off in the sale of sets," the conductor Howard Barlow reminisced, "but it paid off in creating for the company a quality atmosphere. People assumed that Philco sets were the best because we played the best music"; Barlow, "Reminiscences," 1951, pp. 135–36, 150–52, 155, OHRO. If the music was not classical, it at least had to be sufficiently genteel to blend with the "well-modulated voice" of the spokesman for the corporation; *Western Electric News* 20 (Oct. 1931): 31.

78. Henry Souvaine to John F. Royal, 2 Apr. 1937, box 57, folder 4, NBC.

79. NBC, *Broadcast Advertising,* vol. 1: *A Study of the Radio Medium: The Fourth Dimension of Advertising* (New York, 1929), 48; NBC, *Selling Goods—Selling Service: Selling the Consciousness of a Great Ideal,* pamphlet, 16 Apr. 1928, box 3, folder 6, EPHJ; Metropolitan Life, *Radio as an Advertising Medium,* 13–14.

80. See General Motors ads in the *Saturday Evening Post:* 13 Feb. 1926, 104–5; 13 Mar. 1926, 138–39; 13 Nov. 1926, 146–47; 21 May 1927, 73. See also General Motors Corporation, press release, 5 Feb. 1924, GM.

81. See ads in the *Literary Digest:* 15 July 1922, 40; 22 July 1922, 55; 29 July 1922, 55; 12 Aug. 1922, 39; 26 Aug. 1922, 51. See also the *Saturday Evening Post,* 23 Sept. 1922, 76.

82. *Du Pont Magazine* 16 (July–Aug. 1922): 1–2; ibid. (Sept.–Oct. 1922): 12; Irénée du Pont to Stockholders, 1 July 1922, box 3, acc. 1662, DP; C. F. Brown to Irénée du Pont, 18 Oct. 1922, box 3, acc. 1662, DP; *Saturday Evening Post,* 21 Oct. 1922, 52.

83. See ads in the *Saturday Evening Post:* 3 Feb. 1923, 61; 6 Sept. 1930, 62–63; 20 Sept. 1930, 74–

75; 4 Oct. 1930, 34–35. See also *Literary Digest*, 7 Mar. 1923, 79; ibid., 13 Feb. 1926, 69; *Printers' Ink*, 2 Nov. 1922, 133.

84. *Saturday Evening Post*, 7 Jan. 1928, 89; ibid., 20 Oct. 1928, 53; *Literary Digest*, 24 Sept. 1927; ibid., 18 Feb. 1928, 53; F. L. Scott to G. H. Thornley, 29 Apr. 1936, Ford folder, NWA; minutes of creative staff meeting, 4 May 1932, 6; Thomas F. Garbett, *Corporate Advertising: The What, the Why, and the How* (New York, 1981), 7; David L. Lewis, *The Public Image of Henry Ford: An American Folk Hero and His Company* (Detroit, 1976), 177.

85. Lewis, *Public Image*, 176–77; untitled typescript in Ford folder, n.d., pp. 5–7, NWA.

86. Untitled typescript in Ford folder, n.d., 5–7.

87. *Saturday Evening Post*, 25 Oct. 1930, 97–98.

88. AT&T, proceedings of publicity conference, 1919, pp. 46, 60, box 1310, ATT.

89. *Printers' Ink*, 6 Jan. 1927, 187. The quote from *Tide* is reprinted in J. Walter Thompson Company, *News Letter*, 21 Jan. 1929, p. 4, JWT.

90. *Advertising and Selling*, 29 Aug. 1935, 32; Thomas Logan, "Remarks at Advertising Conference," 26 July 1922, GS. Helen Woodward, a former advertising writer, described the attractions of creating institutional advertising: "It's easy to sell the client, it's child's play to write." Thus, in the advertising world "the word Institutional stands . . . for the loveliest velvet there is." Woodward, *It's An Art*, 282.

91. *Advertising and Selling*, 9 Jan. 1929, 18, 66; ibid., 5 Feb. 1930, 84; ibid., 14 Nov. 1928, 25.

92. *Printer's Ink*, 19 Dec. 1929, 4; *Advertising and Selling*, 21 Sept. 1927, 28; George W. Batten Company, *News Letter*, 24 Mar. 1925, pp. 6–8.

93. William Allen White, "How to Sell Service," in National Electric Light Association, *Proceedings of the 49th National Convention* (New York, 1926), 202; *Advertising and Selling*, 23 Feb. 1927, 34.

94. *Saturday Evening Post*, 11 Feb. 1921, 62–63; ibid., 30 Jan. 1926, 124; "Mr. Page on Public Relations," *Long Lines* 19 (Apr. 1940): 1, 28; Federal Communications Commission, *Telephone Investigation, Exhibit 2096E* (Washington, D.C., 1938), vol. 4; Noobar R. Danielian, *AT&T: The Story of Industrial Conquest* (New York, 1939), 193.

95. *Saturday Evening Post*, 3 Dec. 1921, 35; ibid., 27 Mar. 1926, 40–41; ibid., 23 July 1927, 54–55; *Chicago Tribune*, 10 Jan. 1928, 18; ibid., 24 Jan. 1928, 16.

96. Swift & Company, *Year Book, 1919* (Chicago, 1919), 11; idem, *Year Book, 1922* (Chicago, 1922), 7; idem, *Year Book, 1923*, (Chicago, 1923), 7; *Printers' Ink*, 14 Sept. 1922, 125; ibid., 19 Mar. 1925, 161–62; ibid., 3 May 1928, 173; Sicilia, "Selling Power," 450.

97. Tedlow, *Keeping the Corporate Image*, 92; Arthur W. Page, address, General Commercial Conference, May 1930, p. 1, vol. 5, AWP; Noel L. Griese, "AT&T: Origins of the Nation's Oldest Continuous Institutional Advertising Campaign," *Journal of Advertising* 6 (1977): 22; Preston C. Mabon, "The Art of Arthur Page," *Public Relations Journal* 27 (Mar. 1971): 6; F. R. Henderer, *A Comparative Study of the Public Relations Practices in Six Industrial Corporations* (Pittsburgh, 1956), 116; "Summary of Curtis Publishing Company Study of 'What the Public Thinks of Big Business,'" May 1937, box 4, acc. 1662, DP.

98. Thus, when J. Walter Thompson agency leaders in the early 1930s plotted to win for the Johns-Manville Company the institutional status apparently already secured by General Electric, their first instinct was to envision some monumental form of service. How, they pondered, could they relate Johns-Manville "to as big a thing or as big a group of things as the control of sound, shelter, heat and cold"? The "bigness and importance" of these things defined a level of responsibility that qualified Johns-Manville as an institution. Minutes of representatives meeting, 24 Feb. 1931, p. 7, JWT.

99. Whiting Williams, "What Makes Business an Institution?" *Magazine of Business* 55 (June 1929): 658.

100. David Brody, *Workers in Industrial America: Essays in the Twentieth-Century Struggle* (New York, 1980), 71–77; Colin Gordon, *New Deals: Business, Labor, and Politics in America, 1920–1935* (New York, 1994), 163, 256–57, 269; Lizabeth Cohen, *Making a New Deal: Industrial Workers in Chicago, 1919–1939* (New York, 1990), 206–9, 238–46, 289, 315–16. On employer efforts to spread work and provide relief in companies ranging from Eli Lilly to United States Steel, see George David

Smith, *From Monopoly to Competition: The Transformations of Alcoa, 1888–1986* (New York, 1988), 178; James H. Madison, *Eli Lilly: A Life, 1885–1977* (Indianapolis, 1989), 96; Ida D. Tarbell, *Owen D. Young: A New Type of Industrial Leader* (New York, 1932), 150; James Rose, "The United States Steel Duquesne Works, 1886–1941: The Rise of Steel Unionism" (Ph.D. diss., University of California, Davis, 1997), chap. 2, pp. 18, 25; Edward R. Stettinius Jr. to Myron Taylor, 1 Sept. 1936, box 63, ERS.

101. Frankel, *Popularizing Health Conservation,* pamphlet, 1913, p. 16, box 13-05-03, LKF.

102. Few testimonies to the impact of institutional advertisements were so convincing as those that concluded, "No one can calculate the fiscal benefit that has derived from strengthening the company's own morale." See *Printers' Ink,* 22 Aug. 1929, 78–79; ibid., 27 Apr. 1933, 17.

Chapter 6

1. Bruce Barton, *The Public,* pamphlet, 4 Dec. 1935, file 87.2.19, ODY; *Printers' Ink,* 12 Dec. 1935, 17, 20, 24.

2. *Fortune* 19 (Mar. 1939): 83, 148; Paul W. Garrett, "Large Scale Business and the Public," speech ms., 25 Mar. 1939, n.p., GM; idem, "Industry's No. 1 Problem Defined," speech ms., 9 Feb. 1939, p. 1, GM; idem, "National Industrial Conference Board," speech ms., 13 Mar. 1938, n.p., GM; Don Hogate to Paul W. Garrett, 16 Mar. 1938, GM; General Motors Corporation, Department of Public Relations, "Plant City Bulletin," no. 21, 10 Feb. 1939, mimeo, GM.

3. *New York Times,* 5 Dec. 1935, 1, 15; Richard S. Tedlow, *Keeping the Corporate Image: Public Relations and Business, 1900–1950* (Greenwich, Conn., 1979), 99–100; idem, "The National Association of Manufacturers and Public Relations during the New Deal," *Business History Review* 50 (spring 1976): 33; National Association of Manufacturers, "Outline for Remarks on Educational Program," n.d., n.p., box 64, acc. 1662, DP; E. T. Weir to Lammot du Pont, box 54, acc. 1662, DP.

4. Barton, *The Public,* n.p; *Printers' Ink,* 12 Dec. 1935, 17, 20.

5. Tedlow, *Keeping the Corporate Image,* 60–63, 106–10; idem, "National Association," 29, 33.

6. Bruce Barton, "Winning Public Approval," 12 May 1936, BBDO; *Advertising and Selling,* 21 May 1936, 29; *New York Times,* 5 Dec. 1935, 15.

7. For sample versions of the Confession, see *Advertising Age,* 24 May 1937, 10; ibid., 25 Apr. 1938, 1; *Advertising and Selling* 32 (Mar. 1939): 87; *Factory Management and Maintenance* 94 (Mar. 1936): 96–97; *Business Week,* 16 July 1938, 30; Colby Chester, "Business Team Play," enclosed in Verne Burnett to Edward R. Stettinius Jr., 22 Jan. 1936, box 565, ERS.

8. Fred Eldean, "The Next Job of Institutional Advertising," 4 Oct. 1943, n.p., CFK.

9. *Printers' Ink,* 24 June 1937, 60; *Advertising Age,* 28 Oct. 1935, 2; ibid., 24 May 1937, 10; ibid., 25 Apr. 1938, 1, 27; *Market Research* 7 (July 1937): 6; Arthur Kudner, "The Job Ahead: A Talk to Business Men," *Atlantic Monthly* 159 (Mar. 1937): 342–43; *Tide* 10 (July 1936): 35; S. H. Walker and Paul Sklar, "Business Finds Its Voice, Part I," *Harper's Magazine* 176 (Jan. 1938): 119; "What the Public Thinks about the Truth or Untruth of Criticism Directed at Big Business," Apr. 1939, reel 713, JWT. Whenever corporate commitments to expanded public relations initiatives seemed to flag, one could expect a headline such as "Industry Fails to Sell Itself to Waiting U.S." to appear. See H. A. Batten, "Public Relations," speech ms., 28 Apr. 1937, NWA; *Printers' Ink,* 19 Dec. 1935, 92–93; ibid., 7 Jan. 1937, 21, 24; *Advertising and Selling,* 2 Dec. 1937, 31; *People* 1 (Aug. 1937): 21–22, JWT; *Advertising Age,* 3 Jan. 1938, 22.

10. *Printers' Ink,* 21 Jan. 1937, 1; ibid., 24 June 1937, 60; N. W. Ayer & Son, *America Calling,* pamphlet, [ca. 1936], box 34-31, NWA; *Advertising and Selling* 32 (Feb. 1939): 6–7; Bernard Lichtenberg, *Telling the Truth about Business,* pamphlet, 28 Sept. 1936, pp. 2, 5, box 52, ERS; *Atlantic Monthly,* pamphlet, [ca. Nov. 1934], enclosed in Donald B. Snyder to Arthur H. Gilbert, 24 Nov. 1934, box 216, folder 7, WLB.

11. William L. Bird Jr., "The Drama of Enterprise: Du Pont's *Cavalcade of America* and the 'New Vocabulary' of Business Leadership, 1935–1940" (paper presented at the annual meeting of the Society for Cinema Studies, Washington, D.C., May 1990); William L. Bird Jr., "Enterprise and Meaning: Sponsored Film, 1939–1941," *History Today* 39 (Dec. 1989): 24–30.

12. BBDO, *Newsletter,* 21 Feb. 1936; Barton, "Winning Public Approval," n.p.

13. For views of Roosevelt as a tutor in advertising techniques and new media, see *Advertising and Selling,* 27 Apr. 1933, 44–45; ibid., 13 Sept. 1934, 28; ibid., 24 May 1937, 10; ibid., 9 Sept. 1937, 36; ibid., 16 Dec. 1937, 33; *Advertising Age,* 28 Oct. 1933, 16; ibid., 21 June 1937, 49; ibid., 31 Jan. 1938, 33; Ralph Birchard to [Maurice Needham], 23 June 1936, box 66, folder 5, WLB; William Benton to Philip LaFollette, 16 May 1938, box 65, folder 10, WLB; E. T. Weir to L. du Pont, 20 May 1935, box 54, acc. 1662, DP; Wadsworth W. Mount to Alfred P. Sloan Jr., 7 Aug. 1937, enclosed in Mount to L. du Pont, 21 Dec. 1937, box 48, acc. 1662, DP; National Association of Manufacturers, "Outline," p. 127, box 54, acc. 1662, DP.

14. Roland Marchand, *Advertising the American Dream: Making Way for Modernity, 1920–1940* (Berkeley, 1985), 67–72, 83–85. On the same assessment of the public by emerging public relations professionals, see Alan R. Raucher, *Public Relations and Business, 1900–1929* (Baltimore, 1968), 124–28, 133–34; Tedlow, *Keeping the Corporate Image,* 40, 43.

15. *People* 1 (Aug. 1937): 20, JWT.

16. Arthur Brisbane to Charles Sorenson, 21 Mar. 1933, box 10, acc. 572, FM; David L. Lewis, *The Public Image of Henry Ford: An American Folk Hero and His Company* (Detroit, 1976); John M. Staudenmaier, "Henry Ford's Relationship to 'Fordism': Ambiguity as a Modality of Technological Resistance" (draft of paper, 1994), 6.

17. Staudenmaier, "Ford's Relationship to 'Fordism,'" 4, 12; idem, "Making Sense of Henry: Thoughts on the Ford Museum and Greenfield Village" (paper presented at Dibner Institute, Cambridge, Mass., 1993), 5–6, 13. Ford was certainly not alone among corporate leaders in his ambivalence. Theodore Vail, the president of AT&T between 1907 and 1921, had so deplored the luring of country boys to the city that he poured part of his personal fortune into the creation of Lyndonville Institute in Vermont to train farmers' boys to continue in farming occupations. *New York Times,* 18 July 1915, 13; Albert Bigelow Paine, *In One Man's Life: Being Chapters from the Personal and Business Career of Theodore N. Vail* (New York, 1921), 251, 266–70.

A similar nostalgia can be glimpsed in Bruce Barton's novel *The Making of George Groton,* serialized in the *American Magazine* 84 (Nov. 1917): 8–11, 113–18. The hero of this story, in which "an ambitious youth in a small town . . . comes under the admiring eyes of a big business man from the great city," pauses to reflect that "I have known days when I have stood in my office window and watched the lights stream on across Brooklyn Bridge, when I would have given all I owned to be back under the trees in Merwin." The accompanying illustration depicted the conventional small town with its single church steeple.

18. Lewis, *Public Image,* 162, 223–24, 278–82.

19. Henry Ford (in collaboration with Samuel Crowther), *My Life and Work* (Garden City, N.Y., 1923), 188–92; Ford Motor Company, press release, 16 June 1928, box 1, acc. 545, FM; Howard P. Segal, "'Little Plants in the Country': Henry Ford's Village Industries and the Beginning of Decentralized Technology in Modern America," *Prospects* 13 (1988): 183–86, 195; Lewis, *Public Image,* 162. Edwin W. Rice, the president of General Electric from 1913 to 1922, had likewise worried about the "evil effect of draining the normal agricultural forces into industrial development" and of "centralizing great masses of men" in factories. He initiated a plan for the decentralization of GE plants, some of which he proposed placing in "the center of agricultural communities," where they would operate during the "six months of the year in which there is little or no farming work." H.D.S. policy binder, 31 July 1920, DM.

20. *Sacramento Bee,* 3 June 1931, 14; *Chicago Tribune,* 3 June 1931, 19.

21. *Ford News* 12 (June 1932): 3 and back cover; *Business Week,* 2 Sept. 1931, 23; ibid., 22 June 1932, 17; Terry Smith, *Making the Modern: Industry, Art, and Design in America* (Chicago, 1993), 138–40; *Saturday Evening Post,* 24 Jan. 1925, 62–63; ibid., 16 May 1925, 84; ibid., 15 Aug. 1925, 87; ibid., 15 June 1919, 82–83; *Literary Digest,* 12 Sept. 1931, 10.

22. *Fortune* 8 (Dec. 1933): 65; *Ford News* 12 (Aug. 1932): 4; Segal, "Little Plants," 190, 192; *Reader's Digest* 24 (Feb. 1934): 50–51; ibid. 33 (July 1938): 62–64; *Ford Home Almanac,* June 1938, front cover, box 13, acc. 44, FM; Ford Motor Company, "Village Industries," n.d., box 153, acc. 149, FM.

23. Segal, "Little Plants," 198–200; "A Message to All Ford Workers," [1933], box 13, acc. 44, FM; *Printers' Ink,* 2 June 1932, 10, 12.

24. *Alcoa News,* 8 Jan. 1934, 3; ibid., 22 Jan. 1934, 3; U.S. Department of Commerce, *Subsistence*

Gardens (Washington, D.C., 1932), 3–7; Akron Community Gardens, Inc., *Report on Industrial Co-operative Gardening,* pamphlet, [1932], box GA-2, folder 15, BFG. On the context of this program at Goodrich in the 1930s, see Mansel G. Blackford and K. Austin Kerr, *BFGoodrich: Tradition and Transformation, 1870–1995* (Columbus, Ohio, 1996), 111–19.

25.   Robert J. Lynch to Stettinius, 9 May 1934, box 53, ERS; *The Worker in General Motors,* pamphlet, [Dec. 1937], enclosed in L. du Pont to Alfred P. Sloan, 24 Jan. 1938, box 73, acc. 1662, DP.

26.   "Ford Radio Program," circular, 27 Sept. 1934, box 10, acc. 572, FM; "Ford Sunday Evening Hour, October 7, 1934," pp. 81–82, box 15, acc. 44, FM; Lewis, *Public Image,* 313, 317, 326; John W. Spaulding, "The Radio Speaking of William John Cameron," *Speech Monographs* 26 (Mar. 1959): 47.

27.   Lewis, *Public Image,* 317, 326; Spaulding, "Cameron," 47–49; "Interview with Mr. Fred L. Black by Mr. Keith Clark," 10 Mar. 1951, pp. 139–41, box 16, acc. 44, FM; *Propaganda Analysis* 1 (July 1938): 2.

28.   *Printers' Ink,* 27 Dec. 1934, 79–80; W. J. Cameron, "A Series of Talks Given on the Ford Sunday Evening Hour by W. J. Cameron, 1934–35," pp. 12–14, box 42-01, NWA; W. J. Cameron, "Talks on Ford Sunday Hour, 1934–35," box 15, acc. 44, FM.

29.   Spaulding, "Cameron," 50; Lewis, *Public Image,* 326–27; Cameron, "Series of Talks," 21, 24, 64, 69, 76; *Propaganda Analysis* 1 (July 1938): 1, 3.

30.   *Advertising and Selling,* 9 Sept. 1937, 36. For typical criticisms of the "dignity complex," see *Advertising Age,* 21 Sept. 1936, 45; 23 Nov. 1936, 20; 21 June 1937, 49; 31 Jan. 1938, 33; 14 Mar. 1938, 38.

31.   *Advertising and Selling,* 18 Nov. 1937, 38, 48; *Advertising Age,* 28 Feb. 1938, p. 12; *Printers' Ink,* 20 May 1937, 11; Stanley Resor to Lenox R. Lohr, 21 July 1937, box 57, folder 28, NBC.

32.   Charles C. Carr, *Alcoa: An American Enterprise* (New York, 1952), 217; George David Smith, *From Monopoly to Competition: The Transformations of Alcoa, 1888–1986* (New York, 1988), 189, 192–93, 196–201; Winthrop Group, Inc., "Alcoa's Corporate Culture: Enduring Strengths and Embedded Constraints," 1983, pp. 28–29, envelope H-1751, AL; "Alcoa Bible," in-house history and scrapbook, n.d., p. 137, envelope 480, AL; advertising scrapbook, 1937, box 1724, no. 4, AL; C. R. Gibbons to A. B. Norton, 29 Apr. 1937, envelope 1240, AL; *Advertising Age,* 3 Jan. 1938, 12; ibid., 13 June 1938, 10; ibid., 15 Aug. 1938, 20; *Advertising and Selling* 32 (Feb. 1939): 50.

33.   J. Walter Thompson Company, "An Analysis," 1938, box 2, RG 1, JWT; *People* 1 (Sept. 1937), back cover, JWT; "Joe and the Corporate Surplus," box 34-31, NWA; BBDO, *Newsletter,* 24 Oct. 1936, n.p.; ibid., 29 Oct. 1937, 4.

34.   *Saturday Evening Post,* 13 June 1936, 64–65; *Advertising Age,* 31 Jan. 1938, 20; ibid., 21 Mar. 1938, 31; ibid., 20 June 1938, 20; C. E. Lang to Gerard Swope, 11 Feb. 1938, GS; Young & Rubicam, *Second International Research Conference, 1958* (New York, 1958), p. 6, Y&R.

35.   *Advertising Age,* 25 Oct. 1937, 55; ibid., 26 Sept. 1938, 12; *Advertising and Selling* 32 (Feb. 1939): 77, 80; Batten, "Public Relations," n.p.; *New York Times,* 10 Dec. 1936, 36.

36.   Such ads appeared in the *Saturday Evening Post:* 5 Sept. 1936, 64–65; 8 Feb. 1936, 83; 30 Nov. 1935, 54; 16 Jan. 1937, 30–31; 30 Jan. 1937, 34–35; 27 Feb. 1937, 28–29. See also *Du Pont Magazine* 30 (Mar. 1936): back cover; ibid. (Apr. 1936): back cover; ibid. (Sept. 1936): back cover; *U.S. Steel News* 1 (Sept. 1936): n.p.

37.   William D. Kennedy, "Workers Are People," *People* 1 (July 1937): 5, 27, JWT; *Advertising Age,* 22 Nov. 1937, 6. See the covers of *Forbes* on 15 May, 15 Aug. 1937; 15 Jan., 1 Mar., 15 Mar. 1938. See also "The Goodrich Policy of Industrial and Public Responsibility," box GA-2, folder 41, BFG.

38.   *Advertising Age,* 11 Oct. 1937, 28; Roland Marchand, "*Life* Comes to Corporate Headquarters," in *Looking at "Life": America's Favorite Magazine, 1936–1972,* ed. Erika Doss (forthcoming).

39.   *Flash,* 25 Mar. 1938, n.p., JWT; General Motors Corporation, "A Discussion of Current Public Relations Needs with a Specific Recommendation for 'General Motors Concert' Intermission Talks," [1936], pp. 4–5, file 87.2.46, ODY; Edward L. Bernays, *Biography of an Idea: Memoirs of Public Relations Counsel Edward L. Bernays* (New York, 1965), 566.

40.   *Advertising Age,* 17 Jan. 1938, 12; ibid., 7 Feb. 1938, 20; ibid., 25 Apr. 1938, 17; ibid., 22 Nov. 1937, 4; *Forbes,* 1 Apr. 1938, 1; *Printers' Ink Monthly* 37 (July 1938): 17, 55; *Sales Management,* 15 Nov. 1937, 18–20, 86; *Tide* 10 (Aug. 1936): 20; *Advertising and Selling,* 2 Dec. 1937, 48; "The Year 1937:

A Report to All Members of the Johns-Manville Organization by President Lewis H. Brown," box 73, acc. 1662, DP; Marchand, "*Life* Comes to Corporate Headquarters."

41.   Marchand, *Advertising,* 192–93; *Saturday Evening Post,* 26 Sept. 1926, 133.

42.   *U.S. Steel News* 1 (Aug. 1936): inside front cover; ibid. 6 (Apr. 1941): 22–23; *Chrysler Motors Magazine* 5 (May 1938): 13; ibid. 6 (Jan. 1939): 2; *Saturday Evening Post,* 12 June 1937, 39; ibid., 20 Nov. 1937, 43; ibid., 4 May 1940, 103; ibid., 14 Sept. 1940, 93; *Advertising Age,* 1 Mar. 1937, 33.

43.   L. du Pont to J. T. Brown, 10 Nov. 1932, box 3, acc. 1662, DP; William A. Hart to William B. Tracey, 25 Oct. 1932, box 3, acc. 1662, DP; L. du Pont to Herbert C. Calhoun, 5 Mar. 1935, box 45, acc. 1662, DP; C. W. Phellis to Irénée du Pont, 14 Nov. 1922, box 62, acc. 1662, DP; I. du Pont to Phellis, 24 Nov. 1922, box 62, acc. 1662, DP.

44.   Nelson H. De Foe to L. du Pont, 24 Aug. 1932, box 3, acc. 1662, DP; L. du Pont to W. A. Hart, 26 Aug. 1932, box 3, acc. 1662, DP; L. du Pont to A. J. Wilkins, 8 Nov. 1932, box 3, acc. 1662, DP; L. du Pont to Grover A. Whalen, 11 Sept. 1934, box 3, acc. 1662, DP; L. du Pont to Henry J. Schnell, 4 Dec. 1938, box 64, acc. 1662, DP; L. L. L. Golden, *Only by Public Consent: American Corporations Search for Favorable Opinion* (New York, 1968), 242.

45.   Golden, *Only by Public Consent,* 238, 241–42; Charles W. Cheape, *Strictly Business: Walter Carpenter at Du Pont and General Motors* (Baltimore, 1995), 130–32; Robert F. Burk, *The Corporate State and the Broker State: The Du Ponts and American National Politics, 1925–1940* (Cambridge, Mass., 1990), 151–52.

46.   L. du Pont to W. S. Carpenter et al., 14 Jan. 1935, box 20, acc. 1813, DP; T. J. Ross to L. du Pont, 7 Jan. 1935, box 20, acc. 1813, DP.

47.   Du Pont had already engaged in institutional advertising early in the 1920s (see Chapter 5), but that brief venture in identifying the company with the image of the public-spirited chemical engineer came to a decisive halt within a year. As in several other corporations with a "decentralized" divisional structure, the funds for such campaigns at Du Pont were allocated by formula and charged against the budgets of the individual divisions. With no headquarters funds earmarked for the institutional campaign, and with the company's Executive Committee showing only lukewarm support, the advocates of the campaign simply could not override an effective veto by several divisional general managers who refused to contribute to the cost. See C. W. Phellis to Irénée du Pont, 14 Nov. 1922; I. du Pont to Phellis, 24 Nov. 1922: box 62, acc. 1662, DP.

48.   Chaplin Tyler to Jasper Crane, 21 Jan 1935, box 1051, ser. II, pt. 2, DP.

49.   Crane to L. du Pont, 8 Feb. 1935, box 1050, ser. II, pt. 2, DP; W. S. Carpenter to L. du Pont, 8 Feb. 1935, box 1050, ser. II, pt. 2, DP. Carpenter's efforts (and frustrations) in seeking to make the corporation more sensitive to public opinion are effectively recounted in Cheape, *Strictly Business.*

50.   Bruce Barton to L. du Pont, 18 May 1935, box 20, acc. 1813, DP.

51.   Information Bulletin no. 132 KK, 30 Sept. 1935, Advertising Department files, Cellophane Company, DP; Jeffrey L. Meikle, *American Plastic: A Cultural History* (New Brunswick, N.J., 1995), 133–35.

52.   *Tide* 9 (Sept. 1935 suppl.): 14; Meikle, *American Plastic,* 135–36; *Du Pont Magazine* 29 (June 1935): 8; ibid. (Oct. 1935): 16.

53.   Tyler to Crane, 21 Jan. 1935, box 1051, ser. II, pt. 2, DP; BBDO, *Newsletter,* 13 Sept. 1935, 3; ibid., 5 Oct. 1935, 4; *Du Pont Magazine* 29 (Oct. 1935): 16.

54.   *Advertising Age,* 30 Sept. 1935, 29; *Printers' Ink,* 26 Sept. 1935, 82; *Du Pont Magazine* 31 (Feb. 1937): 16; ibid. 32 (Feb. 1938): 16.

55.   Press release, 27 Sept. 1935, box 36, acc. 1410, DP; Information Bulletin no. 166 KK, 27 Dec. 1936, Advertising Department files, Cellophane Company, DP; L. du Pont to W. A. Hart, 28 Feb. 1938, box 4, acc. 1662, DP; *Du Pont Magazine* 30 (Mar. 1936): 14; Golden, *Only by Public Consent,* 243–44; BBDO, *Newsletter,* 5 Oct. 1935, 4; ibid., 16 Nov. 1935, n.p.; ibid., 18 Jan. 1936, n.p.; ibid., 14 Mar. 1936, 11; ibid., 24 Sept. 1937, n.p.

56.   Dixon Ryan Fox to L. du Pont, 3 Apr. 1937; W. S. Forbes to L. du Pont, 13 Sept. 1938: box 4, acc. 1662, DP.

57.   "Commercial Announcement for *Cavalcade* Broadcast of Sept. 15, 1937," box 4, acc. 1662, DP; "'Old Hickory' Commercial Announcement, Revised Aug. 17, 1937," box 4, acc. 1662, DP;

Golden, *Only by Public Consent,* 243; "What Du Pont Customers Say about *The Cavalcade of America,*" attachment to Information Bulletin nos. 9–11, 1936, Advertising Department files, Cellophane Company, DP; Clark-Hooper, Inc., "Co-incidental Radio Advertisement Summary, January thru June, 1937," pp. 3, 30, 41, box 1, folder 1, HC. During the same week, but on other evenings, the *General Motors Concert* gained a 14.6 rating, and *Major Bowes Original Amateur Hour* rated 54.3.

58. L. du Pont to J. W. McCoy, 5 Oct. 1936, box 48, acc. 1662, DP; Cheape, *Strictly Business,* 175–76. Lammot du Pont even berated a younger family member and company executive for too indulgent an attitude toward such trifling corporate activities, reminding him that it remained unjustified "to spend much of the stockholders' money on public relations." A. Felix du Pont to L. du Pont, 28 May 1937; L. du Pont to A. Felix du Pont, 2 June 1937: box 64, acc. 1662, DP.

59. A. L. Tidd to L. du Pont, 10 Feb. 1938; L. du Pont to Tidd, 15 Feb. 1938: box 48, acc. 1662, DP.

60. *Advertising and Selling* 31 (July 1928): 44. As late as 1943 Lammot du Pont still did "not really take much stock in institutional advertising"; L. du Pont to C. G. Shannon, 18 June 1943, box 4, acc. 1662, DP.

61. Walter S. Carpenter Jr., "Comments for the Board of Directors Meeting," 8 Sept. 1937; idem, ibid., 20 Sept. 1937; Carpenter to L. du Pont, 17 Mar. 1939: box 817, acc. 542, DP.

62. Cheape, *Strictly Business,* 117, 121–27, 136, 252. One sign of Du Pont's resistance to prevailing trends was that its Publicity Department, until 1944, continued to be headed by Theodore Joslin, the former presidential press secretary for Herbert Hoover and a holdover from the years of bitter anti-Roosevelt antagonism. Golden (*Only by Public Consent,* 255–57) dates the "modern period" of public relations at Du Pont as beginning in 1944, when Joslin died.

63. Thomas Lamont to M.C.T. [Myron C. Taylor], 29 Jan. 1936; Lamont, "Memorandum for Partners, U.S. Steel," 25 Sept. 1935: box 226, TL. See also Cheape, *Strictly Business,* 70.

64. Bruce Barton to Joseph P. Knapp, 26 Feb. 1930, box 36, BB; Alfred D. Chandler Jr., *Strategy and Structure: Chapters in the History of the Industrial Enterprise* (Cambridge, Mass., 1962), 334.

65. BBDO, *Newsletter,* 26 Oct. 1935, 3.

66. On the resistance of division heads and old-timers to institutional advertising and debates over internal apportionment of the costs, see A. H. Young to A. W. Vogt, 14 Jan. 1936, box 64, ERS; Robert Gregg to W. A. Irvin, 10 Dec. 1937, box 36, ERS; Roy Durstine to Barton, 13 Jan. 1937, box 5, BB.

67. Bruce Barton, "Presentation to United States Steel Company," [Sept. 1935], pp. 25–27, 29, box 558, ERS.

68. Ed Roberts, draft of article on Bruce Barton, n.d., p. 6, BBDO; *Tide* 9 (Dec. 1935): 14.

69. *Saturday Evening Post,* 16 Nov. 1935, 86–87; ibid., 8 Feb. 1936, 66–67; "BBDO Report on Sales and Advertising for the United States Steel Corporation," enclosed in M. Louise MacLeod to Stettinius, 25 Oct. 1935, pp. 18, 25, 28, box 558, ERS; Bruce Barton to Robert Gregg, 31 Jan. 1936, box 558, ERS; Barton to Stettinius, 27 Dec. 1935, box 558, ERS; Horace Vaile to Gregg et al., 26 Mar. 1936, box 36, ERS. In unmistakable Bartonesque rhetoric an internal bulletin of one of the subsidiaries proclaimed, "What we want others to believe we must first believe ourselves"; Carnegie-Illinois Steel Company, "Advertising Bulletin," [ca. 1937], pp. 23, 25, USX.

70. *Saturday Evening Post,* 30 Nov. 1935, 40–41; *Advertising Age,* 16 Dec. 1935, 39; ibid., 20 Jan. 1936, 32.

71. See examples of this series in the *Saturday Evening Post:* 14 Mar. 1936, 80–81; 16 May 1936, 86–87; 26 Sept. 1936, 54–55; 17 Oct. 1936, 86–87.

72. *U.S. Steel News* 2 (Dec. 1937): 20; ibid. 3 (Jan. 1938): 18–19; *Advertising Age,* 25 Apr. 1938, 12.

73. *Tide* 10 (June 1936, suppl.): 1; see also the *U.S. Steel News* covers for June and Sept. 1936 and Oct. 1937.

74. *U.S. Steel News* 2 (Nov. 1937): 23; ibid. 3 (Jan. 1938): 1; ibid. 3 (Mar. 1938): 1; John W. Hill, "Explaining Industry to the Public," 24 Sept. 1938, p. 6, box 39, JWH; J. C. MacDonald, press release, 13 Oct. 1938, reel 16:30A, WDT; Meyer Levin, "The Candid Cameraman," *Esquire* 8 (Nov. 1937): 122, 230, 232; *Motion Picture Daily,* 15 Apr. 1938, clipping, box 48, ERS; J. C. MacDonald to Myron C. Taylor, 4 Oct. 1937, box 48, ERS.

75. *McCall's* 65 (July 1938): 4. Ironically, just when the dramatic films were being produced,

BBDO executives who toured a U.S. Steel mill noted that "blood-sweating bohunks, juggling red-hot metal, are becoming passé in the steel business. Steel workers now flip switches that look like giant editions of the ones that turn on the lights in your house." BBDO, *Newsletter,* 19 Feb. 1937, 6; C. M. Underhill to J. Carlisle MacDonald, 17 Apr. 1937, box 47, ERS. On Standard Oil of Indiana's concurrent product of its own "good-will" film, *Stan,* see *Printers' Ink Monthly* 36 (Feb. 1938): 14–15. On the concept of an "industrial zone aesthetic," see John Stilgoe, *Metropolitan Corridor: Railroads and the American Scene* (New Haven, Conn., 1983), 77, 87–89, 92–93.

76.   *U.S. Steel News* 4 (Apr. 1939): 6–7; ibid. 6 (Apr. 1941): 18–23; ibid. 10 (Oct. 1945): 20–21.

77.   G. L. Lacher to A. H. Young, 11 Feb. 1936, box 64, ERS; Durstine to Barton, 13 Jan. 1937, box 5, BB; Martin Dodge to Walter D. Teague, 4 Nov. 1936, 2 June 1937, reel 16:30A, WDT; *Advertising Age,* 27 Dec. 1937, 2; ibid., 10 Jan. 1938, 29; ibid., 21 Feb. 1938, 37; ibid., 25 Apr. 1938, 12; *U.S. Steel News* 2 (Nov. 1937): 21–24; ibid. (Dec. 1937): 20; ibid. 5 (July 1940): cover; ibid. 6 (Apr. 1941): 18–23.

78.   Durstine to Barton, 13 Jan. 1937, box 5, BB; J.C.M. [J. Carlisle MacDonald] to Stettinius, 11 May 1937, 23 June 1937, box 47, ERS; press release, Department of Public Relations, Tennessee Coal, Iron, and Railroad Company, 7 Oct. 1937, box 48, ERS; press release, Carnegie Illinois Steel Corporation, 19 June 1937, box 48, ERS; Edward R. Stettinius Jr., address, 27 Jan. 1938, p. 20, box 52, ERS.

79.   *Advertising Age,* 10 Jan. 1938, 29. Portions of this statement were lifted verbatim from Barton's 1935 proposal to U.S. Steel; see Barton, "Presentation," 36.

80.   Alfred P. Sloan Jr. to Charles Kettering, 31 Aug. 1931, CFK; L. du Pont to Sloan, 19 Jan. 1931, carton 1, "10 Point Program" folder, GMB; Sloan to L. du Pont, 21 Jan. 1931, carton 1, "10 Point Program" folder, GMB.

81.   *Advertising Age,* 25 Apr. 1938, 27. Garrett scolded his new colleagues for ads in a recent issue of the *Saturday Evening Post.* Although General Motors had published a lavish two-page institutional message in this issue, two of its divisions, Chevrolet and LaSalle, had each presented one-page ads that carried no identification with the parent company. See Paul Garrett, "A Bigger and Better General Motors," speech ms., 3 Oct. 1931, GM.

82.   Garrett to Kettering, 5 Aug. 1931, 18 Sept. 1931, 28 Nov. 1933; Florence A. Wilkinson to General Motors, 11 Sept. 1933; Minnie E. Richards to General Motors, 9 Sept. 1933: CFK. See also Garrett to Bernays, 5 Sept. 1933, ELB.

83.   Garrett to Kettering, 12 Oct. 1931, 22 Dec. 1931, 11 Mar. 1932, 2 May 1932, and enclosures, CFK.

84.   General Motors Corporation, "Press Release for 'The Advertiser,'" GM. For more extended analyses of customer research at General Motors, see Sally Clarke, "Consumers, Information, and Marketing Efficiency at GM, 1921–1940," *Business and Economic History* 25 (fall 1996): 186–95; Roland Marchand, "Customer Research as Public Relations: General Motors in the 1930s," in *Getting and Spending: European and American Consumption in the Twentieth Century,* ed. Susan Strasser, Charles McGovern, and Matthias Judt (New York, in press).

85.   Henry G. Weaver, "Personal Interviews vs. Direct Mail Questionnaires," 18 May 1933, pp. 1, 4, 6, box 18, ERS; "Notes on Executive Committee Minutes," 11 Aug. 1932, carton 2, GMB; press release, 14 Oct. 1933, GM; Alfred P. Sloan Jr., "The Proving Ground of Public Opinion," *Printers' Ink,* 21 Sept. 1933, 92–93; General Motors Corporation, *24th Annual Report . . . for Year Ended December 31, 1932,* HCR.

86.   *Fortune* 19 (Mar. 1939): 138; Arthur J. Kuhn, *GM Passes Ford, 1918–1938: Designing the General Motors Performance-Control System* (University Park, Penn., 1986), 219–21. See also Clarke, "Consumers."

87.   Garrett, "Bigger and Better," 2; Bernays, *Biography,* 547.

88.   Notes on Executive Committee minutes, 11 Aug. 1932, GMB; Weaver, "Personal Interviews," 1, 4, 6; [idem], "False Teeth and Chewing Gum: Thought Starter No. 80," n.d., p. 5, box 592, ERS; idem, "The Proving Ground of Public Opinion," *Journal of Consulting Psychology* 5 (1941): 92–93. A trade journal observed that GM was reaping public goodwill by inferring that General Motors was "actually interested in what the individual thinks and . . . anxious to accept his advice"; "General Motors Ask the Buyer for Opinions," *Canadian Advertising Data,* Nov. 1932, 14, 25. I am indebted to Daniel Robinson for calling this article to my attention.

89. General Motors Corporation, *The Philosophy of Customer Research*, pamphlet, [1933], NYPL; *Saturday Evening Post*, 28 Apr. 1934, 38–39.

90. *Advertising Age*, 19 May 1934, 23; "Customer Research: Final Report of 1933 Study," 1933, CFK; *Fortune* 19 (Mar. 1939): 138, 141; Charles Francis McGovern, "Sold American: Inventing the Consumer, 1890–1940" (Ph.D. diss., Harvard University, 1993), 377; Charles F. McGovern, "Consumption and Citizenship in the United States, 1900–1940," in Strasser, McGovern, and Judt, eds., *Getting and Spending* (in press).

91. Attachment to H. G. Weaver to O. E. Hunt, 8 Oct. 1932, CFK; General Motors, *Philosophy of Customer Research*, 2. Weaver's diagram later gained recognition in a textbook on business psychology; see Edward K. Strong Jr., *Psychological Aspects of Business* (New York, 1938), 175.

92. Sloan is quoted in Ed Cray, *Chrome Colossus: General Motors and Its Times* (New York, 1980), 321.

93. Thus, GM claimed to carry out far more directly and practically what Lizabeth Cohen describes as government gestures under the New Deal to give "a real voice to consumers" and to take consumers' interests "better into account"; Cohen, "Making Citizen Consumers through Depression and War," in Strasser, McGovern, and Judt, eds., *Getting and Spending* (in press).

94. *Saturday Evening Post*, 24 Oct. 1936, 48–49; Neil H. Borden and Martin V. Marshall, *Advertising Management: Text and Cases*, rev. ed. (Homewood, Ill., 1959), 398–99.

95. "Customer Research: Final Report," n.p.; *Fortune* 19 (Mar. 1939) 51, 141; *Saturday Evening Post*, 23 June 1934, 30–31. On the range and depth of early 1930s concerns within GM, see the correspondence of GM executives in the "10 Point Program" folder, carton 1, GMB.

96. Garrett, "Bigger and Better," n.p.; General Motors, *Annual Report, 1932*, 20; idem, *25th Annual Report . . . for the Year Ended December 31, 1933*, p. 24, HCR.

97. General Motors Corporation, Research Division, "An Experiment in Advertising and Publicity," 1936, pp. 5–9, GM; Sloan to Kettering, 18 May 1934, CFK; Garrett to Kettering, 19 Sept. 1934, CFK; "Topics for Public Relations Committee Meeting," 11 Nov. 1932, CFK; "A 1933 Publicity Plan for General Motors," uncatalogued reports, CFK; *General Motors World* 13 (Oct. 1934): 5; minutes of Public Relations Committee meeting, 20 Sept. 1933, pp. 6–10, 17, box 19, ERS; Garrett to Stettinius, 25 Sept. 1933, box 19, ERS; *Printer's Ink*, 17 Sept. 1931, 102.

98. Paul W. Garrett, "The Importance of the Public," pp. 4–5, in "White Sulphur Springs Conference of GM, 1934," folder 77-7.4-1.13-2, CSM; Sloan to Owen D. Young, 10 May, 14 June 1934, file 87.2.145, ODY; *Scientific Monthly* 39 (July 1934): 67–78; *General Motors World* 13 (June 1934): 4; ibid. (July 1934): 6; press release, 26 May 1934, CFK; Bernays, *Biography*, 553.

99. Press releases, 1 Oct. 1934, 6 Aug. 1936, GM; *Broadcasting*, 15 Dec. 1935, 33; *Printers' Ink*, 17 Oct. 1935, 106; *Advertising Age*, 5 Aug. 1935, 23; Garrett to Kettering, 15 May 1935, CFK; press release, 30 Sept. 1935, CFK.

100. *Fortune* 19 (Mar. 1939): 45–46; General Motors Corporation, *27th Annual Report . . . for the Year Ended December 31, 1935*, p. 5, HCR; Borden and Marshall, *Advertising Management*, 397; Garrett, "Importance of the Public," 4–5. The phrase "really coterminous" is *Fortune*'s; the emphasis in Garrett's remarks is mine.

101. Sloan to L. du Pont, 16 Apr. 1935; L. du Pont to Sloan, 23 Apr. 1935; Carpenter to Sloan, 2 July 1935; Sloan to Carpenter, 8 July 1935: box 821, ser. II, pt. 2, DP.

102. General Motors Corporation, "Discussion of Current Public Relations Needs"; *Saturday Evening Post*, 16 Sept. 1936, 27–28; ibid., 24 Oct. 1936, 48–49.

103. Garrett to Carpenter, 1 May 1936; C. R. Brown to Carpenter, 7 May 1936: box 821, ser. II, pt. 2, DP.

104. Garrett to Carpenter, 1 May 1936, box 821, ser. II, pt. 2, DP; Sloan to General Motors Employees, 15 Oct. 1936, box 566, ERS; Cray, *Chrome Colossus*, 283, 321. See the ads in the *American Federationist*: 43 (Apr. 1936): 345; (May 1936): 455; (June 1936): 576; (July 1936): 680; (Dec. 1936): 1231.

105. Alfred P. Sloan Jr., "The Broadened Responsibilities of Industry's Executives," in *For Top-Executives Only: A Symposium*, ed. J. George Frederick (New York, 1936), 358–59, 362, 370; Donaldson Brown to Sloan, 9 May 1938, box 821, ser. II, pt. 2, DP.

106. Brown to Sloan, 9 May 1938, box 821, ser. II, pt. 2, DP.

107. Garrett, "Importance of the Public," 5–7; idem, "Industry's No. 1 Problem Defined," speech ms., 9 Feb. 1939, p. 8, GM.

108. Roy C. Witner to Henry Souvaine, 25 Mar. 1937, box 57, folder 4, NBC; Weaver to Kettering, 16 Dec. 1937, CFK. For ads in this series, see the *Saturday Evening Post:* 16 Jan. 1937, 30–31; 30 Jan. 1937, 34–35; 27 Feb. 1937, 28–29.

109. "Topics for Public Relations Committee Meeting," n.p.

110. *GM Folks* 1 (May 1938): inside front cover; Garrett, "Industry's No. 1 Problem," 8.

111. *GM Folks* 1 (May 1938): n.p.; ibid. (Oct. 1938): inside front cover; ibid. 2 (Sept. 1939): back cover; Don Hogate to Garrett, 16 Mar. 1938, GM.

112. *From Dawn to Sunset,* produced by Jam Handy, Inc., for Chevrolet Motor Company, 1937. I am indebted to Rick Prelinger of Prelinger Associates, New York City, for an opportunity to view this film from his collection.

113. Alfred P. Sloan Jr., *Shall We Have More—or Less?* pamphlet, 22 May 1936, pp. 1–3, HML; General Motors Corporation, *The Worker in General Motors,* pamphlet, [Dec. 1937], enclosed in L. du Pont to Sloan, 24 Jan. 1938, box 73, acc. 1662, DP; J. Handley Wright and Byron H. Christian, *Public Relations in Management* (New York, 1949), 112.

114. S. H. Walker and Paul Sklar, "Business Finds Its Voice, Part III," *Harper's Magazine* 176 (Mar. 1938): 432–33; General Motors Corporation, "With Faith in Indianapolis," ad, Indianapolis newspapers, 18 Dec. 1936, GM; General Motors Corporation, "A Record Investment in Progress," proof of ad, Nov. 1936, GM.

115. Hogate to Kettering, 17 Apr. 1936, CFK; minutes of meeting of Detroit Public Relations Committee, 17 Apr. 1936, CFK; "Suggestions for Improvement of GM PR in Detroit," [1936], pp. 33, 40, CFK; Paul Willard Garrett, *As Others See Us,* pamphlet, 27 June 1936, GM; Hogate to Garrett, 16 Mar. 1938, GM.

116. Garrett to Kettering, 22 Oct. 1937, CFK; "Home Address: Main Street U.S.A.," newspaper ad, Oct. 1937, GM; *Neighbor and Customer in Every Community,* pamphlet, n.d. [1938], GM; press release, 4 Apr. 1938, GM; *GM Folks* 1 (July 1938): back cover.

117. Paul W. Garrett, "National Industrial Conference Board," speech ms., 13 Mar. 1938, n.p., GM; idem, "Industry's No. 1 Problem," 8; Hogate to Garrett, 16 Mar. 1938, GM; Garrett, *As Others See Us,* n.p. On the "Dayton Plan," see also Peter Drucker, *The Concept of the Corporation,* 2d ed. (New York, 1972), 94; *Fortune* 19 (Mar. 1939): 150; Karen Miller, "Amplifying the Voice of Business: Hill and Knowlton's Influence on Political, Public, and Media Discourse in Postwar America" (Ph.D. diss., University of Wisconsin, Madison, 1993), 141–42.

118. "General Motors Comes to Linden," ad, New Jersey newspapers, 25 May 1937, GM; "Shake, Syracuse!" ad, Syracuse newspapers, 24 Sept. 1936, GM; General Motors Corporation, "Yesterday Has Built for Today and Tomorrow," proof of ad, [1937], GM; Paul Garrett, "Industry's Public Relations Job and the Personnel Executive's Part in It," speech ms., [1938], n.p., GM; *Fortune* 19 (Mar. 1939): 45.

119. Paul W. Garrett, *Management: Tell What You Stand For,* pamphlet, 26 Sept. 1944, pp. 16–17, BL.

120. John M. Shaw, memorandum for W. J. O'Connor, 4 Sept. 1930, box 1, JMS.

121. *Advertising Age,* 6 July 1936, 36; 12 Oct. 1936, 38; 7 Sept. 1937, 1.

122. Tedlow, *Keeping the Corporate Image,* 59. For examples, see *Advertising Age:* 18 May 1936, 12; 14 Dec. 1936, 24; 27 Dec. 1937, 17; 21 Feb. 1938, 2; 22 Aug. 1938, 15. See also *Advertising and Selling* 31 (Oct. 1938): 40–41; ibid., 15 Feb. 1939, 6–7; *New York Times,* 17 Oct. 1936, 31; S. H. Walker and Paul Sklar, "Business Finds Its Voice, Part II," *Harper's Magazine* 176 (Feb. 1938): 329.

123. BBDO, "The DEVIL—11 Wall," *The Wedge* 34, no. 2 (1934); BBDO, "No-Man's Land," *The Wedge,* 34, no. 5 (1934); N. W. Ayer, *What Is a Capitalist?* and *Why Business Is Big,* pamphlets, 1936, box 34-31, NWA.

124. Young & Rubicam, *Standard Practice,* 1936, pp. 118–19, Y&R; *Advertising Age,* 5 July 1937, 20; ibid., 20 Sept. 1937, 18; ibid., 4 Oct. 1937, 30; ibid., 1 Nov. 1937, 2; ibid., 12 Sept. 1938, 2; *Advertising and Selling* 31 (Oct. 1938): 42; Tedlow, *Keeping the Corporate Image,* 172, 174; *Tide* 10 (Apr. 1936): 15, 18; enclosure in C. H. Lang to C. E. Wilson, 23 Sept. 1938, GS.

125. Donald S. Napoli, *Architects of Adjustment: The History of the Psychological Profession in the United*

States (Port Washington, N.Y., 1981), 49; Leonard W. Doob, "An 'Experimental' Study of the Psychological Corporation," *Psychological Bulletin* 35 (Apr. 1938): 220–22.

126. Irwin Ross, *The Image Merchants: The Fabulous World of Public Relations* (Garden City, N.Y., 1959), 259; Psychological Corporation, "A Study of Public Relations and Social Attitudes," *Journal of Applied Psychology* 21 (1937): 591, 593, 599; Psychological Corporation, "The Eighth Nation-Wide Social and Experimental Survey," 1943, box 4, acc. 1662, DP; William A. Hart to L. du Pont, 18 Apr. 1938, box 4, acc. 1662, DP; H. Lang to C. E. Wilson, 23 Sept. 1938, GS; *Fortune* 10 (Oct. 1937): 167.

127. Psychological Corp., "Eighth Nation-Wide Survey," pp. 1, 5.

128. Elmo Roper, "A Survey of Attitudes toward and Opinions about Ford Motor Company," box 22, acc. 5, FM; Curtis Publishing Company, *The Court of Public Opinion,* pamphlet (Philadelphia, April 1937), box 56, ERS.

129. *Fortune* 19 (Mar. 1939): 83, 148; Kuhn, *GM Passes Ford,* 235; "Paul Garrett," biographical file, GM; Paul W. Garrett, "Large Scale Business and the Public," speech ms., 25 Mar. 1939, n.p; idem, "Industry's No. 1 Problem," p. 1; idem, "National Industrial Conference Board," n.p.; Hogate to Garrett, 16 Mar. 1938, GM; "Plant City Bulletin," no. 21, 10 Feb. 1939, mimeo, GM.

130. John W. Hill, eventually the head of the Hill-Knowlton Public Relations firm, was first hired by Republic Steel and the American Iron and Steel Institute in 1933. United States Steel hired a public relations director in the immediate wake of its decision in late 1935 to undertake institutional advertising with Bruce Barton. Du Pont energized its dormant public relations operation by participating in regional fairs in 1935 and 1936 and mounting an institutional advertising campaign with BBDO. International Harvester officially established a public relations department in 1937, as did Pittsburgh Plate Glass in 1939. See *Tide* 10 (15 Oct. 1936): 21; Kenneth Henry, *Defenders and Shapers of the Corporate Image* (New Haven, Conn., 1972), 37; John W. Hill, *The Making of a Public Relations Man* (New York, 1963), 44; Irwin Ross, *The Image Merchants* (New York, 1959), 34, 162; Tedlow, *Keeping the Corporate Image,* 104, 175–77. On the rise of public relations professionals in the late 1930s, see also Miller, "Amplifying the Voice of Business," 39–41, 68–69.

131. *Forbes,* 1 May 1939, 12; *Fortune* 19 (Mar. 1939): 88; *Advertising Age,* 25 Apr. 1938, 1–2; Richardson Wood, "The Corporation Goes in Politics," *Harvard Business Review* 21 (autumn 1942): 61; Market Research Corporation of America, *Industrial Relations, Public Relations, Economic Research, Market Research,* pamphlet, [1938], p. 17, box 53, FRS.

132. *Fortune* 19 (Mar. 1939): 83, 85–86. On conversation with the masses as a "feminine" proposition, see Andreas Huyssen, *After the Great Divide: Modernism, Mass Culture, Postmodernism* (Bloomington, Ind., 1986), 44–50; Roland Marchand, "Advertising Expertise and the Decline of the 'Trickle Down' Theory," in *Proceedings, Thirty-third Annual Conference of the American Council on Consumer Interests,* ed. Vickie L. Hampton (Columbia, Mo., 1987), 9–12.

Chapter 7

1. Walter Dorwin Teague, "Industrial Art and Its Future," speech ms., [1936], p. 3, box 79, WDT.

2. Two of the best analyses of changing styles and modes of display in world's fairs in the United States are John G. Cawelti, "America on Display: The World's Fairs of 1876, 1893, 1933," in *America in the Age of Industrialization,* ed. Frederic C. Jaher (New York, 1968), 317–63; and Neil Harris, "Museums, Merchandising, and Popular Taste: The Struggle for Influence," in *Material Culture and the Study of American Life,* ed. Ian M. B. Quimby (New York, 1978), 140–74.

3. Chrysler press release, 27 Apr. 1939, T. J. Ross Scrapbooks, vol. 334, ILL; Chaplin Tyler, "Visit to Texas Centennial Exposition," enclosed in Tyler to Charles K. Weston, July 1936, box 51, ser. II, pt. 2, DP.

4. See illustrations in the *Electrical World:* 7 June 1884, 185–86; 13 Sept. 1884, 83; 27 Sept. 1884, 105; 18 Oct. 1884, 117.

5. *Electrical World,* 7 June 1884, 185; ibid., 11 Oct. 1884, 132; Blake McKelvey, "Rochester at the World's Fair," *Rochester History* 26 (July 1964): 1; *Young Henry Ford Went to the Fair,* pamphlet, 1939, box 1005, NYWF; David L. Lewis, *The Public Image of Henry Ford: An American Folk Hero and His*

Company (Detroit, 1976), 118, 297; David B. Sicilia, "Selling Power: Marketing and Monopoly at Boston Edison, 1886–1929" (Ph.D. diss., Brandeis University, 1991), 213.

6. Sicilia, "Selling Power," 209, 213–16, 218–19, 317–22; Eastman Kodak Company, *Trade Circular* 6 (Oct. 1905): 1, EK; Eastman Kodak Company, "Kodak Overseas," blue binder, n.d., EK; Douglas Collins, *The Story of Kodak* (New York, 1990), 99–100.

7. *Harvester World* 3 (Jan. 1912): 26. The head of the National Cash Register Company, J. H. Patterson, for instance, provided two weeks vacation and all expenses for department heads, foremen, and six hundred women workers to attend the 1904 World's Fair at St. Louis. Part of his agenda, along with the promotion of company morale, was the expectation that these citizens of Dayton would "come back with the determination to force the School Board to give us manual training in our schools." American Institute of Social Service, *Weekly Commercial Letters Service,* 13 July 1904, box 41, CMc. On the sporadic desire not to incur the expenses of participation, usually overridden by the fear of being upstaged by competitors, see E. M. Barton to F. P. Fish, 21 Aug. 1902, box 1326, ATT.

8. James W. Buel, *The Magic City* (St. Louis, 1894), n.p.; John Allwood, *The Great Exhibitions* (London, 1977), 87; photograph no. 1354 (1908), HHP; *Western Electric News* 4 (May 1915): 16–17; Frank Morton Todd, *The Story of the Exposition* (New York, 1921), vol. 4, opposite pp. 166 and 206; *Remington Notes* 3 (1915): n.p., box 6, WF.

9. *Telephone Switchboard in Operation in the Exhibit of the American Bell Telephone Company in the Electricity Building, World's Fair, Chicago,* pamphlet, [1893], box 1061, ATT; *Exhibit of the American Bell Telephone Company, Electricity Building, Columbian Exposition, Chicago, 1893,* pamphlet, [1893], pp. 12, 18, 25, box 1061, ATT.

10. *The General Electric Company at the Pan-American Exposition, August 12, 1901,* pamphlet, historical file L 4527, GES; David E. Nye, *Electrifying America: Social Meanings of a New Technology* (Cambridge, Mass., 1990), 33–43; Carolyn Marvin, "Dazzling the Multitude: Imagining the Electric Light as a Communications Medium," in *Imagining Tomorrow: History, Technology, and the American Future,* ed. Joseph J. Corn (Cambridge, Mass., 1986), 204.

11. "World's Fair, Chicago, GE Exhibits at," [1893], historical file L 487–91, GES; *Electrical World,* 7 June 1884, 56; ibid., 16 Aug. 1884, 52; ibid., 20 Sept. 1884, 96; ibid., 27 Sept. 1884, 108; Robert W. Rydell, *World of Fairs: The Century-of-Progress Expositions* (Chicago, 1993), 19.

12. Neil Harris, *Humbug: The Art of P. T. Barnum* (Chicago, 1973), 57, 73, 75, 79, 81–82.

13. David E. Nye, *American Technological Sublime* (Cambridge, Mass., 1994), 129; Benjamin C. Truman, *History of the World's Fair* (1893; reprint, New York, 1976), 321–26; Pennsylvania Railroad Company, *The Pennsylvania Railroad at the Louisiana Purchase Exposition, St. Louis, Missouri, 1904* (Philadelphia, 1905), 8, 10; Mark Bennitt, ed., *History of the Louisiana Purchase Exposition* (1905; reprint, New York, 1976), 635; David R. Francis, *The Universal Exposition of 1904* (St. Louis, 1913), 384; Charles M. Kurtz, *The Saint Louis World's Fair of 1904: An Illustrated Handbook* (St. Louis, 1903), 23.

14. Postum Company, *A Trip through Postumville,* pamphlet, 1920, n.p., KGF; *Printers' Ink,* 11 May 1922, 22.

15. Postum, *Trip through Postumville,* n.p.; idem, *The Door Unbolted,* pamphlet, 1906, p. 3, KGF; idem, *There's a Reason,* pamphlet, n.d., pp. 1, 5, 7, KGF.

16. Postum, *Trip through Postumville,* n.p.

17. Ibid.; Postum, *There's a Reason,* frontispiece and pp. 1, 4; Marge and Warren Pshea, oral history, interview by Elizabeth Adkins, 26 Feb. 1991, p. 22, KGF.

18. Robert C. Alberts, *The Good Provider: H. J. Heinz and His 57 Varieties* (Boston, 1973), 124–26.

19. Gertrude Beeks, "Notes on Investigation Trip, 1901," pp. 12–14, 23, file 3B, box 27, NMc; Leroy Fairman, *The Growth of a Great Industry,* pamphlet, 1910, pp. 17, 21, 33, HHP; Alberts, *Good Provider,* 124–25; 153–56; Stephen Potter, *The Magic Number: The Story of "57"* (London, 1959), 22; Roland Cole, "How Heinz Advertises Idea behind Plant and Product," *Printers' Ink Monthly* 5 (July 1922): 19–20, 101.

20. Alberts, *Good Provider,* 131–32. Beneath its famous six-story electric sign in New York City, Heinz also publicized its corporate image through a display room "where attractive young women

packed vegetables in clear glass jars." See Mildred Friedman, Steven Heller, Caroline Hightower, et al., *Graphic Design in America: A Visual Language History* (Minneapolis, 1989), 37.

21. *Printers' Ink,* 27 July 1922, 163–64; Postum, *Trip through Postumville,* n.p.; Armour and Company, *Souvenir,* pamphlet, 1893, n.p., CHS.

22. Louise Carroll Wade, *Chicago's Pride: The Stockyards, Packingtown, and Environs in the Nineteenth Century* (Chicago, 1987), 369–71; Catherine Campbell Cocks, "'A City Excellent to Behold': Urban Tourism and the Commodification of Public Life in the United States, 1850–1915" (Ph.D. diss., University of California, Davis, 1997), 317.

23. Armour, *Souvenir,* n.p.

24. Armour and Company, *Seeing Armour's,* pamphlet, [1917], pp. 3–4, CHS; idem, *Seeing Armour's,* pamphlet, [1918], pp. 1, 4, CHS; idem, *Containing Facts about the Business and Organization,* pamphlet, 1917, pp. 5–7, CHS; Swift & Company, *Visitors' Reference Book,* pamphlet, [1913], n.p, CHS; idem, *Year Book, 1910* (Chicago, 1910), p. 13, CHS; idem, *A Visit to Swift & Company,* pamphlet for mailing, [1918], n.p., CHS; idem, *Little Journeys through the Plants of Swift & Company,* pamphlet, 1920, pp. 1, 21, 52, 93, NYPL.

25. Lewis, *Public Image,* 40, 53–55, 118, 498n.88; John M. Staudenmaier, "Making Sense of Henry: Thoughts on the Ford Museum and Greenfield Village" (paper presented at the Dibner Institute, Cambridge, Mass., 1993), 3.

26. Lewis, *Public Image,* 118, 162, 498n.88; Staudenmaier, "Making Sense."

27. Charles Ripley, *Romance of a Great Factory* (Schenectady, N.Y., 1919), 9–11, 13, 18, 55, 63–64, 97, 111–12.

28. Printers' Ink, *Fifty Years: 1888–1938* (New York, 1938), 302; *Printers' Ink Monthly* 12 (Mar. 1926): 27; *Printers' Ink,* 14 Nov. 1929, 94. On the nineteenth-century legacy of this penchant for the picture of the factory as advertisement, see Pamela Walker Lurito, "Advertising's Smoky Past: Themes of Progress in Nineteenth-Century American Advertisements," in *The Popular Perception of Industrial History: Essays from the Lowell Conference on Industrial History, 1985,* ed. Robert Weible and Francis R. Walsh (Lanham, Md., 1989), 184–86. For the persistence of this instinct to display the factory in advertisements, see *Saturday Evening Post,* 3 Mar. 1928, 170–71; ibid., 10 Mar. 1928, 132–33.

29. *Edison Sales Builder* 2 (June 1915): 56; *Western Electric News* 4 (May 1915): 1–2, 16–17; Todd, *Story of the Exposition,* 4:297.

30. United States Steel Corporation, *Description of Exhibits of United States Steel Corporation and Subsidiary Companies, Palace of Mines and Metallurgy, Panama-Pacific International Exposition,* pamphlet (San Francisco, [1915]), pp. 5, 17, 19, 54, USX.

31. "The Reminiscences of Frank Vivian," oral history, 1952, pp. 7–10, 14–15, 31, FM; *Ford Times* 8 (July 1915): 455; Lewis, *Public Image,* 118.

32. U.S. Steel pointed out that its exhibits were intended to demonstrate not only advances in the process of manufacture but also "the advanced activities and interests of the Corporation" in employee welfare and working conditions. It put on display a typical "change house" with lockers and showers for employees when they left work. Large illustrations depicted the "flower plots inside the millyards" and the employee flower and vegetable gardens. Ford supplemented its main display with "before and after" models of workers' housing to demonstrate the wonderful effects of the Ford five-dollar day on workers' living standards. U.S. Steel, *Description of Exhibits,* 47, 51; Lewis, *Public Image,* 118.

33. *Collier's,* 2 June 1934, 13; Cawelti, "America on Display," 354. Chrysler is quoted in "Sample Press Release," attached to Norman W. Grett to J. E. Fields, 13 Dec. 1931, folder 1-3377, CP; Firestone Tire & Rubber Company, press release, 20 June 1932, folder 1-5600, CP.

34. *Collier's,* 2 June 1934, 12–13; Jeffrey L. Meikle, *Twentieth Century Limited: Industrial Design in America, 1925–1939* (Philadelphia, 1979), 3, 153–54; Cawelti, "American on Display," 354; *Printers' Ink,* 15 June 1933, 48; *Long Lines* 12 (June 1933): 9.

35. Cawelti, "America on Display," 347–48; "Chicago World's Fair Centennial Celebration," July 1928, p. 6, box 5, folder 8, JR; unsigned to George K. Burgess, 21 Aug. 1928, box 5, folder 8, JR. On the competitive undercutting of the original plan of collective exhibits, see also Lenox Lohr to Rufus Davis, 30 Apr. 1931, folder 354, LL.

36. *Westinghouse Electric News* 1 (May 1915): 10–11; ibid. (Oct. 1915): 14–15; "Trade Paper Advertising, 1915," folder 3589, IH; *Architectural Forum* 56 (May 1932): 496A.

37. AT&T, *Exhibit of the American Bell Telephone Company, Electricity Building, Columbian Exposition, Chicago, 1893,* pamphlet, 1893, pp. 11–12, box 1061, ATT; idem, "Bell Telephone Exhibit at the Panama-Pacific Exposition," 1915, p. 6, box 1061, ATT; idem, "The Bell System at a Century of Progress," n.p., box 1061, ATT; untitled manuscript on AT&T at the fairs, 1915, p. 3, case N, no. 22700-10D, ATT; Cawelti, "America on Display," 346, 351–52; T. J. Ross Jr. to E. Ross Bartley, 4 June 1932, folder 1-3378, CP; Ross to Norman Grett, 14 Apr. 1932, folder 1-3378, CP; *Architectural Forum* 56 (May 1932): 496D; H. D. Morrow, "The Ford Exposition," 1934, n.p., box 2, acc. 450, FM.

38. Aluminum Company of America, *Aluminum on Display at the Century of Progress Exposition,* pamphlet, n.d., envelope 163, AL; Ford Motor Company, "1934 Report on the Fair," 1934, pp. 10, 35, box 7, acc. 1109, FM; Timken Steel and Tube Company, *A Trip through the Timken Steel Exhibit,* pamphlet, n.d., box 3, CPL; "The Kraft Mayonnaise Kitchen," postcard, 1933, RG 14, SG 35, acc. 85-121, KGF.

39. Rydell, *World of Fairs,* 116, 122; Lewis, *Public Image,* 300. *Automotive Industries,* 2 June 1934, 685, estimated $2 million for Ford and $3 million for General Motors.

40. Market Analysis, Inc., "Third Attendance Survey of New York World's Fair," 13 Nov. 1939, pp. 28–29, box GA-2, folder 19, BFG; "World's Fair: A Study of Circulation and Reactions," box 16, acc. 146, FM.

41. Lewis, *Public Image,* 297–98; "The Reminiscences of Fred L. Black," oral history, 1954, p. 197, FM.

42. Lewis, *Public Image,* 298–301; F. L. Black to Fred Campsall, 30 June 1934, box 1540, acc. 285, FM.

43. Lewis, *Public Image,* 297–89; Morrow, "Ford Proposition," n.p.; Jos. A. Small to C. C. Cheadle, 6 June 1934, box 2, acc. 450, FM; *Literary Digest,* 18 Aug. 1934, 6.

44. Walter Dorwin Teague, "Designing Ford's Exhibit at a Century of Progress," *Product Engineering,* Aug. 1934, p. 282, box 2, acc. 450, FM; Ford Motor Company, *Out of the Earth,* pamphlet, [1934], folder 16-269, CP.

45. *Advertising Arts* 4 (July 1933): 15, 18. On the photographs of the River Rouge plant by Sheeler and Bourke-White, see Terry Smith, *Making the Modern: Industry, Art, and Design in America* (Chicago, 1993), 112–13; 192–94; Karen Lucic, *Charles Sheeler and the Cult of the Machine* (London, 1991), 89–95; Mary Jane Jacob, "The Rouge in 1927: Photographs and Paintings by Charles Sheeler," in Detroit Institute of Arts, *The Rouge: The Image of Industry in the Art of Charles Sheeler and Diego Rivera* (Detroit, 1978), 11–18.

46. *Saturday Evening Post,* 28 June 1924, 56–57; ibid., 15 Nov. 1924, 82–83; ibid., 10 Jan. 1925, 82–83; *Ford News,* 8 Feb. 1924, 1, 4; ibid., 1 Aug. 1924, 6; Lewis, *Public Image,* 187; "See the Giant Ford Works in Miniature," 1924 institutional folder, acc. 19, FM; "From Raw Materials to Finished Product," 1924 institutional folder, acc. 19, FM. On the impact of the tour of the River Rouge on visitors, see John M. Staudenmaier, "Clean Exhibits, Messy Exhibits: Henry Ford's Technological Aesthetic," working paper, 1993, pp. 3–4. According to one writer, the factory seemed "one huge, perfectly-timed, smoothly operating industrial machine of almost unbelievable efficiency." Staudenmaier notes that "deeply emotional, quasi-religious responses" to the symbolic power of the Rouge plant, by visitors ranging from German engineers to the Mexican muralist Diego Rivera, were "not unusual."

47. *New Outlook* 164 (Sept. 1934): 59; *How Firestone Gum-Dipped Tires Are Made,* pamphlet, n.d., folder 15-130, CP; *Firestone Dealer,* Apr. 1933, p. 10, clipping, folder 1-5599, CP; press release, 24 Apr. 1933, folder 1-559, CP; Ford Motor Company, "Comments on Advertising Value to Ford Motor Co. of Various Exhibits in Ford Exposition, and Suggestions for Future Exhibits," typescript, [1934], p. 36, FM; Edsel Ford to J. Park Van Zandt, 30 Nov. 1931, box 397, acc. 6, FM; *Your Part in the Ford Exposition,* pamphlet, 1934, box 2, acc. 450, FM; *Mimeo Flashes,* 21 Sept. 1934, box 1540, acc. 285, FM; *General Motors World* 11 (Nov. 1932): 5; "Reminiscences of Fred L. Black," 193, 197; Lewis, *Public Image,* 297–98.

48. Lewis, *Public Image,* 286; Walter Dorwin Teague to Edsel Ford, 14 June 1934, box 167, acc.

6, FM. On Teague's passion for unity, in both aesthetic style and dramatic structure, see his "Exhibition Technique," *American Architect and Architecture* 151 (Sept. 1937): 32.

49.   Walter Dorwin Teague, "Industrial Art and Its Future," speech ms., 1936, p. 3, box 79, WDT. By 1937 Teague was claiming "four or five years" of intensive "exhibit experience"; Teague, "Exhibition Technique," 33. For his emphasis on internal exhibits, see also Teague to William A. Hart, 11 June 1936, reel 16:32A, WDT; Teague to Robert Gregg, 5 Apr. 1937, reel 16:30A, WDT. For a more extensive account of the impact of the rising cadre of industrial designers on corporate fair exhibits, see Roland Marchand, "The Designers Go to the Fair: Walter Dorwin Teague and the Professionalization of Industrial Exhibits, 1933–1940," *Design Issues* 8 (fall 1991): 4–17.

50.   Erika Doss, *Benton, Pollock, and the Politics of Modernism: From Regionalism to Abstract Expressionism* (Chicago, 1991), 67, 74, 79, 87–88; *General Motors World* 12 (Mar. 1933): 7; *GE Monogram* 10 (May 1933): 15; press release, 6 June 1933, box 60A, WWA; Vicki Goldberg, *Margaret Bourke-White: A Biography* (New York, 1986), 87, 104–7, 110–12, 143, 148, 155; Ellen Wiley Todd, *The "New Woman" Revised: Painting and Gender Politics on Fourteenth Street* (Berkeley, 1993), 90–91; Karal Ann Marling, *Wall-to-Wall America: A Cultural History of Post Office Murals in the Great Depression* (Minneapolis, 1982), 17–19, 34–36; Matthew Baigell, *The American Scene: American Painting of the Thirties* (New York, 1974), 43, 55.

51.   Minutes of creative staff meeting, 1 Feb. 1933, pp. 1–2, JWT; Harry M. Adler to AT&T, 4 Mar. 1938, file 22700-10-A, ATT.

52.   Jon M. Williams and Daniel T. Muir, *Corporate Images: Photography and the Du Pont Company, 1865–1972* (Wilmington, Del., 1984), 47; *Sales Management,* 1 Sept. 1937, 2–3; Goldberg, *Bourke-White,* 143; *Alcoa News,* 28 May 1934, 1.

53.   On expressions of absorption and "engagement" in corporate photography of workers, see David E. Nye, *Image Worlds: Corporate Identities at General Electric, 1890–1930* (Cambridge, Mass., 1985), 83. Through such images, Alcoa attempted to insist that "even in the most modern of aluminum equipment, craftsmanship plays its part"; *Aluminum News-Letter* 1 (Mar. 1934): 3.

54.   Visitors to the Ford exhibit were even recruited to disseminate this lesson by taking home or mailing small sectioned boxes, covered with cellophane, in which tiny samples of a dozen of the earth's basic materials—from iron ore and bauxite to cork and soybeans—were neatly compartmentalized and labeled for the collector's edification. "Man must go to the earth for all materials," box of samples for mailing, folder 16-269, CP.

55.   Walter Dorwin Teague, "What Can We Do with an Exhibit to Magnetize the Crowd?" *Sales Management,* 1 Jan. 1937, 63.

56.   Ford, "Comments on Advertising Value," 4, 15, 20, 22, 26–27, 31, 36; *General Motors World* 12 (Nov. 1933): 6–7; AT&T, "Bell System at a Century of Progress," 5.

57.   *GE Monogram* 10 (Jan. 1933): 11; ibid. (Apr. 1933): 12; ibid. (June 1933): 17; General Electric Publicity Department, "General Electric in a Century of Progress," mimeo, [1933], pp. 1–2, L 5335, GES. The Westinghouse House of Wonders differed from the GE exhibit mainly in its emphasis on visitor participation in manipulating various devices to obtain baffling or astonishing results. Ford, "Comments on Advertising Value," 5–6. On the origins of the House of Magic appellation for GE laboratories and its use in the popularization of GE for radio audiences, see Roland Marchand and Michael L. Smith, "Corporate Science on Display," in *Scientific Authority and Twentieth-Century America,* ed. Ronald Walters (Baltimore, 1997), 160–64.

58.   *General Motors World* 13 (July 1934): 6; R. F. Schreitmueller to R. H. Grant, 10 June 1933, CFK.

59.   Allen Orth, oral history, interview by T. A. Boyd, 26 Aug. 1960, pp. 2, 5, CFK.

60.   Alfred P. Sloan Jr. to Owen D. Young, 10 May 1934, 14 June 1934, file 87.2.145, ODY; *Scientific Monthly* 39 (July 1934): 67–78; *General Motors World* 13 (June 1934): 4; ibid. (July 1934): 6; press release, 26 May 1934, CFK; Edward L. Bernays, *Biography of an Idea: Memoirs of Public Relations Counsel Edward L. Bernays* (New York, 1965), 553.

61.   *Telephone,* 10 June 1933, 8–9; C. T. Smith, "Exhibiting Telephone Progress at the World's Fair," *Bell Telephone Quarterly* 13 (Jan. 1934): 5, 21. See also "Report on the Bell Telephone Exhibit at the Texas Centennial Exposition," 1936, n.p., box 1061, ATT.

62.   S. L. Andre to A. W. Page, 15 Mar. 1934, box 1061, ATT; Smith, "Exhibiting Telephone Progress," 8–10; G. S. Fulcher to Director of Exhibits, 11 Sept. 1933, folder 1-6178, CP.

63. *Bell Telephone News* 23 (July 1933): 14; Rydell, *World of Fairs,* 126–27. The reporter for the *Bell Telephone News,* an AT&T employee, observed that listeners would "hang on the caller's words with an avid interest, laughing aloud, or with mouths slightly agape, as completely engrossed as if they were watching a play." During the day of his visit, he noted, two girls calling their mothers had burst into tears.

64. Minutes of creative staff meeting, 3 Jan. 1934, pp. 1–3, JWT. Even corporations that had not participated in the Century of Progress Exposition soon invested heavily in exposition displays. Du Pont entered the major exhibit arena for the first time with a $115,000 display and a thirty-person staff at the Texas Centennial Exposition in 1936; Standard Oil of Ohio, according to *Advertising Age,* invested "virtually its entire advertising appropriation" in its demonstrations at the Great Lakes Exposition in Cleveland in 1937. "Status of 1936 Texas Centennial Advertising Appropriation . . . as of 10-23-36," box 55, acc. 500, ser. II, pt. 2, DP; R. H. Coleman to W. A. Hart, n.d., box 56, acc. 500, ser. II, pt. 2, DP; *Advertising Age,* 4 Jan. 1937, 14; Leonard S. Reich, *The Making of American Industrial Research: Science and Business at GE and Bell, 1876–1926* (New York, 1985), 94.

65. Smith, "Exhibiting Telephone Progress," 5; AT&T, "Bell System at a Century of Progress," 16–17; "Report on the Bell Telephone Exhibit at the Texas Centennial Exposition," n.p.; A. W. Page, memorandum, 14 Nov. 1933, box 1061, ATT; S. L. Andre to A. W. Page, 15 Mar. 1934, box 1061, ATT; Ford, "Comments on Advertising Value," 1–42; Coleman to Hart, n.d, box 56, acc. 500, ser. II, pt. 2, DP; "Case History and Final Report, Texas Exhibit," [1936], box 51, ser. II, pt. 2, DP; Fred Black to Edsel Ford, 9 June 1934, box 1540, acc. 285, FM; "Hourly Attendance for Exhibit, Texas Centennial," [1936], attendance records binder, box 2, acc. 450; Ross Federal Service, Inc., "Comments Overheard at Ford Exhibit, Texas Centennial," [1936], box 2, acc. 450, FM.

66. *Printers' Ink,* 15 June 1933, 47–48; *Automotive Industries,* 2 June 1934, 685; minutes of creative staff meeting, 3 Jan. 1934, pp. 1–3, JWT. In "Twenty-two Million Gold Fish," printed in the Thompson meeting minutes, the speaker promised that his survey of consumer reactions to the fair would "supply a fresh method by which principles of modern merchandising may be lifted out of the realm of opinion into matters of demonstrable fact." See also *Advertising and Selling,* 23 Sept. 1937, 68–70.

67. *Printers' Ink,* 15 June 1933, 47–48. The second observer is quoted from Cawelti, "America on Display," 352. See also minutes of creative staff meeting, 3 Jan. 1934, p. 11, JWT.

68. General Electric Company, untitled typescript, 8 May 1934, folder 1-6177, CP; *Automotive Industries,* 2 June 1934, 684–85, was prompted to report that "animation is an even more important attraction of automotive exhibits this year than last. It may be said to be the keynote."

69. Carl J. Hasbrouck to William A. Hart, 3 Dec. 1935, box 53, ser. II, pt. 2, DP; Harvey Watts, "Report," 1 Aug. 1936, box 5, ser. II, pt. 2, DP; Chaplin Tyler, "Visit to Texas Centennial Exposition," 1936, pp. 6–7, box 21, ser. II, pt. 2, DP; "Memo for Nov. 1936 Du Pont Presentation," n.d., reel 16:21A, WDT; C. C. Cheadle to F. L. Black, box 1, acc. 450, FM; Teague to Black, 8 Feb. 1936, box 1, acc. 533, FM.

70. Smith, "Exhibiting Telephone Progress," 2, 4, 6–7, 13–14, 18; C. T. Smith, "Memo for Mr. A. W. Page," [ca. Dec. 1933], n.p., box 1061, ATT; *Bell Telephone Quarterly* 19 (Jan. 1940): 59–70; Ford, "1934 Report on the Fair," pp. 5–7, 11–12, 22, 24, 32–33, box 7, acc. 1109, FM; Teague to Edsel Ford et al., 23 June 1936, box 1, acc. 450, FM; E. P. H. James to E. C. Carlson, 4 May 1934, box 24, folder 5, NBC.

71. Roland Marchand, *Advertising the American Dream: Making Way for Modernity, 1920–1940* (Berkeley, 1985), 66–72.

72. Minutes of creative staff meeting, 3 Jan. 1934, p. 12, JWT. Smith, "Exhibiting Telephone Progress," 3; Ford, "1934 Report on Fair," 10; oversize scrapbook, acc. 77.242, DPP.

73. T. W. Witherspoon to Paul W. Sampson, 1 July 1939, box 35, ser. II, pt. 2, DP; "Dallas Exhibit: Report of Wilburn McKee," n.d., box 11, ser. II, pt. 2, DP; Watts, "Report"; Teague to William A. Hart, 22 June 1936, reel 16:21A, WDT.

74. Carl J. Hasbrouck to L. W. Blaisdell, 4 Dec. 1935, reel 16:23A, WDT; Walter Dorwin Teague, presentation to U.S. Steel, Sept. 1936, reel 16:30A, WDT; "Report by George D. McCaffrey," in minutes of board of directors meeting, 2 Feb. 1938, NYWF; Cawelti, "America on Display," 351; Teague, "What Can We Do?" 63. On the use of the female visitor to illustrate the

need to simplify, see Lenox Lohr, address, 19 Jan. 1930, p. 3, folder 200, LL; minutes of creative staff meeting, 3 Jan. 1934, pp. 1–2, JWT.

75.   "Newspaper Memorandum," 26 Feb. 1936, Y&R; *Advertising and Selling,* 13 Sept. 1934, 53. On the emphasis on low intelligence by the advertising trade press, see *Printers' Ink,* 8 Apr. 1926, 90–91; 7 June 1928, 101; 12 June 1930, 142–42; 19 Nov. 1931, 105. For an extended discussion of this issue, see Marchand, *Advertising,* 53–72, 306–11.

76.   Marchand, *Advertising,* 66–69; Truman, *History of the World's Fair,* 322; "Reminiscences of Frank Vivian," 27.

77.   *U.S. Steel News* 4 (Apr. 1939): 29; *Westinghouse Magazine* 11 (Oct. 1939): 9.

78.   John Mills to A. W. Page, 17 Sept. 1936, file 22700-10-A, ATT; B. F. Goodrich Company, *Highlights: New York's 1940 World's Fair,* pamphlet, n.d., box GA-2, folder 18, BFG; A. M. Erickson, "Outline Description of Wilson Exhibits Building," [1939], file 351, NBG.

79.   *Detroit Free Press,* 27 Jan. 1936, 2; 29 Jan. 1936, 5; 30 Jan. 1936, 3.

80.   Thus, the Ford Motor Company shipped to Atlantic City the "Human Ford" exhibit (a car that replied to questions with a human voice), its "car in the clouds" optical illusion display, and the demonstration of the rapid assembly and disassembly of a V-8 motor from its 1934 Century of Progress display; the Texas Company later transported to the resort's boardwalk its history of oil display, a diorama and map with flashing lights, from the 1936 Texas Centennial Exposition. See *Du Pont Magazine* 30 (midsummer 1936), 6–7; Du Pont Advertising Department, "Information Bulletin," 6 Aug. 1936, n.p., DP; *Bulletin* (Chamber of Commerce of Atlantic City), 15 Feb. 1933, n.p.; ibid., 23 Oct. 1935, 1; ibid., 31 Mar. 1937, 1; *Westinghouse Magazine* 7 (Feb. 1935): 1; C. C. Cheadle to F. L. Black, 12 May 1937, box 1, acc. 450, FM; Lewis, *Public Image,* 301, 303.

81.   *General Motors World* 13 (July 1934): 6; Orth, oral history, 2.

82.   T. O. Richards to Charles Kettering, 17 Mar. 1936; Paul Garrett to Allen Orth, 19 Mar. 1935: CFK.

83.   Garrett to Sloan and Kettering, 25 June 1934, CFK; Garrett to Kettering, 19 Sept. 1934, CFK; Kettering to Sloan, 19 Mar. 1936, CFK; Garrett to Kettering, 29 Oct. 1936, CFK; Paul Garrett, "The Importance of the Public," speech ms., 1934, p. 4, folder 77-7.4-1.13-2, CSM; San Antonio, Texas, newspaper, 18 Feb. 1937, clipping, Parade of Progress 1937 folder, CFK.

84.   General Motors Corporation, *Souvenir Edition: General Motors Parade of Progress,* pamphlet, [1936], CFK; idem, press release (Greensboro, N.C.), 4 June 1936, GM; *Miami Herald,* 19 Feb. 1936, 12A; *General Motors World* 15 (Feb. 1936): 3. The early account in *General Motors World* indicated a crew of forty, but the press release of 4 June put the number at fifty, as did "Souvenir Itinerary, Parade of Progress, 1937," CFK.

85.   On the Goodrich Silver Fleet, see "Silver Fleet," [1929], box GA-2, folder 56, BFG; minutes of creative staff meeting, 15 Feb. 1933, p. 9, JWT; Philip J. Kelly, *The Making of a Salesman* (New York, 1965), 93. On the Ford tent shows, see Lewis, *Public Image,* 209; C. C. Cheadle to J. Crawford, 16 Feb. 1931, box 394, acc. 6, FM; folders 810a, 813c, box 395, acc. 833, FM. Although General Motors sought to help local dealers capitalize indirectly on visits of the Parade of Progress, it deliberately downplayed any sales intent (sales solicitation was prohibited on the local Parade grounds) and stressed the mixture of education and entertainment that the free shows of the Circus of Science provided for the public. In this emphasis it differed from Westinghouse's six traveling "circuses," which also featured "marvels of science" exhibits adapted from the company's Chicago display but more oriented toward the sale of appliances. *Westinghouse Magazine* 7 (Feb. 1935): 1.

86.   Automobile Quarterly Magazine, *GM: The First 75 Years* (New York, 1983), 82; press release (Greensboro, N.C.), 4 June 1936, GM. On special visiting hours for African Americans, see *Daily News* (Greensboro, N.C.), 1 June 1936, 7; *Durham Sun,* 27 May 1936, 2.

87.   *Miami Herald,* 16 Feb. 1936, 5A; ibid., 18 Feb. 1936, 1; *Miami Daily News,* 18 Feb. 1936, 5; Automobile Quarterly, *GM,* 82; T. A. Boyd, *Professional Amateur: The Biography of Charles Franklin Kettering* (New York, 1957), 218–19. The Parade actually opened in Lakeland, Florida, on 11 February but designated the Miami visit as its official premiere.

88.   *Miami Herald,* 24 Feb. 1936, 1; Stuart W. Leslie, *Boss Kettering* (New York, 1983), 258; Kettering to Sloan, 19 Mar. 1936, CFK; General Motors, *Souvenir Edition; General Motors World* 15 (Feb. 1936): 3–4; *Advertising Age,* 2 Feb. 1936, 2.

89. Except for occasional visits to small towns in remote regions (El Centro, far from any large population center, counted only about 9,000 inhabitants), the Parade shunned towns of less than 10,000 people.

90. John W. Reedy, oral history, interview by T. A. Boyd, 24 Aug. 1960, p. 3, CFK; Public Relations Dept. to Kettering, 18 Jan. 1938, CFK; *Tide* 10 (Feb. 1936): 20; *General Motors World* 15 (Feb. 1936): 4.

91. C. A. Lewis, "Eighth Operating Report of the Parade of Progress," Aug. 1938, p. 1, CFK; idem, "Ninth Operating Report of the Parade of Progress," Jan. 1939, p. 10, CFK; *Orlando Morning Sentinel,* 19 Mar. 1936, p. 10, clipping, CFK; ibid., 20 Mar. 1936, p. 14A, clipping, CFK; *Miami Daily News,* 19 Feb. 1936, p. 12, clipping, CFK; San Antonio newspaper, 18 Feb. 1937, n.p., clipping, CFK; Orth to Garrett, 21 July 1936, CFK.

92. Orth to Garrett, 16 Mar. 1937, CFK; Garrett to Orth, 23 Mar. 1937, CFK; J. M. Jerpe to C. A. Lewis and Victor Borella, 6 July 1937, CFK; Lewis, "Ninth Operating Report," 7–10; press release, 16 May 1937, GM.

93. Jerpe to Lewis and Borella, 6 July 1937; Garrett to Kettering, 23 Mar. 1936, CFK; Kettering to Garrett, n.d, CFK; Orth to Garrett, 16 Mar. 1937, CFK; Paul Garrett, "Notes for Talk: Previews of Progress," 2 Mar. 1938, GM. On the development of the General Motors "jes' folks" motif in public relations between 1936 and 1938, see also Chapter 6.

94. "General Motors Institutional Advertising," Case Study Adv. 759, p. 44, HBSA; Leslie, *Boss Kettering,* 69; Boyd, *Professional Amateur,* 217; Charles F. Kettering, "Science and the Future Automobile" (1916), in *Prophet of Progress: Selections from the Speeches of Charles F. Kettering,* ed. T. A. Boyd (New York, 1961), 61, 67–68, 71–75; Orth, oral history, 2, 6; General Motors, *Souvenir Edition.*

95. *Advertising and Selling* 32 (June 1939): 51; Julian Lewis Watkins, *The One Hundred Greatest Advertisements: Who Wrote Them and What They Did,* 2d ed., rev. (New York, 1959), 123; Lewis, "Ninth Operating Report," 6–7; *Fortune* 19 (Mar. 1939): 49; Paul Garrett, "Large Scale Business and the Public," speech ms., 25 Mar. 1939, GM. On examples of actual boys "set to dreaming," see Jerpe to Kettering, 2 Dec. 1936, 17 May 1939, CFK; Bob Hurley to Dear Sirs, 9 June 1939, CFK.

96. *Advertising and Selling* 32 (Feb. 1939): [57]; Watkins, *One Hundred Greatest Advertisements,* 123.

97. During its last year the Parade of Progress completed a triumphal "Broadway run" in New York City, where it camped on the future site of the GM exhibit at the coming New York World's Fair; it was a main attraction of the major preview held for that fair. A review in the *Washington Times* near the end of the Parade's run grasped just the effect intended by this style of institutional advertising. "Gone was the pompous, autocratic atmosphere so usually associated with industrial tycoons," reported the newspaper. Through the circus atmosphere of banners, canvas tents, and blaring music, General Motors had created "one of the most refreshing exhibitions ever staged of the growing intelligence of Big Business in its relations to the man in the street." Lewis, "Ninth Operating Report," 11–12, and attached clipping (*Washington Times,* 8 Nov. 1938); Paul Garrett, "Introductory Remarks, GM Family Party," speech ms., Apr. 1938, CFK; idem, "Notes for Talk"; news releases, 16 Apr. 1938, May 1938, CFK; Neil H. Borden and Martin V. Marshall, *Advertising Management: Text and Cases* (Homewood, Ill., 1959), 416; *GM Folks* 1 (June 1938): n.p.; Orth, oral history, 3.

98. On the Casino of Science of 1939 and 1940, see *Futurama,* pamphlet, n.d., n.p., file 408, NBG; *Press Guide, General Motors Highways and Horizons Exhibit, 1940,* pamphlet, p. 5, file 381, NBG.

99. *Advertising and Selling,* 23 Sept. 1937, 70; Teague, "Designing Ford's Exhibit at a Century of Progress," *Product Engineering* (Aug. 1934): 282, box 2, acc. 450, FM; "Principal Assignments Executed for the FMC by W. D. Teague and Staff," n.d., reel 16:31, WDT; Teague to Robert Gregg, 5 Apr. 1937, reel 16:30A, WDT; oversize scrapbook, acc. 77.242, DPP.

100. Martin Dodge to E. I. Du Pont Company, 23 July 1937, box 34, ser. II, pt. 2, DP; *Forbes,* 1 May 1939, 12; Bernard Lichtenberg, "Business Backs New York World Fair to Meet New Deal Propaganda," *Public Opinion Quarterly* 2 (Apr. 1938): 314–20; Peter Michelson and V. E. Scott, "Preliminary Suggestion for Participation by the General Electric Company in the New York World's Fair," July 1937, GS; A. D. Marshall to Peter Michelson and V. E. Scott, 6 Aug. 1937, GS.

101. "Outline for Extension of 'Wonder World of Chemistry,'" 1939, acc. 77.242, DPP; *Westinghouse Magazine* 10 (Nov.–Dec. 1938): 7; Walter Dorwin Teague, "World's Fair, 1939: Its Influence

on Advertising and Design," *Advertising and Selling* 31 (Oct. 1938): 32. See also "Railroads at the New York World's Fair, 1939," box 486, acc. 1810, PRR.

102. Michelson and Scott, "Preliminary Suggestion"; Warren I. Susman, "The People's Fair," in *Culture as History: The Transformation of American Culture in the Twentieth Century,* ed. Warren I. Susman (New York, 1984), 213; Alice G. Marquis, *Hopes and Ashes: The Birth of Modern Times* (New York, 1986), 188, 195; Ed Tyng, *Making a World's Fair* (New York, 1958), 26.

103. Walter Dorwin Teague, explanatory caption in oversize scrapbook, acc. 77.242, DPP; idem, "Suggestions for Rebuilding 'The March of Chemistry,'" box 51, ser. II, pt. 2, DP; Teague to William A. Hart, 22 June 1936, reel 16:21A, WDT.

104. Teague, "Suggestions for Rebuilding"; Brooks Darlington to Hart, 24 Jan. 1939, box 36, ser. II, pt. 2, DP; David J. Rhees, "Making the Nation Chemically Conscious: The Popularization of Chemistry in America, 1914–1940" (paper presented at the annual meeting of the History of Science Society, Chicago, Dec. 1985), 12–13; Ford Motor Company, "Benefits Received from Our Participation in the New York World's Fair, 1939," [1939], box 2, acc. 554, FM.

105. *What to See Today at the Chrysler 5-Star Show: 60 Minutes of Magic,* pamphlet, May 1939, T. J. Ross Scrapbooks, vol. 330, ILL; *Chrysler Motors Magazine* 6 (June 1940): 6.

106. David E. Nye, "Ritual Tomorrows," in *Making Exhibits of Ourselves* (forthcoming), 16–17; *The General Electric Building, New York World's Fair, 1940,* pamphlet, [1940], box 1005, NYWF; *Business Week,* 4 Nov. 1939, 22, 27; *Bell Telephone Quarterly* 19 (Jan. 1940): 59–60; *Pacific Telephone Magazine,* 1939, p. 23, box 1061, ATT; "Script for 15-Minute Interview over Radio Station WRL," 16 May 1940, box 44, acc. 1410, DP. See also Emerson Evans to Matthew N. Chappell, 19 July 1939, box 34, ser. II, pt. 2, DP, for the observation, based on "four or five visits" to the Du Pont exhibit, that "the magic element in this process will make a more striking appeal than the present emphasis on research and will link it closer to the spectator's experience, while at the same time mak[ing] the spectator acutely conscious of Du Pont research." This remark pointedly describes the shift from the operational aesthetic to impression management.

107. *Advertising and Selling* 32 (July 1939): 34–35; *The Middleton Family at the New York World's Fair,* RP.

108. *Middleton Family.* Treadway's comment appears in one of the cartoon-sequence versions of the story in magazine ads; see *Saturday Evening Post,* 19 Aug. 1939, 81.

109. *Saturday Evening Post,* 15 Apr. 1939, 62–63; ibid., 24 June 1939, 101; ibid., 19 Aug. 1939, 81; *Westinghouse Magazine* 11 (Oct. 1939): 9.

110. *Advertising and Selling* 32 (Feb. 1939): 22–23; *Young Henry Ford Went to the Fair,* pamphlet, 1939, box 21, acc. 445, FM; "Ford Cycle of Production, 1940, Revised," enclosed in H. L. McClinton to Fred Black, 18 June 1940, box 21, acc. 554, FM; *The Ford Exposition, New York World's Fair,* pamphlet, n.d., box 1005, NYWF.

111. N. W. Ayer & Son, "Four New Movies Released by Ford," press release, 18 July 1940, box 5, acc. 450, FM; press release, n.d., box 21, acc. 554, FM; Edward Mabley, "Transportation Pageant," 19 Oct. 1937, reel 16:23A, WDT; Walter D. Teague, "Ford Exposition, 1940," reel 16:23A, WDT; Lewis, *Public Image,* 305–7. Like the GM Parade of Progress exhibits, which contrasted modern superhighways with historical dioramas of the village smithy and "Grandpa's Ol' Dobbin parked before the corner saloon of bygone days," the Ford shows recounted the history of transportation to invite snickers of amusement at the quaint "inadequacies" of the past. See *Miami Herald,* 18 Feb. 1936, 1; ibid., 19 Feb. 1936, 14A; *Miami Daily News,* 18 Feb. 1936, 5; ibid., 19 Feb. 1936, 10, 14; *Durham Sun,* 25 May 1936, 9A; *General Motors World* 15 (Feb. 1936): 4; General Motors, *Souvenir Edition.*

112. Press releases, 6, 13 May 1939, box 14, acc. 544, FM; Henry Billings, "Mural Decoration for the Entrance Hall of the Ford Motor Building," enclosed in Billings to Teague, 21 Oct. 1938, box 1, acc. 554, FM; Gerald Wendt to Teague, 23 June 1938, box 1, acc. 554, FM; Marquis, *Hopes and Ashes,* 212.

113. Billings, "Mural Decoration"; Plummer Whipple to Fred Black, [1939], box 3, acc. 56, FM; press releases, 6, 13 May 1939, box 14, acc. 554, FM; *Ayer News File,* 10 Feb. 1929, NWA; Teague, "Suggestions for Rebuilding."

114. *Sales Management*, 1 July 1939, 60; George F. Pierrot to H. G. McCoy, 21 May 1939, box 3, acc. 56, FM.

115. *Journal American New York*, 11 June 1939, 3; *Variety*, 26 Apr. 1939; *San Antonio Express*, n.d., clipping, file 381, NBG. Statistics on the Futurama's popularity appear in Market Analysts, Inc., "Ratings of Exhibits," enclosed in Sanford Griffith to C. E. O'Neil, 14 Mar. 1940, box 9, RG 3, JWT; *Sales Management*, 1 July 1939, 26, 60–61. On a rating system of 3 points for overall first choice, 2 for second, and 1 for third, the Market Analysts survey arrived at a rating of 1,659 for General Motors, followed by 514 for General Electric and only 347 for Ford.

116. *New York Post*, 26 Oct. 1939; *New York Sunday Mirror*, 30 Apr. 1939; *New York Journal American*, [ca. 21 June 1939]: clippings, file 381, NBG.

117. For a more extensive account of the background that Norman Bel Geddes brought to Futurama, see Roland Marchand, "The Designers Go to the Fair, II: Norman Bel Geddes, the General Motors 'Futurama,' and the Visit to the Factory Transformed," *Design Issues* 8 (spring 1992): 23–40.

118. An excellent interpretive study of Bel Geddes's role in the Shell advertising campaign appears in Jeffrey L. Meikle, *The City of Tomorrow: Model 1937* (London, 1984). For examples of Shell ads that cited Bel Geddes as an authority on traffic and planning, see *Saturday Evening Post*, 10 July 1937, 40–41; 17 July 1937, 71.

119. *Flash*, 5 Nov. 1937, 1; *People* 1 (Sept. 1937): 1–3, JWT; Meikle, *City of Tomorrow*, 11, 19–22; Bruce Bliven, "Metropolis: 1960 Style," *New Republic*, 29 Sept. 1937, 211–12.

120. Meikle, *Twentieth Century Limited*, 207; *People* 1 (Sept. 1937): inside front cover, JWT; "Notes Taken in Meeting with Mr. Geddes," 10 Nov. 1936, file 356, NBG; "Notes of Meeting with Mr. Geddes," 12 Nov. 1936, file 356, NBG. On the collapse of the Goodyear sponsorship, see Norman Bel Geddes to J. W. Dineen, 24 Feb., 16 Mar. 1938, file 381, NBG; Norman Bel Geddes, "Autobiog.," typescript of unpublished biography, AE-84, chap. 80, pp. 1–2, NBG.

121. Bel Geddes, "Autobiog.," AE-84, chap. 80, p. 5; ibid., AJ-17, chap. 80, pp. 3–4, NBG; Norman Bel Geddes, AMI series, second draft of autobiography, chap. 76, p. 9, NBG.

122. Norman Bel Geddes, "Draft of Presentation," with penciled corrections, 30 Mar. 1938, file 381, NBG; Paul Garrett, "Survey on World's Fair," 15 Dec. 1939, GM; *GM Folks* 2 (Mar. 1939): n.p.

123. General Motors Corporation, press release, 15–16 Apr. 1939, file 384, NBG; ibid., 29 Apr. 1939, file 381, NBG; *Press Guide, General Motors Highways and Horizons Exhibit, 1940*, pamphlet, pp. 9–10, file 381, NBG; Normal Bel Geddes, chart of specifications for preliminary model, [1938], file 381, NBG; Bel Geddes to Frances Waite Geddes, 9 Nov. 1938, personal correspondence, NBG.

124. Worthen Paxton to Bel Geddes, 1 Nov. 1938; "Notes on Airplane Trip, Nov. 2, 1938," file 381, NBG; notes on meeting, 1 Nov. 1938, file 381, NBG; untitled manuscript, file 381, NBG; Paxton to Richard Grant, 12 July 1938, file 381, NBG; Bel Geddes to Frances Waite Geddes, 2 Nov. 1938, personal correspondence, NBG; Morton Eustis, "Big Show in Flushing Meadows," *Theatre Arts Monthly* 23 (Aug. 1939): 571; Marquis, *Hopes and Ashes*, 210.

125. *BBDO Bulletin*, 19 May 1937, n.p., BBDO; Bel Geddes to Frances Waite Geddes, 16 Nov. 1938, personal correspondence, NBG.

126. "Description of the General Motors Building and Exhibit for the New York World's Fair," 8 Sept. 1939, pp. 1–2, file 381, NBG; Peter Schladermundt, "What Is Design," p. 14, in Bel Geddes, "Autobiog.," AJ-17, chaps. 74–75; Robert Coombs, "Norman Bel Geddes' Highways and Horizons," *Perspecta* 13/14 (1971): 12–13; Douglas Haskell, "To-morrow and the World's Fair," *Architectural Record* 88 (Aug. 1940): 71; Meikle, *Twentieth Century Limited*, 201.

127. *New York Sun*, 29 Apr. 1939, n.p., and *Syracuse (N.Y.) Post Standard*, 19 May 1939, n.p., clippings, file 381, folder I, NBG; *Christian Science Monitor*, 8 July 1939, p. 6, clipping, file 397, NBG; Eustis, "Big Show," 571; Coombs, "Geddes' Highways and Horizons," 15–16; Norman Bel Geddes, *Miracle in the Evening: Autobiography*, ed. William Kelley (Garden City, N.Y., 1960), 262.

128. "Description of the General Motors Building," 4–5; *Press Guide, 1940*, 10–12; Coombs, "Geddes' Highways and Horizons," 15–16; Eustis, "Big Show," 572.

129. See clippings from *Nantucket (Mass.) Inquirer-Mirror*, n.d.; *San Antonio Express*, n.d.; *New York Sun*, 29 Apr. 1939; *Milledgeville (Ga.) Times*, 18 May 1939: file 381, NBG. See also General Motors Corporation, press release, 15–16 Apr. 1939, file 384, NBG.

130. *Press Guide, 1940,* 13; Bel Geddes et al., untitled memo beginning "This exhibit . . . ," [7 Apr. 1938], p. 10, file 381, NBG; *New York Sun,* 19 Apr. 1939, clipping, file 381, NBG; Bel Geddes, "Autobiog.," AE-84, chap. 77, p. 1; "A Comprehensive Description of the General Motors Highways and Horizons Exhibit," CFK.

131. Eustis, "Big Show," 571; *A Greeting to Our Guests,* pamphlet, n.d., n.p., file 408, NBG.

132. *Press Guide, 1940,* 13, "Sound Chair Script, Futurama," 1939, p. 1, file 381, NBG; Stuart Chase, "Pattern for a Brave New World," *Cosmopolitan,* Dec. 1939, 39.

133. General Motors Corporation, press release, 15–16 Apr. 1939, file 384, NBG; "Description of the Conveyor Ride Models," n.p., file 381, NBG; *Press Guide, 1940,* 2; Sloan to Bel Geddes, 31 Mar. 1939, file 381, NBG; *1960 Calling!* pamphlet, n.d., file 381, NBG; E. B. White, *Essays of E. B. White* (New York, 1977), 114–15.

134. "Description of Conveyor Ride Models," n.p.; Norman Bel Geddes Company, notes on meeting, 1 Nov. 1938, file 381, folder I, NBG; *Charlotte (N.C.) Observer,* 18 June 1939, and *New York World-Telegram,* 13 July 1939, clippings, file 381, NBG.

135. "Description of the General Motors Building," n.p.

136. Ibid., 31–33; Bel Geddes et al., untitled memo beginning "This Exhibit . . .", 22; "Comprehensive Description," n.p.; Folke Kihlstedt, "Utopia Realized: The World's Fairs of the 1930s," in *Imagining Tomorrow: History, Technology, and the American Future,* ed. Joseph J. Corn (Cambridge, Mass., 1986), 108; New York Museum of Science and Industry, *Exhibition Techniques* (New York, 1940), 42.

137. In a similar vein, Jeffrey Meikle (*Twentieth Century Limited,* 197) notes Teague's comment that "people must *flow* in an exhibit" and observes that by 1939 designers had consciously come to see exhibition buildings as "machines for processing people."

138. Ford, "Comments on Advertising Value," 25–26; Worthen Paxton to Richard H. Grant, 10 Oct. 1938, file 381, NBG; Bel Geddes, "Autobiog.," AE-84, chap. 77, p. 1; *Press Guide, 1940,* 20; Bel Geddes et al., untitled memo beginning "This Exhibit . . . ," 10, 13; White, *Essays,* 114. The *New York World Telegram* of 13 July 1939 confirmed Bel Geddes's success when it described the soundtrack as "a quiet, intimate voice, tensely dramatic, yet direct and almost confidential"; clipping, file 381, NBG.

139. Schladermundt, "What Is Design," 14–15; emphasis mine. On the importance of controlling the movement of fair crowds to ensure their viewing of displays in the right order, rather than allowing them to "wander at will," see Teague, "Exhibition Technique," 31–32.

140. Nye, "Ritual Tomorrows," 5; *New York Journal American,* 11 June 1939, p. 37, clipping, file 381, NBG.

141. *Bell Telephone Quarterly* 19 (Jan. 1940): 60; Norman Bel Geddes, "The Proposed Exhibit," n.d., p. 3, file 381, NBG; idem, *Miracle in the Evening,* 324.

142. In fact, as the GM exhibit designer Allen Orth had earlier reminded company officers, an emphasis on the factory and assembly lines might invite the audience to recall those labor issues that had been "so much in the limelight" as a result of the sit-down strikes at General Motors; Orth, "Technical Suggestions Relative to New York World's Fair—1939," 1 July 1937, p. 5, CFK.

143. Teague to Hart, 4 Jan. 1937, reel 16:21A, WDT; "Chemical Memorandum," n.d., box 64, acc. 1662, DP; "Program for Focal Exhibit of Means of Communication," [1939], p. 2, box 57, NYWF.

144. For all the evidence of enthusiasm for Futurama, it is still difficult to say how successfully it conveyed GM's intended messages. Its effort to celebrate the wonders of the free enterprise system was overshadowed by its visionary qualities. And many of these visions of the future, including the exhibit's centerpiece, the superhighway system, would obviously have to be realized by the public sector; GM was certainly not offering to build such a system itself. As Walter Lippmann put it, General Motors had "spent a small fortune to convince the American public that if it wishes to enjoy the full benefit of private enterprise in motor manufacturing, it will have to rebuild its cities and highways by public enterprise"; Lippmann, "A Day at the World's Fair," *New York Herald Tribune,* 6 June 1939, 25.

If that had indeed been the focus of General Motors' strategy, we might argue that the federal highway programs of the 1950s proved that Futurama had truly attained its long-run objective. But there is no evidence that GM focused on so specific a goal. Moreover, the emphasis on public planning that such a goal entailed would have been difficult to divorce from the notion of a larger role for federal social and economic planning, to GM executives an anathema associated with the New Deal. Bel Geddes obviously believed in a vision of large-scale public planning, and he had even imagined Franklin Roosevelt opening the Futurama exhibit until horrified GM executives icily buried Bel Geddes's suggestion. It seems more plausible to conclude that the monumental theatricality, futuristic aura, and crowd-pleasing aspects of the Bel Geddes plan were the primary attractions for GM leaders, and for the sake of these they overlooked the designer's emphasis on planning. See Bel Geddes, "Autobiog.," AE-83, chap. 79, p. 4; ibid., AE-84, chap. 76, pp. 1–3; Norman Bel Geddes Company, "Minutes of Meeting of Norman Bel Geddes & Company," 5 Apr. 1938, file 389, NBG; "Minutes of Meeting, GMC," 17 July 1938, file 381, NBG; *Detroit Home Newspaper,* 18 June 1939, clipping, file 381, NBG.

145. Paul G. Hoffman to Bel Geddes, 2 July 1940, file 384, NBG; Norman Bel Geddes, *Magic Motorways* (New York, 1940), 4.

Chapter 8

1. *GM Folks* 5 (July 1942): 2–5; J. F. Pedder to C. S. Trigg, 22 Aug. 1942, file 79-10.1-144, FR; *Dayton Daily News,* 21 June 1942, clipping, attached to Frank C. Lyons to Charles Kettering, 25 June 1942, CFK.

2. *Dayton Daily News,* 21 June 1942, clipping; *Arms for Victory* poster, n.d., file 79-10.1-144, FR; *Plowshares,* printed program, n.d., file 79-10.1-144, FR; *General Motors and Its Employes Present "Arms for Victory,"* pamphlet, [1942], file 79-10.1-144, FR.

3. *Plowshares,* script no. 1 (with penciled changes and comments), [1942], p. 109, file 79-10.1-145, FR.

4. *Plowshares,* script, revised draft, [ca. Mar. 1942]), file 79-10.1-145, FR; *GM Folks* 5 (July 1942): 2.

5. *Plowshares,* script no. 1, pp. 1–4, 6, 9; *Arms for Victory* poster; *Dayton Daily News,* 21 June 1942, clipping, p. 8.

6. *Cheers from the Camps,* pamphlet, 1942, enclosed in Paul Garrett to Kettering, 3 June 1942, CFK; Alfred P. Sloan Jr. to Kettering, 5 June 1942, CFK; General Motors Corporation, press releases, 23 June, 28 July, 25 Aug. 1942, CFK. One radio executive wrote that he found the show "instructive and entertaining, with just enough of the heartthrob in it to have the right effect"; David Hale Salpern to E. E. Trefethen Jr., 21 June 1943, carton 15, HJK.

7. "Summary Report of 'Arms for Victory' Promotion and Ticket Distribution," 30 Sept. 1942, file 79-10.1-144, FR; General Motors Corporation, press releases, 7 Aug. 1942, 25 Oct. 1942, 14 Jan. 1944, CFK; *Dayton Daily News,* 21 June 1942, clipping; H. W. Anderson to F. C. Evans, 28 Feb. 1944, box 821, ser. II, pt. 2, DP; *GM Folks* 6 (Jan. 1943): 23, 26.

8. David Glassberg, *American Historical Pageantry: The Uses of Tradition in the Early Twentieth Century* (Chapel Hill, N.C., 1990), 2, 226, 283, 285–86; Bausch & Lomb Optical Company, *Seeing It Through,* pamphlet, [ca. 1944]), p. 48, BL; David O. Woodbury, *Battlefronts of Industry: Westinghouse in World War II* (New York, 1948), 100; J. Carlisle MacDonald, "Public Relations in a Traditional Period," speech ms., 11 Jan. 1944, USX; Eastman Kodak Company, press releases, 18 June 1942, 11 Aug. 1943, EK.

9. Elizabeth Fones-Wolf, "Industrial Recreation, the Second World War, and the Revival of Welfare Capitalism, 1934–1960," *Business History Review* 60 (summer 1986): 245–49, 255–57; John Bodnar, "Moral Patriotism and Collective Memory in Whiting, Indiana, 1920–1992," in *Bonds of Affection: Americans Define Their Patriotism,* ed. John Bodnar (Princeton, 1996), 296; *Collier's,* 11 July 1942, 68–69; ibid., 28 Nov. 1942, 47; Chrysler Corporation, press release, 21 Jan. 1942, box 53, folder 4, ILL; idem, *To All Employees,* pamphlet, 11 June 1942, box 55, folder 5, ILL; *G.F. [General Foods] News Letter* 3 (Dec. 1942–Jan. 1943): 1; *The Lamp* 26 (Dec. 1943): 20–21; *GM Folks* 7 (Mar. 1944): 12–13; *Modern Millwheel* 7 (Dec. 1943): 24–25; *195 Bulletin [AT&T]* 16 (Apr. 1942): 13; ibid. (Oct. 1942): 4–5, 21; *Long Lines* 23 (Feb. 1944): 14–16; ibid. (Mar. 1944): 14–15; Alex Osborn, "42 Ways to Advertise in Wartime," [1942], BBDO.

10. *Life,* 12 Oct. 1942, 110–11; *Fortune* 19 (Mar. 1939): 150. For sample descriptions of corpo-

rate wartime shows, see *Alcoa News,* 20 July 1942, 4; *Ford Times,* 2 Apr. 1943, 5; *GM Folks* 6 (Dec. 1943): 25; Eastman Kodak Company, press release, 19 June 1942, EK. An observer of one wartime corporate campaign described it as "a morale-building program which would cause every member of the organization from president to janitor to feel himself an integral part of the war effort and produce accordingly"; Mabel G. Flanley, "Tuning in on the Home Front," speech ms., 13 May 1942, BPL.

11. *GM Folks* 6 (Apr. 1943): 12; Paul Garrett, *Management: Tell What You Stand For,* pamphlet, 26 Sept. 1944, pp. 4–5, BL. See also *Collier's,* 26 Aug. 1944, 82.

12. Paul Fussell, *Wartime: Understanding and Behavior in the Second World War* (New York, 1989), 153, 156, 161. See also Bruce Catton, *The War Lords of Washington* (New York, 1948), 28, 36–37.

13. On the problems and tensions involved in conversion to war production and the reasons for deliberate delay, see Richard S. Tedlow, *Keeping the Corporate Image: Public Relations and Business, 1900–1950* (Greenwich, Conn., 1979), 114, 139; Gregory Hooks, *Forging the Military-Industrial Complex: World War II's Battle of the Potomac* (Urbana, Ill., 1991), 98–99, 112.

14. Ronald E. Stromberg, "American Business and the Approach of War, 1935–1941," *Journal of Economic History* 13 (winter 1953): 63, 69, 76; Catton, *War Lords,* 46; Elizabeth Fones-Wolf, *Selling Free Enterprise: The Business Assault on Labor and Liberalism, 1945–1960* (Urbana, Ill., 1994), 26; Charles E. Wilson, "Can We Save Free Enterprise?" *American Magazine* 132 (Nov. 1941): 37.

15. E. E. Lincoln, "Confidential Special Five-Year Forecast, 1941–1945," 17 Apr. 1940, box 43, acc. 1662, DP.

16. C. E. Wilson to Sloan, 19 Sept. 1940; W. S. Carpenter Jr. to Sloan, 18 Apr. 1941: box 837, ser. II, pt. 2, DP.

17. Edgar A. Smith to Group Executives and Divisional General Managers, 21 May 1941, box 837, ser. II, pt. 2, DP; S. D. Hopkins to General Managers, 14 Jan. 1942, CFK; Alan Clive, *State of War: Michigan in World War II* (Ann Arbor, 1979), 23–25.

18. "Report of General Motors Press Conference," 10 Jan. 1942, p. 11, CFK; Paul Garrett, *Public Opinion and the War,* pamphlet, July 1942, p. 2, DPL; Clive, *State of War,* 20; *Plowshares,* script no. 1, p. 15.

19. Alan Brinkley, *The End of Reform: New Deal Liberalism in Recession and War* (New York, 1995), 121; Bennett H. Wall and George S. Gibb, *Teagle of Jersey Standard* (New Orleans, 1974), 297, 307–8, 314–17; Hooks, *Forging the Military-Industrial Complex,* 106, 109, 112; George David Smith, *From Monopoly to Competition: The Transformation of Alcoa, 1888–1986* (New York, 1988), 214–16, 232.

20. *Advertising and Selling* 32 (Oct. 1939): 19. In January 1942 rumors circulated that Washington might impose an "advertising blackout." An agency executive later cast an eye back on "the dire forebodings of just a year ago, when many in advertising . . . feared . . . a complete collapse." *Advertising and Selling* 35 (Jan. 1942): 9; ibid. 36 (May 1943): 13.

21. Ibid. 32 (Oct. 1939): 38.

22. Ibid. 35 (Jan. 1942): 9; Du Pont Company, "Advertising Clinic," [18 Sept. 1941], pp. 8, 11, 13, unprocessed files, DP; Howell John Harris, *The Right to Manage: Industrial Relations Policies of American Business in the 1940s* (Madison, Wisc., 1982), 7–8, 48, 58.

23. Wilson, "Can We Save Free Enterprise?" 36–37, 64–65. "This is the Dangerous Decade," Wilson announced. Too many people now believed that "private enterprise has failed" and that it was "time for the government to take over" (64).

24. Du Pont, "Advertising Clinic," 8; Bruce Barton, "Advertising: 1942 and After," [ca. Nov. 1941], pp. 18–19, box 75, BB; *Advertising and Selling* 35 (Jan. 1942): 17. On the "siege mentality" within advertising trade journals on the eve of war, see also Mark H. Leff, "The Politics of Sacrifice on the American Home Front in World War II," *Journal of American History* 77 (Mar. 1991): 1307, 1309.

25. Psychological Corporation, "The Eighth Nation-Wide Social and Experimental Survey," 1943, pp. 1, 3–5, box 4, acc. 1662, DP; William L. Bird Jr., "The Drama of Enterprise: Du Pont's *Cavalcade of America* and the 'New Vocabulary' of Business Leadership, 1935–1940" (paper presented at the annual meeting of the Society for Cinema Studies, Washington, D.C., May 1990), 1. At Du Pont, company officers deplored the apparently "defeatist" attitudes of British businessmen

who put up "little defense of the enterprise system" and seemed to be "willing . . . to accept, more or less fatalistically, a post-war socialistic regime." E. E. Lincoln to J. E. Crane, 14 July 1942; Bronson Batchelor to Lammot du Pont, 17 Nov. 1942: box 43, acc. 1662, DP.

26. George Romney, untitled pamphlet, Oct. 1942, acc. box 382, FM.

27. *Advertising and Selling* 35 (July 1942): 15; ibid. (Sept. 1942): 17; John Benson, "The Place of Advertising in a War Economy," speech ms., [1942], pp. 14–15, attached to Benson to Thomas D'Arcy Brophy, 29 May 1942, box 7, folder 9, TDB; James D. Scott, "Advertising When Consumers Cannot Buy," *Harvard Business Review* 21 (winter 1943): 215; Frank Fox, *Madison Avenue Goes to War: The Strange Military Career of American Advertising* (Provo, Utah, 1975), 40–41; Leff, "Politics of Sacrifice," 1312. The full implications of Morgenthau's policy were not immediately clear, but within a few months the advertising trade press, attentive to every nuance of the Treasury Department's discourse and behavior, confidently concluded that even extensive institutional advertising by companies with no products to offer wartime consumers would clearly qualify as deductible. One trade journal even went so far as to conclude that "all advertisers seemingly have Carte Blanche"; *Tide,* 15 Sept. 1942, 52. A similar tax policy existed during World War I; see Chapter 3.

28. Benson, "Place of Advertising," 4–5; Tedlow, *Keeping the Corporate Image,* 139. Improved morale would result both from direct messages in corporate institutional ads and from their corollary financial support of a comforting, familiar amplitude of media fare. Benson emphasized advertising's "cheering effect upon the masses" and warned that its curtailment would remove "familiar landmarks" from people's daily lives and "shock them with the fear of losing normal satisfactions by which men live."

29. Robert Griffith, "The Selling of America: The Advertising Council and American Politics, 1942–1960," *Business History Review* 57 (autumn 1983): 390–93; Fox, *Madison Avenue,* 21–22; Harold B. Thomas, "The Background and Beginning of the Advertising Council," in *The Promise of Advertising,* ed. C. H. Sandage (Homewood, Ill., 1961), 16–18, 33, 35. Thomas, the chairman of the War Advertising Council, proclaimed in January 1942 that all the organization's other purposes had been "completely submerged to the one objective of helping to win this war." But he could not refrain from pointing out the need for "preserving some foundation under the private enterprise structure, else, what are we fighting for?"

30. War Advertising Council, minutes of the meeting of the Board of Directors, 10 June 1943, box 4, folder 8, TDB; Thomas Brophy to Mr. Weir and Mr. Link, 5 Apr. 1945, box 49, folder 4, TDB; War Advertising Council, *4 Ways to Show Your Colors,* pamphlet, [1943], pp. 2–4, box 3, ser. 13/2/305, AC; idem, "Indoctrination Meeting," 12 Jan. 1945, pp. 5–6, box 4, ser. 13/2/305, AC; Thomas, "Background and Beginning," 23–24, 39; *Advertising and Selling* 35 (Mar. 1942): 22; ibid. (Nov. 1942): 26; *JWT Service News Letter,* 1 July 1943, 7, JWT.

31. Griffith, "Selling of America," 390–93; War Advertising Council, "Words that Work for Victory," annual report, Mar. 1943–44, p. 3, box 1, ser. 13/2/201, AC; idem, "Preliminary Organization Report," 27 July 1942, p. 3, box 1, ser. 13/2/201, AC; idem, *From War to Peace,* pamphlet, 1945, n.p., box 1, ser. 13/2/300, AC; idem, "Indoctrination Meeting," 5–6; *Sales Management,* 15 Feb. 1946, 128–29; Advertising Council, "Questions and Answers about the Advertising Council," [ca. 1946], pp. 4, 6, 8, box 1, FC.

32. *195 Bulletin [AT&T]* 17 (Apr. 1943): 8; C. E. Wilson to General Managers, 27 Sept. 1943, file 87-11.4-3, CFK; J. Carlisle MacDonald, "U.S. Steel's Public Relations and the War," speech ms., 12 Jan. 1943, n.p., USX. See also "Message of March 17, 1946," in U.S. Steel, *The Radio Story of the Industrial Family That Serves the Nation: United States Steel* (Pittsburgh, 1947), 58; Douglas Alan Fisher, *Steel in the War* (New York, 1946), 8–34, 144–57; Charles W. Cheape, *Strictly Business: Walter Carpenter at Du Pont and General Motors* (Baltimore, 1995), 200.

33. General Motors Corporation, memo to General Managers, 27 Sept. 1943, CFK; Wesley W. Stout, *A War Job "Thought Impossible"* (Detroit, 1945); idem, *Bullets by the Billion* (Detroit, 1946); General Motors Corporation, *Allison War Album* (Indianapolis, 1944); idem, *Buick at Its Battle Stations* (Detroit, 1944); idem, *The Tale of the Tremendous Trifle* (Bristol, Conn., 1944).

34. *Advertising and Selling* 35 (Feb. 1942): 56; Robert B. Westbrook, "Fighting for the American Family: Private Interests and Public Obligations in World War II," in *The Power of Culture: Critical Essays in American History,* ed. Richard Wightman Fox and T. J. Jackson Lears (Chicago, 1993), 202; Elmo Roper, "First Installment of Survey on Freedom from Want Campaign," Apr. 1943, p. 4, reel 444, JWT.

35. *Business Week,* 8 Jan. 1944, 52; *Advertising and Selling* 35 (Nov. 1942): 32; Fox, *Madison Avenue,* 32, 56–57, 68–69; General Motors Corporation, *Mobilizing America's Economic Strength,* pamphlet, 15 Oct. 1940, pp. 3–4, FL.

36. *Life,* 22 Nov. 1943, 5; *Saturday Evening Post,* 18 Mar. 1944, 64–65; Thomas, "Background and Beginning," 22; James Webb Young, "What Shall We Do about It," speech ms., 14 Nov. 1941, box 1, ser. 13/2/282, AC; Henry J. Kaiser, "Address to American Academic of Political Science," pp. 9–10, enclosed in Adline Hovgard to Kaiser, 20 Oct. 1942, carton 12, HJK; Kaiser to C. F. Calhoun, 6, 7 Sept. 1942, carton 12, HJK; John B. Hughes, "News and Views," radio script, 7 Oct. 1942, n.p., carton 13, HJK; Henry J. Kaiser, speech ms., 1 Mar. 1944, carton 24, HJK. Donaldson Brown, a leading GM executive, urged recognition of "the right to work" as the fifth freedom; Henry Weaver, the head of GM's consumer research, liked the proposal of the conservative radio commentator Fulton Lewis Jr. for "freedom of individual enterprise" as the fifth freedom. General Motors Corporation, "War Production Shorts," attached to Paul Garrett to Editor, 13 June 1942, CFK; Henry Weaver, "Thought Starters," attached to Weaver to Kettering, 9 Aug. 1943, CFK.

37. *Successful Grocer* 22 (Aug. 1943): 14–16; "Proceedings, Thirty-second Annual Meeting, Association of National Advertisers," 12 Nov. 1941, p. 33, box 1, GCC; "Talk Delivered by Paul B. West," 26 Apr. 1945, pp. 2–3, box 7, folder 11, TDB; Henry C. Link, "Advertising: A Major Post-War Power for Social Security and against Inflation," 18 Nov. 1943, box 109, acc. 554, FM.

38. Less frequently, as in Black & Decker's "Here's Why American Free Enterprise Works" or Youngstown Sheet and Tube's "Free Enterprise at Work" ads, the company would preface its story of wartime contributions with a headline vaunting free enterprise. *Saturday Evening Post,* 11 Mar. 1944, 59; *Business Week,* 8 Jan. 1944, 74.

39. *Successful Grocer* 22 (June 1943): 7; ibid. (Aug. 1943): 4, 14, 32, 40–42; *Progressive Grocer* 21 (Dec. 1942): 32; *Good Housekeeping* 119 (Aug. 1944): back cover; ibid. (Oct. 1944): inside front cover; ibid. (Dec. 1944): 16; *Ladies' Home Journal* 61 (Sept. 1944): 51; ibid. (Oct. 1944): 14; *McCall's* 71 (July 1944): inside front cover; ibid. (Aug. 1944): inside front cover; *Life,* 6 Nov. 1944, 20.

40. *Progressive Grocer* 21 (Dec. 1942): 32; Garrett to Editor, 2 Oct. 1944, General Motors, New York, 1944 file, CFK.

41. General Motors Corporation, press release, 26 Oct. 1944, CFK; *Country Gentleman* 114 (Jan. 1944): 21. Sloan had warned as early as 1936 that "regimentation of industry" represented a dangerous "step" along the road to state socialism; Alfred P. Sloan Jr., *Shall We Have More—or Less?* pamphlet, 22 May 1936, p. 9, HML. General Motors had introduced the regimentation theme in somewhat oblique anti–New Deal advertisements in 1936, but this language seemed even more effective once the war was under way.

42. *Saturday Evening Post,* 11 Nov. 1944, 59; Fox, *Madison Avenue,* 70–71, 75, 85–86; *Fortune* 27 (May 1943): 16; *Life,* 9 Oct. 1944, 67, 121; *Kodakery,* 1 June 1943, 4; *Saturday Evening Post,* 17 Apr. 1943, inside front cover. See also Westbrook, "Fighting for the American Family," 203, 207, 213–15. Westbrook stresses the Norman Rockwell imagery of the war period and the "homely fragments" of life, which he conceptualizes as a "familial" notion of war aims.

43. Fussell, *Wartime,* 127–28.

44. *The Lamp* 25 (Apr. 1943): 1; *Saturday Evening Post,* 17 June 1944, 60; *Advertising and Selling* 36 (Feb. 1943): 14. "The Kid in Upper 4," in the New Haven Railroad's prize-winning ad, was a raw new recruit who already missed hamburgers, his dog, and a "lot of little things" back home; *Collier's,* 9 Jan. 1943, 49.

45. *Saturday Evening Post,* 27 Feb. 1943, 7; ibid., 17 Apr. 1943, inside front cover; ibid., 12 June 1943, inside front cover; *Fortune* 27 (May 1943): inside front cover. Although such free-enterprise messages were wholly embedded in narratives of the prosaic comforts and opportunities of small-town life, apparently not all readers unwittingly ingested the ideology along with the nostalgia. One serviceman from the agency that had produced the Nash-Kelvinator ad wrote back to remark that the "average guy" among the GIs "smells the propaganda in that one." This was true, he said, even of "fellows you might not imagine had the wit to detect the ulterior motive behind these ads." Responses to the agency on the success of the Nash-Kelvinator ads among servicemen were mixed. Some thought that their fellow GIs viewed them as authentic and liked the attempt at sympathy with the serviceman's viewpoint. Others reported that the series "seems 'corny' even to the corniest 'G.I.'" and scoffed at the notion that "we're fighting mostly for cheap hamburgers by the bag." But apparently no one thought to ask one pertinent question: Why did no Nash-Kelvinator

serviceman-protagonist express a yearning to go back to a job at the Nash-Kelvinator factory? See Sgt. Harry Hartwick to Raymond Rubicam, 9 May 1944; Edgar B. Van Winkle to Rubicam, n.d.; Lt. Comdr. T. J. Smith to Rubicam, 29 May 1944; Edwin A. Kirschner to Rubicam, 3 June 1944; Robert L. Harrison to Rubicam, n.d.; Capt. A. G. Layng to Rubicam, 26 May 1944: all in Letters from Soldiers file, Y&R.

46. *Saturday Evening Post,* 12 Feb. 1944, 66.

47. *U.S. Steel News* 4 (Oct. 1940): back cover; Paul Garrett, *Propaganda for Democracy,* pamphlet, 7 Dec. 1939: 4, 14, 19, box 7B, CSM; *Life,* 12 Oct. 1942, 63; *GE Monogram* 21 (Apr. 1944): 16, 20, 25, box 67, folder 25B, ODY; "Tentative Program, Du Pont Advertising Clinic," 24 Aug. 1932, p. 2, box 14, ser. II, pt. 2, DP; J. Walter Thompson Company, *News Bulletin,* 27 Mar. 1945, 1–2.

48. *Life,* 2 Oct. 1944, 9; *U.S. Steel News* 8 (July 1943): 20; *Alcoa News,* 17 Mar. 1941, 2. In a series of film "playlets" intended as "screen editorials," William Bird notes, the National Association of Manufacturers told stories of the immigrant "Joe Karnac" and the all-American pilot "Bill Smith" in "recognizable, human situations" characterized by "familiar scenes" and the "comedy, drama, and homely philosophy of 'regular folks'"; Bird, "Enterprise and Meaning: Sponsored Film, 1939–1949," *History Today* 39 (Dec. 1989): 29.

49. *Kraftsman* 2 (Feb.–Mar. 1944): 10; ibid. (Apr.–May, 1944): 16; ibid. (June–July, 1944): 16; General Electric Company, "People Are Talking," reproduction of ad, Dec. 1943, GEF; R. S. Peare to O. D. Young, 6 June 1943, folder 9.3, OYGE.

50. General Motors Corporation, "Adv. 521-RR," n.d., p. 8, GM; Garrett to Executive Group, 16 Mar. 1944, file 87-11.5-31, CFK. For examples of these ads, see *Country Gentleman* 114 (Mar. 1944): 41; (Apr. 1944): 46; (May 1944): 33; (Aug. 1944): 3; (Oct. 1944): 36.

51. V. L. Simpson, "Talk on Film 'Soldiers of the Soil,'" 22 July 1943, box 14, ser. II, pt. 2, DP; Theodore G. Joslin and William A. Hart to W. S. Carpenter Jr., 30 Aug. 1943, box 832, acc. 542, DP.

52. Information Bulletin no. 198, 27 Dec. 1943, Cellophane Division, unprocessed files, DP; Du Pont, "Du Pont Presents—Soldiers of the Soil," 1943, mimeo, Cellophane Division, unprocessed files, DP; William S. Dutton to Carpenter, 25 Jan. 1943, box 833, DP; *Why You'll Want To Show This Picture,* pamphlet, n.d., box 14, ser. II, pt. 2, DP; Simpson, "Talk on Film"; caption on back of still photograph from *Soldiers of the Soil,* box 2, acc. 72.341, DPP.

53. For examples of Rockwellesque imagery, see *Advertising and Selling* 35 (Feb. 1942): 29–30; ibid. (Oct. 1942): 12; *Saturday Evening Post,* 21 Apr. 1945, 71; *Life,* 8 Nov. 1943, 21.

54. *Saturday Evening Post,* 6 May 1944, 71; ibid., 20 May 1944, 97; War Advertising Council, "Wartime Advertising Awards," n.p., box 6, ser. 13/2/305, AC.

55. *The Lamp* 25 (Apr. 1943): 1; *Country Gentleman* 11 (Jan. 1944): 21; *Advertising and Selling* 36 (May 1943): 70; *Good Housekeeping* 117 (Nov. 1943): 173.

56. Ayer News File, 14 Dec. 1941, pp. 1–2, NWA.

57. *Advertising and Selling* 35 (Apr. 1942): 16; "Survey of Opinions Concerning Modern Advertising Volunteered by Combat Personnel Coming through an Air Forces Station," n.d. box 109, acc. 554, FM.

58. "Survey of Opinions." See also Raymond Rubicam to William H. Skirm, 4 May 1944; Capt. D. V. Cleary to Rubicam, 16 May 1944; Lt. J. W. Link to Rubicam, 2 June 1944; Lt. Comdr. T. J. Smith to Rubicam, 29 May 1944; Major Frederick L. Devereaux Jr. to Rubicam, 21 May 1944; Lt. (jg) George Hand Jr. to Rubicam, 28 May 1944; Sgt. Harry Hartwich to Rubicam, 9 May 1944; Cpl. Ted Pittenger to Rubicam, 6 May 1944; Capt. R. B. Wilder to Rubicam, 20 May 1944: all in Letters from Soldiers file, Y&R.

59. Walter S. Carpenter Jr., then president of Du Pont, and Henry Ford were most vehement. See Carpenter to Hart, 1 Nov. 1943, box 821, acc. 542, DP; Carpenter to H. Brayman and Hart, 10 Feb. 1945, box 821, acc. 542, DP; Hart to Carpenter, 5 Mar. 1945, box 821, acc. 542, DP; Glen Perry to Brayman, 13 Feb. 1945, box 833, ser. II, pt. 2, DP; David L. Lewis, *The Public Image of Henry Ford: An American Folk Hero and His Company* (Detroit, 1976), 381–82; John W. Thompson, "Report on Three National Surveys," [ca. 1944], box 109, acc. 149, FM; untitled memo, ca. 1944, box 105, acc. 149, FM; John Thompson, "Reminiscences," 1952, pp. 57–58, FM.

60. *Advertising and Selling* 35 (Feb. 1942): 56; ibid. (Apr. 1942): 16; ibid. (May 1942): 20; ibid.

(June 1942): 14; ibid. (Oct. 1942): 28; ibid. 36 (Feb. 1943): 113; ibid. (May 1943): 14; *Tide,* 15 Oct. 1942, 12; Fox, *Madison Avenue,* 38, 45–47; Glen Perry to Harold Brayman, 3 Feb. 1945, box 33, ser. II, pt. 2, DP.

61. *GM Folks* 5 (Feb. 1942): inside front cover. On the use of the phrase "people's war" or "little man's war," see *Advertising and Selling* 35 (Mar. 1942): 21; "Free Men Fight," radio script, 7 Aug. 194, enclosed in M. H. Aylesworth to Bruce Barton, 7 Aug. 1942, box 2, BB.

62. *Ford Times,* 1 Aug. 1943, 8; *Saturday Evening Post,* 15 Aug. 1944, 78; ibid., 5 May 1945, inside front cover. See also *Chrysler War Work Magazine* 9 (Feb. 1943): 14.

63. *Advertising and Selling* 35 (Mar. 1942): 21; *Kodakery,* 15 June 1943, 4; ibid., 29 June 1943, 4; Eastman Kodak Company, press releases, 3 Sept. 1943, 20 Apr. 1944, 20 June 1944, EK. On the concurrent rise of cultural pluralism in the labor movement, see Gary Gerstle, *Working-Class Americanism: The Politics of Labor in a Textile City, 1914–1960* (New York, 1989), 289–302 and passim. On the movies, see Richard Lingeman, *Don't You Know There's a War On? The American Home Front, 1941–1945* (New York, 1970): 184; Clayton R. Koppes and Gregory D. Black, *Hollywood Goes to War: How Politics, Profits, and Propaganda Shaped World War II Movies* (New York, 1987), 69, 152, 304, 310. Before the war was over, even Puerto Ricans and Native Americans would receive corporate tributes; as far as I have been able to determine, African Americans did not gain such recognition in general-circulation publicity, although a few did in company magazines. The Ford Motor Company, which counted African Americans as over 11 percent of its total workforce by 1942 (compared to about 3 percent at Chrysler and General Motors), gave some attention to black workers in its publications but never cast them as representative workers. Indicative of the continuing invisibility of African Americans was a photograph in *GM Folks* for July 1943; accompanying the company's message that "It takes all kinds of People" to accomplish wartime production, the photograph included no black workers. A. J. L. to Edsel Ford, [ca. 6 May 1942], box 383, acc. 6, FM; *GM Folks* 6 (July 1943): 14–17.

64. *The Lamp* 27 (Dec. 1945): 8; *Advertising and Selling* 35 (Feb. 1942): 96–97. Although listener surveys had demonstrated that radio would never be able to convert the majority of the population to "serious" music, the hope for such a transformation of the benighted public seemed to spring eternal. On this issue, see Roland Marchand, *Advertising the American Dream: Making Way for Modernity, 1920–1940* (Berkeley, 1985), 88–92.

65. Harrison B. Summers, ed., *A Thirty-Year History of Programs Carried on National Radio Networks in the United States, 1926–1956* (1958; reprint, New York, 1971), 83–84, 91–92, 123–24, 133; Orrin E. Dunlap Jr., *Radio in Advertising* (New York, 1931), 102; *GM Folks* 6 (Aug. 1943): 7; ibid. (Sept. 1943): 10; ibid. (Nov. 1943): 26; Donald Cord Meyer, "The NBC Symphony Orchestra" (Ph.D. diss., University of California, Davis, 1994), 160–62.

66. Brinkley, *End of Reform,* 121; Henrietta M. Larson, Evelyn H. Knowlton, and Charles S. Popple, *History of Standard Oil Company (New Jersey): New Horizons, 1927–1950* (New York, 1971), 433–52; Michele H. Bogart, *Advertising, Artists, and the Borders of Art* (Chicago, 1995), 274–75.

67. *Fortune* 38 (Sept. 1948): 102; Maren Stange, *Symbols of Ideal Life: Social Documentary Photography in America, 1890–1950* (New York, 1989), 141; Stephen W. Plattner, *Roy Stryker: U.S.A., 1943–1950* (Austin, Tex., 1983), 11–14, 18.

68. Plattner, *Roy Stryker,* 17–18, 21–23; *Fortune* 38 (Sept. 1942): 102; Richard Eells, *The Corporation and the Arts* (New York, 1967), 159–60; Stange, *Symbols,* 133.

69. Bogart, *Advertising, Artists,* 274–75; *Tide,* 15 July 1942, 56; *The Lamp* 26 (June 1944): cover; ibid. (Sept. 1944): cover; ibid. 27 (Dec. 1945): cover and pp. 8–10. Among the artists commissioned by SONJ were Thomas Hart Benton, Adolf Dehn, Ernest Fiene, Millard Sheets, Lawrence Beall Smith, and Frederic Taubes.

70. L. L. L. Golden, *Only by Public Consent: American Corporations' Search for Favorable Opinion* (New York, 1968), 297; Michele H. Bogart, *Public Sculpture and the Civic Ideal in New York City, 1890–1930* (Chicago, 1989), 155–56.

71. Neil Harris, *Cultural Excursions: Marketing Appetites and Cultural Tastes in Modern America* (Chicago, 1990), 357, 367–73; James Sloan Allen, *The Romance of Commerce and Culture: Capitalism, Modernism, and the Chicago-Aspen Crusade for Cultural Reform* (Chicago, 1983), xiii, 31–32; Eells, *Corporation and the Arts,* 199–20; T. J. Jackson Lears, "Uneasy Courtship: Modern Art and Modern

Advertising," *American Quarterly* 39 (spring 1987): 149–41. This association with high art enabled Paepcke, in Neil Harris's phrase, "to create a new corporate style . . . for his young company." The notion that the fusion of corporate strategy with modernistic high art laid the basis for a pervasive trend in corporate visual style, however, seems dubious. As Michele Bogart has observed, the effectiveness of the Container Corporation ads and the power of this imagery lay in its idiosyncrasy, in "the perception that its specific strategies were unrepeatable"; Bogart, *Advertising, Artists,* 268–69.

72.   *Tide,* 15 July 1942, 56; *GM Folks* 6 (Sept. 1943): 10; General Motors Corporation, press release, 30 July 1943, CFK.

73.   Sloan to Carpenter, 2 May 1944, box 837, ser. II, pt. 2, DP; Carpenter to Sloan, 25 Apr. 1944, box 837, ser. II, pt. 2, DP; Alfred Alosin to Paul Garrett, 24 Apr. 1944, box 837, ser. II, pt. 2, DP; Ayer News File, 25 Apr. 1940, p. 1, NWA; R. B. Jewett, "A Review of the Telephone Hour, April–September, 1940," pp. 28, 30–31, box 11, ser. 1, folder 10-040, ATT. On similar internal considerations at Ford and Du Pont, see R. A. G. to J. R. Davis, 29 Dec. 1944, FM; W. A. Hart to Carpenter, 24 June 1943, box 821, ser. II, pt. 2, DP. For Sloan's earlier calls for tunefulness, see Sloan to N. H. Aylesworthy, 2 Jan., 15 Apr. 1935, box 41, folder 46, NBC.

74.   General Motors Corporation, minutes of meeting, Public Relations Policy Group, 22 Dec. 1942, p. 3, CFK; middle commercial, *Watch the World Go By,* 13 Sept. 1943, box 2, acc. 149, FM. On the idea of a "republican" technology compatible with the concept of know-how as an element in a democratic mode of progress, see John Kasson, *Civilizing the Machine: Technology and Republican Values in America, 1776–1900* (New York, 1976), 14–26, 22, 40–41, 48. John A. Kouvenhowen, *The Arts in Modern Civilization* (New York, 1948), 13–19, uses the term "democratic-technological vernacular" for a quality with similar connotations as those of know-how.

75.   *GM Folks* 6 (June 1943): 6; Fox, *Madison Avenue,* 79–80. It was free enterprise, averred an ad by 114 electric companies in 1943, that explained the initiative and know-how demonstrated by "those doggoned kids!"—the GI mechanics who had repaired an abandoned French tank on the fighting front in North Africa. It also had inspired the "ordinary folks" who, having seen a job that needed to be done, had built and managed America's private electric companies. See *Saturday Evening Post,* 18 Mar. 1944, 64–65; *Time,* 5 July 1943, 49.

76.   Paul Garrett to Editor, 1 Apr. 1942, pp. 1, 3, 7–8, file 87-11.4-22, CFK; O. E. Hunt, untitled report, 10 Feb. 1942, enclosed in C. E. Wilson to Carpenter, 12 Feb. 1942, box 837, ser. II, pt. 2, DP; Harris, *Right to Manage,* 72–89, 132; Catton, *War Lords,* 91–93, 98; Brinkley, *End of Reform,* 206–9; Clive, *State of War,* 33.

77.   Harris, *Right to Manage,* 84; Nelson Lichtenstein, "'The Man in the Middle': A Social History of Automobile Industry Foremen," in *On the Line: Essays in the History of Auto Work,* ed. Nelson Lichtenstein and Stephen Meyer (Urbana, Ill., 1989), 169–70, 177–78.

78.   Lichtenstein, "Man in the Middle," 161; Sloan to Kettering, 25 Oct. 1944, file 87-11.5-33, CFK; C. E. Wilson to Kettering, 13 Mar. 1944, file 87-11.4-35, CFK.

79.   When a middle manager urged that more be done to "combat the prejudice against the managers of industry" stemming from the 1930s, GM's Alfred Sloan agreed that nothing compared in significance to the "engineering, management, planning . . . that must come from a comparatively limited number at the top." Perhaps reflecting on the need to bind foremen to top management, Sloan observed that while the company certainly needed to "sell" the idea that "it is leadership that counts," a single reservation should be noted—that "this ability or know-how . . . extends quite a way down into the organization itself." Boyd to Garrett, 26 Sept. 1944; Sloan to Boyd, 29 Sept. 1944: CFK.

80.   Minutes of meeting, Public Relations Policy Group, 3–4; "Good News from the Production Front," [Apr. 1943], CFK; Garrett to T. A. Boyd, 9 Oct. 1944, file 87-11.5-33, CFK.

81.   Henry Weaver, "Interpreting the Mass Production Idea," enclosed in Weaver to Kettering, 29 May 1942, CFK; "Public Problems Confronting General Motors as We Go into 1943," attached to Garrett to Kettering, 9 Jan. 1943, CFK; General Motors Corporation Customer Research Staff, *Thought Starters Regarding Free Enterprise and Why,* pamphlet, Thought Starters Series, no. 113, [ca. 1942], NYPL.

82.   Garrett to Boyd, 9 Oct. 1944, CFK; Charles F. Kettering, *As Ket Sees It,* pamphlet, [1945], esp. radio talks of 17 Oct. 1943 and 23 Apr. 1944, NYPL; *Country Gentleman* 114 (Mar. 1944): 41; ibid. (Apr. 1944): 46.

83. *McCall's* 71 (June 1944): 61; *Saturday Evening Post,* 3 June 1944, 56; *GM Folks* 6 (Feb. 1943): inside back cover; ibid. (Mar. 1943): inside back cover; ibid. (Aug. 1943): 5; ibid. 7 (May 1944): back cover; *Life,* 29 Nov. 1943, 46–47.

84. Middle commercials, *Watch the World Go By,* 6, 18 Aug. 1943; 2, 12, 19, 20, 26, 29, 30 Sept. 1943; 3 Jan. 1944: box 2, acc. 149, FM.

85. *Time,* 2 Oct. 1944, 34; ibid., 6 Nov. 1944, 51; *Saturday Evening Post,* 11 Nov. 1944, 52; ibid., 28 Apr. 1945, 37; *Country Gentleman* 114 (Dec. 1944): 27. See also Dodge Division, Chrysler Motors, press release, 13 Jan. 1943, MSO 355, ILL.

86. Benson, "Place of Advertising," 12–13; *Bell Telephone Magazine* 21 (June 1942): 133; ibid. 22 (winter 1943–44): 210.

87. *Good Housekeeping* 115 (Oct. 1942): 96–97.

88. Fox, *Madison Avenue,* 86.

89. Aluminum Company of America, scrapbook, 1941, file 1725, AL; Fox, *Madison Avenue,* 87.

90. *The Wedge* 53, no. 2 (1941): n.p., OYGE; *Life,* 24 Aug. 1942, 3: *Saturday Evening Post,* 13 May 1944, 76; ibid., 3 Apr. 1944, 49; ibid., 3 July 1944, 73; *Newsweek,* 17 Jan. 1944, 48–49; ibid., 3 Apr. 1944, 49; ibid., 3 July 1944, 73; *Time,* 18 Oct. 1943, 34; ibid., 20 Nov. 1944, 89; *Collier's,* 21 Nov. 1942, 5; ibid., 13 Nov. 1943, 50; B. F. Goodrich Company, souvenir of first TV broadcast, [1943], box GA-2, folder 6, BFG; *Progressive Grocer* 22 (Oct. 1943): 1; *The Lamp* 25 (Oct. 1943): 29.

91. *GE Monogram* 19 (July 1942): back cover; ibid. 20 (Jan. 1943): n.p.; *Collier's,* 11 July 1942, 37.

92. *Advertising and Selling* 35 (July 1942): 26; ibid. 36 (Jan. 1943): 26; ibid. (June 1943): 26; Chad F. Calhoun to Henry J. Kaiser, 18 Dec. 1942, carton 12, HJK; *Tide,* 1 Aug. 1942, 44; ibid., 15 Aug. 1942, 14; *Life,* 9 Oct. 1944, 9; ibid., 3 Apr. 1943, 29; *Good Housekeeping* 117 (Nov. 1943): 173.

93. *Collier's,* 22 Aug. 1942, 65; ibid., 3 Oct. 1942, 3; ibid., 31 Oct. 1942, 9. See also *Newsweek,* 17 Jan. 1944, 48–49.

94. *Saturday Evening Post,* 6 May 1944, 94; ibid., 17 June 1944, 75; *McCall's* 71 (Aug. 1944): 71; *Collier's,* 19 Sept. 1942, 2; *Good Housekeeping* 116 (Apr. 1943): 149; *Country Gentleman* 114 (Apr. 1944): 89.

95. B. F. Goodrich Company, "Television Broadcast Book," 7 Sept. 1943, box GA-2, folder 6, BFG; *Advertising and Selling* 35 (Sept. 1942): 25; *Collier's,* 18 July 1942, 5; ibid., 15 Aug. 1942, 5; ibid., 19 Dec. 1942, 5.

96. *Saturday Evening Post,* 13 May 1944, 76; middle commercial, *Watch the World Go By,* 18 Aug. 1943, 29 Sept. 1943, 7 Jan. 1944, box 2, acc. 149, FM; *Collier's,* 3 Oct. 1942, 3.

97. General Motors Corporation, "War Production Shorts," attached to Garrett to Editor, 13 June 1942, CFK.

98. Jeffrey L. Meikle, *American Plastic: A Cultural History* (New Brunswick, N.J., 1995), 162–65; C. E. Wilson to B. E. Hutchinson, 28 Nov. 1942, CFK; Wilson to Lammot du Pont, 27 Nov. 1942, CFK.

99. Wilson to Hutchinson, 28 Nov. 1942, CFK; Wilson to L. du Pont, 27 Nov. 1942, CFK; General Motors Corporation, minutes of meeting, Public Relations Policy Group, 22 Dec. 1942, p. 7, CFK; minutes of General Motors Engineering Policy Group meeting, 13 Apr. 1943, n.p., CFK.

100. J. R. Davis, address (excerpts), 23 Nov. 1944, box 105, acc. 149, FM; John Thompson, "Reminiscences," 1952, p. 83, FM; Ford Motor Company, untitled report on soldiers' reactions, n.d., p. 30, box 19, acc. 149, FM; General Motors Corporation, press release, [Jan. 1944], CFK. For Kettering's similar message to the farm community, see his "Postwar Thinking vs. Postwar Dreaming," *Country Gentleman* 114 (Jan. 1944): 11, 73.

101. *Mademoiselle* 18 (Mar. 1944): 205.

102. *GM Folks* 7 (Oct. 1944): 1, 18; *Arab World* 1 (autumn 1944): 34, clipping, carton 34, HJK; *Fortune* 28 (Oct. 1943): 258; *Business Week,* 29 Jan. 1944, 92.

103. For examples of both the eagerness for and anxieties about postwar planning, see "Memo No. 105: To All General Managers," 25 Jan. 1943, CFK; "Notes of Meeting No. 7 of Post-War Planning Policy Group," 3 May 1943, CFK; C. E. Wilson to All General Managers, 23 Jan., 3 July, 13 Sept. 1943, CFK; Donaldson Brown to Post-War Planning Group, 11 Jan. 1943, CFK; Sloan to

O. E. Hunt, 7 Nov. 1944, file 87-11.5-33, CFK; Norman Bel Geddes to John W. Thomas, 5 June 1942, box 478, NBG; R. C. Sickler to R. A. Applegate, 13 Oct. 1943, box 14, ser. II, pt. 2, DP; Ben Duffy to William A. Hart, 7 Feb. 1945, box 14, ser. II, pt. 2, DP; "Advertising Clinic Suggestions," 26 Aug. 1943, box 14, ser. II, pt. 2, DP; "Advertising Clinic Notes," 15 Dec. 1944, box 14, ser. II, pt. 2, DP; Lammot du Pont, "Post-War Planning and the Chemical Industry," speech ms., June 1943, unprocessed files, Cellophane Division, DP.

104. Marion B. Folsom, "Planning—from the Bottom up . . . for Peace," speech ms., 16 Aug. 1943, EK; *Advertising and Selling* 36 (Jan. 1943): 44; Donaldson Brown to Pyke Johnson, 27 Feb. 1943, CFK; Brown to Post-War Planning Policy Group, 11 Jan. 1943, CFK; Alfred P. Sloan, Jr., "The Challenge," speech ms., 10 Dec. 1943, CFK; E. V. Rippingilee to O. E. Hunt, 3 June 1943, CFK; Henry C. Link, "Advertising: A Major Post-War Power for Social Security and against Inflation," 18 Nov. 1943, p. 4, box 109, acc. 554, FM; Edward L. Bernays, *Biography of an Idea: Memoirs of Public Relations Counsel Edward L. Bernays* (New York, 1965), 350.

105. *Time,* 22 May 1944, 92; ibid., 20 Nov. 1944, 89; *Life,* 17 May 1943, 54; ibid., 22 May 1944, 92.

106. *Business Week,* 28 Aug. 1943, 23; ibid., 11 Mar. 1944, 25; "Glimpses into the Wonder World of Tomorrow," Information Bulletin no. 141, 9 Sept. 1943, unprocessed files, Cellophane Division, DP.

107. *Time,* 26 June 1944, 73. That corporations succeeded in portraying themselves simultaneously as the designers of a high-tech future and as the denizens and guardians of the idyllic American small town was certainly one of their more notable accomplishments in image creation during World War II. Americans, without giving up the ideal of progress, could find special comfort in nostalgic wartime idealizations of the simple life. Basically unified in support of the war as a national necessity but disinclined to ponder or idealize the war's purposes, Americans fought the war—as many have observed—simply to get it over. See Fox, *Madison Avenue,* 75–79; Fussell, *Wartime,* 139–42; Westbrook, "Fighting for the American Family," 198, 203, 207, 213–15. Advertisers seem to have found little resistance to their promises that the sacrifices made during this ordeal should lead to a better life (improved technology) in the context of getting back home (to Main Street).

108. *Saturday Evening Post,* 29 Apr. 1944, 81; ibid., 13 May 1944, 76; *Fortune* 27 (June 1943): 32; ibid. 28 (Aug. 1943): 205; *Life,* 23 Nov. 1943, 1. Alcoa remained the striking exception to this trend, depicting a monumental futuristic metropolis in the background of its ad "Out of the Sky Comes the Earth's Great New Employer," in the *Saturday Evening Post,* 29 Apr. 1944, 89.

109. *Business Week,* 11 Jan. 1941, 3; *Saturday Evening Post,* 20 May 1944, 68; ibid., 27 May 1944, 64; ibid., 24 June 1944, 50; *Country Gentleman* 114 (June 1944): 27; ibid. (July 1944): 32; ibid. (Dec. 1944) 32.

110. *Fortune* 27 (May 1943): 167; ibid. 29 (Mar. 1944): 67; *McCall's* 71 (Apr. 1944): 120; *Saturday Evening Post,* 25 Mar. 1944, 95; *Modern Millwheel* 7 (Christmas 1943): 25.

111. Fox, *Madison Avenue,* 77, 79; *Good Housekeeping* 117 (July 1943) 60; ibid. (Sept. 1943): 143; *Country Gentleman* 114 (Jan. 1944): 21; *Fortune* 29 (Mar. 1944): 67.

112. *Saturday Evening Post,* 18 Aug. 1945, 50; ibid., 6 May 1944, 71, 73; *Fortune* 29 (Mar. 1944), 67; *Business Week,* 12 Feb. 1944, 55; *Ladies' Home Journal* 61 (Feb. 1944): 146.

113. *Saturday Evening Post,* 14 June 1941, 116; Terry Smith, *Making the Modern: Industry, Art, and Design in America* (Chicago, 1993), 110–11.

114. *Advertising and Selling* 35 (Feb. 1942): 165; ibid. 36 (June 1943): 93; Hearst Newspapers, untitled oversize pamphlet, [ca. 1942], folder 15.4, OYGE; *Saturday Evening Post,* 22 May 1943, 47; ibid., 22 Apr. 1944, 88; Thomas D. Brophy to W. C. Dickerman, 31 Dec. 1943, box 7, folder 7, TDB.

115. See, for example, *Advertising Age,* 13 Dec. 1937, 12; *Life,* 3 Mar. 1941, 3; *U.S. News and World Report,* 17 Aug. 1945, 1; *The Lamp* 27 (Apr. 1945): 2, 5; *Steel Facts,* no. 3 (Jan. 1935): 5; ibid., no. 10 (Dec. 1935): 1; *Forbes,* 14 Nov. 1942, 26–27; *U.S. News,* 21 June 1946, 1; John W. Hill, "Organization for Public Relations," speech ms., 30 Nov. 1942, p. 6, box 39, JWH; *General Motors Executive Bulletin* 1 (Apr. 1944): 8, file 87-11.5-32, CFK; Archibald J. Allen, *Up from the Ranks* (Cincinnati, 1965), xxiii. The head of AT&T even claimed that "workers and management are largely the same people in America, only at different stages of their careers"; *Bell Telephone Quarterly* 22 (winter 1943–44): 213.

116. Charles F. Kettering, "American Crossroads," radio talk, 27 Aug. 1944, in Kettering, *As Ket Sees It,* pamphlet, [1945], NYPL; *Fortune* 30 (Nov. 1944): 66.

117. *Saturday Evening Post,* 17 June 1944, 60.

118. Paul Garrett, *A Case Example in Public Relations,* pamphlet, 4 Dec. 1945, HML; Garrett to Editor, 2 Oct. 1944, CFK; *GM Folks* 6 (Oct. 1943): 4–5; Garrett, "How Can We Build Good Public Relations?" n.d., n.p., GM. On the Cincinnati failure, see the *Cincinnati Enquirer:* 1 July 1944, 1; 11 July 1944, 18; 21 July 1944, 1; 23 July 1944, 1–2; 3 Sept. 1944, 1; 5 Sept. 1944, 1; 9 Sept. 1944, 1. See also C. E. Wilson to L. P. Fisher, 4 Sept. 1943, file 87-11.4-34, CFK; Sanford M. Jacoby, "American Exceptionalism Revisited: The Importance of Management" (paper presented at the annual meeting of the Social Science History Association Convention, New Orleans, Oct. 1987), 32.

119. Middle commercial, *Watch the World Go By,* 28 Mar., 5 Apr. 1943, box 383, acc. 6, FM; *In the Service of America,* pamphlet, n.d., box 109, acc. 149, FM; *Ford Times,* 11 June 1943, 5; *Ford News* 21 (Mar. 1941): 72, 80; Howard P. Segal, "'Little Plants in the Country': Henry Ford's Village Industries and the Beginning of Decentralized Technology in Modern America," *Prospects* 13 (1988): 207–8.

120. See, for instance, *Ladies' Home Journal* 61 (Feb. 1944): 146; *Newsweek,* 24 Jan. 1944, 10.

121. Fussell, *Wartime,* 155. On such local rallies, parades, and celebrations, see Eastman Kodak Company, press releases, 19 June 1942, 11 Aug. 1943, EK; Procter & Gamble Company, *Presentation of the Army-Navy Production Award, Wolf Creek Ordinance Plant, Milan, Tennessee,* pamphlet, 1942, BL; *GM Folks* 6 (Dec. 1943): 25.

122. *Ford News* 21 (Aug. 1941): 214; *Ford Times,* 2 Apr. 1943, 1, 8; ibid., 11 June 1943, 11; ibid., 1 Aug. 1943, 8; ibid., 28 Apr. 1944, 3.

123. *GM Folks* 6 (May 1943): cover, 14; ibid. 7 (July 1944): 15; *Alcoa News,* 5 June 1944, 1; General Motors Corporation, *Grow More for '44 . . . ,* pamphlet, [1944], box 7A, CSM; *Chrysler War Work Magazine* 10 (Mar. 1944): 2, 4–6; U.S. Steel, *Radio Story,* cover and pp. 3, 9, 13, 17, 19; Swift & Company, *Year Book, 1943* (Chicago, 1943), 17–18, 29; Fones-Wolf, "Industrial Recreation," 245, 248, 255.

Conclusion

1. Paul W. Garrett, *Public Relations—Industry's No. 1 Job,* pamphlet, 22 Apr. 1938, GM; idem, *Management—Tell What You Stand For,* pamphlet, 26 Sept. 1944, 16–17, BL.

2. Paul Garrett, "Industry: Thoroughfare to Victory," speech ms., 15 Dec. 1941, box 7B, CSM; J. Carlisle MacDonald, "U.S. Steel's Public Relations and the War," speech ms., 12 Jan. 1943, USX.

3. J. Carlisle MacDonald, *The Public Relations Job Ahead,* pamphlet, 7 Jan. 1948, p. 5, USX; Richardson Wood, "The Corporation Goes into Politics," *Harvard Business Review* 21 (autumn 1942): 68; Karen S. Miller, "Amplifying the Voice of Business: Hill and Knowlton's Influence on Political, Public, and Media Discourse in Postwar America" (Ph.D. diss., University of Wisconsin, Madison, 1993), 127–30; Elizabeth Fones-Wolf, *Selling Free Enterprise: The Business Assault on Labor and Liberalism, 1945–1960* (Urbana, Ill., 1994), 6–10, 171–80; Richard Tedlow, *Keeping the Corporate Image: Public Relations and Business, 1900–1950* (Greenwich, Conn., 1979), 140–41; *Sales Management,* 20 Nov. 1947, 78.

4. Paul Garrett to T. A. Boyd, 9 Oct. 1944, CFK; *GM Folks* 6 (Apr. 1943): 12; Paul Garrett, *Public Opinion and the War,* pamphlet, July 1943, p. 8, DPL. On the sense of having arrived at a new plateau of public appreciation, see also Fred Eldean, "The Next Job for Institutional Advertising," 4 Oct. 1943, CFK; and Howell John Harris, *The Right to Manage: Industrial Relations Policies of American Business in the 1940s* (Madison, Wisc. 1982), 94.

5. B. W. Keithley to Advertising Sections, 21 Feb. 1945, box 14, ser. II, pt. 2, DP; W. A. Thompson to Owen D. Young, 13 Oct. 1943, file 9.3, OYGE; R. S. Pears to Young, 5 Feb. 1945, file 9.3, OYGE; Opinion Research Corporation, *The Public Looks at Alcoa: A Survey for the Aluminum Company of America,* pamphlet, 1946, 5–6 8–9, envelope 1411, AL.

6. Mansel G. Blackford, *A History of Small Business in America* (New York, 1991), 58, 63–64, 74–75. On the advantages of large businesses in conversion to war production and reconversion after World War II, see Gregory Hooks, *Forging the Military-Industrial Complex: World War II's Battle of the Potomac* (Urbana, Ill., 1991), esp. 135–39, 141–49, 150–51, 156–57.

7. Paul Garrett, "How Can We Build Good Public Relations?" n.d., n.p., GM; idem, "Industry: Thoroughfare to Victory"; Thomas Lamont, "Memorandum for T.W.L.," 14 Apr. 1942, box 228, TL. A survey by the Psychological Corporation indicated that the percentage of Americans who thought that "the business people, the manufacturers, are doing a good job for the most part to help win this war" had advanced from a promising 80 percent in April of 1942 to an auspicious 88 percent in November. See Gordon Cole and Albert D. Freiberg, "Third Draft of Dialogue for the Fourth A.N.A. Study," [ca. Dec. 1942], box 1, GCC; Thomas C. Cochran, "The Sons of the Trust Busters: The Corporation and the American Dream," in *Twentieth-Century Pessimism and the American Dream,* ed. Raymond C. Miller (Detroit, 1961), 80.

8. A. E. Winger to Harold Thomas, attachment to minutes of meeting of 17 Aug. 1944, pp. 1–2, AC; War Advertising Council, *The War Advertising Council: What It Is, What It Is Doing, and Why It Is Important to American Business,* pamphlet, [1943], AC; idem, press release, 1 Nov. 1945, box 6, ser. 13/2/305, AC; R. S. Repplier, "Business Gears Itself for Continuing Public Service," n.d., box 1, ser. 13/2/282, AC.

9. Alvin von Auw, *Heritage and Destiny: Reflections on the Bell System in Transition* (New York, 1983), 23; Richard Eells, *The Corporation and the Arts* (New York, 1967), viii, x, 176; Peter F. Drucker, *The Concept of the Corporation,* 2d ed. (New York, 1972), 5.

10. Bruce Barton, "Improvement of Public Opinion about United States Steel," 9 Jan. 1950, p. 10, box 80, BB.

11. Western Electric Company, "Concerning a Neighbor of Yours," scrapbook of newspaper ads, 1920–1922, ATT; *American Magazine* 121 (June 1936): 134.

12. AT&T, *A Bridge of Voices: A Selection from More than 900 Messages on the "Telephone Hour," 1940–1958* (Philadelphia, [1958]), 7, 10; *Long Lines* 19 (Apr. 1940): 1; General Motors Corporation, "Neighbor and Customer in Every Community," attachment to press release, 4 Apr. 1938, GM.

13. James C. Collins and Jerry I. Porras, *Built to Last: Successful Habits of Voluntary Companies* (New York, 1944), 8–9, 23, 30–31, 73.

14. Drucker, *Concept of the Corporation,* 5; Edward Littlejohn, "The Heirs of the Robber Barons: The Businessman's Role in Contemporary Society," in Miller, ed., *Twentieth-Century Pessimism,* 26; Cochran, "Sons of the Trust Busters," 80.

15. On the capacity of business corporations to set social and political priorities and exercise paternal responsibility in solving social problems, see William J. Ahfeld, "Pragmatic Limits on Business Involvement," *Public Relations Journal* 27 (May 1971): 6–9; David Vogel, "Why Businessmen Distrust Their State: The Political Consciousness of American Corporate Executives," *British Journal of Political Science* 8 (Jan. 1978): 72–76; Fones-Wolf, *Selling Free Enterprise,* 5–6, 67.

SOURCES FOR ILLUSTRATIONS

Chapter 1

Fig. 1.1 Arthur Young, "Nearer, My God to Thee," *The Masses* 5 (Dec. 1913): 17.

Fig. 1.2 Marshall Field & Co., *The Store of Service,* pamphlet, n.d., Chicago Historical Society.

Fig. 1.3 Wanamaker Co., *The Golden Book of the Wanamaker Stores* (Philadelphia, 1911), 56h.

Figs. 1.4, 1.5 *Cassier's Magazine* 28 (Sept. 1905): 351, 356.

Fig. 1.6 *Everybody's Magazine* 42 (Apr. 1920): 125.

Fig. 1.7, 1.8 W. G. McLoughlin Collection.

Fig. 1.9, 1.10 *Ladies' Home Journal* 36 (July 1919): 60; (Sept. 1919): 101.

Figs. 1.11, 1.12 *Saturday Evening Post,* 28 June 1924, 123; 19 July 1924, 103.

Fig. 1.13 Collections of the Henry Ford Museum and Greenfield Village.

Fig. 1.14 *Ladies' Home Journal* 39 (May 1922): 127.

Fig. 1.15 *Harper's Weekly,* 19 Dec. 1896, 1256.

Fig. 1.16 *The Metropolitan,* 1909. Courtesy MetLife Archives.

Fig. 1.17 Hugh McAtmney, *The Master Builders* (New York, 1913), 5.

Fig. 1.18, 1.19 *System* 24 (Sept. 1913): n.p.; (Oct. 1913): 398.

Chapter 2

Fig. 2.1 *Country Life in America* 14 (July 1908): 323.

Fig. 2.2 Ibid. 16 (Sept. 1909): 550.

Fig. 2.3 Ibid. 18 (Aug. 1910): 476.

Fig. 2.4, 2.5 Ibid. 16 (Oct. 1909): 588; 17 (Dec. 1909): 238.

Fig. 2.6 *Western Electric News* 4 (May 1915): cover. Property of AT&T Archives; reprinted with permission of AT&T.

Fig. 2.7 *Country Life in America* 19 (Mar. 1911): 391.

Fig. 2.8 Ibid. 25 (Mar. 1914): 94.

Fig. 2.9 *Weavers of Speech.* Property of AT&T Archives; reprinted with permission of AT&T.

Page numbers in italic refer to illustrations.

Blackford, Mansel, 10, 358
Bliven, Bruce, 302
Bluestone, Daniel, 41
Bogart, Michele, 167
bolshevism, 88, 98, 101
Bon Marché (Paris), 15–16, 115
Boston, 11, 14, 250
Boston Edison Company, 251
Boston Manufacturing Company, 28
Boucicaut, Aristide and Marguerite, 15
boundaries, 15, 17, 45–46; within business, 3–4; cultural, 14; gendered, 15
Bourke-White, Margaret, 239, 271, 274, *308*, 333
Bracker, Leone, 141–42
Bradley Fertilizer Company: trade card, *29*
Brandes, Stuart, 23
Brennan, Walter, 326
"Bringing the Hand-shake Back to Our Factories," 113
Brisbane, Arthur, 207
Brody, David, 98
Brophy, Thomas, 350
Brown, Donaldson, 132, 238–39, 245, 346
Bruere, Henry, 24, 25
Buffalo, 250
Buick, 131–32
Bunyan, John, 163
Bureau of Corporations, 42
Burleson, Albert, 56
Burroughs Adding Machine Company, 90–91; ad, *33*
business: democracy, 75; expansion, 8; and religion, 11
"Business Backs New York World Fair to Meet New Deal Propaganda" (Lichtenberg), 292
Business Barometer, 247
business bigness, 237, 327, 360; meatpackers and, 96; mistrust of, 49. *See also* big business; corporate bigness
Business Week, 293, 295
Byoir, Carl, 90

Cadburys (Birmingham), 15, 115
Cadillac, 131–32, 138
Cadman, Rev. S. Parkes, 36
Calkins, Earnest Elmo, 187
Cameron, William J., 210–11
Canada: AT&T in, 50–51; private utilities in, 50, 56
"Can We Save Free Enterprise?" (Wilson), 319

capitalism, 3, 319; industrial, 29. *See also* welfare capitalism
Caples, John, 134, 198
Carnegie, Andrew, 164, 225
Carnegie Steel Company, 22
Carpenter, Walter S., 219, 222–23, 318, 434n59
Casino of Science, 291
Cassandre, A. M., 335
Cassatt, Alexander, 43
Caterpillar Tractor, 104
The Cavalcade of America, 220–23
Cawelti, John, 265, 267
Cellophane, 346–47; ads, *347*
centralization: of public relations, 239; U.S. Steel and, 228. *See also* decentralization
Century of Progress Exposition (Chicago), 265–80, 283; AT&T at, 69, 85, *278;* Du Pont and, 218; Ford at, 208–9, 268–76, *269–70,* 280; General Motors at, 235, *266,* 284, 288; Kraft at, 267, *268*
CF&I. *See* Colorado Fuel and Iron Company (CF&I)
Chamber of Commerce (U.S.), 98, 213
Chandler, Alfred D., Jr., 103–4, 131
Charlotte Observer, 306
Chase, Stuart, 305
Cheape, Charles, 223
Cheers from the Camps, 313
Chevrolet, 131–32, 138, 241–42, 267–68, 276, 302; ad, *359*
Chicago, 260, 362; and Marshall Field's, 11, 13, 38; and McCormick Reaper Company, 15, 23. *See also* Century of Progress Exposition (Chicago); Columbian Exposition (Chicago)
Chicago Commons, 183
Chicago Evening Post, 24
Chicago Telephone Company, 110
Chicago Tribune, 16, 24
The Child, 183
Chrysler, Walter, 265
Chrysler Corporation, 207, 293, 324, 337, 356; ads, 339, *340,* 349; and fair exhibits, 250, 266–67
Chrysler Motors Magazine, 217, 293
church, 2–3, 9, *9,* 38, 45–46, 363. *See also* religion
Cincinnati, 33, 354–55
CIO (Committee for Industrial Organization), 216, 224, 227
Circus of Science, 284, 288
Cities Service Cavaliers, 193
Cities Service Concert Orchestra, 193
Civic Federation of Chicago, 23

Civilian Advisory Commission, 88
class. *See* social class
Cleveland, 33, 283. *See also* Great Lakes Exposition (Cleveland)
clocks, 38; Metropolitan Life's, 38, *39*
coal strike, 42
coal trust, 42
Coca-Cola, 267
Cochran, Thomas, 359
Coffin, Charles F., 149–51
Cohen, Lizabeth, 110
Colgate, Bayard, 102
Colgate & Company, 102
collectivism, 346
Collier's, 42, 265
Colorado Fuel and Iron Company (CF&I), 16–17, 98; employee magazines, 16, 109; Ludlow massacre and, 16–17, 88, 98, 109, 115
Columbian Exposition (Chicago), 249–50, 254–55; AT&T at, 253; meatpackers at, 259
commercialism, 2, 246, 336, 362
commercial sponsors, 192
Committee on Public Information (CPI), 89–90
common folk imagery, 211–18, *240,* 321, 326, 331, *334,* 335–36, 350, *352,* 362; AT&T and, 82, 85, 96, *214;* Barton and, 171; and corporate leaders, 144; Du Pont and, 220, *221,* 222; General Motors and, 231–32, 239–45, 288; Metropolitan Life and, 186, *186;* Swift and, 96, *97;* Westinghouse and, 297–98; during World War II, 324–29, 346. *See also* Main Street imagery
communications, 108, 111, 117; breakdown in, 108, 115; downward, 110; external, 363; in General Motors, 137, 239; internal, 101, 104, 117
communities: island, 3; local, 2, 4, 9, 361; manufacturing, 22; model, 15
community, 45, 116, 363, 370n8; and AT&T, 73–74; awareness of, 4; company and, 354–57, 359, 361; corporation and, 316; General Motors and, 138–39, 236, 243–44, 286, 291, 361; pageants, 312, 316; U.S. Steel and, 226
company: as employee, 80; as institution, 41, 250, 293; reputation, 26; role in society, 164; spirit, 15. *See also* corporations
company culture. *See* corporate culture
company founders: and corporate identity, 26–28, 31–32, *32–33*

17; and employee representation, 114–18; expenditures on, 22; fair exhibits and, 116, 265; as feminine, 25; Heinz, 115, 258–59; in institutional ads, 116; internal tensions created by, 25; International Harvester, 21–26, 42, 111; McCormick Reaper Company, 23–24; Metropolitan Life, 182–83, 185, 187; NCR, 17–21, 45, 115; paternalism and, 16, 109, 114–16; public image of, 17, 118; Pullman Company, 114; strikes and, 24; Swift, 25; turnover and, 114–16; U.S. Steel, 21–23, 394n95; wartime (WW II), 316; Westinghouse, 316; for women, 23, 182

welfare workers, 25

Wellville Post, 110

West, Paul, 322

Western Electric Company, 67, 81, 111, 113, 150, 154, 362, 379n9, 391n67; ads, *112, 168,* 170; employee magazines, 111, 113; fair exhibits, 61, *62,* 81, 263; as institution, 199; research laboratories, 194

Western Electric News, 62, 108, 110, 393n79

Western Union, 57; building, 36

Westinghouse, George, 42, 378n118

Westinghouse Company, 109, 150, 199; ads, 216–17, *217, 296–97;* common folk imagery and, 297–98; consumers, 282; ethnic imagery and, 216–17; fair exhibits, 253–54, 267, 276–77, 282, 292, 295–98, *296–97,* 425n85; film and, 295–98; Link Audit and, 247; war pageant, 316; welfare programs, 316

Westinghouse Electric News, 109–11, 393n79

What Is a Capitalist? (Ayer), 246

White, E. B., 305, 310

White, William Allen, 199

White Sulphur Springs (W. Va.), 230

Why Business Is Big (Ayer), 246

WIB (War Industries Board), 89–90

Wiebe, Robert, 3

Willard, Daniel, 89, 119

Williams, Whiting, 201

Williamson, Oliver, 3

Willow Run plant, 355

Wilson, Charles E., 318, 319

Wilson, Charles Erwin, 318, 344

Wilson, Woodrow, 56, 91

window displays, 173

women, 44, 64, 282, 324, 341; in ads, *65, 68,* 68, 70–72, *70–72, 75–76, 76–77, 78,* 157, *158–59,* 177, *251;* charity work, 25; as consumers, 72, 282–83; as customers, 14; Du Pont and, 358; employees, 14, 23, 66, 316; factory tours and, 255; fair exhibits and, 282–83; at Heinz, 256–57; at Metropolitan Life, 182; as stockholders, 23, 77; and telephone use, 69–72; welfare programs for, 23, 182; welfare workers, 25; workers, 25, 33, 256; workforce of, 115, 182. *See also* feminine

Wood, Grant, 328, 350

Wood, Robert E., General, 389n41

Woolworth, Frank, 41

Woolworth building, 36, 38–39, *40,* 41

work councils, 116–17

workers, 8, 46, 214–16; in ads, *75, 100, 215, 238, 240;* blue collar, 109, 162, 340; ethnic, 331; General Motors, 237–38, 242, 354; Heinz, 256; morale, 98, 110–11, 214, 354; shortages of, 88; U.S. Steel, 227; white collar, 108, 129; women, 25, 33, 256. *See also* employees; workforce

workforce: at CF&I, 16; female, 115, 182; and welfare programs, 16; during World War II, 316

working class, 181, 183

working conditions, 14, 20, 25

workmen's compensation, 181–82

Works Progress Administration (WPA), 273, 295–96

world-of-tomorrow images, 341–47

World's Columbian Exposition. *See* Columbian Exposition (Chicago)

World's Fair. *See* New York World's Fair

World's Fair and Louisiana Purchase

Exposition (St. Louis), 250, 254–55, 420n7

World's Work, 83

World War I, 80–81, 83, 88–89, 115, 166, 316, 319, 349; AFL unionization during, 116; Atterbury during, 118; Barton during, 134; employee bargaining during, 119; government control of railroads during, 119; mobilizing for, 89–91; munitions traders during, 219; welfare programs, 356

World War II, 5, 82, 312–56, 358, 360; advertisements, 324, 330–31; advertising, 320–22, 326, 330–31, 333, 338, 343; Alcoa during, 319, 326, 341; Armour during, 322–23; AT&T during, 321, 330, 333; Barton during, 319; big business during, 319–20, 322, 326, 330, 335, 349; common folk imagery during, 324–29, 346; corporate image during, 321–22, 346, 358; corporate imagery during, 313, 336, 341, 346, 348; employees during, 316–17; free enterprise during, 317–20, 322–24, 339, 341, 343, 354–55, 360; General Motors during, 318, 321, 337–38; institutional advertising during, 317, 319–21; morale during, 318, 321, 356; panoramas and, 107; public relations during, 317–18, 320, 331, 357–58, 360

WPA, 273, 295–96

Wright, Helena, 29

Yates, JoAnne, 104, 110

yearbooks, 95

YMCA, 11

York (Pa.), 326

Young, Arthur: cartoon by, *9*

Young, James Webb, 322

Young, Owen D., 89, 150–51, 154, 156, 161, 164

Young & Rubicam, advertising agency, 246, 282, 330

Youngstown Sheet and Tube, 433n38

Your Baby, 183

Zahavi, Gerald, 110, 114

Designer:	Steve Renick
Compositor:	G&S Typesetters, Inc.
Text:	10.85/12 Bembo
Display:	Gill Sans
Printer/Binder:	South China Printing Company Ltd.